Neo-Chinese
Style
Clubs

ARTPOWER

Neo-Chinese Style Clubs
Copyright © Artpower International Publishing Co., Ltd.

ARTPOWER™

Designer: Chen Ting
Chief Editor: Weng Danzhi

Address: Room C, 9/F., Sun House, 181 Des Voeux Road
Central, Hong Kong, China
Tel: 852-31840676
Fax: 852-25432396

Editorial Department
Address: 13B, Zijing Ge, Fa Zhan Xing Yuan, No. 1, Mintian
Road, Futian District, Shenzhen, China
Tel: 86-755-82913355
Fax: 86-755-82020029

Web: www.artpower.com.cn
E-mail: artpower@artpower.com.cn

ISBN 978-988-68243-8-2

No part of this publication may be reproduced or utilised in any form by any means, electronic or mechanical, including photocopying, recording or by any information storage and retrieval system, without prior written permission of the publisher.

All images in this book have been reproduced with the knowledge and prior consent of the designers and the clients concerned, and every effort has been made to ensure that credits accurately comply with information applied. No responsibility is accepted by producer, publisher, or printer for any infringement of copyright or otherwise arising from the contents of this publication.

Printed in China

PREFACE

When it comes to the furnishings, either the Chinese scroll landscape painting, the great calligraphy works, or the artfully-outlined blue and white porcelain has brought the implicit and sophisticated charm which gently undulates in an attractive manner to all places and times.

None of these numerous art descendants aren't the spiritual support bequeathed by the Chinese civilization with a long long history. Nowadays they also bring us the feelings of the highbrow or vulgar culture at that time.

As time goes by, the rise and fall of various dynasties have gone with the wind. Our forefathers have bequeathed such an elegant life full of reading and appreciation of art, allowing us to enjoy romantic love, or cultivate ourselves and hereby become better in our quiet life far from fame and fortune. There is also a great deal of ancient artistic charm, making us easily feel the same as what was in the past. Even though the science and technology have made huge progress today, our state of mind and thoughts can't match our forefathers' vision and imagination in the old days.

Borrow the Chinese traditional art as a clue for the design, but it is not about the form of it. It only makes us to treat the nature in a view referring to the tradition, hoping to trigger people's longing for the classic civilization by applying the traditional and antique beauties. Just like this time, there is a very unique style which combine the ramification of Chinese traditional civilization with the exotic style, uniting them in an organic whole so as to further highlight the oriental spirit and make the people thinking more. No tasting of a Chinese atmosphere, no knowledge about it's profound culture accumulation. Chinese style is a chance for those who are graceful and who deeply comprehend the Chinese culture, to trace back the history.

Along with the ethnic consciousness revival, neo-Chinese style appears. Chinese style is endowed with a strong humanistic color that decorative elements emerge in endlessly, including animals, figures... or to draw the religious ideology of all ages in a certain aspect; it is also an attitude! Neo-Chinese is not an elements pile-up, and it is also not a completed ancient style restoring, but by using features of Chinese style to express a pursuit for the graceful, elegant and abundant oriental spirit. According to the modern requirement for aesthetics, the creation of the projects with traditional style lets the traditional art keep in the later generation's mind, for the design, for the east.

Gao Xiong

Dao He Design Studio

CONTENTS

006　Tang Qian Moon Clubhouse

016　Ji Pin Hui

026　Beijing Whampoa Club

034　The Club of Joy

062　Tender Luxury

070　Zen Spa Club

078　Hefei Humble-home Senior Club

084　Sales Center of Xing Fu Li

092　Zi Yue Ya Zhu Business Club

102　Show Upper River Town Club

116　Enterprise Club of COSCO

122　Yuanxiong Jinhuayuan Sales Center

132　Pavilion 2012

140　Xinjiang Nanshan Club

152　Panjin Oriental Ginza Center City Club

160　Shenyang Oriental Ginza Center City Club

168　The Villa Club of Sun Golden Town

176	Jincheng Club
182	Sanya Peninsula Blue Bay Reception Club
192	Chao Huang Ge Club
196	Lake Clubhouse
202	SocietyM
212	Bingo Billiard Club
224	Rizon Jet at Biggin Hill airport
234	Ru Yi Club — Hidden Luxury
240	U-PARK Sales Center
250	Sales Center of Nanning Ronghe MOCO Community
256	Longhu Shi Ji Feng Jing Club
260	Zhengzhou Postal VIP Club
266	Green Park Club
274	Harbin Bincai Group Sales Center
286	Fuzhou Show Property Beyond Club
294	Maple Country Club (MCC)
304	Green Weaving Club House

Tang Qian Moon Clubhouse

Design Agency: Dao He Design Studio
Designer: Gao Xiong
Client: Tang Qian Moon Real Estate
Location: Fuzhou, China
Area: 350 m²
Photographer: Shi Kai , Li Lingyu

With a modern way to interpret the new connotation of Chinese style, to subvert the traditional positioning concept of the clubhouse, we give the clubhouse new space mission with the iconic Chinese elements: a haven of peace and tranquility, within easy reach of the high-end. This is Tang Qian Moon Clubhouse, Which highlights the "New Chinese poetic inhabitation" as its marketing spirit. Without obvious introduction, without grand scale of momentum, hidden in the down town, Wusi Road section is small in the city.

When I entered into the club and saw the moon model on the space and echoing lotus lamp in soft loading, the thought flashed through my mind that the bright moon pours down soft rays on the lotus, and I can 't help but blurt out: the moonlight, such as frost, dancing on the water.

Walking every corner of the clubhouse, I only find the spatial pattern of division adopts semi-enclosed partition. It is not only to achieve a visual rich, but also to get a little more relaxed atmosphere to interact. Unconventional adjustment of the details takes both privacy and sociability of the clubhouse into account.

The habit is something striking into marrow that freely dispose of your behavior and thinking, and unconsciously become a part of life. In the clubhouse, semi-enclosed partition can be seen everywhere. Through the yarn mill material of glass, vague figure like soft yarn overlying the bright moon surface in the clear and scant-started night, appears ethereal and distant. I think this is an intelligent design, with the logo of a situation and the integration of the space aesthetic feeling, creating an immersed sense. It seems near but not, far but not, and you personally experience an imaginary beautiful scene, which seems to be out of reach, but just a turn around, you are there. Being in some green plants, petals sway, full of lightness and loveliness when figure walks. When you open the curtain, rings on the round-backed armchairs are clearly visible. Dust under the sun is that paradoxical precipitate. The cold restrained Lotus hand seat undoes Zen, and what it scattered is the enlightenment of life.

In departure, I reviewed the article "I love lotus" on the wall again. Design even so uses its style to be right for different people in the competitive market. Good design can speak. It is not contaminated even growing in the muddy pond, and does not seem seductive even been washing off in clear water for years. It can be both appreciated distantly and touched blasphemously.

【爱莲说】

水陆草木之花，可爱者甚蕃。晋陶渊明独爱菊。自李唐来，世人盛爱牡丹。予独爱莲之出淤泥而不染，濯清涟而不妖，中通外直，不蔓不枝，香远益清，亭亭净植，可远观而不可亵玩焉。予谓菊，花之隐逸者也；牡丹，花之富贵者也；莲，花之君子者也。噫！菊之爱，陶后鲜有闻。莲之爱，同予者何人？牡丹之爱，宜乎众矣。

008

009

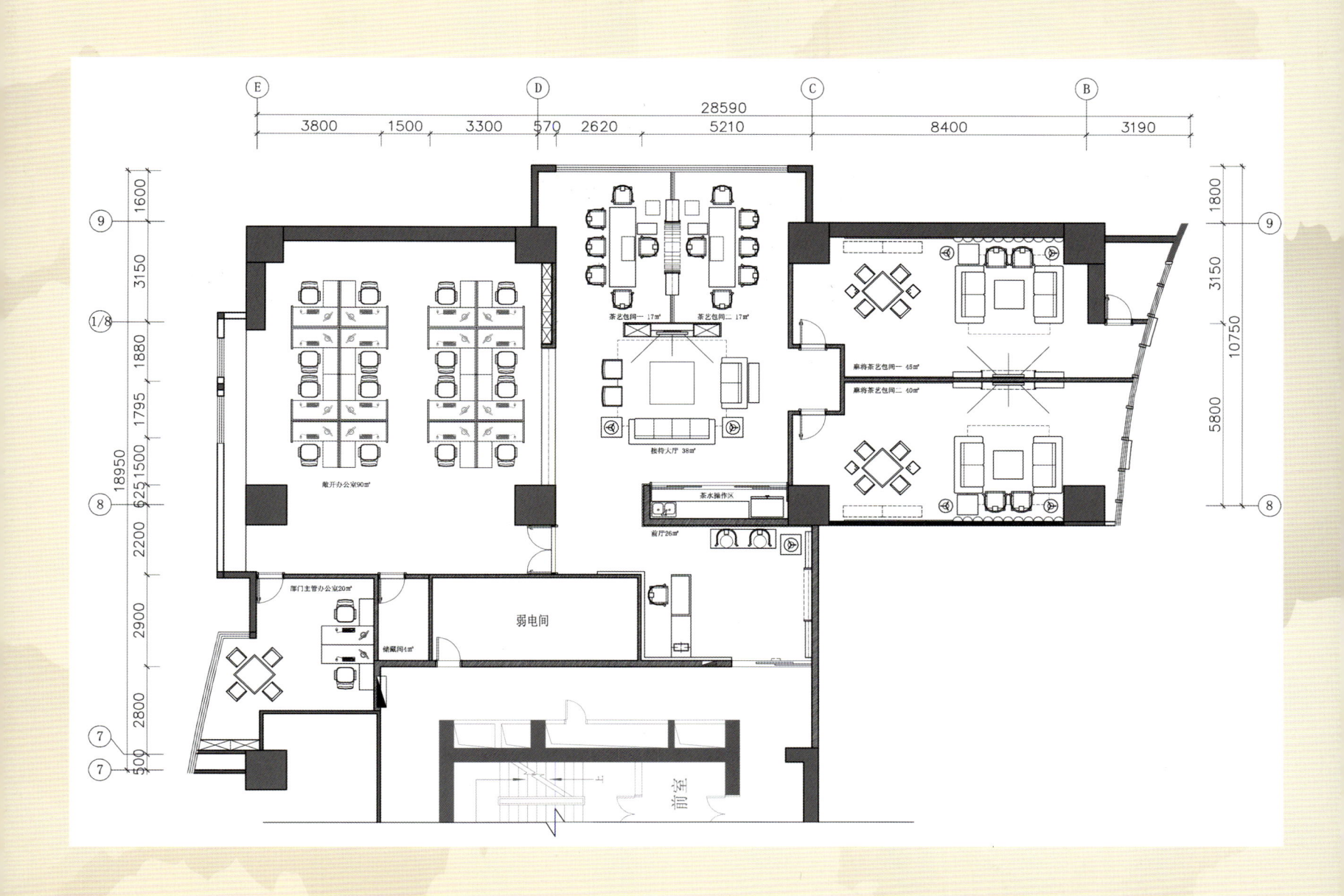

010

011

予独菊，花之君子者也。噫，菊之爱，陶后鲜有闻，莲之爱，同予者何人。牡丹之爱，宜乎众矣。

亭亭净植，可远观而不可亵玩焉。

水陆草木之花，可爱者甚蕃。
晋陶渊明独爱菊。
自李唐来，世人盛爱牡丹。

013

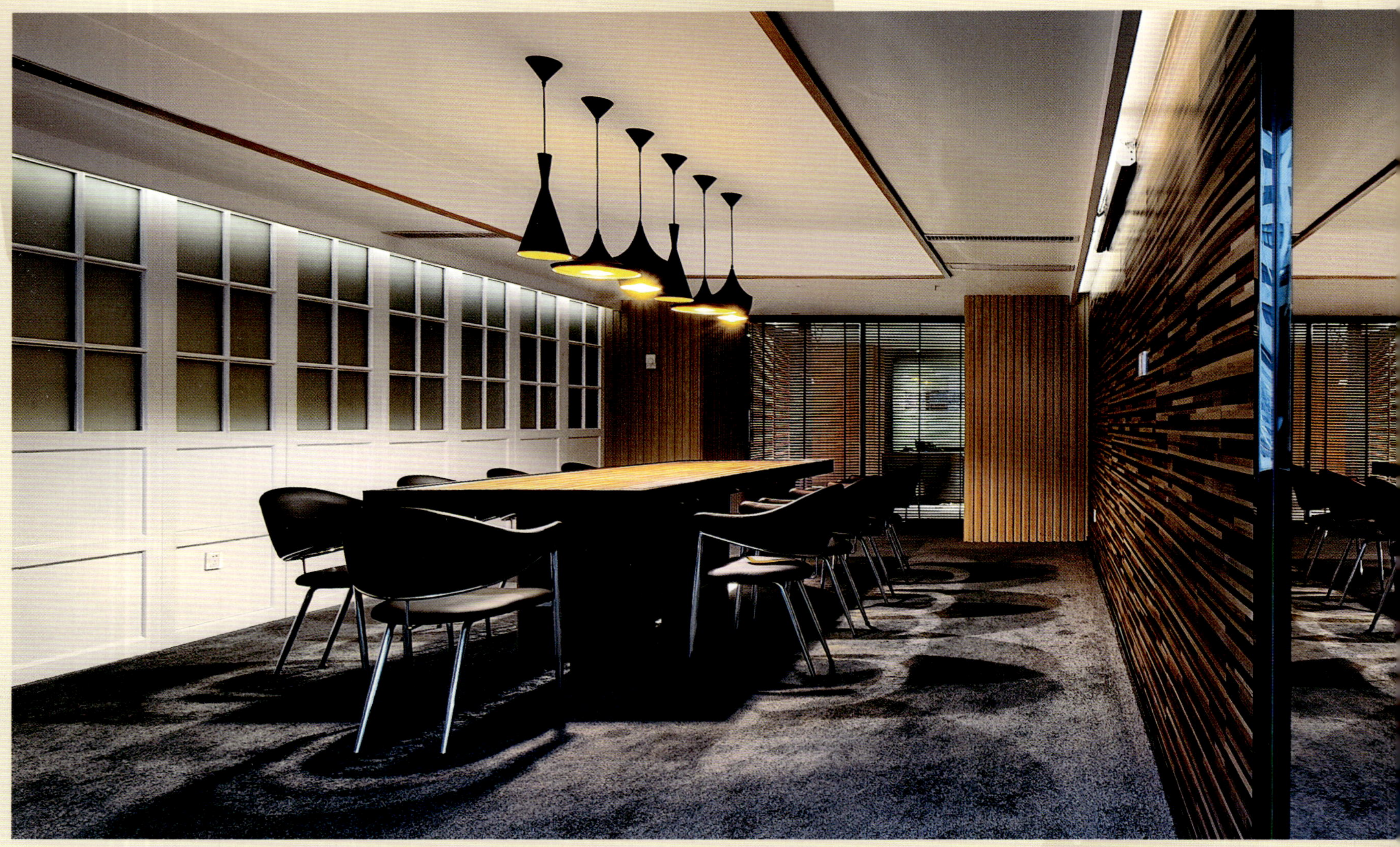

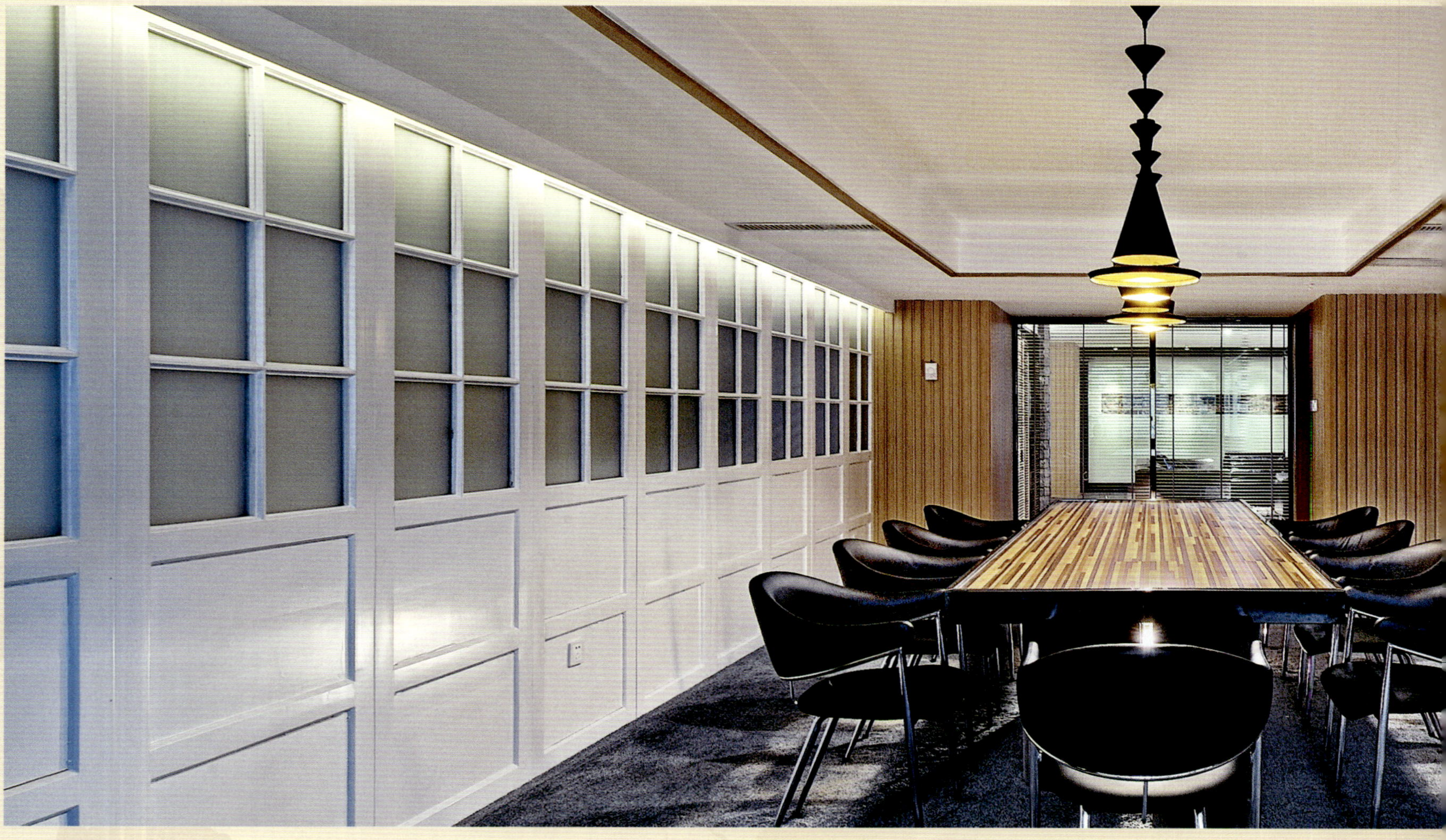

015

Ji Pin Hui

Design Agency: Dao He Design Studio

Designer: Gao Xiong

Location: Fuzhou, China

Area: 250 m²

Photographer: Zhou Yuedong

The Perfection Gift

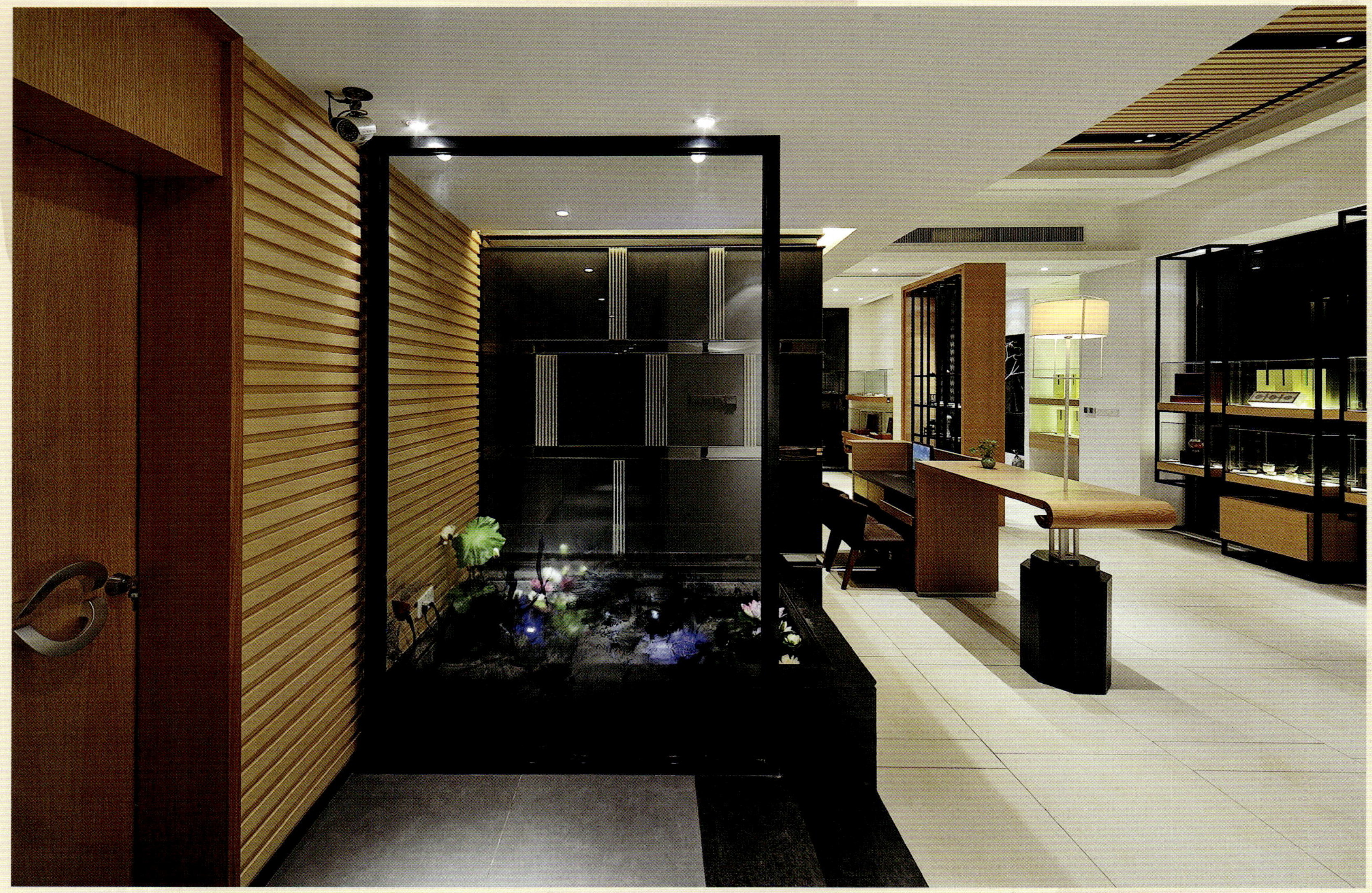

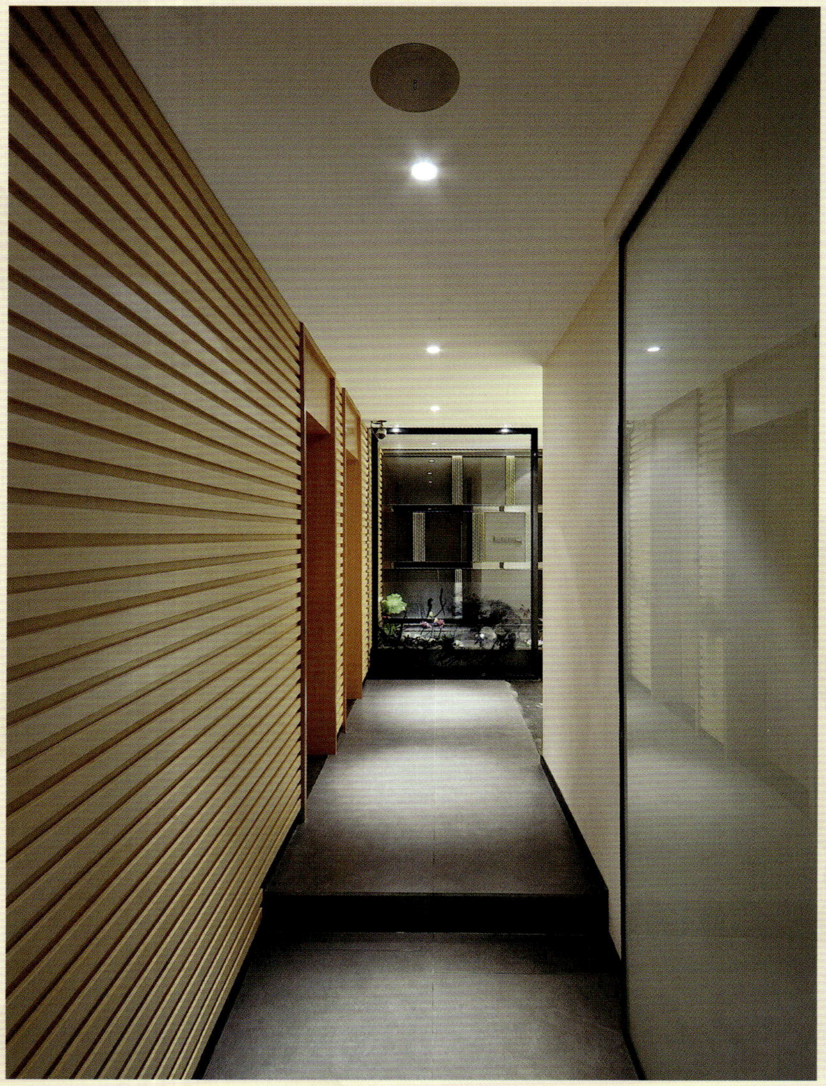

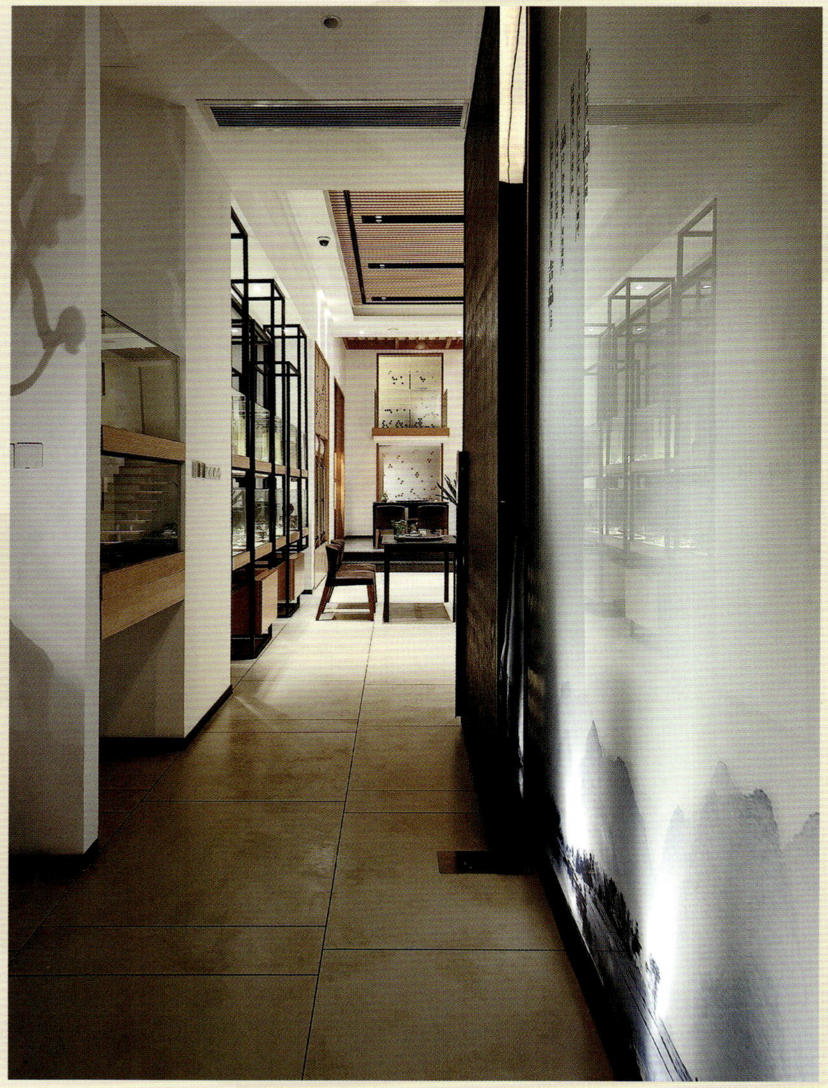

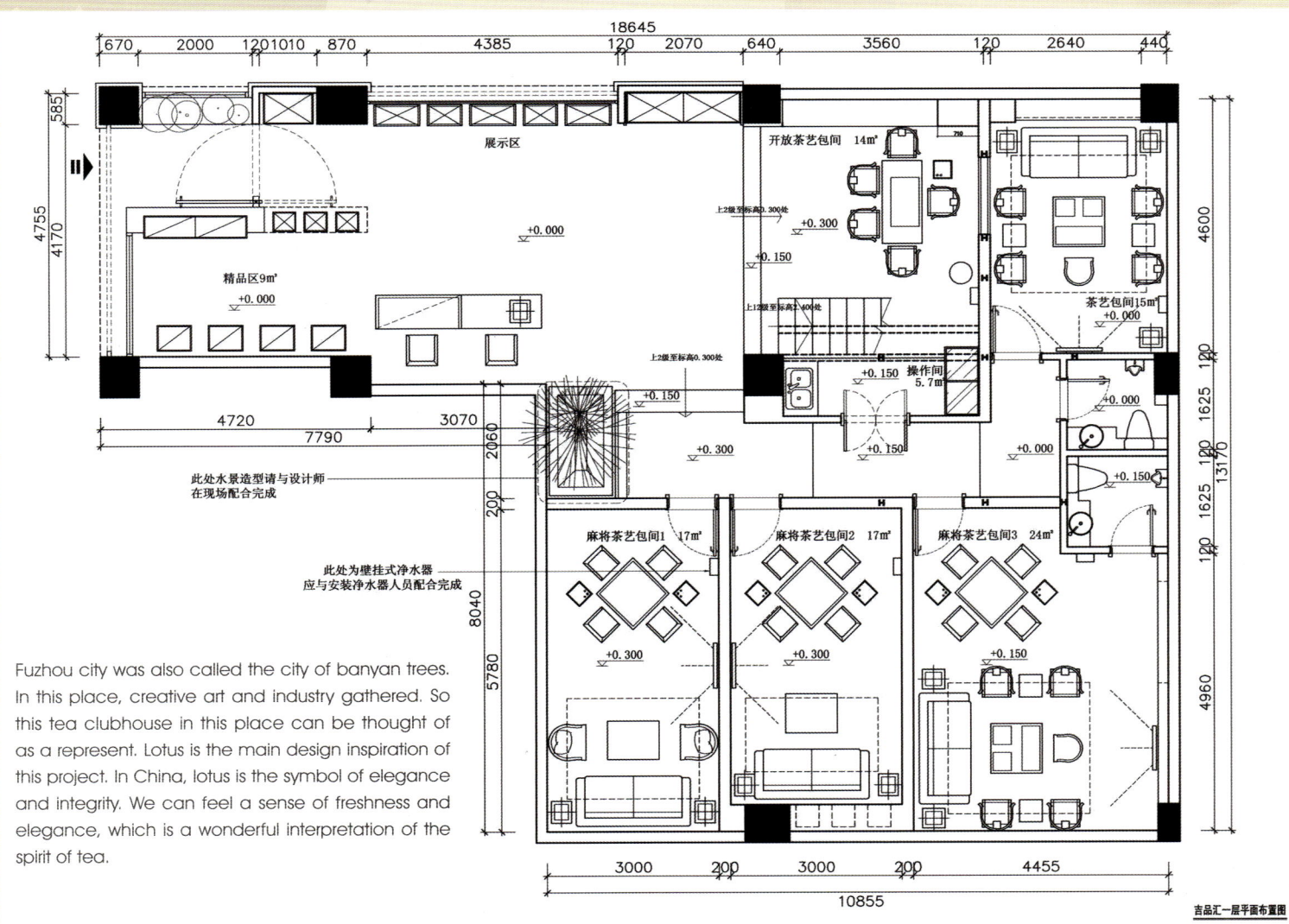

Fuzhou city was also called the city of banyan trees. In this place, creative art and industry gathered. So this tea clubhouse in this place can be thought of as a represent. Lotus is the main design inspiration of this project. In China, lotus is the symbol of elegance and integrity. We can feel a sense of freshness and elegance, which is a wonderful interpretation of the spirit of tea.

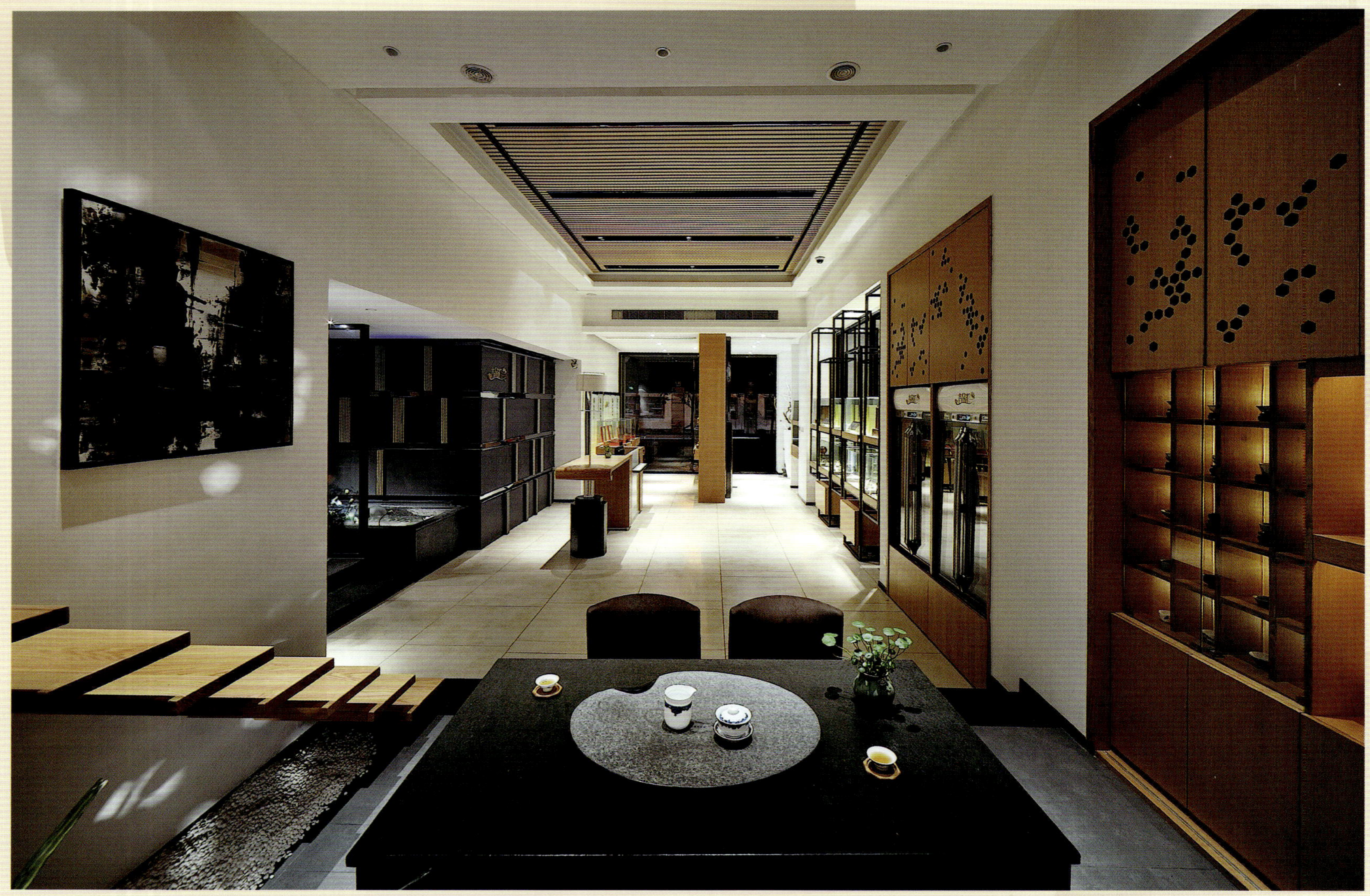

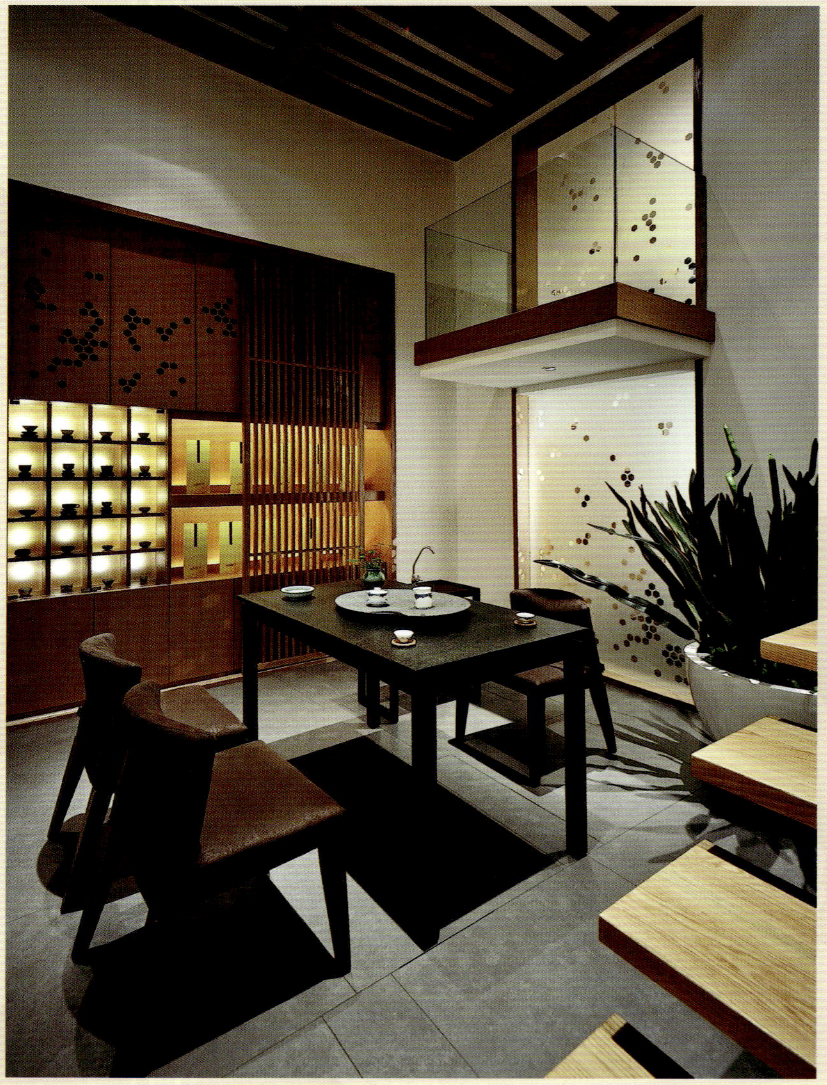

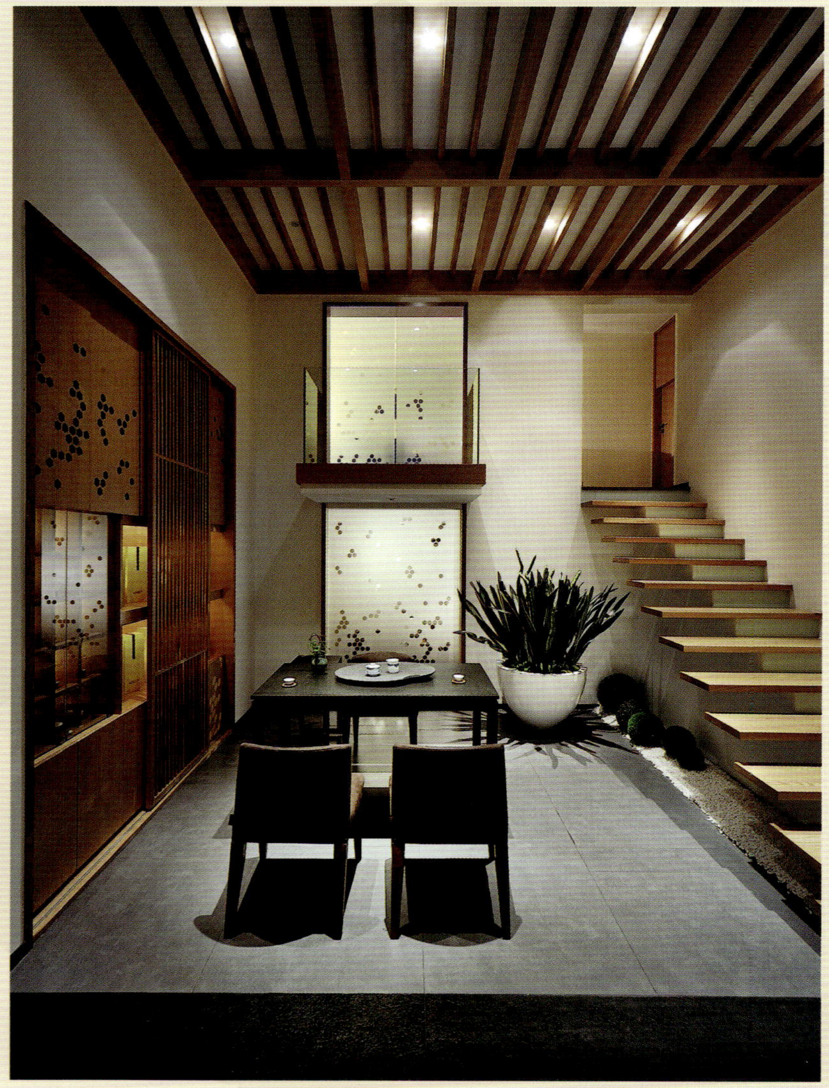

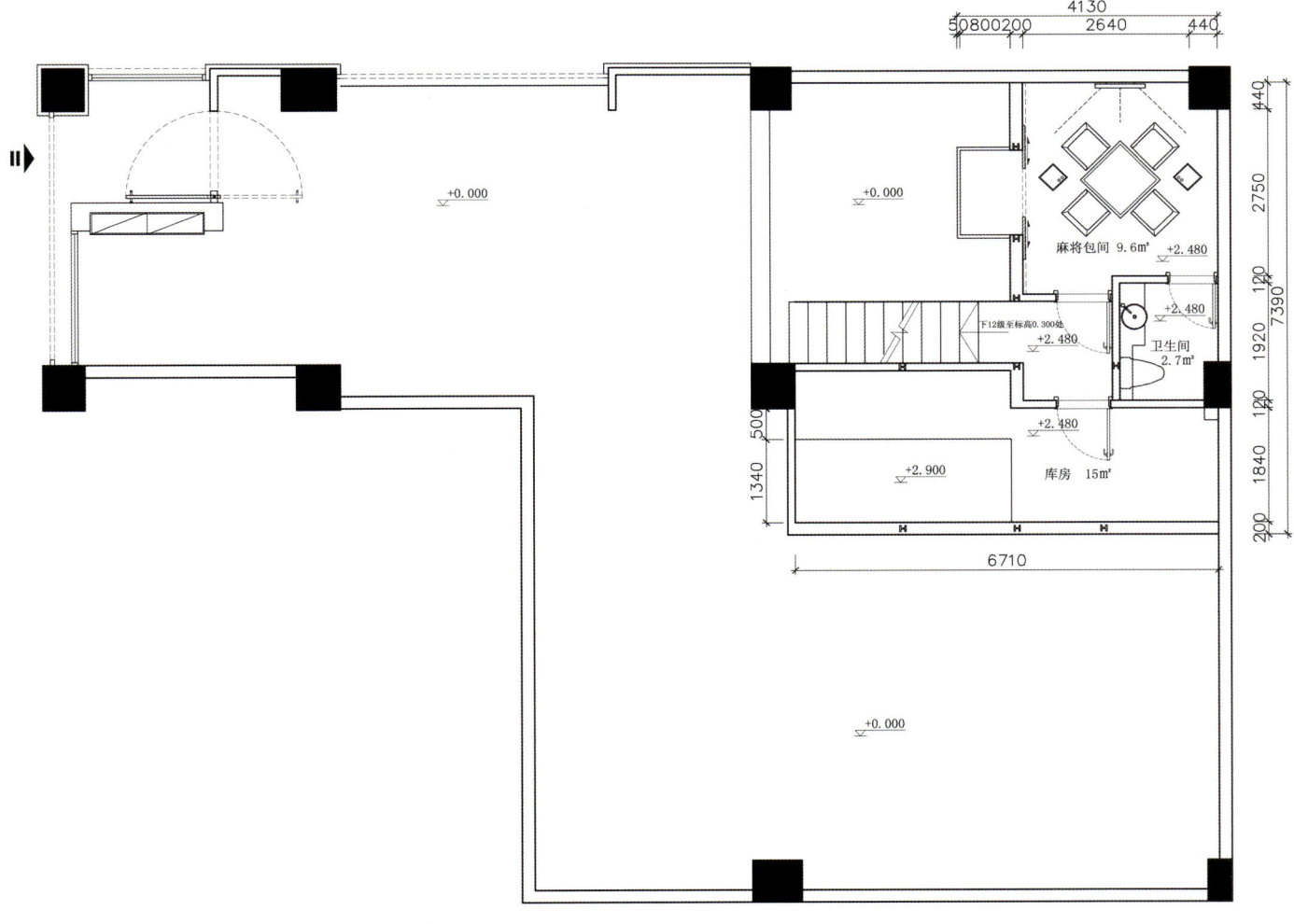

吉品汇二层平面布置图

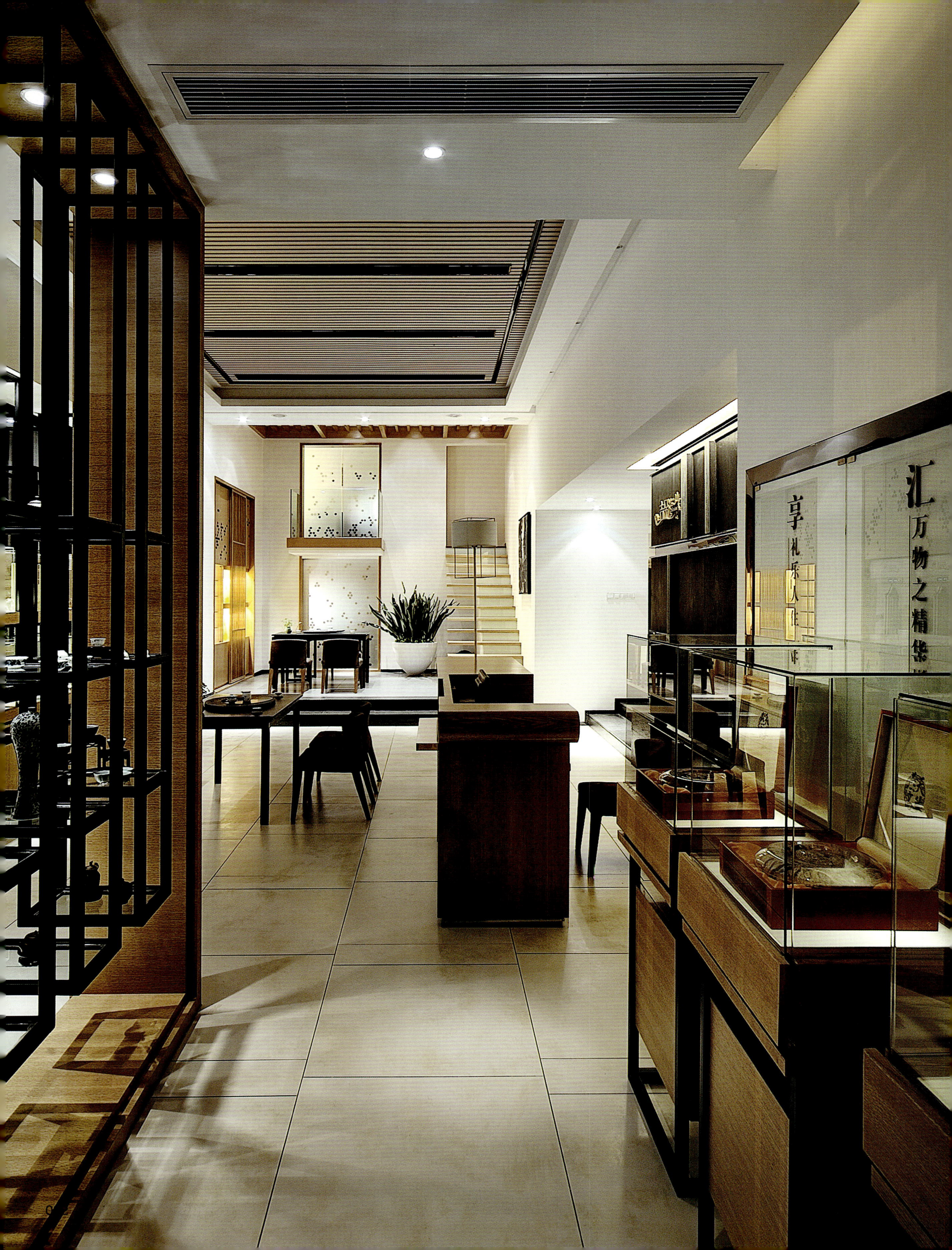
汇
万物之精
享
礼乐人

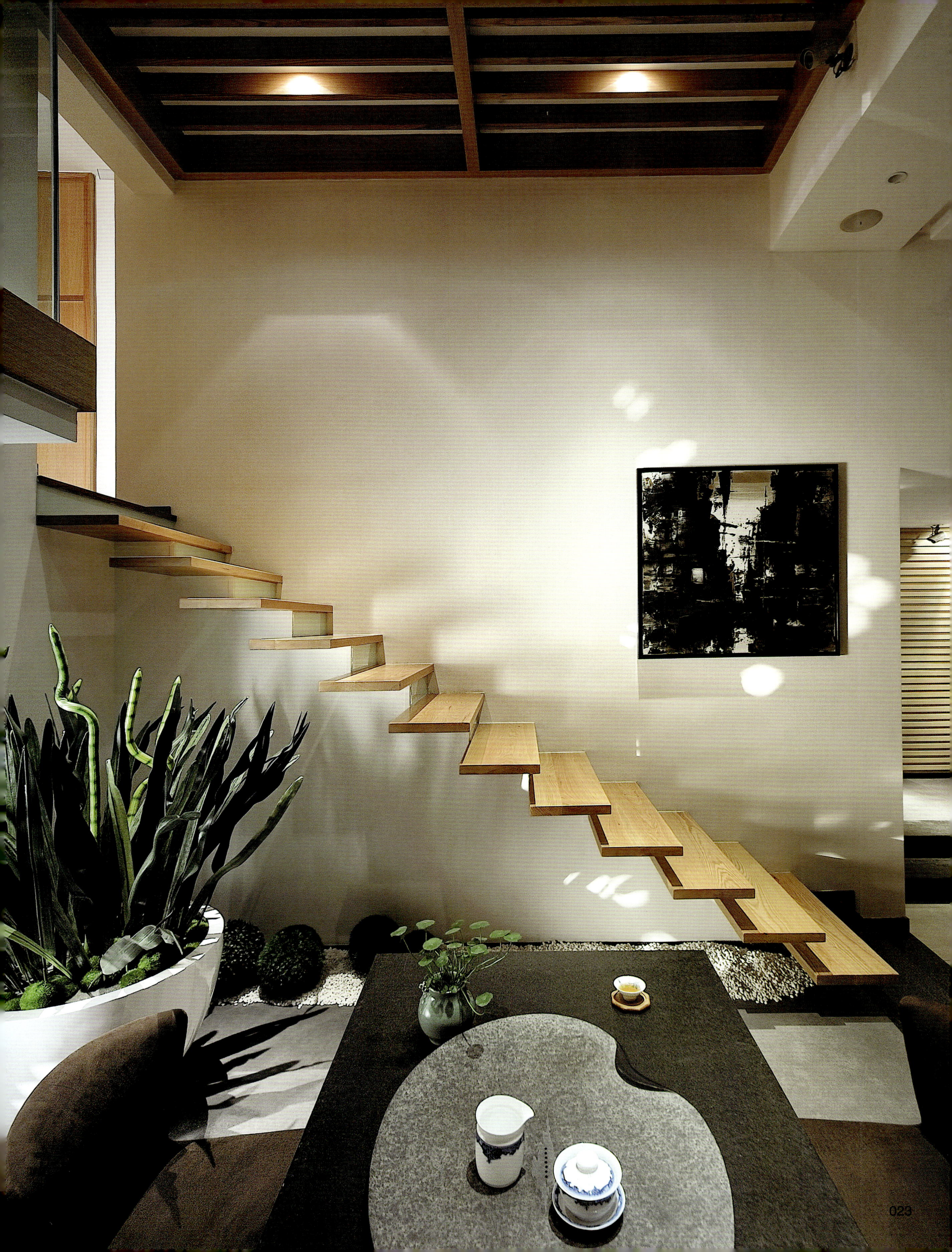

024

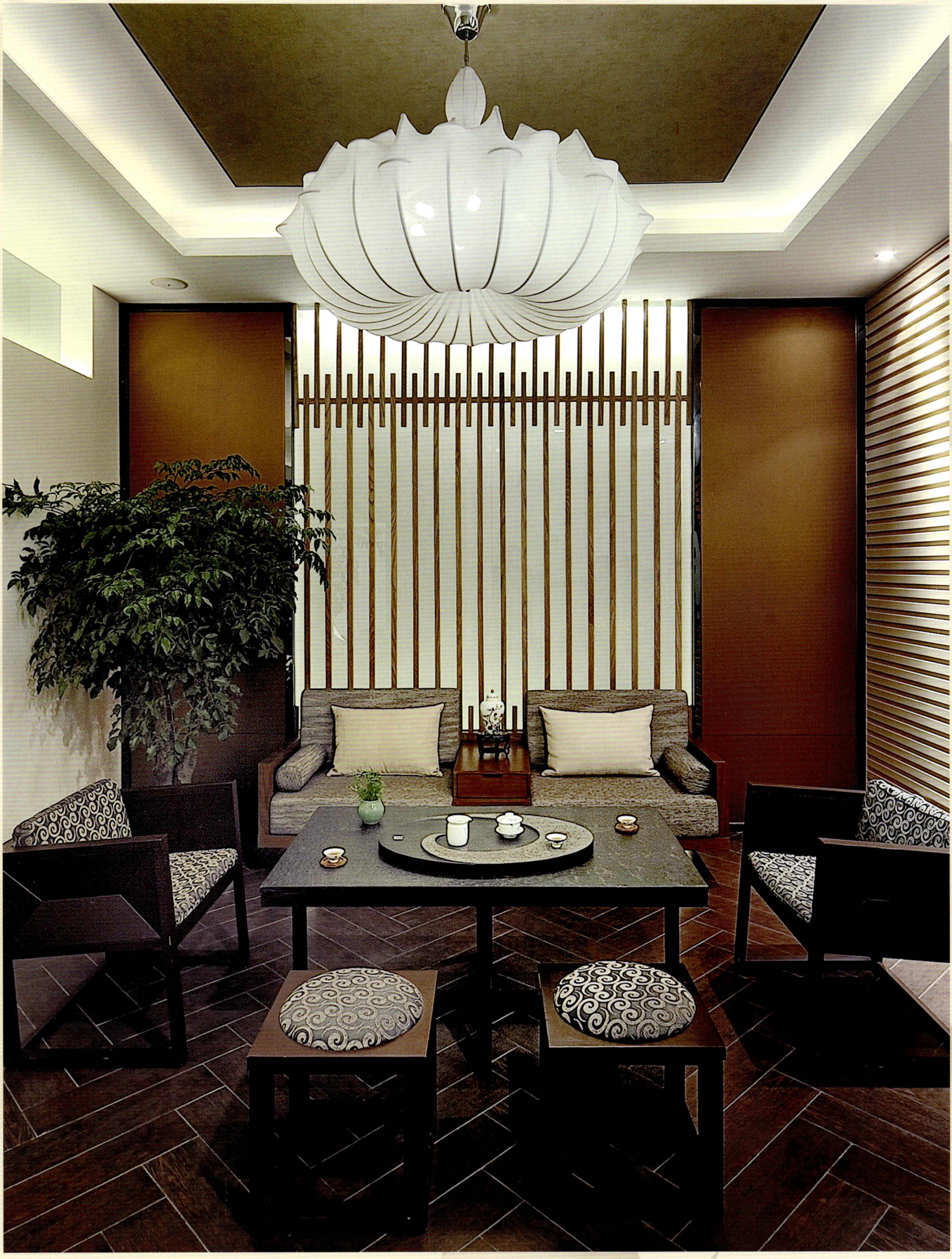

Beijing Whampoa Club

Design Agency: Neri&Hu Design and Research Office
Designer in Charge: Lyndon Neri and Rossana Hu
Project team members: Andrew Roman (Associate – in charge), Erika Lanselle, Windy Zhang
Client: Beijing Financial Street Holdings in collaboration with Whampoa Club
Location: Beijing, China
Area: 2,080 m²
Photographer: Derryck Menere

Beijing Whampoa Club is situated in a reconfigured traditional Chinese courtyard house amidst a cluster of modern curtain wall high rises on Beijing's financial street. From the onset, the overriding question concerning the design was how to "properly" engage the traditional Chinese courtyard typology with a restaurant whose aim is to contrast a modern dining experience with traditional Chinese cooking techniques. To address this, Neri & Hu explored different ways of occupying the traditional courtyard house, providing a constant juxtaposition of new/old, fresh/stale, light/dark, open/enclosed, exemplifying the culinary concept in an architectural experience.

Upon entering the restaurant and traveling through the corridors, one is surrounded by a completely white space. Solemn and serene, the purity of the space draws attention to the Chinese construction details rather than obscuring it with colorful imagery, as in history. The white corridors provide rest for the eyes before their transition to the various decadent destinations.

In contrast with the white corridors, the Bar is all black. Here, the traditional Chinese screen has been replaced and re-interpreted with a custom-made pattern – rings of water overlapping one another, drawing in the water from the courtyard.

The Private Dining Rooms are each a different color, framed by lacquered custom screens. The decadence of Chinese culture is evident with the northernmost room – historically the most auspicious – the most elaborate.

The project site is actually a courtyard house re-built that one used to stand, with a parking garage trenched below. For this reason the structures are considered "semi-historical." As commentary on this recent demolition trend and disregard for historic preservation, the first courtyard was hollowed out and opened to the level below, resulting in a physical lowering. Glass was then installed to create a reflection pool filled with water, a peaceful setting in memory of courtyard houses long gone.

The Grand Staircase showcases images glorifying the preparation of food. Moving along the staircase, one can experience, stage by stage, the lengthy preparation process involved in Chinese cuisine. Upon arrival below, one is seated to then experience the food itself.

027

Light streams through the 'broken' courtyard above and reverberates across thousands of stainless steel discs in the Public Dining Room. The steel discs reflect one's own image as well as allowing glimpses of the gutted courtyard above: a reminder. This lower courtyard is framed by a single stream of water – creating a dialogue with the pool above — as well as ebonized wood screens which function to recreate the halls and house that traditionally surround a courtyard. Spaces beyond the screen allow for semi-private dining and the opportunity to look back into the courtyard.

029

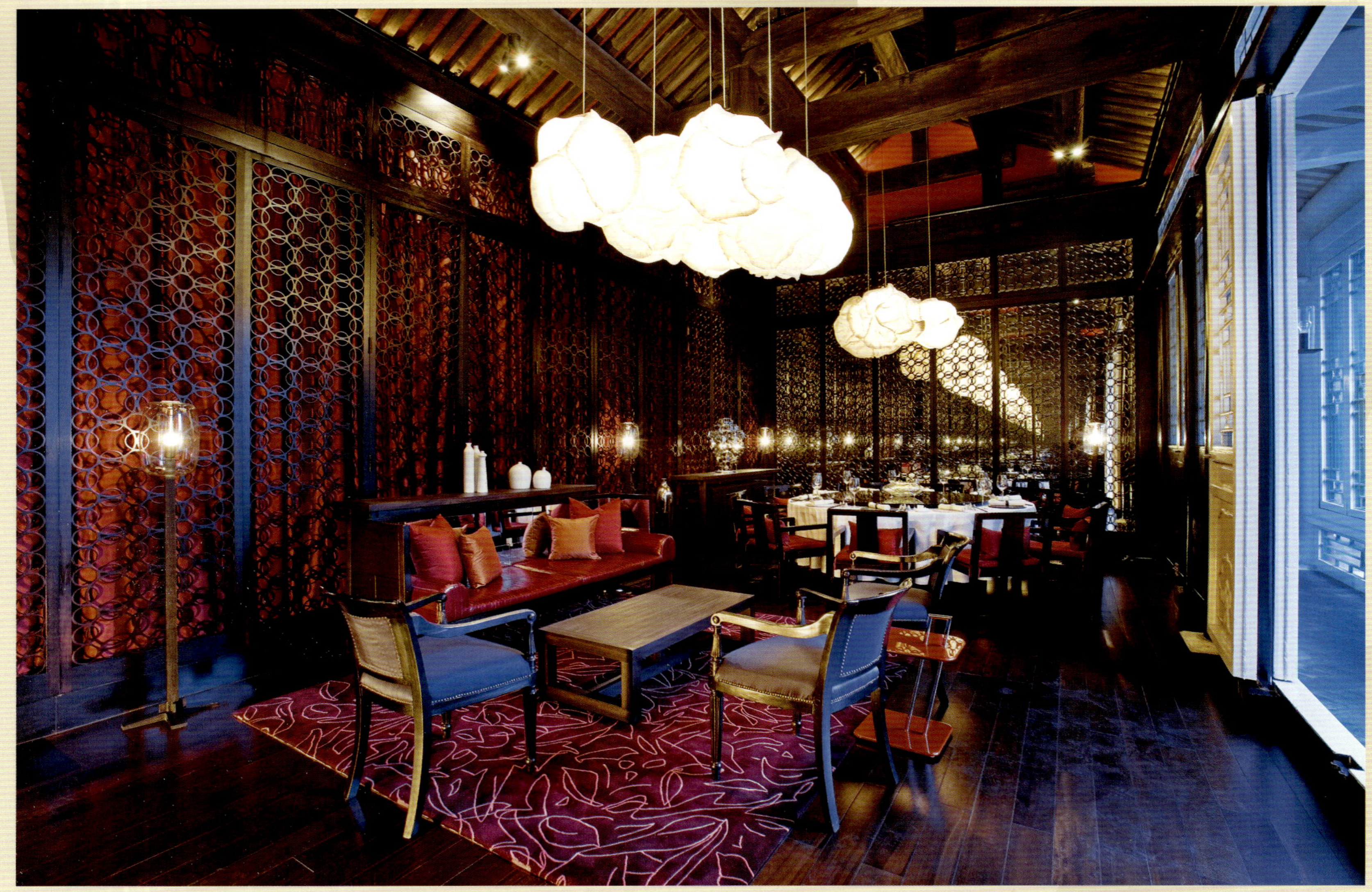

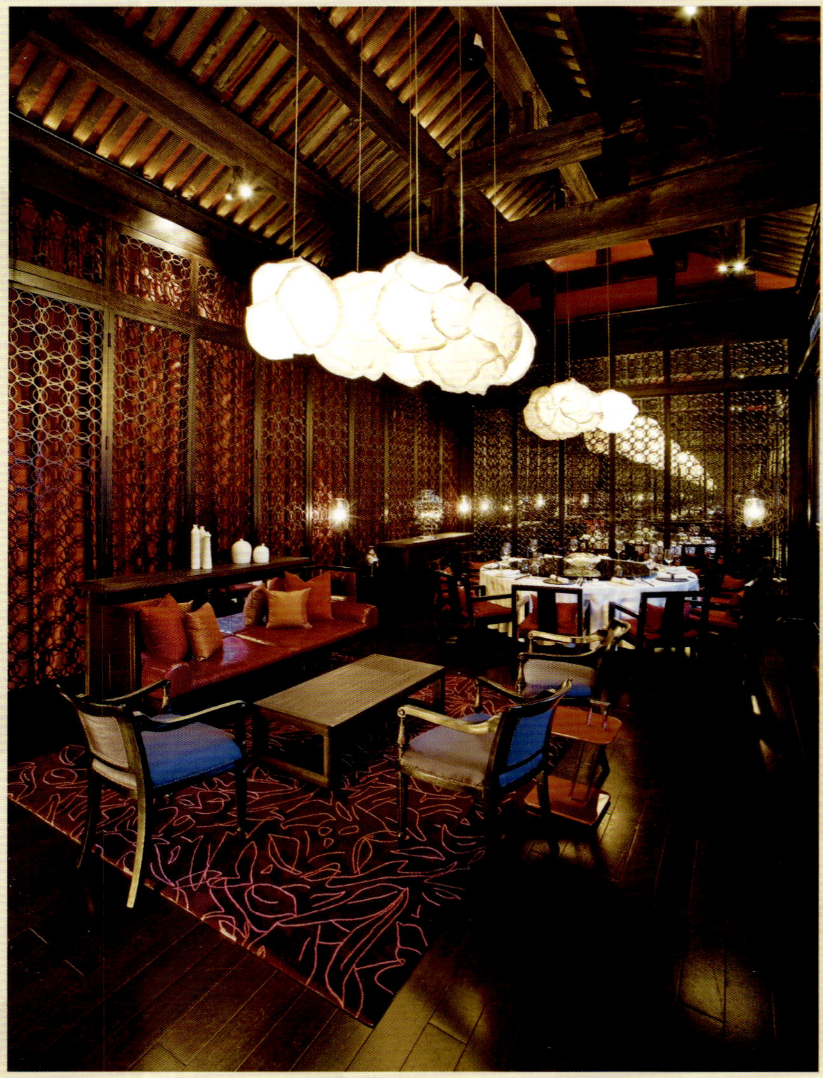

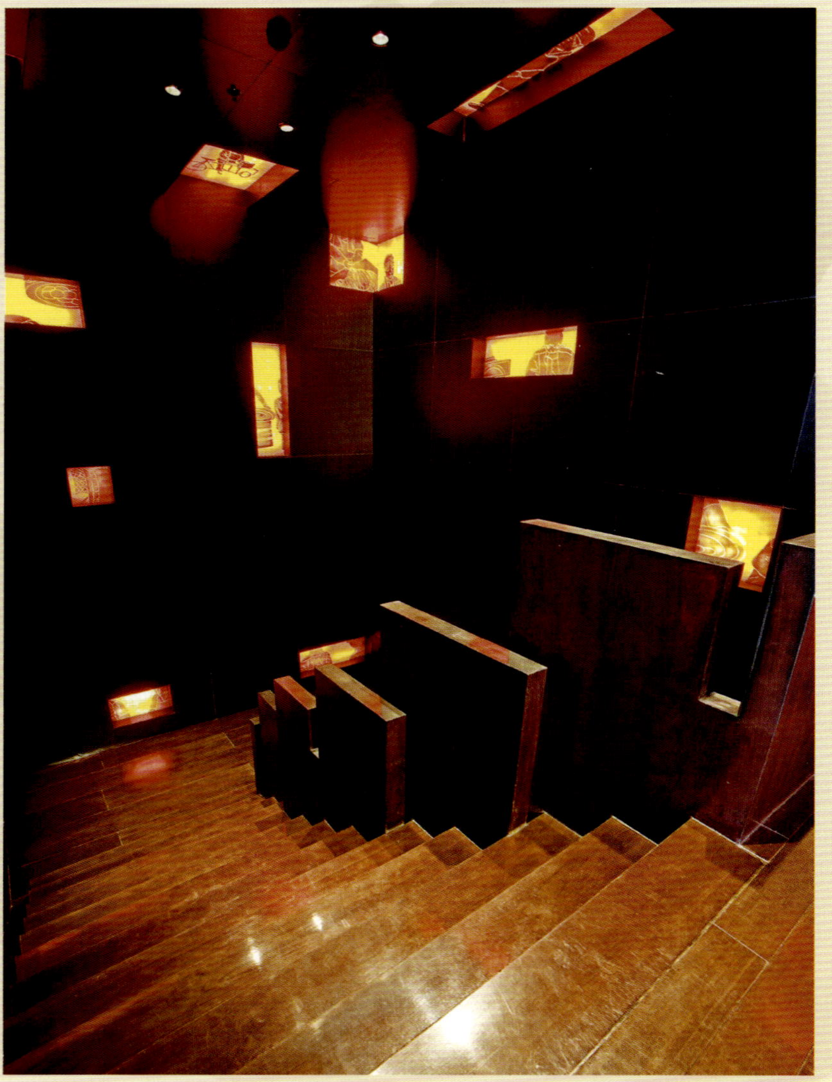

031

032

033

The Club of Joy

Design agency: Shenzhen Horizon Space Design Co., Ltd.
Designer: Han Song
Location: Ningbo, China
Area: 850 m²
Photographer: Jiang He Photography

Based on Park Hyatt Hotel, this project is on the natural scenic spot of Dongqian Lake in Ningbo, exclusively possessing cultural landscapes such as small putuo, carved stone group of the southern song dynasty etc., which is an unparalleled geographical advantage.

The club perfectly matches Park Hyatt Hotel on space and vision. In the space, we strengthen oriental sense of propriety and superiority by traditional Chinese architectural space sequence; on the vision, we use exquisite materials and innovative technology details with contracted match of black and white color to show Dongqian Lake's artistic conception of misty rain and inkwash painting.

We adhere to Park Hyatt Hotel's consistent high quality in hardware and intelligent system, which accidentally makes the customers feel Park Hyatt's nature character.

For example, once you enter the club, all the curtains slowly open for you and sunshine spills into inside; when you press the switch, the toilet door will automatically hide into the wall; the intelligent closestool works autoinductively.

People shall have comfortable experience of high quality everywhere.

We set up independent exclusive high-end customer reception space, where there is independent wine bar and toilet. Please enjoy the honorable and exclusive reception services.

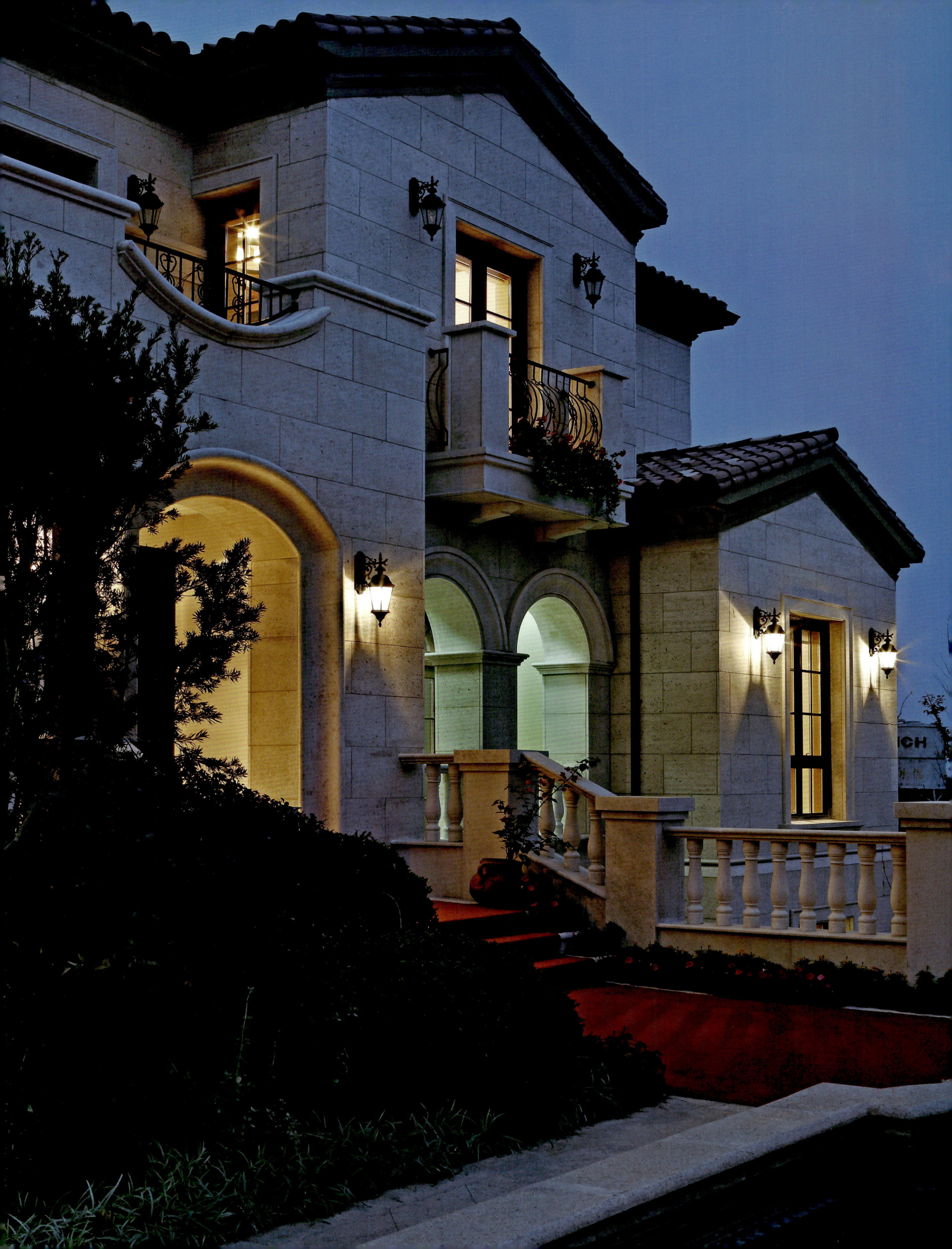
ICH

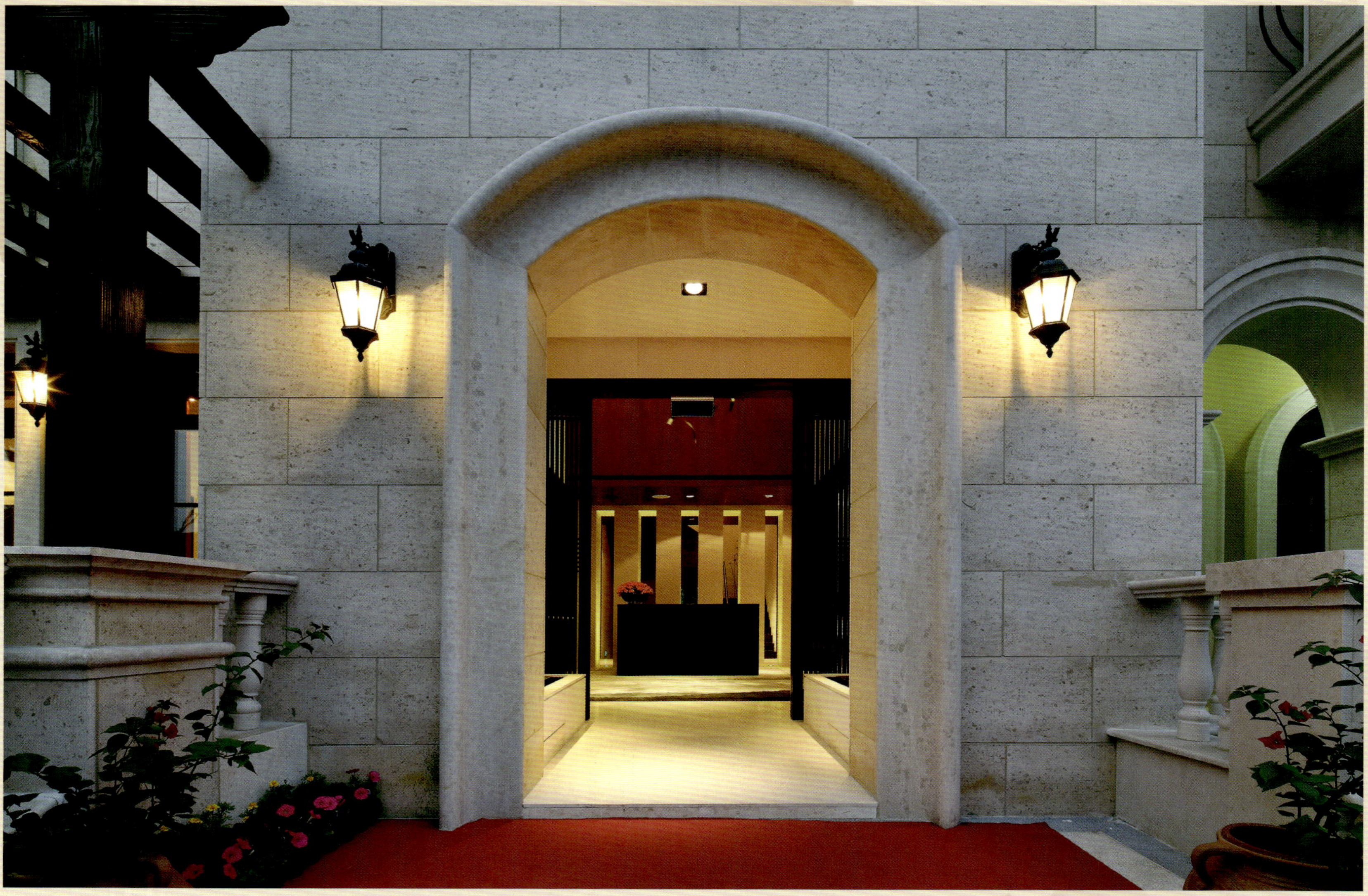

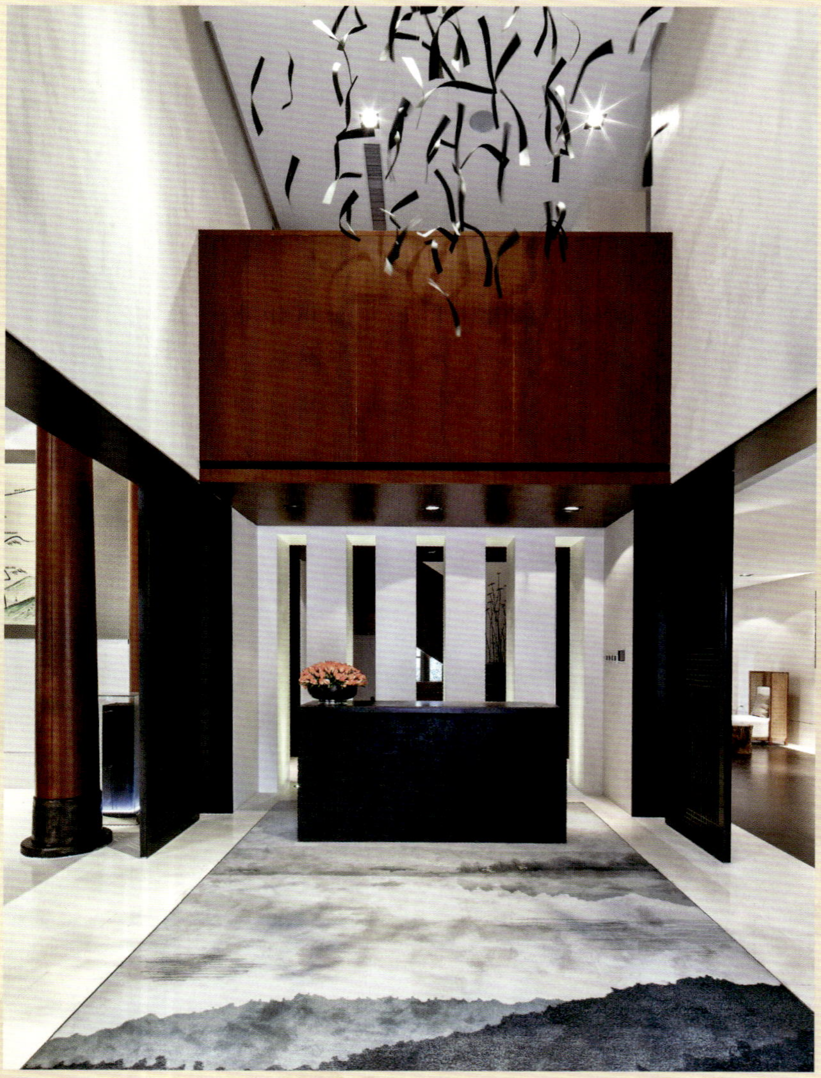

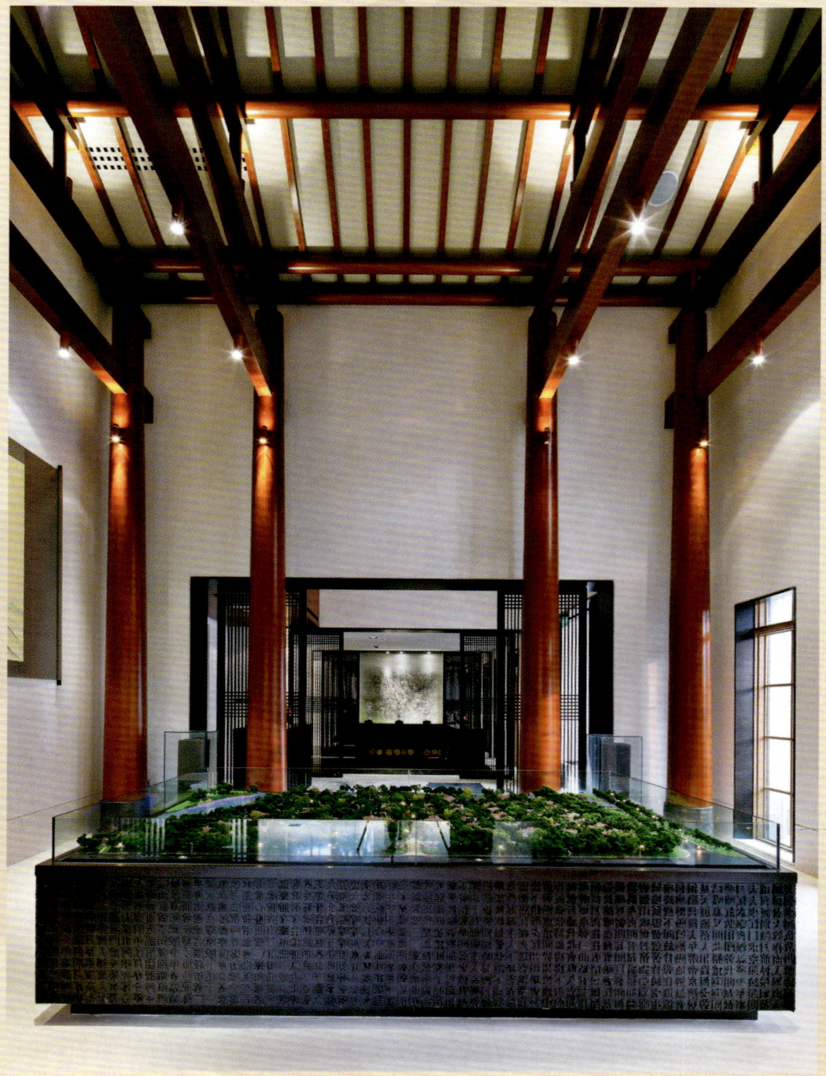

037

038

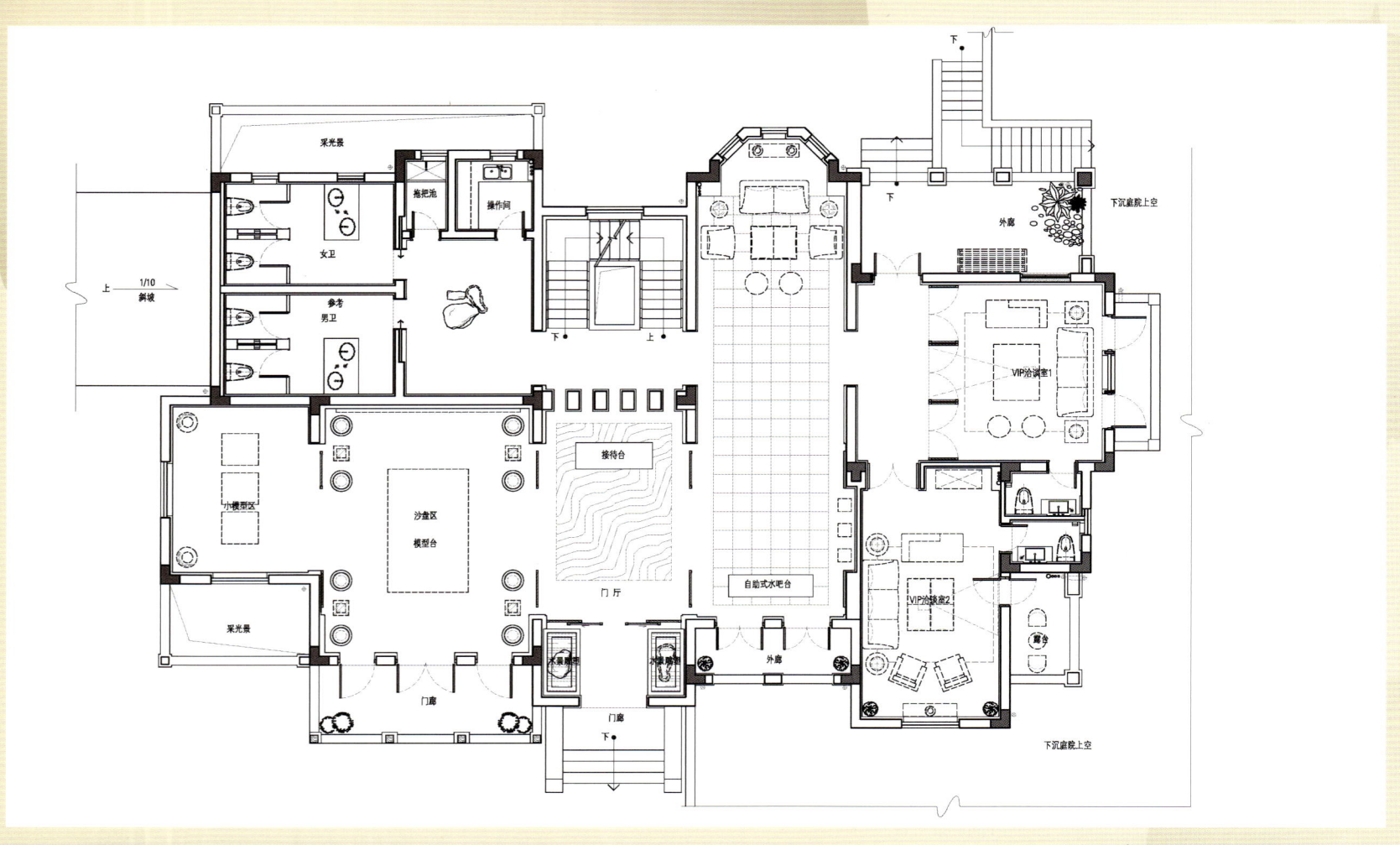

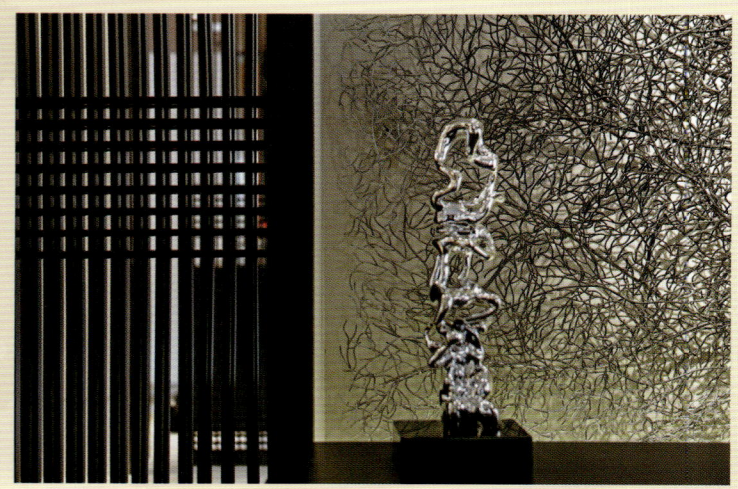

We disassemble and subdivide multiple functions of a space to ensure every space is perfect, and the quality sense is greatly enhanced.

In order to increase the new experience of the function, namely adding cultural and artistic temperament to business practices, we have designed a small private collection museum involving china, furniture, modern Chinese painting, jade and so on in the underground. The museum not only greatly improves the quality but also brings customers new visual and psychological experience. In it, you will be free from earthly restraints, with worries and distracting thoughts disappearing completely. You do fully feel the pleasure of being alone.

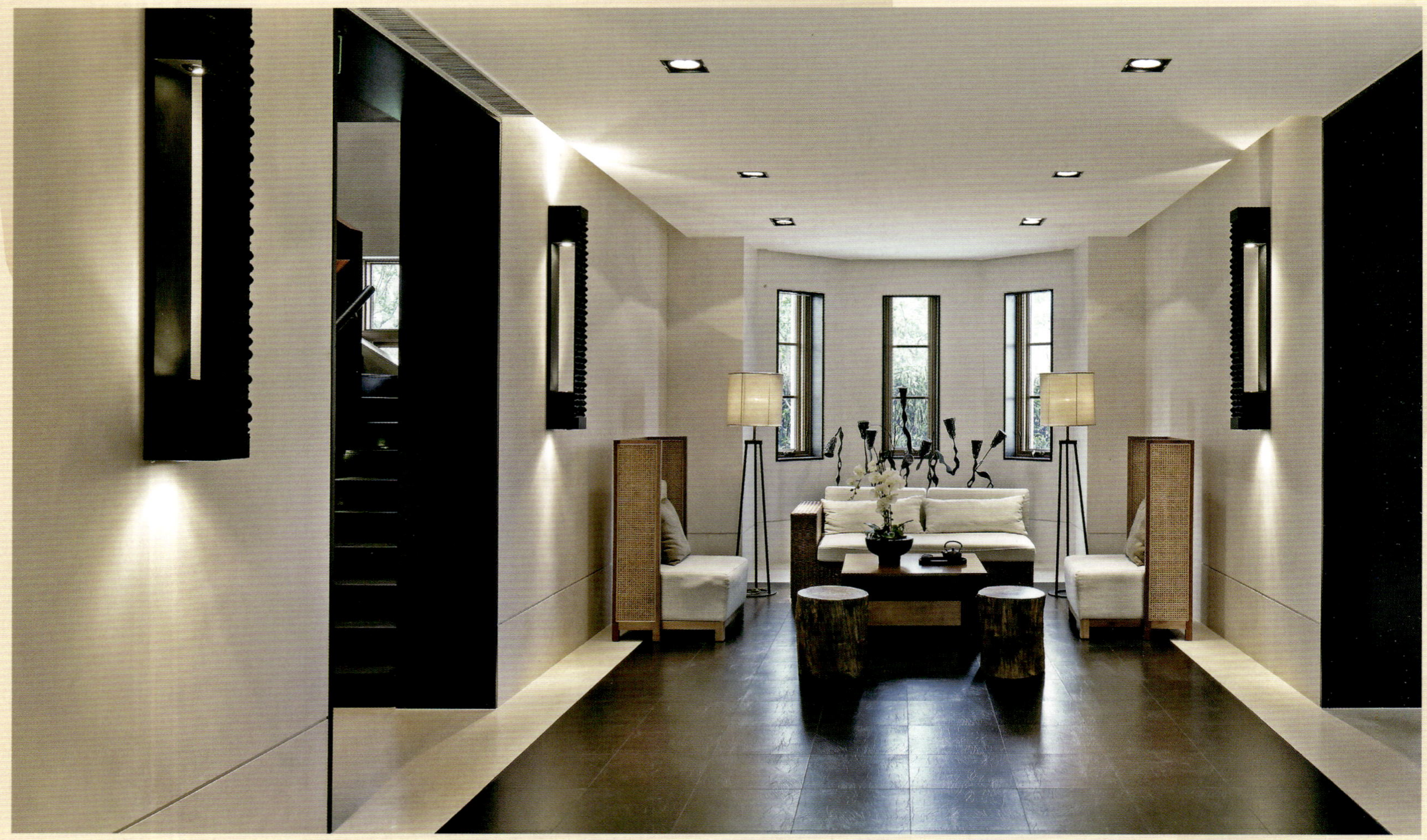

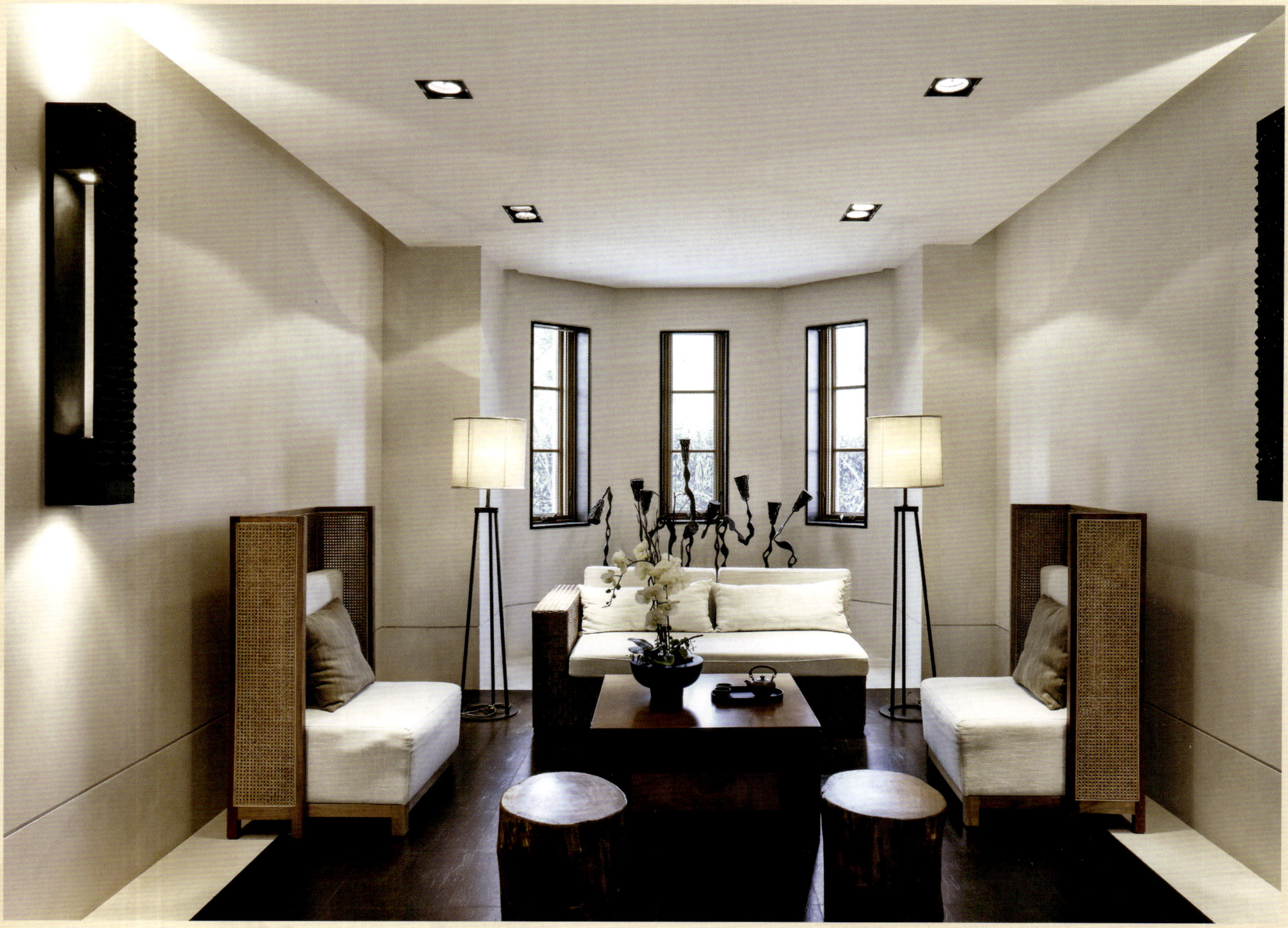

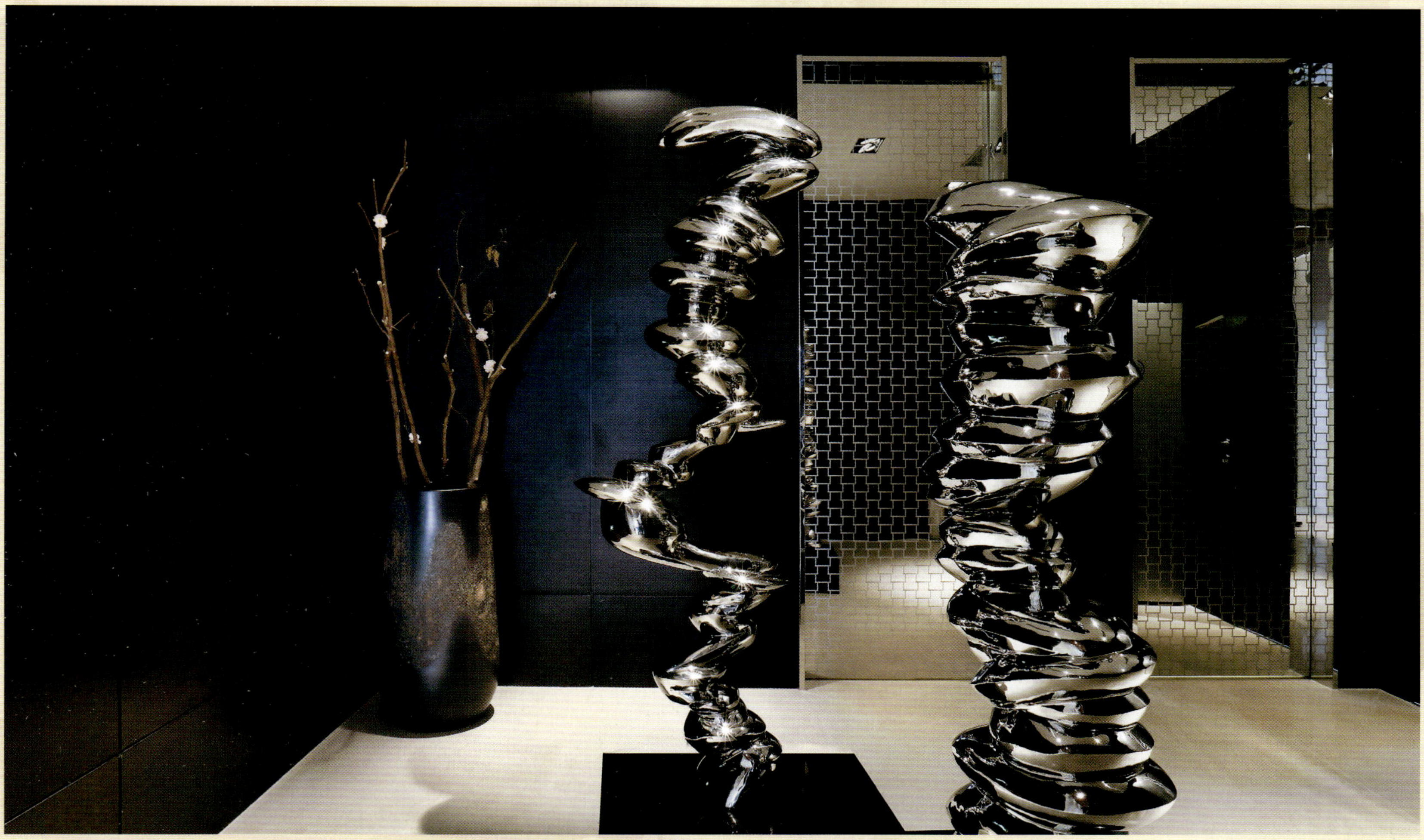
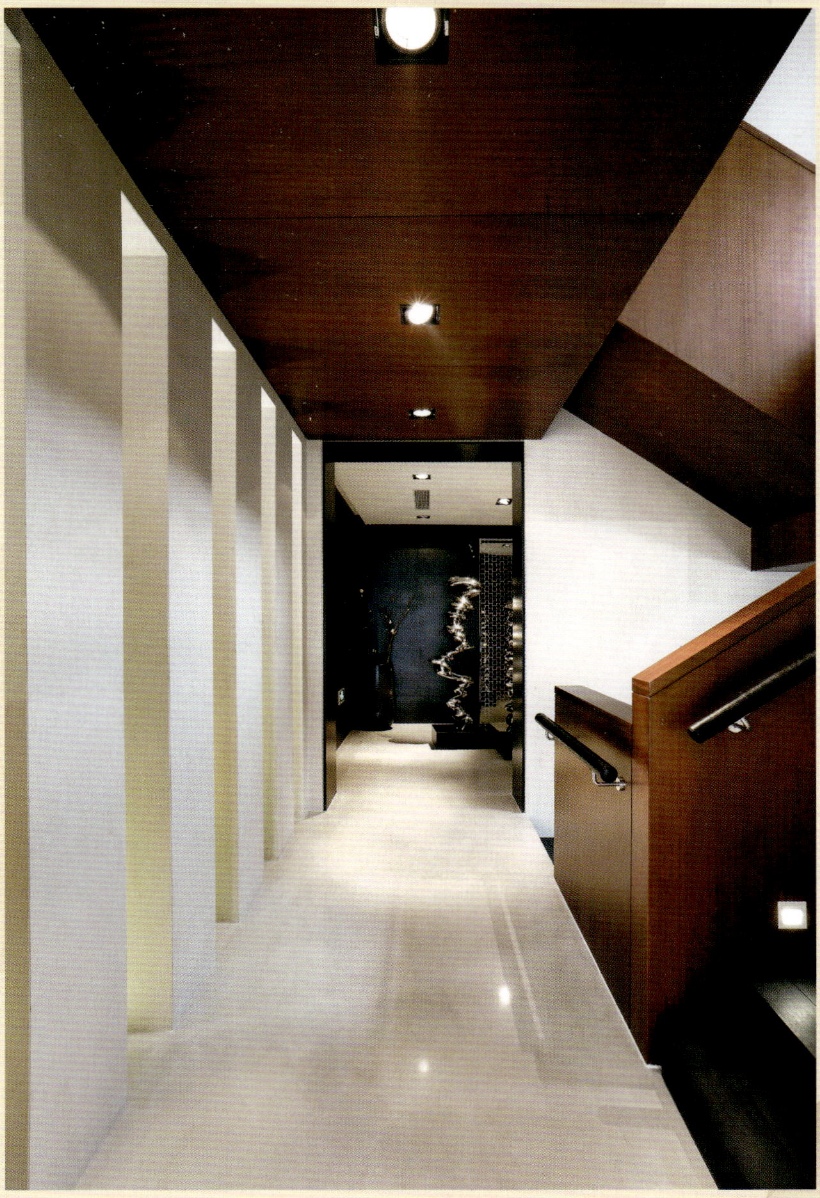
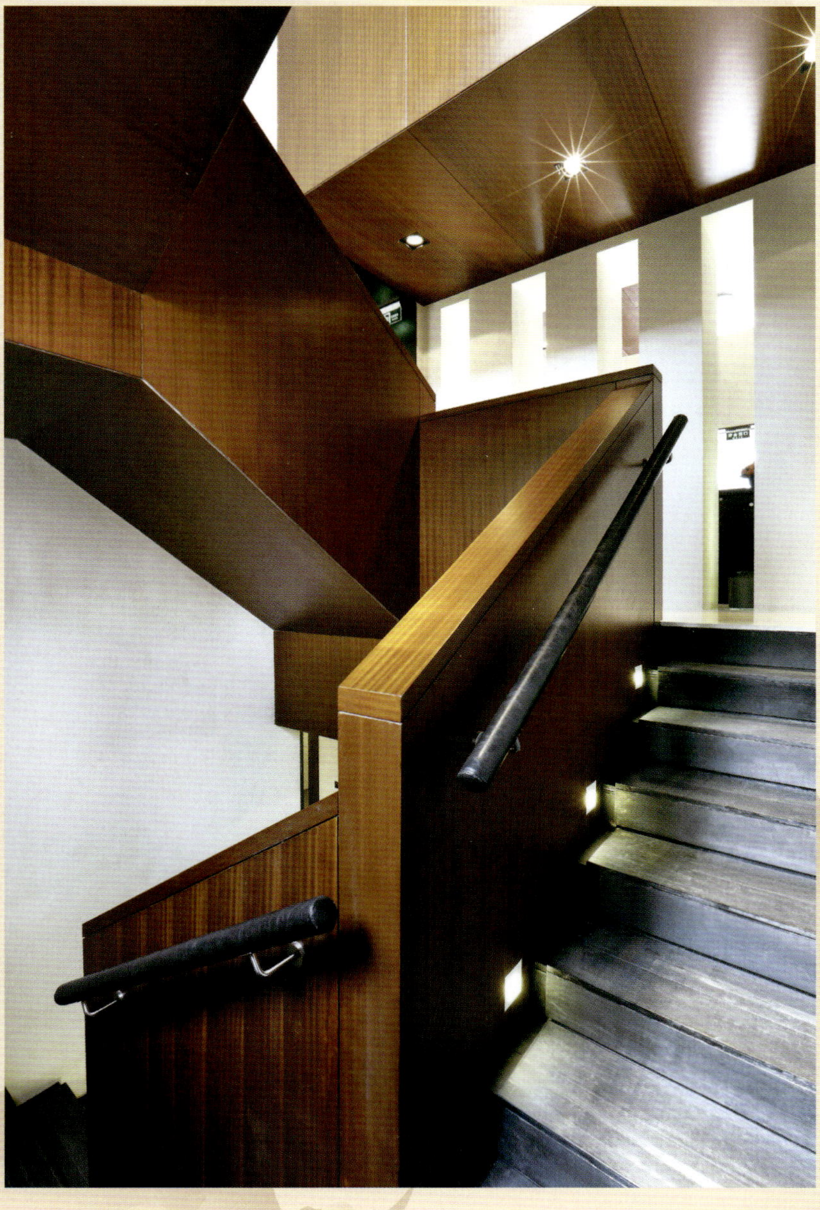

042

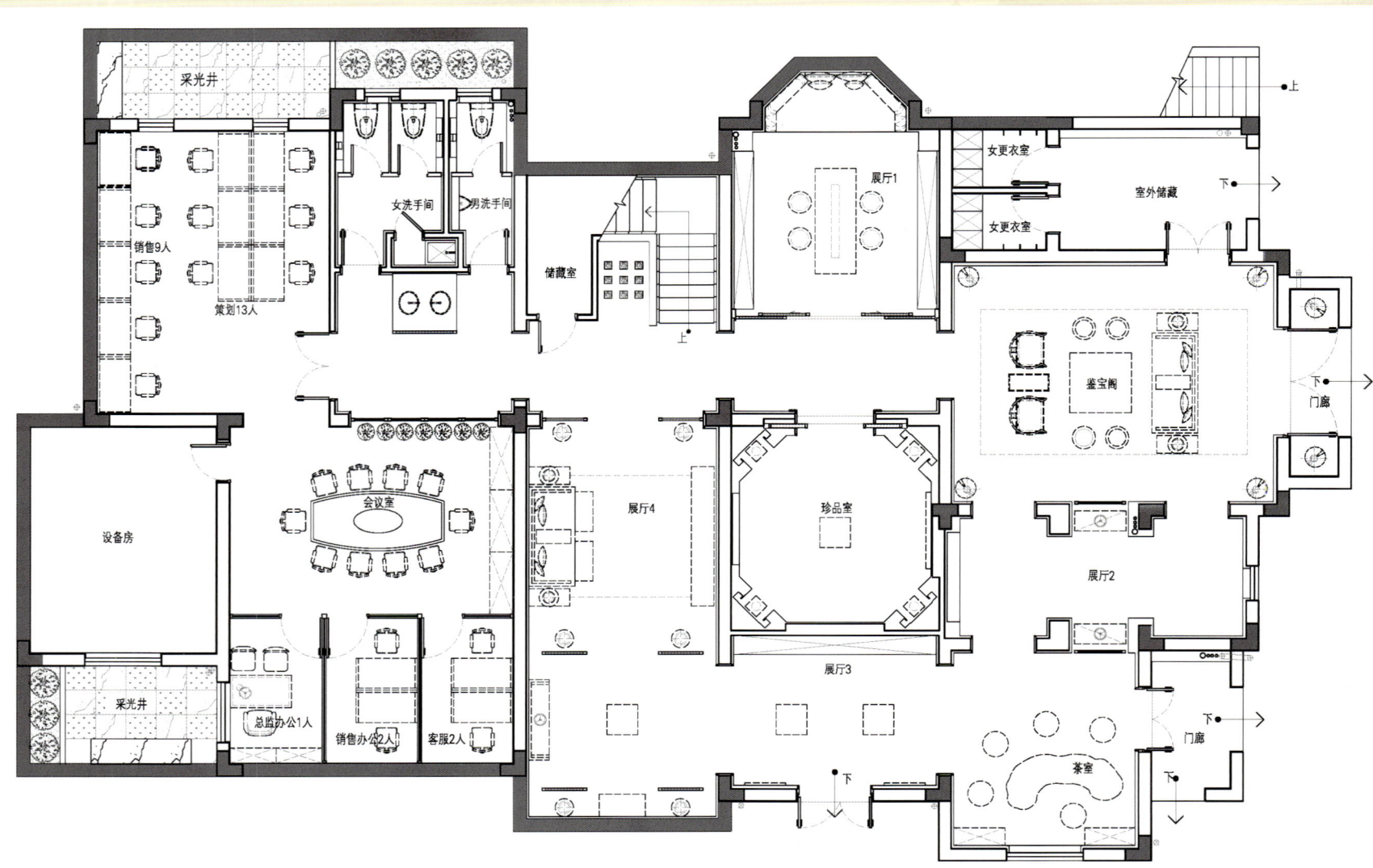

043

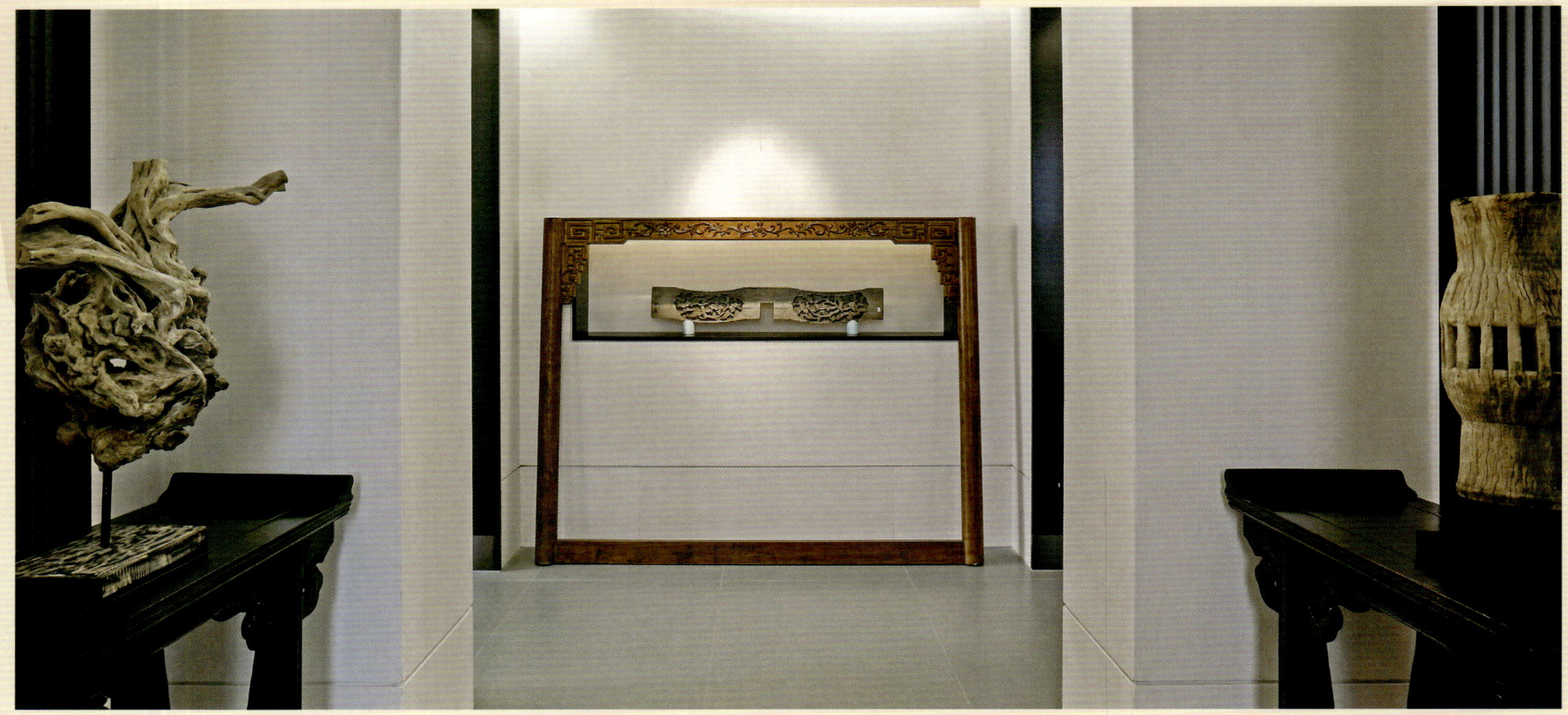
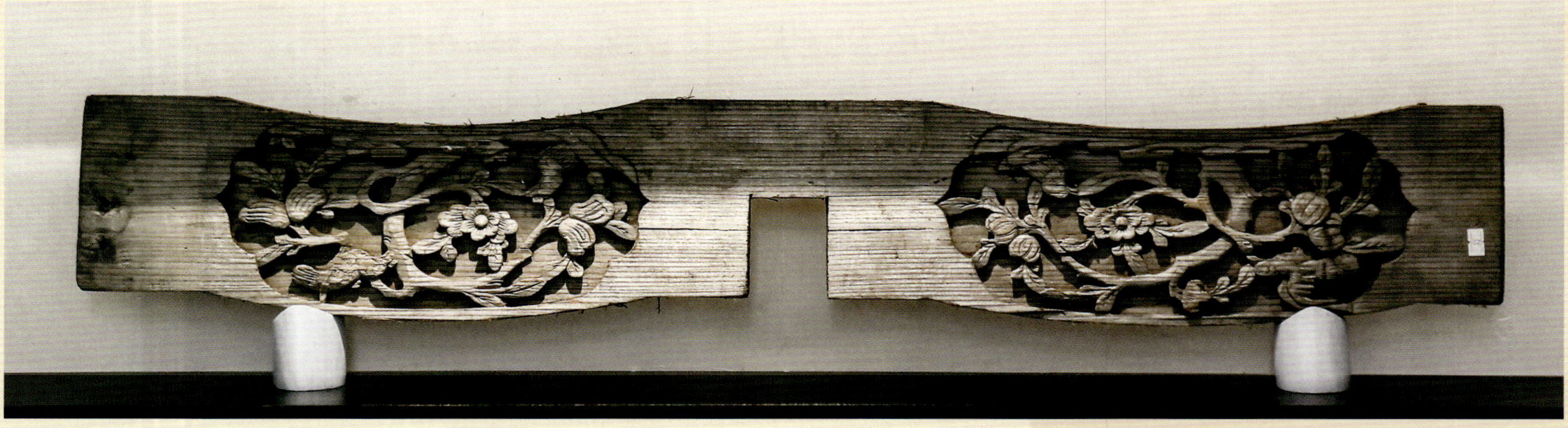
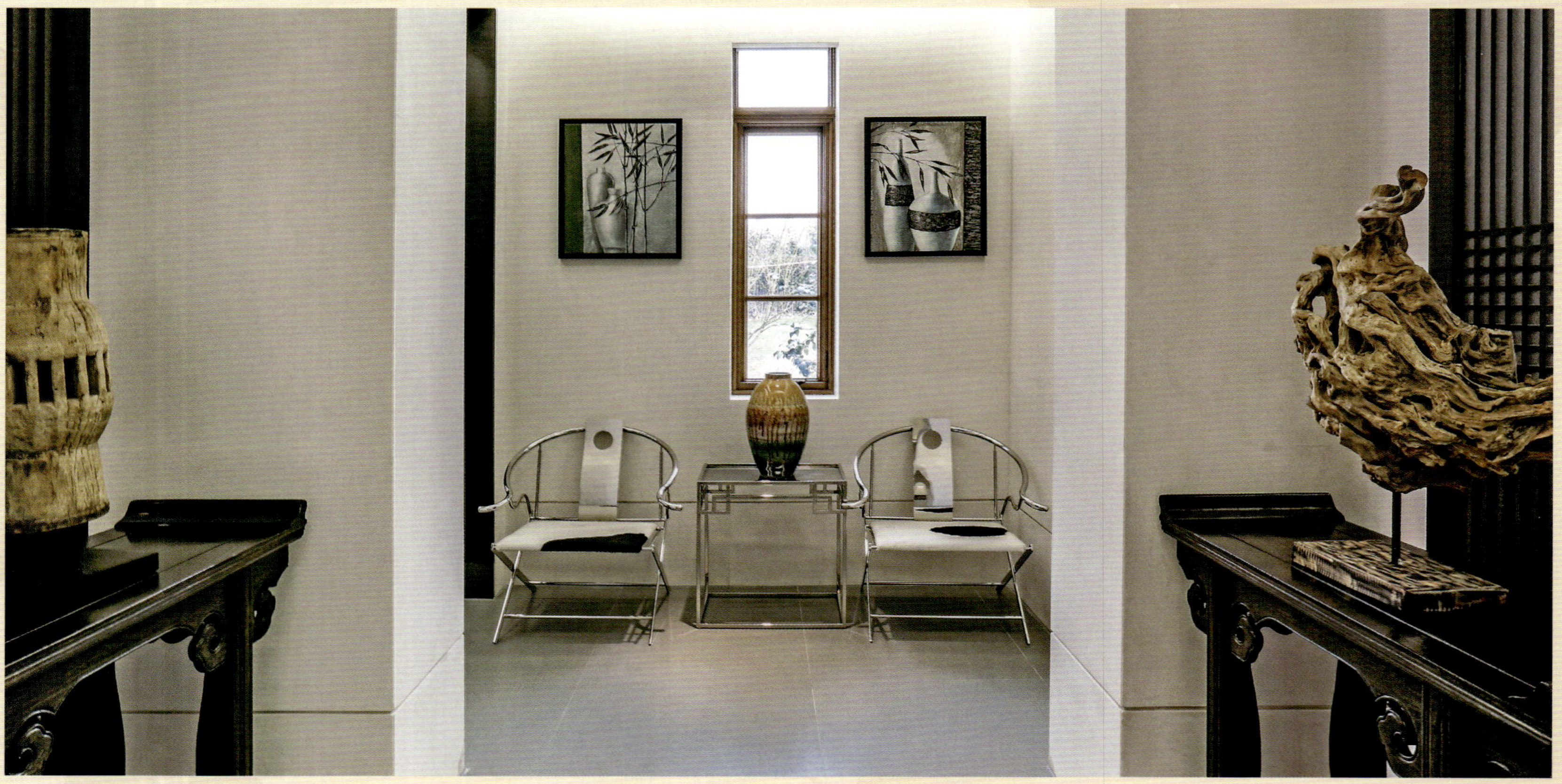

045

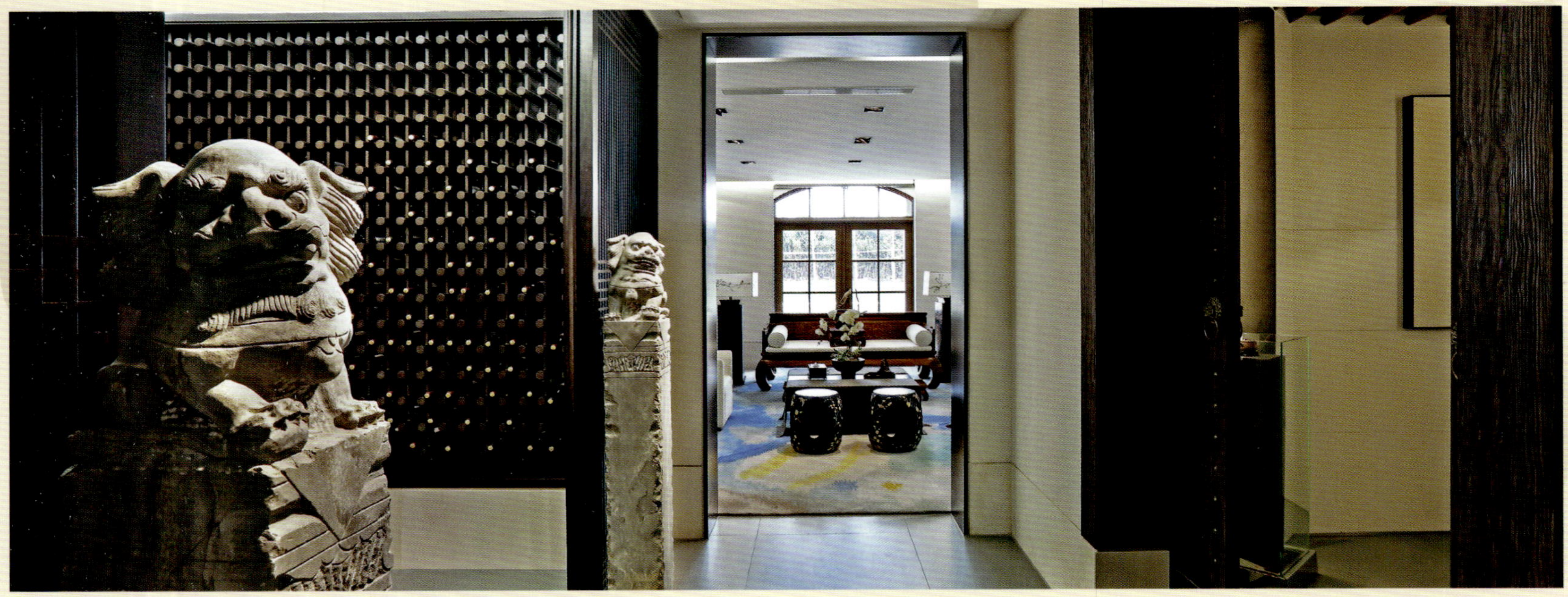

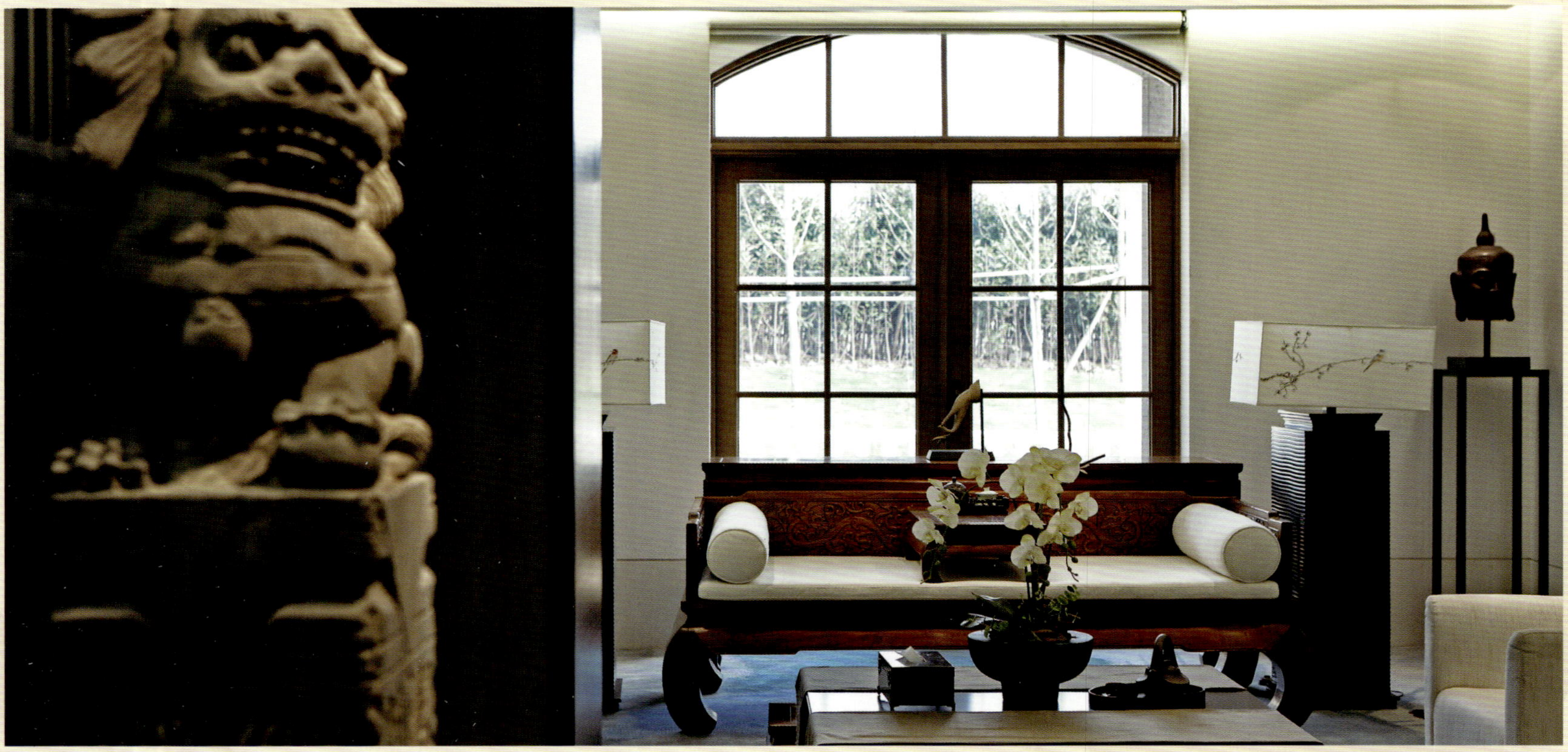

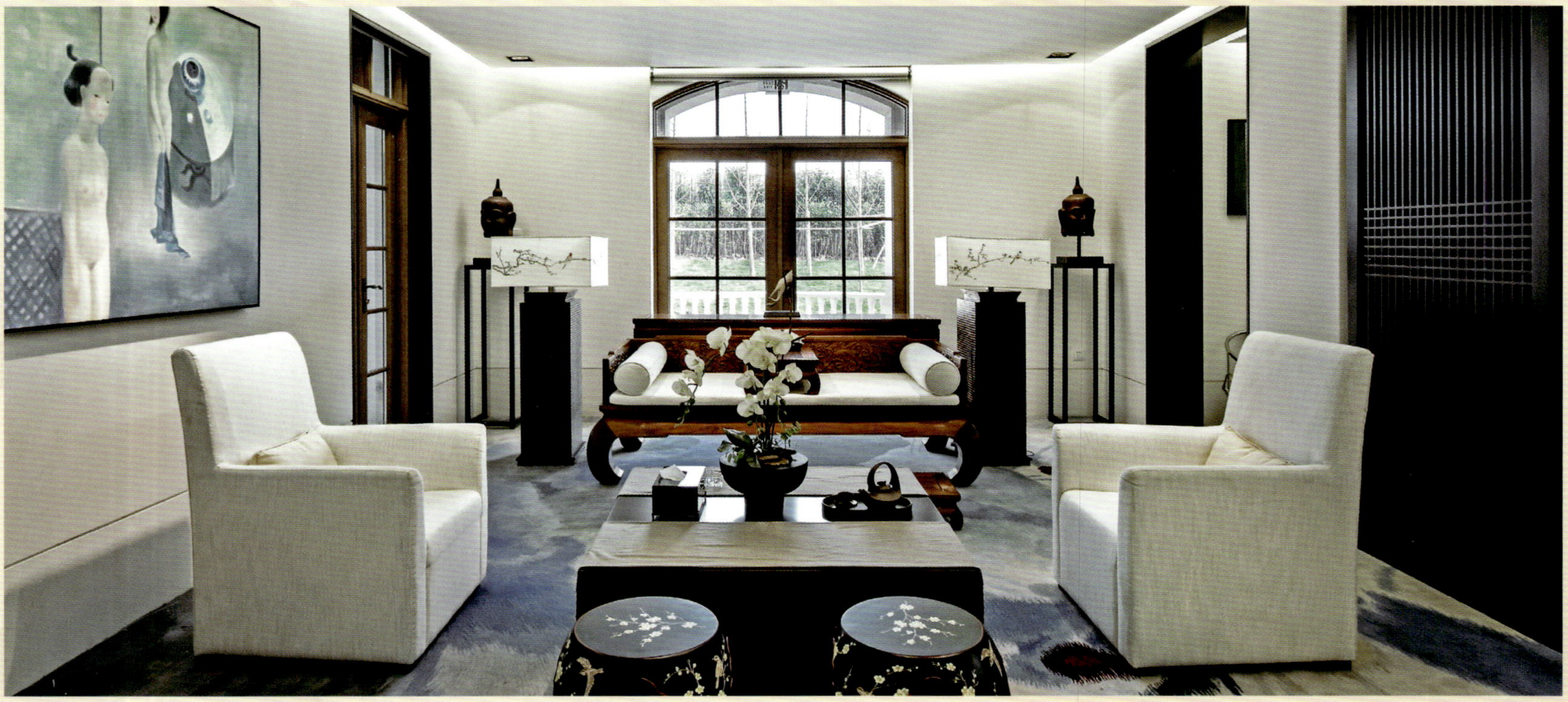

047

048

049

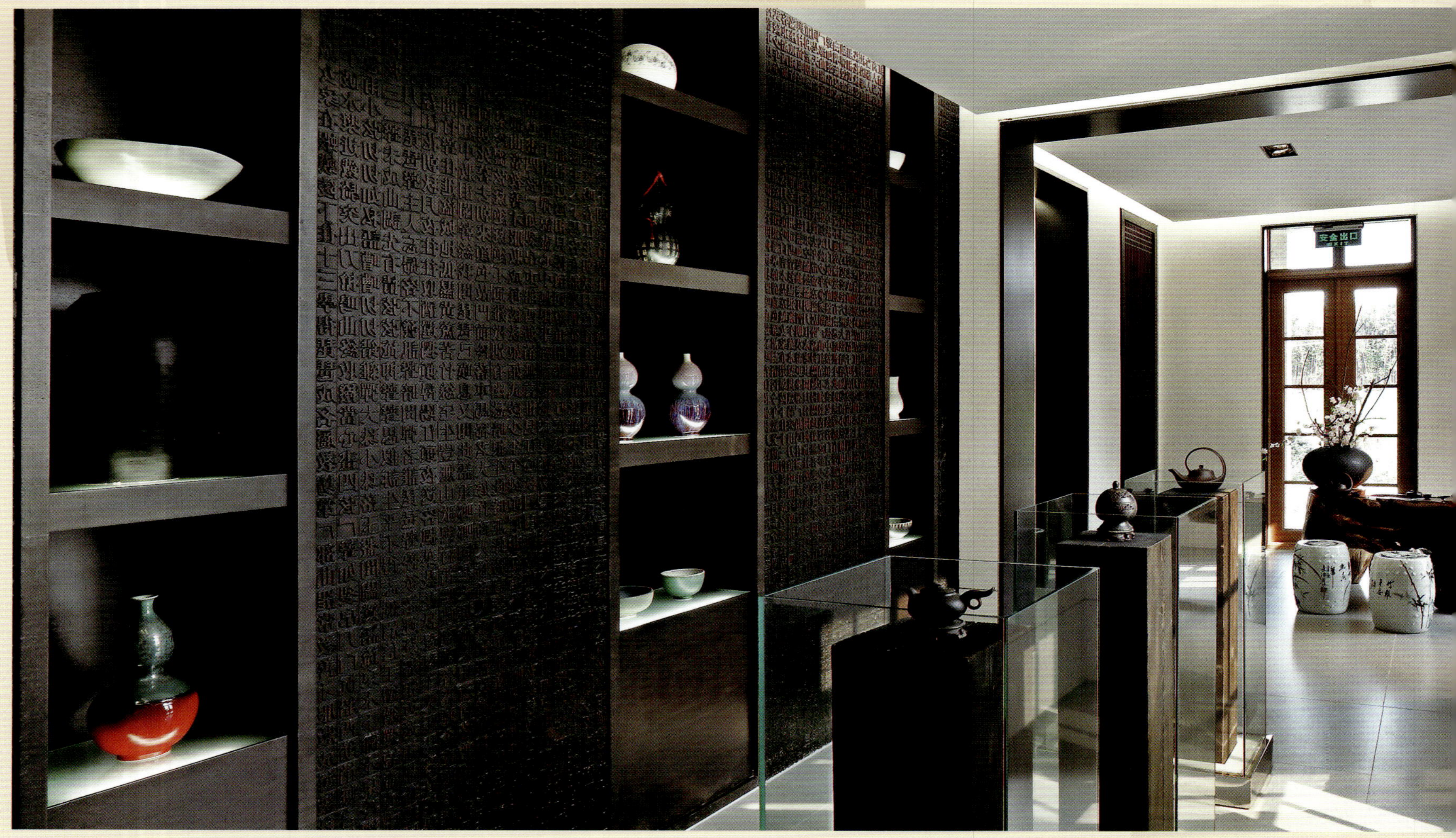
安全出口

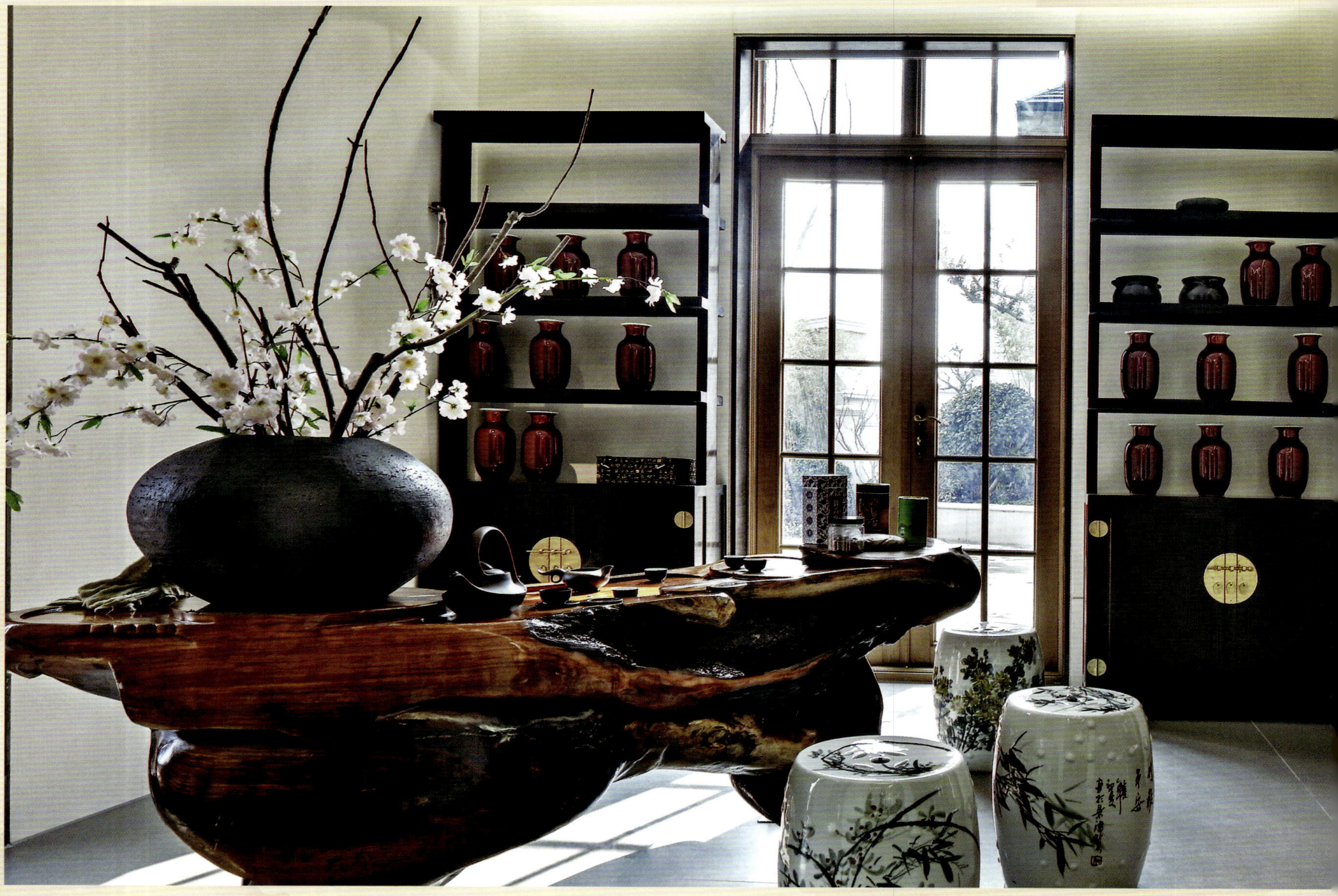

051

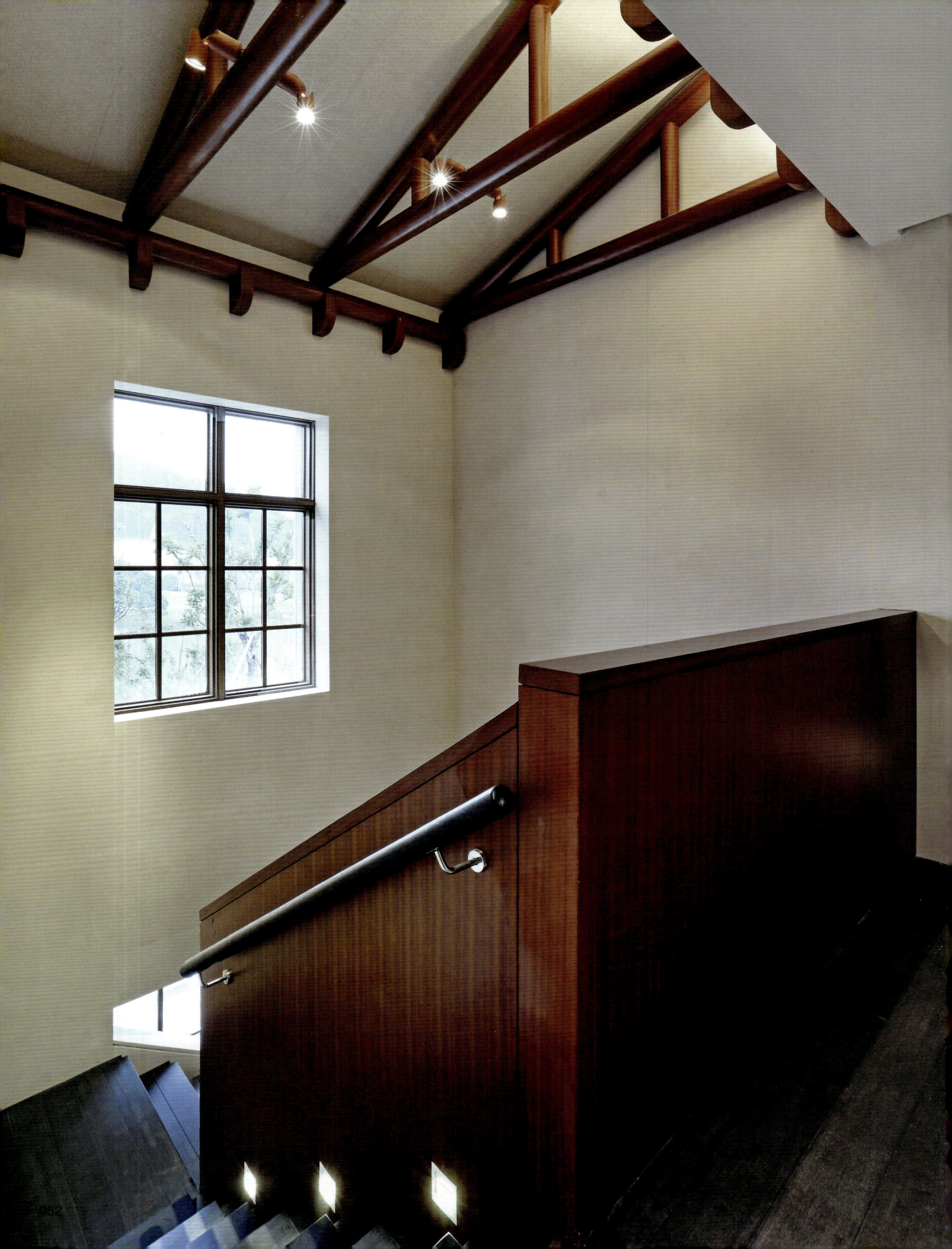

053

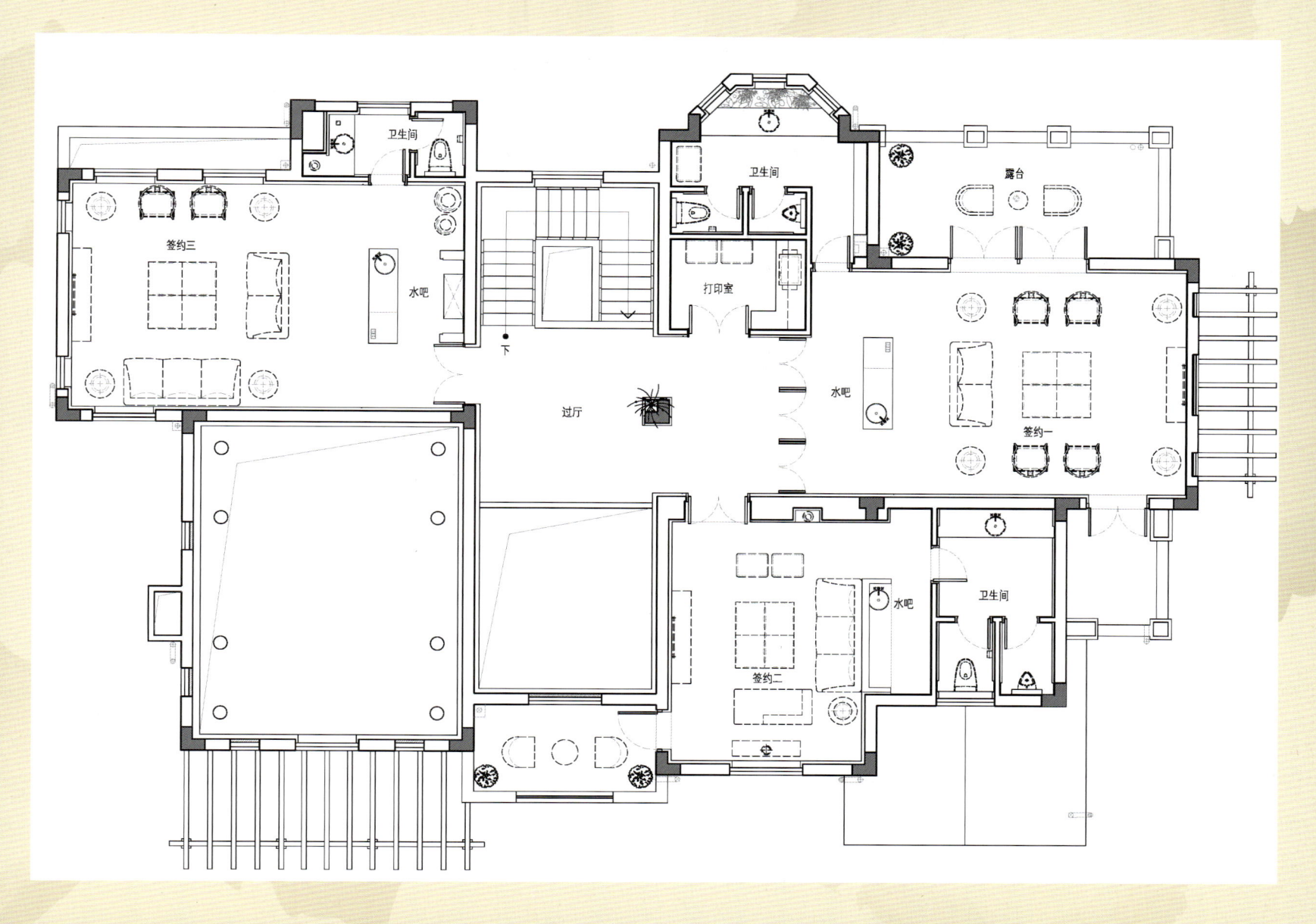

054

055

056

057

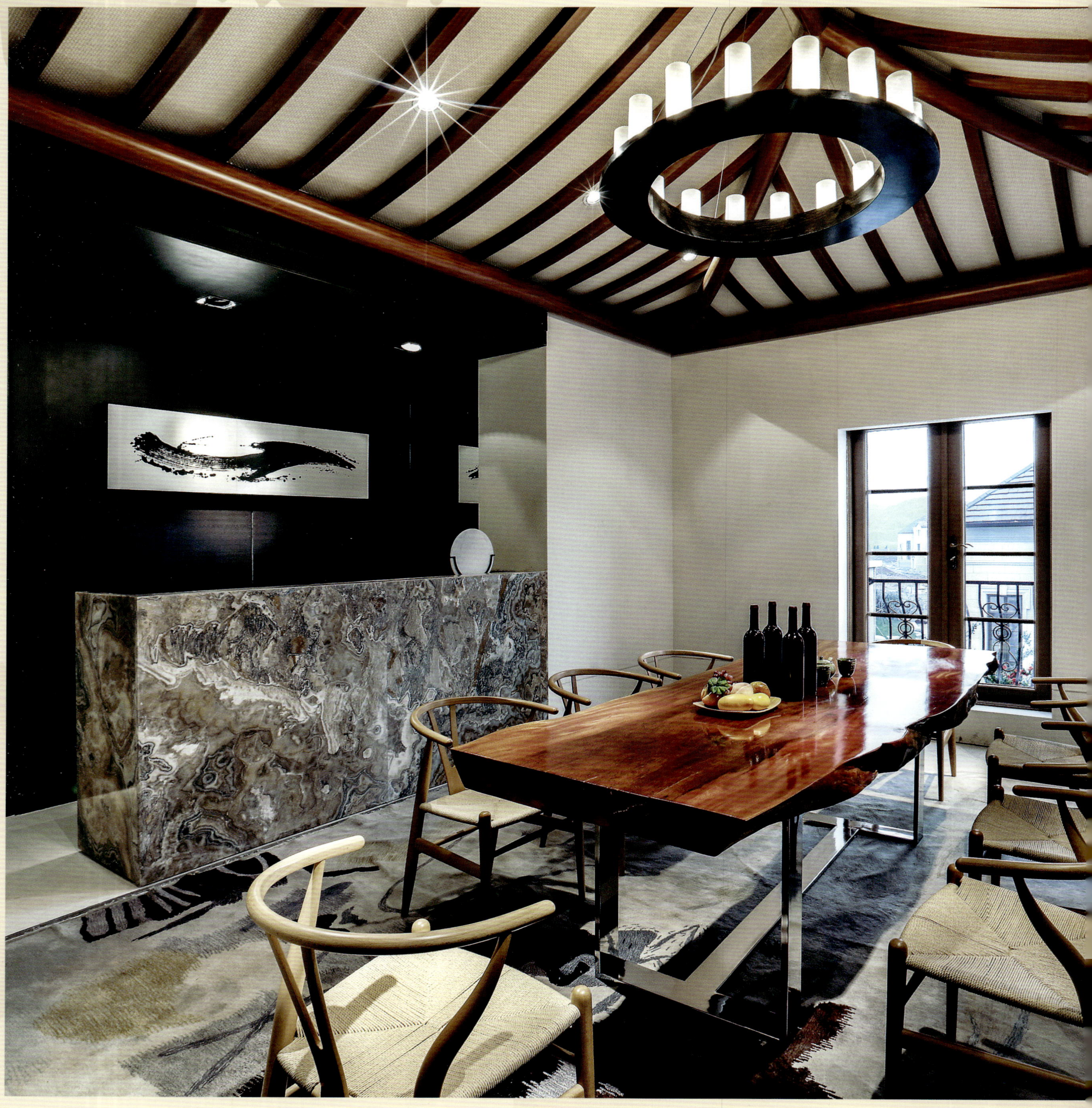

059

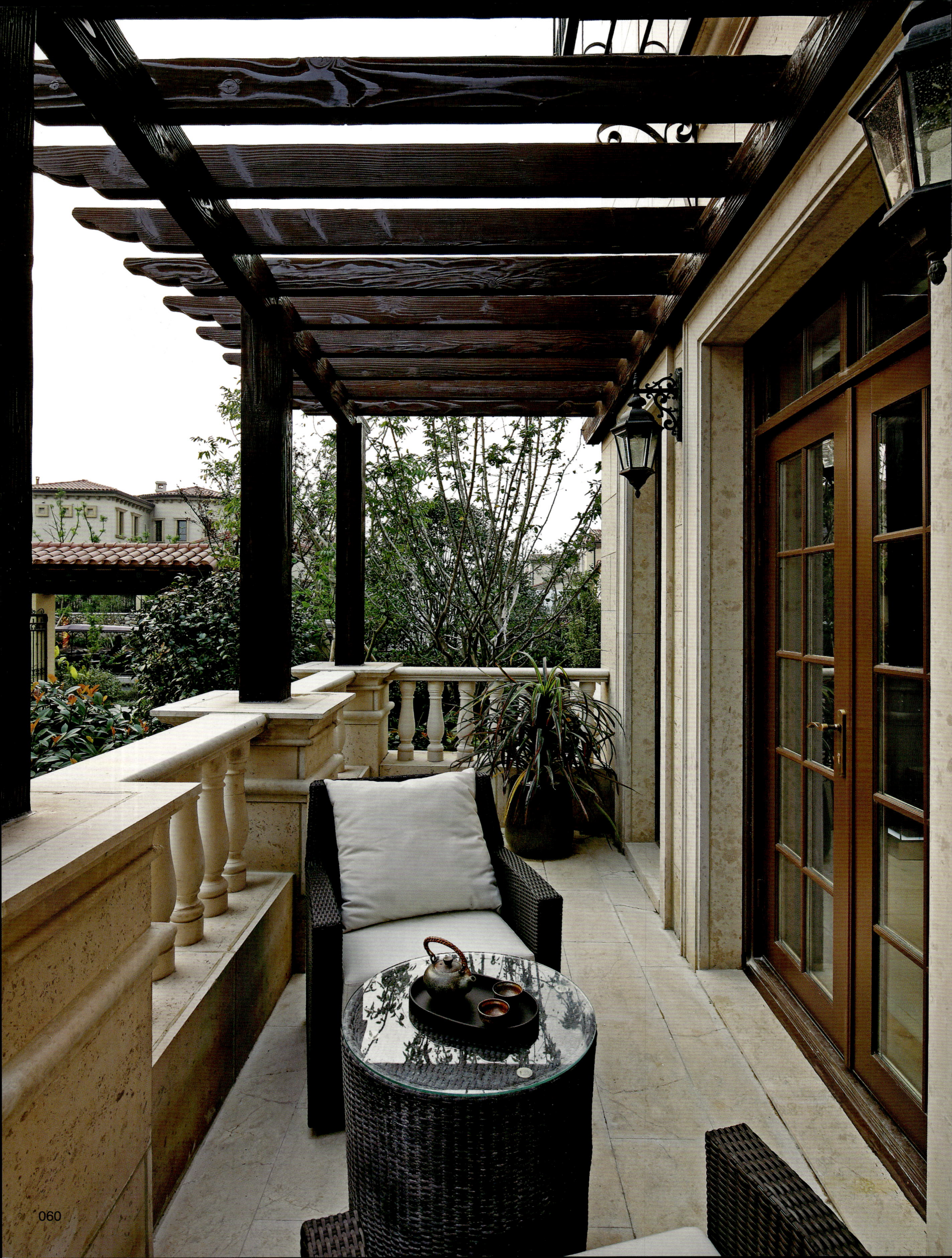

061

Tender Luxury

Designer: Hank M. Chao
Participants: Wang Yingjian, Hu Xinyue
Location: Shanghai, China
Area: 700 m²
Photographer: Maoder Chou

The form of luxury is mostly concentrated in a pile on the appearance of complex, a bit like Western rococo visual dazzling combination of that kind. But is this the only way out of the luxury expression? Or we have other options that can be more reserved expression of the so-called gorgeous? So we have a relatively quieter but equally effective way to express a sense of luxury space.

The project is located by the side of the Huangpu River, Pudong Shanghai, which is a new developed land surrounded by well-planned landscape package. For the entrance that we deliberately emphasized the depth of field and separated it by the pool to cut the moving lines of the rear leading to the toilets. To project the flow texture of the water, we placed the dynamic projection of water ripples on the toilet wall facade, which have a visual linkage of Huangpu River on both indoor and outdoor view. Turning to the seating area, we used bookcase hanging from the ceiling but not to the down floor as a separator. It does not completely block the space, but yet still can have the visual part of the penetrating sense. Metal curtain is also used in this kind of soft segment space. Besides, the bar is designed by using the practices of the carved handling, with straight lines around which makes a strong contrast. The background served as a foil to the aspen woods to make the light and shadows looming, inadvertently spilled on the ground to increase the poetic sense, just like a stone in the forest. For the walkway leading to the VIP room we set the same projection wave on the ground, and this kind of dynamic way introduces a more interesting process of entering the room, and also makes up the design defect of limitation to "hardware" which can not be interacted with people. The fireplace is also placed in the VIP room to increase the visual sense of warmth.

The overall color presents calm and restrained tone to respond to the concept that deliberately avoided the extravagant sense, but through the material is an appearance of a more deep gorgeousness. The wide amount of high ceiling and the released space is a performance of another luxury - waste of the scale, the kind of waste which can not be achieved for the visual tension by a small space, as the designer, is trying to convey a visual expression through this project.

063

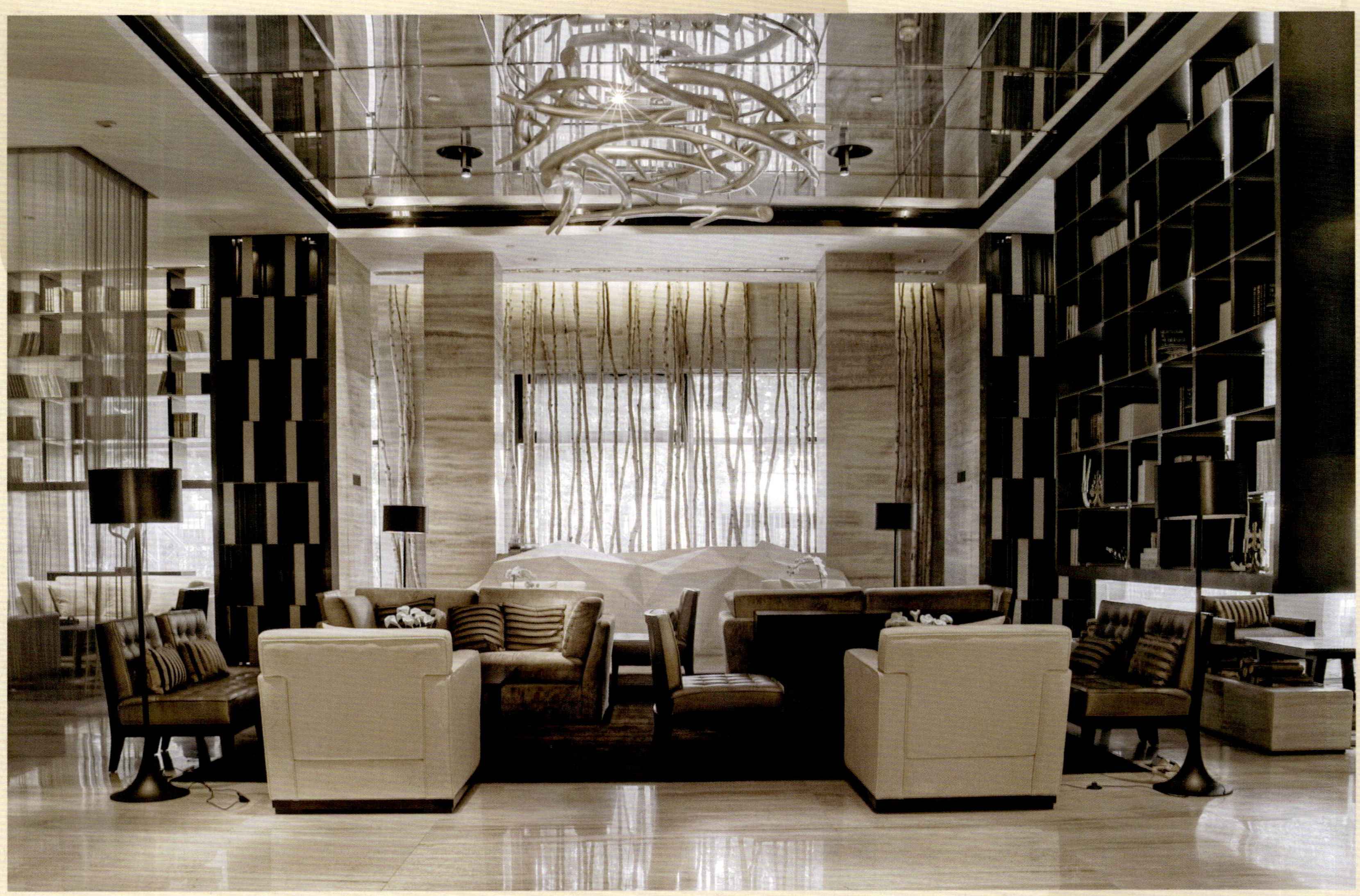

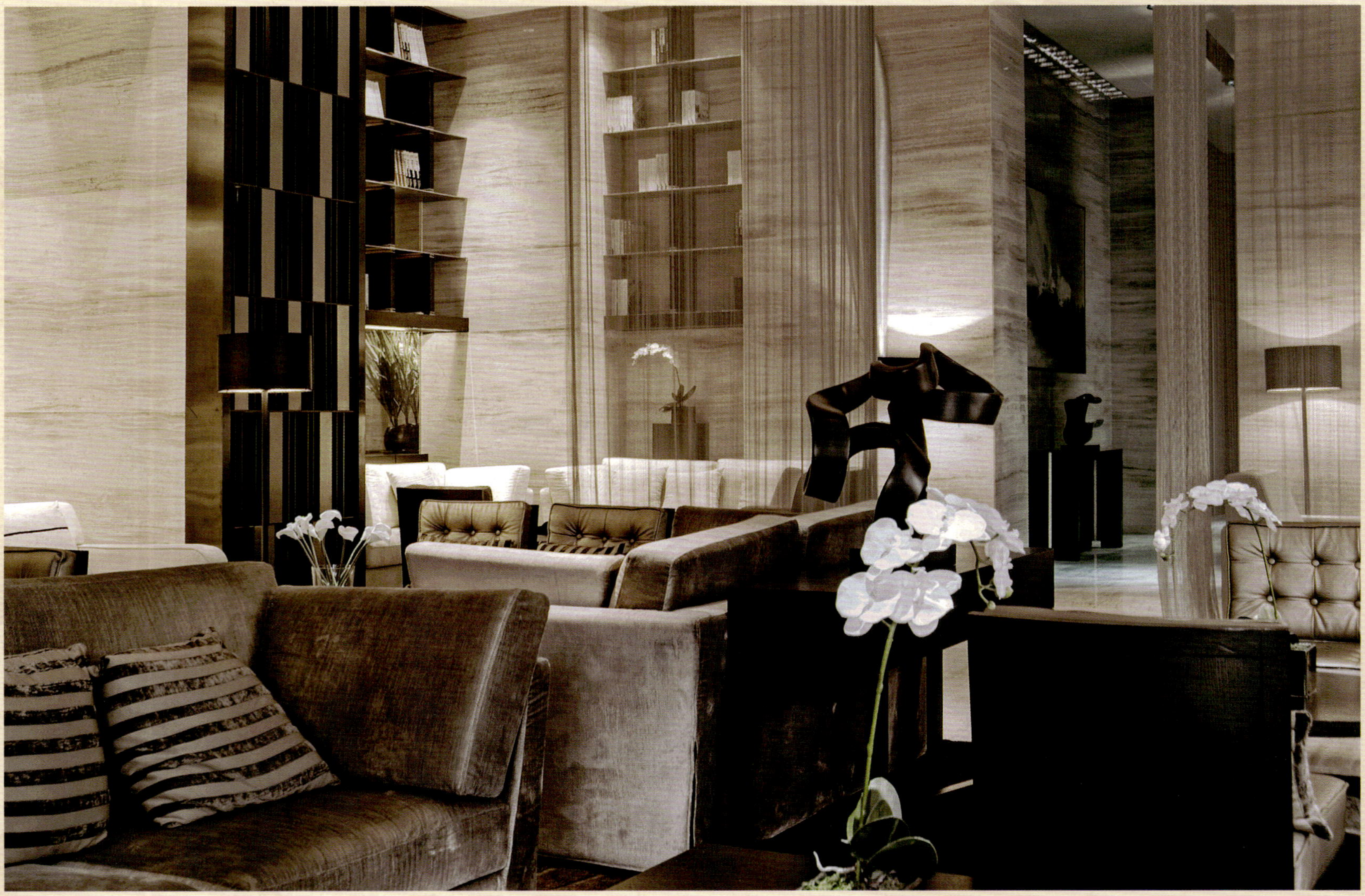

065

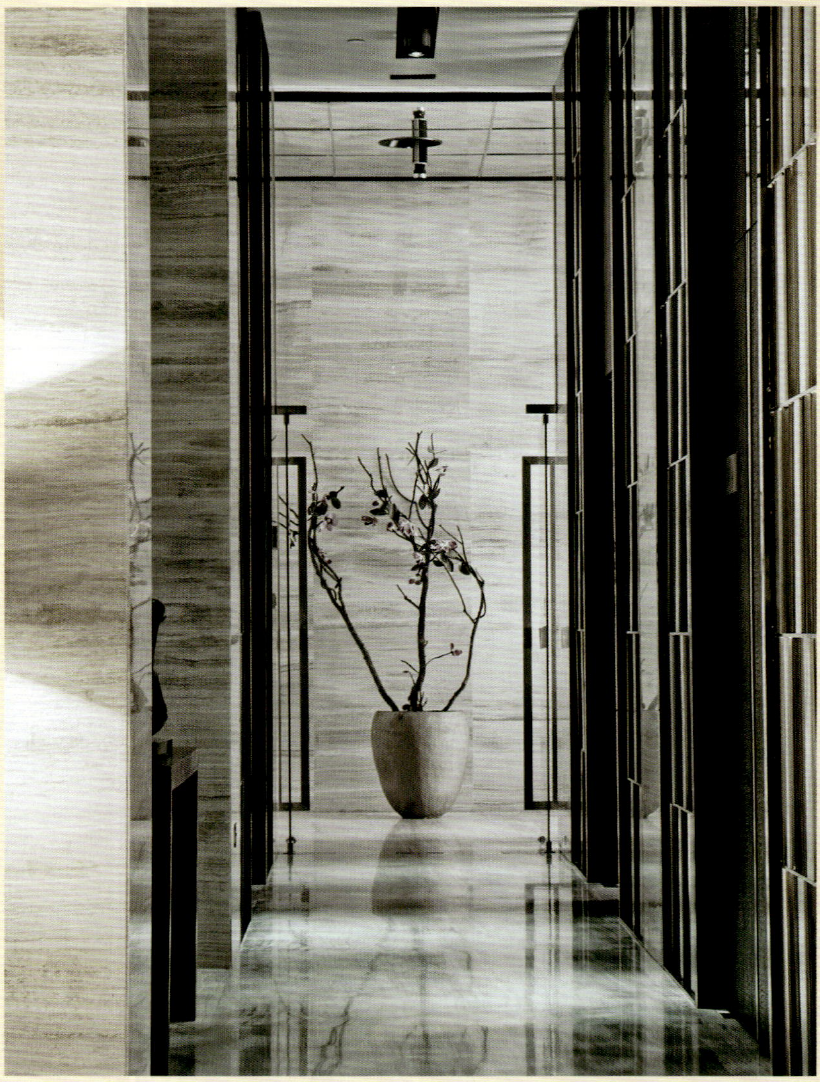

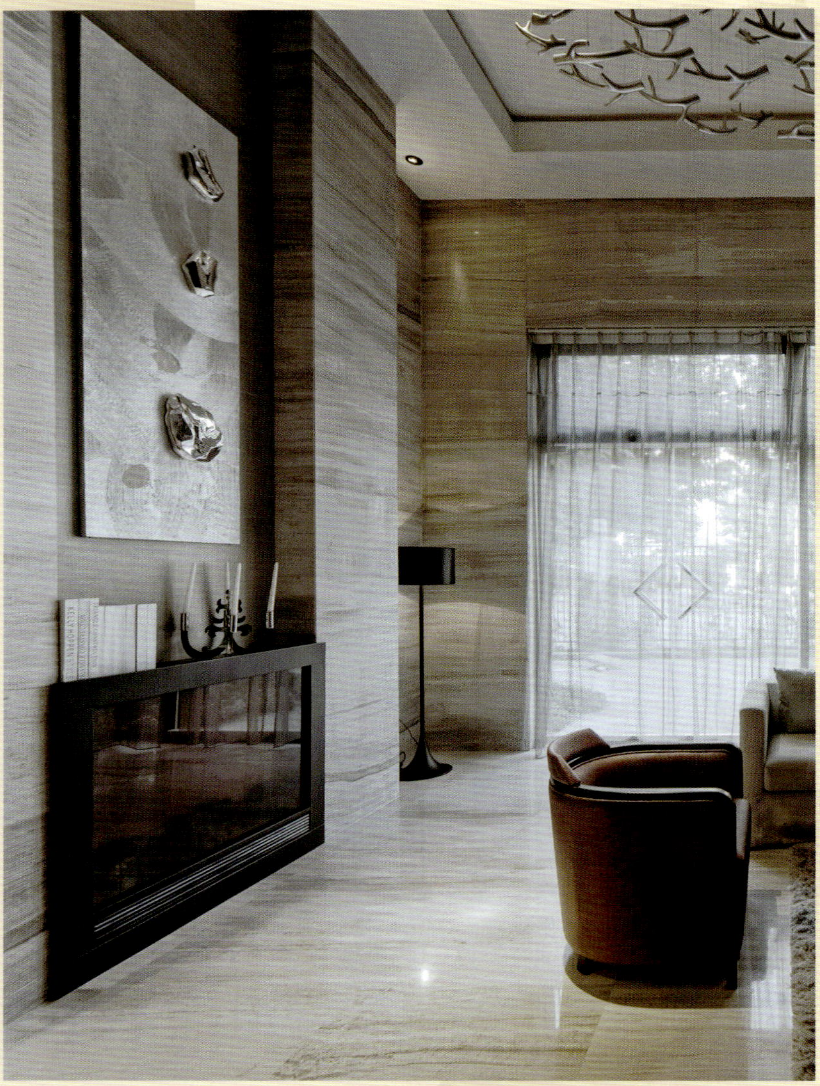

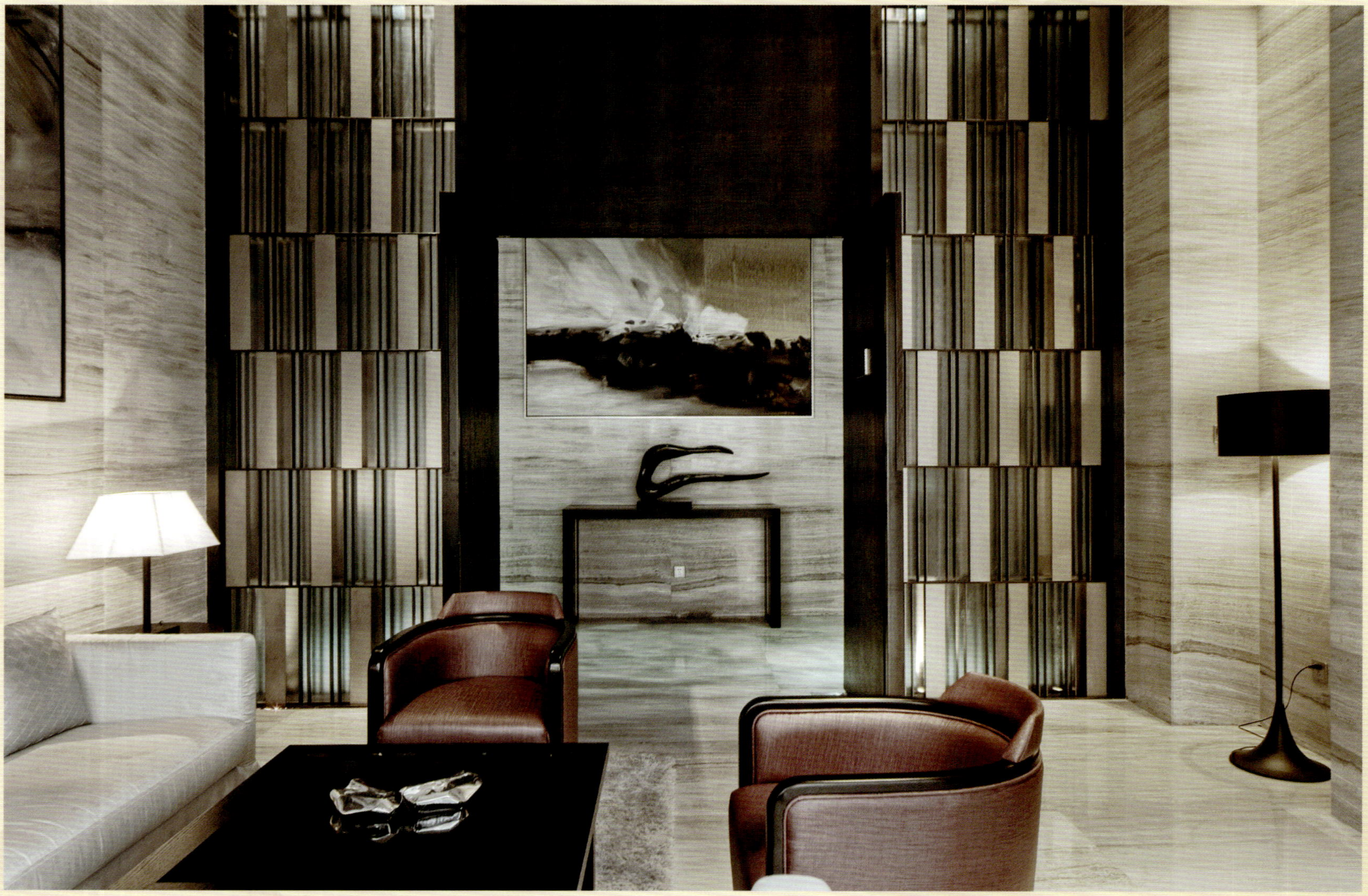

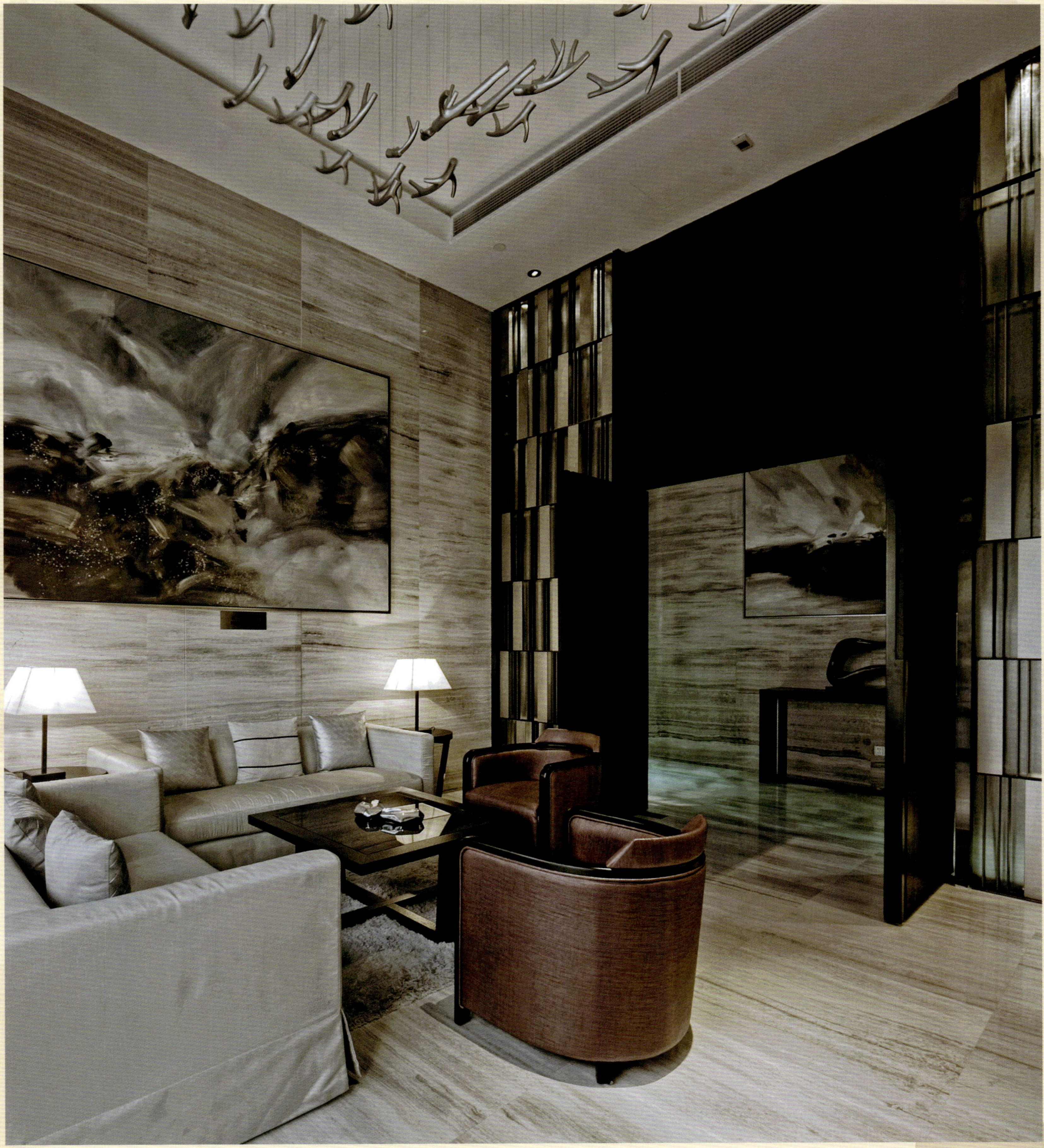

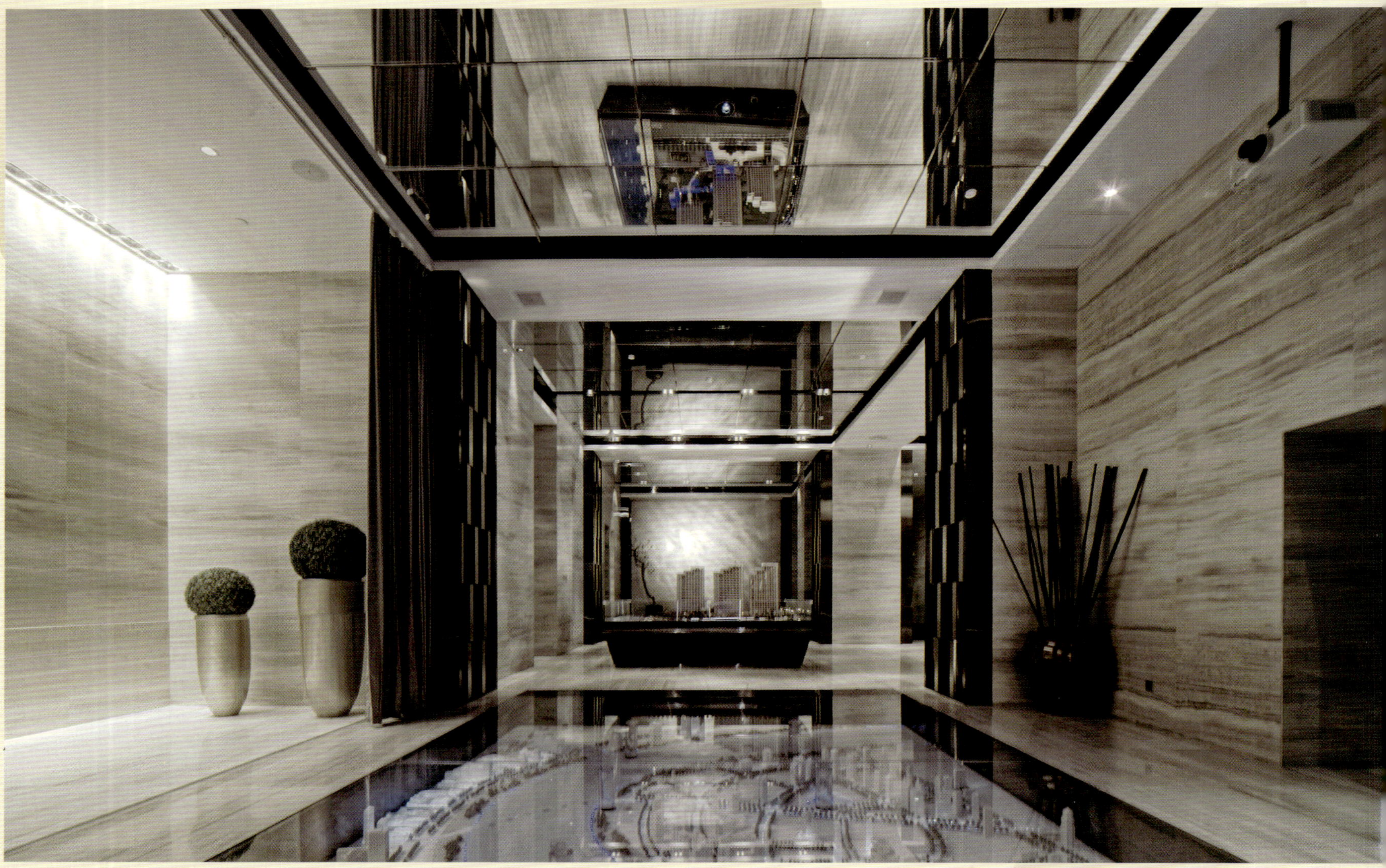

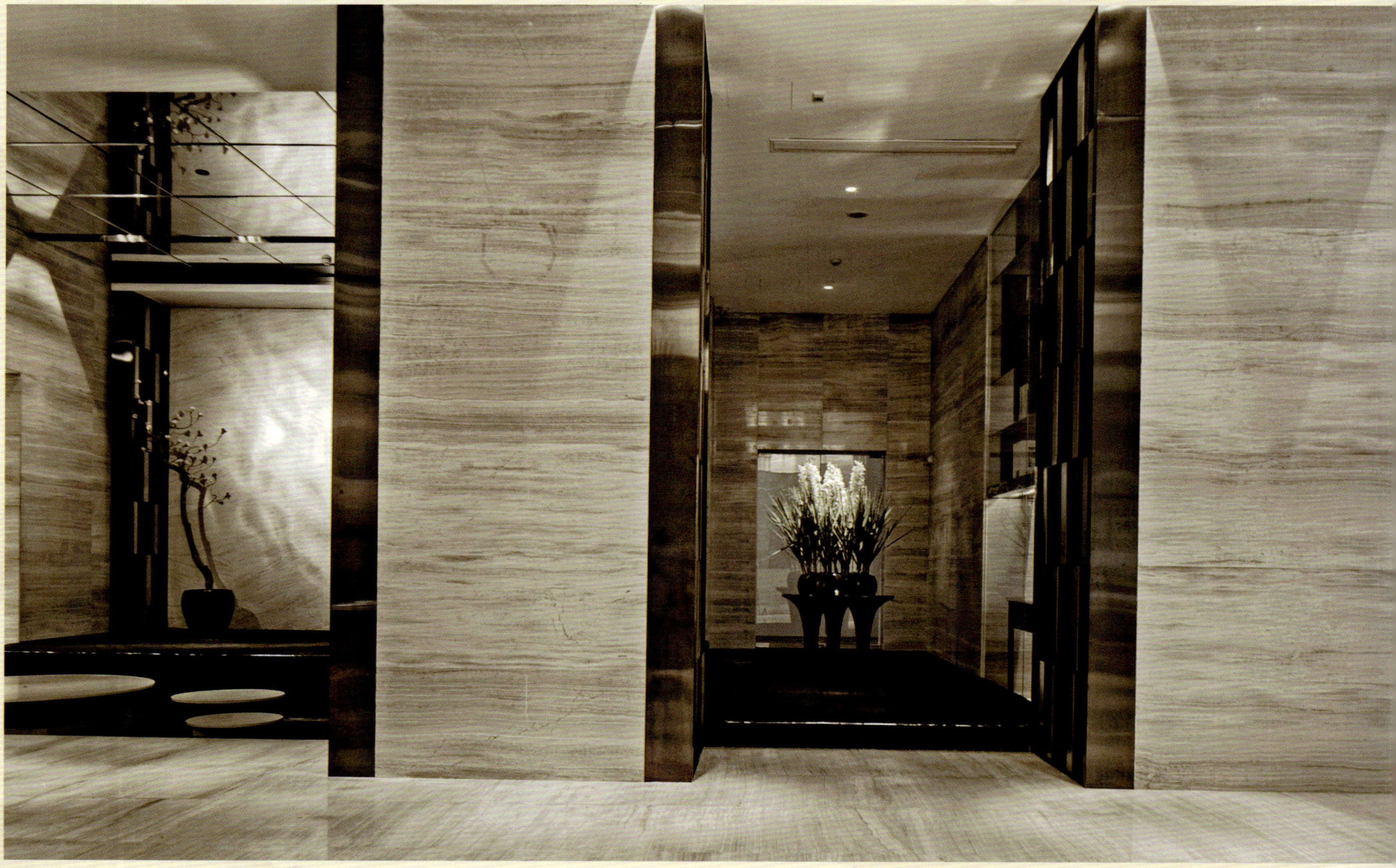

069

Zen Spa Club

Design Agency: Xiao's Design
Designer: Xiao Aibin
Client: Nanyuan Hotel
Location: Suzhou, China
Area: 2000 m²
Photographer: Xiao Aihua

The Spa, located in Suzhou Nanyuan Hotel, will give you a sense of far from the madding crowd, and you will completely loose yourself in this beautiful space. Surrounded by the flowers and green trees, listening to the soft music, watching the beautiful scenery, your whole heart and body will enjoy a thoroughly relaxation.

The Spa is totally a neo-orientalism design. The decoration and the design can express an intensive oriental culture.

071

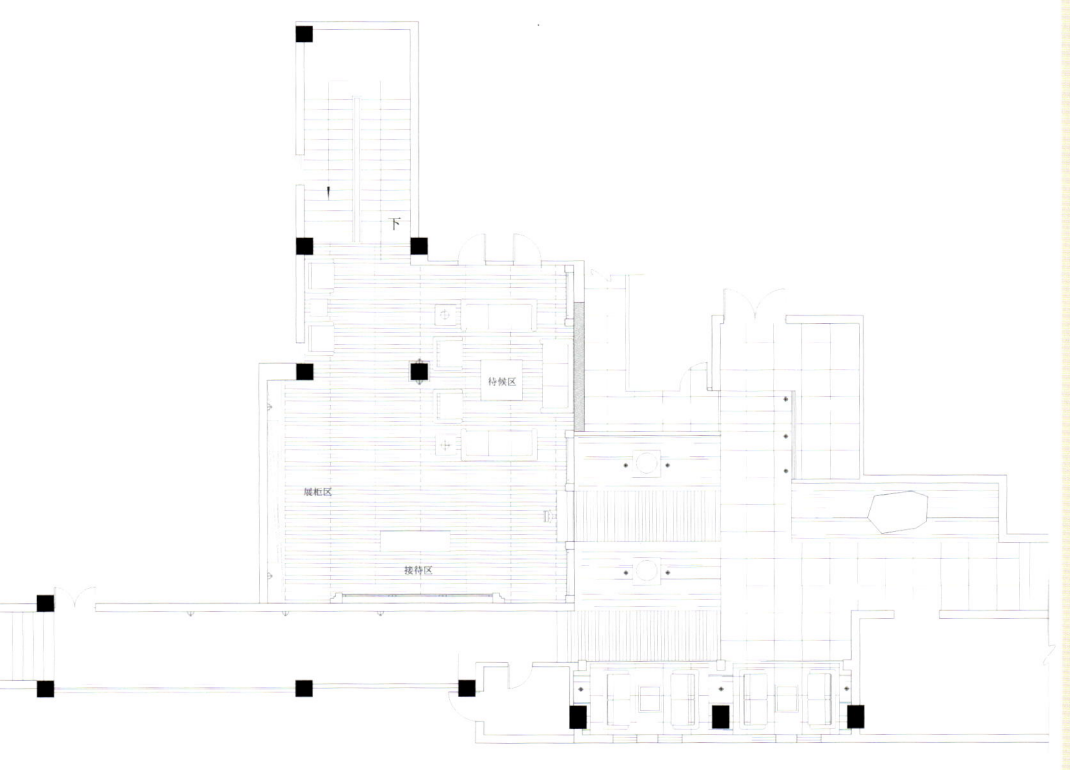

072

073

074

075

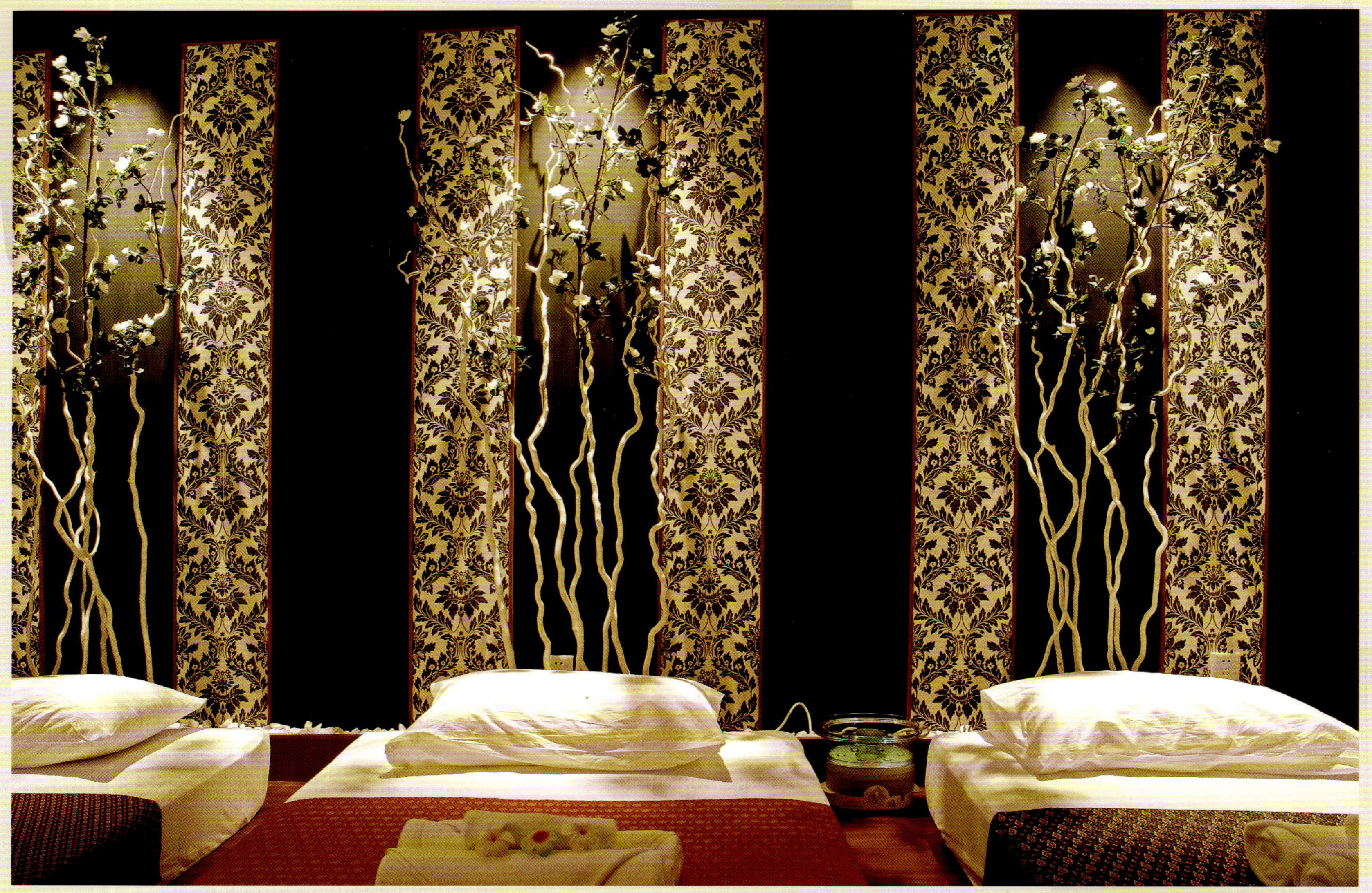

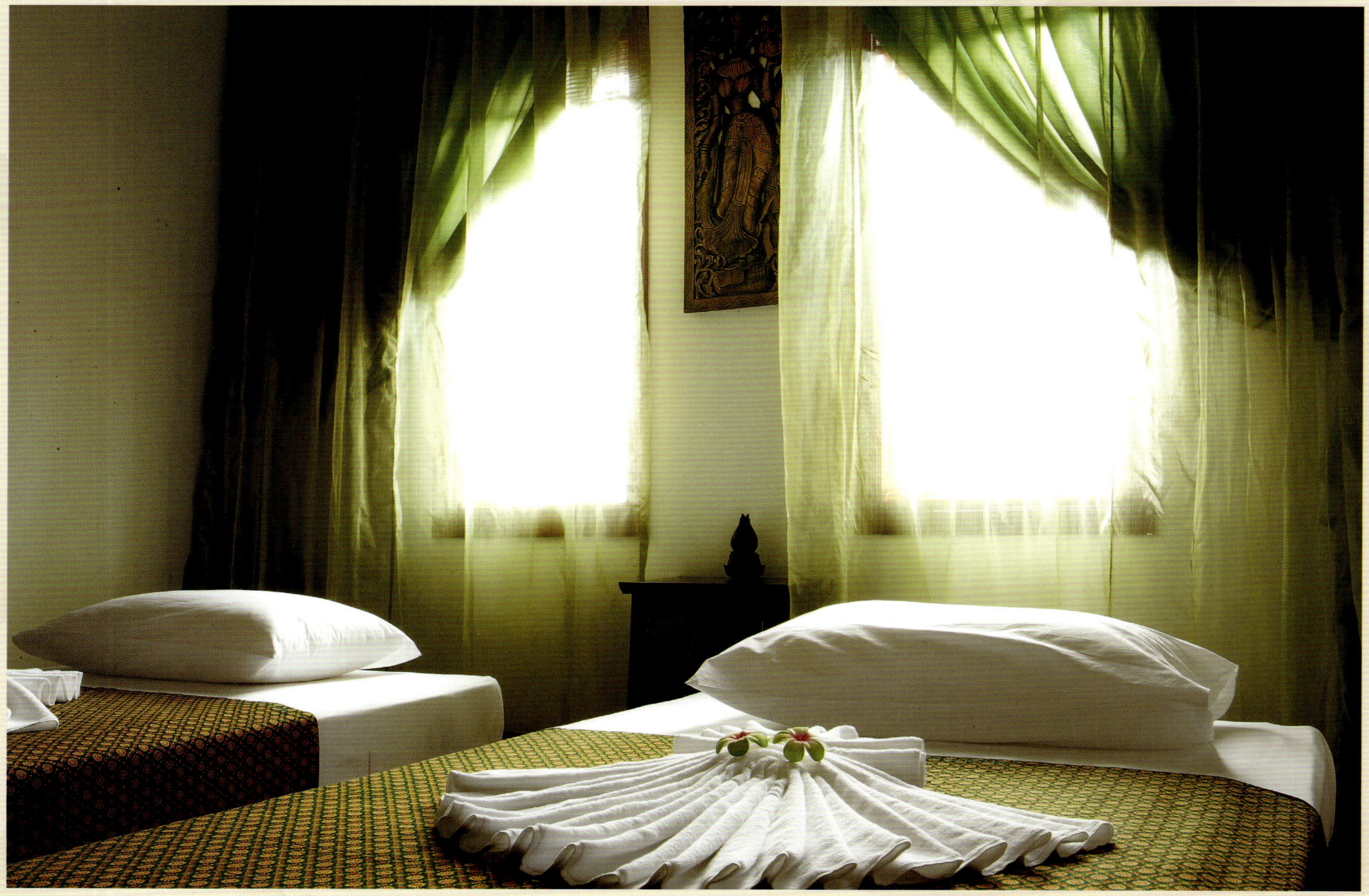

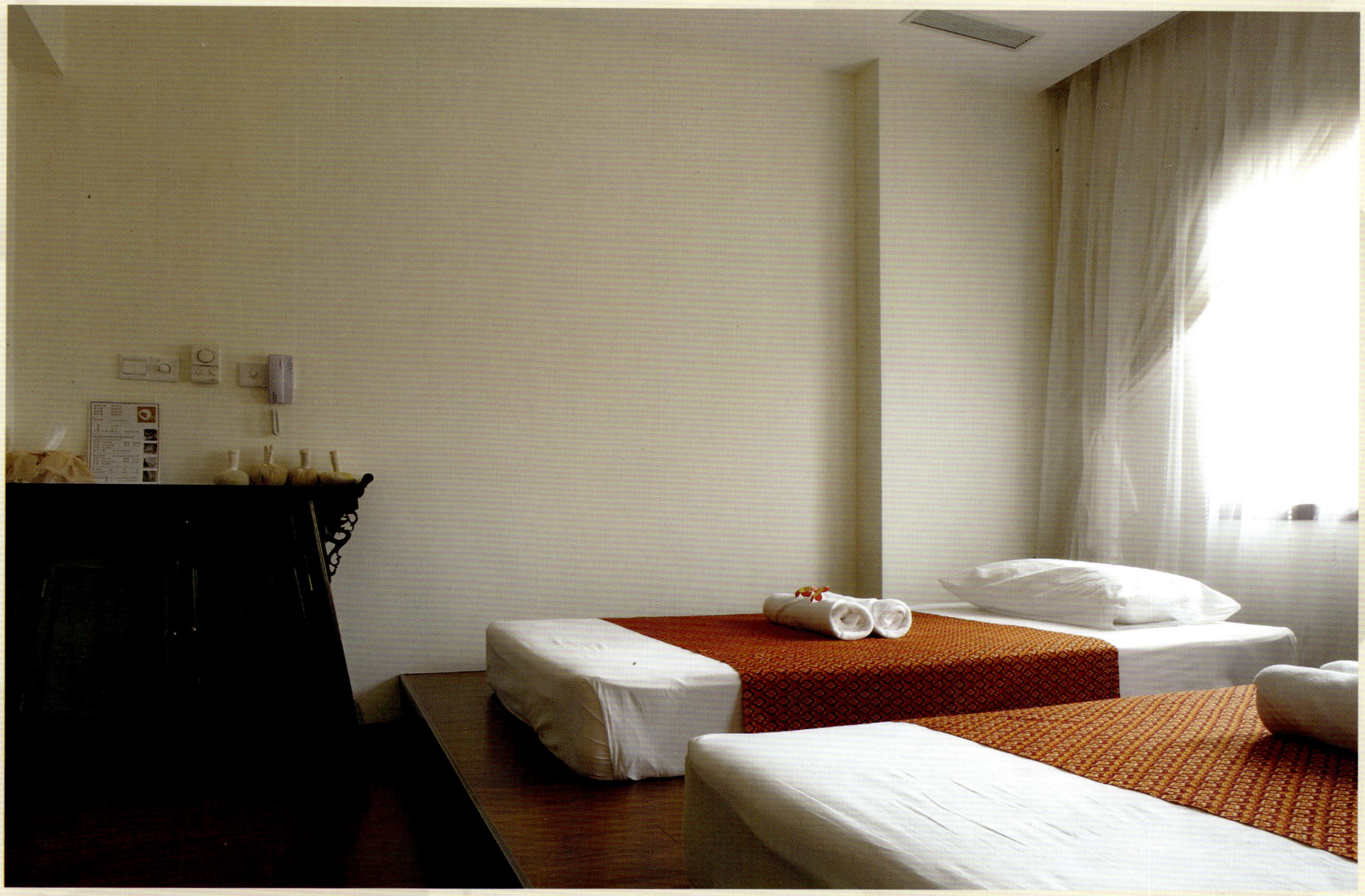

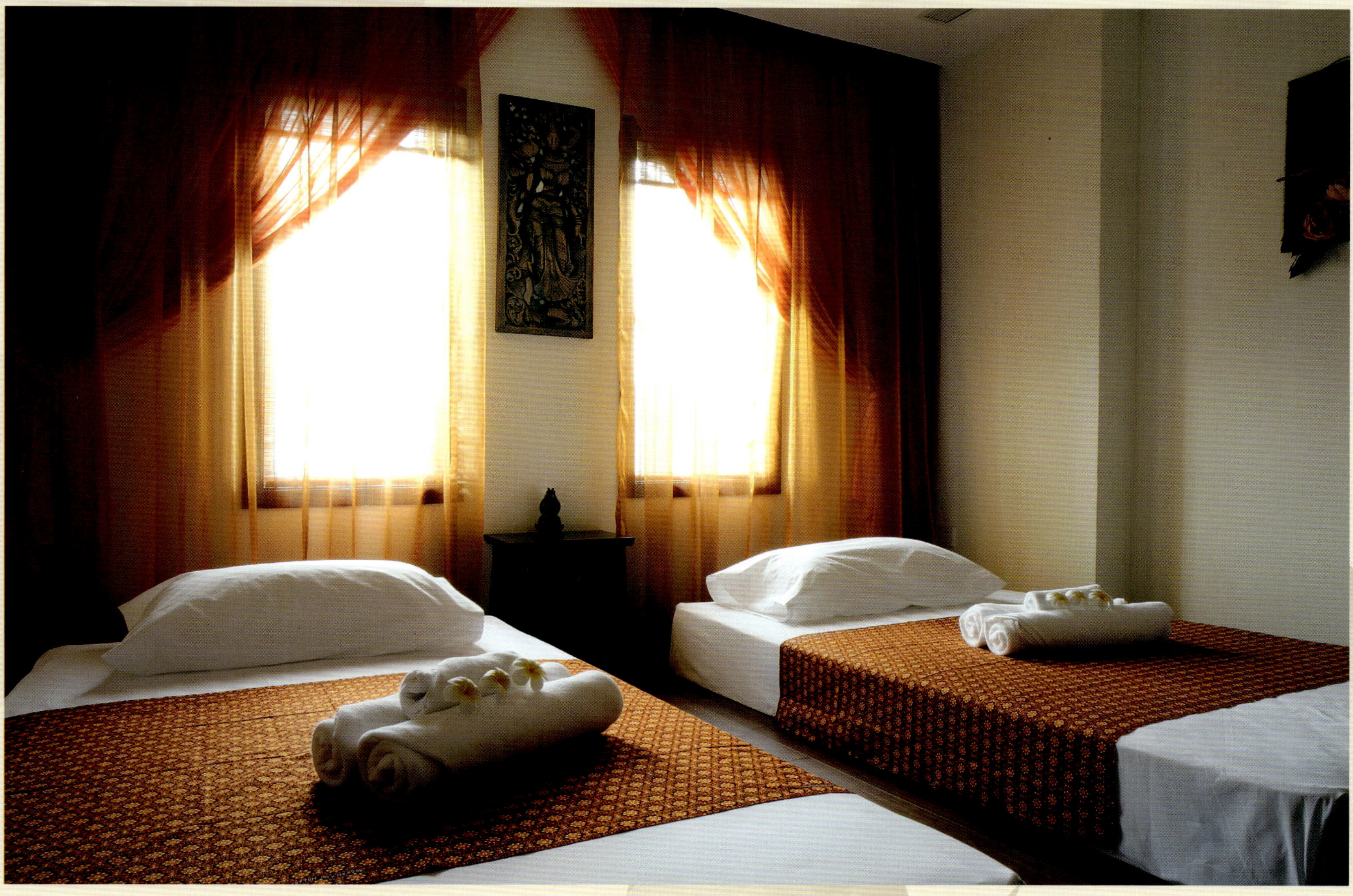

Hefei Humble-home Senior Club

Design Agency: Da Tang Shi Jia
Designer: Huang He
Location: Hefei, China

Through the analysis of the space, designers hope to completely integrate the typical Chinese characteristic elements such as "hall", "gallery", "lorry", "well" into the building with the modern materials. By the transformation of the space, they create the scene of new landscape and unripe brightness of each step. The "patio" is the unique space created specially by designers. In the interplay of light and shadow, people are so affectionate as to forget to return. And the designers use the most simple Chinese materials and elements to build the space and make our atmosphere "zen". At the same time, the adoption of plenty of bluestone and old copper gives people an illusion of space and time.

Unique and delicate architecture opuscule is also the focus of the design. Stone Buddhists, which have different appearance but look the same calm and tranquil, seem to tell us that "nothing is left", leaving us some kind of tranquility. Washstand and sink made of the inkstone not only have practical function but also leave people unforgettable memories. The light effect used in a stage offers people a feeling that the change of space and emotional comb completely integrate into the same space and time.

079

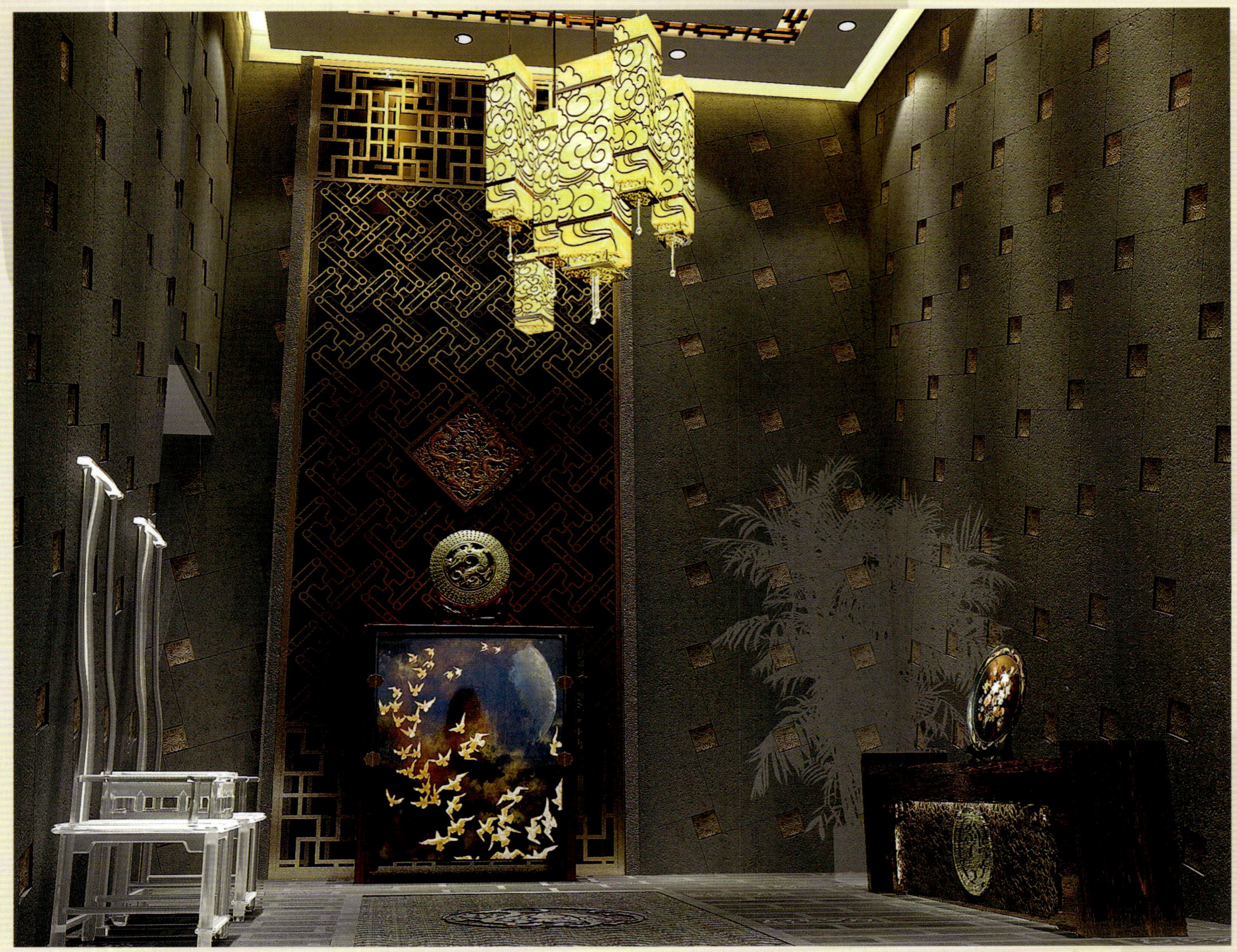

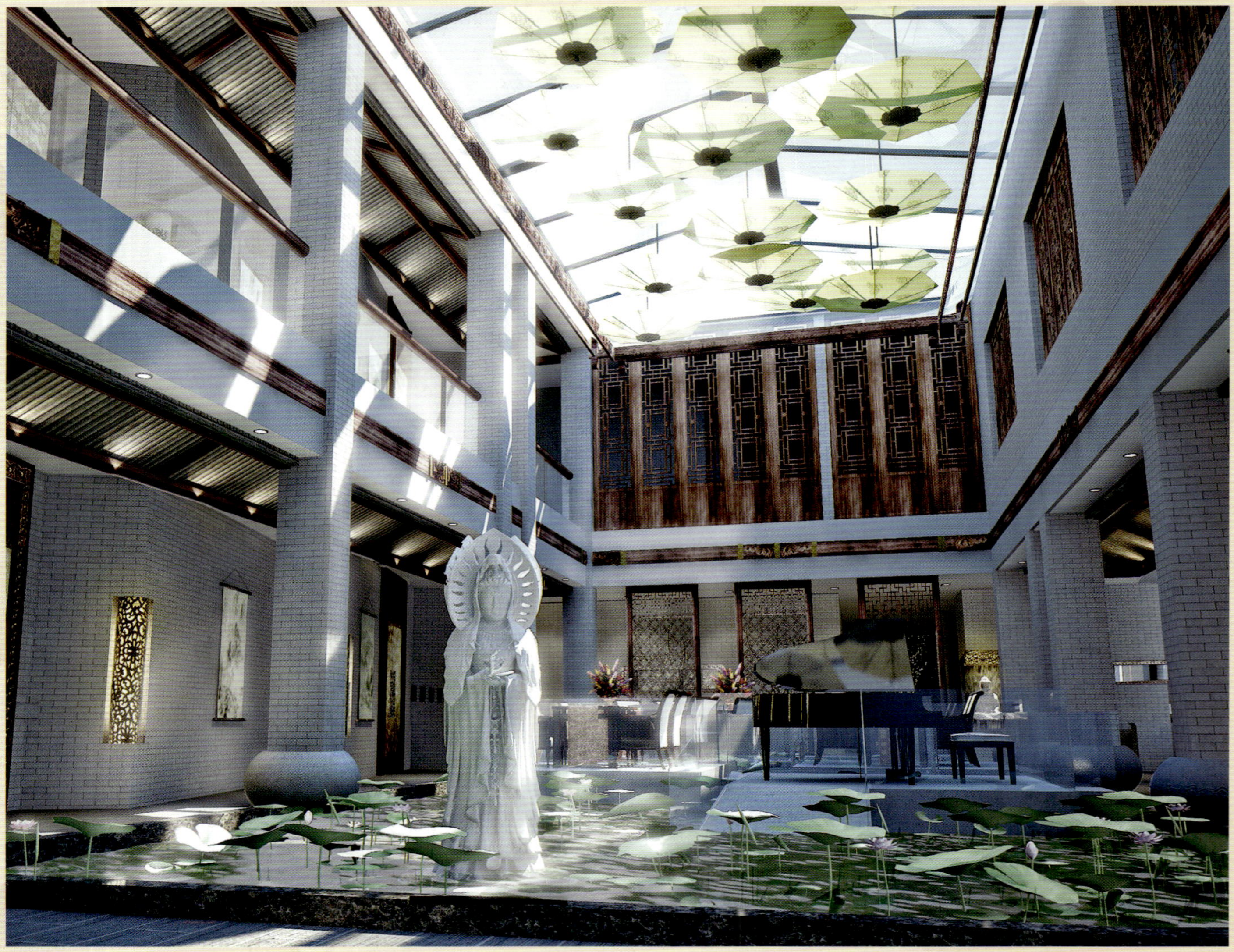

081

082

083

Sales Center of Xing Fu Li

Designer: Tsung-Jen Lin

Design Team: Ben-Tao Li, Qiang Han, K. Kei

Client: Capital Domain

Location: Yiwu, Zhejiang, China

Area: 760 m²

Photographer: Wang Jishou

Recognized by United Nations and world banks, the City of Yiwu houses the world's biggest small goods market, having seemingly arisen over night, and is now the center of trading for small goods in the world. The people of Yiwu, once workers on the farming fields, dared to change their fates and stepped into the world of business and landed on success. "Breakthrough Innovations" is this city's most valued essence. The city strongly encourages young entrepreneur, and with that in mind, the Lahas Zone was idealistically conceived and designed, centering a green environment that can incorporate services, offices, and exhibitions all into living comfortably.

For the successful implementation of such a green zone for innovations, Capital Domain commissioned avant-garde architect of the natural styles, Tsung-Jen Lin to create the showroom that will symbolize Lahas Zone. Differing from past sale centers, Lahas Zone was comprehensively renovated from an old factory building instead of a new building on the Lahas Zone site in accordance with maintaining green. Facing the many challenges of the old structure, while maintaining the integrity of recycle design and adhering to the developers intentions, Lin has created Chinese stylized models of living for the post contemporary age. Lin believes that the principles of green design are in the recyled use of the property and how to utilize an abandoned building undergoing a program change to its full potential. The design for this abandoned factory would also have to consider long term use beyond just a showroom, to incorporate a club like setting for future use in the effort to be true to green design. The plan is to continue transforming the space's functionality in the future, section by section, to maximize its recycle output and a continuing renew to program. However, the current main purpose was to utilize minimal construction to achieve a showroom with an air of "Subtle Happiness". (The idea of "Subtle Happiness" or "Syoukakkou" came from the famous author Haruki Murakami, which means: Though it's subtle and maybe pedestrian, it's a feeling of happiness that you're completely sure of.)

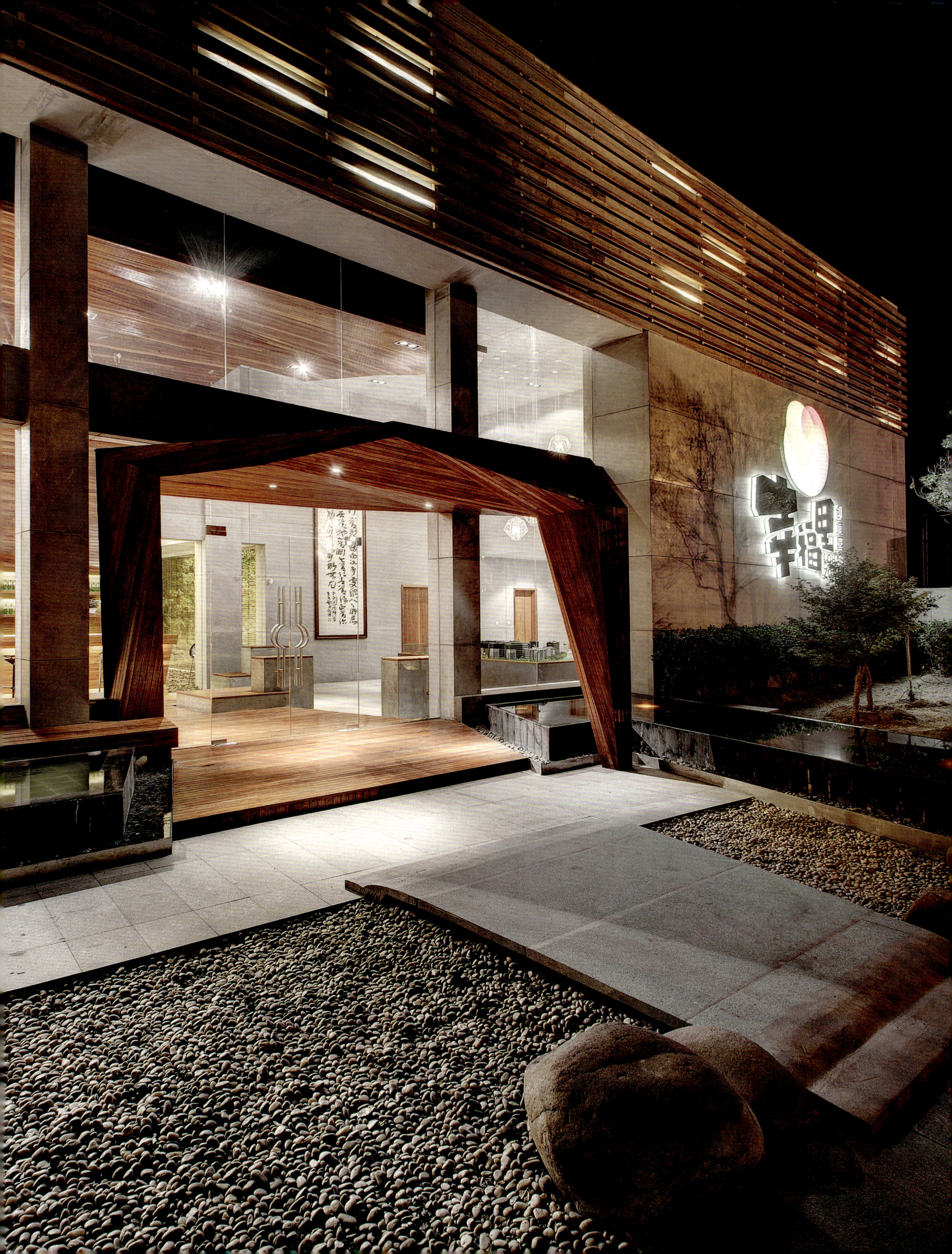

086

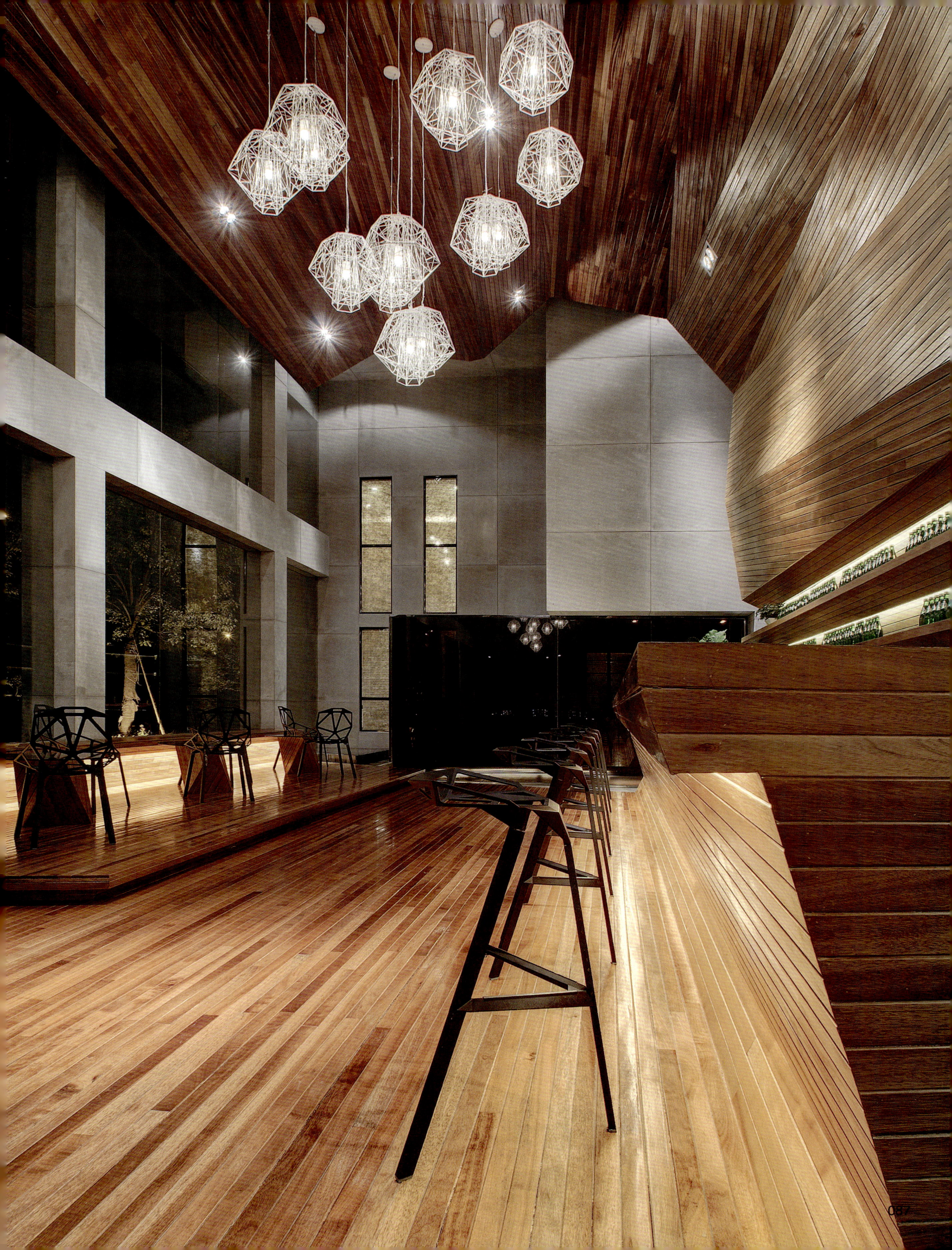

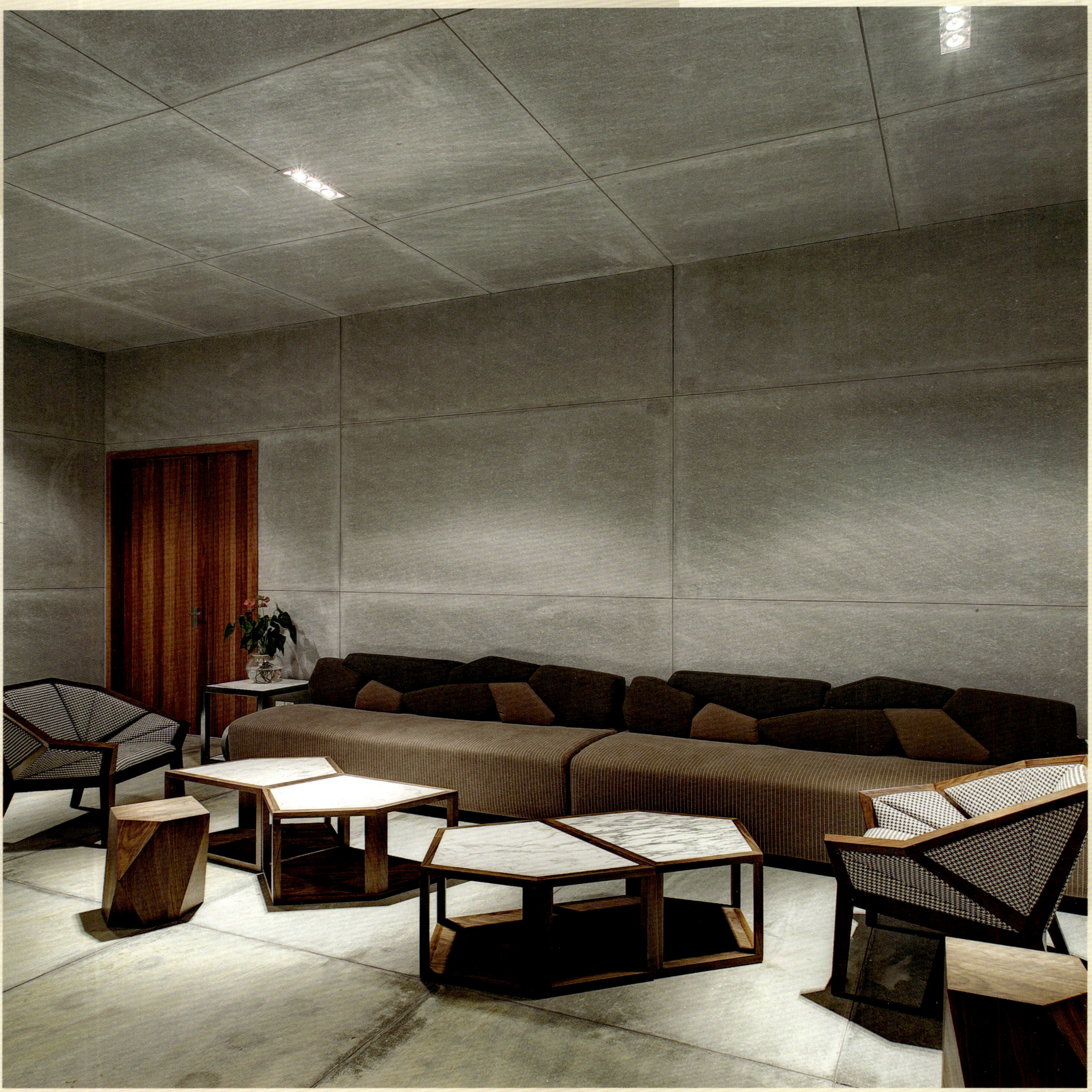

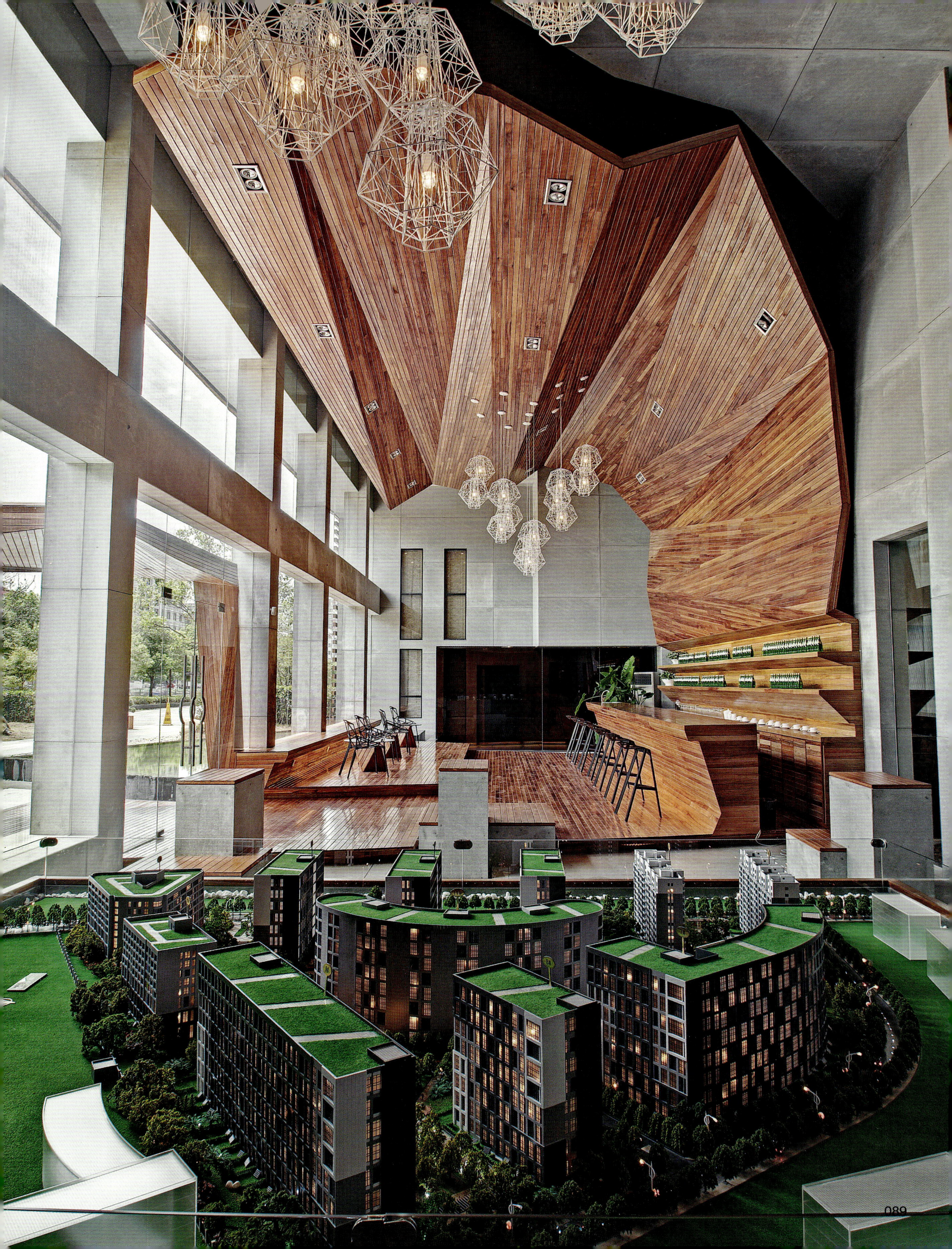

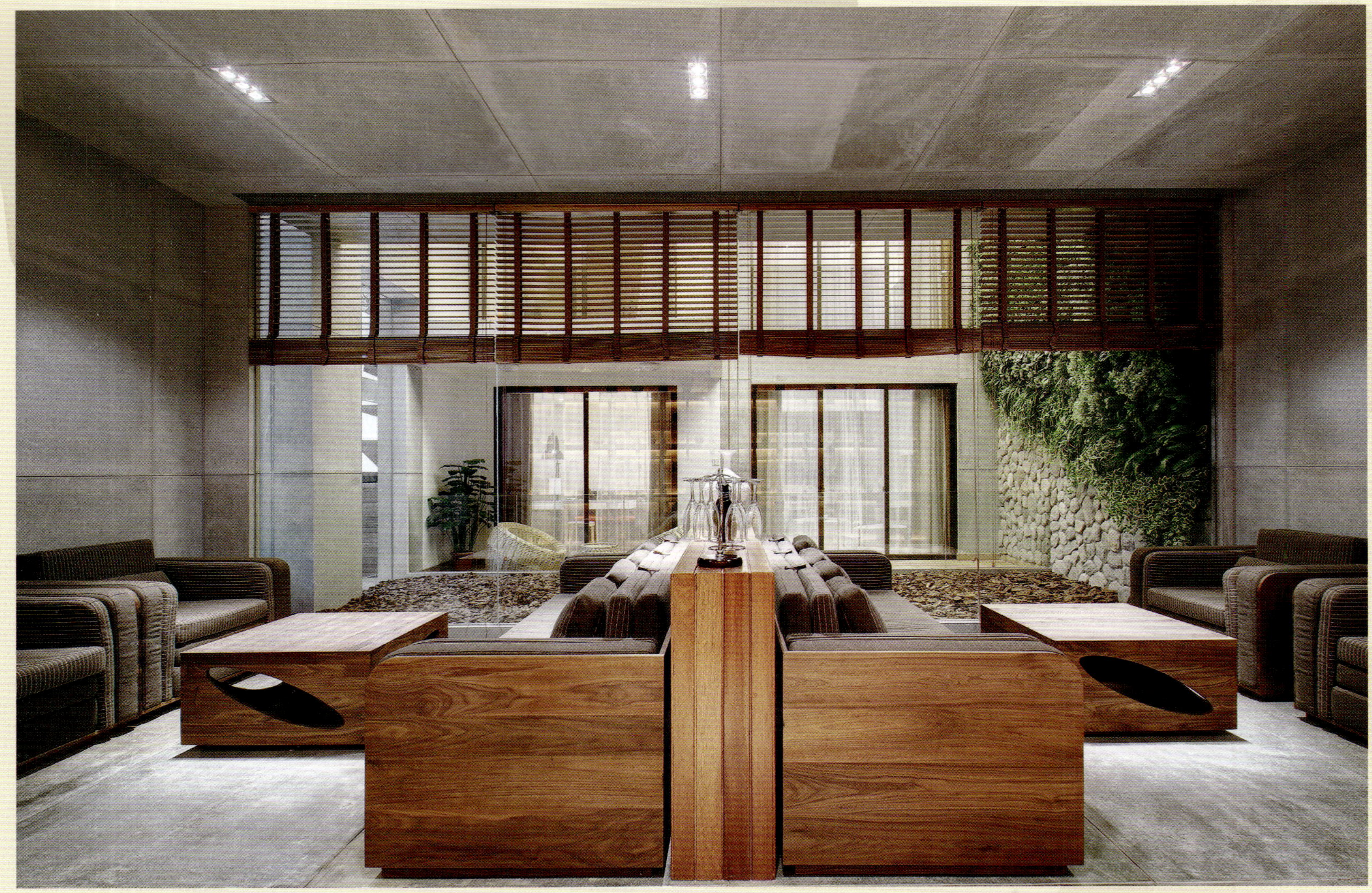

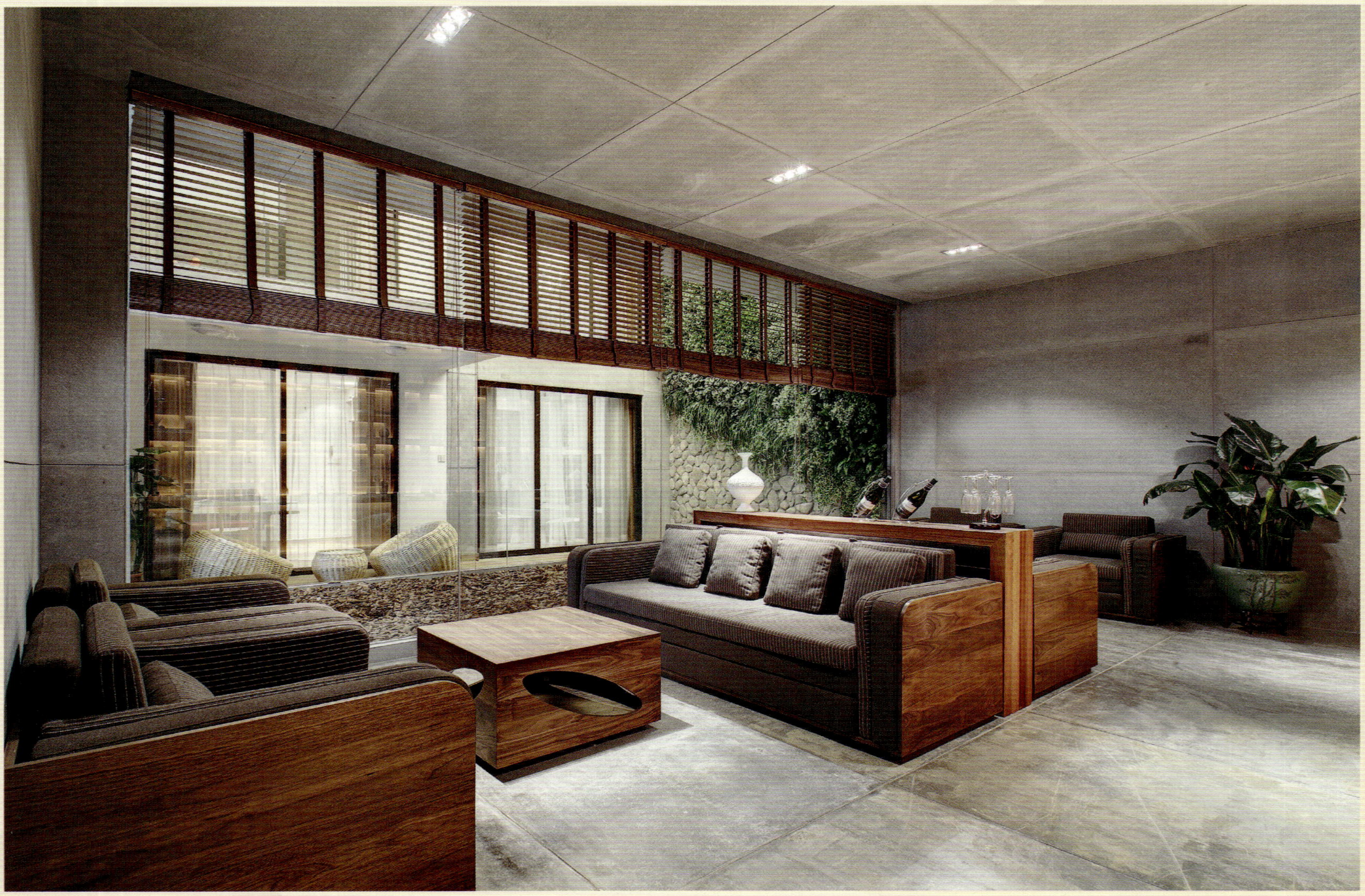

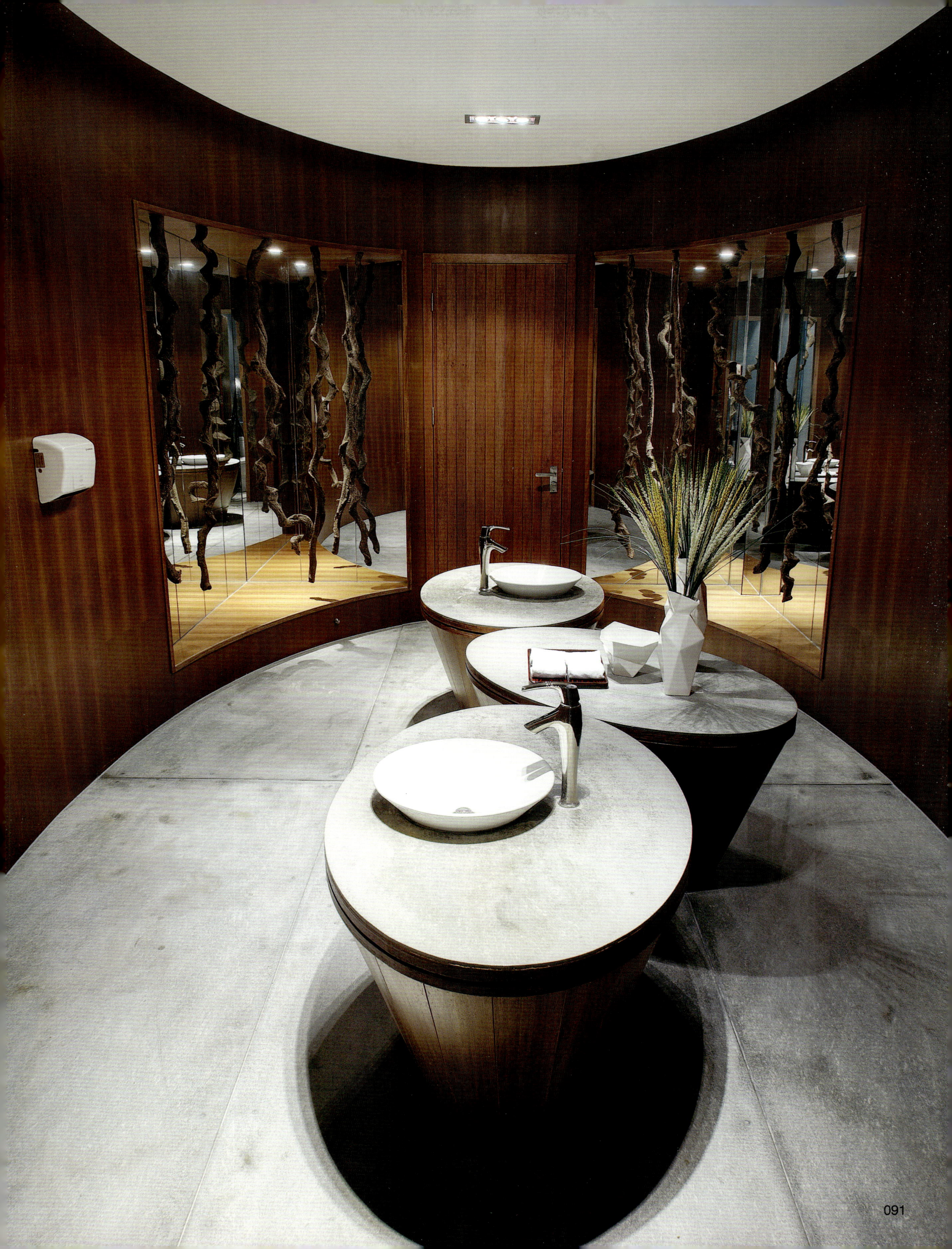

Zi Yue Ya Zhu Business Club

Design Agency: DARA
Designer: Jiang Peng
Client: Zi Yue Ya Zhu Business Club
Location: Beijing, China
Area: 1000 m^2
Photographer: Yun Wei

The courtyard complex is lingering in the minds of every Beijinger. This project reflects the designer's abundant understanding and experiences about courtyard architecture and interior design. The club is surrounded by the prospered Old Gulou Street and Bell Tower, which is an unparalleled geographical advantage. The lobby is serving as a banqueting suite for VIPs. The dining room is available for over a dozen people to have dinner at the same time, and the grand crystal chandelier and exotic old white dining table are drawing people's attention.

The sunvo mural, a piece of artwork by a well-known artist, makes the entire room dignified; the wooden seats, which reflect Chinese and Western elements, mix and match with the Western buckled chair, adding visual interests to the room. Cigar room's inspiration comes from the Palace of Gathering Excellence of the Forbidden City. Blue and sauce yellow echo the Royal style; exquisite handmade silk carpet and the Moroccan-style chandelier again reflect the charm of fusion. Jade Hall, full of subtropical feel, is based on a green tone.

093

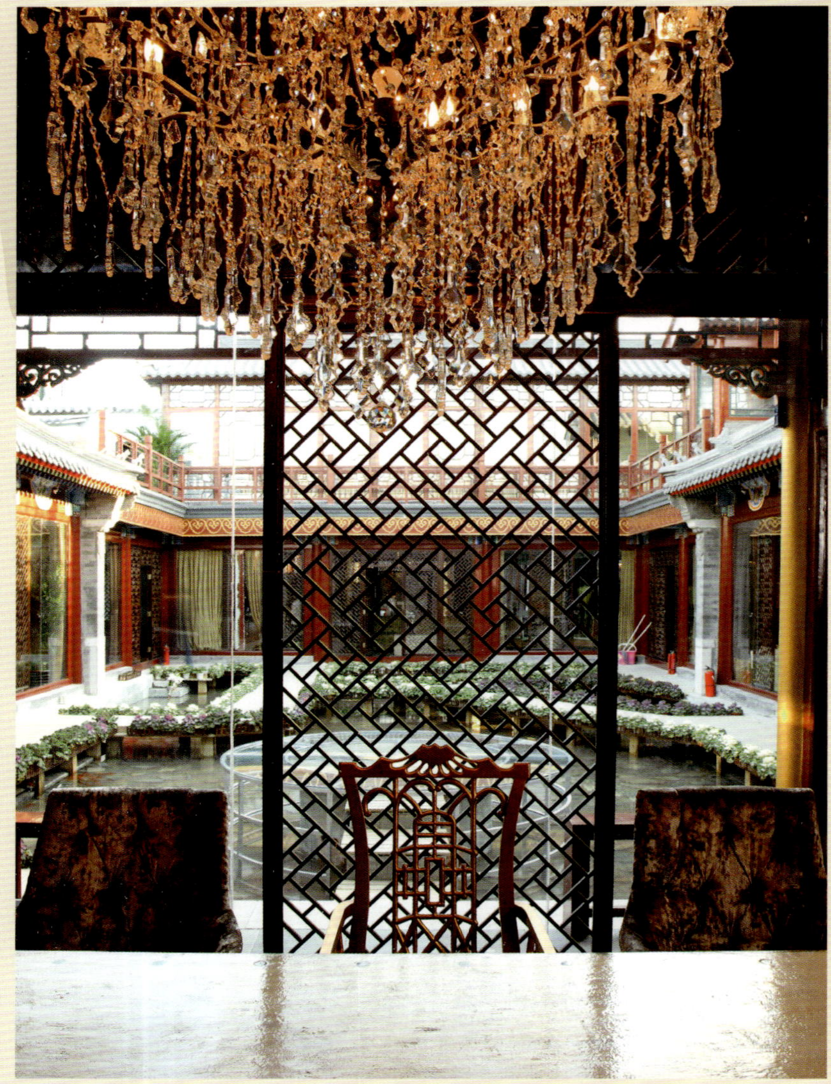

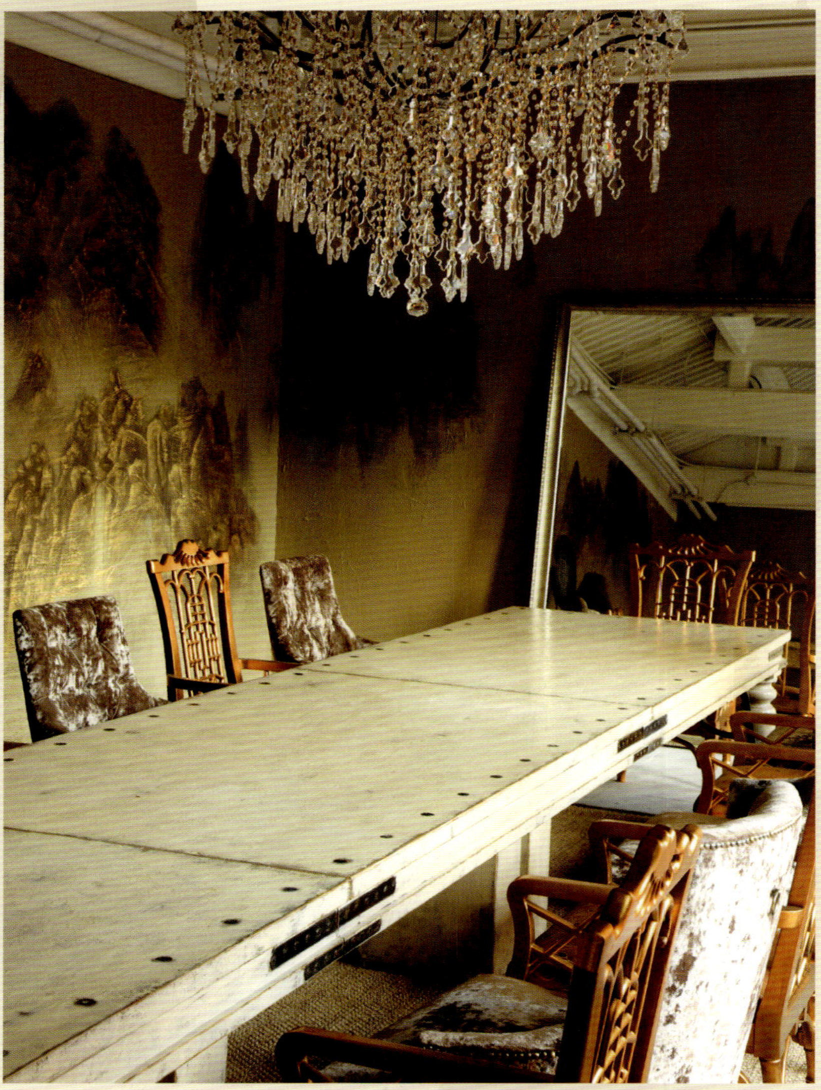

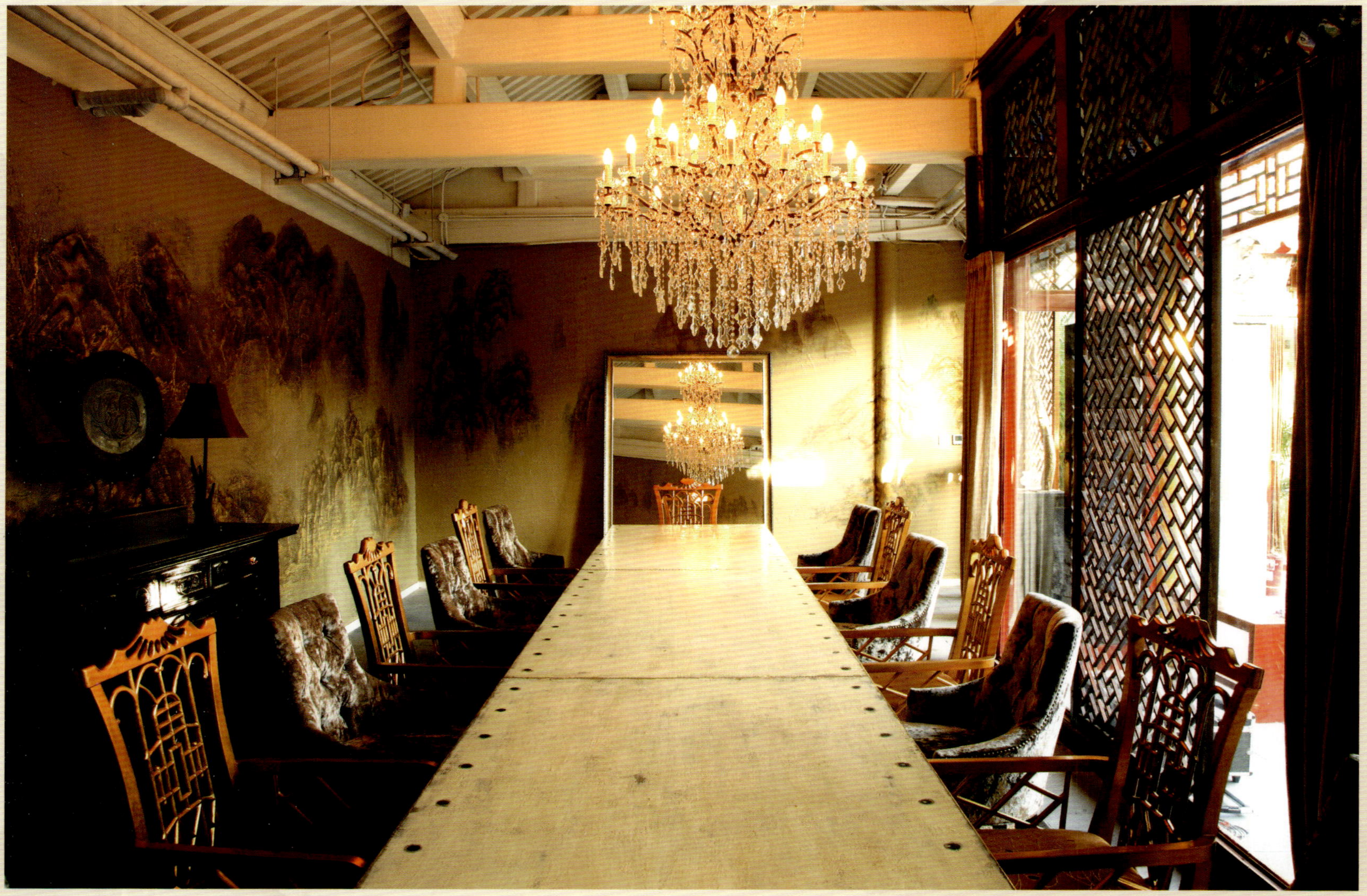

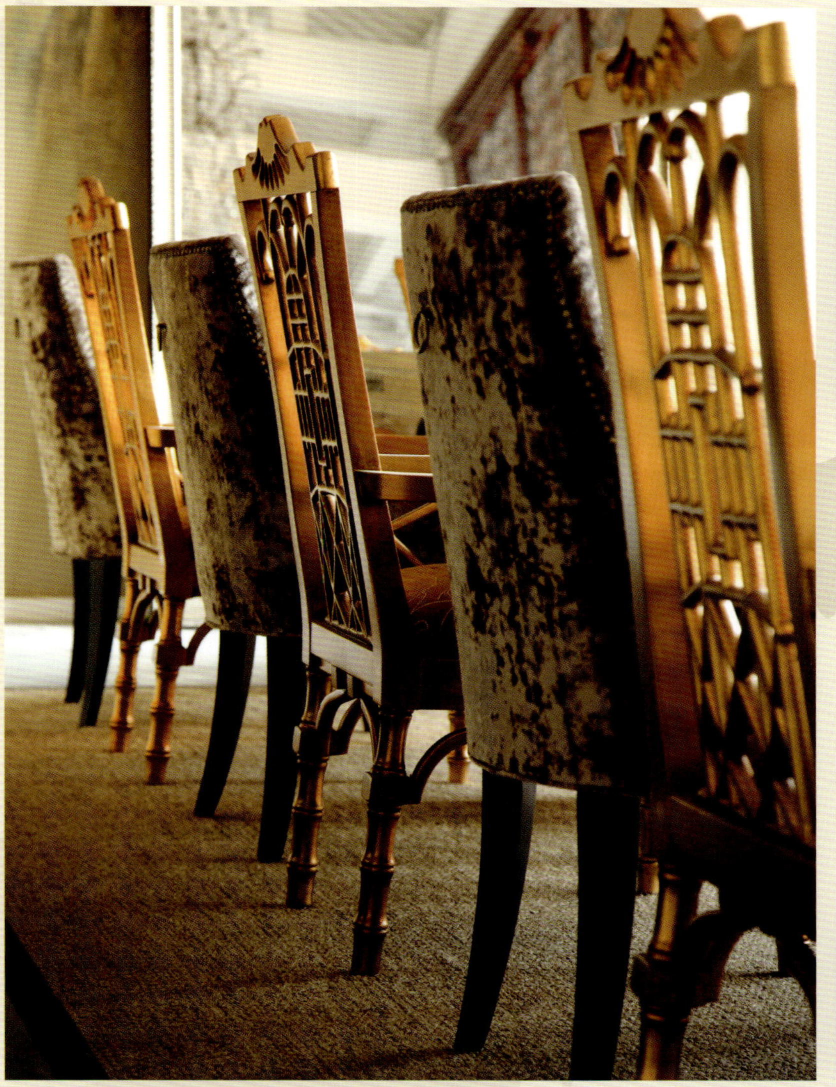

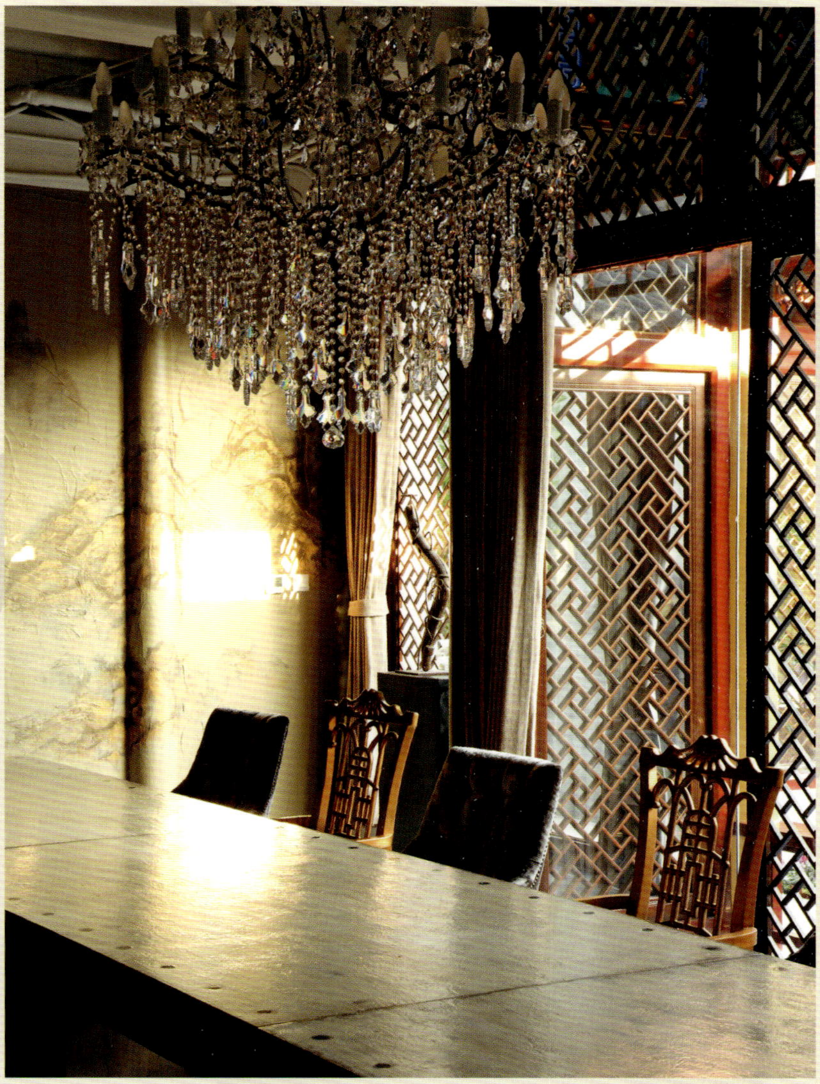

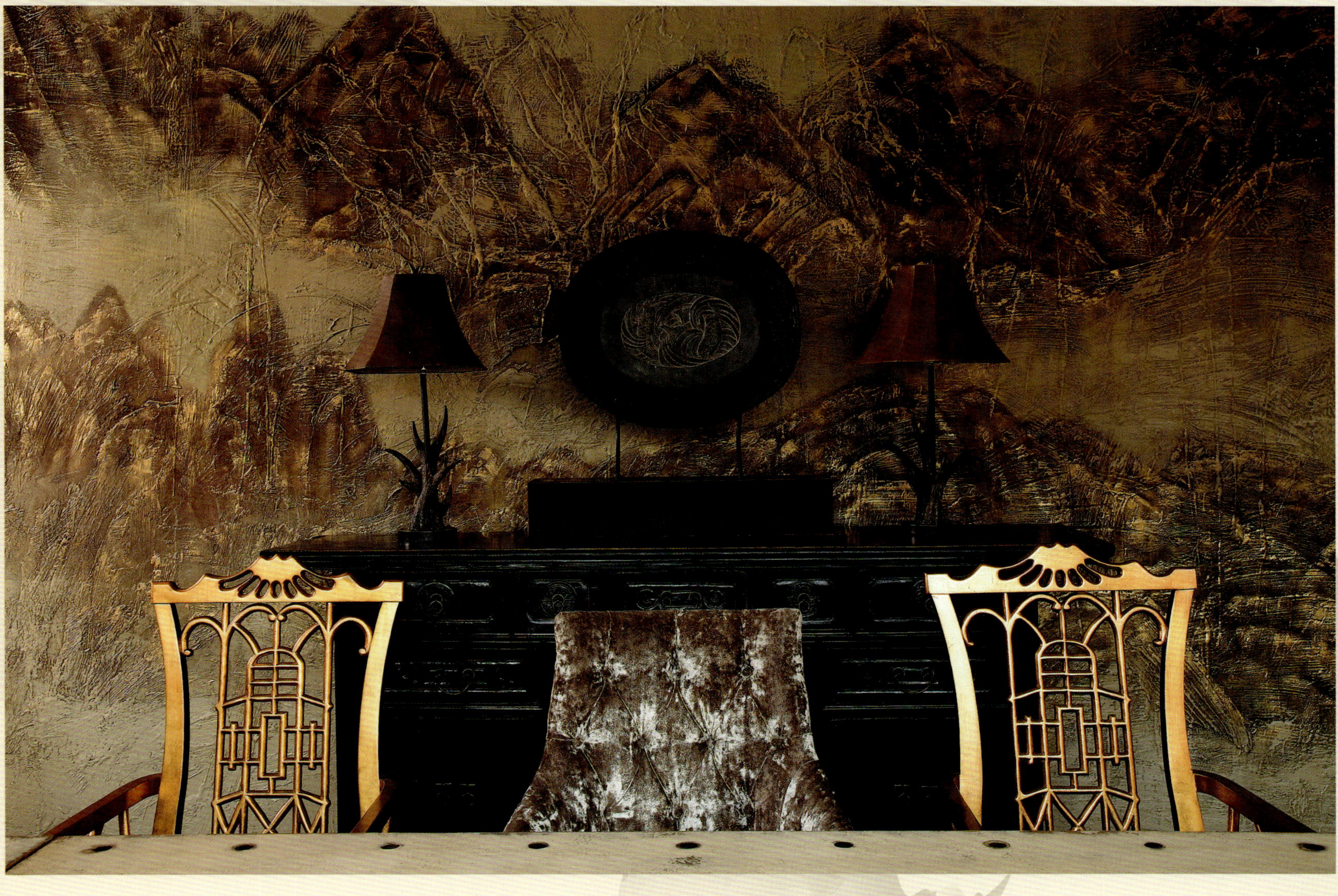

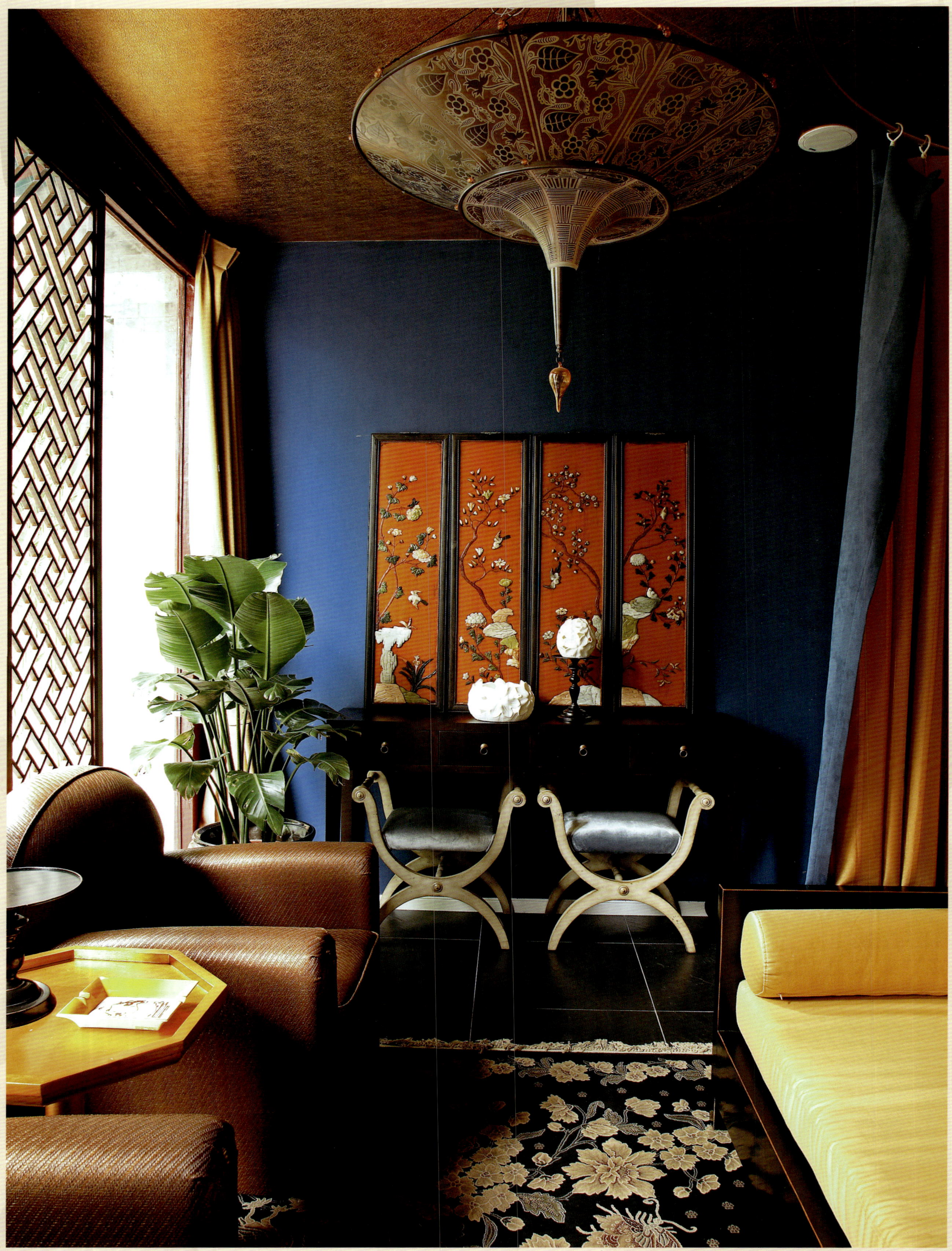

097

098

099

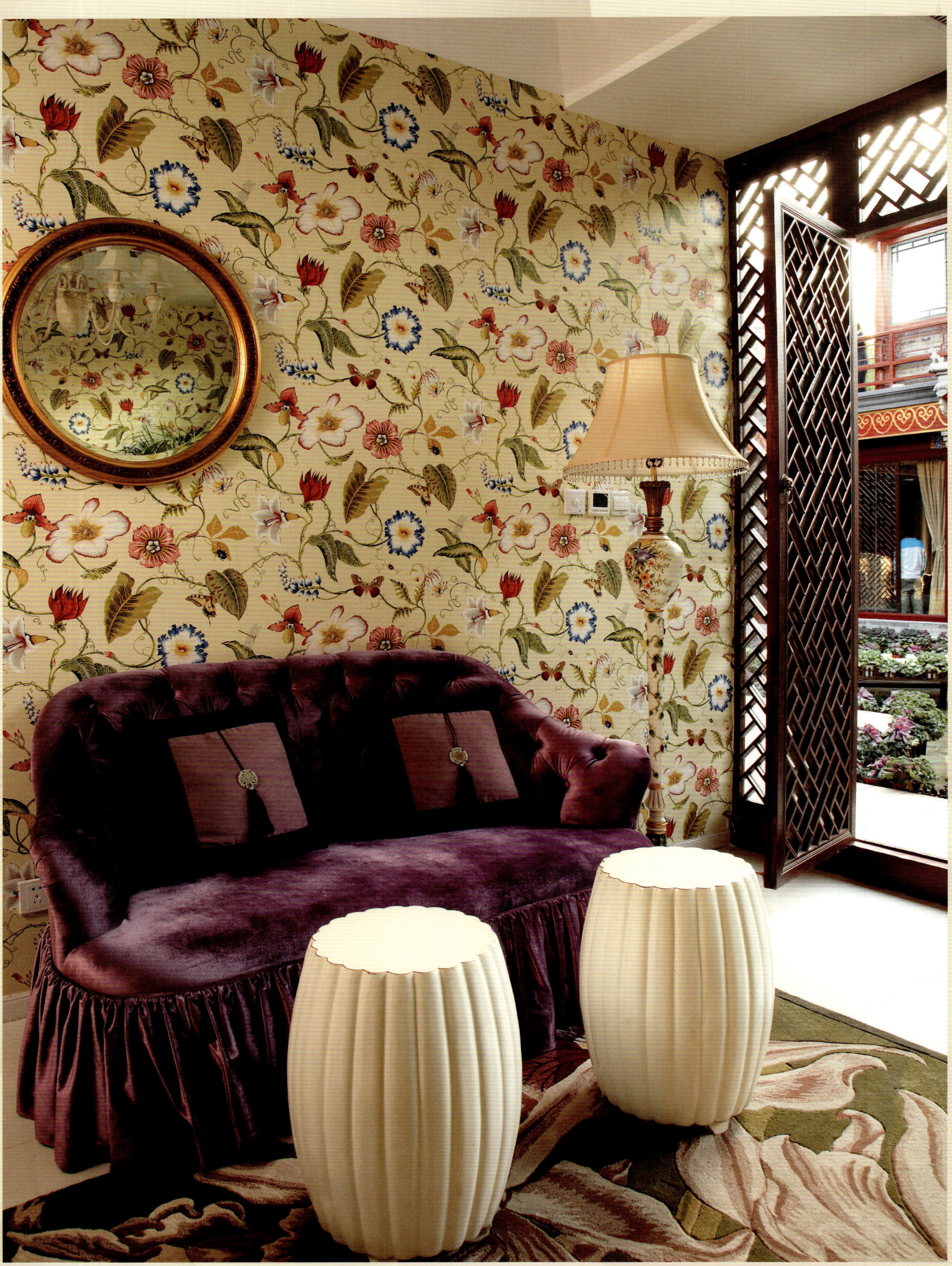

101

Show Upper River Town Club

Design Agency: Shenzhen Pinki Design Consultant Co., Ltd.
Designer: Liu Weijun
Location: Fuzhou, China
Area: 4660 m²
Theme: Charming Oriental

"Charming Oriental" will be built in the overall planning which integrates the surrounding environment and scenery to reflect Chinese ideology, culture and traditions. It clearly expresses developer's concept of building a "museum" of Fuzhou modern culture. Combined with Gang-tou River historical context, it shows the unique domestic culture.

Each room of Charming Oriental demonstrates the designer's remolding and innovating from traditional concepts. It is simple in form but rich in content. It is full of cultural connotation to achieve harmony with nature, architecture, and integration with nature. There is not only the building but also the scenes, dry landscape, raindrop curtain, water-wave-ceiling and Chang Ta-qian's splash-ink landscape painting, making the rooms pure and majestic. The combination of traditional and modern design, together with the landscape of Suzhou Garden, presents full expression of the chamber with modern oriental charm.

The chamber is divided into four levels. The main level is a meeting area for the display and leisure with an indoor swimming pool in Chinese architectural style; the second and third levels are an common area for multiple purposes; the fourth level is a combination of building displaying area and multi-function leisure area. The setout of the chamber takes the plum blossom as the design element throughout the entire space, such as carpet, tissue boxes, pillows, and etc. Traditional Chinese bird cage, artwork, floor lamps, and furniture are placed symmetrically to illustrate the Oriental charm and verve.

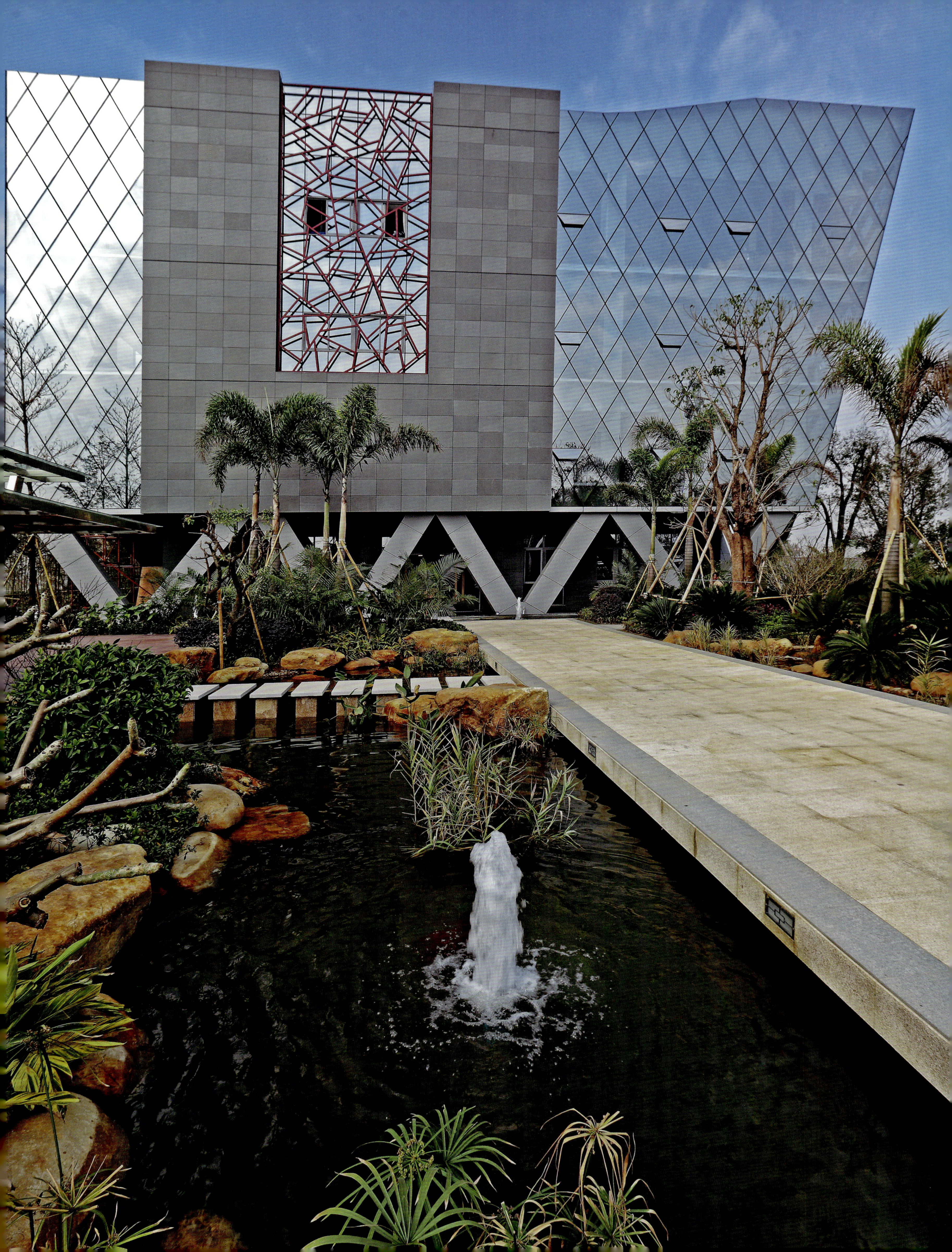

104

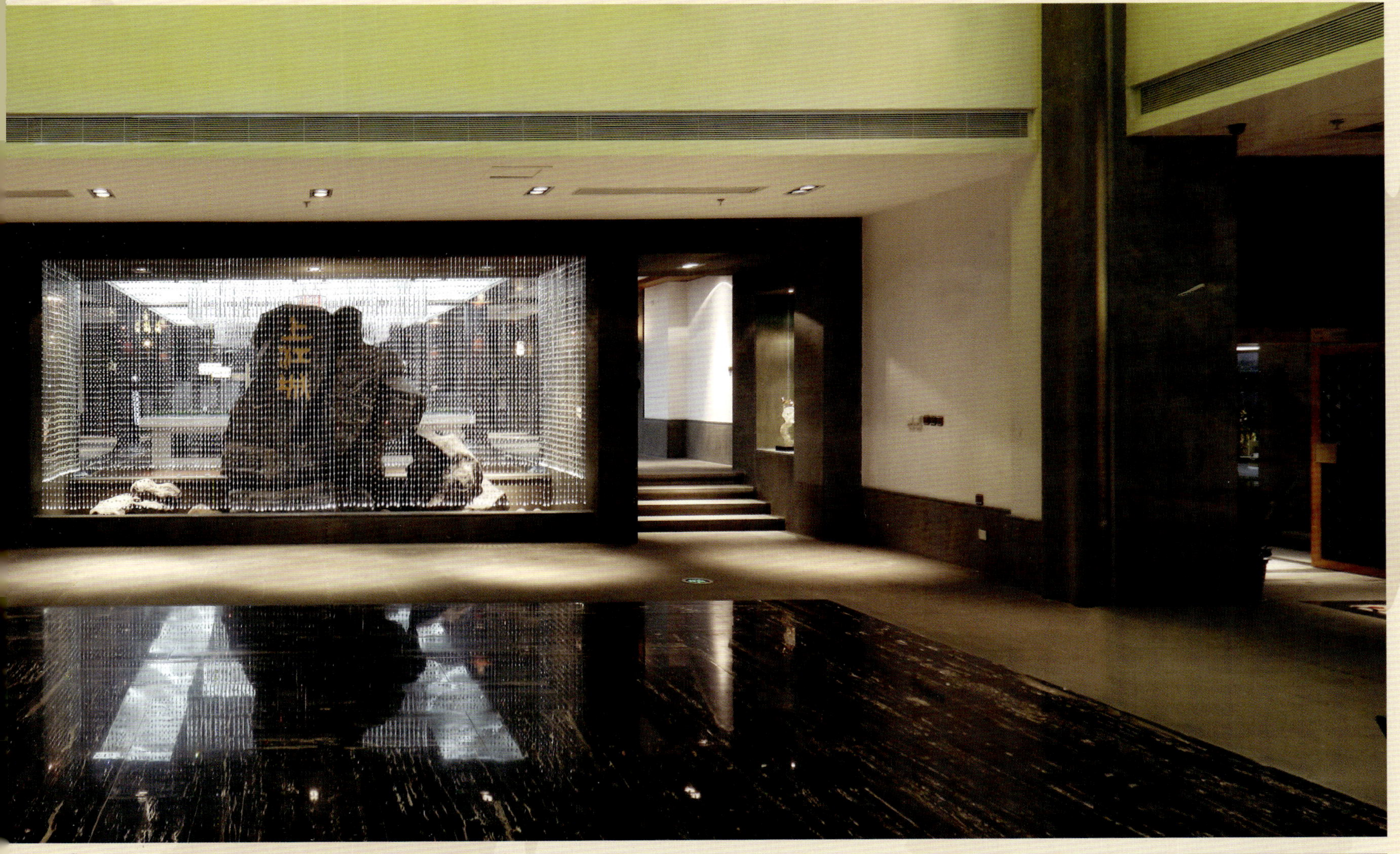

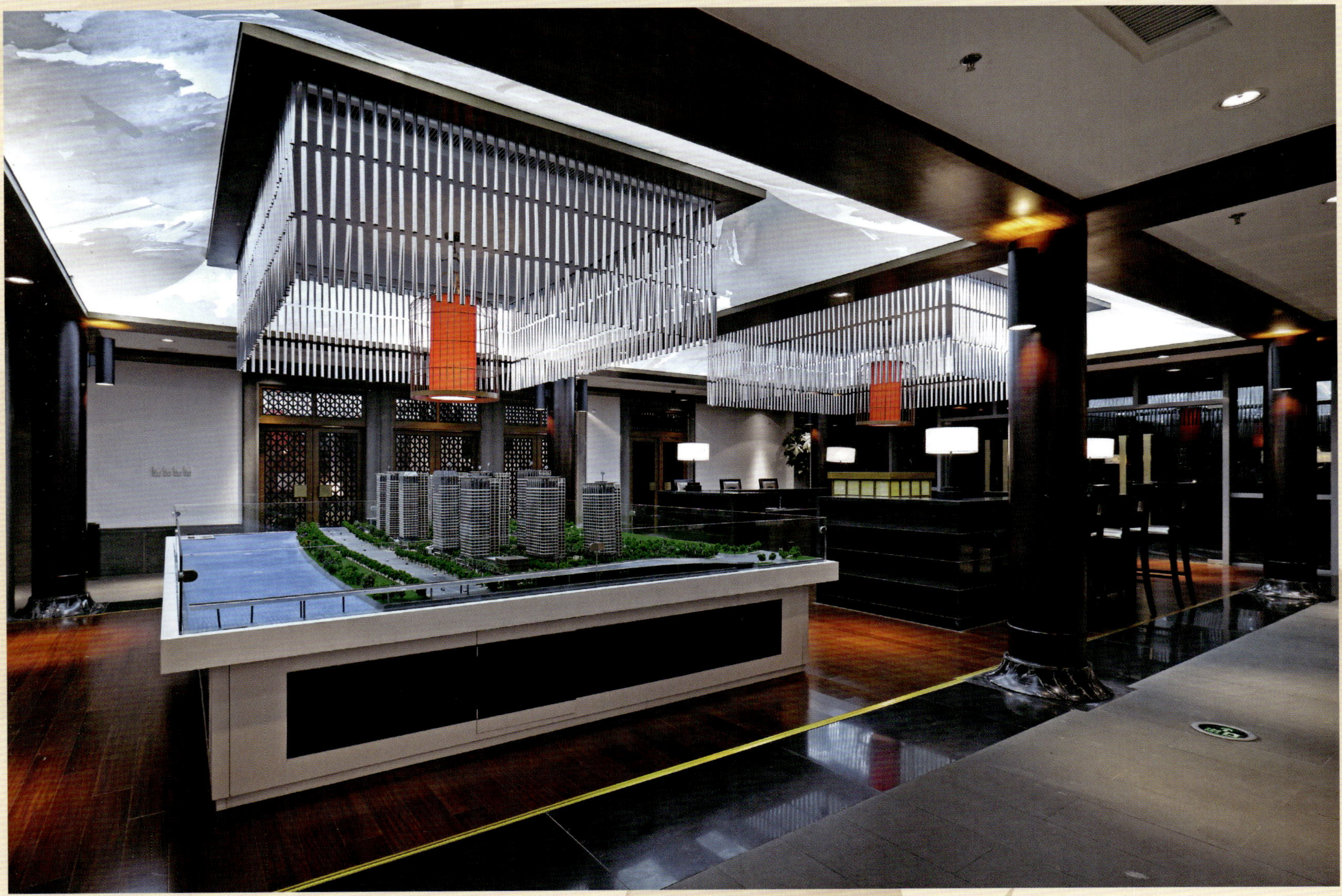

106

二层平面布置图
SC: 1:150

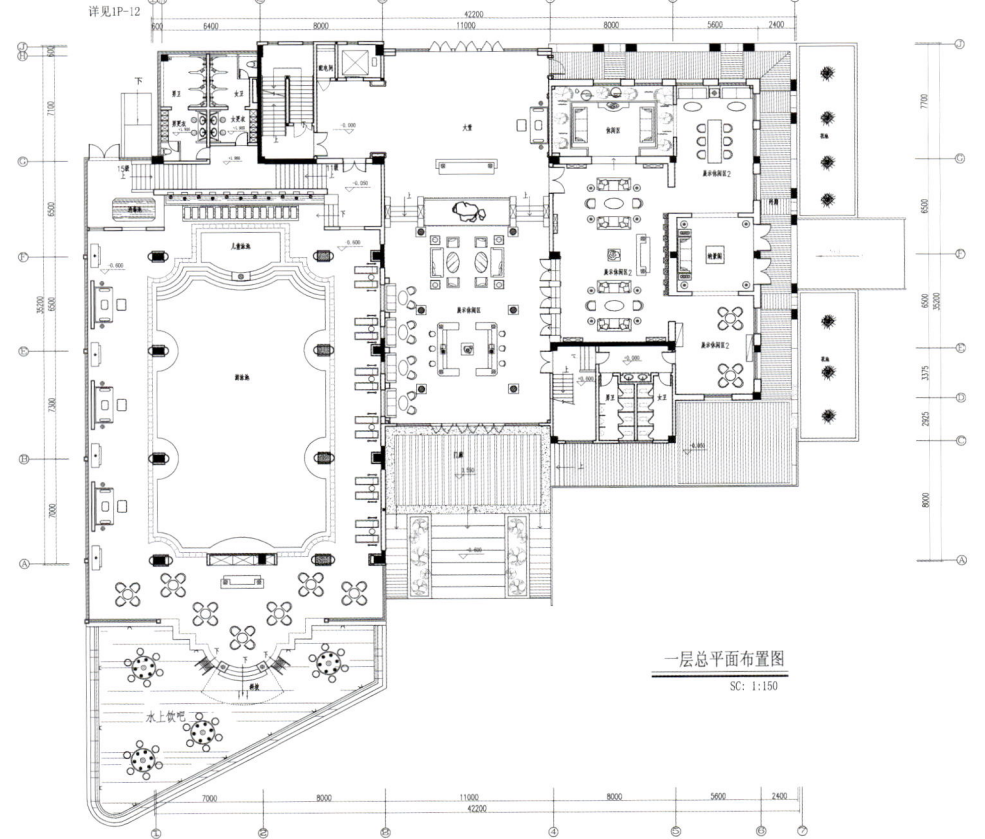

一层总平面布置图
SC: 1:150

107

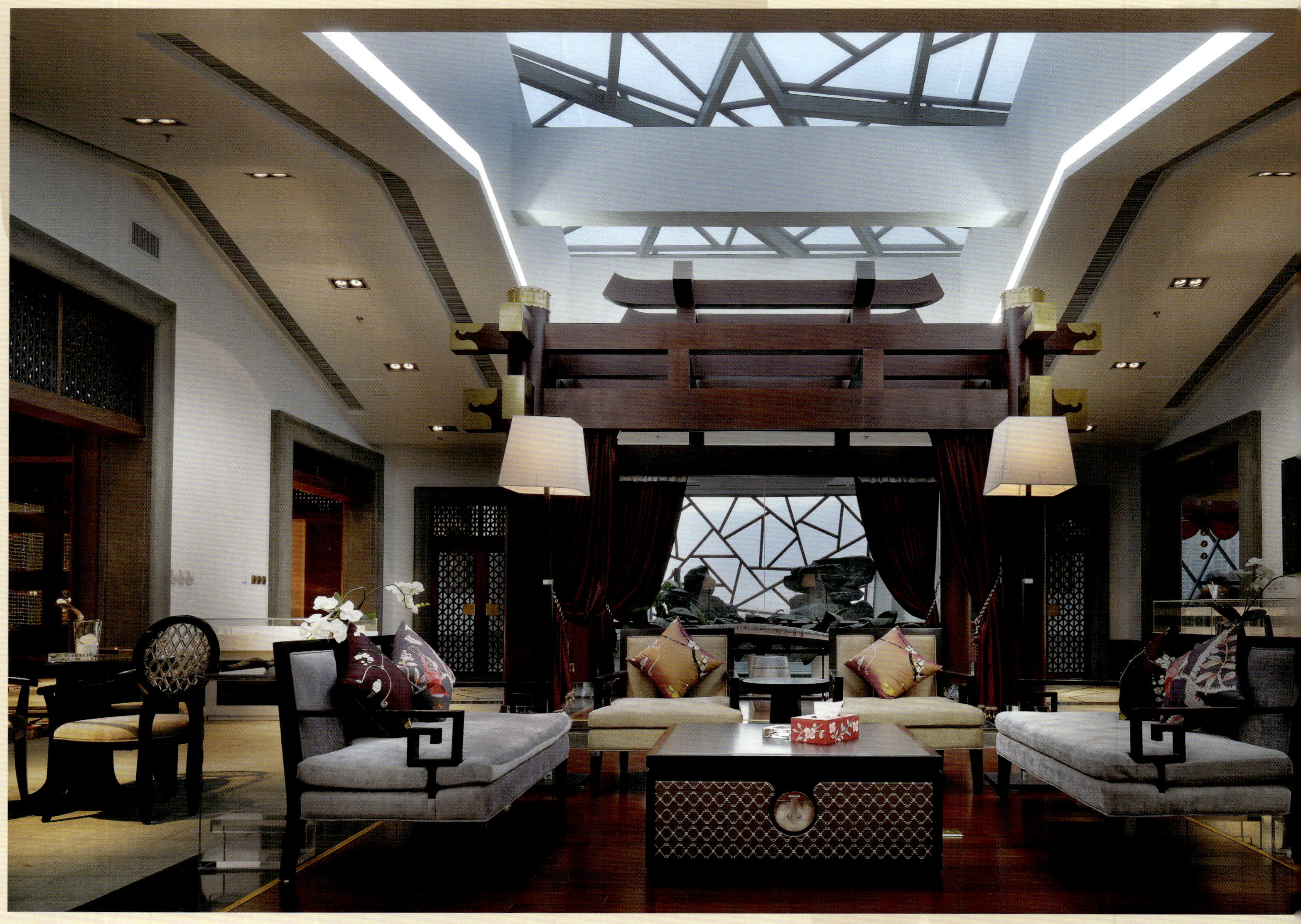

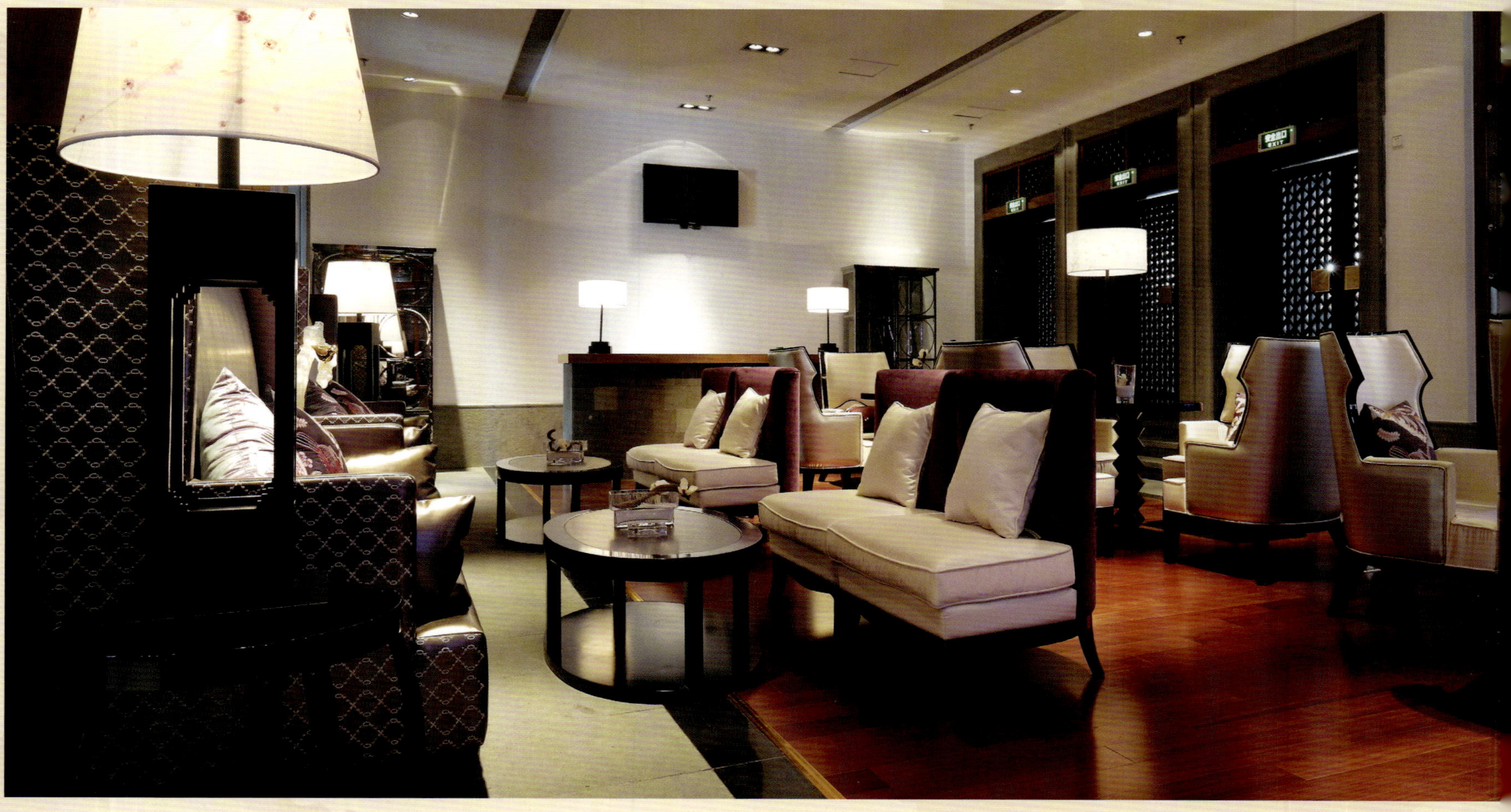

109

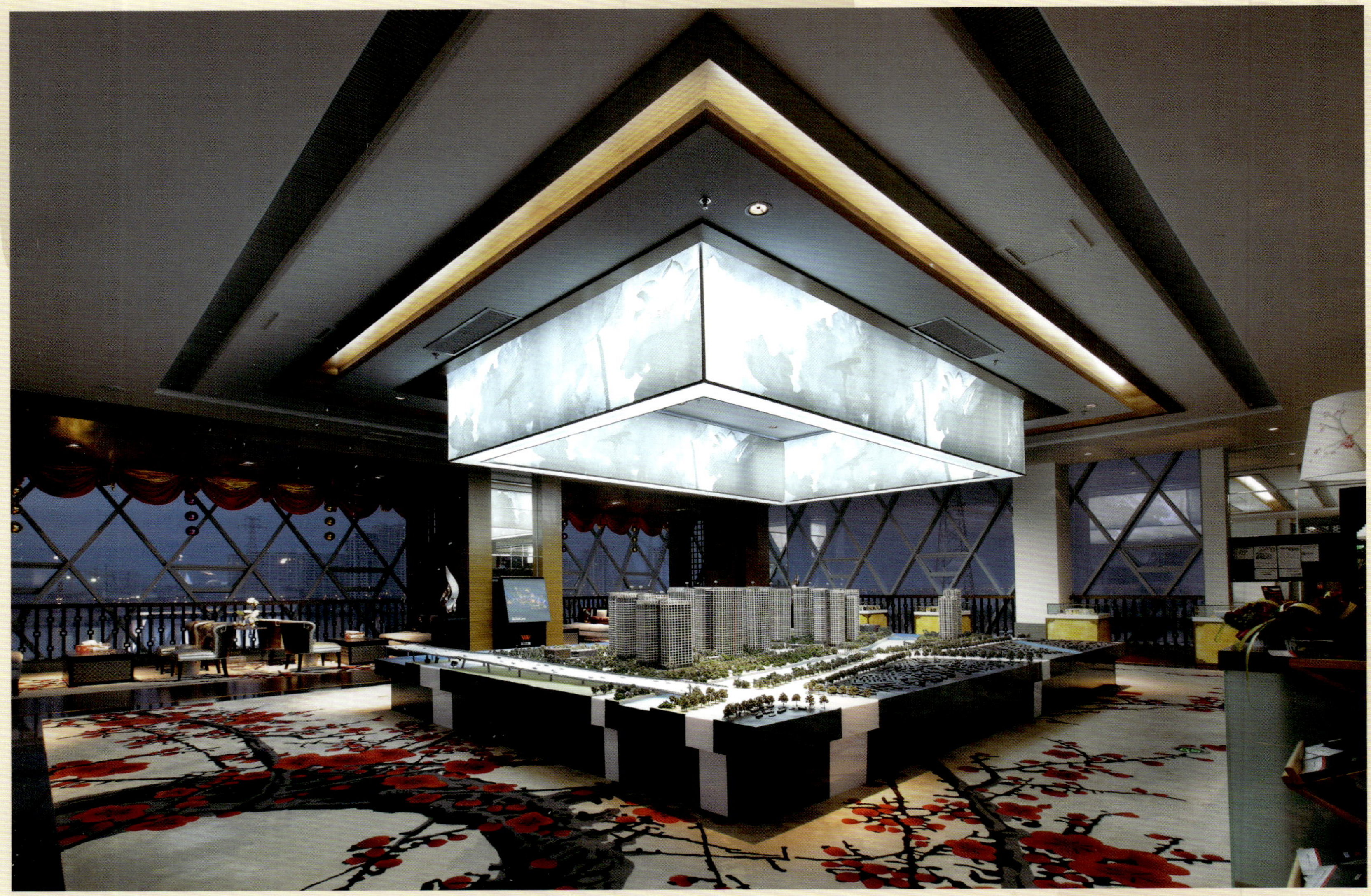

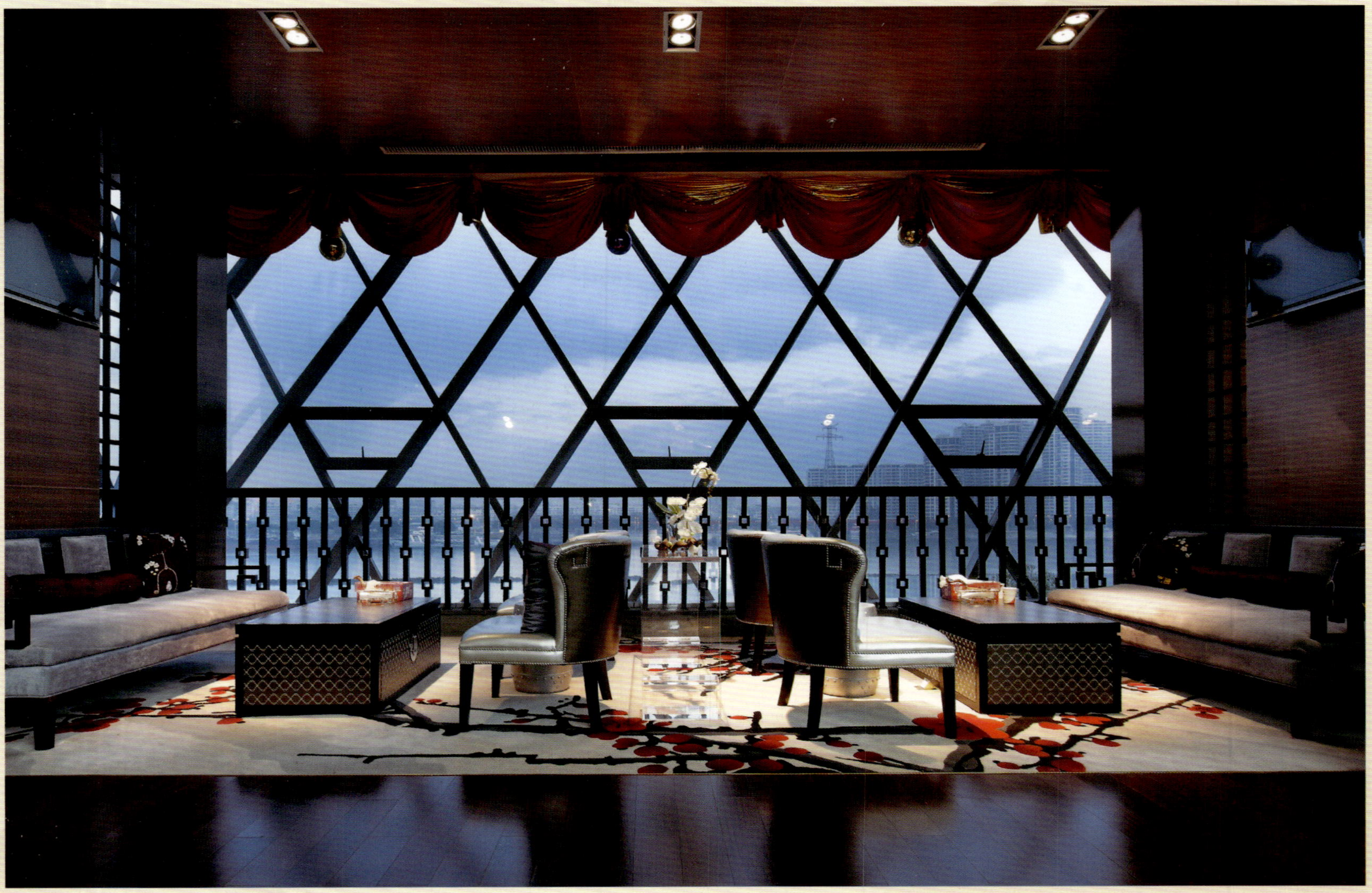

111

112

四层平面布置图
(面积:约1250㎡) SC: 1:150

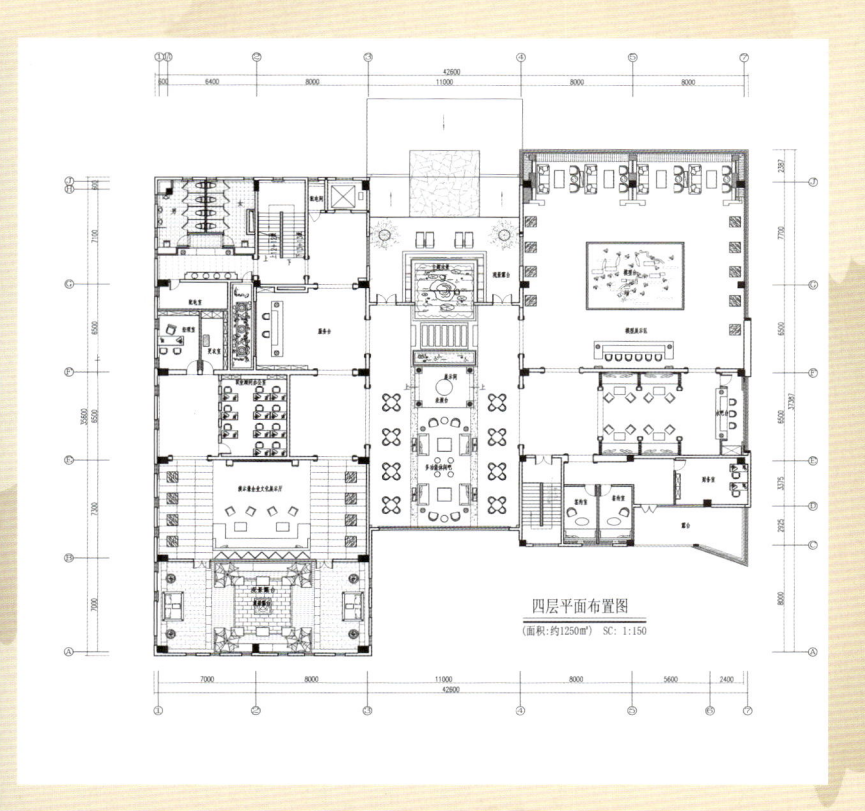

113

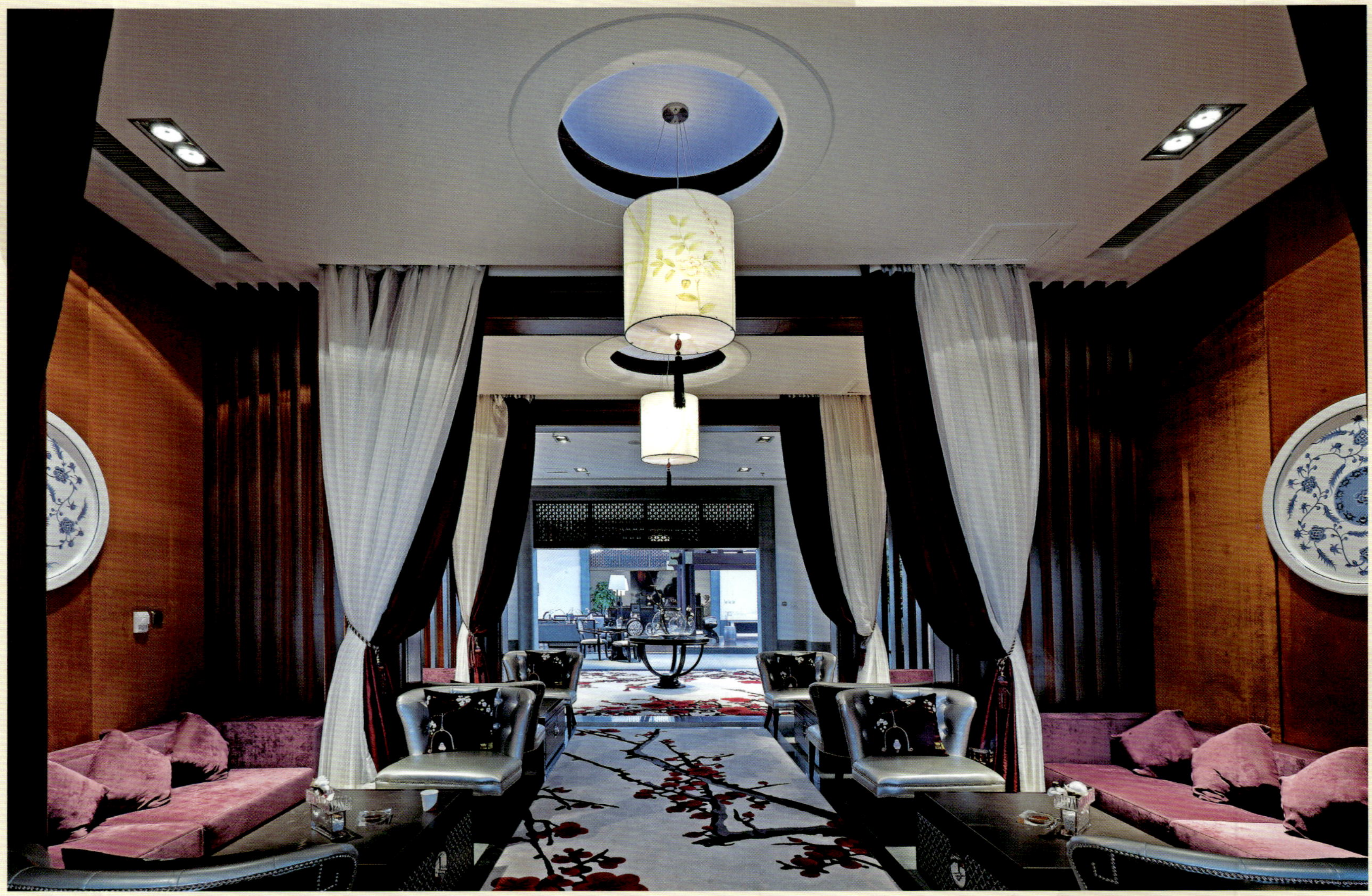

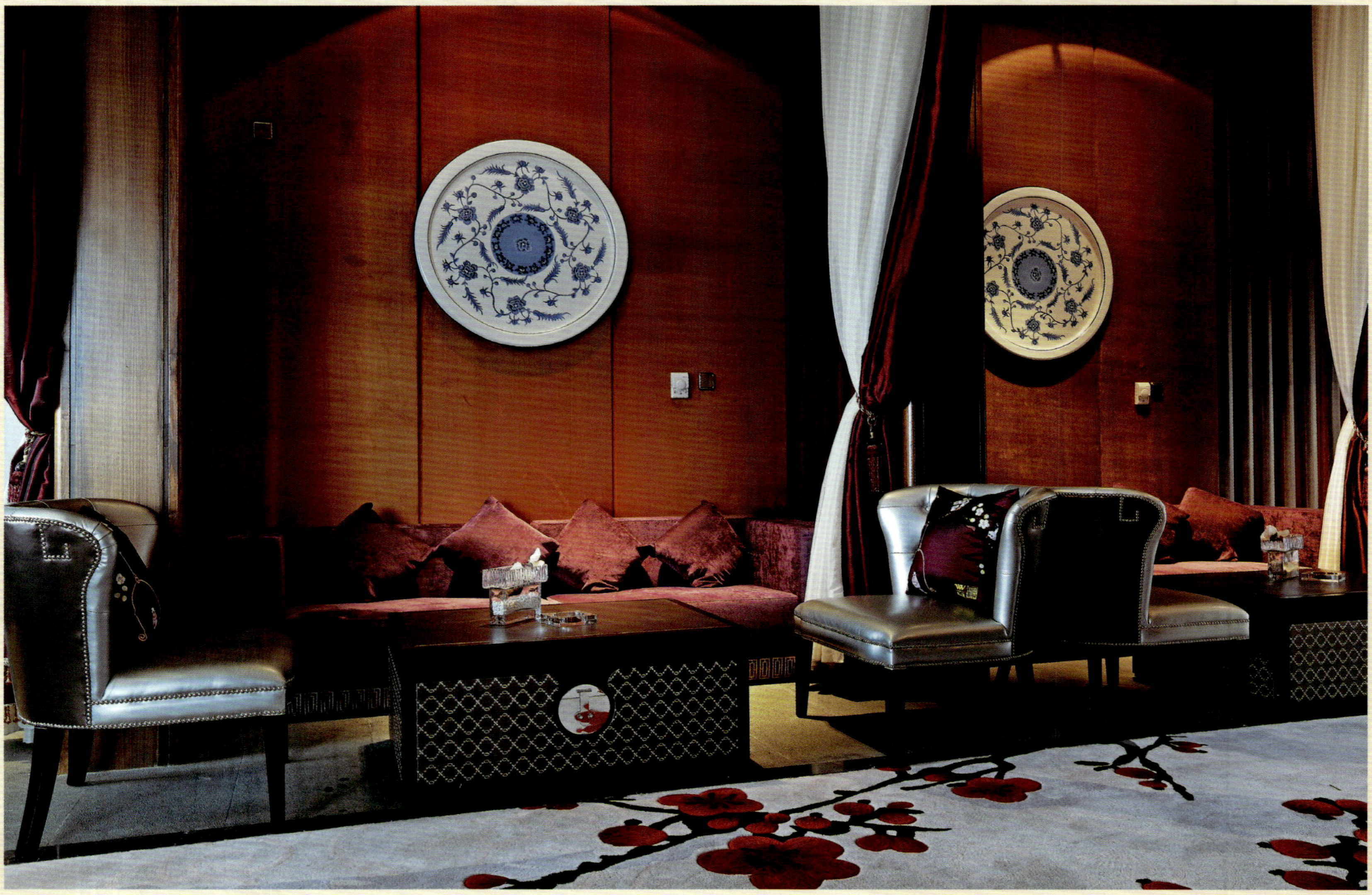

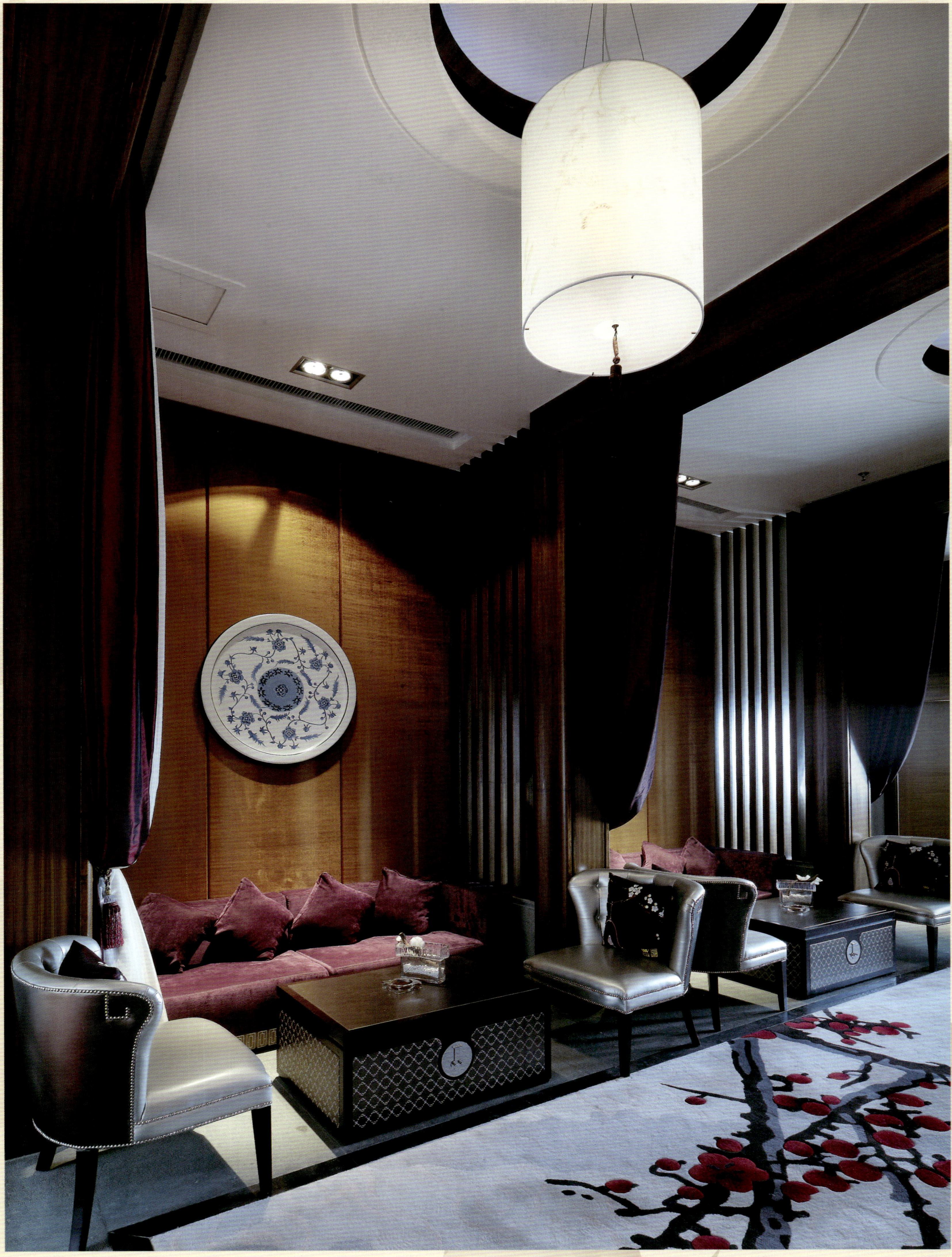

Enterprise Club of COSCO

Designer: Lydia Lu
Decoration Design: MoGA Decoration Design
Client: China Ocean Shipping(Group) Company
Location: Shanghai, China
Area: 300 m²

With a good Location near Huangpu Rive, it has a great view of the Oriental Pearl and the Bund scenic.

Armarni Casa's furniture extremely conveys the concept of simpleness, elegance and luxury. Shell plate, copper wallpaper, leather ceiling and imported silver enrich the space with low-key luxury.

117

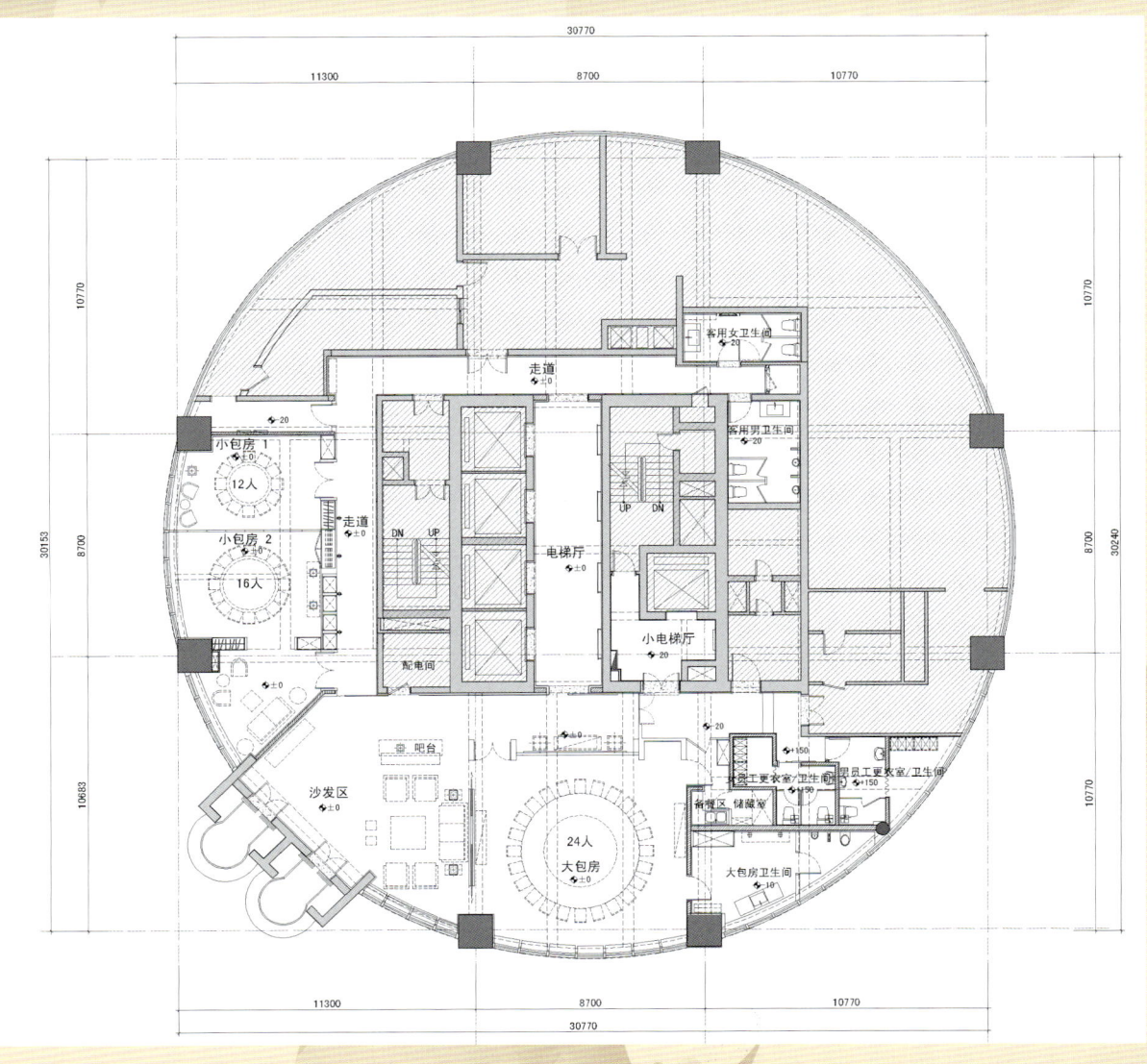

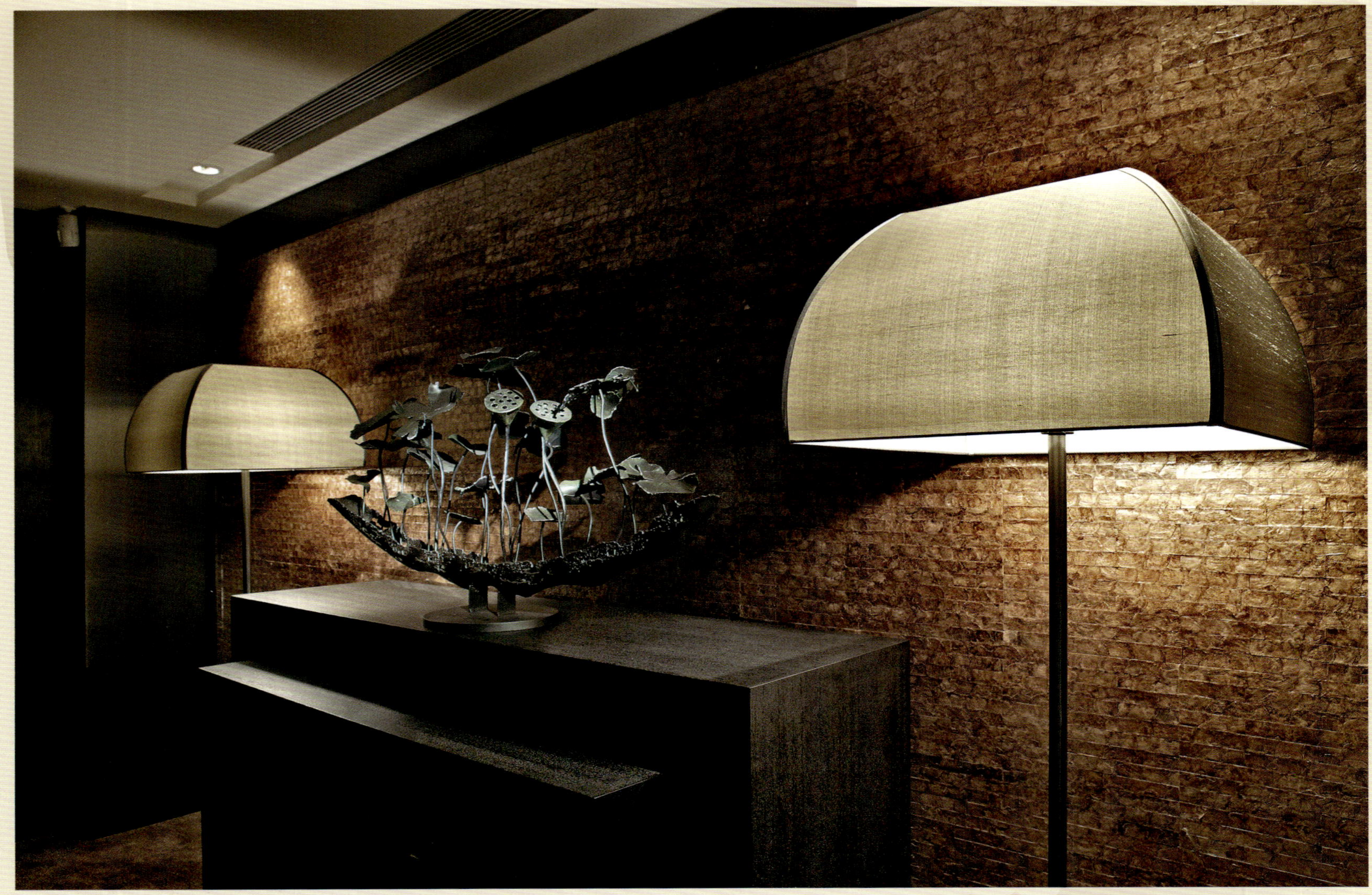

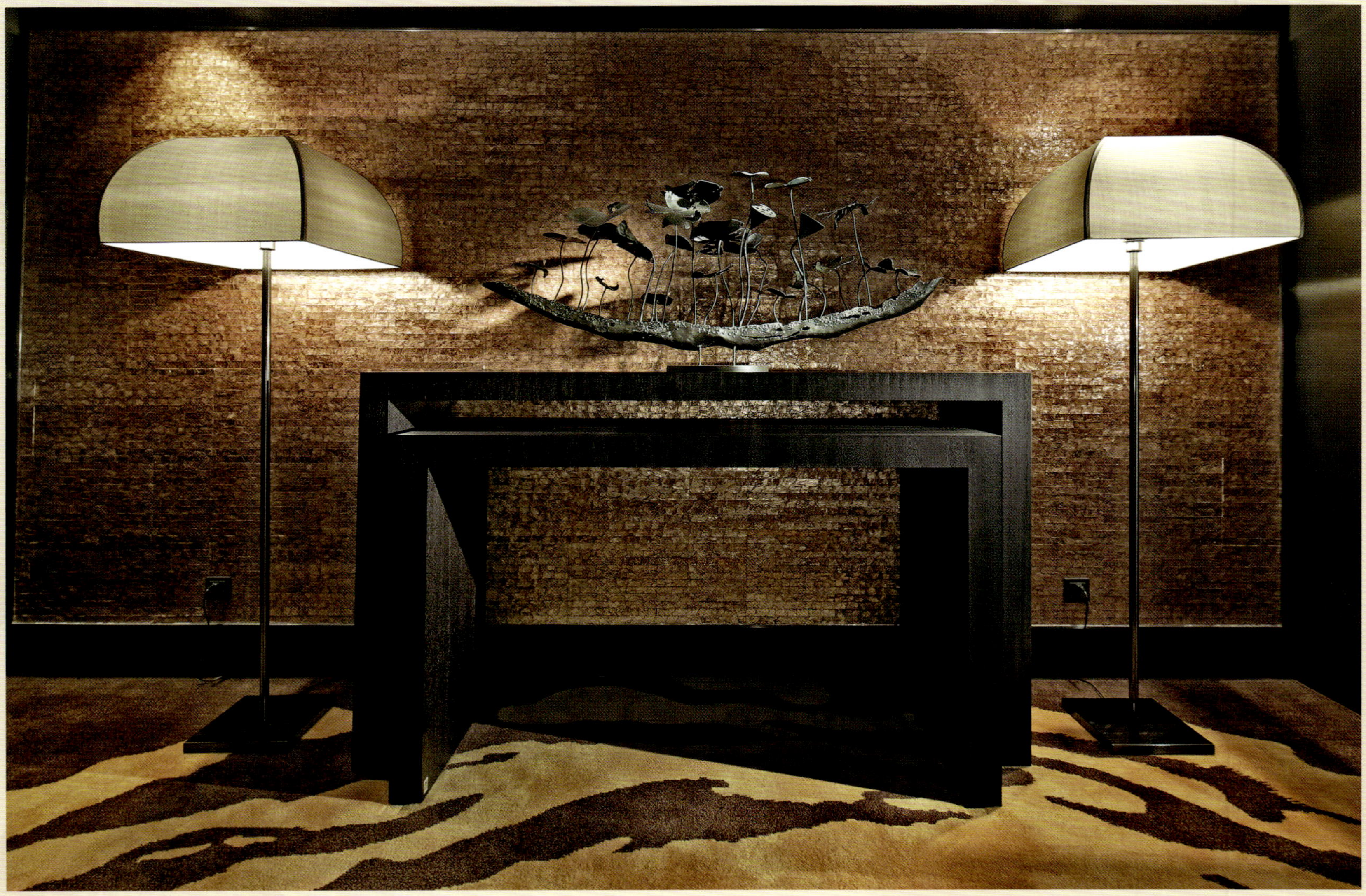

119

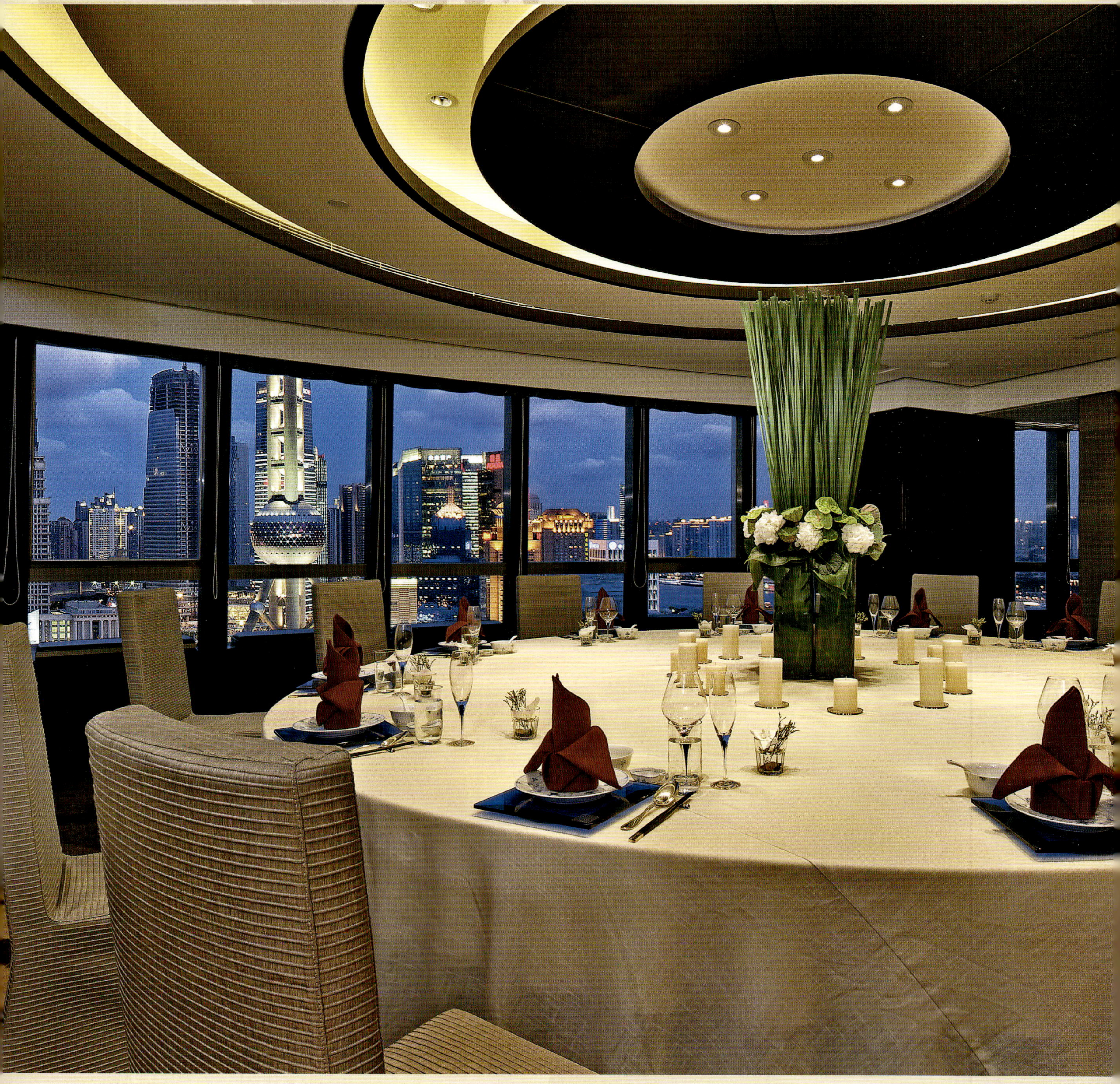

121

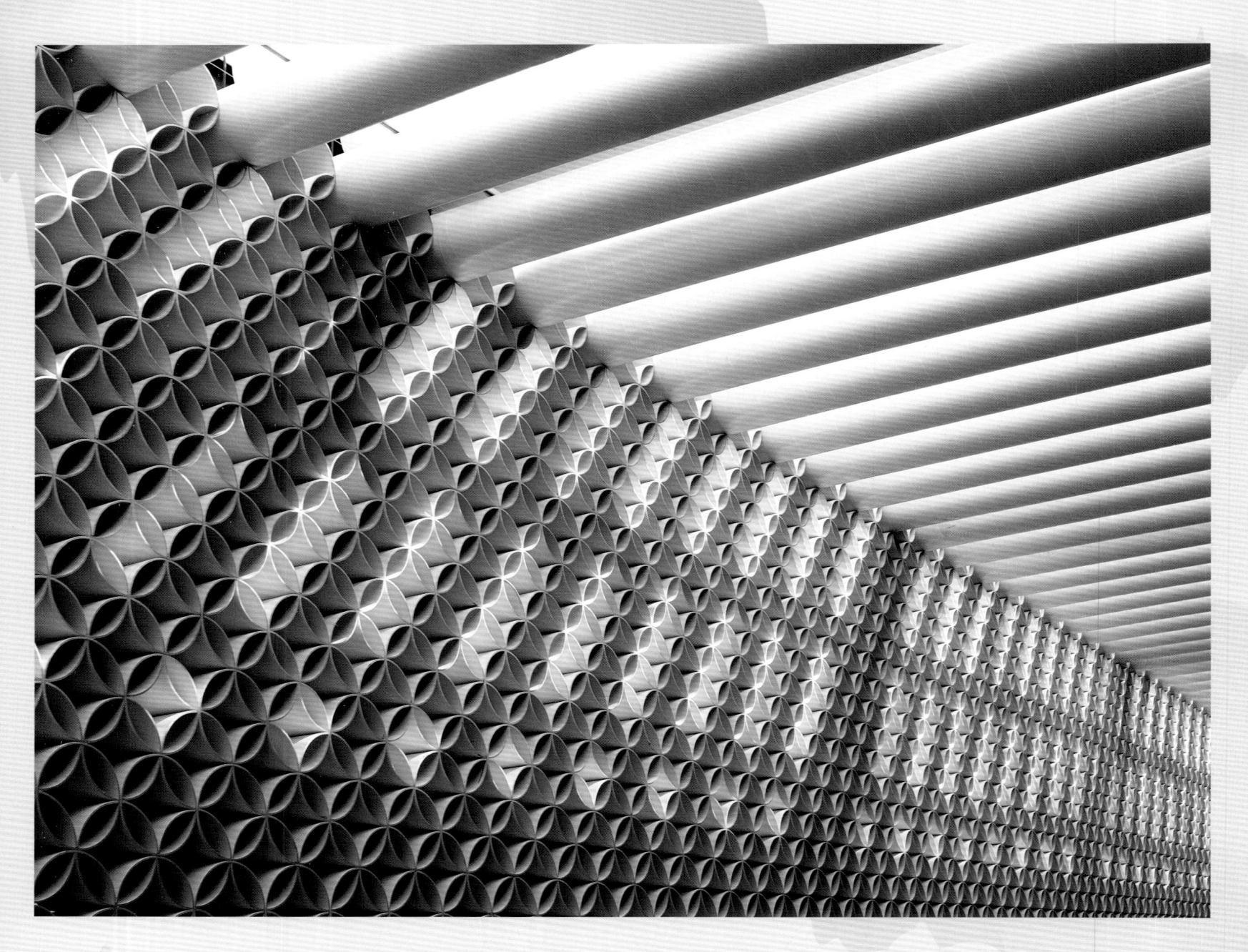

Yuanxiong Jinhuayuan Sales Center

Design Agency: Sherwood Design
Designer: Huang Shuheng
Location: Taipei, China
Area: 1153 m²
Photographer: Wang Jishou

This sales center mainly adopts the European nobility style, the pure white space plus the natural light from outside, just like the noble and holy ceremonly space. The designer uses the contemporary design technique to show an elegant and classic space.

And the most wonderful part of this sales center is in the middle of this space. It is a complete white wall with various designs. This could be a creative thought by the Sherwood designers.

123

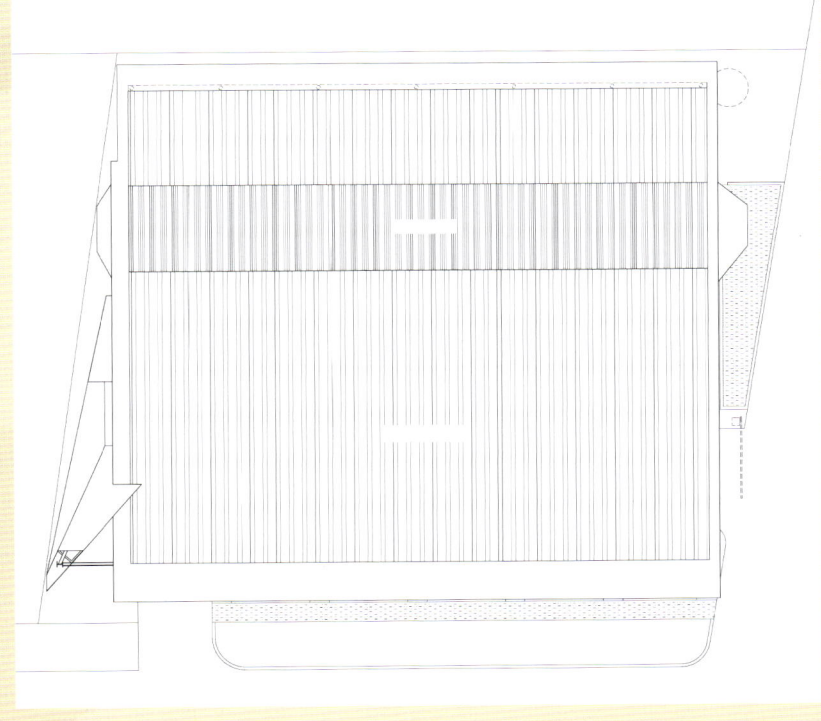

124

125

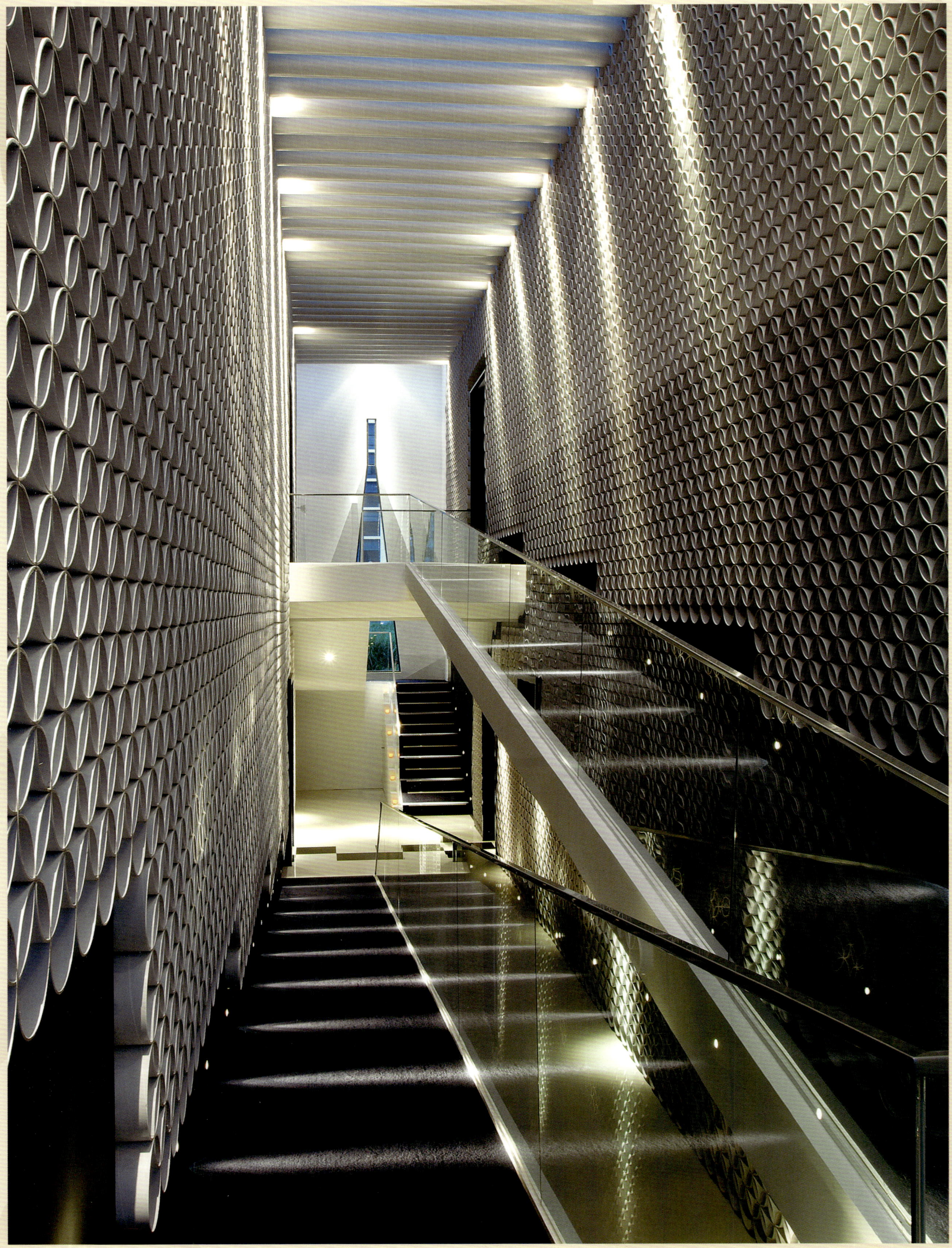

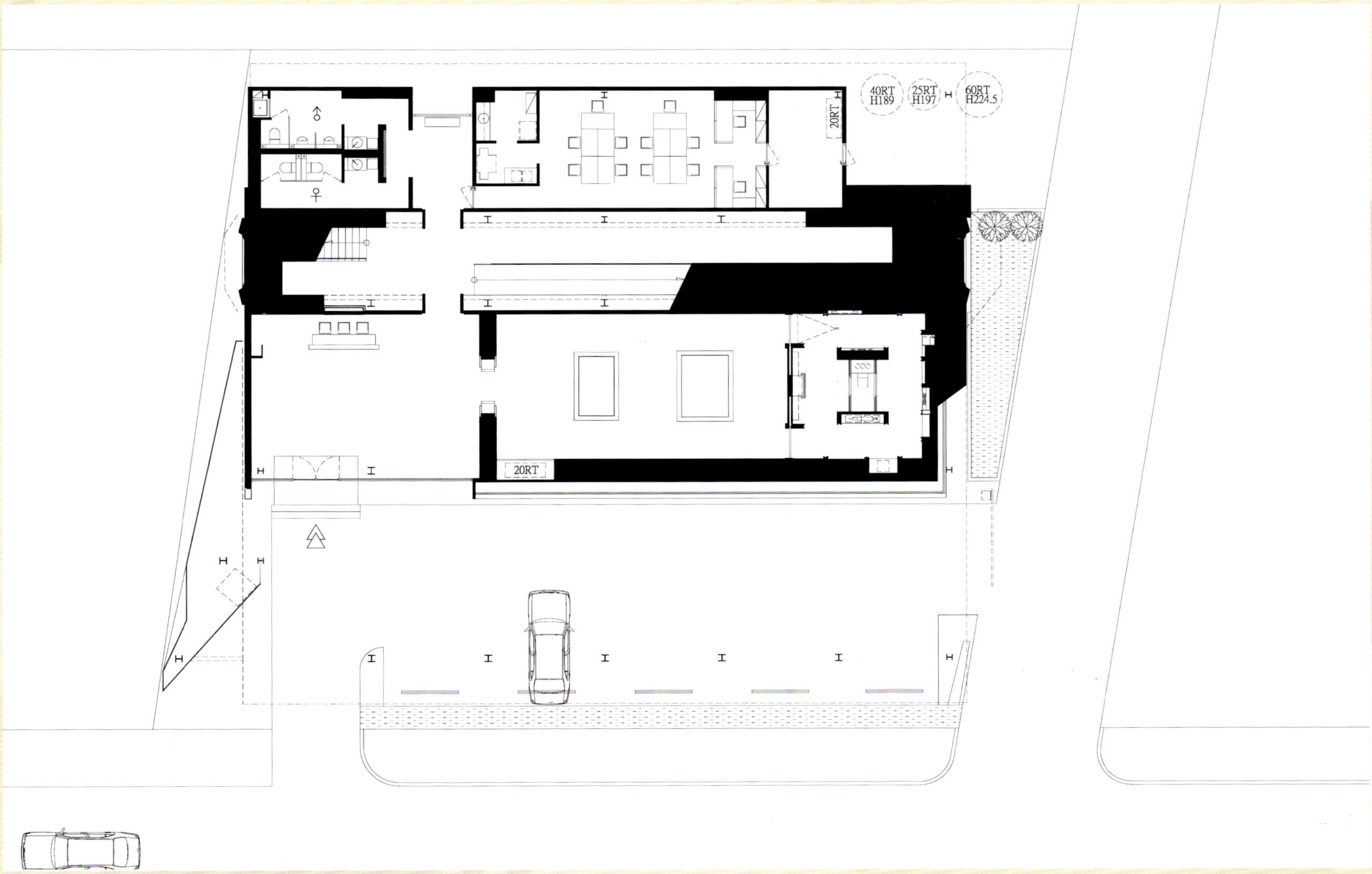
40RT
H189
25RT
H197
60RT
H224.5
20RT
20RT

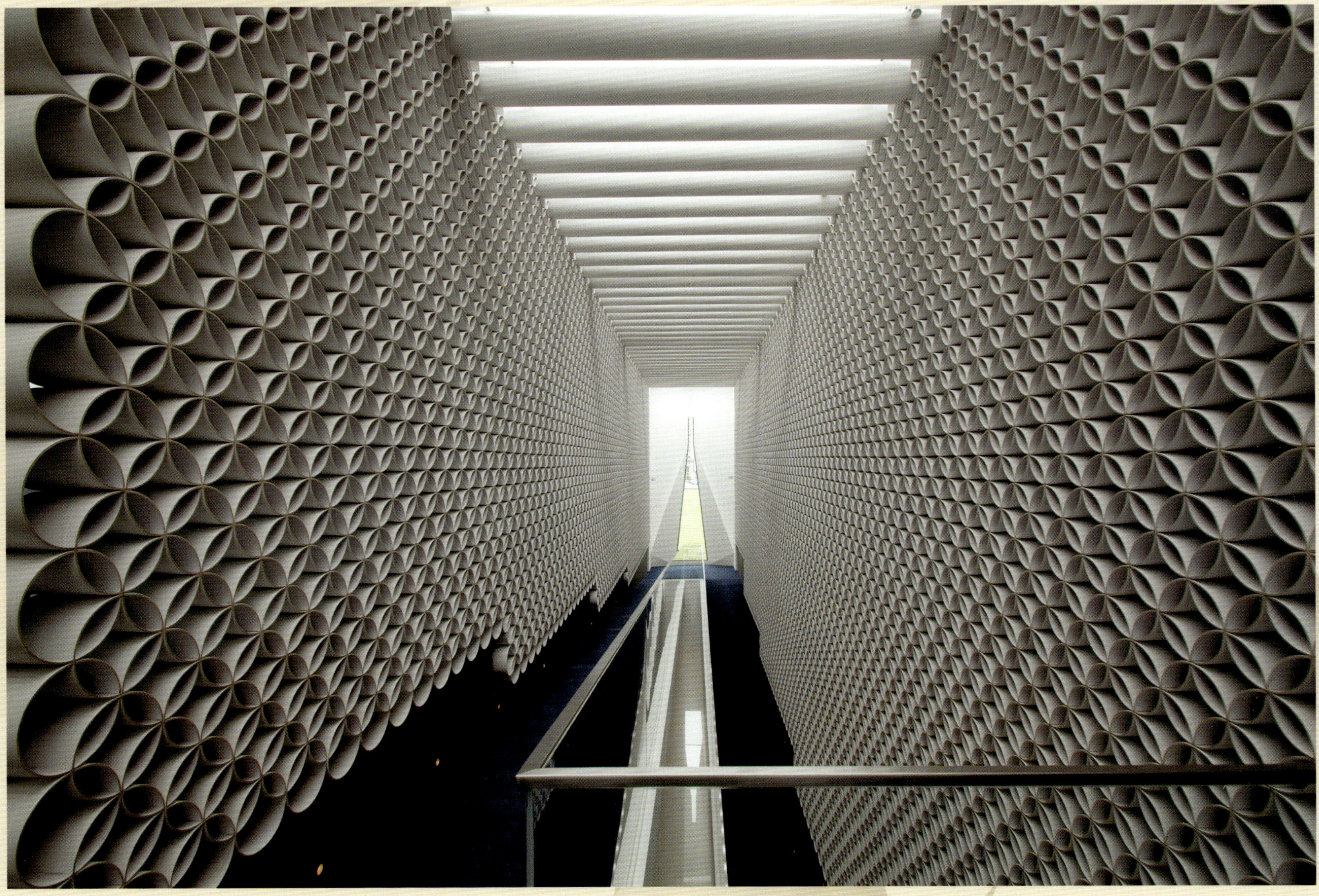

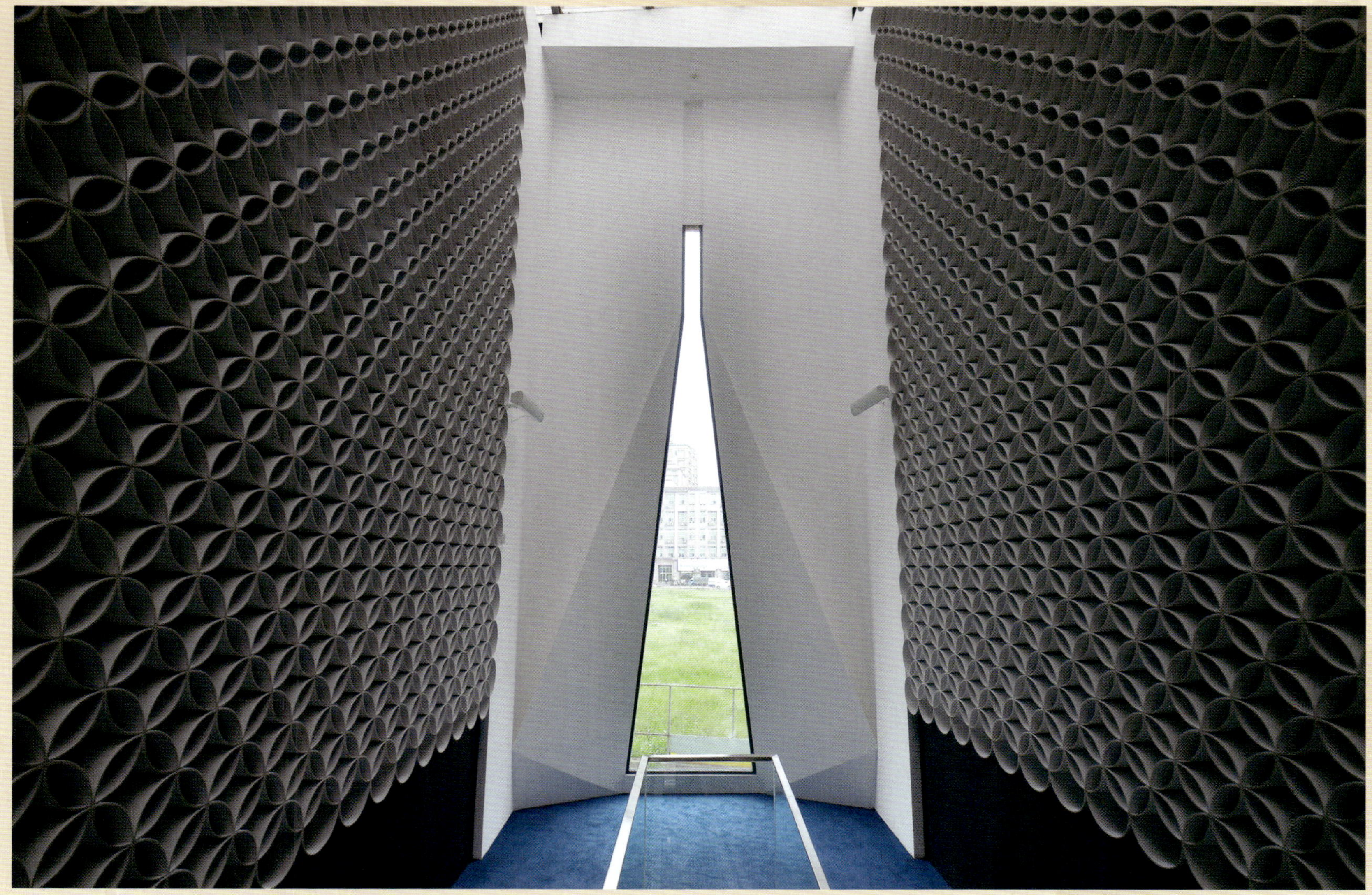

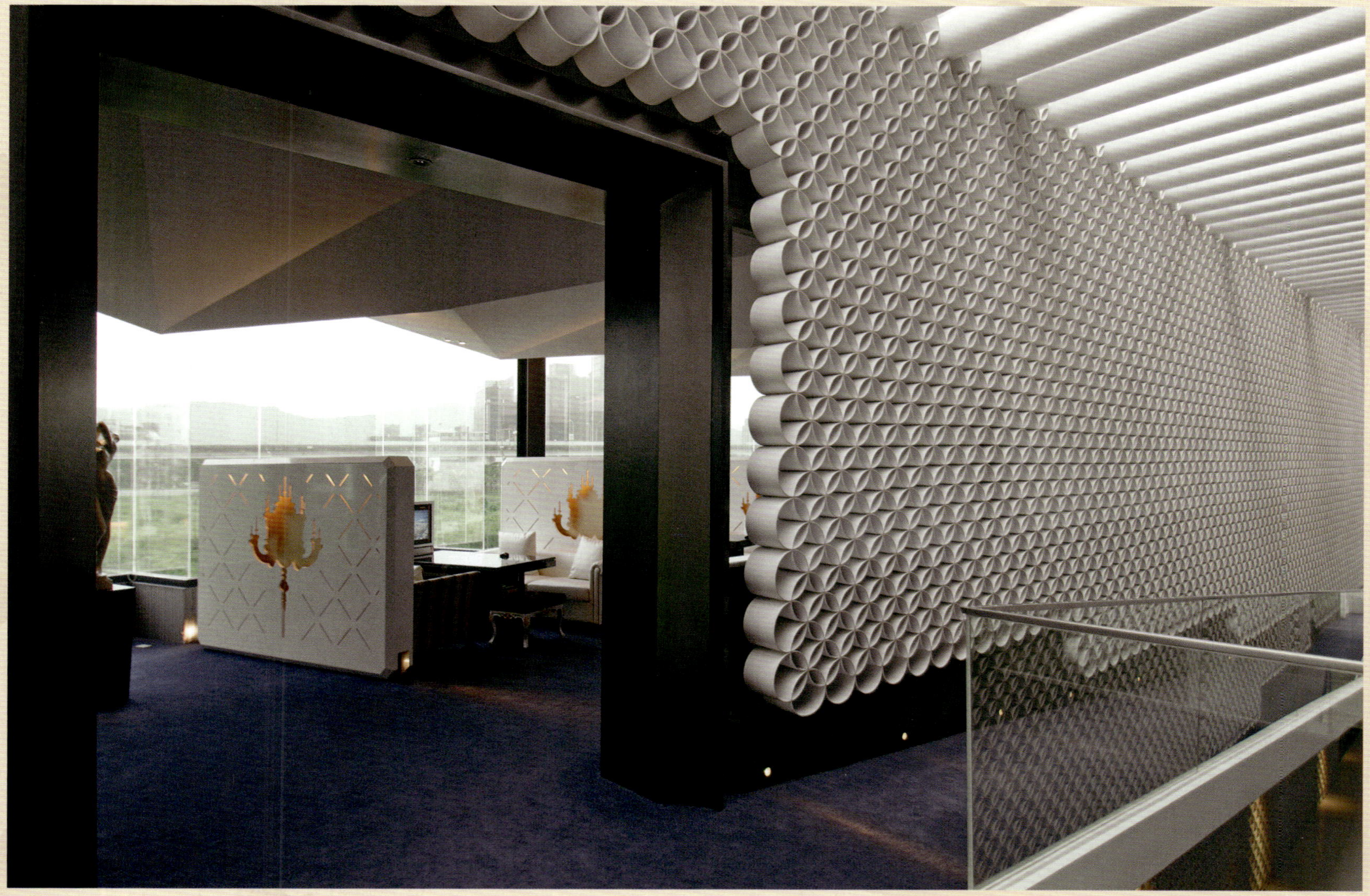

129

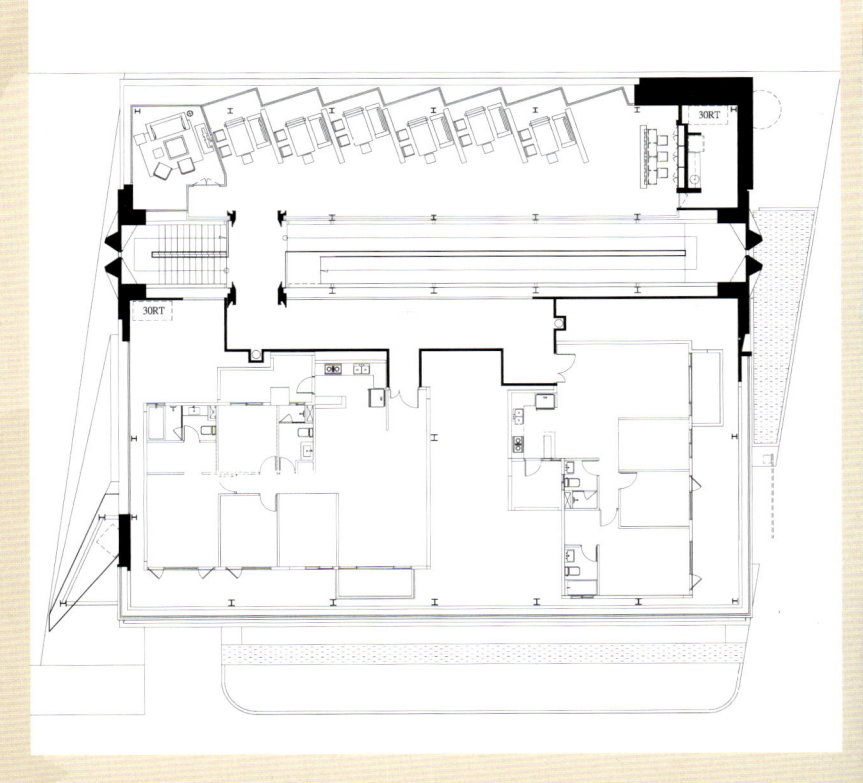

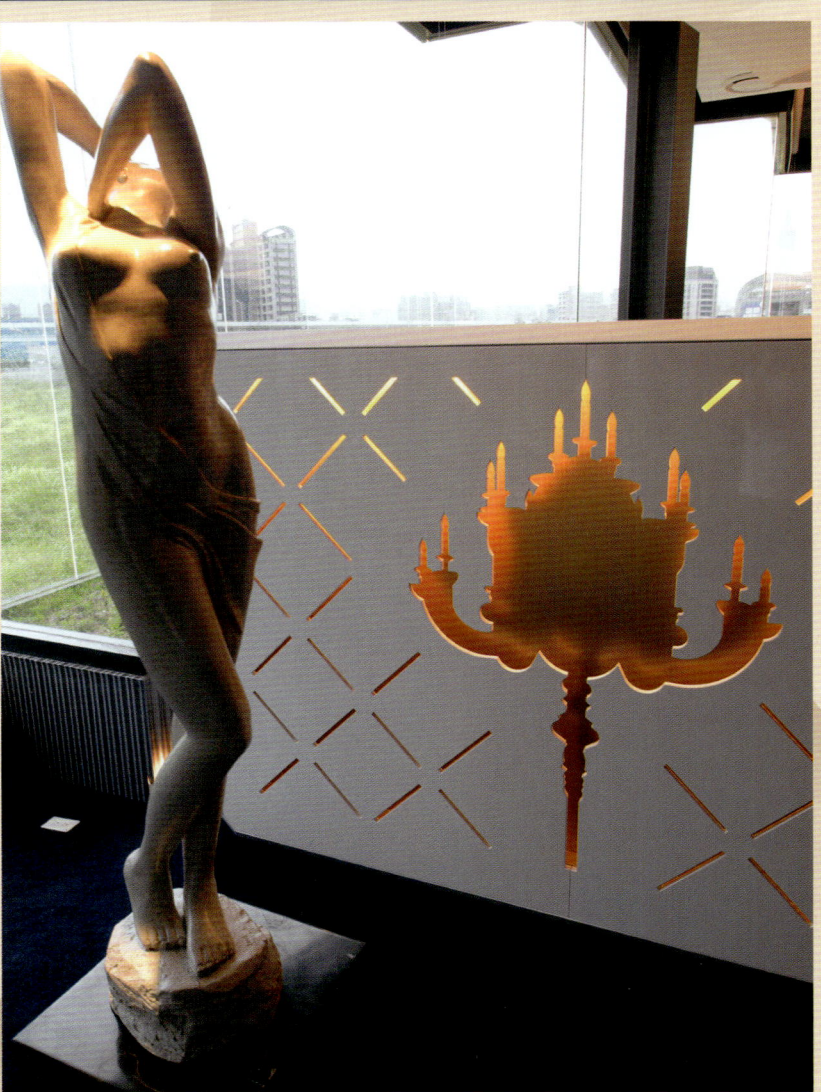

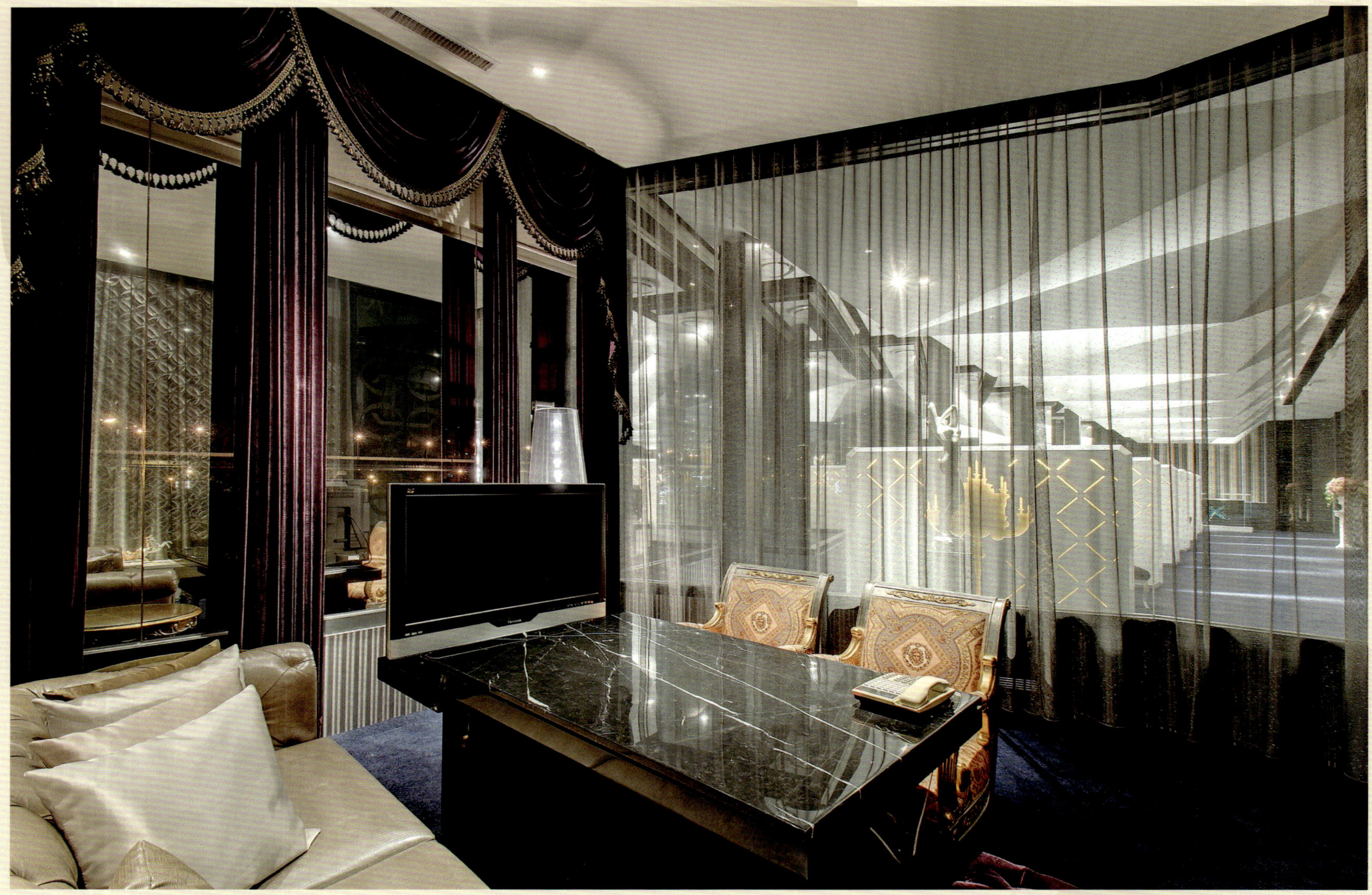

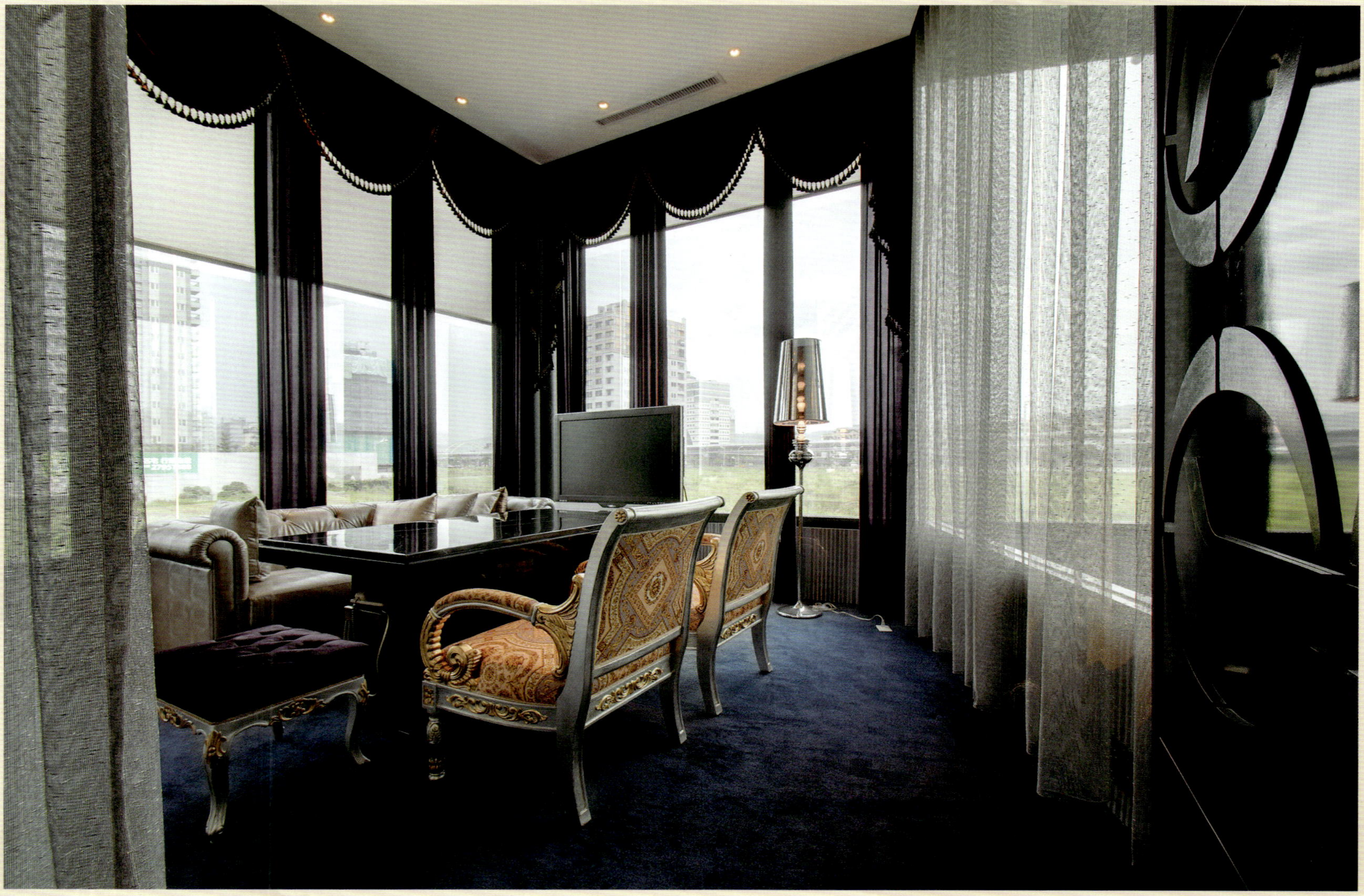

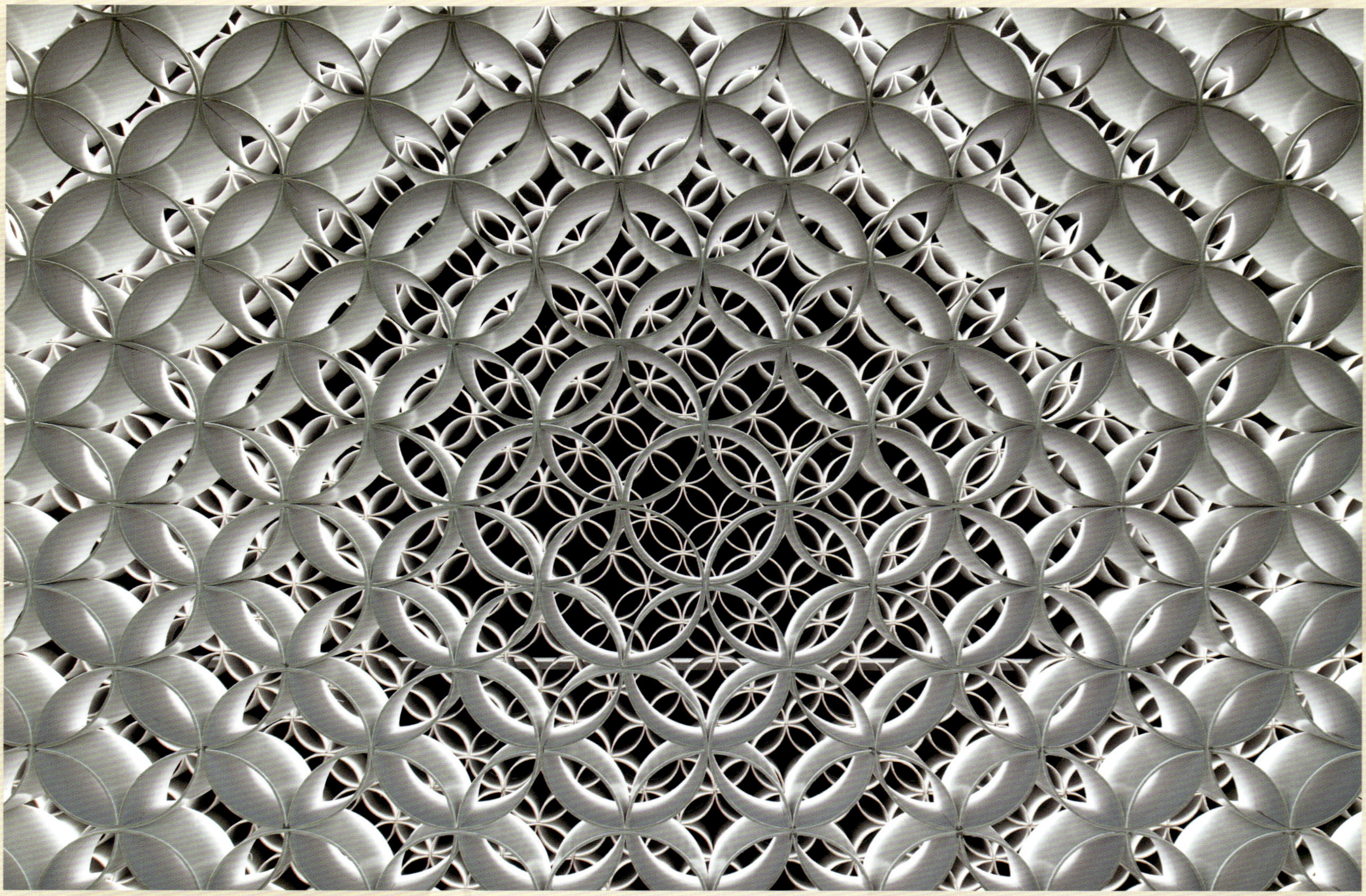

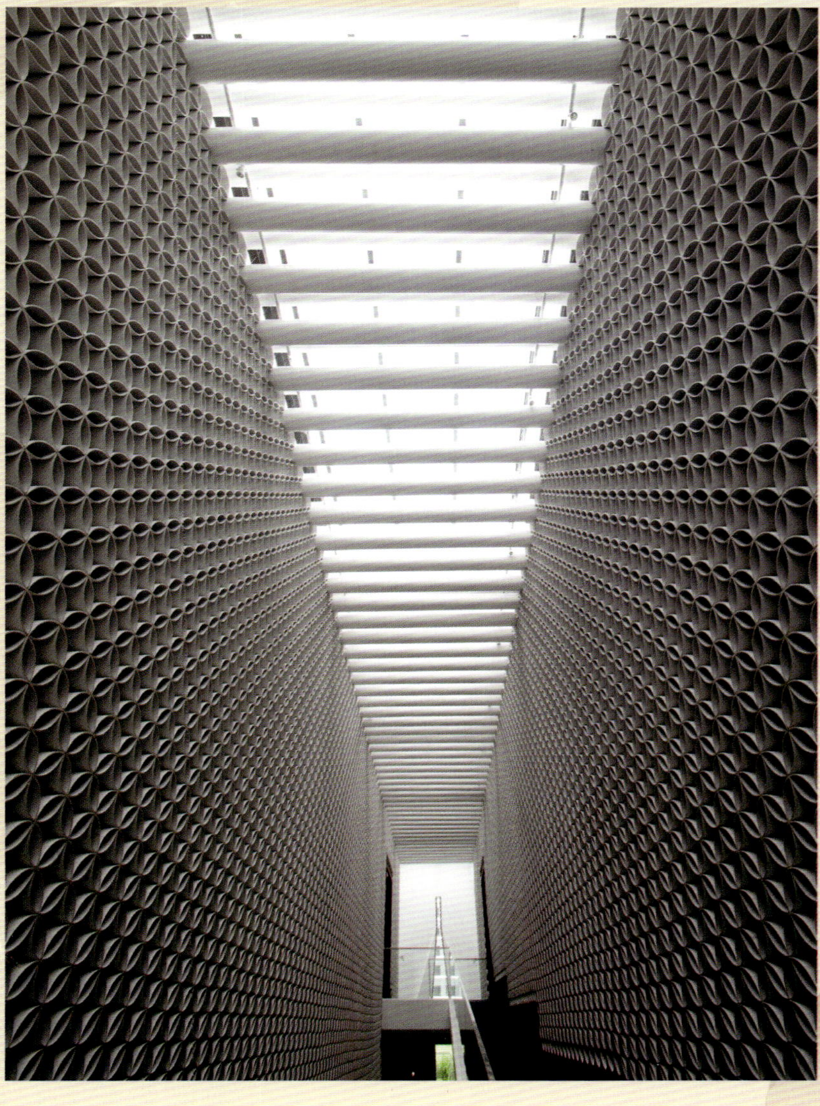

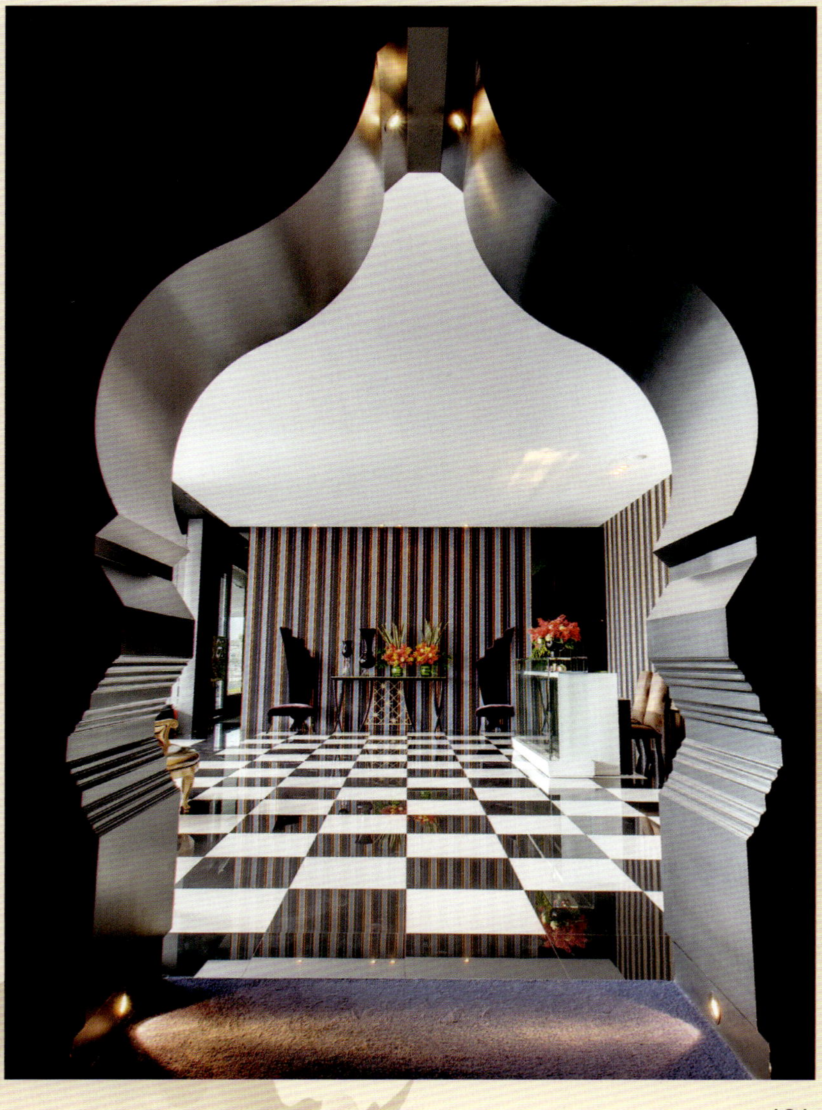

Pavilion 2012

Architect: Pitsou Kedem

Design Team: Pitsou Kedem, Irene Goldberg, Raz Melamed

Photographer: Amit Geron

A structure is used by a real estate company as a sales office for residential project they are building. The project examines the line between architecture, marketing and consumption.

The architect chose to relate it to the project as a contemporary pavilion and attempted to combine, within one building, modern, minimalistic, architectural principles and thereby create a building that is almost an object or a piece of sculpture akin to a small, architectural pavilion. At the same time, the architect attempted to cope with consumer principles relevant to the period, the need to sell and the reasons for the structures construction — marketing, marketing, and marketing.

It is interesting to see the mutuality between pure architecture which, despite everything, manages through purity and constraint to serve the brand needs of a large real estate company which usually seeks ways to stand out, to be bigger and more grandiose. The architecture succeeds in bringing to the world of aggressive marketing used by real estate companies a structure, which despite its temporary nature (it will be demolished in a year's time), also brings with it qualities associated with permanence.

The structure arouses curiosity and draws attention whilst still maintaining its monochromatic restraint and quiet strength. It uses reflecting pools to strengthen its look and to create illusions and reflections and combines central, internal courtyards with trees bursting out from two dimensional, white spaces which suggest the volume and the space inside the structure.

A geometric pattern of vertical wooden lines serves as a "skin" that divides the spaces or as a texture which is imprinted, using special techniques, on the outside. The sun's rays, striking the wall, create a repeating, three dimensional illusion. The pavilion succeeds in fulfilling both of its functions — architectural and marketing. The structure was designed and built in just three months. It was built entirely from a metal skeleton (lightweight construction), most of which was built in the factory and transported to the site for erection and finishing touches.

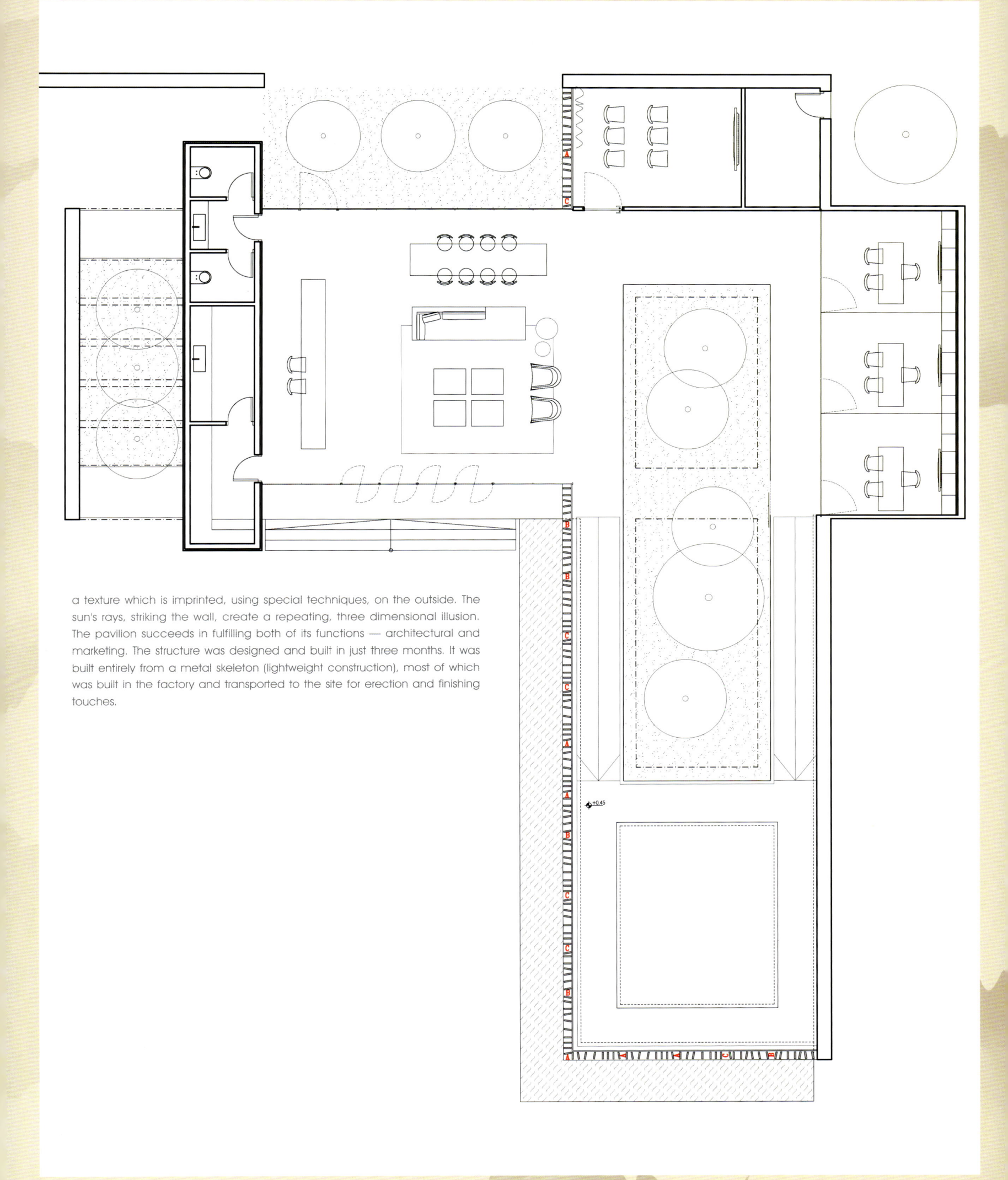

134

135

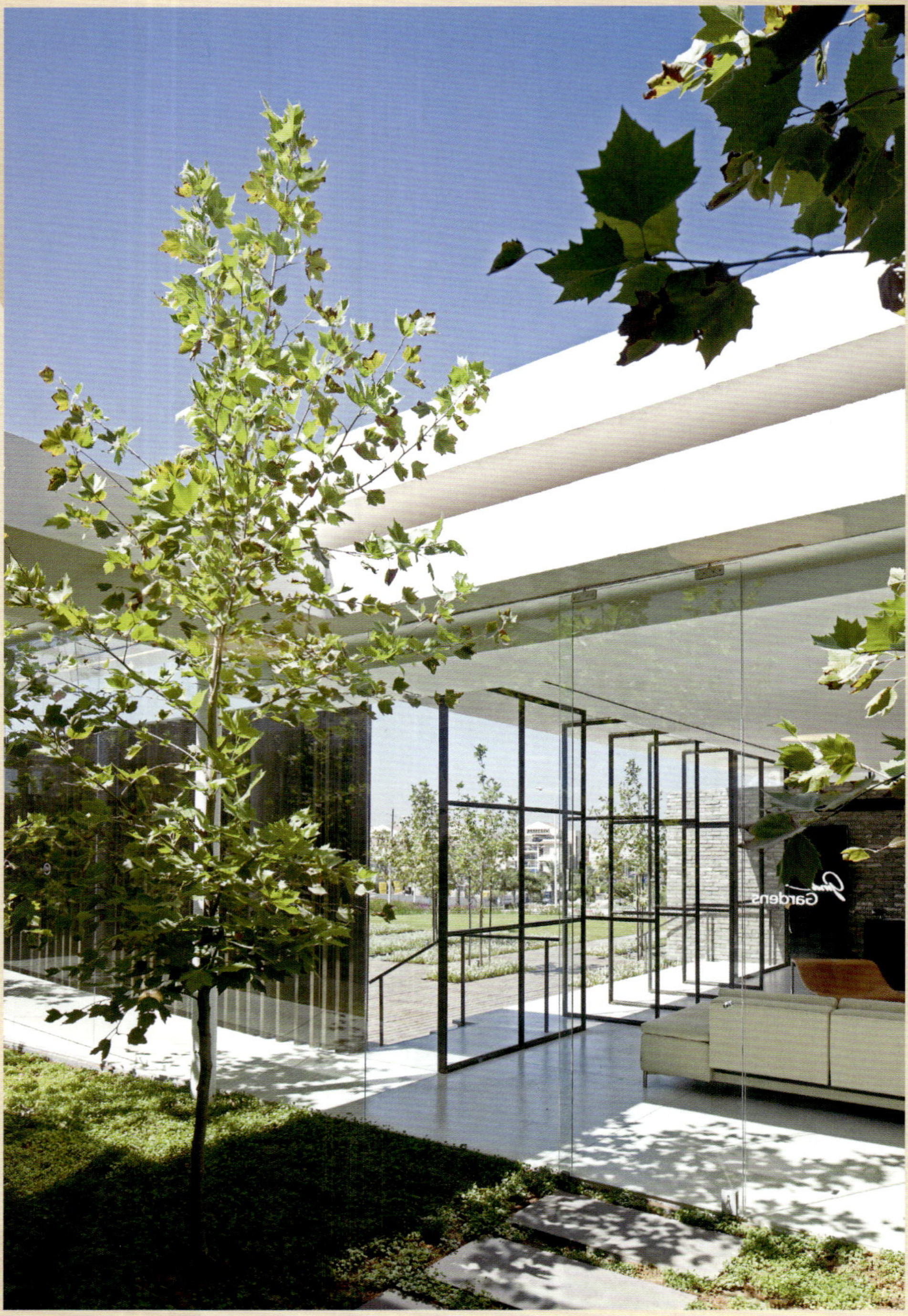

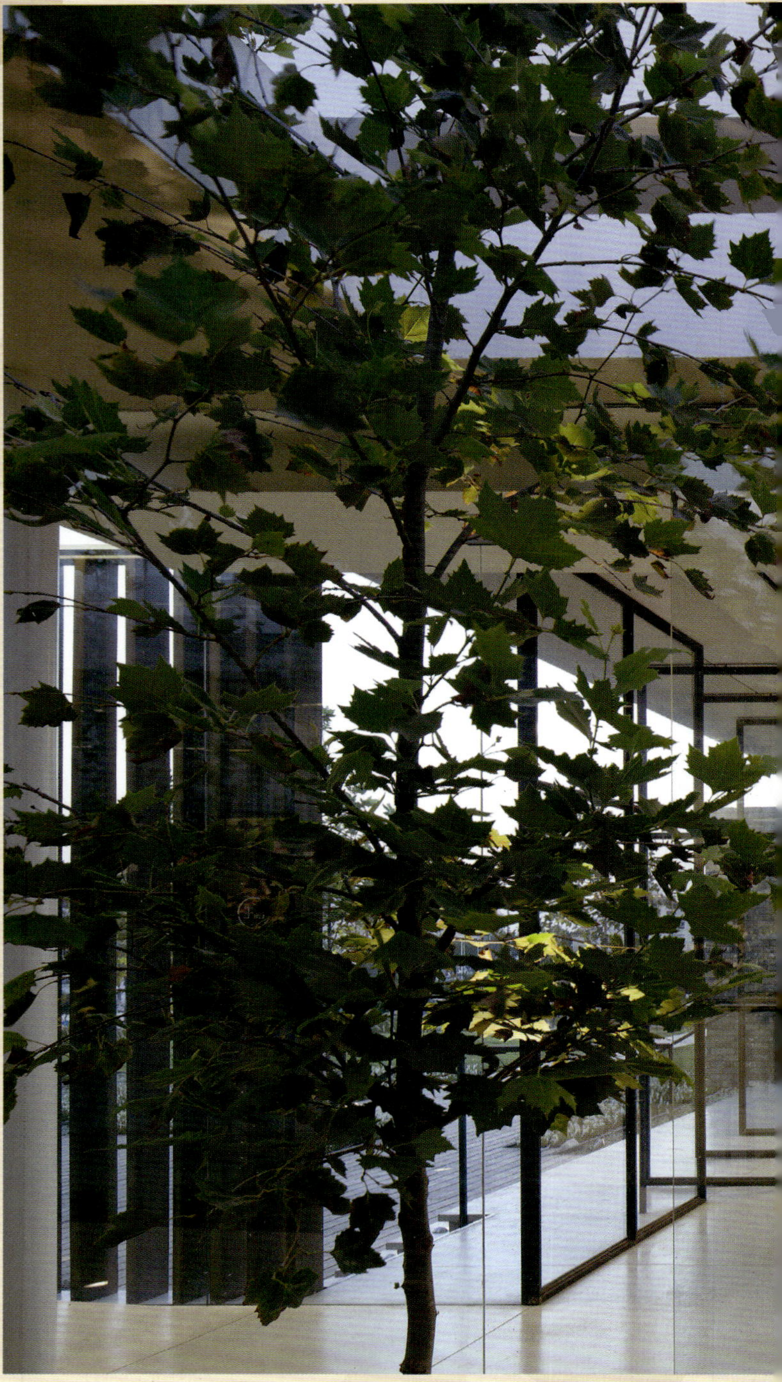

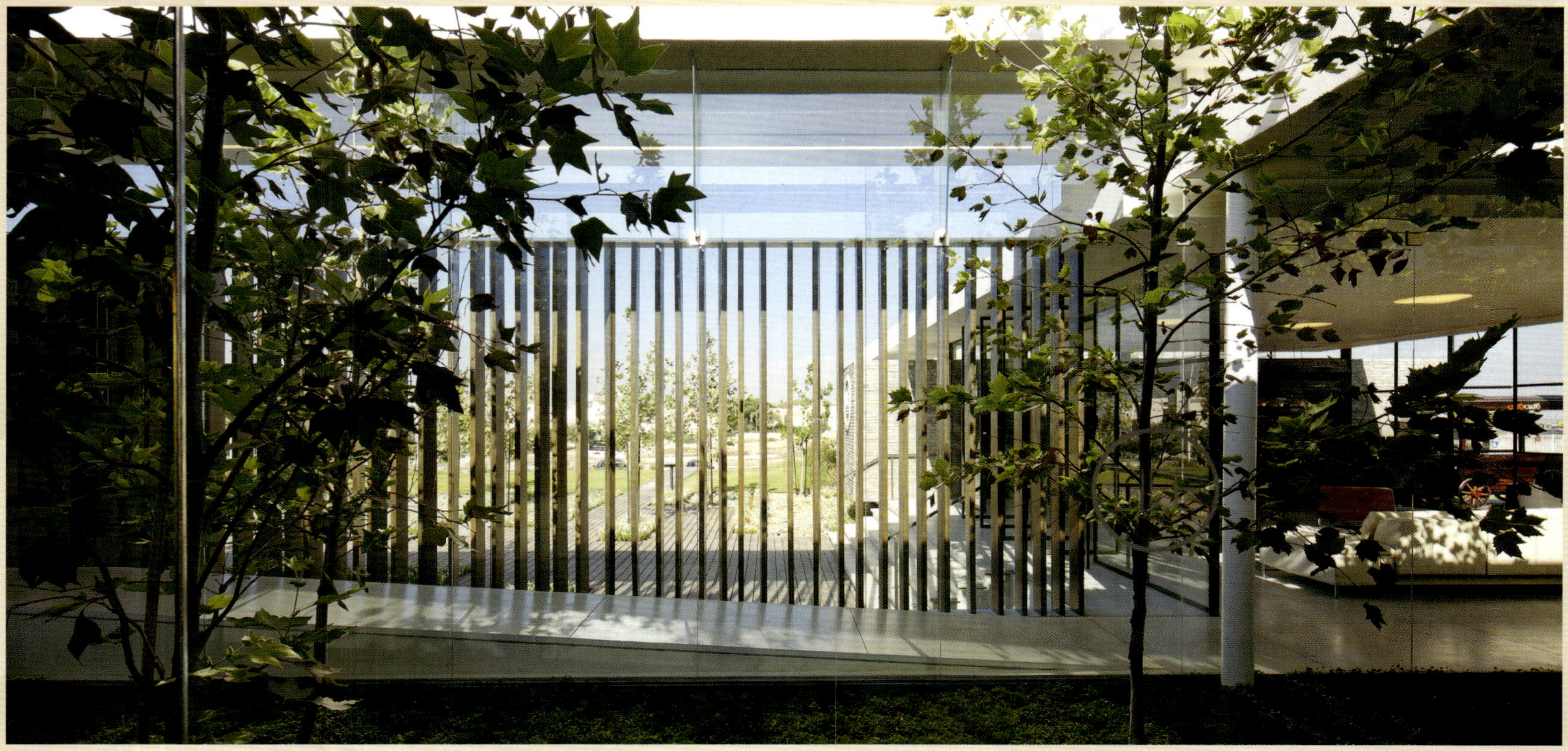

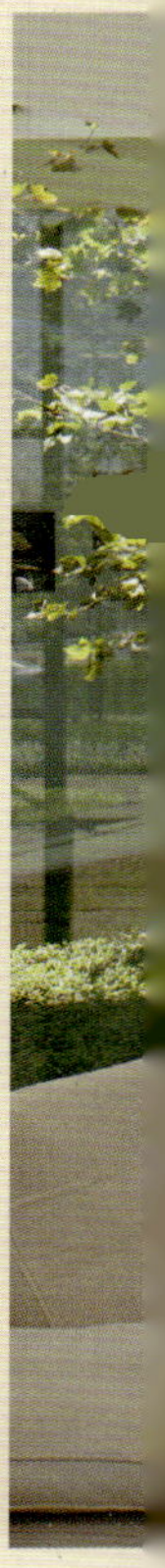

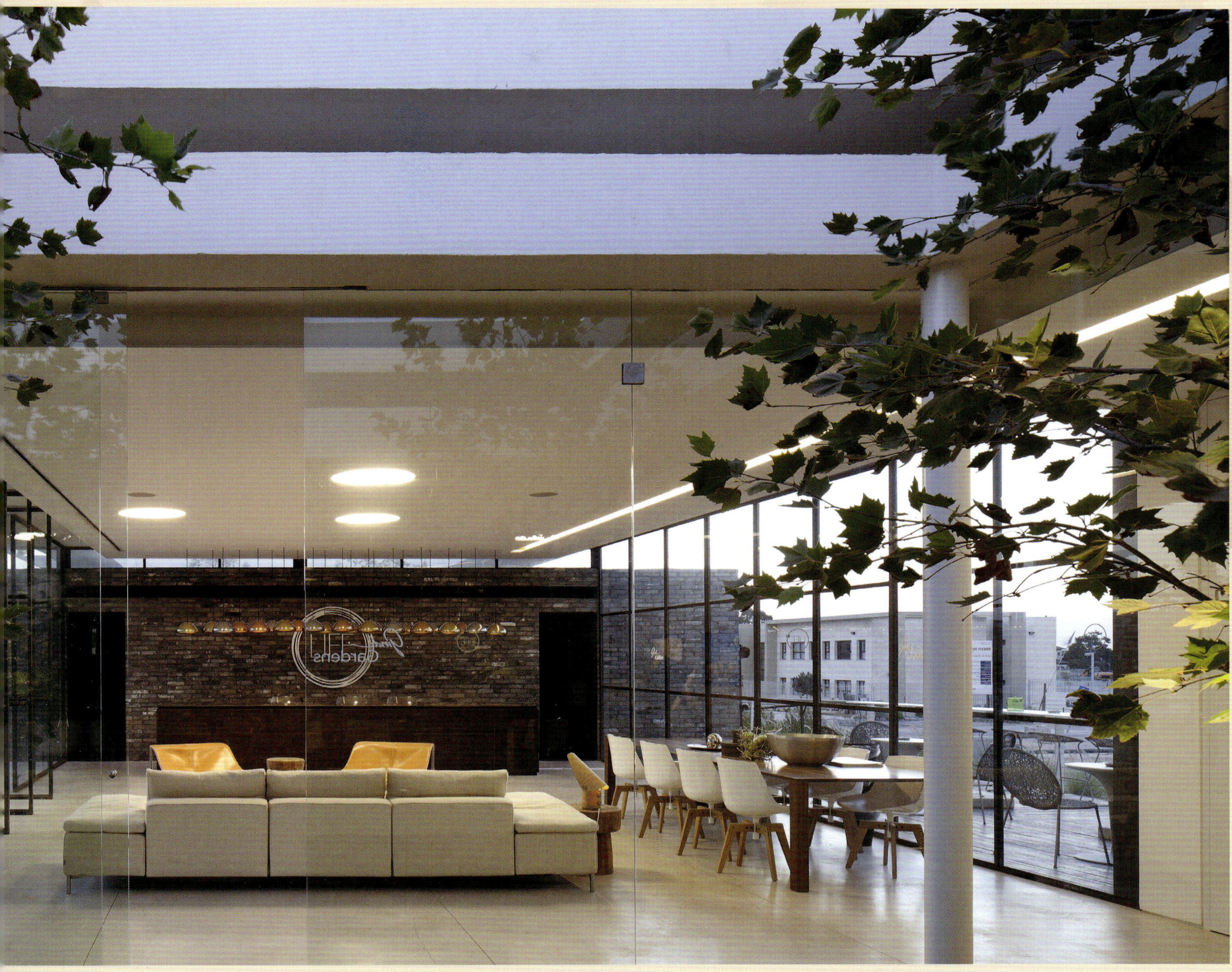

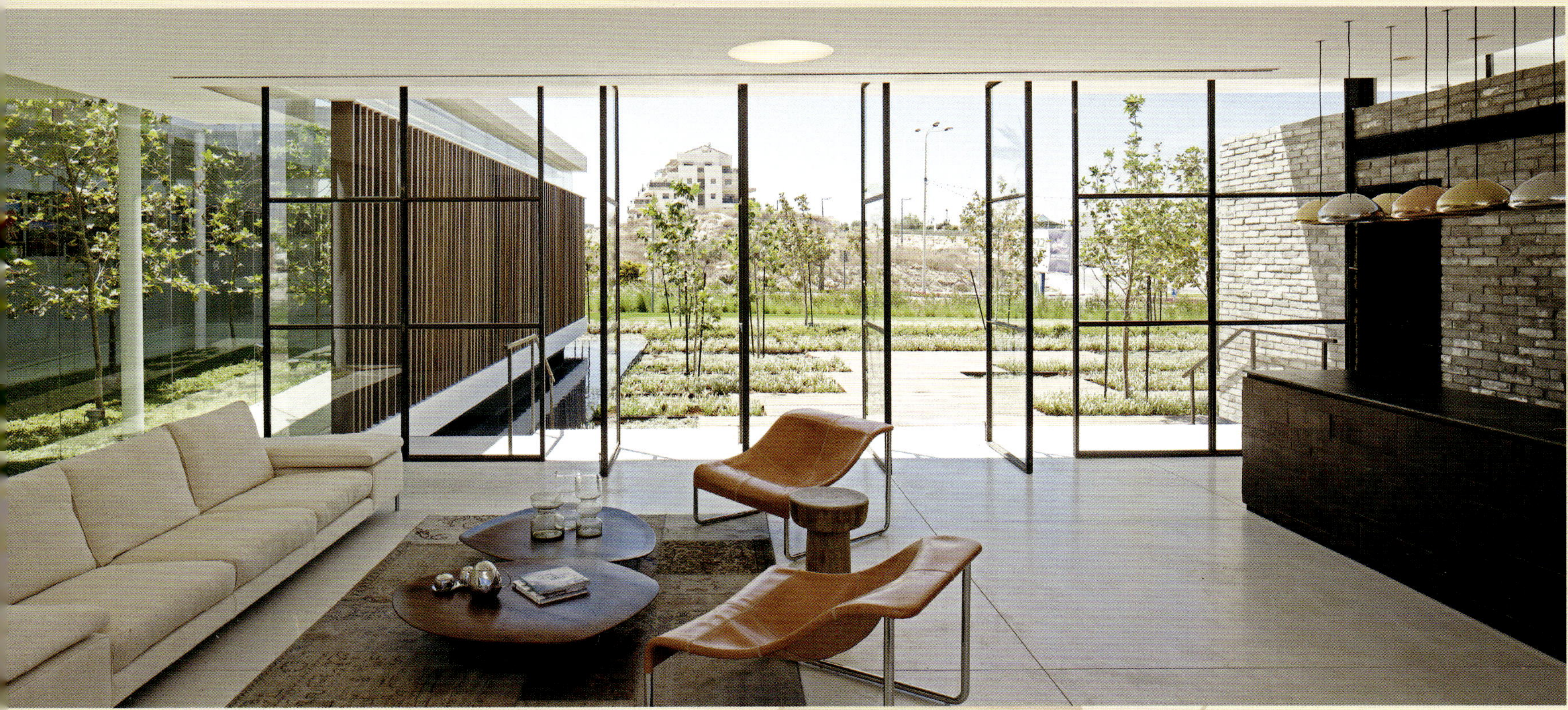

138

139

Xinjiang Nanshan Club

Design Agency: Xiao's Design

Location: Xin Jiang, China

Area: 2200 m²

Photographer: Xu Yourong

Located in the mysterious Xin Jiang, this project was designed for the horse racing lovers. This building is a simple form in its nature, taking the traditional siheyuan form, and the designer try to make the main aspect facing the stud-farm. It is very convenient for the visitors to watch the horse racing program as well as to enjoy the beautiful scenery outside.

141

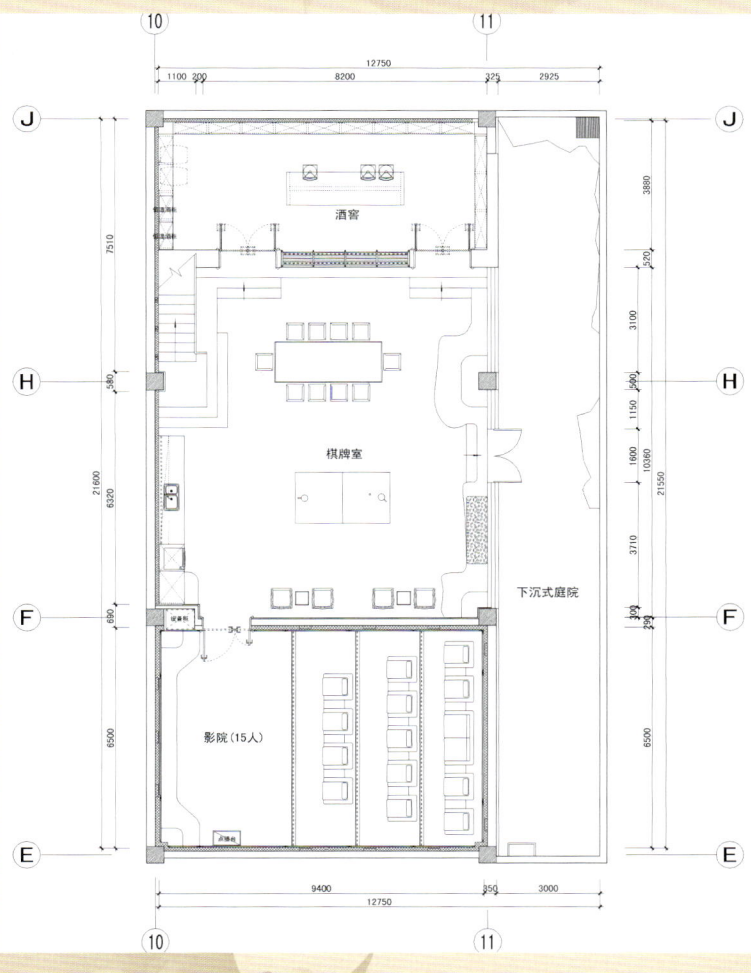

142

143

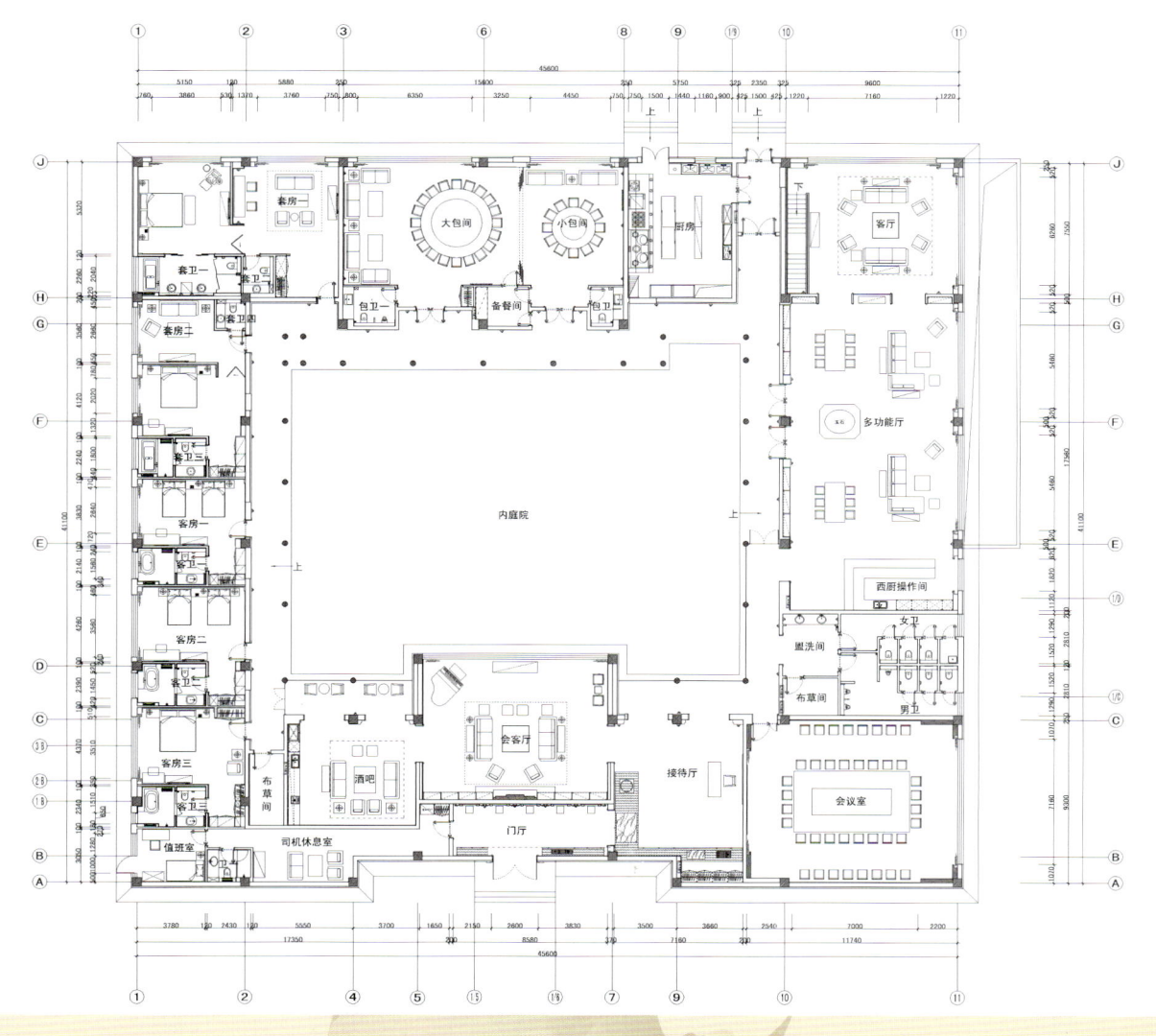

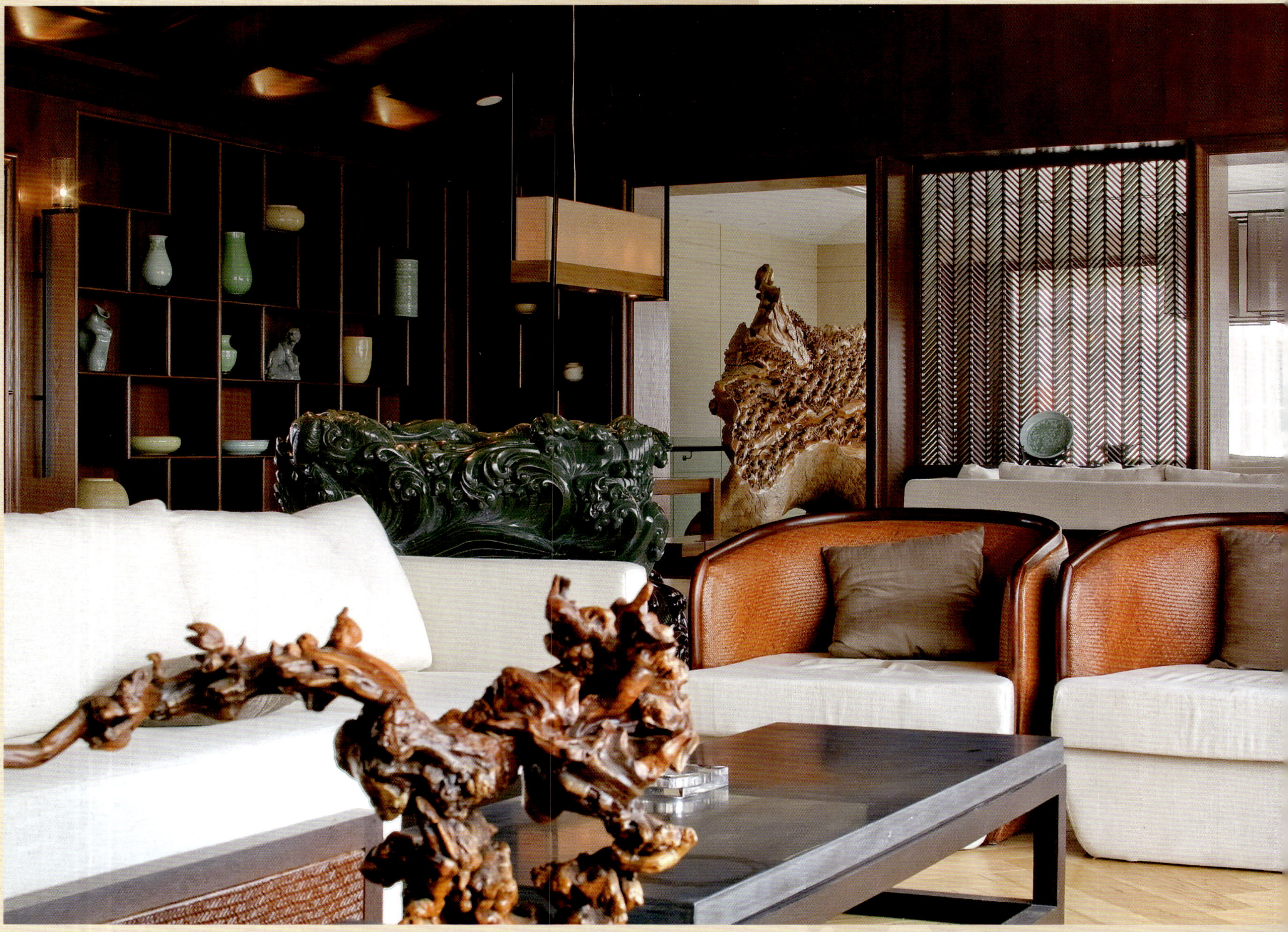

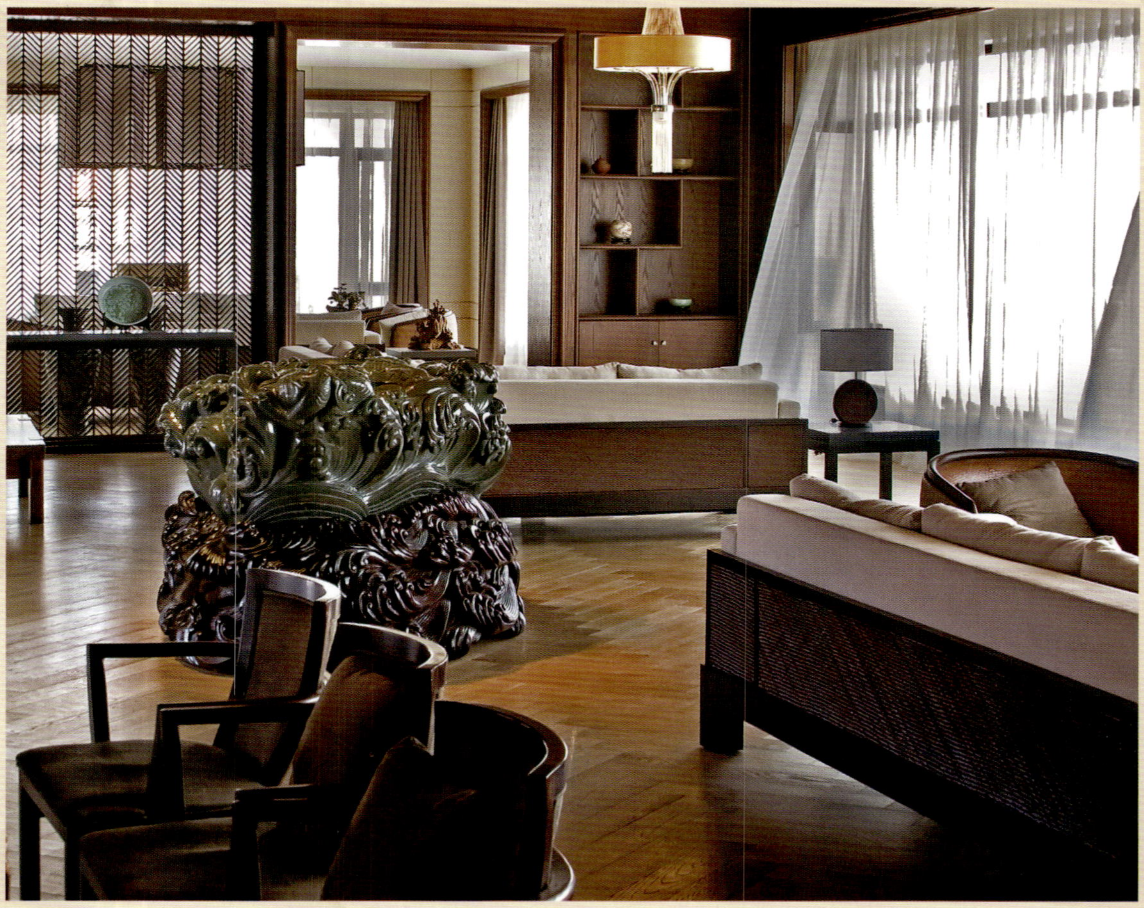

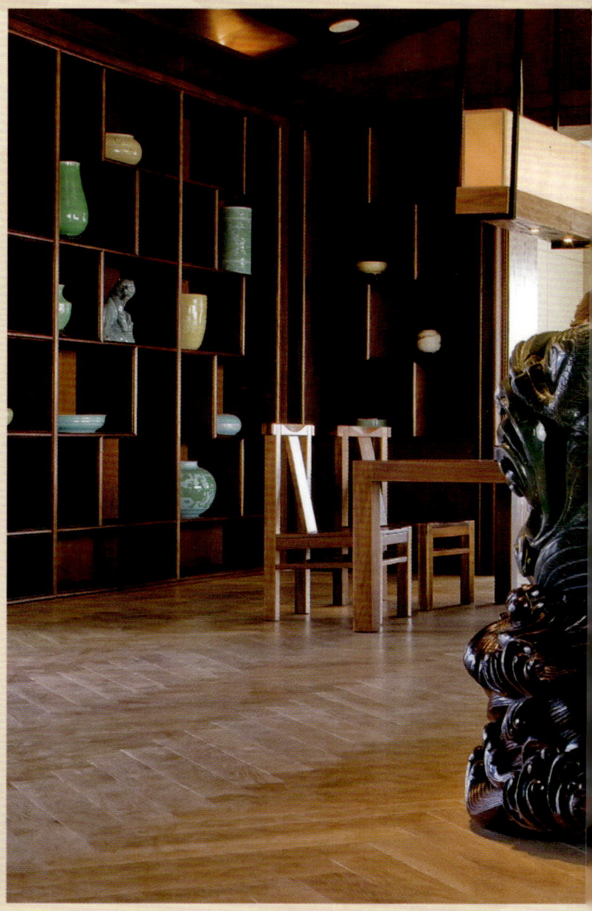

145

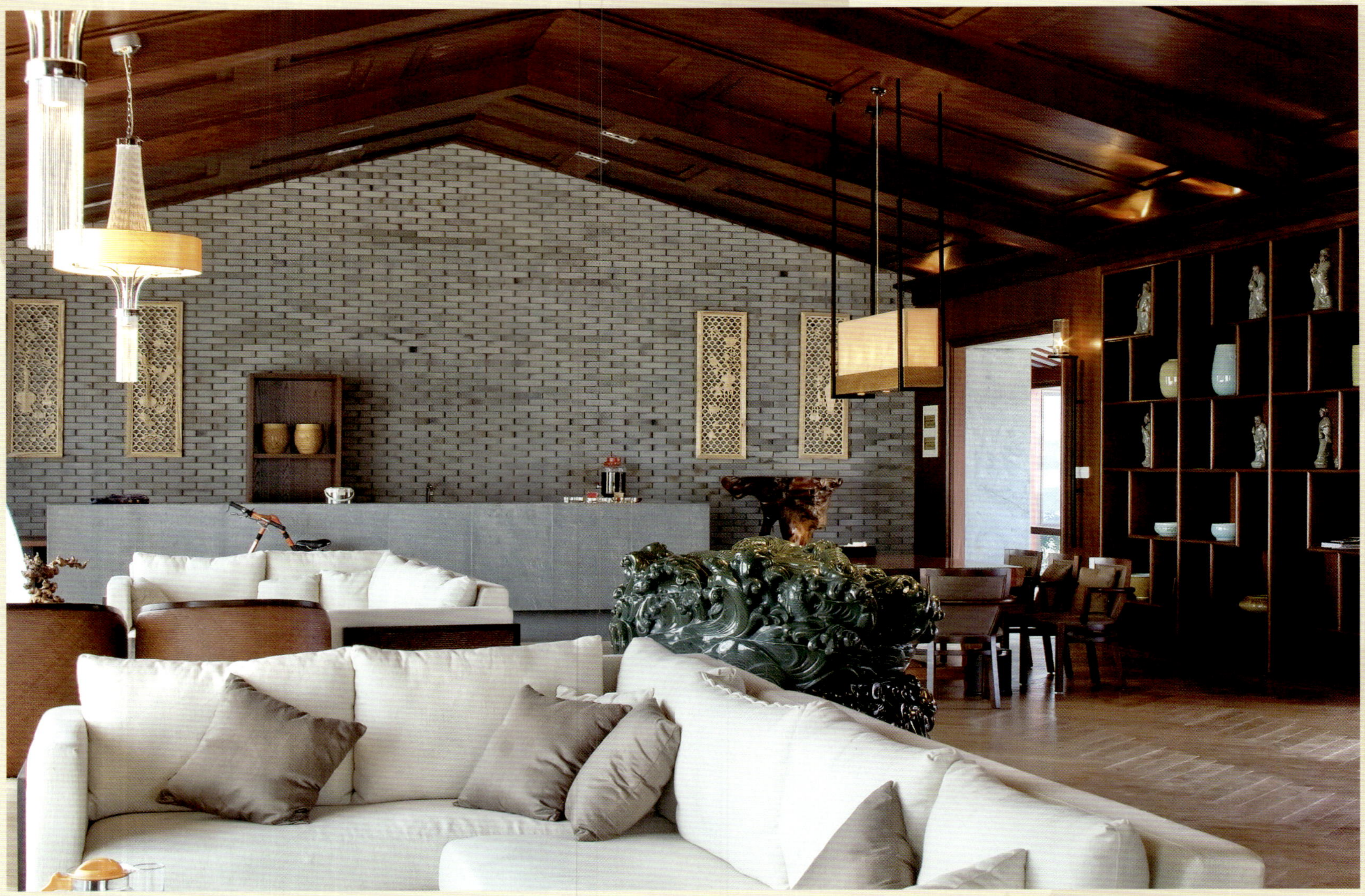

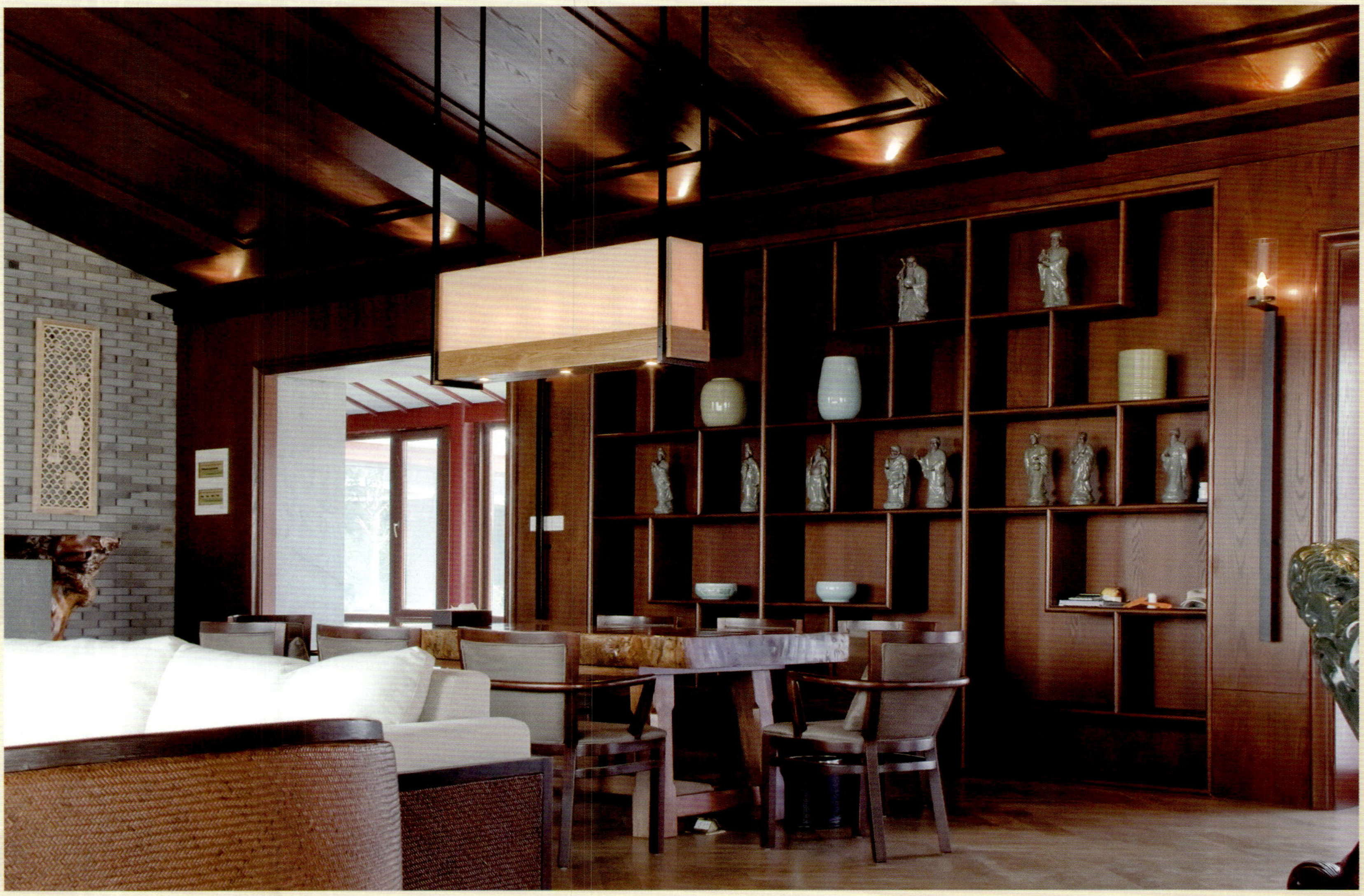

147

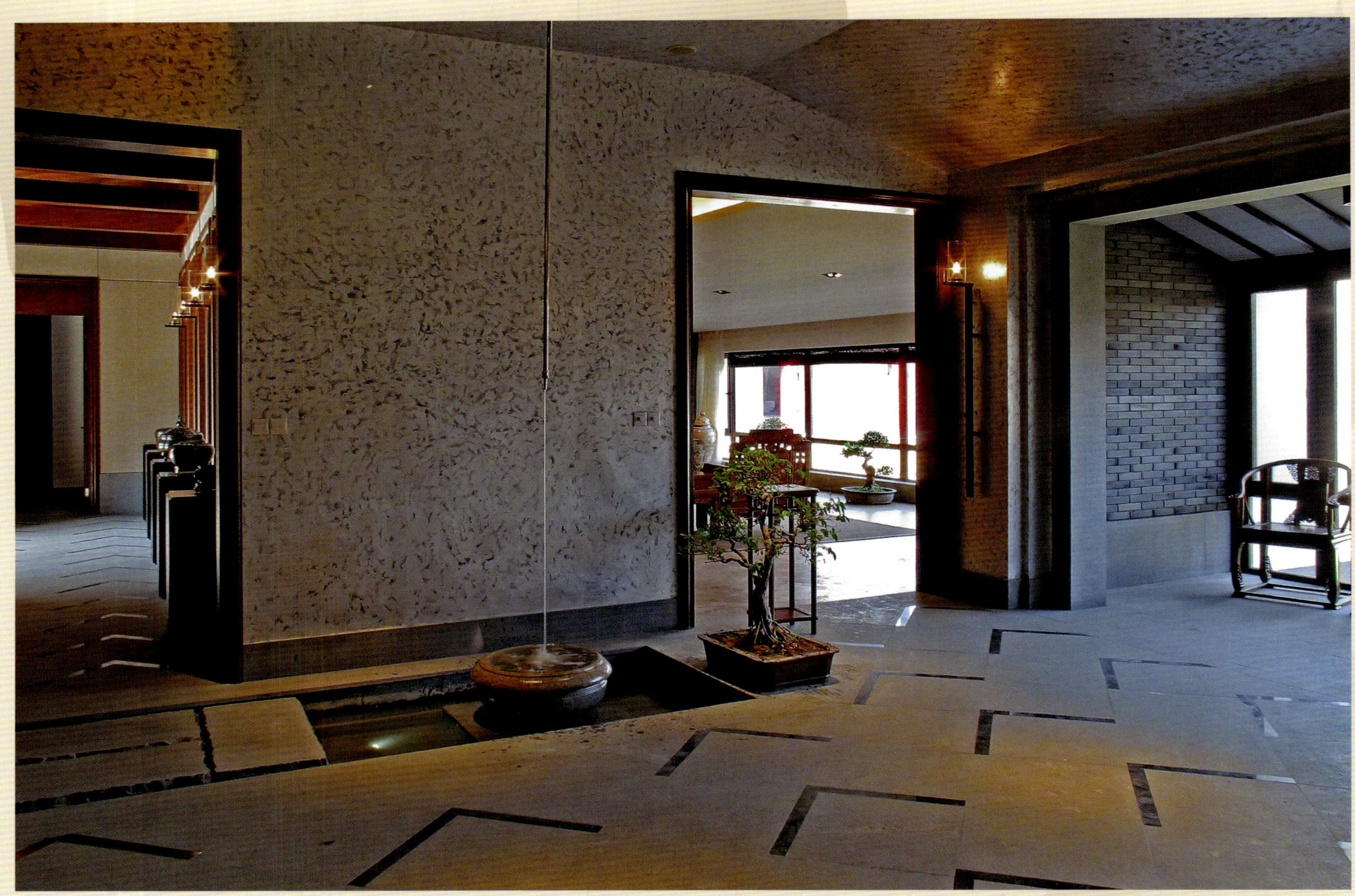

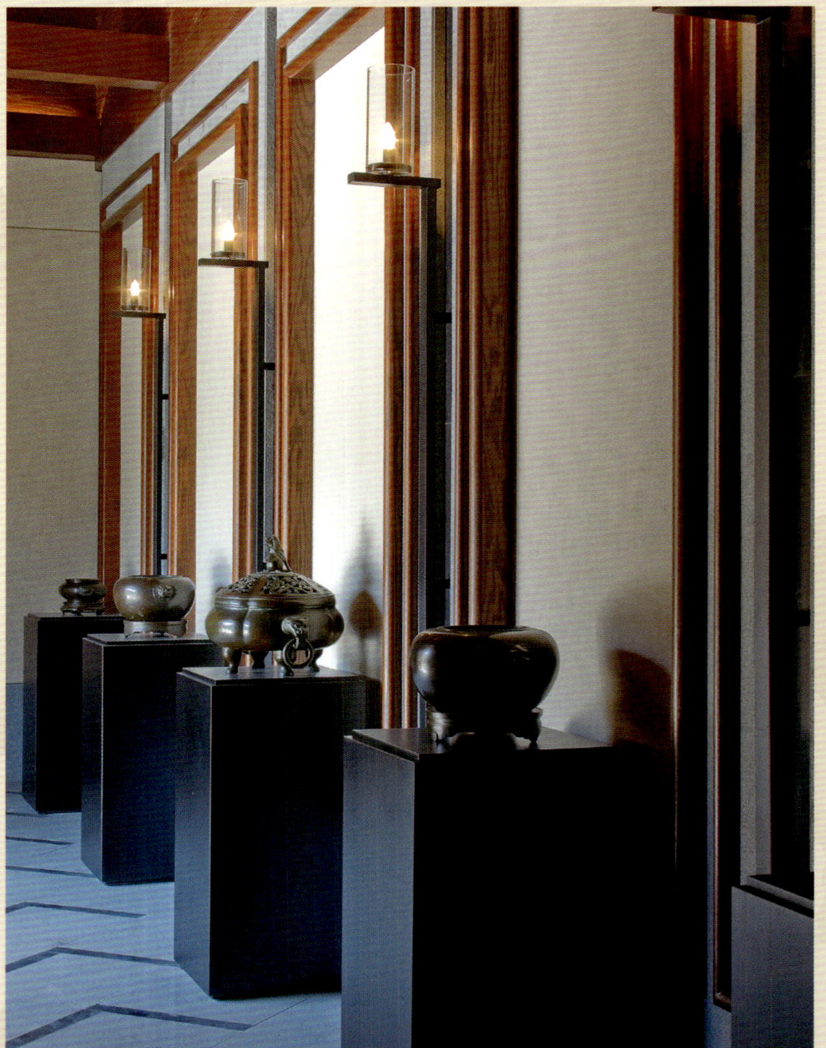

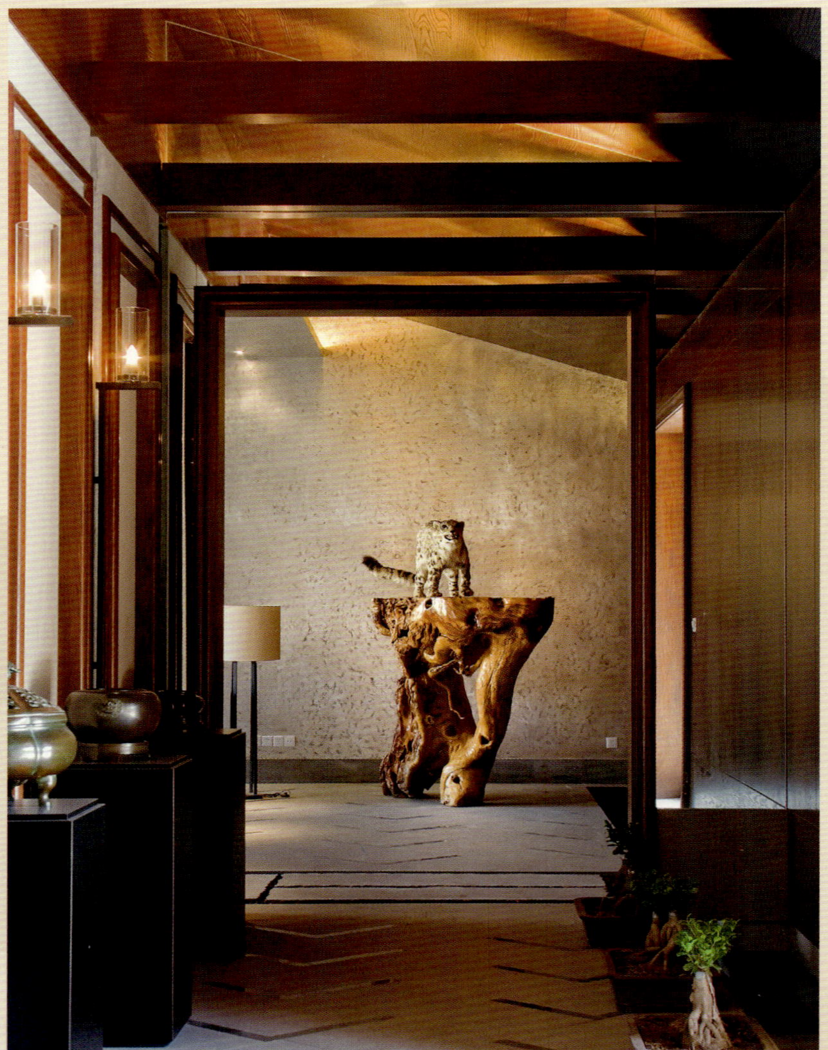

149

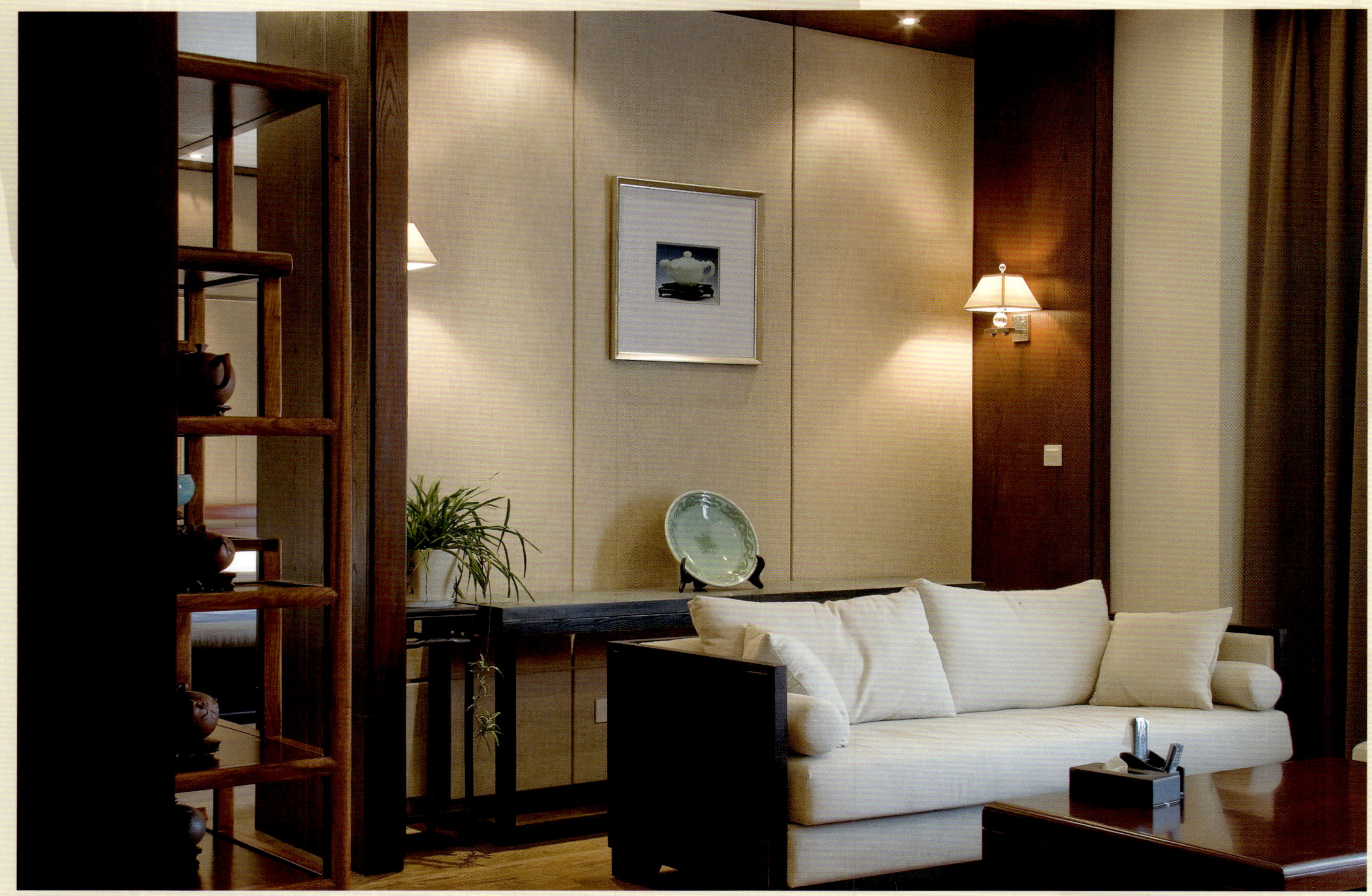

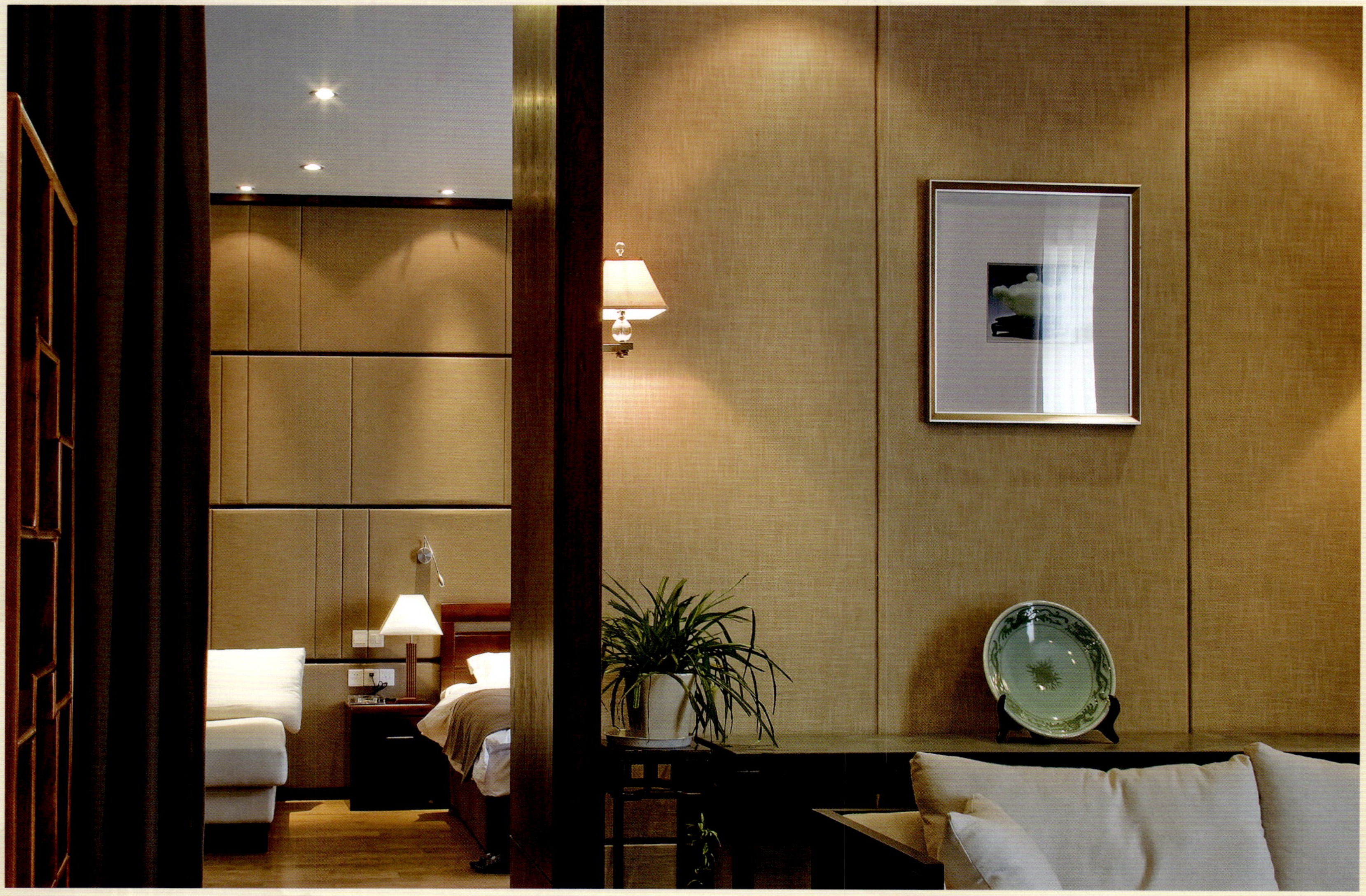

151

Panjin Oriental Ginza Center City Club

Design Agency: Shenzhen Huge Rock Interior Design Co., Ltd.
Location: Panjin, Liaoning, China
Area: 3500 m²
Photographer: Chen Zhong

Located in Liaoning, the chamber of the Orient Ginza Central City has elegant and quiet surroundings and extremely oriental charm. What it builds is a noble and intimate atmosphere. Contracted modern fashion sense and abstract stripping of oriental elements are deeply rooted in the whole space, containing a profound oriental atmosphere and owning esthetic sentiment of the present. Designers draw inspiration from oriental traditional elements, and boldly join "destroying" and "negative", thus create a new concept. In traditional symbol, we find elements of abstract expression, and find the most sensitive area to wantonly express a kind of art strength beyond the superficial culture and art, which virtually enhances the mystery tension of the space.

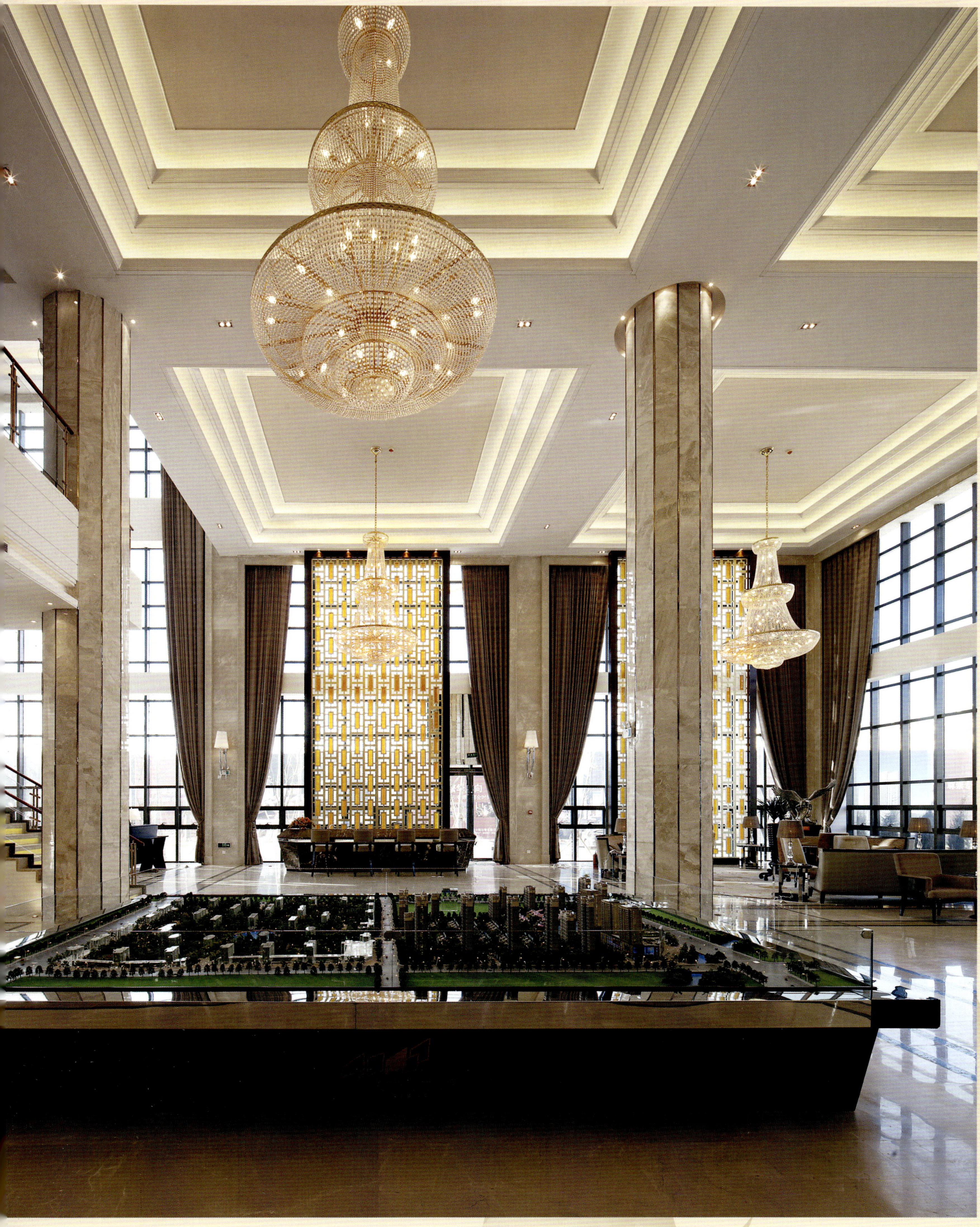

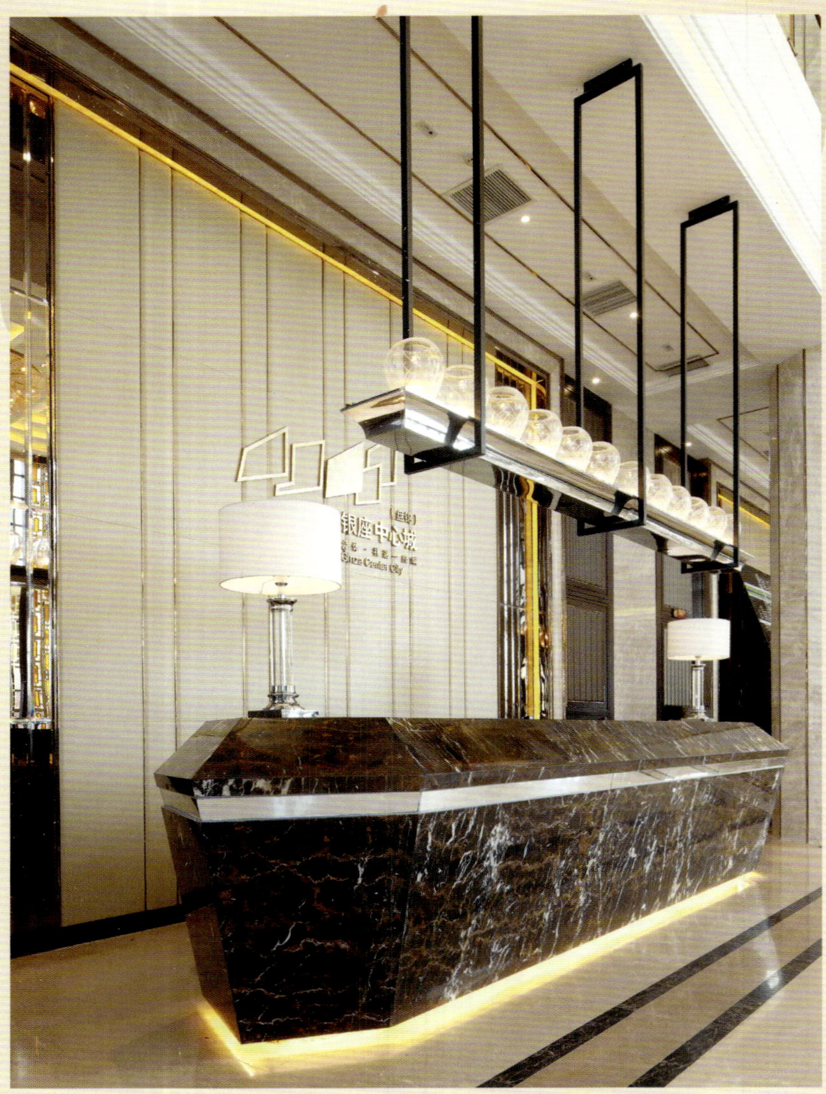
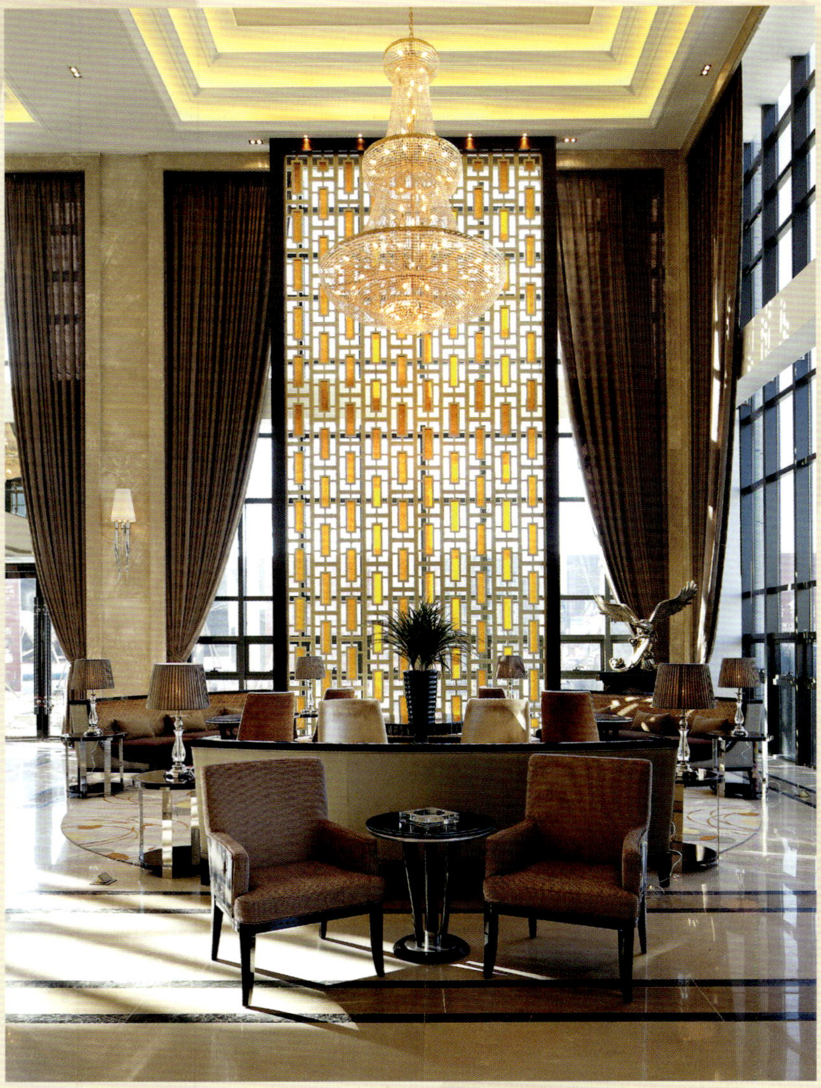
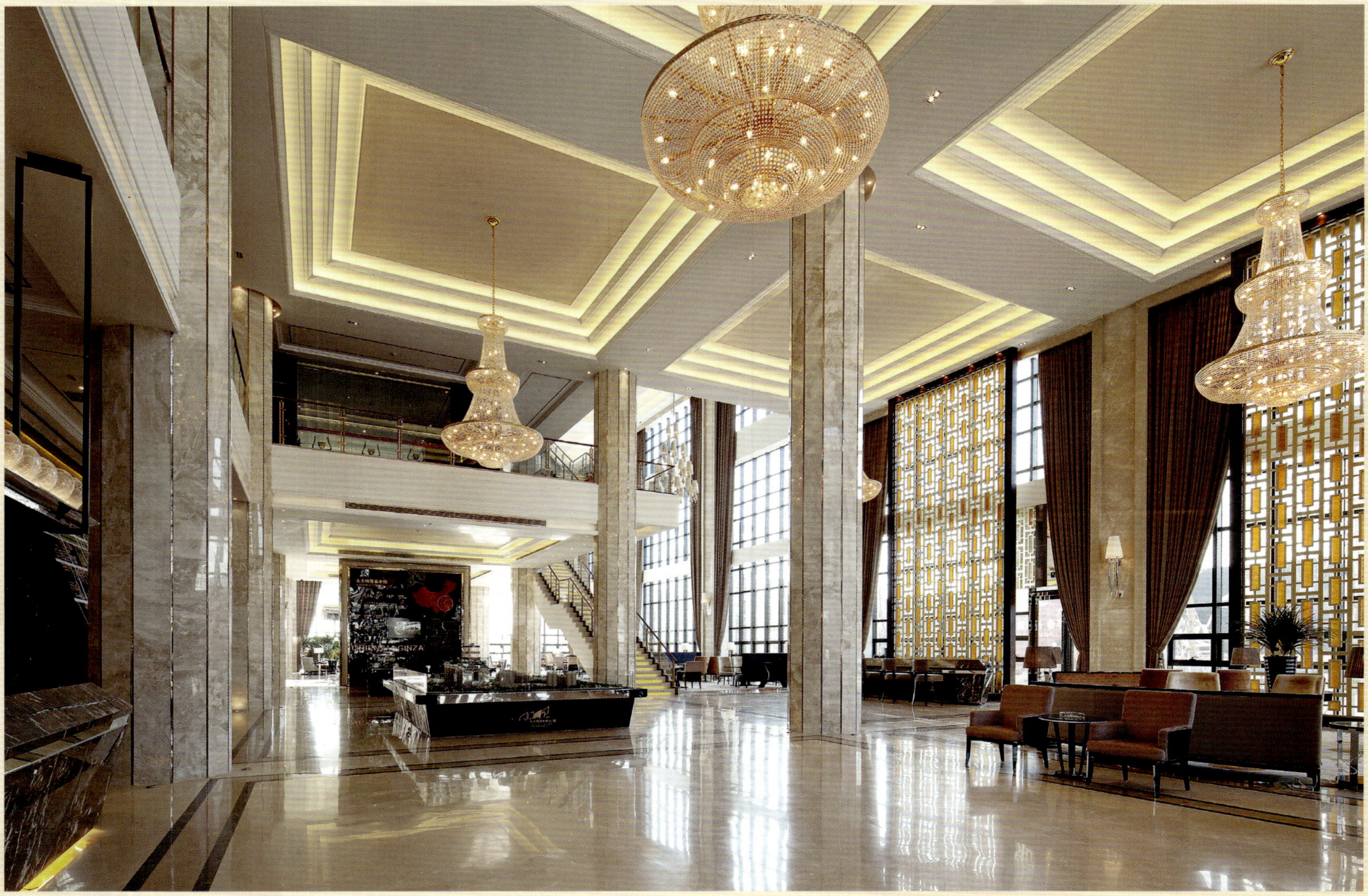

FURNITURE PLAN
Scale 1:100   一层 平面布置图

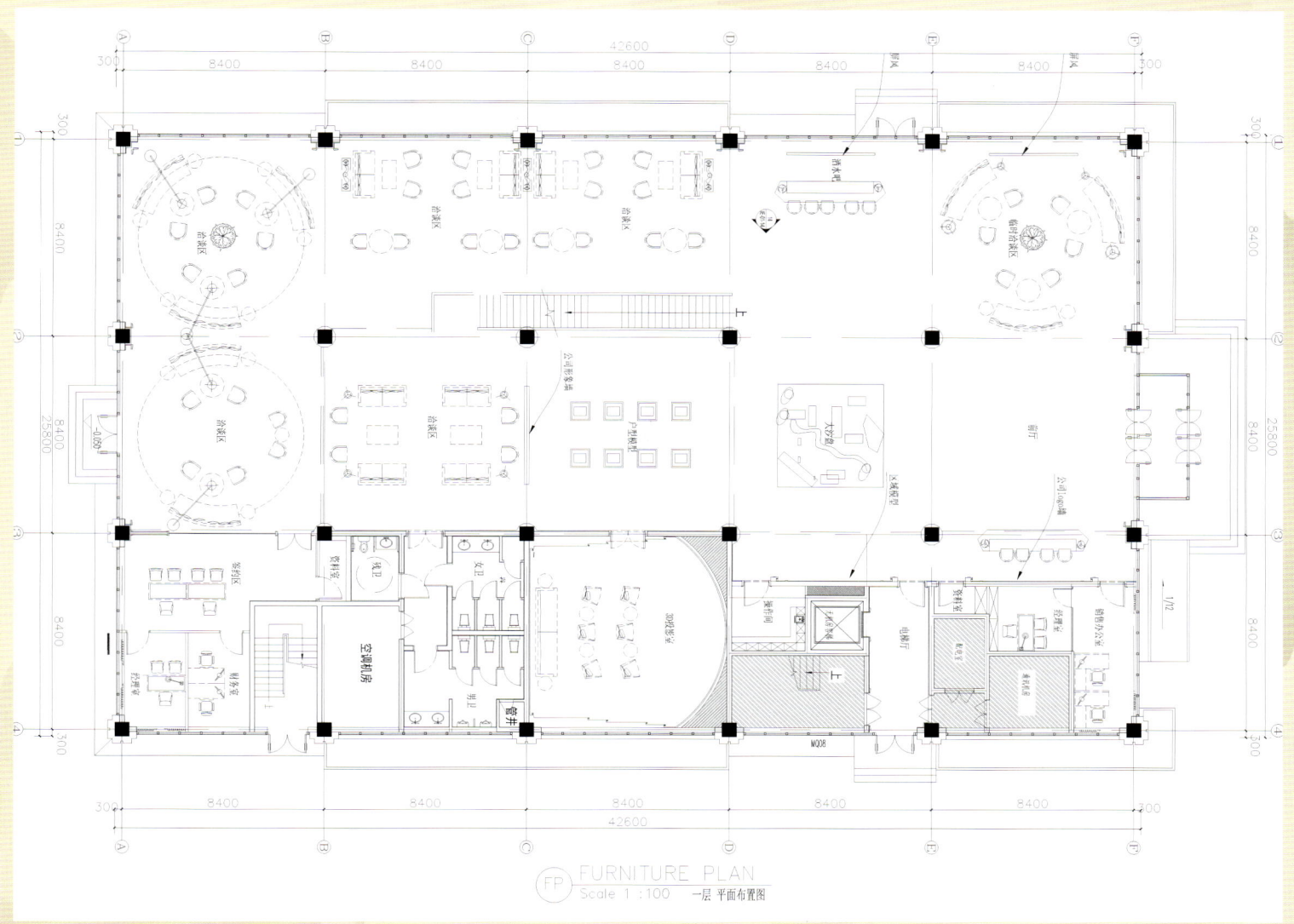

156

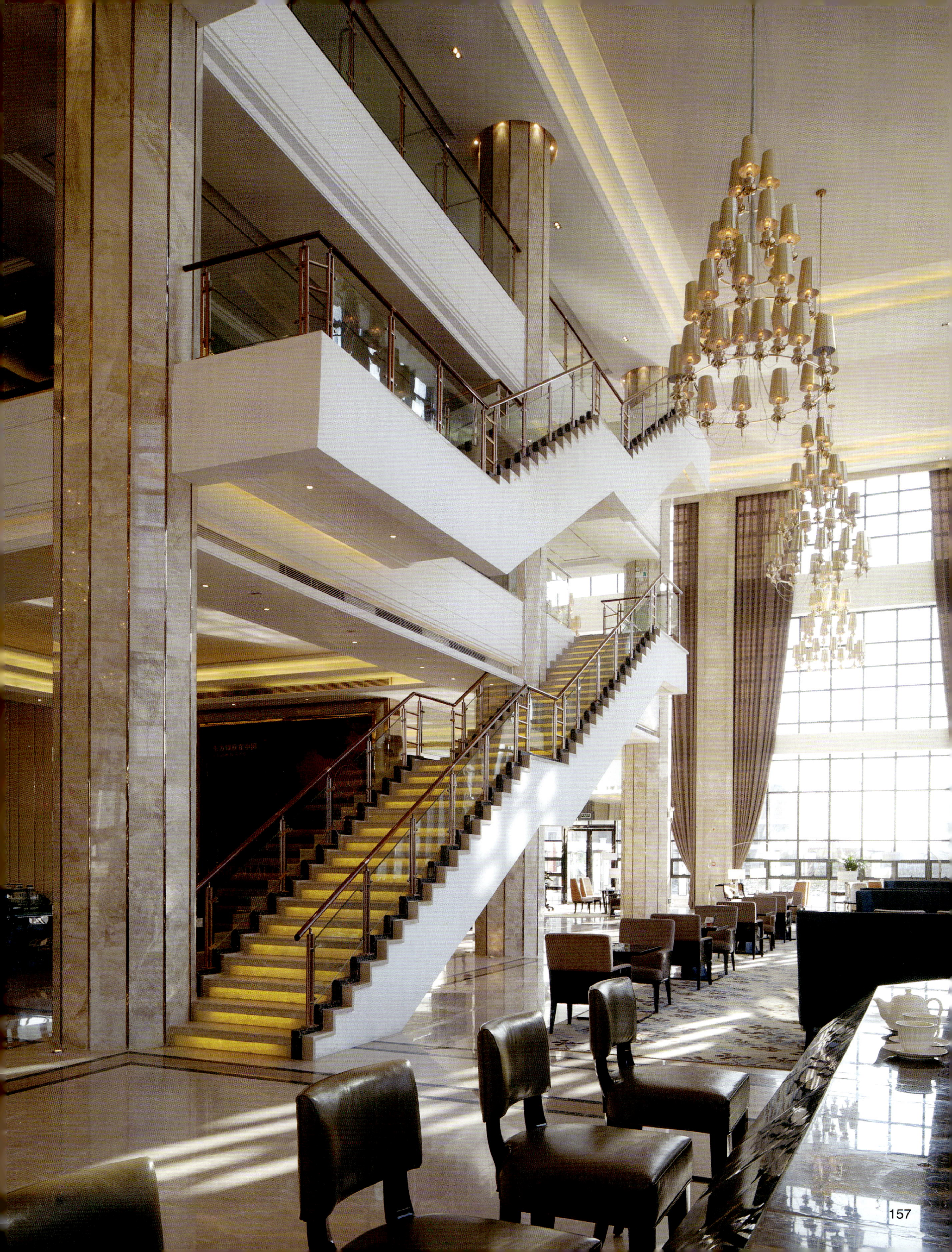

FURNITURE PLAN
Scale 1:100 二层平面布置图

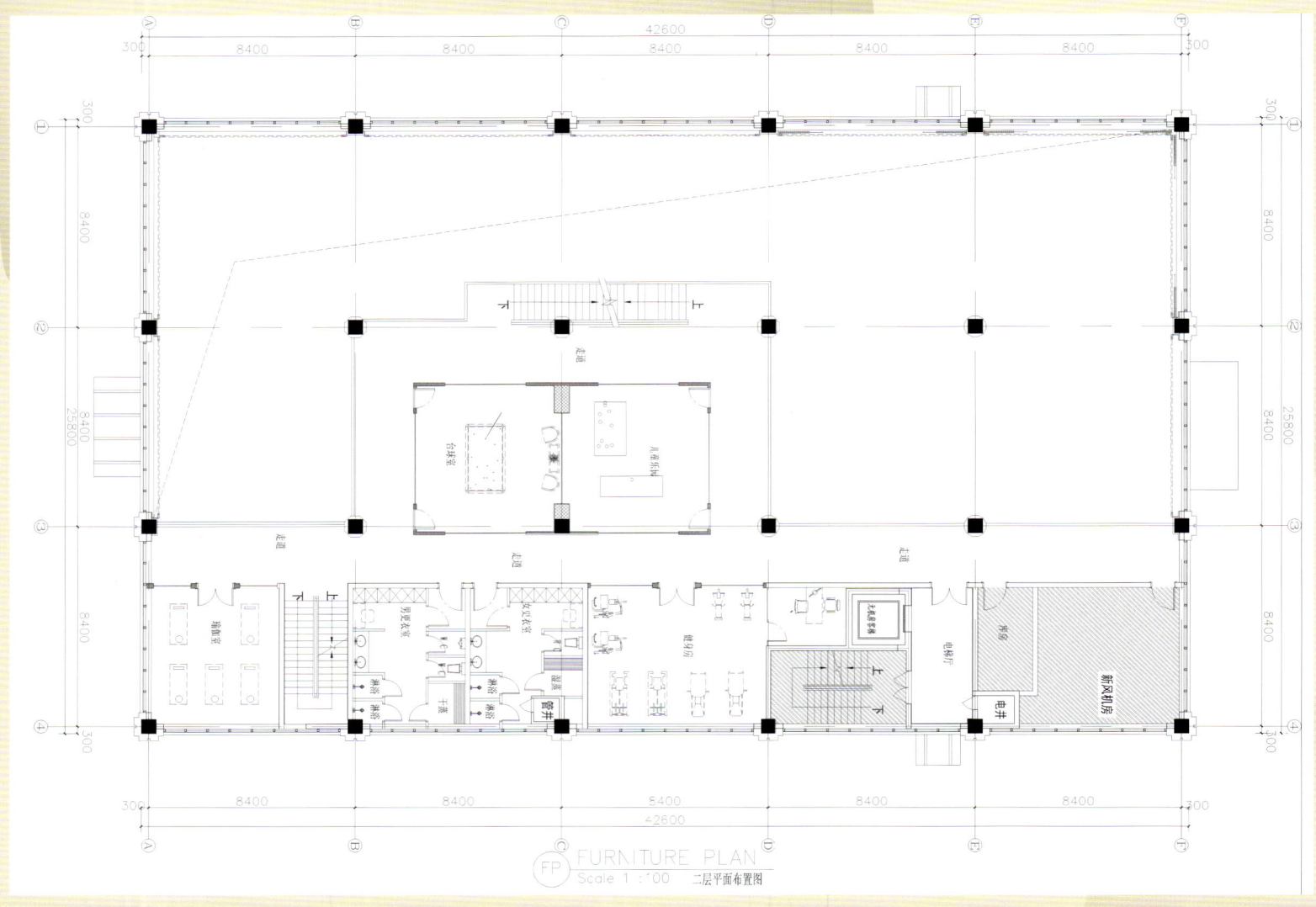

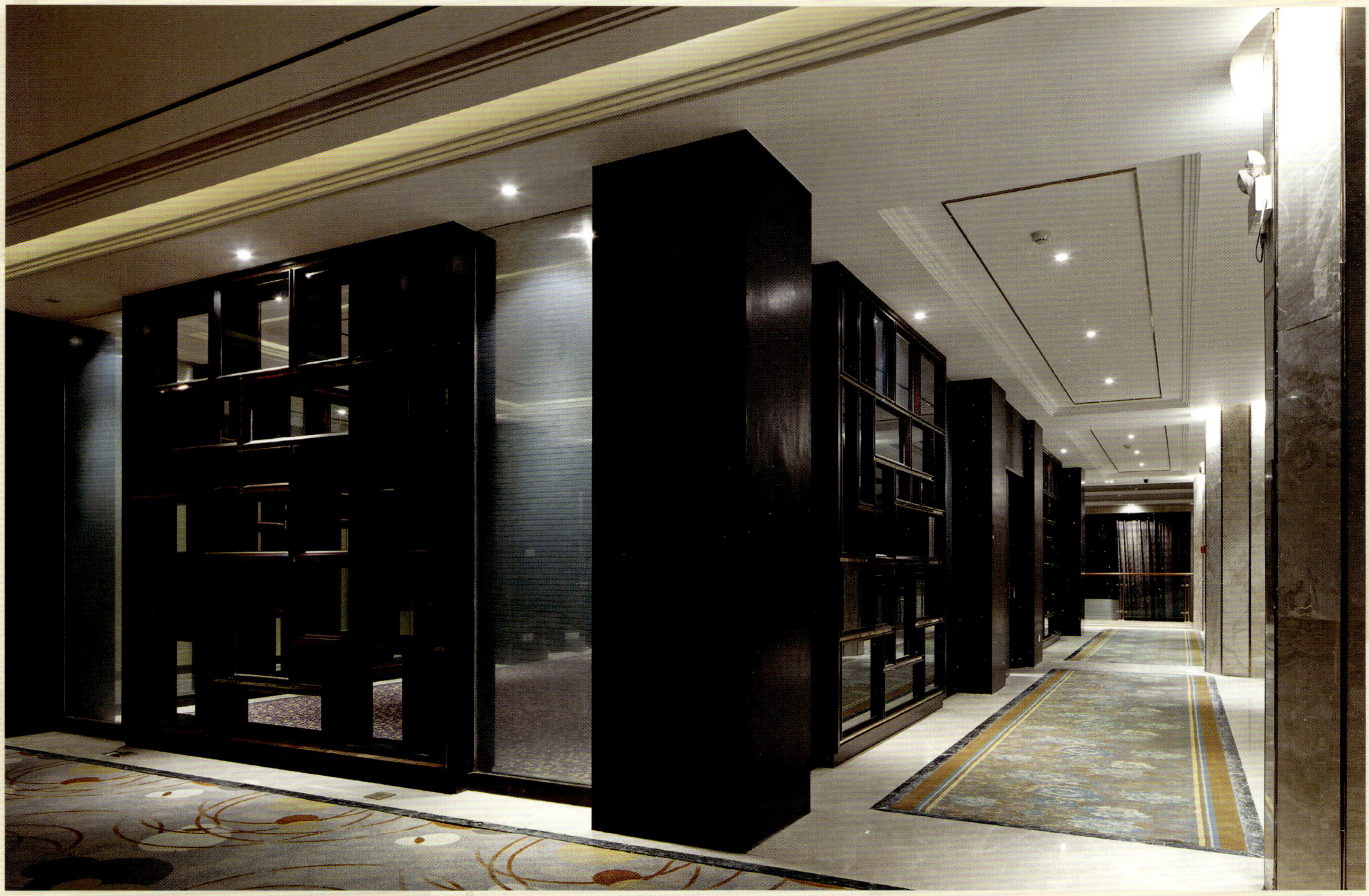

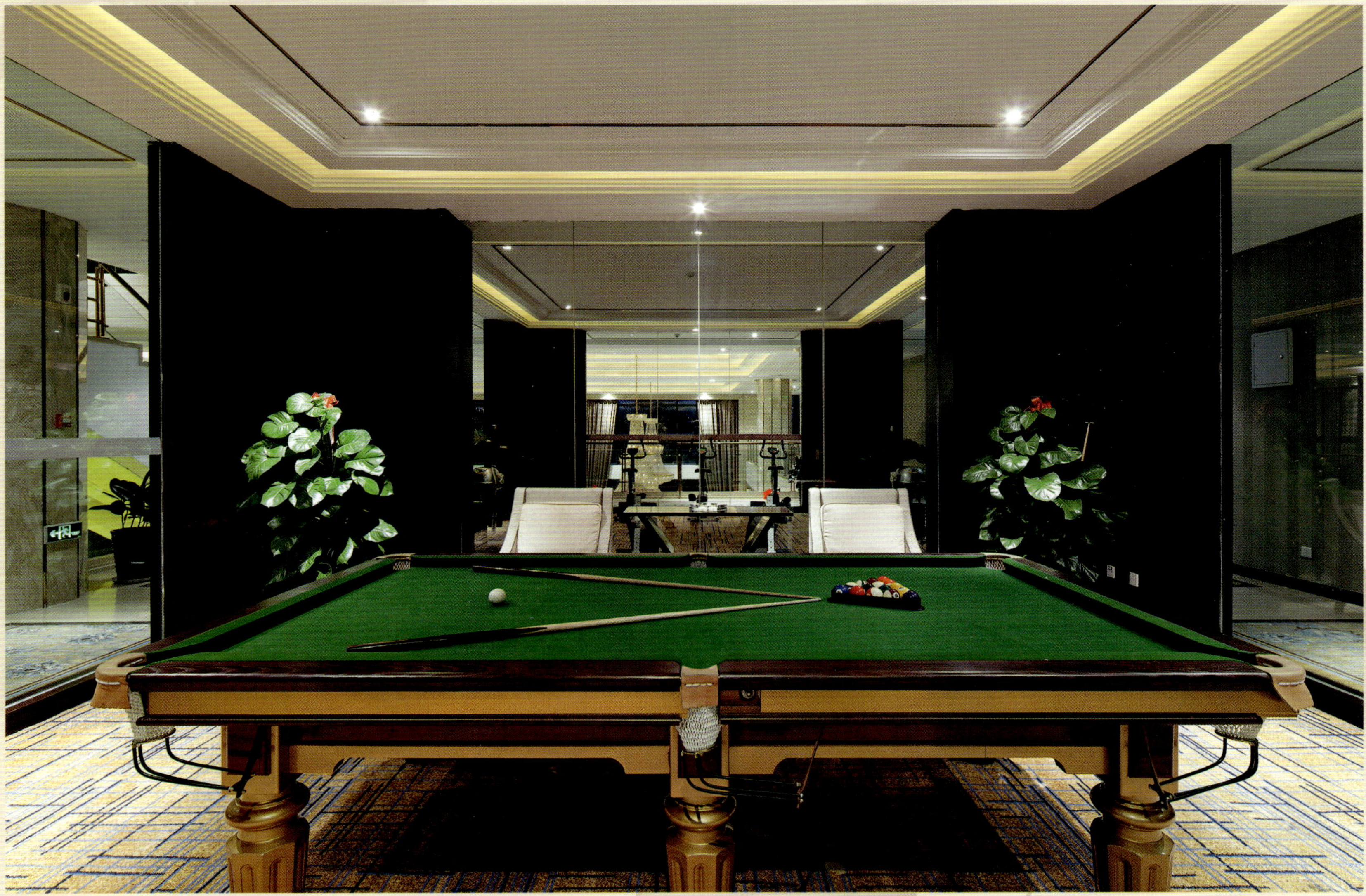

Shenyang Oriental Ginza Center City Club

Design Agency: Shenzhen Huge Rock Interior Design Co., Ltd.
Designer: Zhong Xingjian
Location: Shenyang, Liaoning, China
Area: 3000 m²
Photographer: Chen Zhong

In order to express the luxurious temperament, we adopt neoclassicism to design the building, which advocates a kind of revivalism complex, namely, to find the details of life that can be combined with European medieval art on display in modern life. Classical and fashionable elements collided, forming a new design language. Loose appearance but intensive spirit is the main characteristic of neoclassicism. Paying attention to adornment effect, we use modern methods and materials to restore the classical temperament, so neoclassicism has the dual aesthetic effect of classicism and modernism. And the perfect combination make people not only enjoy the material civilization but also get spiritual consolation at the same time.

161

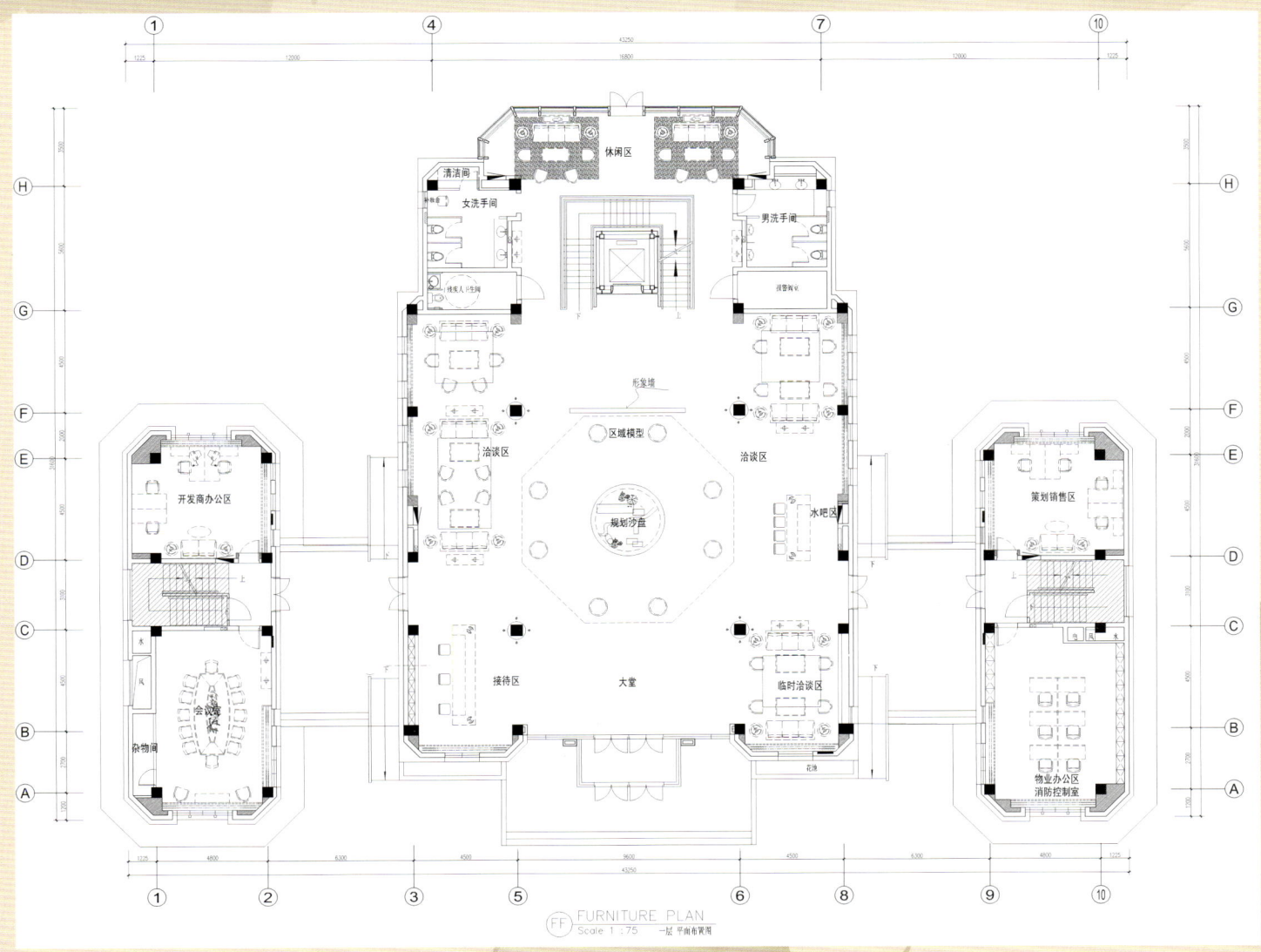

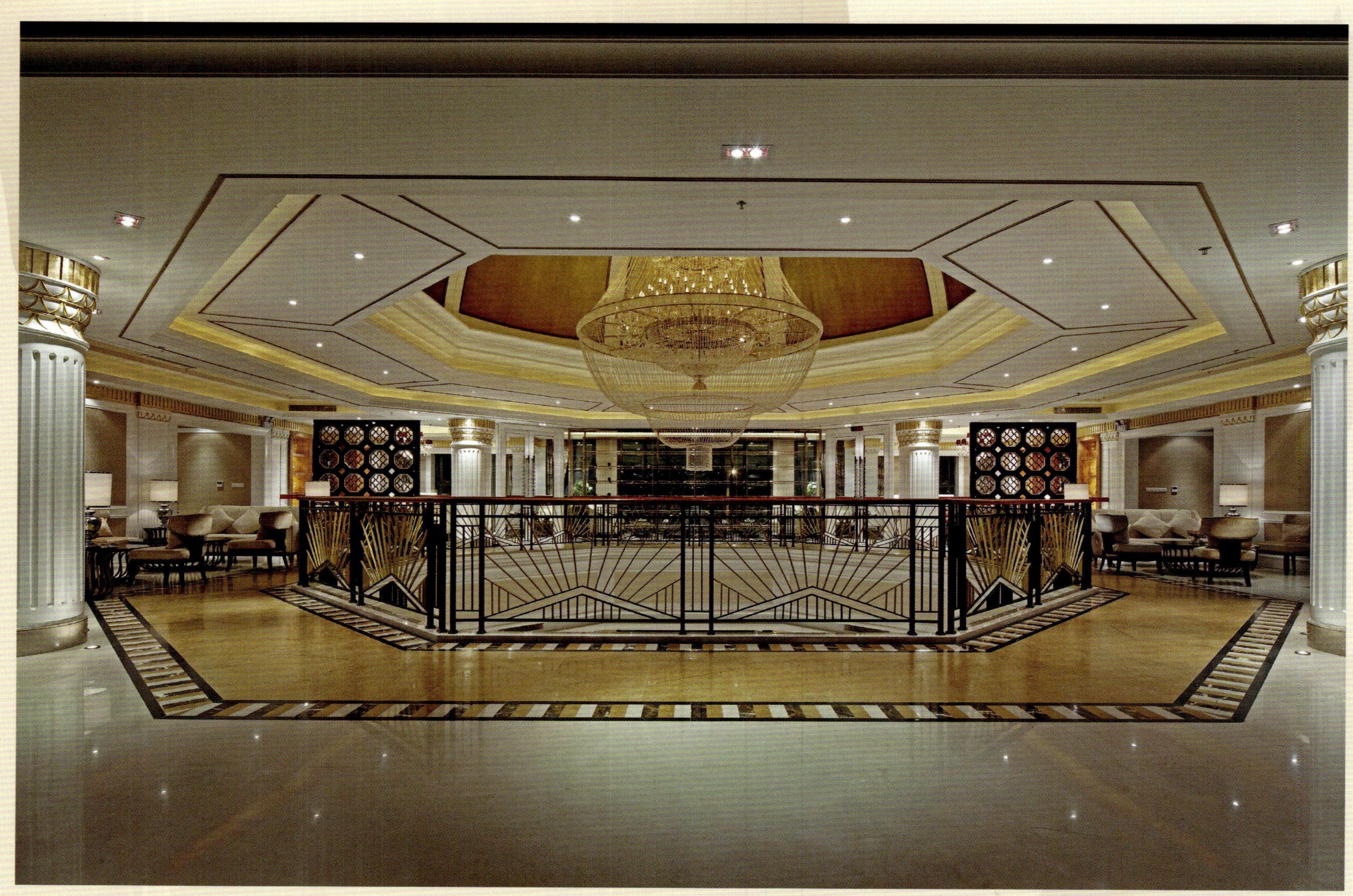

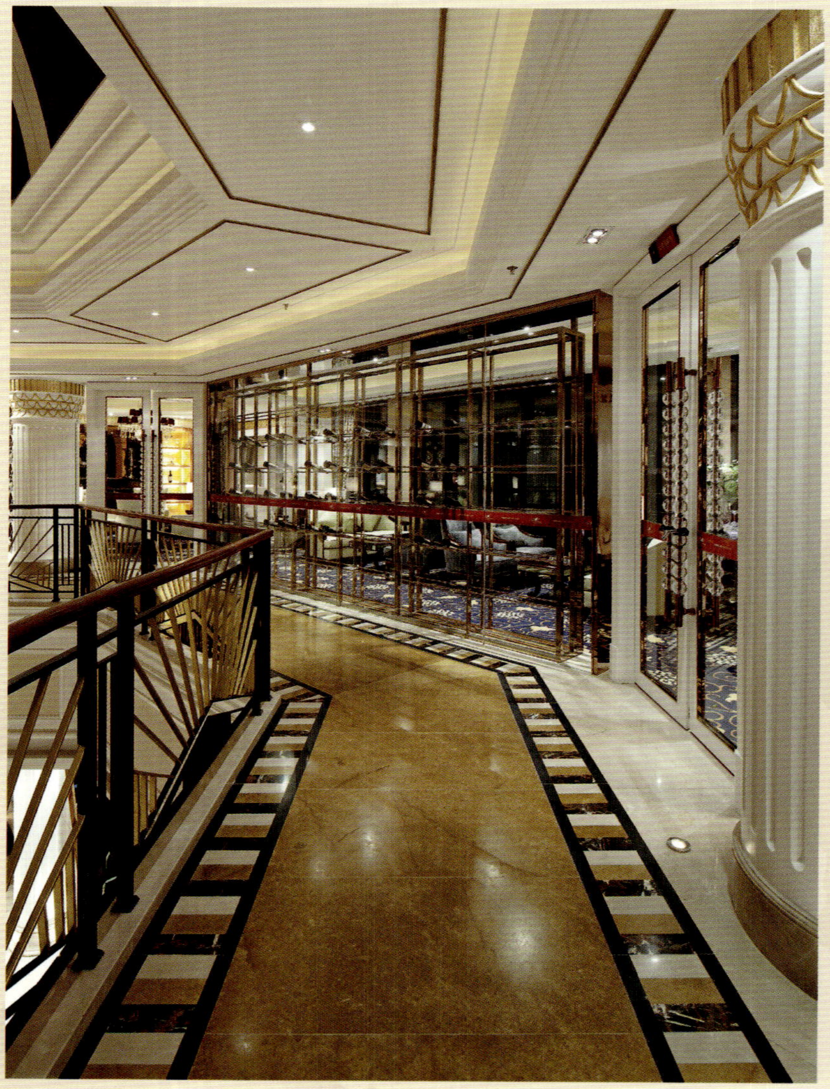

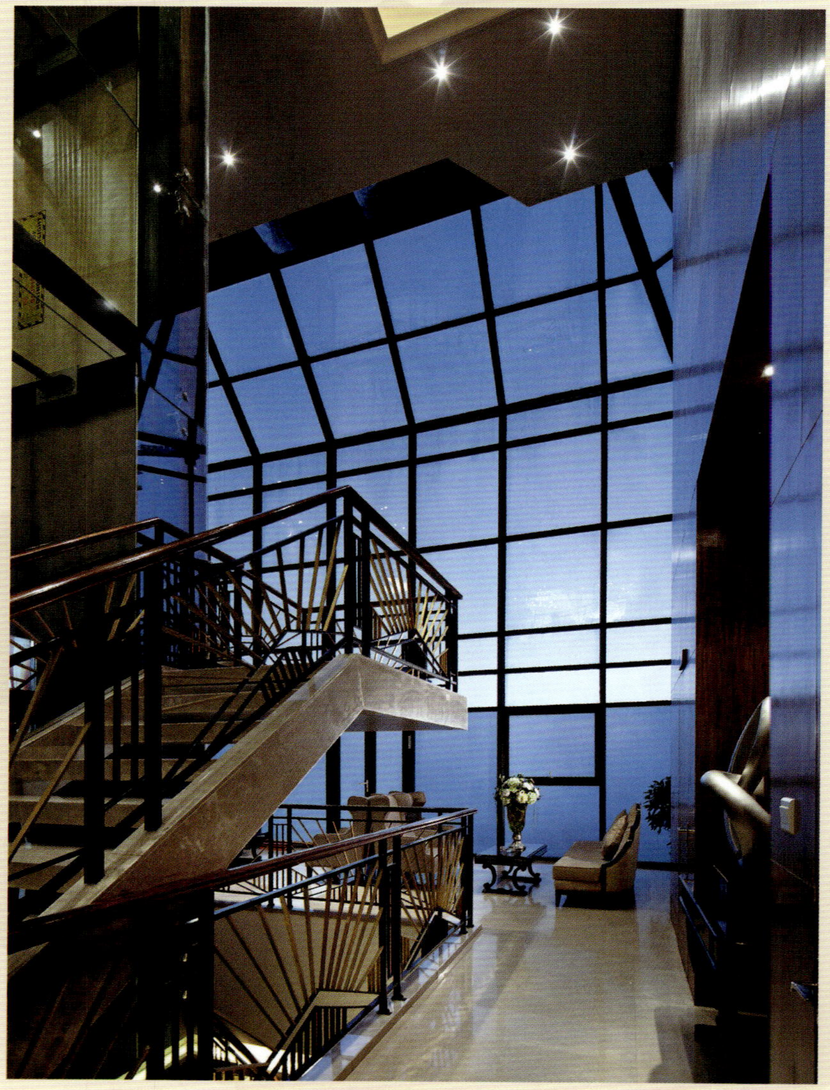

FURNITURE PLAN
Scale 1:75   二层 平面布置图

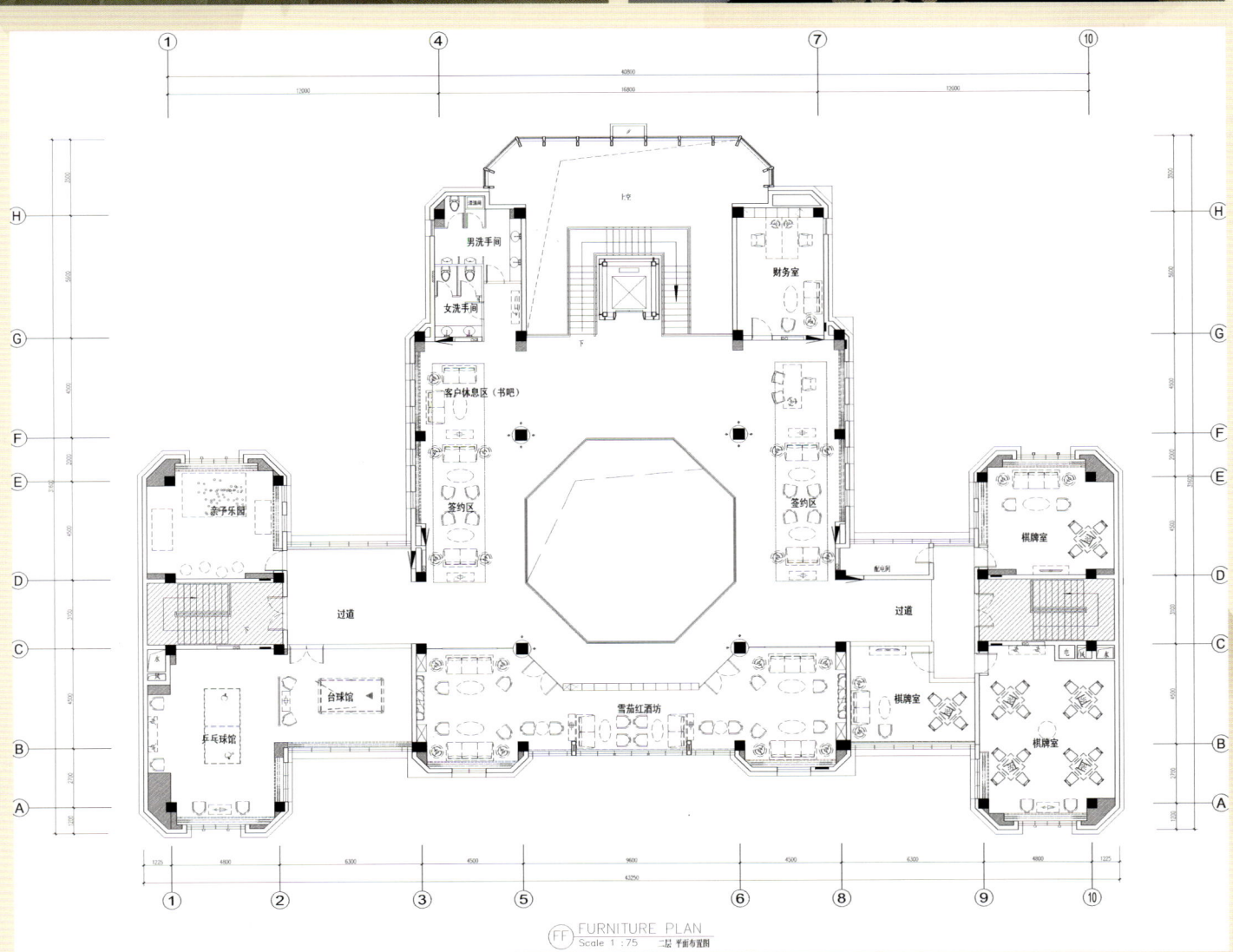

163

164

165

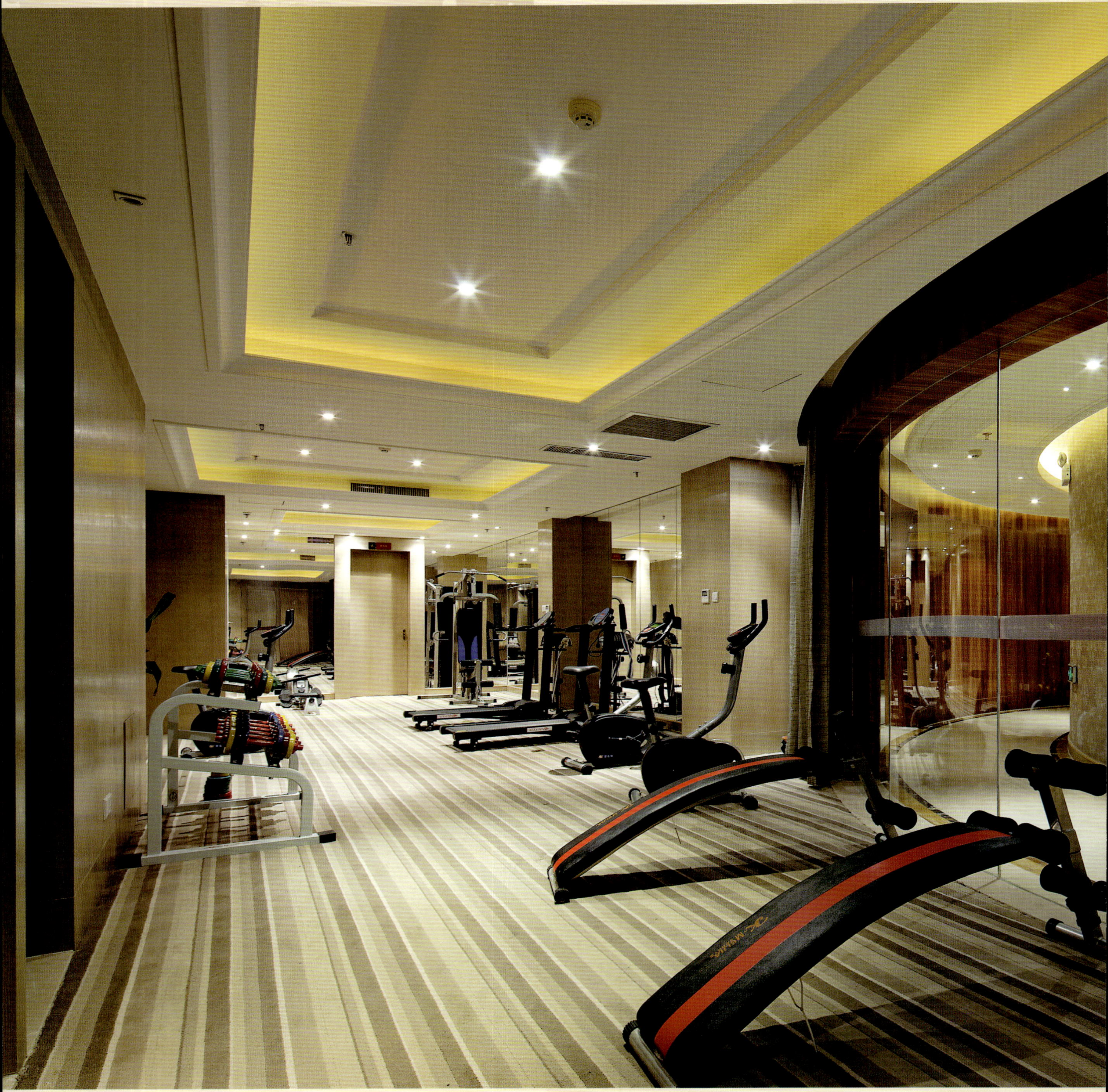

FURNITURE PLAN
Scale 1:75 平面索引布置图

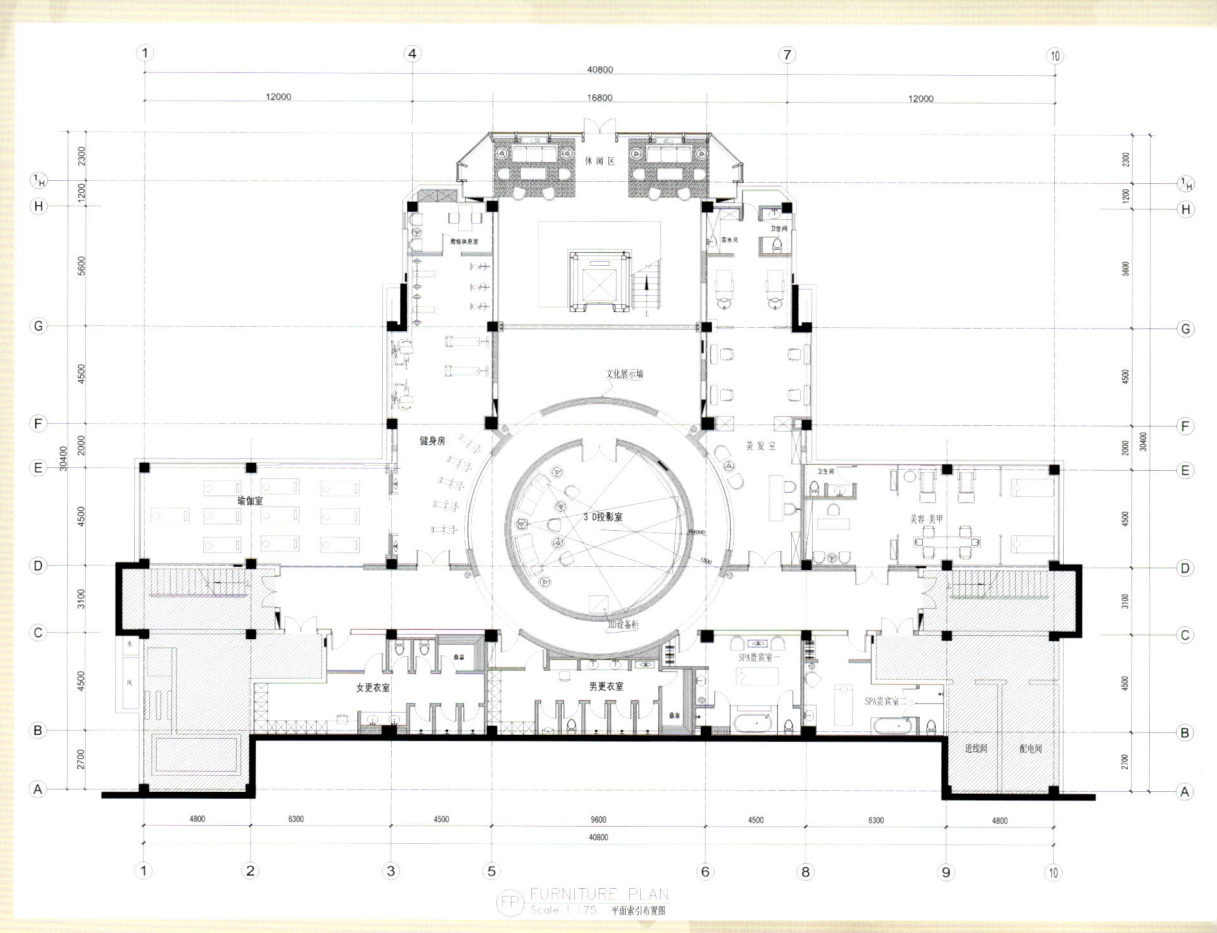

167

The Villa Club of Sun Golden Town

Design Agency: Shenzhen Pinki Design Consultant Co., Ltd.

Designer: Liu Weijun

Client: Xi'an Guo Zhong Star City Real Estate

Location: Xi'an, China

Area: 600 m²

The chamber is planned to be a detached villa, and is an important part of the project value. It will become an important symbol of offering clients a space to enjoy luxury life. Designers view the chamber as a representative of the upper-class life of xi 'an, which is not only the most dazzling pearl, but also an oasis of modern metropolis with rich culture and sight.

According to the project of high-end, taste and status symbol meaning of clients, daily life and banquet requirements, designers divide the chamber into three levels. The main level is the private club of openness; the second level is the private living space; the third level is the private leisure and writing space.

The private club is close to the concept of a reception or art exhibition hall. When you enter the club and pass through the hallway equipped with shoe-changing room, the first place you come is deputy hall and living room mainly for negotiating. Here, you can see floor window for panorama view that has three sides and a total of 29 meters in length, and the landscape pool and sinking between the deputy hall and living room which plays the role of functional partition and transition. And the theme wall paved by culture stone at the hand escalator position makes the space of negotiating more approachable.

When you pass through the door of the theme wall, there are early restaurant and a main restaurant accommodating 6 to 8 and 12 people respectively. Next to the

169

restaurants is a big kitchen of 22 square meters, which shows the master's high demands for cooking and warm and considerate service for guests. By the side of the restaurants, humanized passage for the disabled is set up through to the water bar, where you can drink and smoke a cigar. On the whole, the main level of private club contains a central courtyard gallery around good lighting, a water bar, early restaurant, a main restaurant, a home theatre, high tea area and etc. It has jumped out from the concept of the traditional big and unsuitable blocking-pattern ostentation and extravagance. In a word, the chamber is the one with comprehensive living facilities, complete equipment, and communication atmosphere of rich cultural ambience.

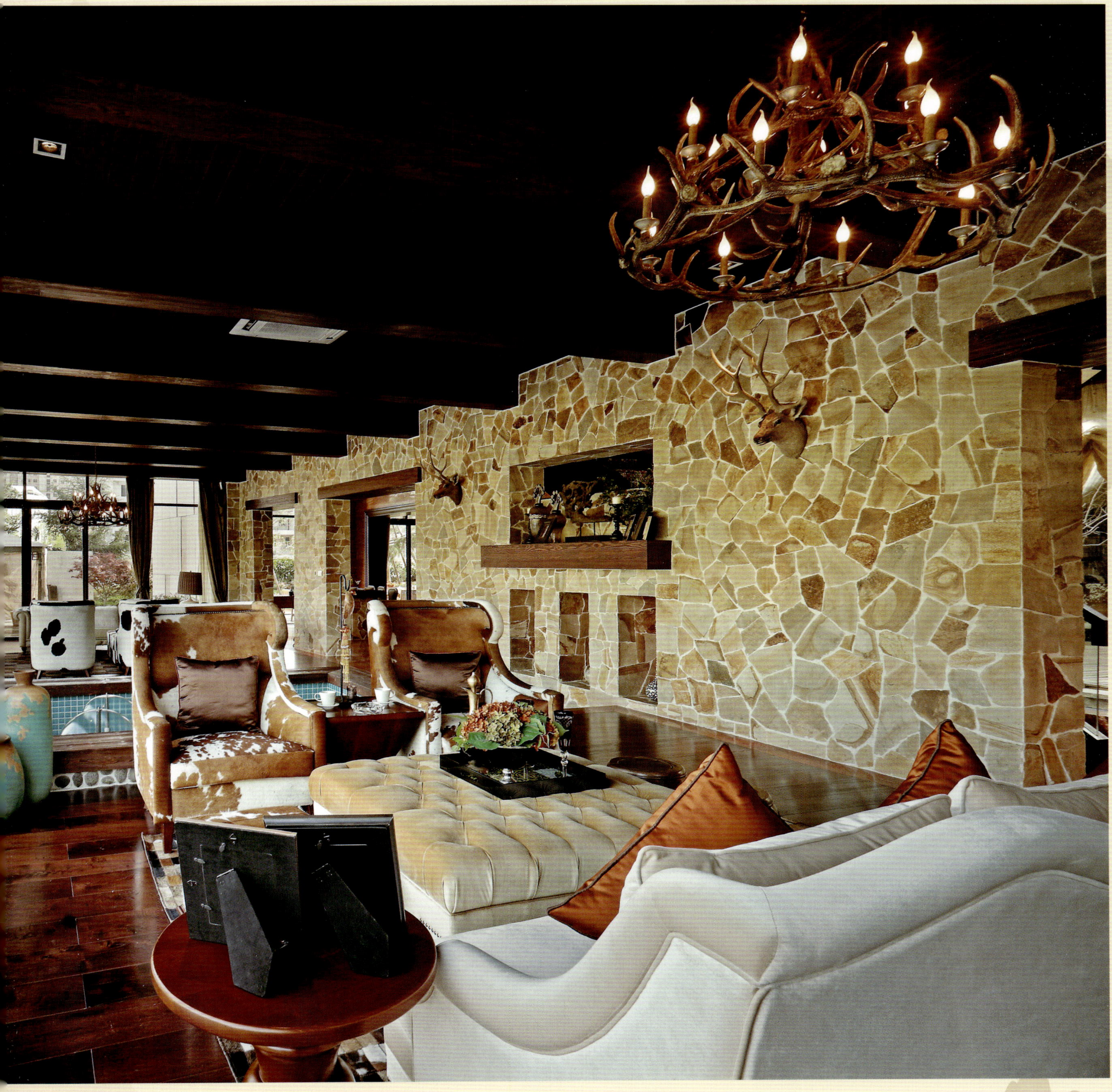

172

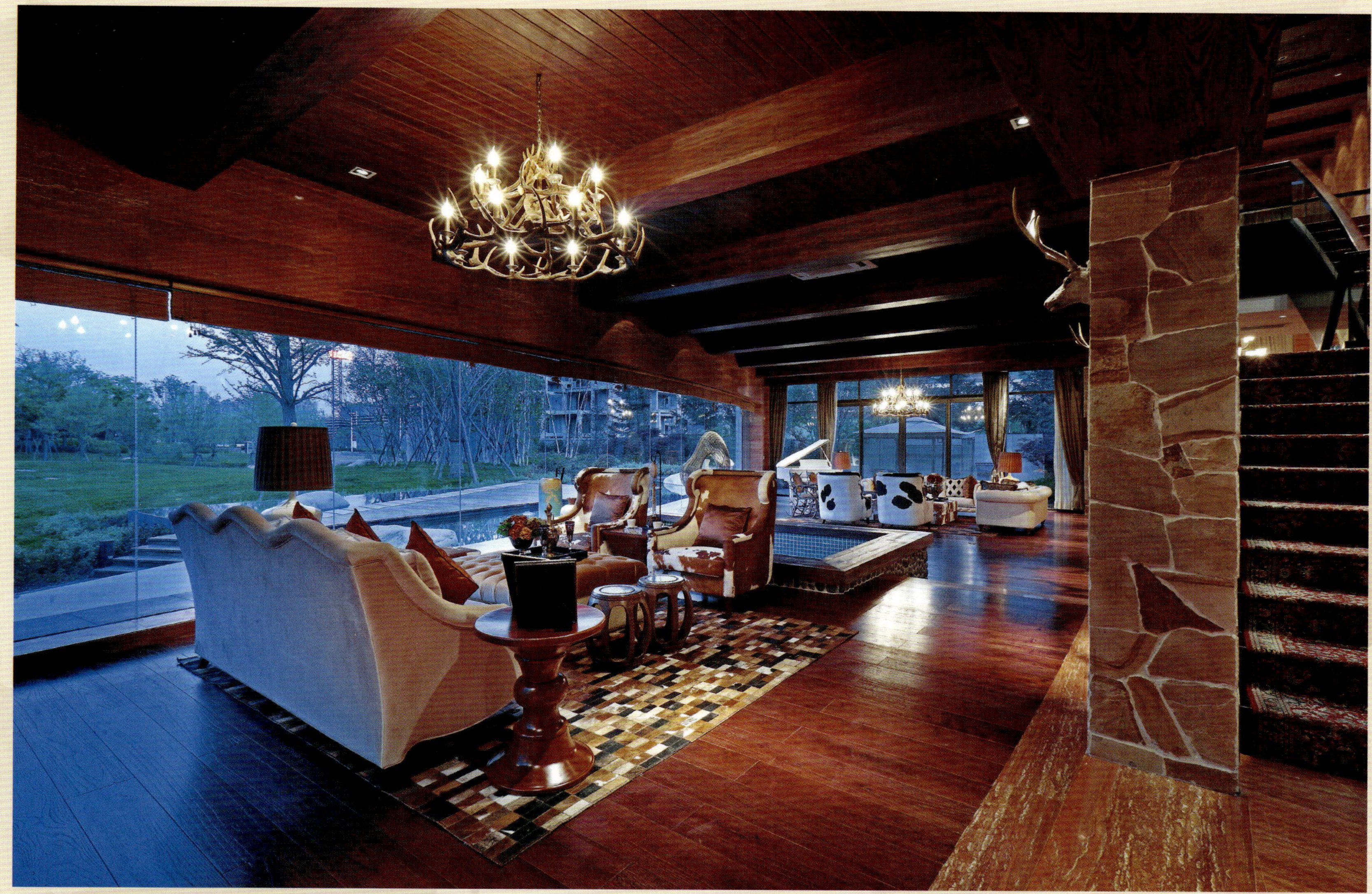

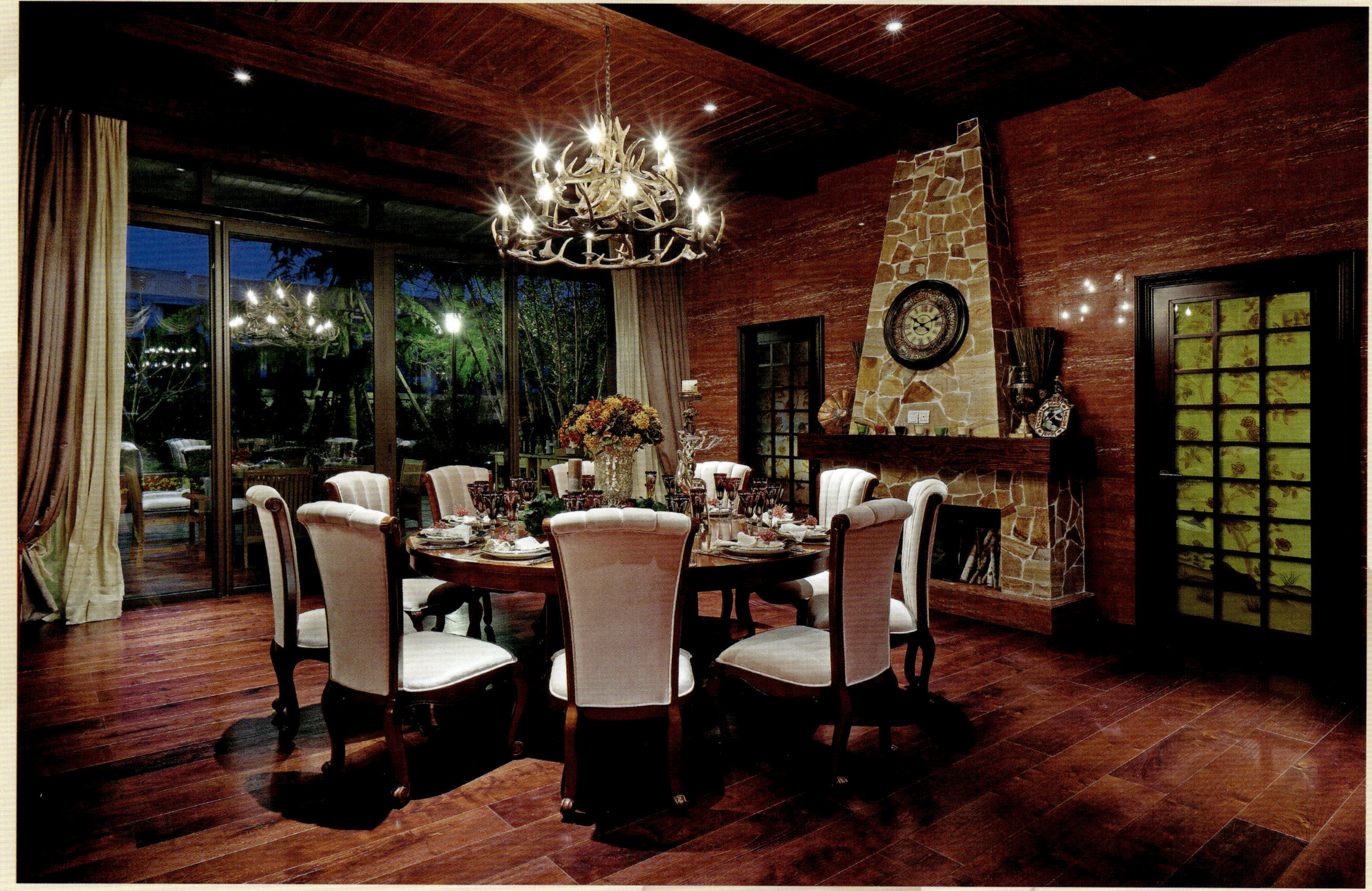

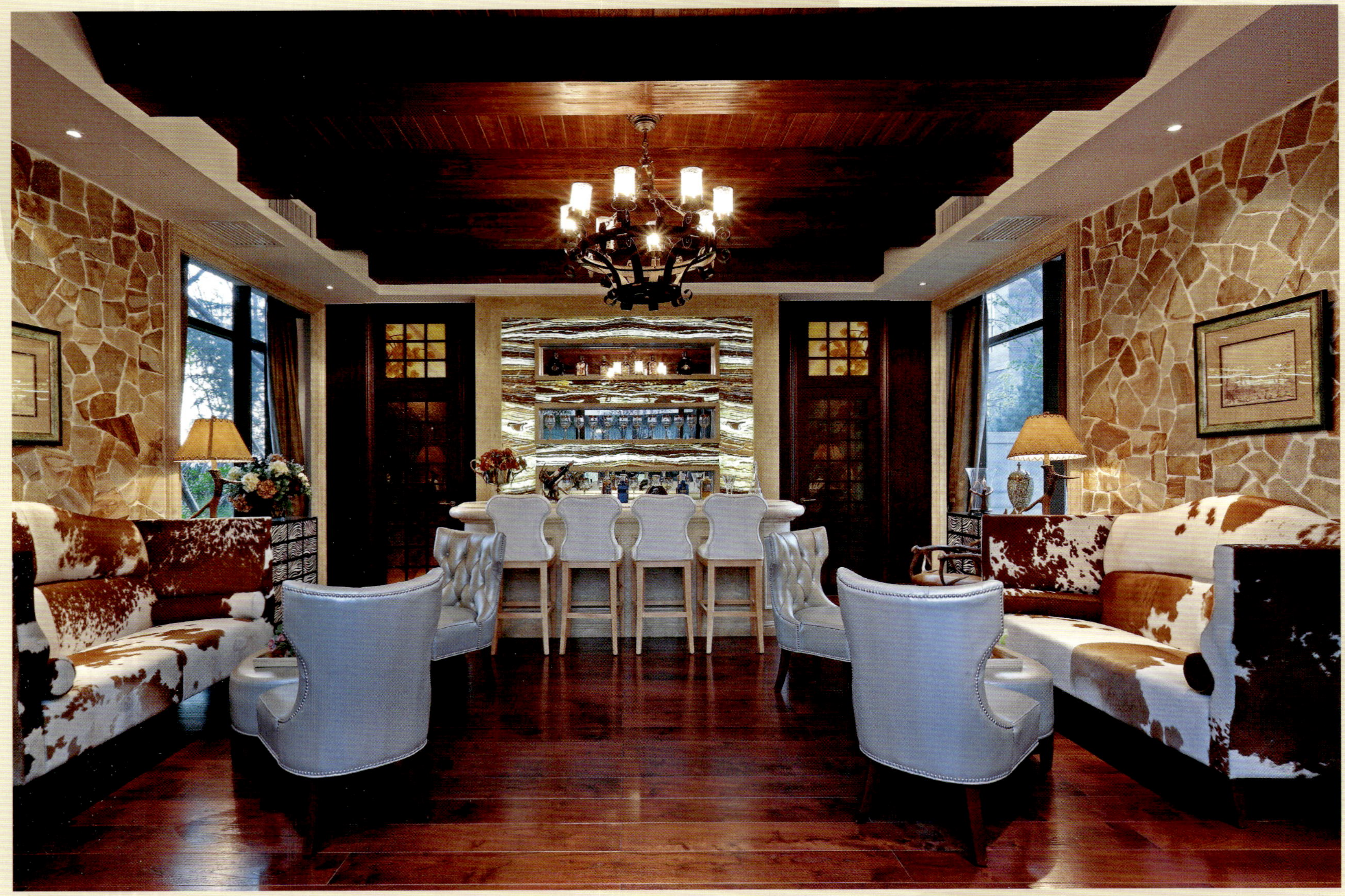

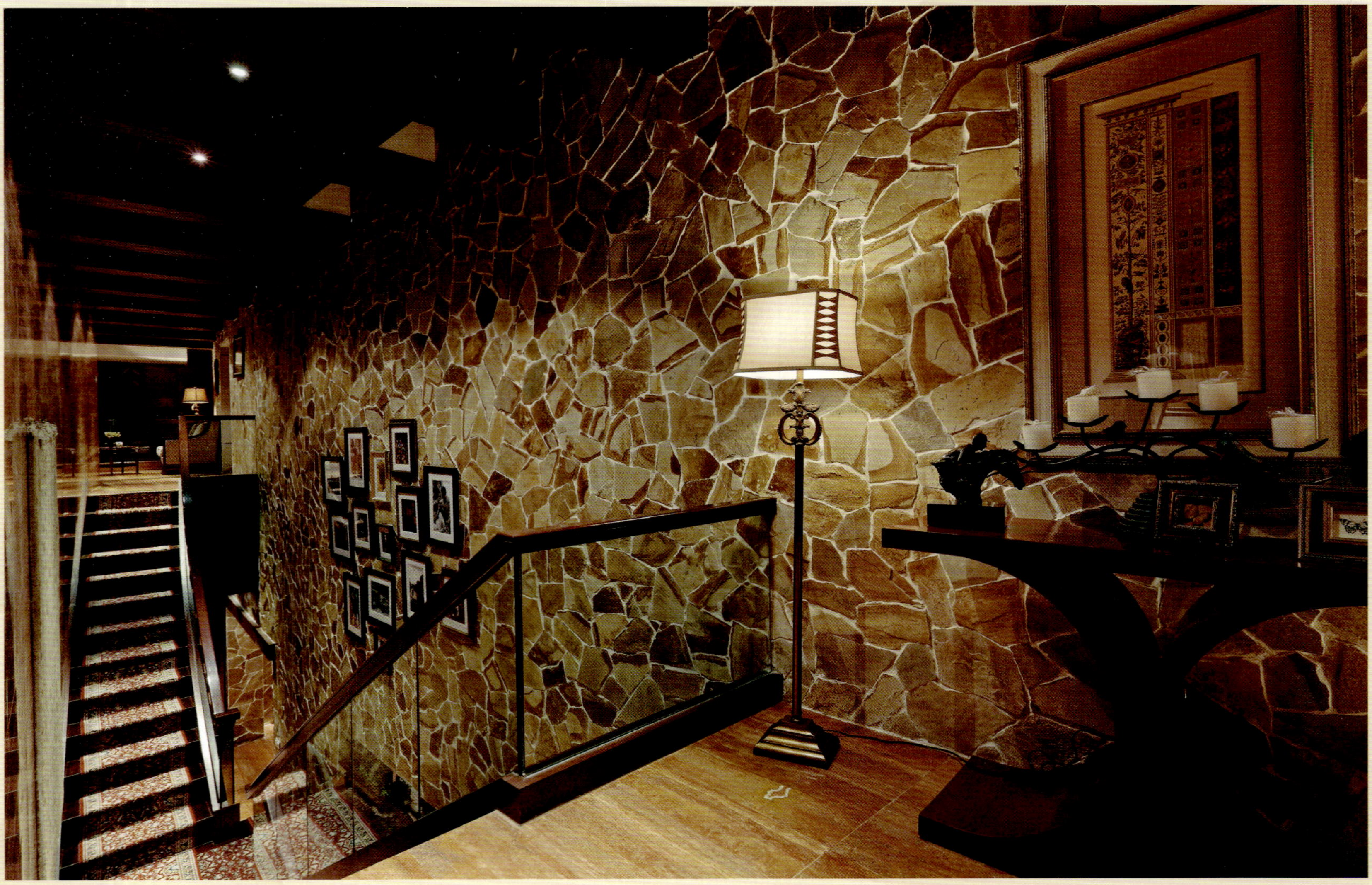

175

Jincheng Club

Design Agency: Hong Kong Fong Wong Architects & Associates

Client: Zhonghai Real Estate

Location: Chengdu, China

Area: 800 m²

Photographer: Jiang Guozhen

The design of this project was inspired by the history of ancient Silk Road. The clubhouse is located in the first post house of Silk Road — Cuqiao. As we know, the silk comes from the cocoon, the designer took the cocoon as its basic idea. By abstracting and analyzing the form and characteristics of the cocoon, there forms a unique theme pattern applied in the interior design. It intends to bring an atmosphere implying a cocoon pupating into a butterfly for this space.

The designer adopted the Art Nouveau style to create a modern and elegant place for the visitors to rest both their body and mind.

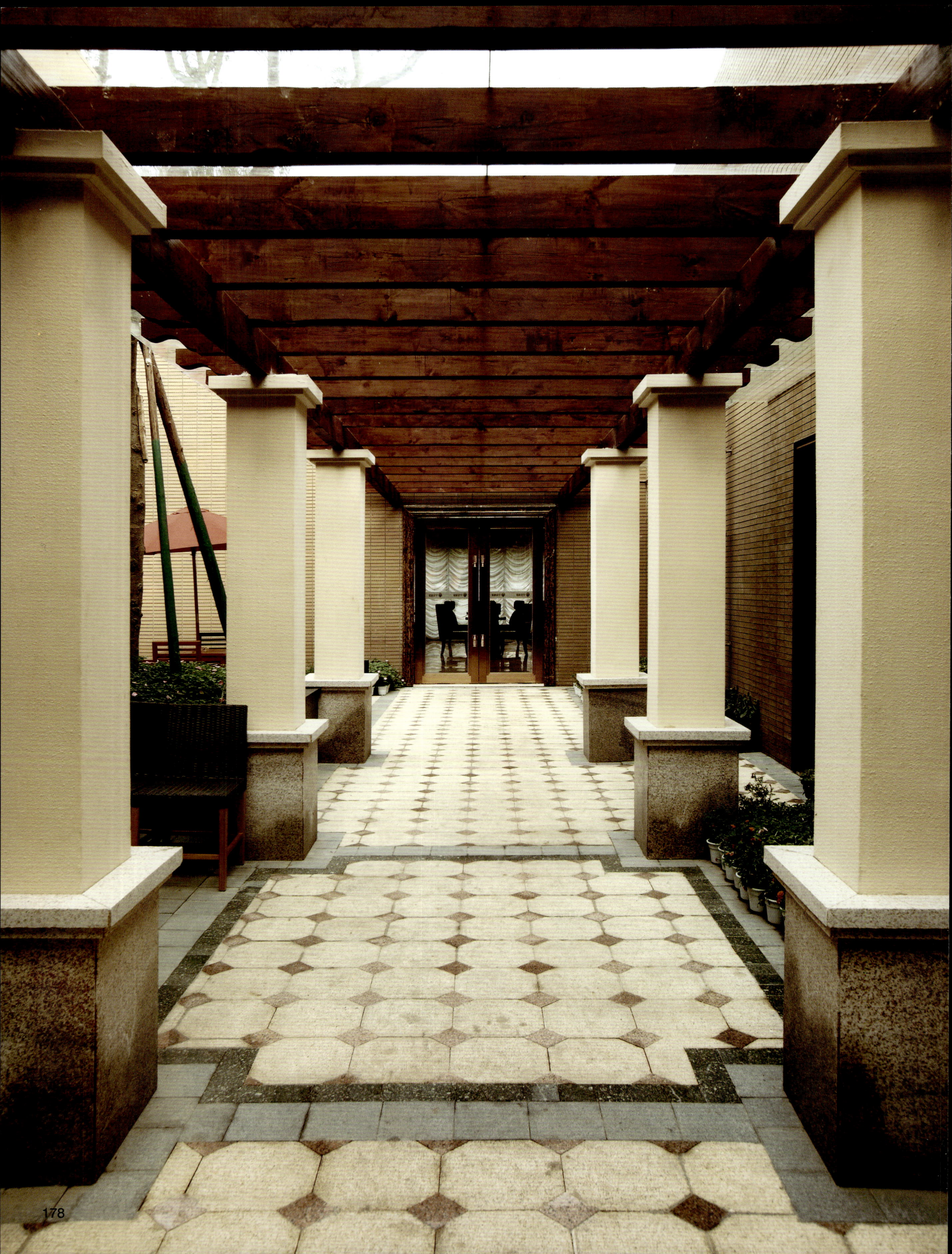

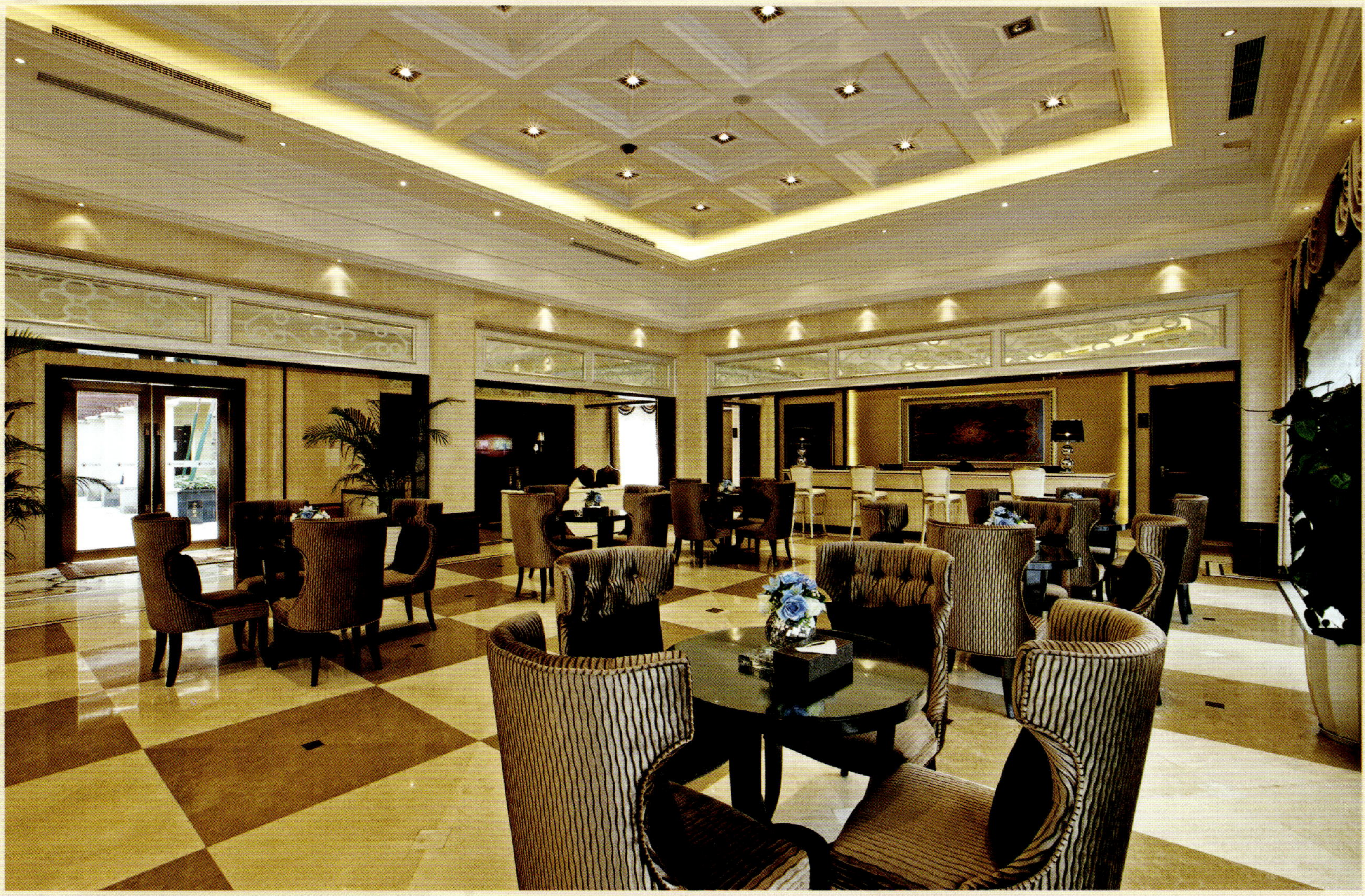

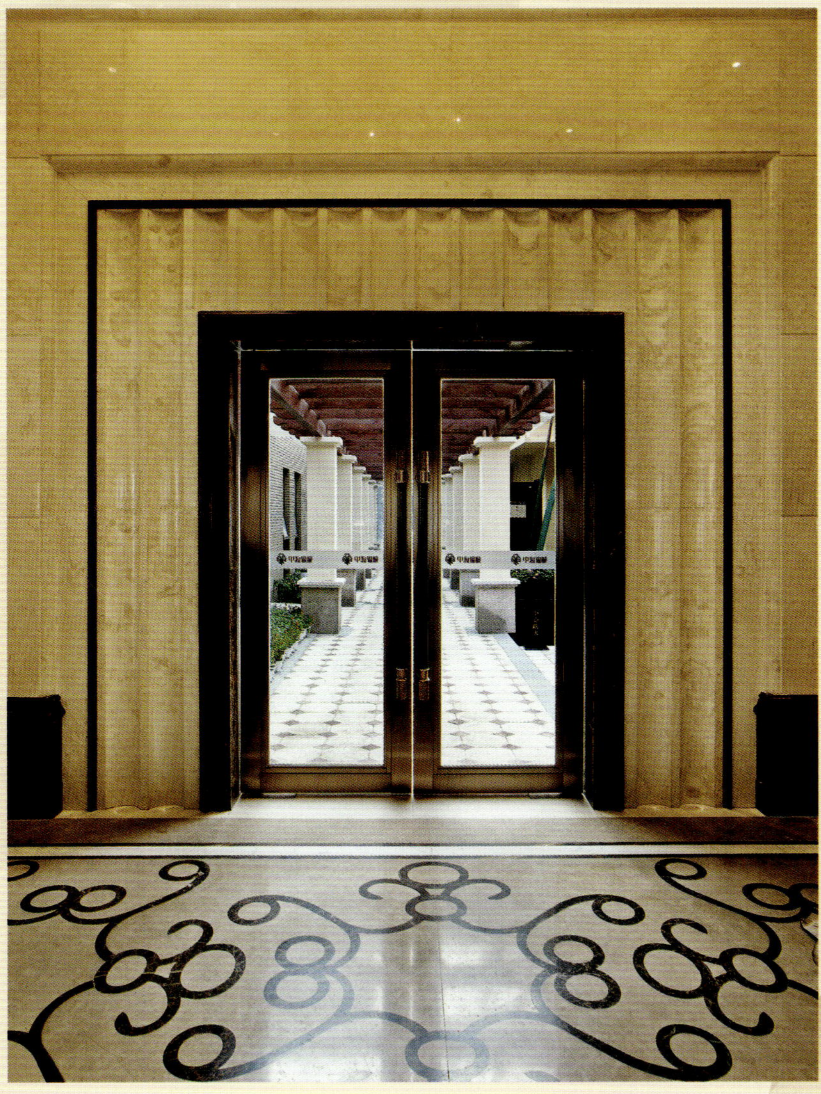

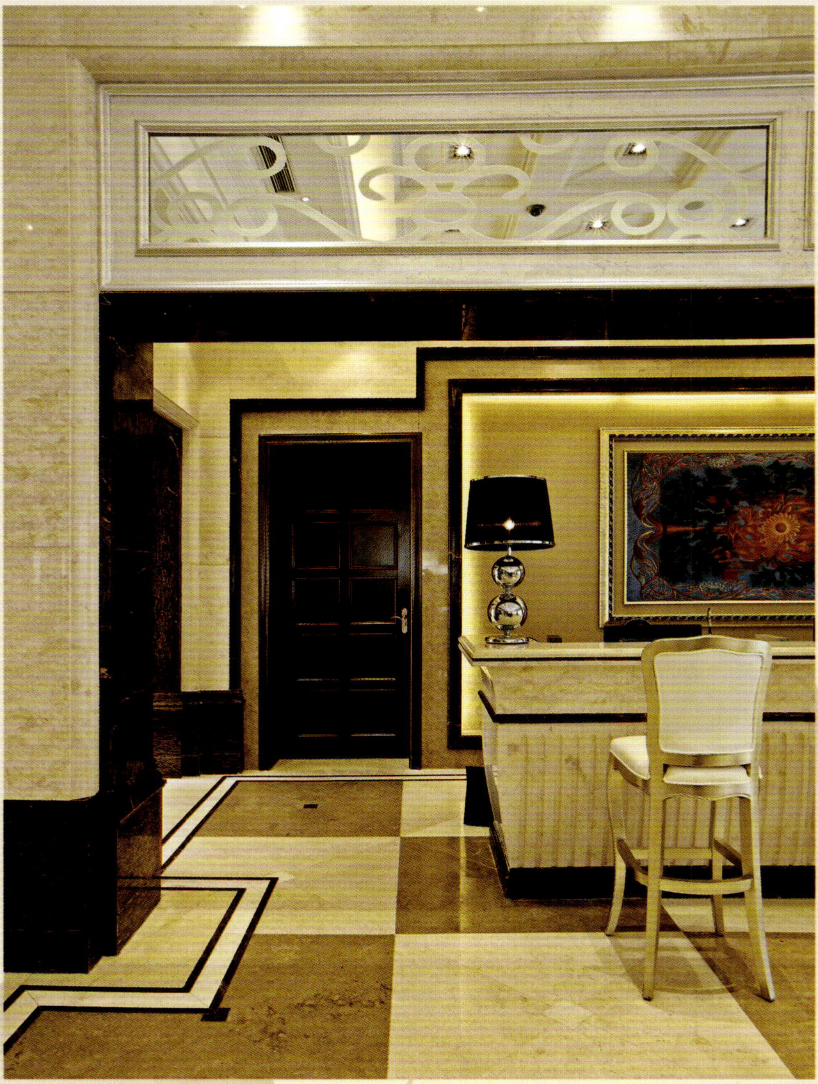

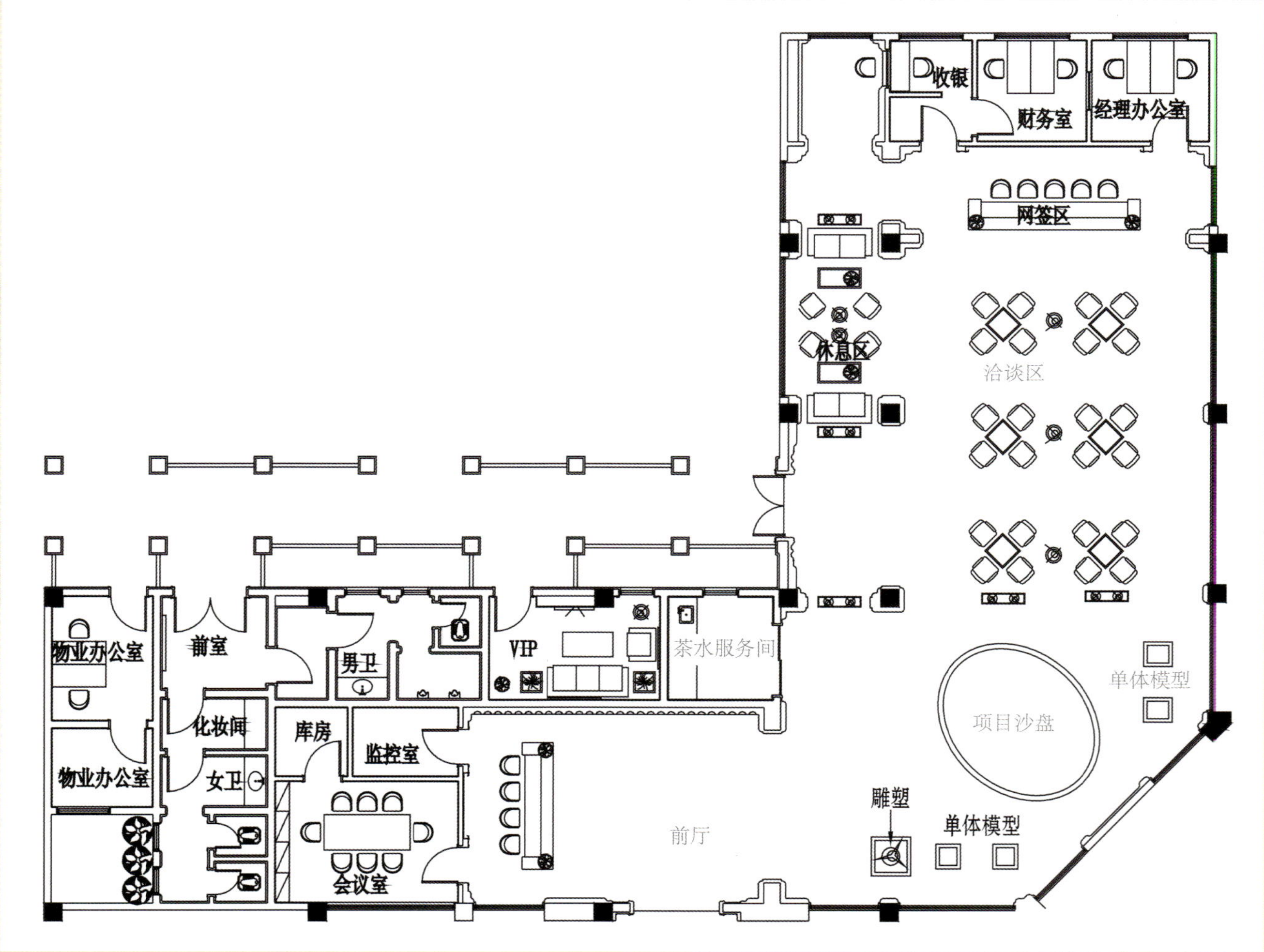
收银
财务室
经理办公室
网签区
休息区
洽谈区
物业办公室
前室
男卫
VIP
茶水服务间
化妆间
库房
监控室
物业办公室
女卫
会议室
单体模型
项目沙盘
雕塑
单体模型
前厅

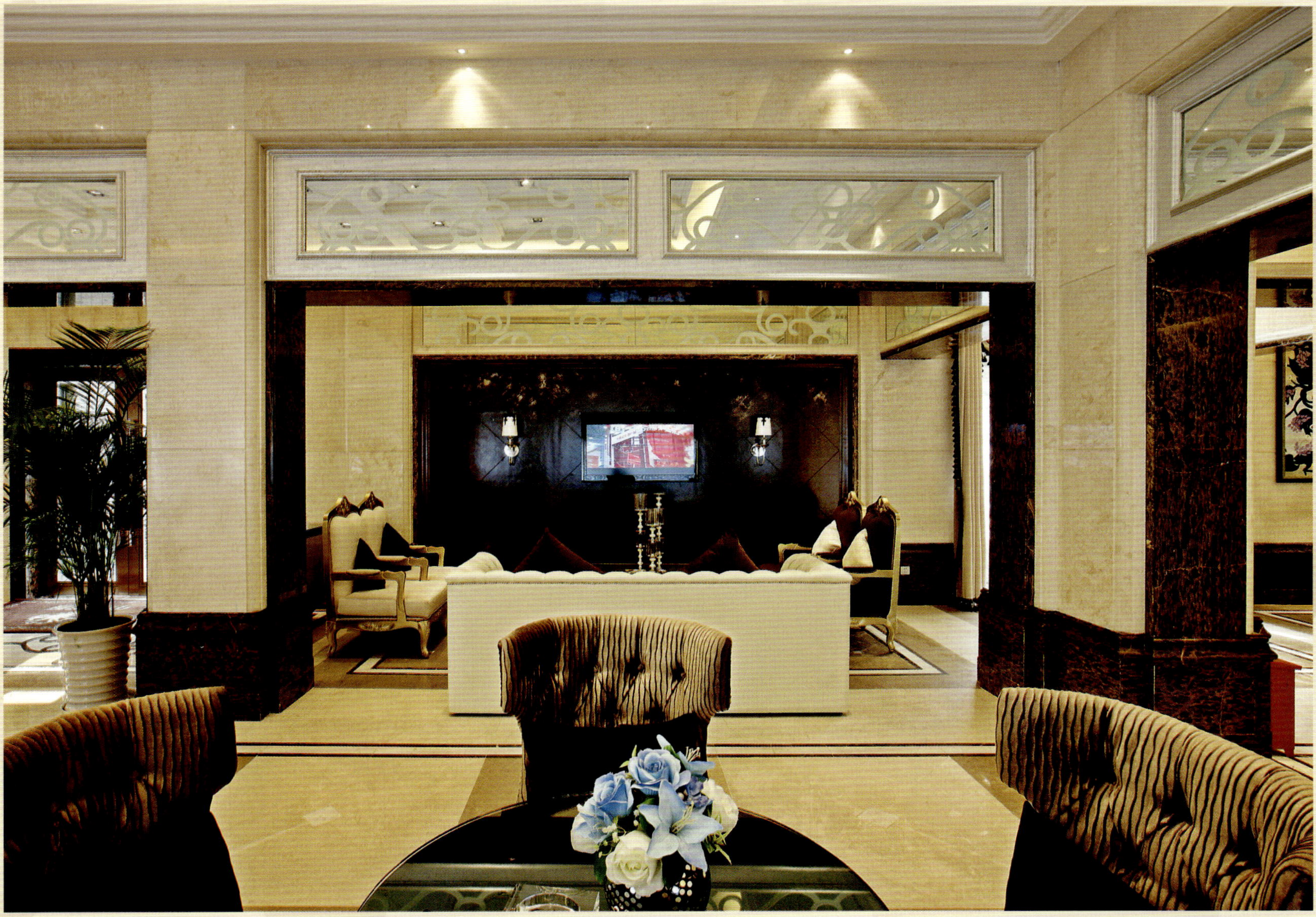

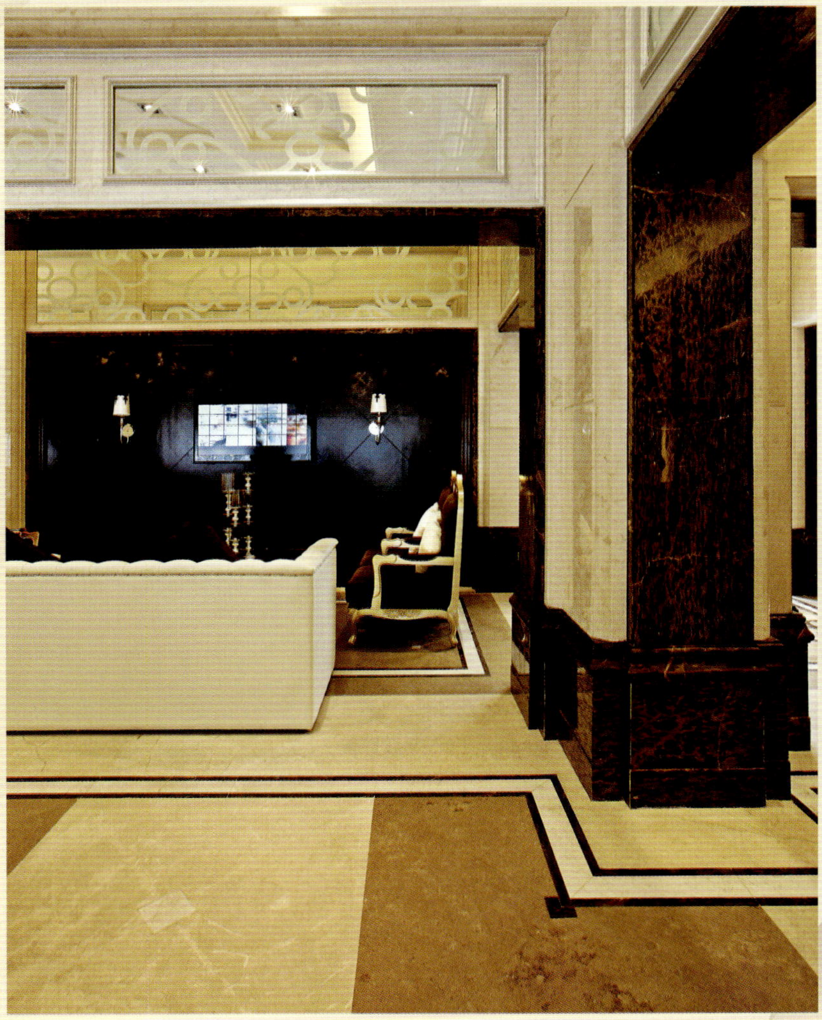

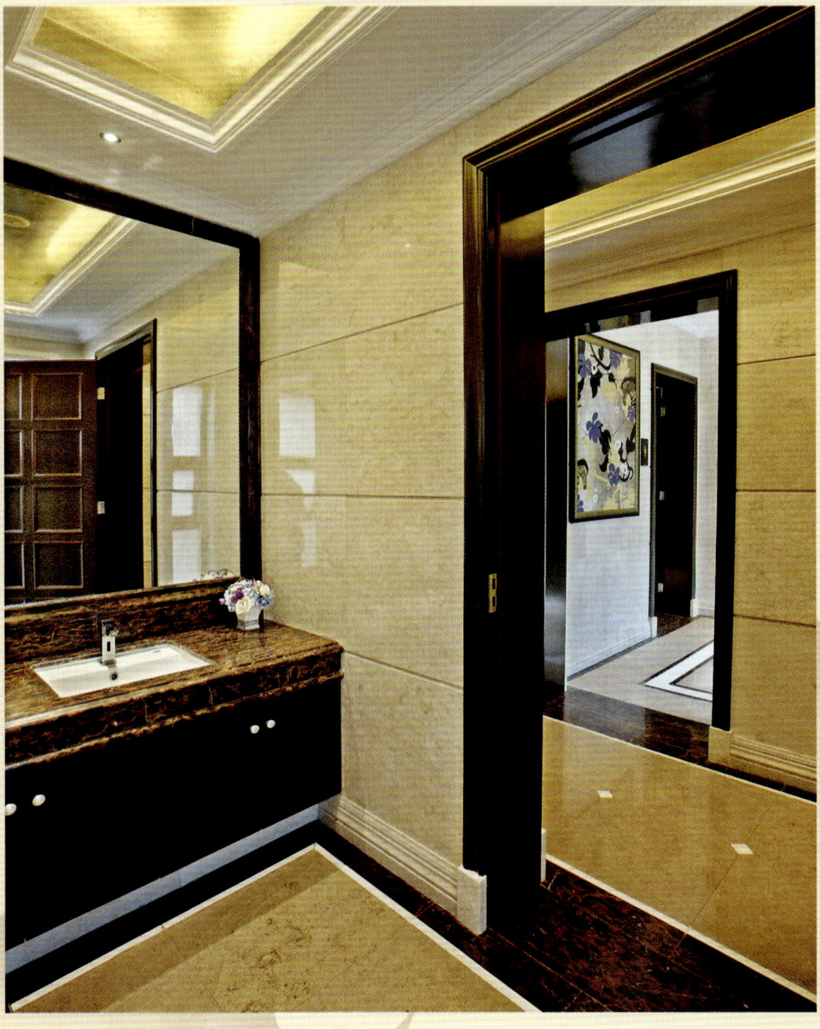

Sanya Peninsula Blue Bay Reception Club

Design Agency: Symmetry international space
Designer: Zakia Zhang
Client: Sanya Run Feng Construction Co., Ltd.
Area: 939 m^2

Architectural image description: architectural concept is that a white sail boat travels in the sea; façade propped up by the white tensioned membrane as mast; the end of the water is deep bowl-shaped; connecting to it, water platform of the open VIP area is made of wooden louvers, like a bow sampan. Real indoor space is more like a luxury yacht.

Spatial configuration description: the ground floor 1F is arranged with audio-visual room and virtual model room; 2F is an open vip discussion area, separated from the noisy sales area by the patio gallery. In the deepest of the building, the silver chandelier overhang before the background of jade, creating a gorgeous yet leisurely atmosphere for the entire bar.

Process design description: stepping up the stairs from 2F, the highest point is the deep and boundless pool. When you transfer into the gallery, both sides are respectively independent open-VIP area and sales discussion area. In the rear of the discussion area, there are stairs down into the multimedia audio-visual room, where an overall project introduction will be given. The last side is intensive-decoration model rooms.

Lighting and light design: architectural lighting emphasizes the overall outer contour, the wavy wood grill, white tensioned membrane, as well as the giant bowl-shaped pool; the indoor takes the soft but gorgeous light distributed by the jade as the

183

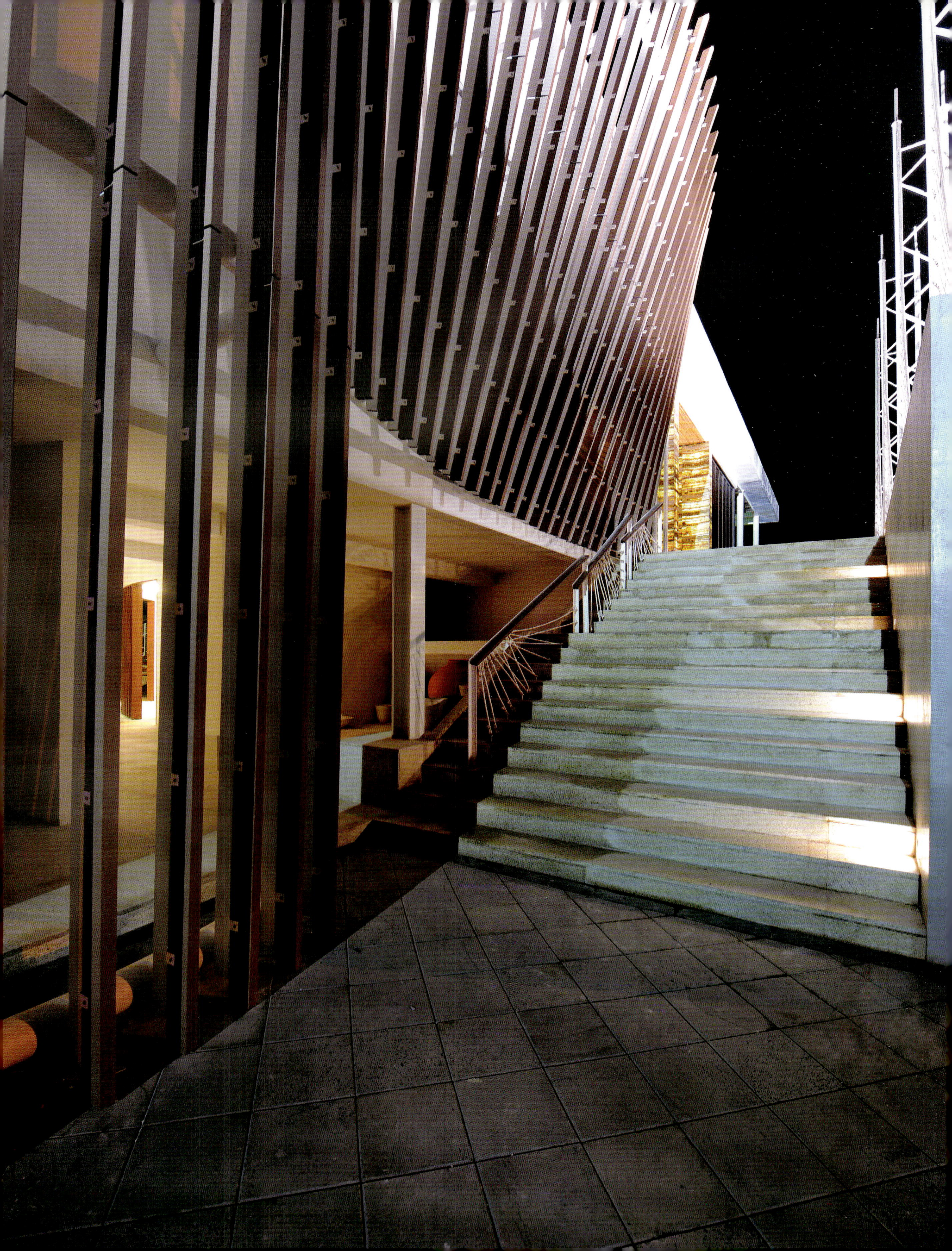

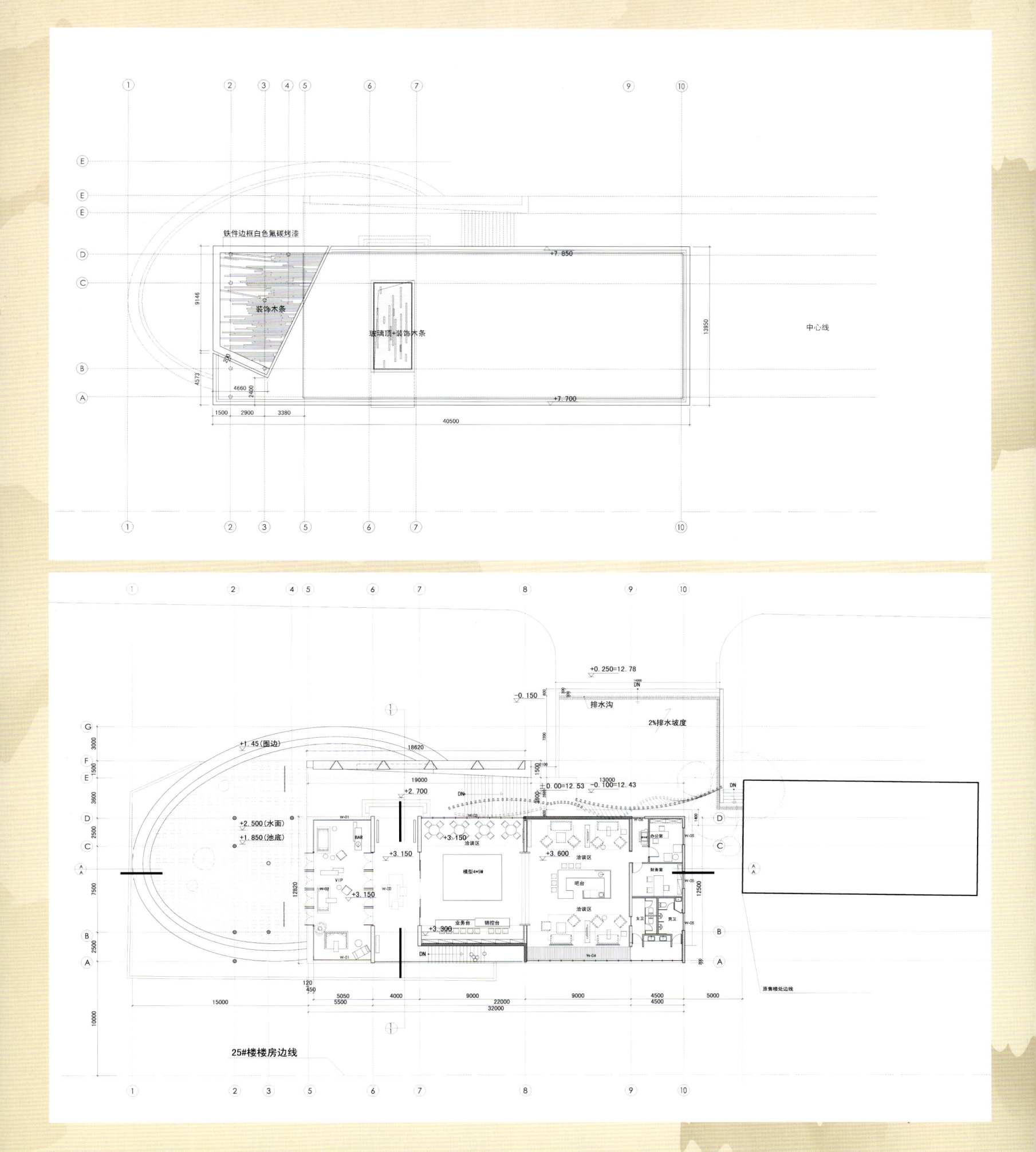

background, accompanied with a dreamy and gorgeous atmosphere created by a champagne-color metal ceiling lamp.

Design and application of materials: Putting the little black ceramic tiles into herringbone shape on the ground, with manual and natural tonality, the concert and the contrast will make their characters more significant, under the colorful texture and gorgeous luster of the Cappucine Onyx on the wall.

Carbon concept: From the combination of physical and spatial relationships, it uses a large number of floating eaves to achieve adequate shaded effects and finally make an environment of "cool enough to reduce air conditioning usage".

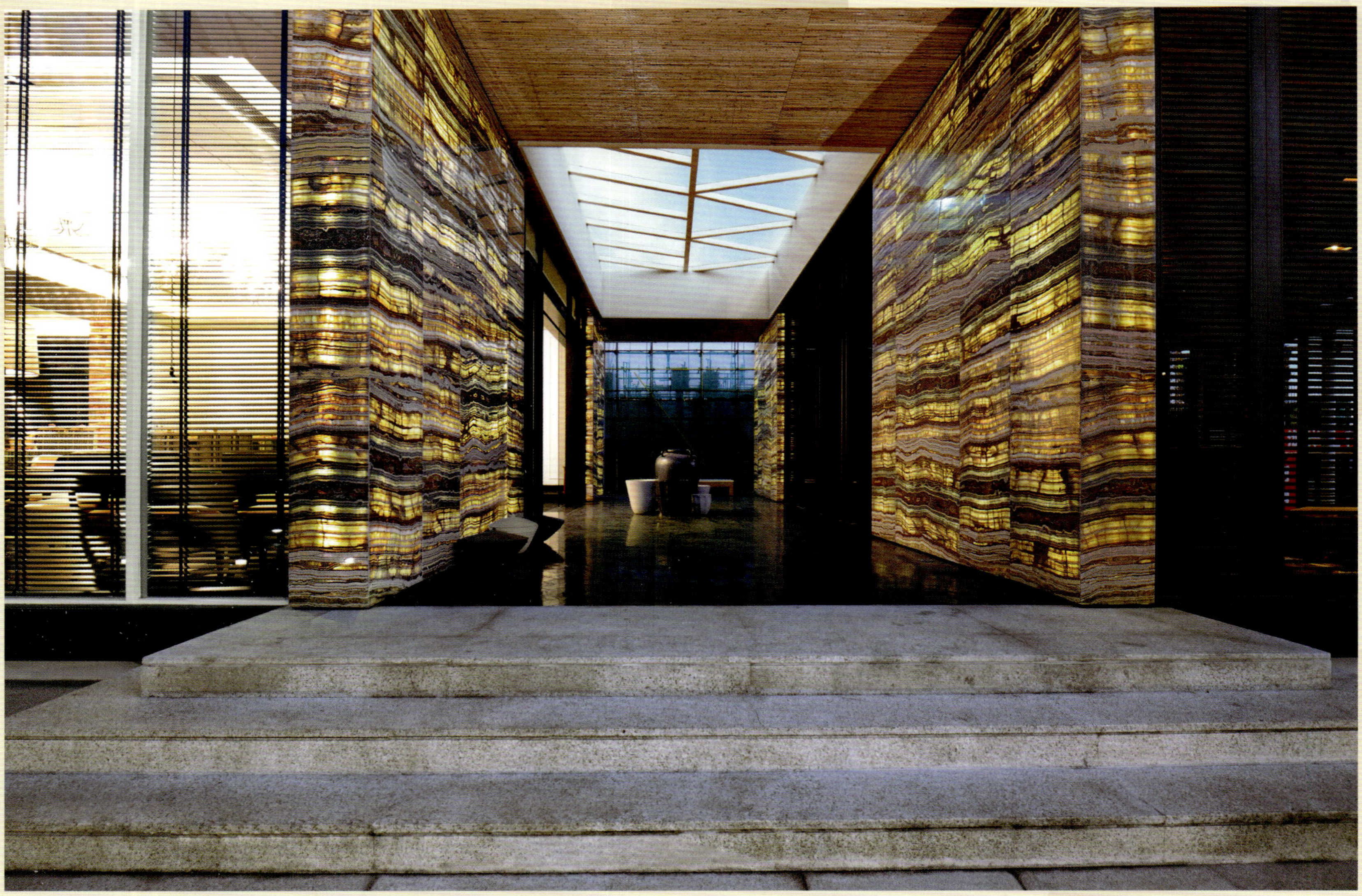

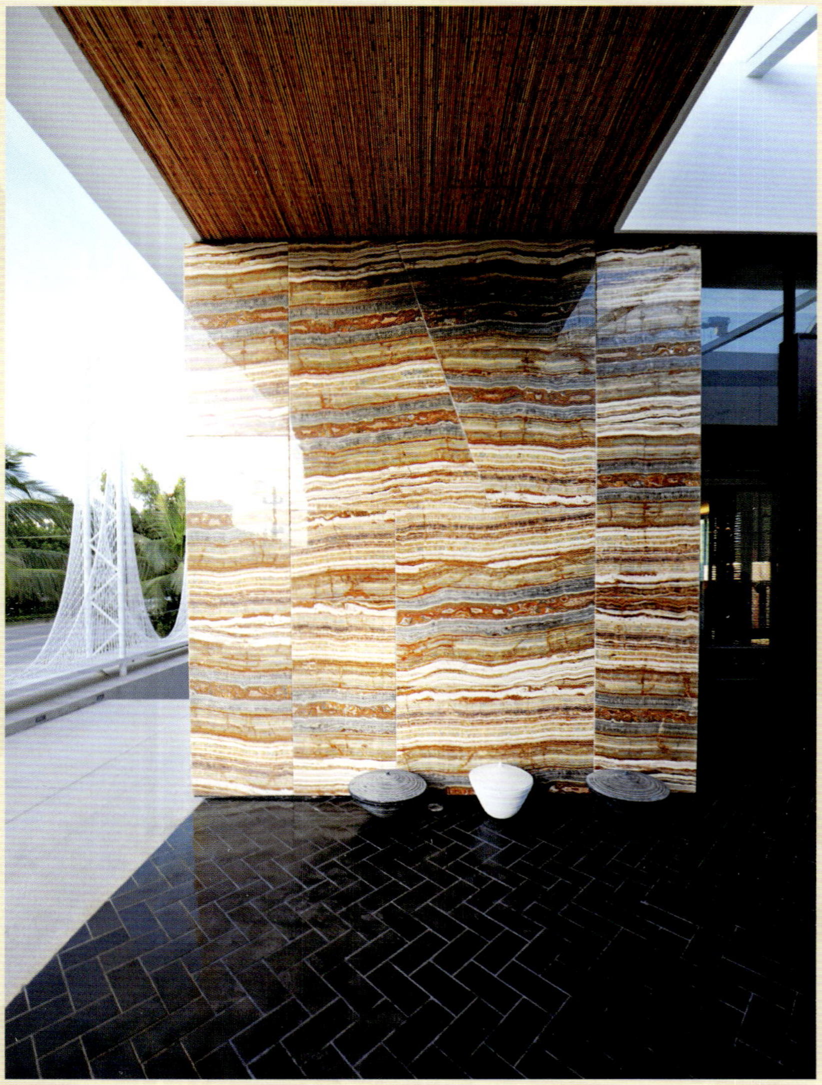

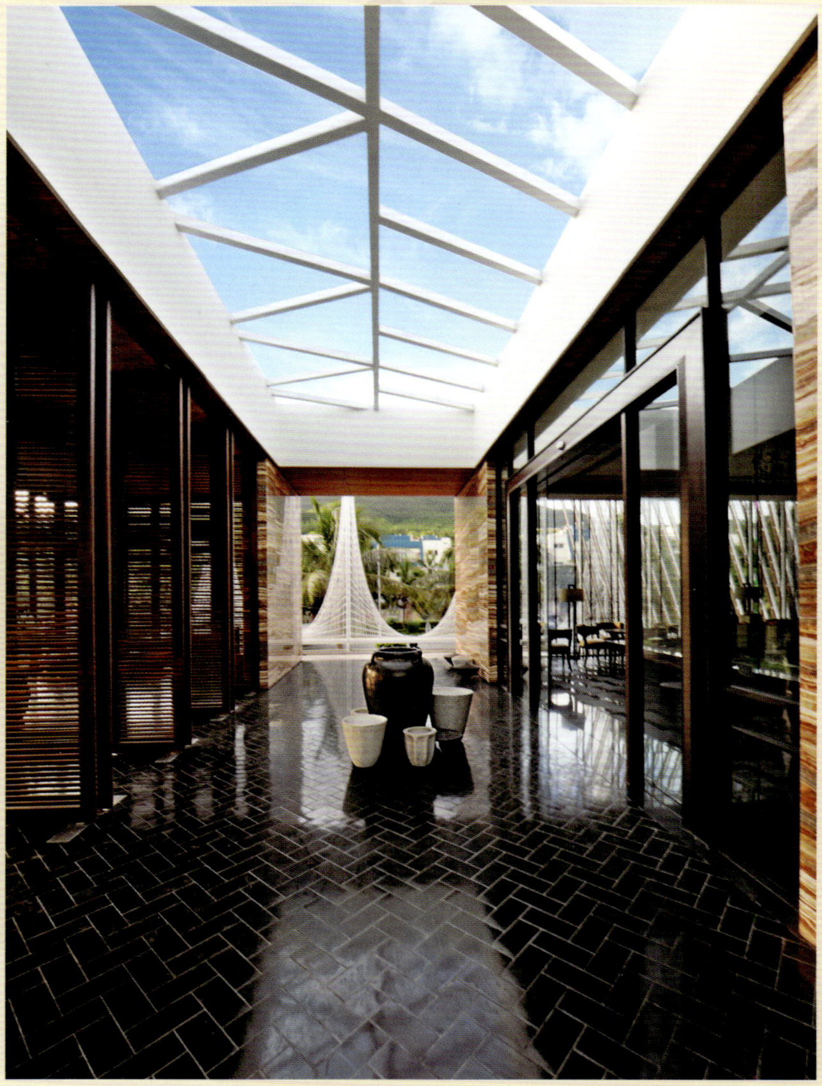

25#楼楼房边线

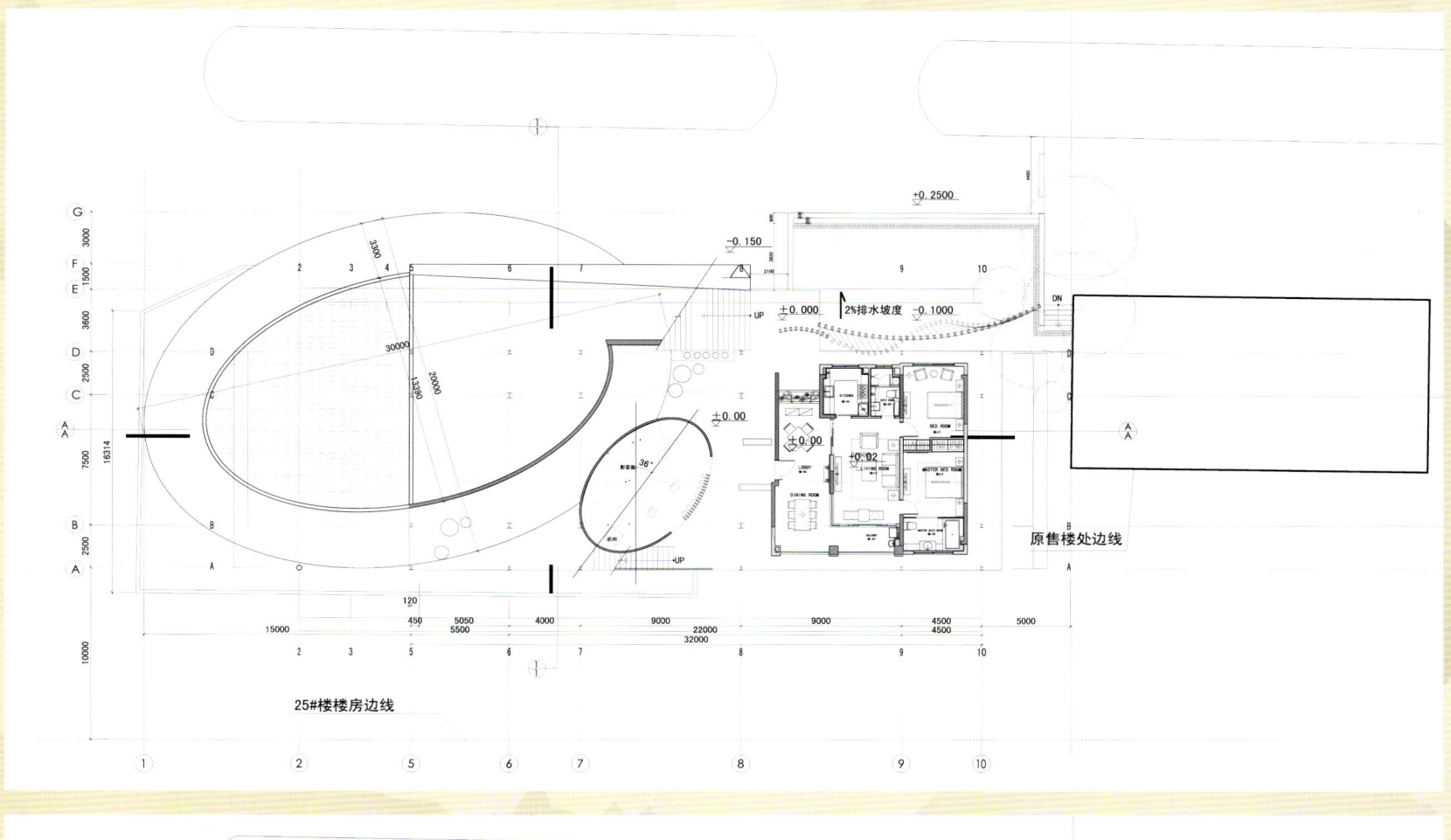

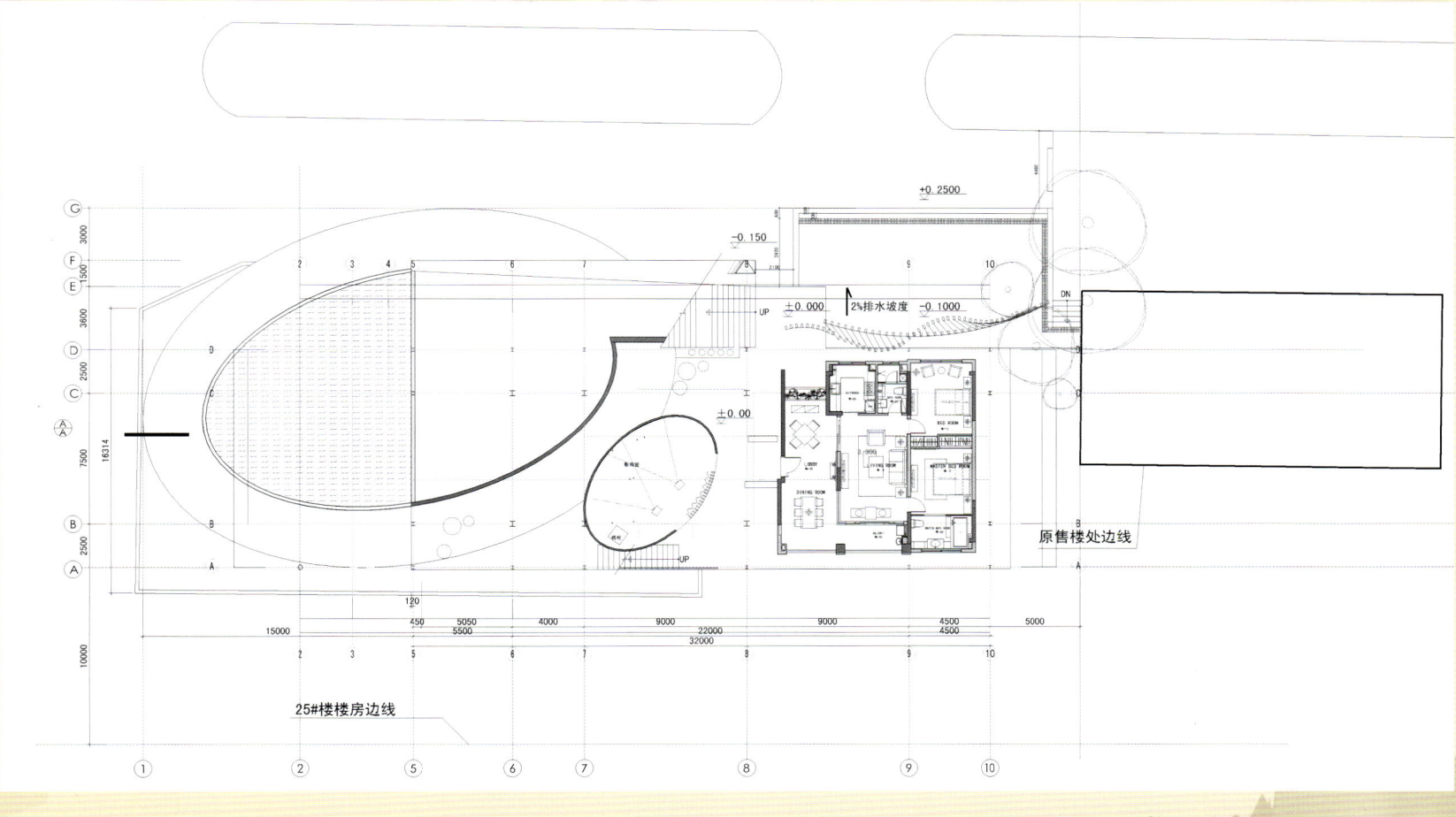

原售楼处边线

187

188

189

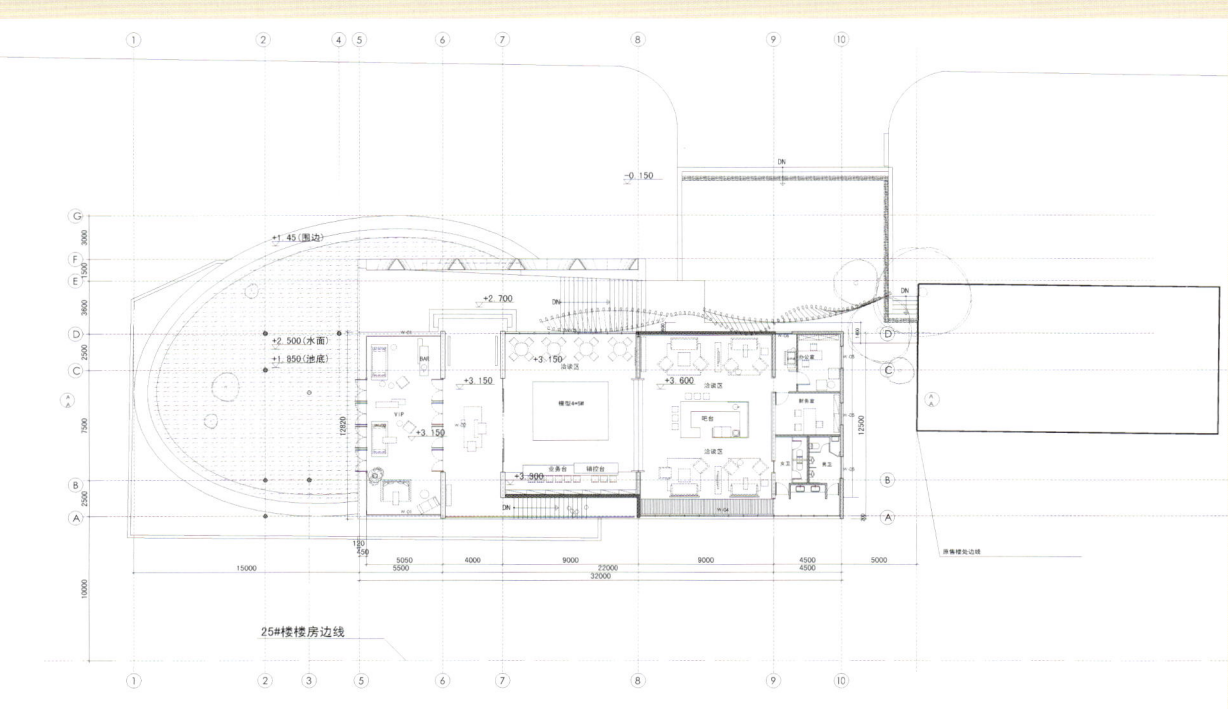

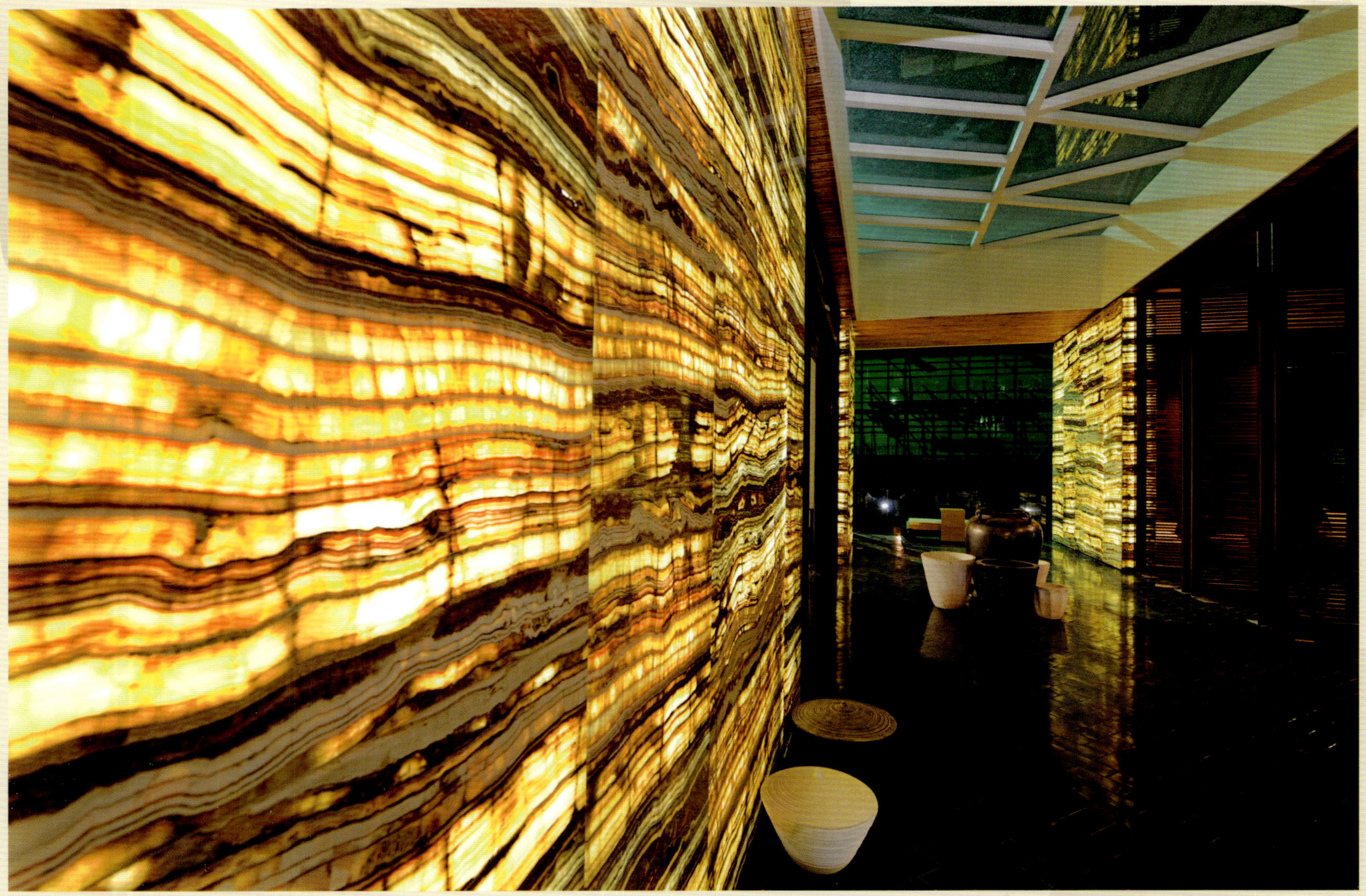

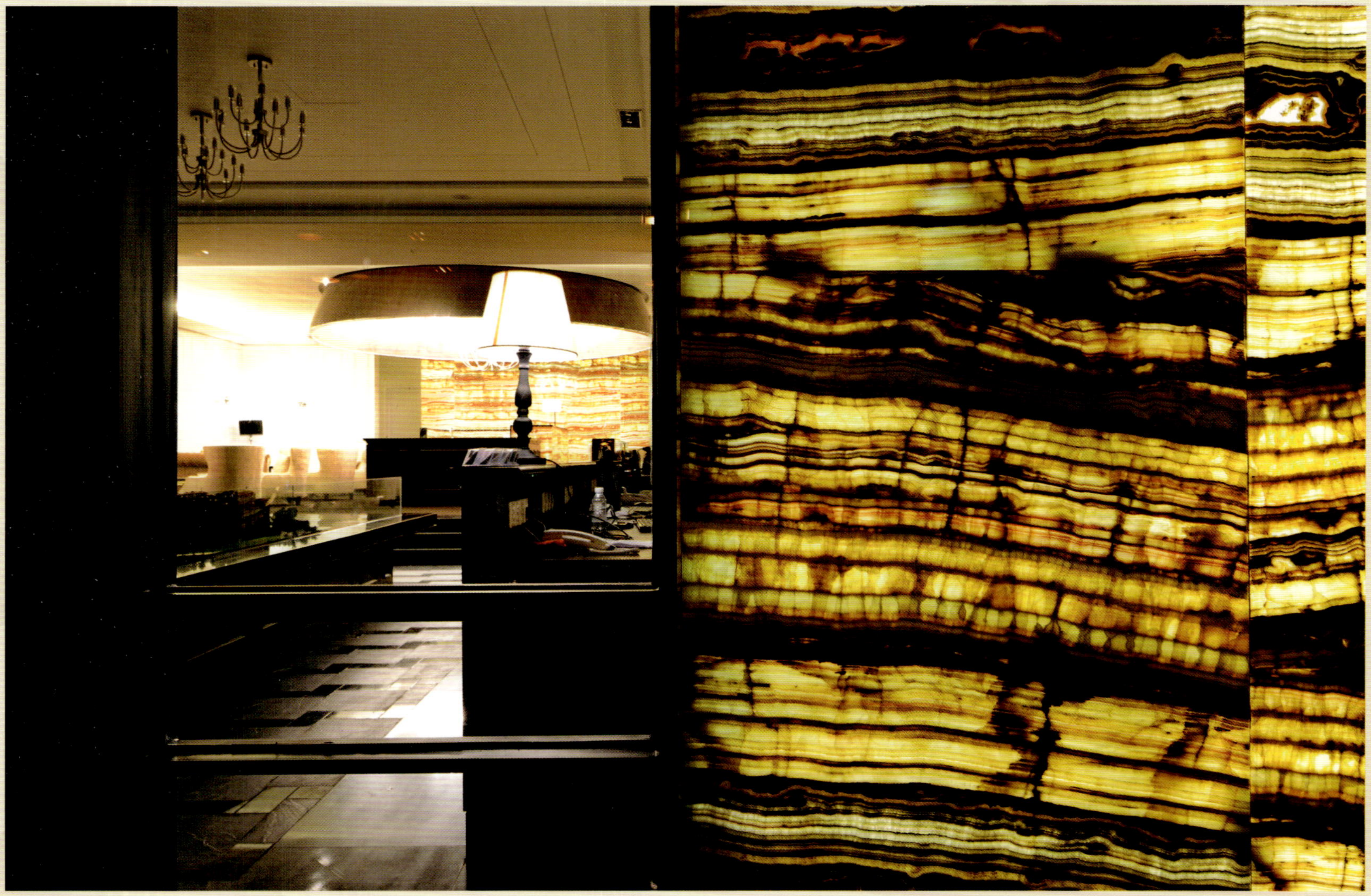

191

Chao Huang Ge Club

Design Agency: Da Tang Shi Jia
Location: Sichuan, China
Area: 3000 m²

Chao Huang Ge Club of Chengdu is one of the famous brands of high-end business club in western China, where it has the leader position and play an important role in the whole industry. It has been the business center of upper-class society. The owner is very harsh and strict with this case. He demands to build a "plain" European business environment so as to enhance and maintain the brand position in the industry.

With full understanding of European culture and deep love of its architecture, designers find a breakthrough of the design soon. They make interpretation and analysis of the space, and decide that the entire space is to build an intimate and elegant business atmosphere. According to that thought, they decide to divide the space into indoor area and outdoor area, which will be perfectly unified together.

The concept of front room space is used throughout the design, not only in the luxury suites and lobby but also in public toilets, and it becomes one of highlights of the whole design. The lighting design is special in the entire business club, making the whole atmosphere closer to a kind of luxurious "comfort", which shows the designers' higher talent.

193

194

195

Lake Clubhouse

Design Agency: Joey Ho Design Limited
Designer: Joey Ho, Daphne Ng, Douglas Fung
Client: Sun Hung Kai Real Estate Agency Co., Ltd.
Location: Guangzhou, China
Area: 13200 m^2
Photographer: Wu Yongchang, Ray Lau

Situated alongside natural lakes and green scenery, the Lake Clubhouse incorporates a new model of prestigious club, sports club, family club and spa. The central medium is to take the element of water surface as a point of reflection on more tranquil and calm ways of living. The figurative concept is to build the clubhouse on the surface of lake to create the light-filled sensation and grant a floating atmosphere for the activities happened in the whole area.

Housed at the middle of the Lake Clubhouse attaching with an external pool, a swimming pool is the centerpiece of the entire clubhouse to connect a loop for various components to be distributed fluidly on the conceptual lake where visitors can move freely through different experiences in the order the water flows.

Sensuously marching through the clubhouse, one sees the decorative elements and furnishings such as specially-treated glass surface, vertical strips of glass, straight lines of the timber and furniture, the crystal lamp and the soft carpet that were meticulously chosen for enhancing the nature of water — fluid, serenity, refraction, formless state and sparkle — the senses the designer intentionally wants visitors to experience about.

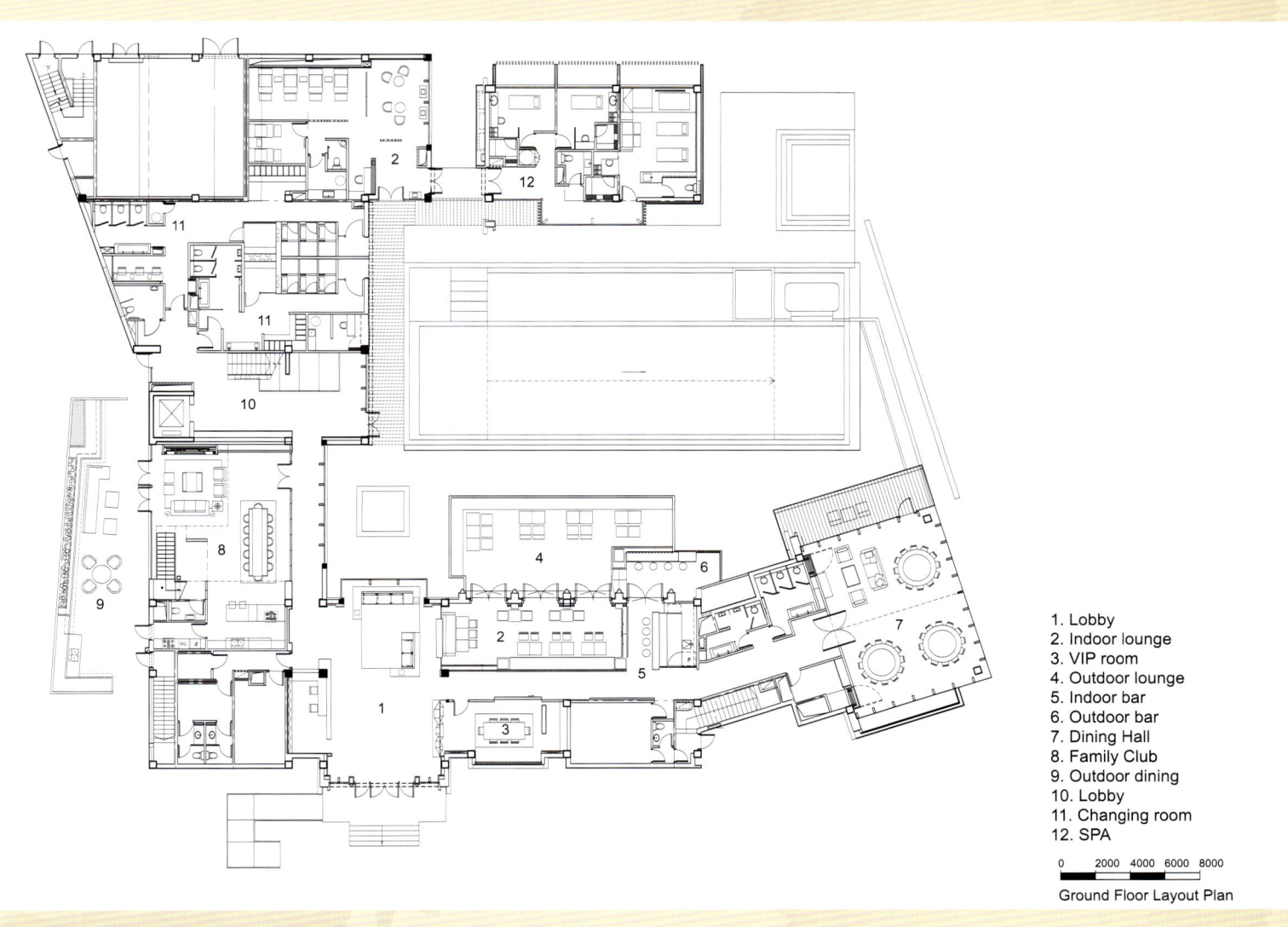

1. Lobby
2. Indoor lounge
3. VIP room
4. Outdoor lounge
5. Indoor bar
6. Outdoor bar
7. Dining Hall
8. Family Club
9. Outdoor dining
10. Lobby
11. Changing room
12. SPA

Ground Floor Layout Plan

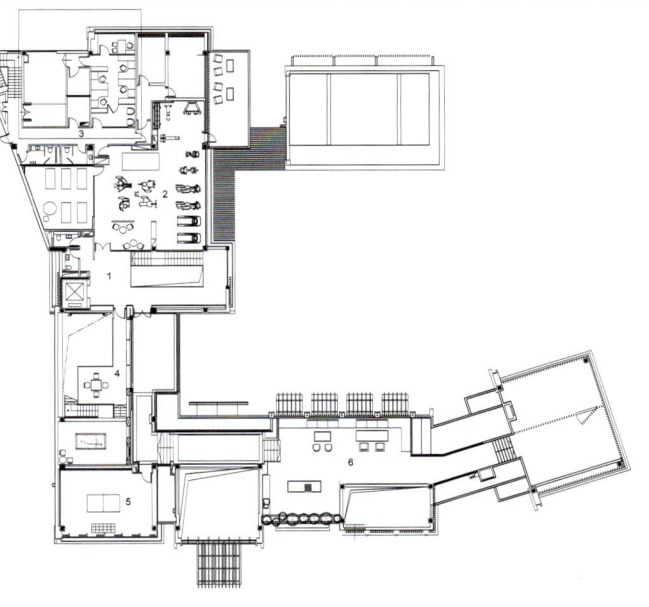

1. Lobby
2. Sports club
3. Office
4. Family club
5. Sports Room
6. Outdoor BBQ area

1st Floor Layout Plan

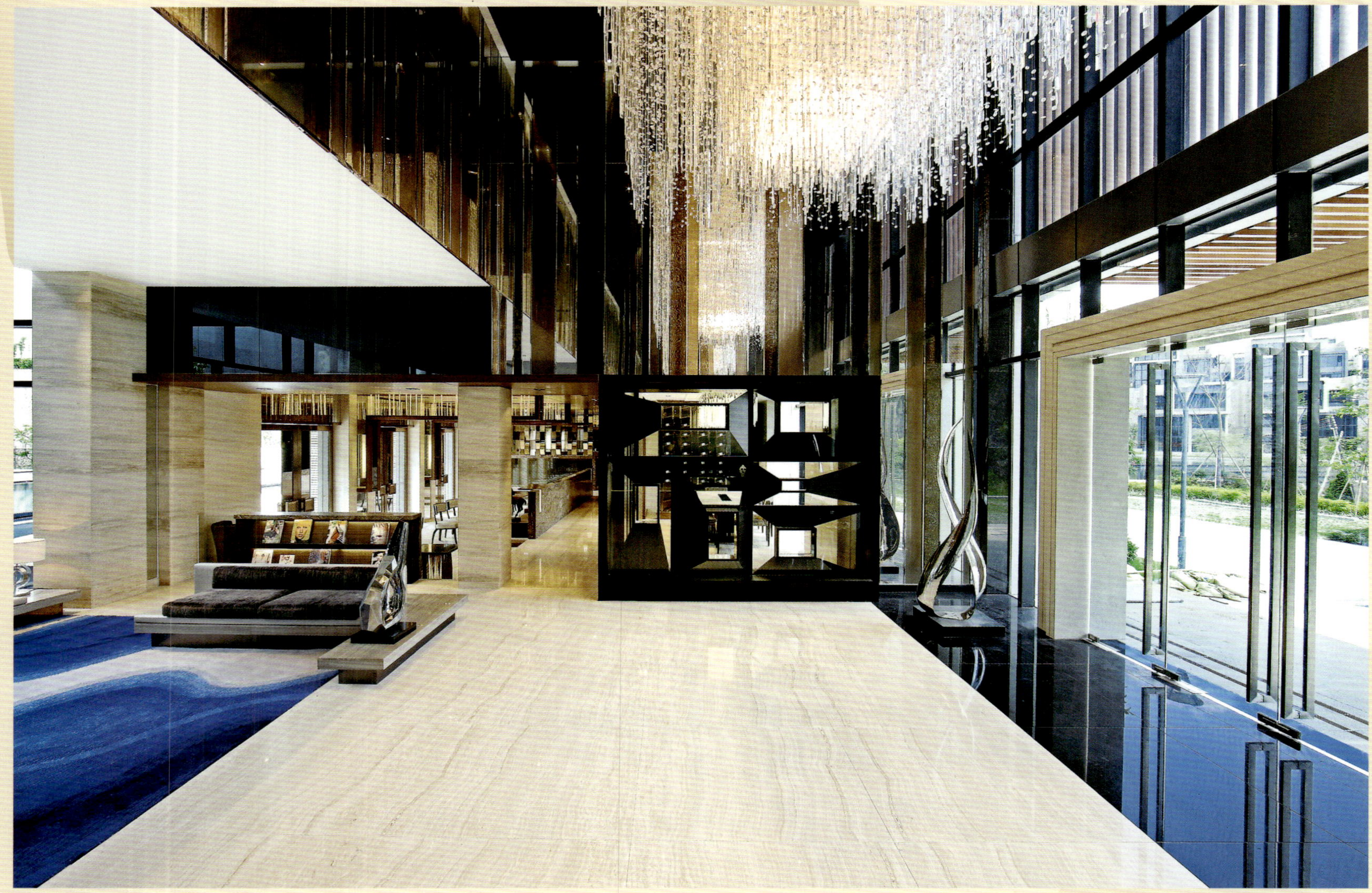

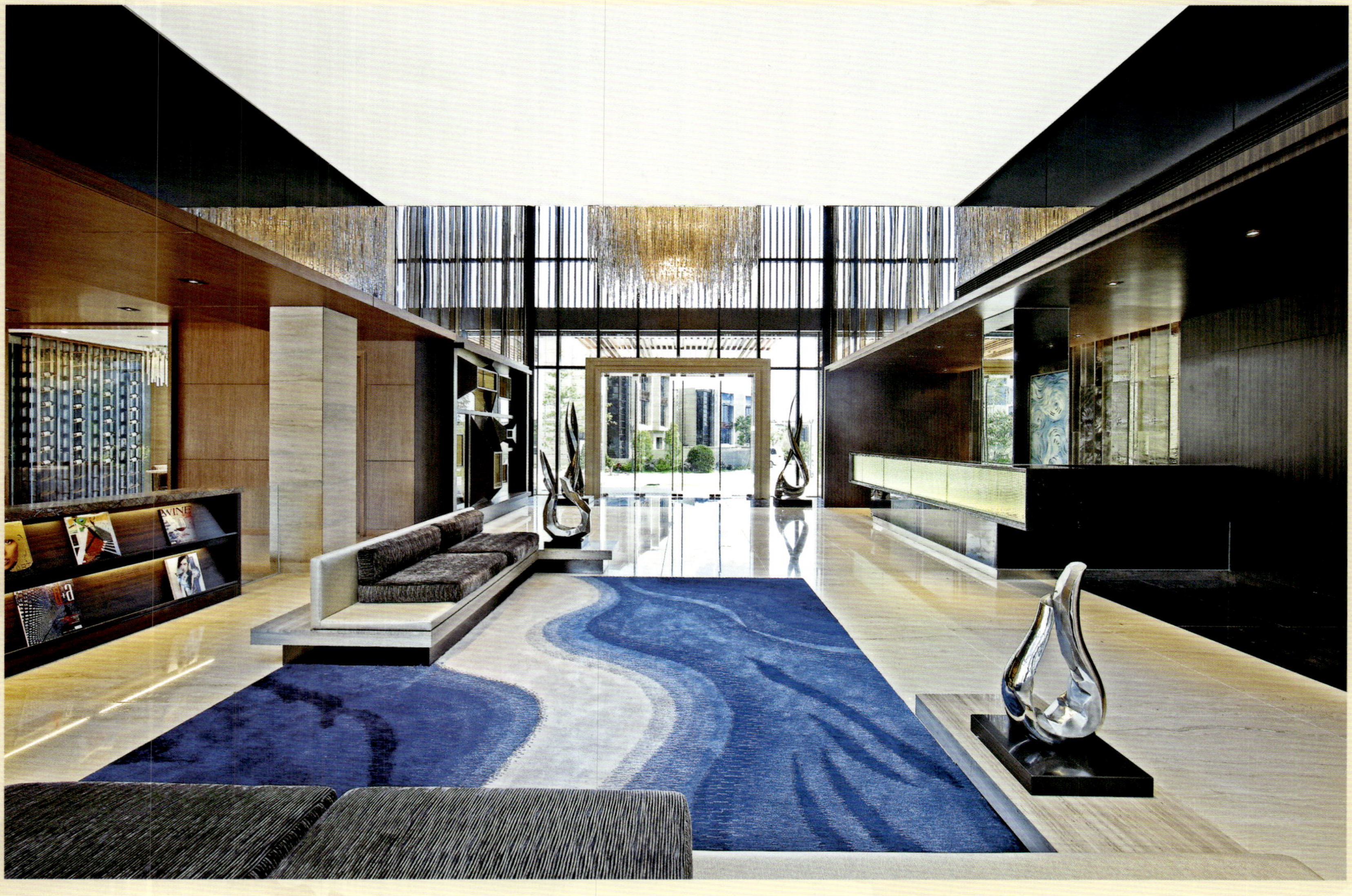

199

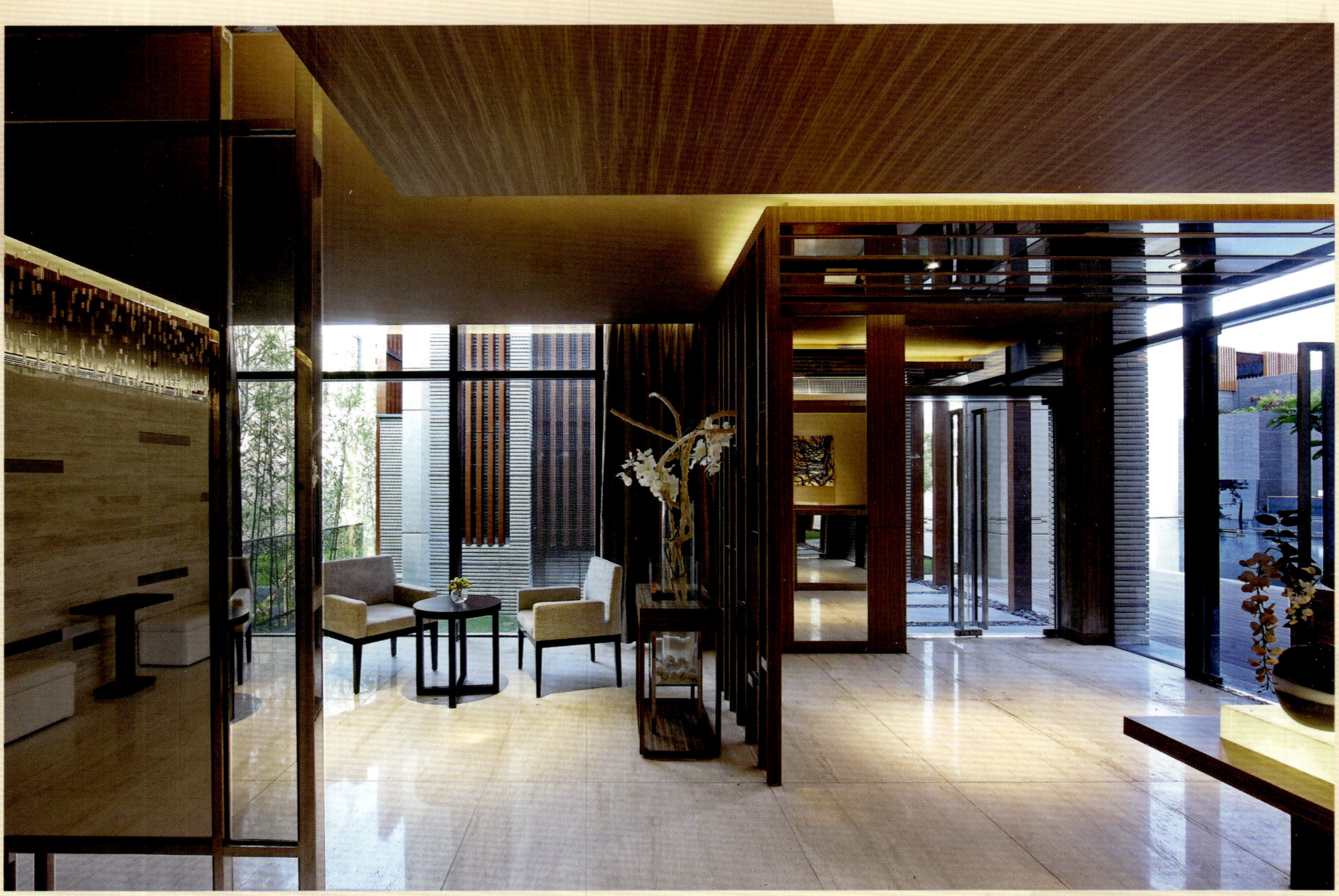

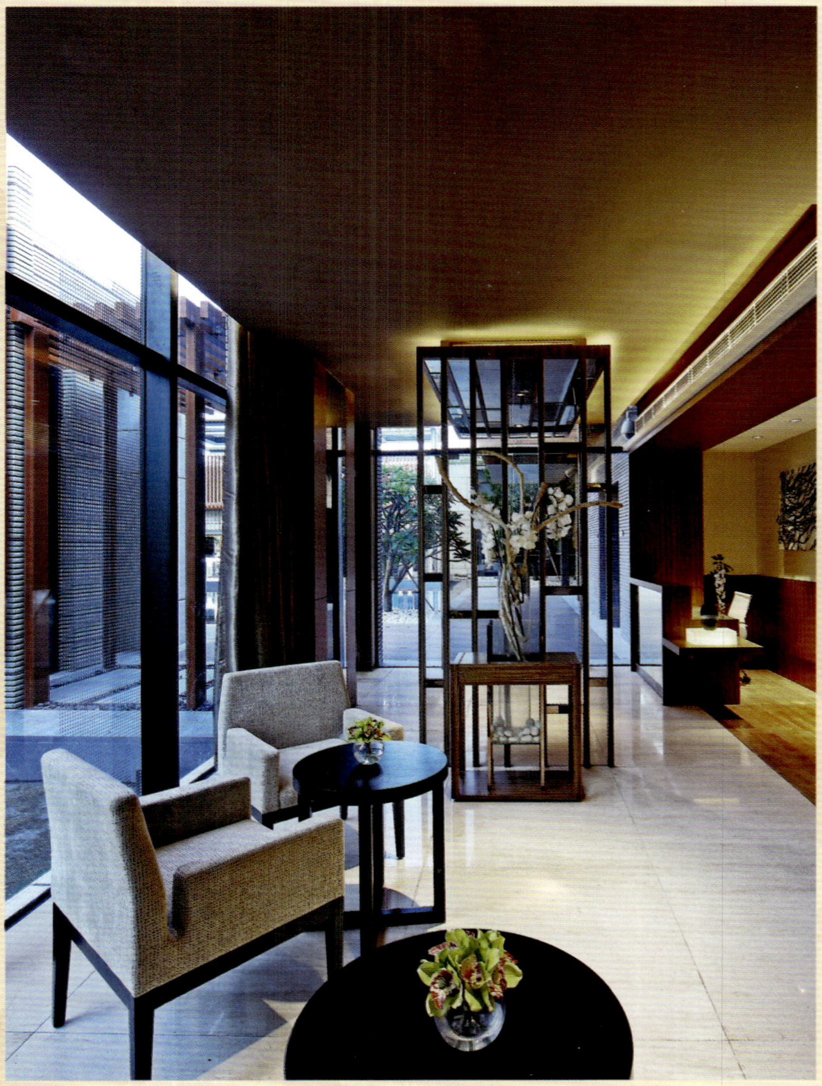

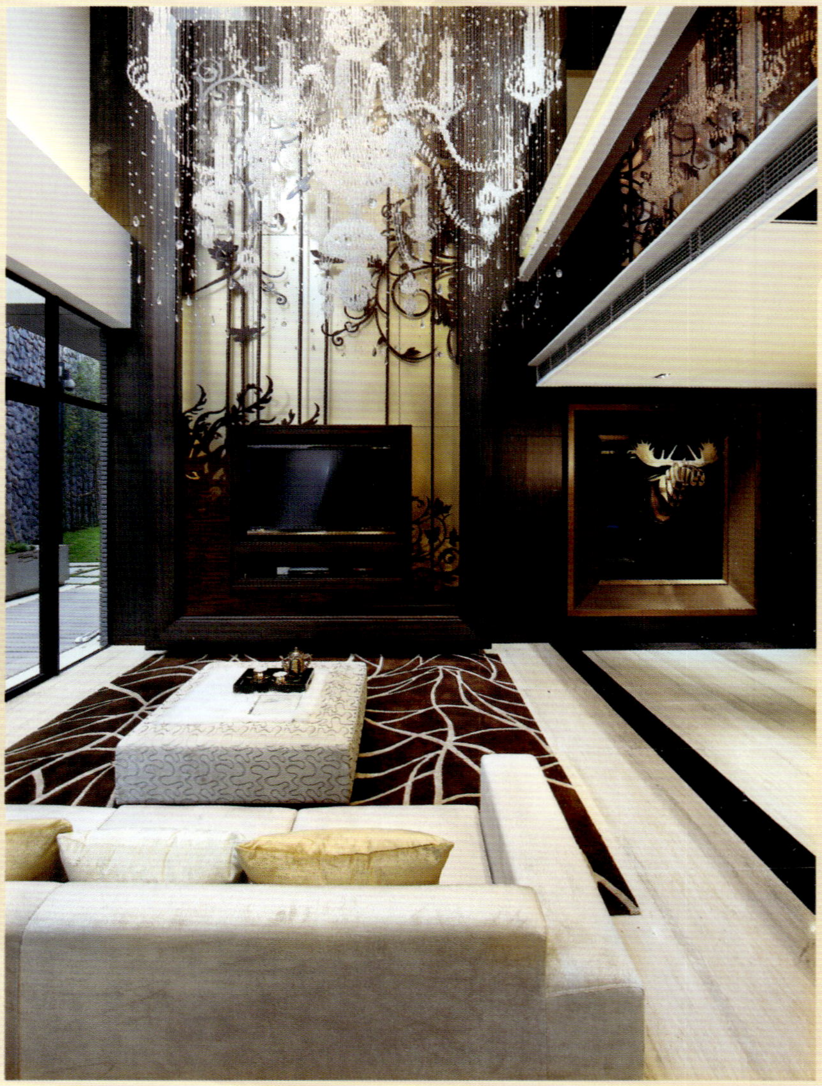

201

SocietyM

Design Agency: Concrete
Client: CitizenM
Location: Glasgow
Area: 585 m^2
Photographer: Ewout Huibers for Concrete

Heart of SocietyM is the club room. A place where you can work, meet, play and relax. The space is designed as a modern and inspiring gentlemen's club. Two large cabinets run parallel along the space and are filled with books and artworks for inspiration. Divers seating facilities, vitra style living room, working desks and a wooden robust library table are created to work, meet, play or read. A bar serves the best coffee and two working booths are there for the ones who need to work a bit more concentrated. The cabinets are made of white film faced plywood: the same principle as CitizenM but in a different colour. The wooden bamboo floor creates a warm atmosphere while the black ceiling creates intimacy. The printed carpets are pixelated images of old Persian carpets: a gentlemen's club item modernised

The club room can be used by the members of SocietyM. At the entrance each member has a private mailbox which serves as a safe as well. 84 Different second hand mailbox letter plates emphasise the idea of each individual member.

203

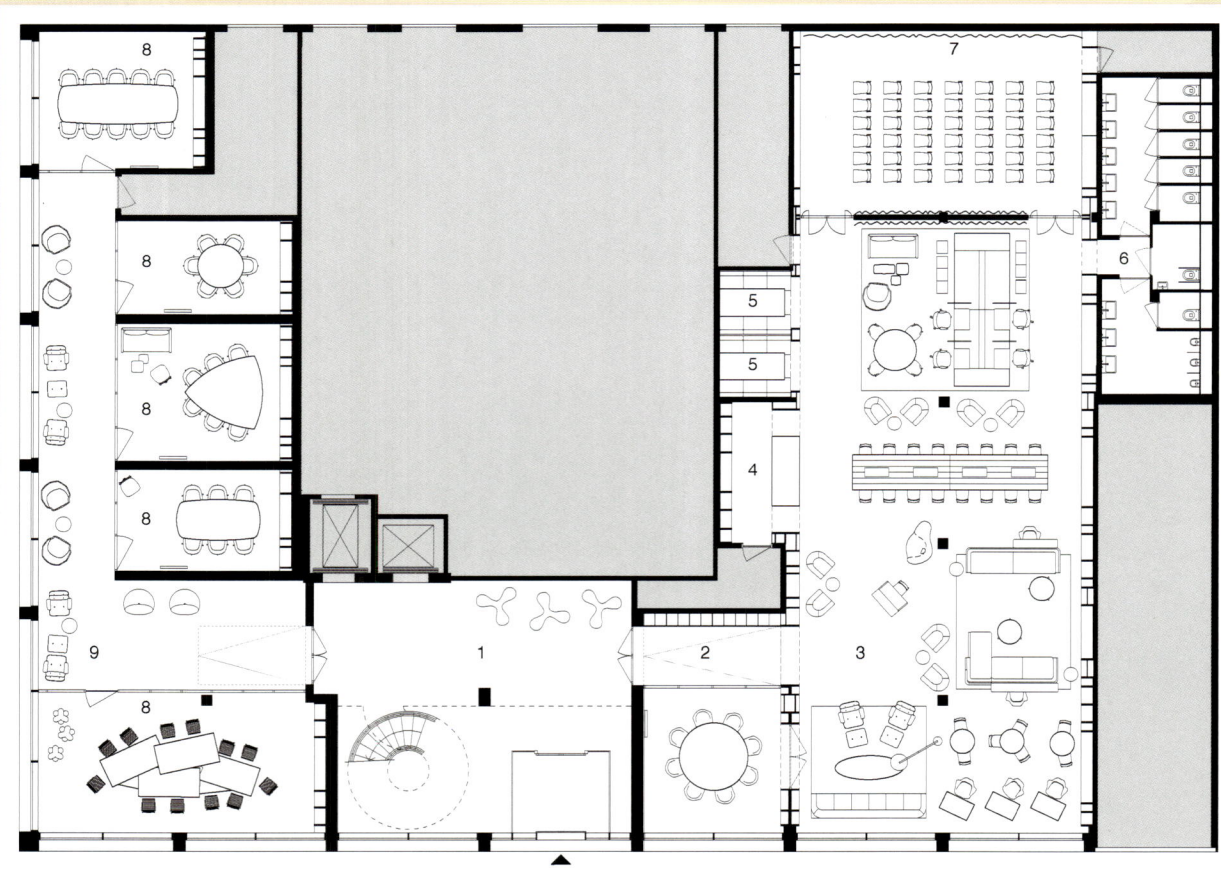

1 entrance CitizenM and societyM
2 mailbox wall members
3 club room to work meet and play
4 bar
5 working booths
6 restrooms
7 screening room
8 creating space
9 corridor for informal meet, wait and call

205

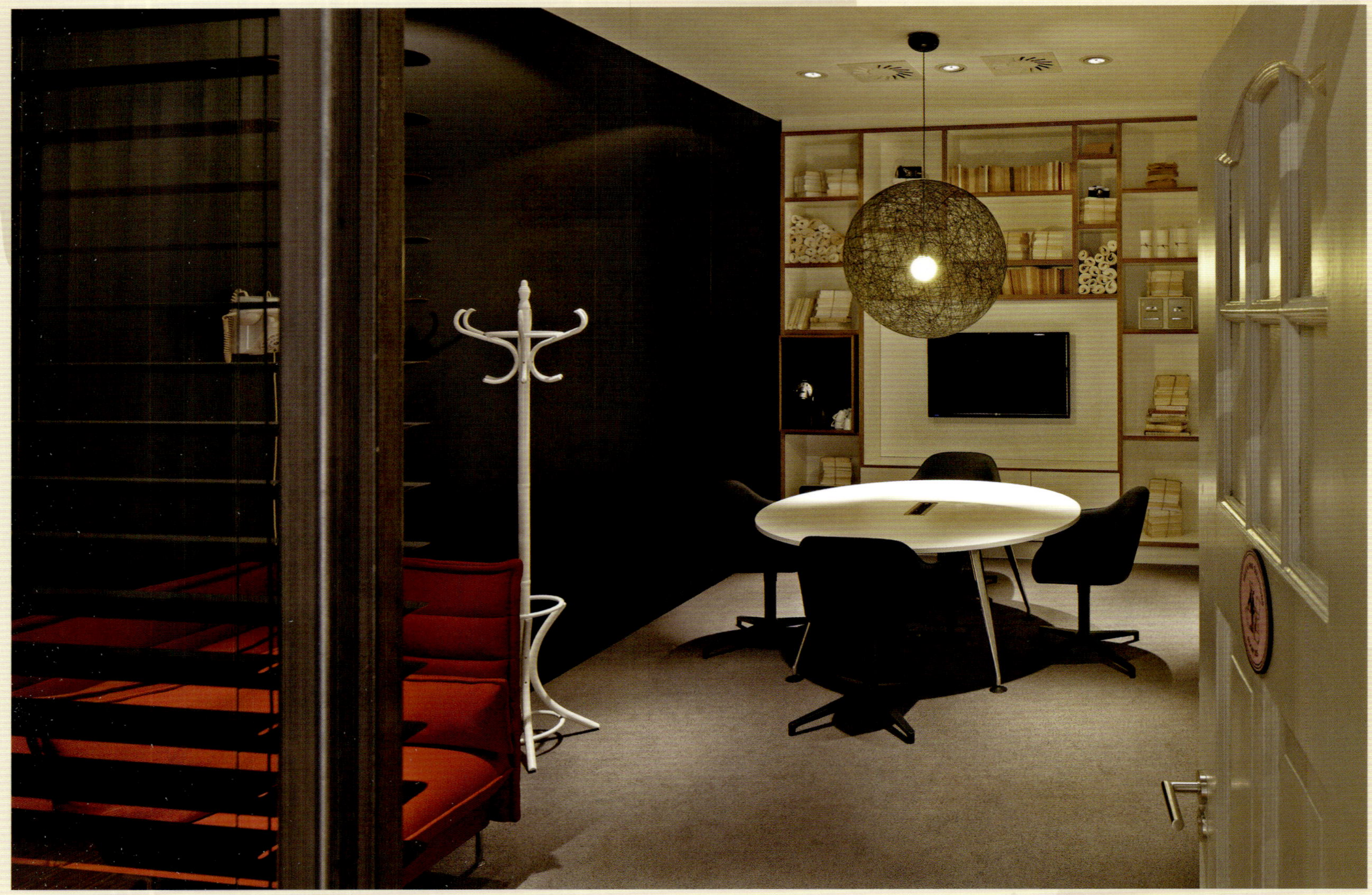

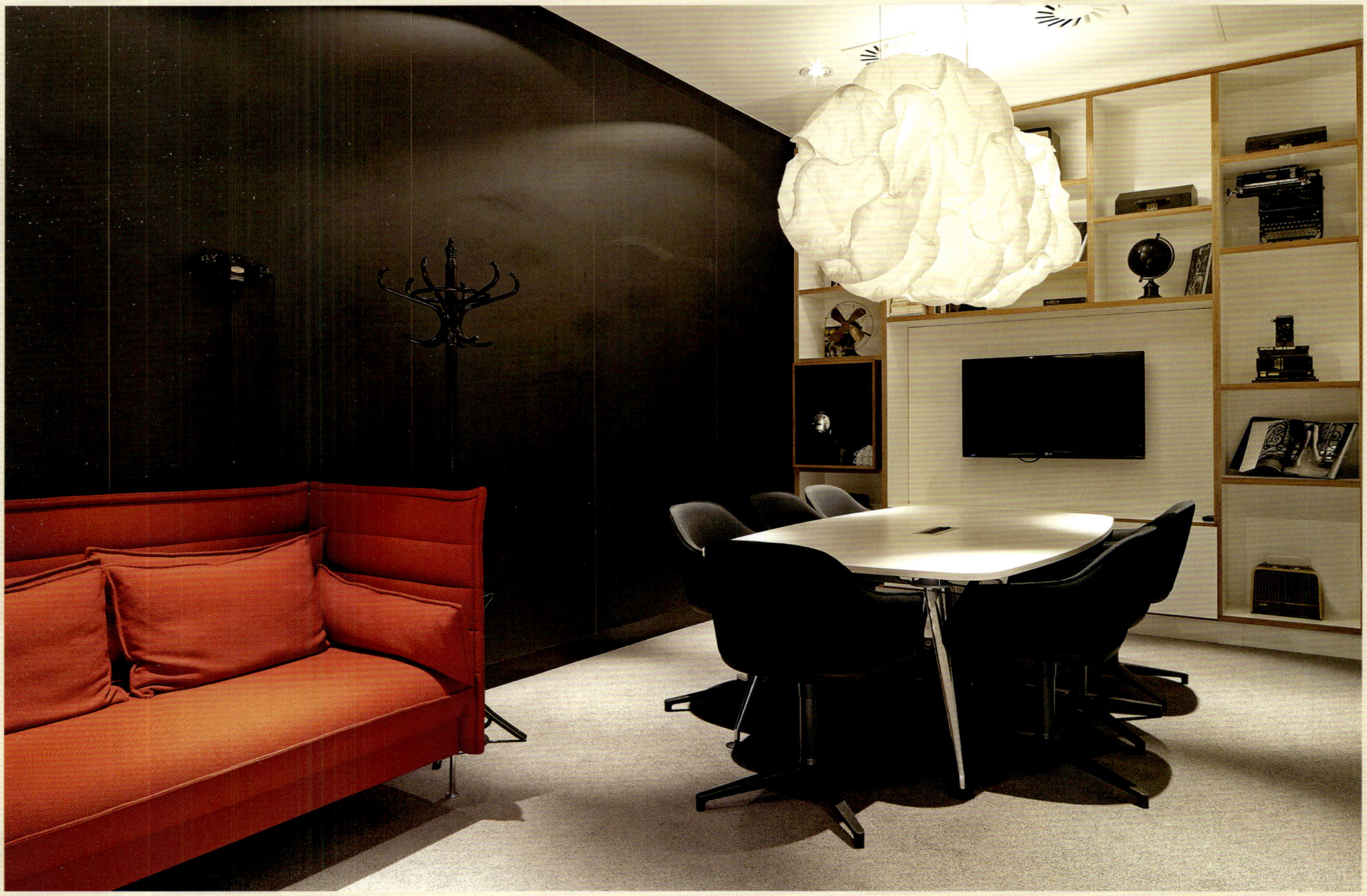

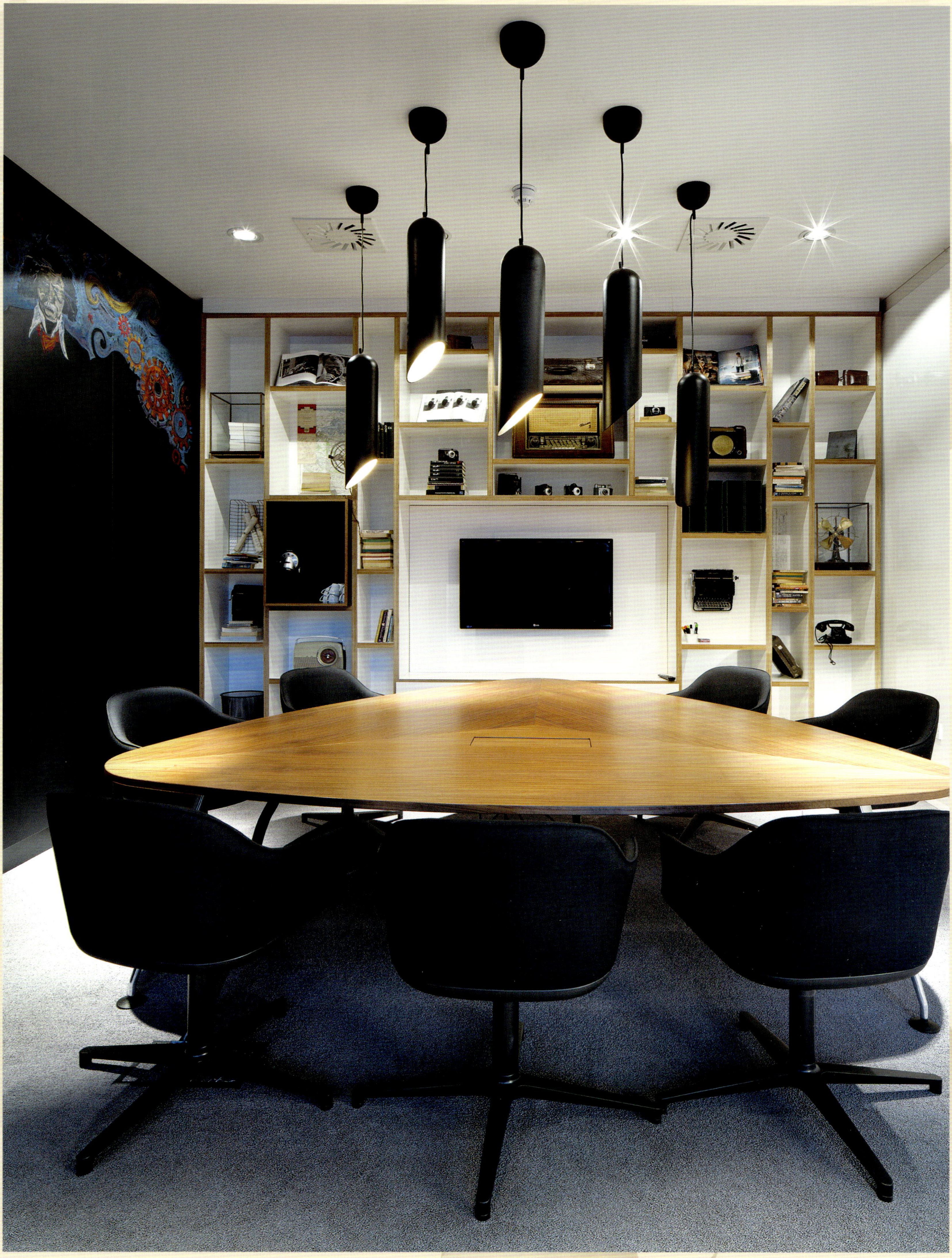

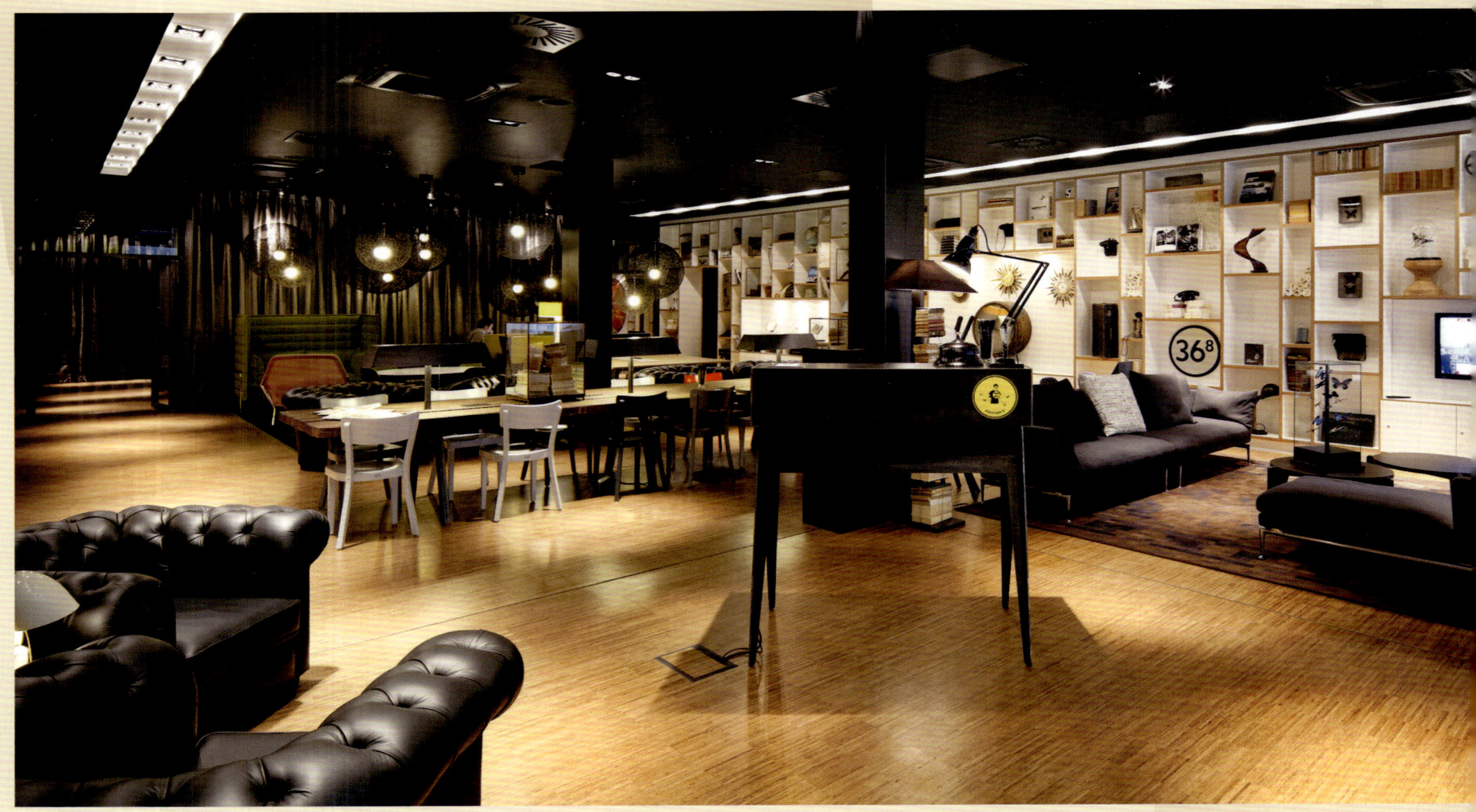

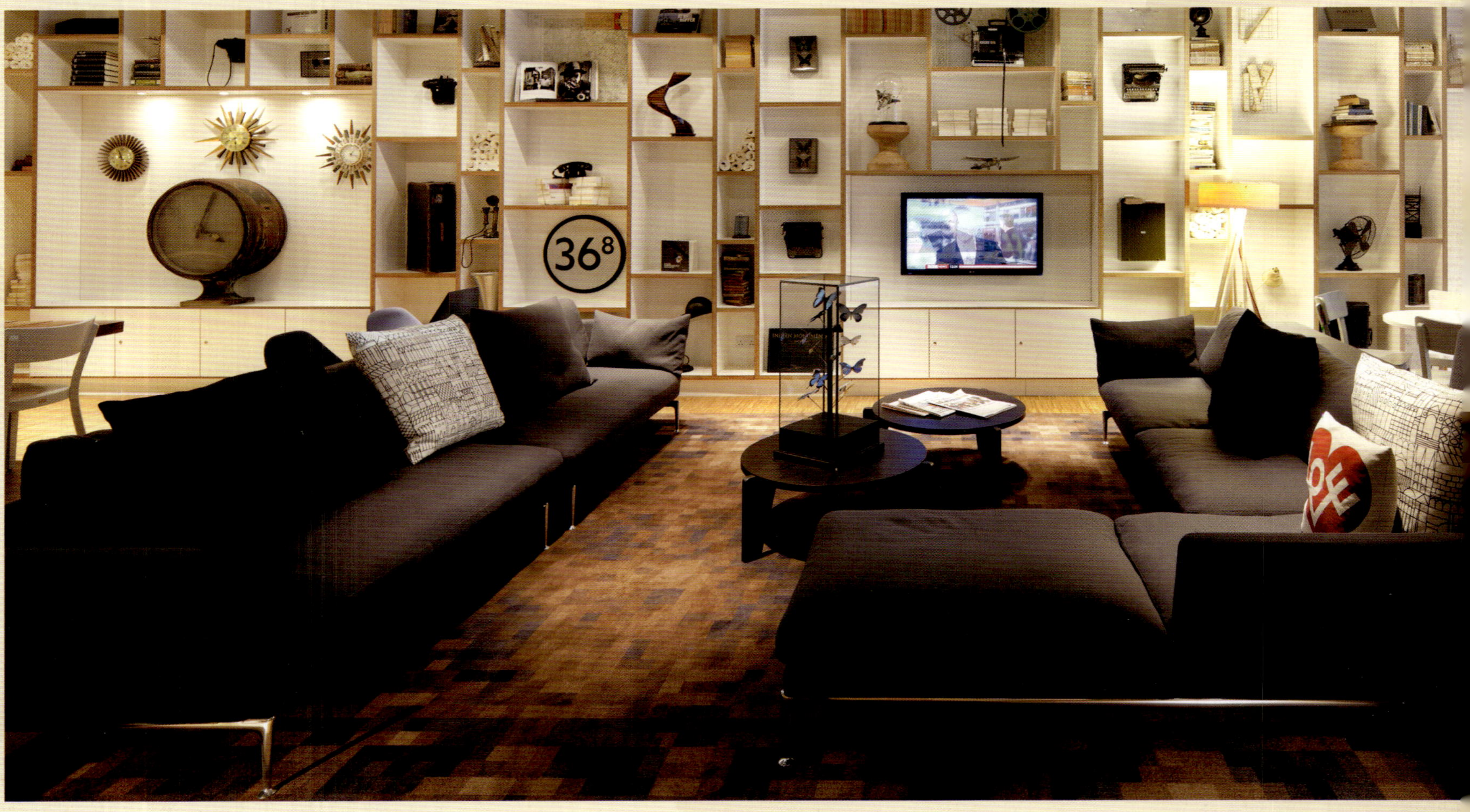

209

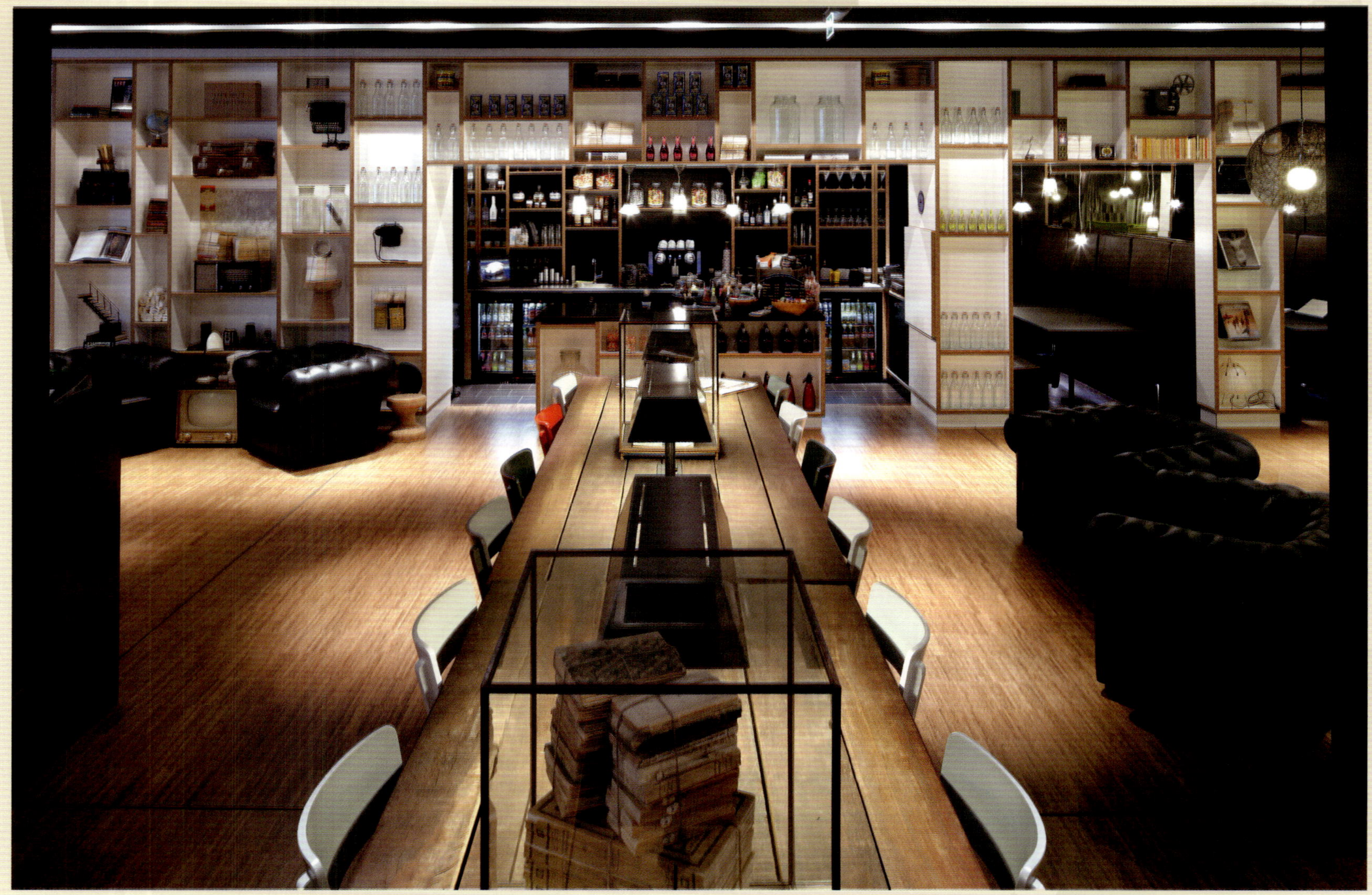

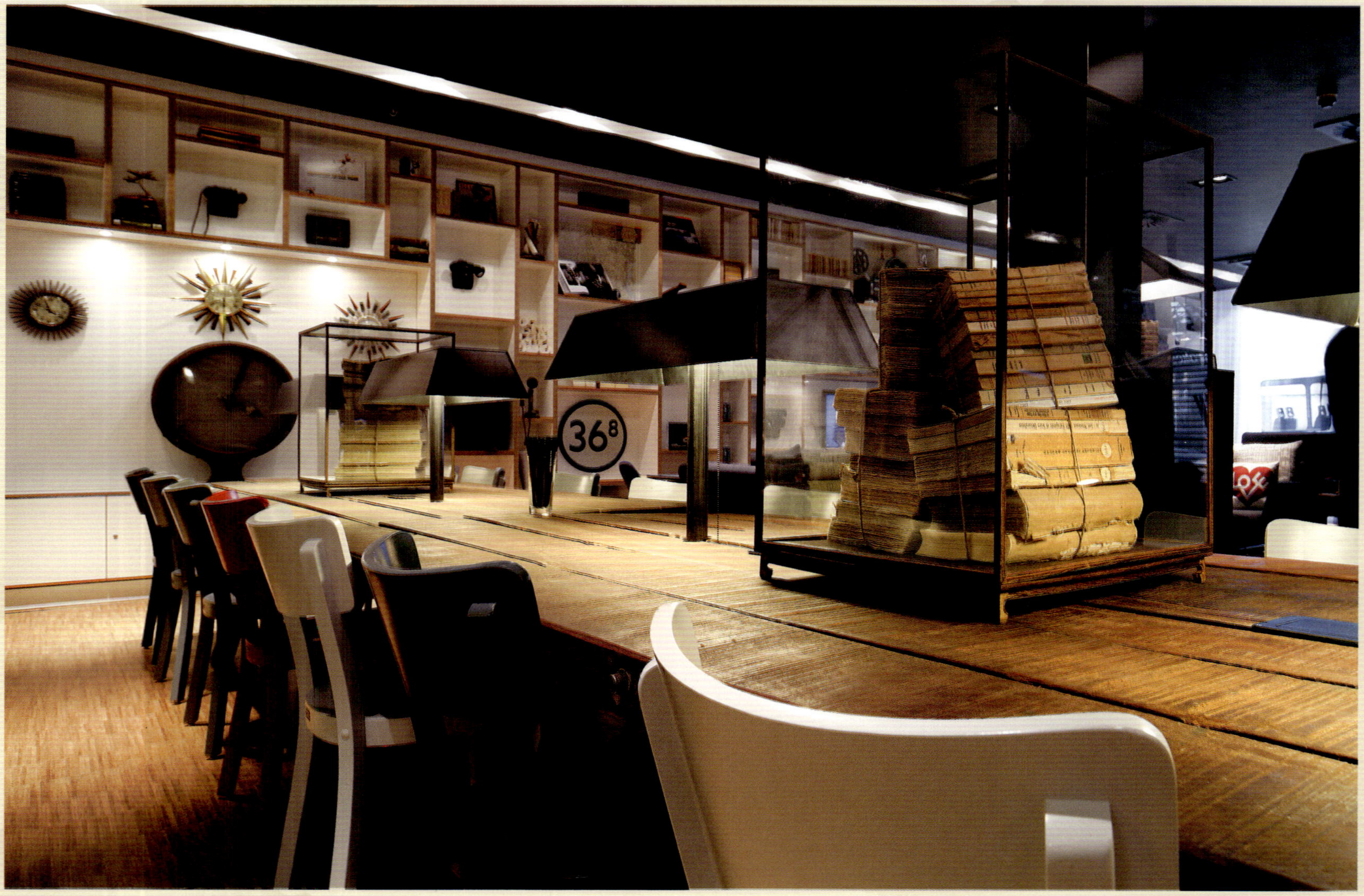
368

211

Bingo Billiard Club

Design Agency: Dao He Design Studio
Designer: Gao Xiong
Location: Fuzhou, Fujian, China
Area: 800 m²
Photographer: Zhou Yuedong

Geometry cutting has been boldly used in building the front table of entrance and both sides of the rod cabinet. The painted PVC pipes in background reduce the visual drop, and put the logo into it to emphasize the modern geometry model. The wall of leisure waiting area, which is made up of several tilted parquets as a partition, is the continuation of the main area. Therefore, the entire space has been expanded, and enhances those interactive works of the lights and shadows. On the other side, the personal tutor area is surrounded by two leisure bars. It is not an enclosed space, as the wall of left-hand aisle is made of wood as the front table. There are some display cabinets as well.

On designing of linear and block surface, the tough and masculine style are all over the whole space. It has been positioned in the modern fashion style of recreational billiards club by the appearance of light and shadow. That beauty of difference arises in the entire club, which attracts you to have a try even though you are not a billiard lover.

赛格台球-省体店平面布置图

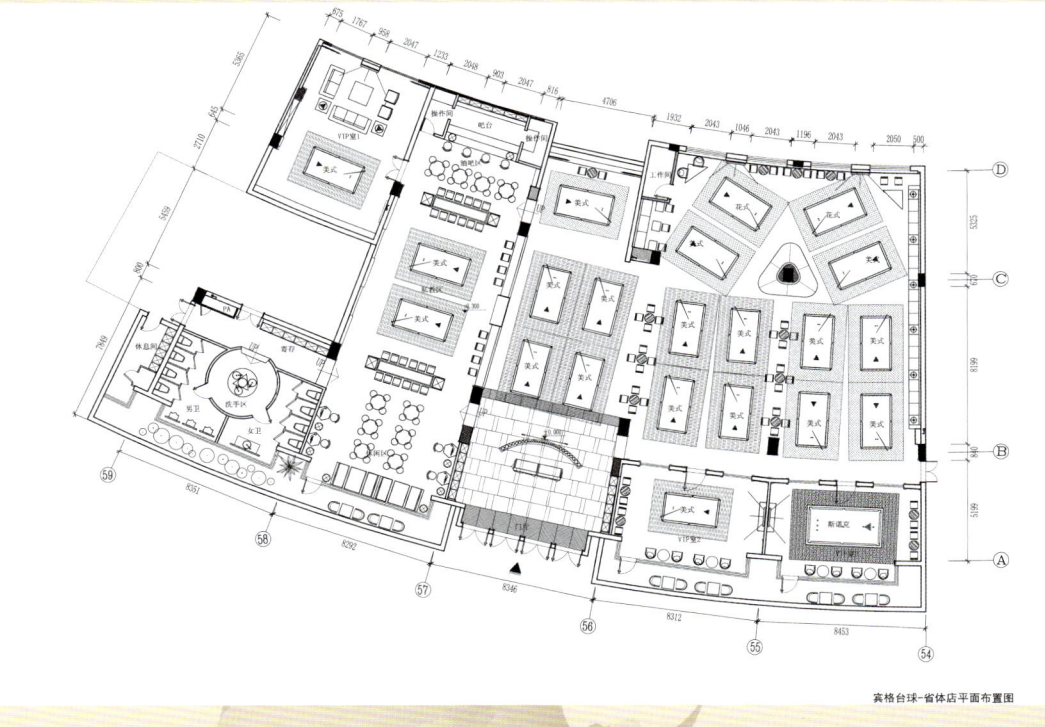

213

前台进门A立面图
SCALE:1:30

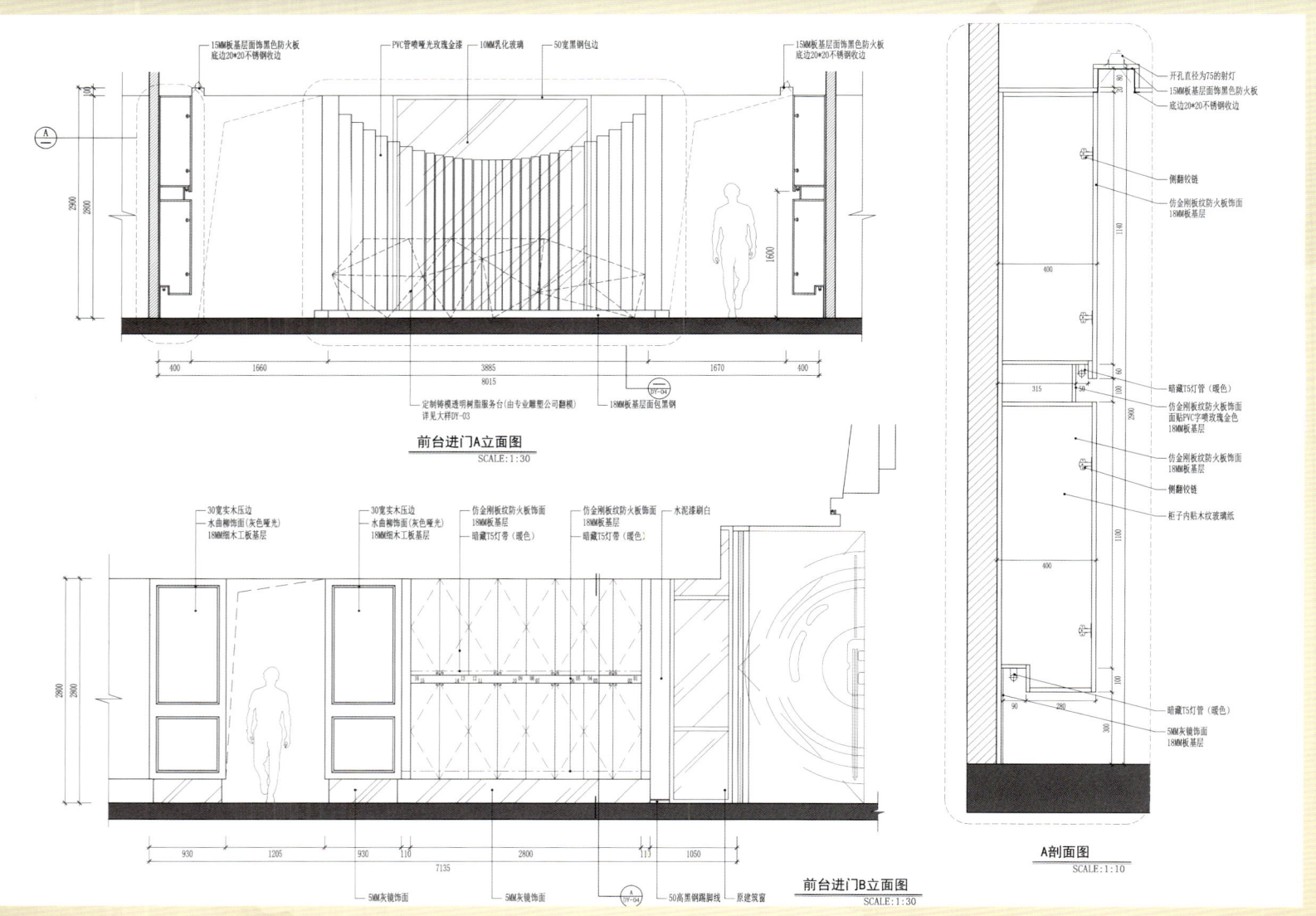

前台进门B立面图
SCALE:1:30

A剖面图
SCALE:1:10

吧台A立面图
SCALE:1:30

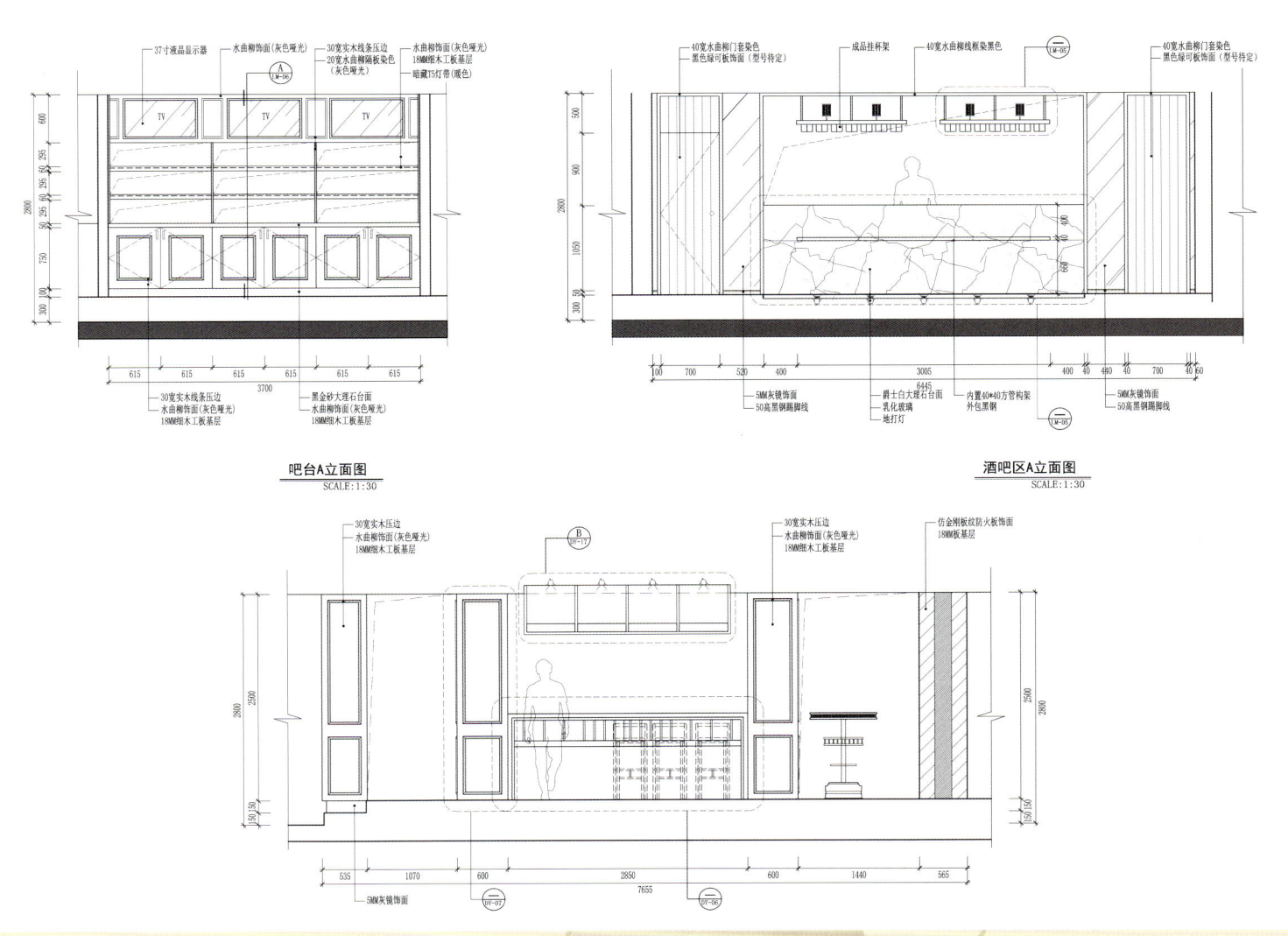

酒吧区A立面图
SCALE:1:30

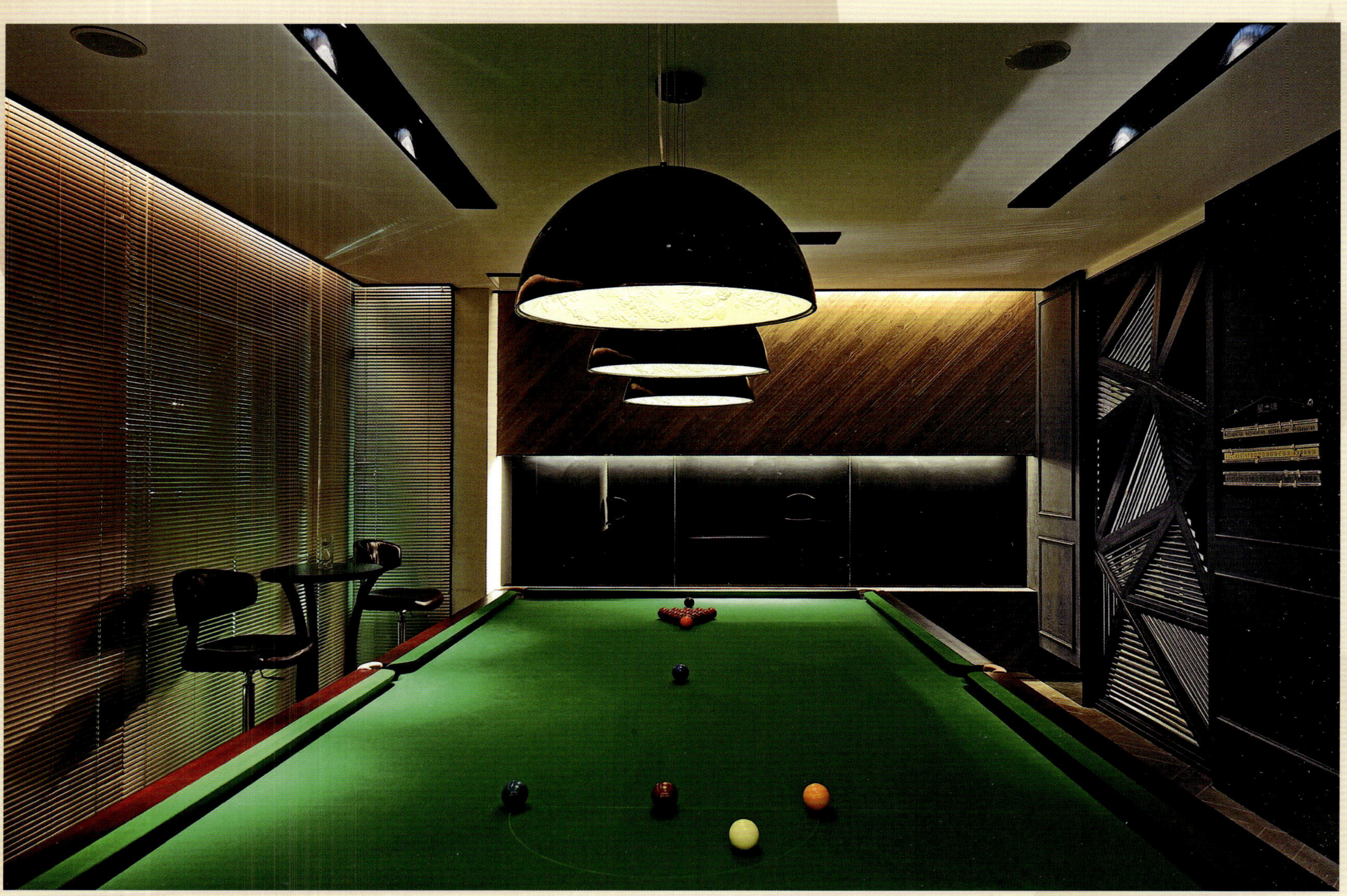

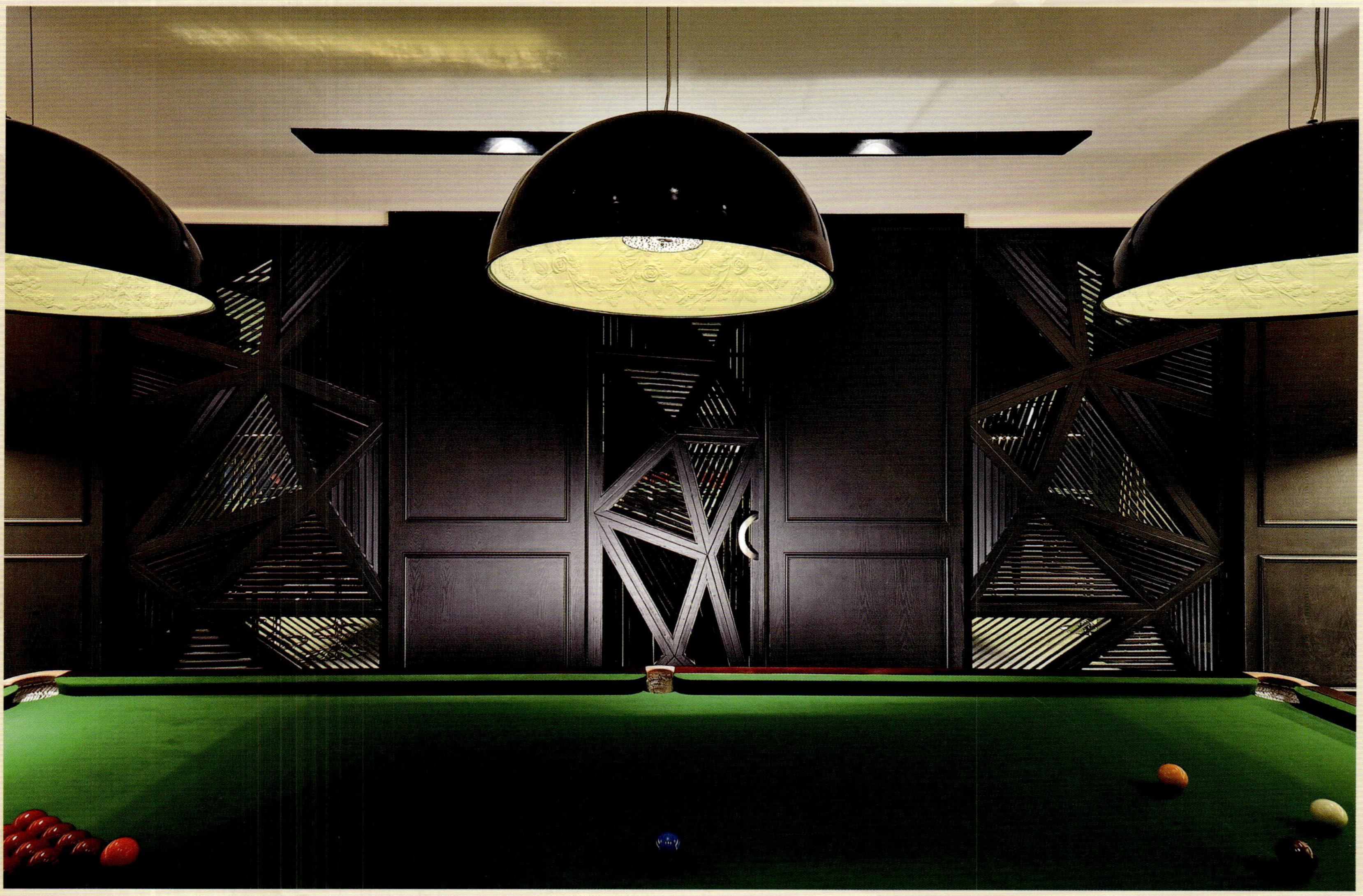

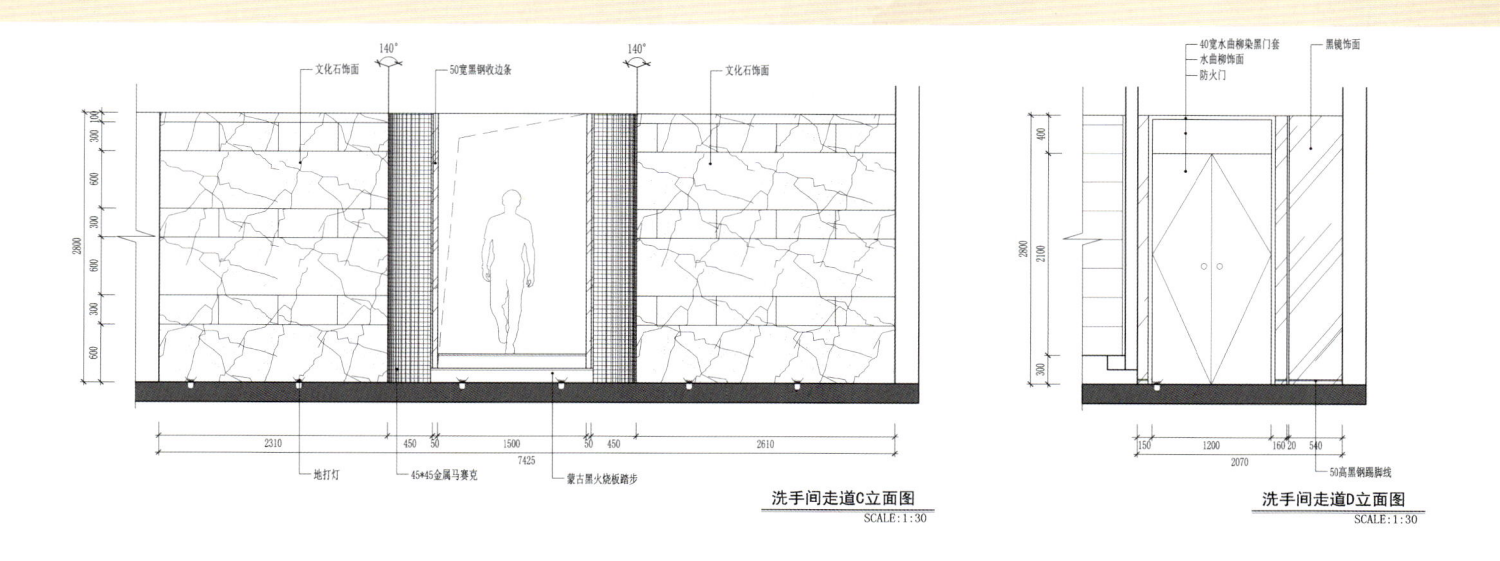

洗手间走道C立面图
SCALE:1:30

洗手间走道D立面图
SCALE:1:30

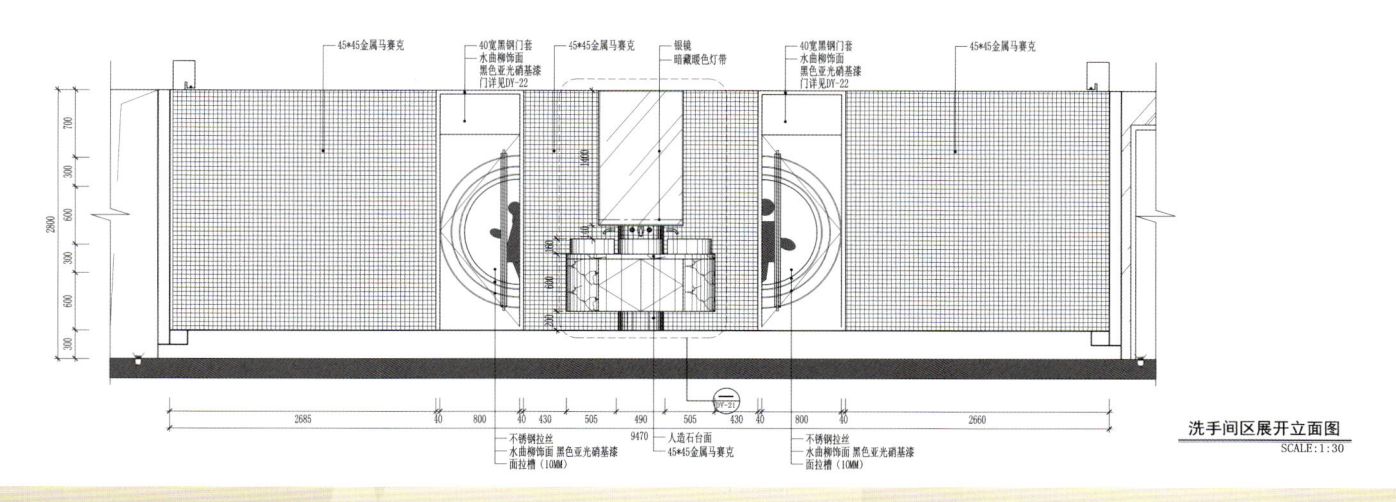

洗手间区展开立面图
SCALE:1:30

217

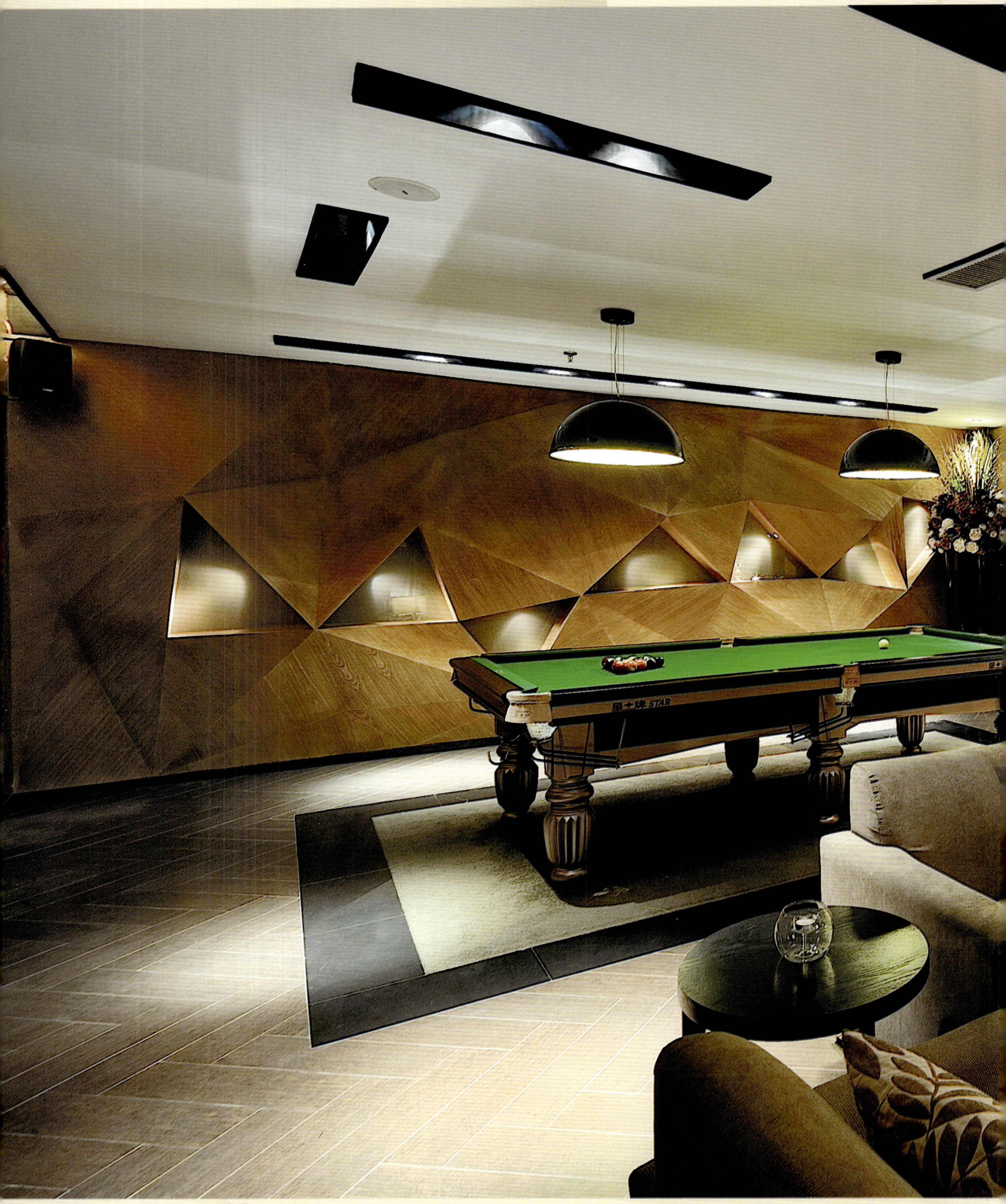
STAR

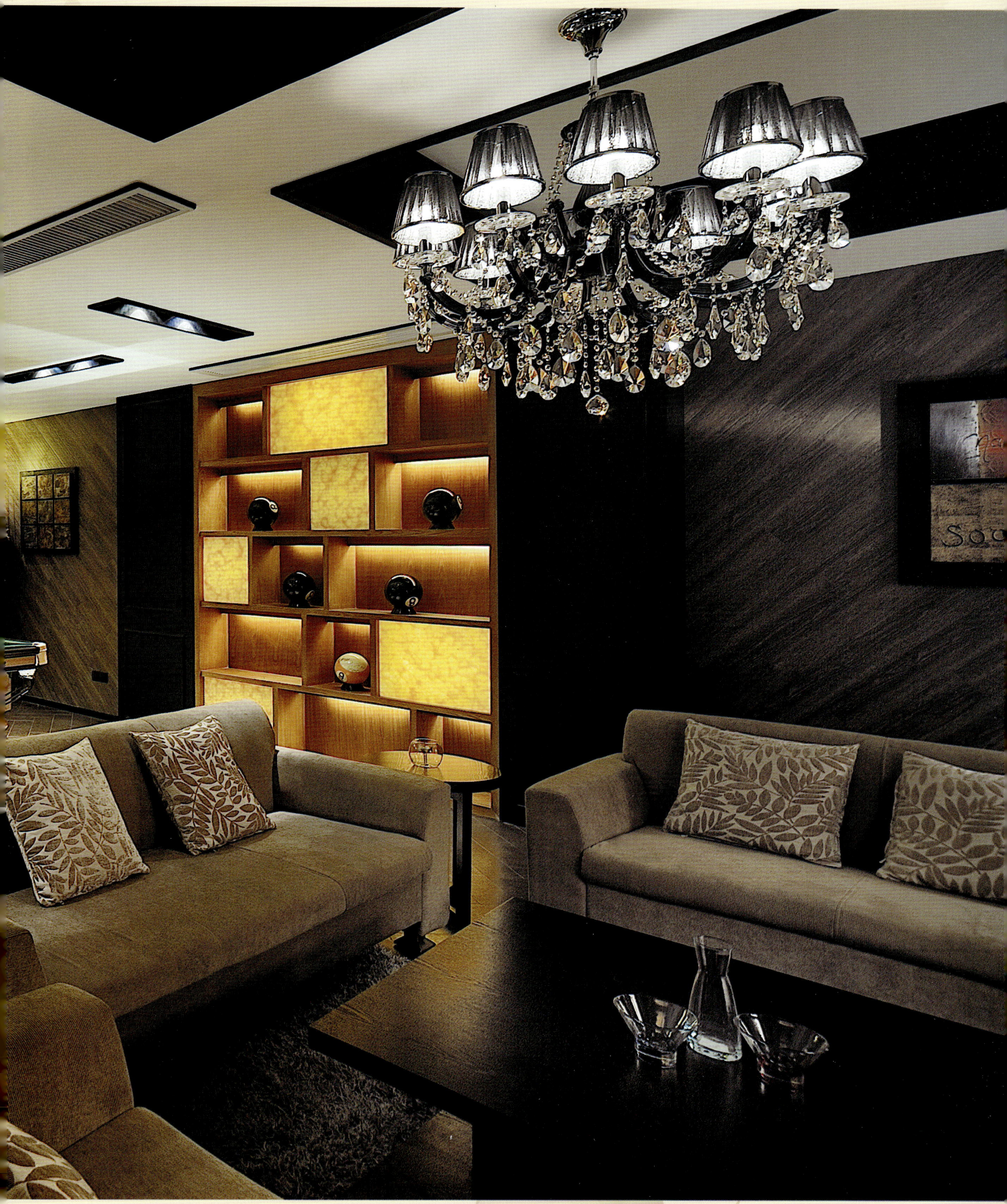

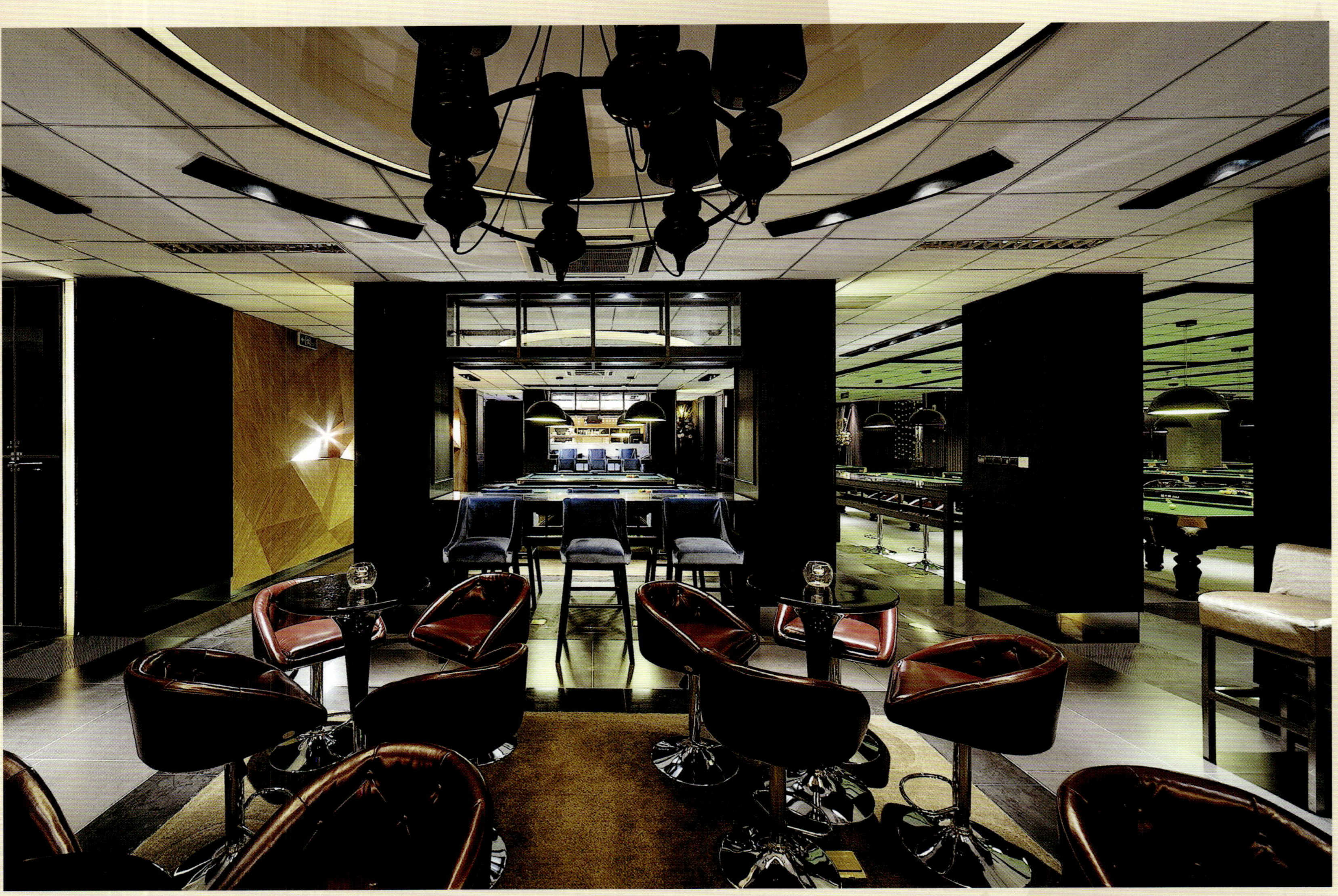

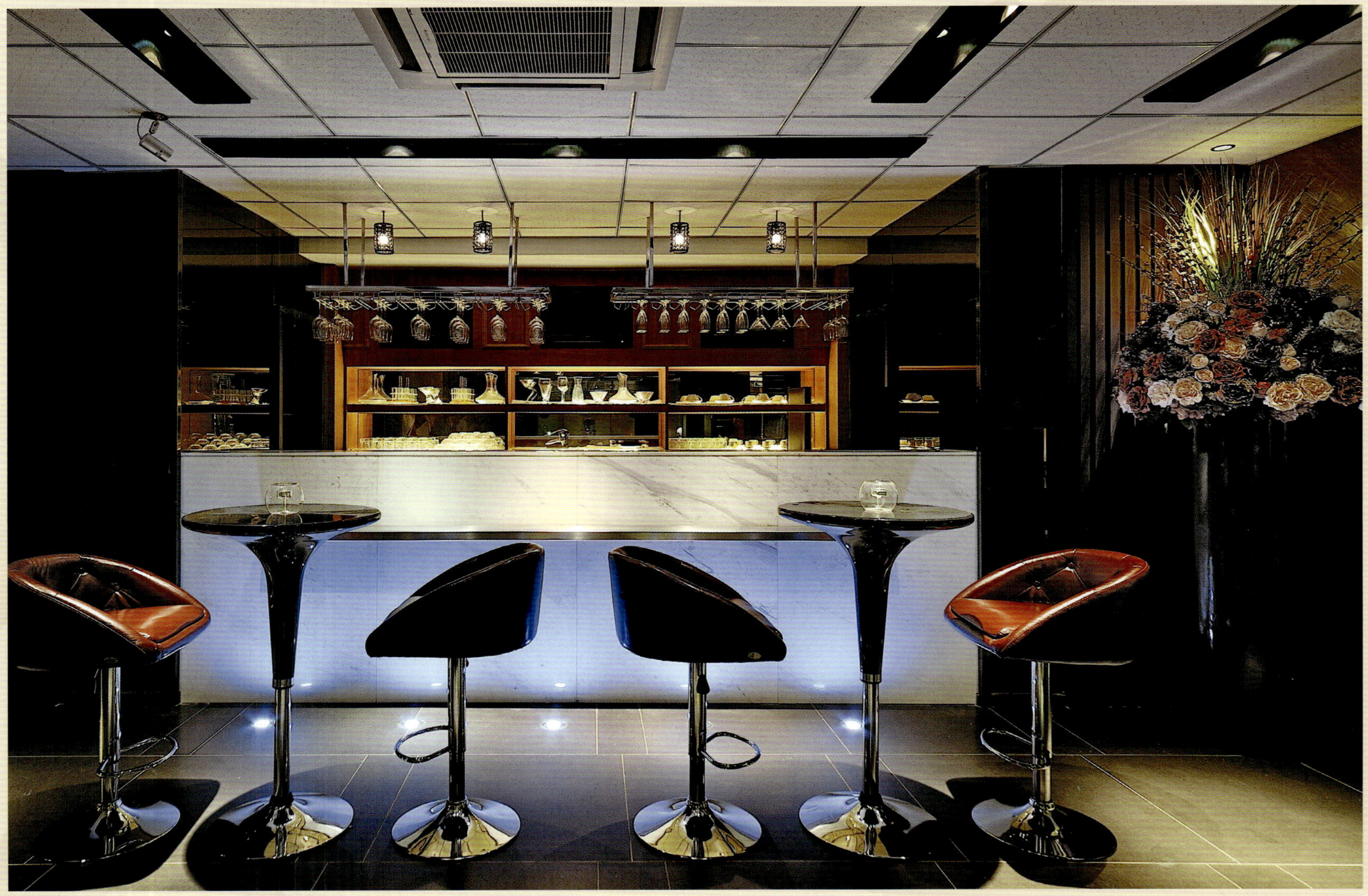

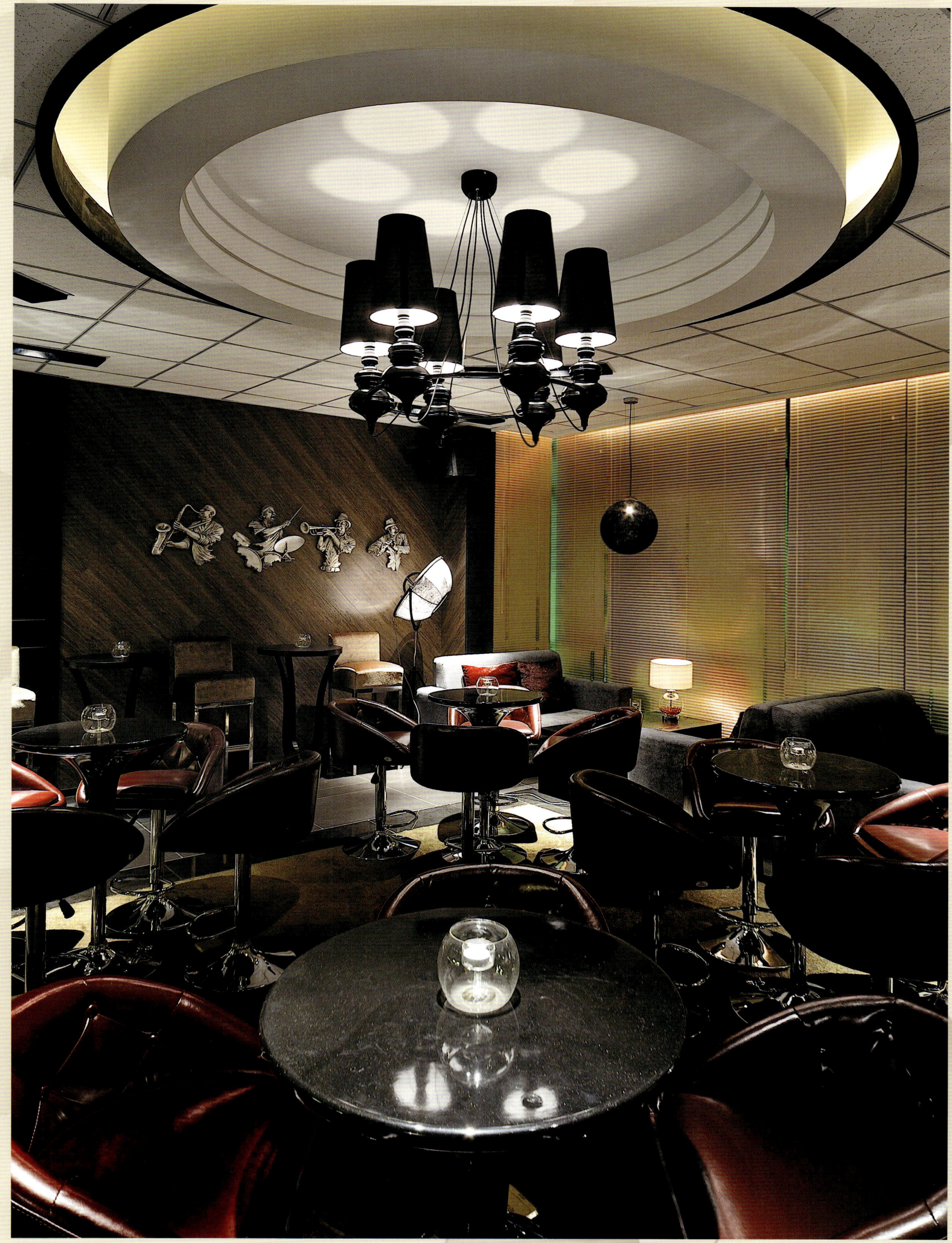

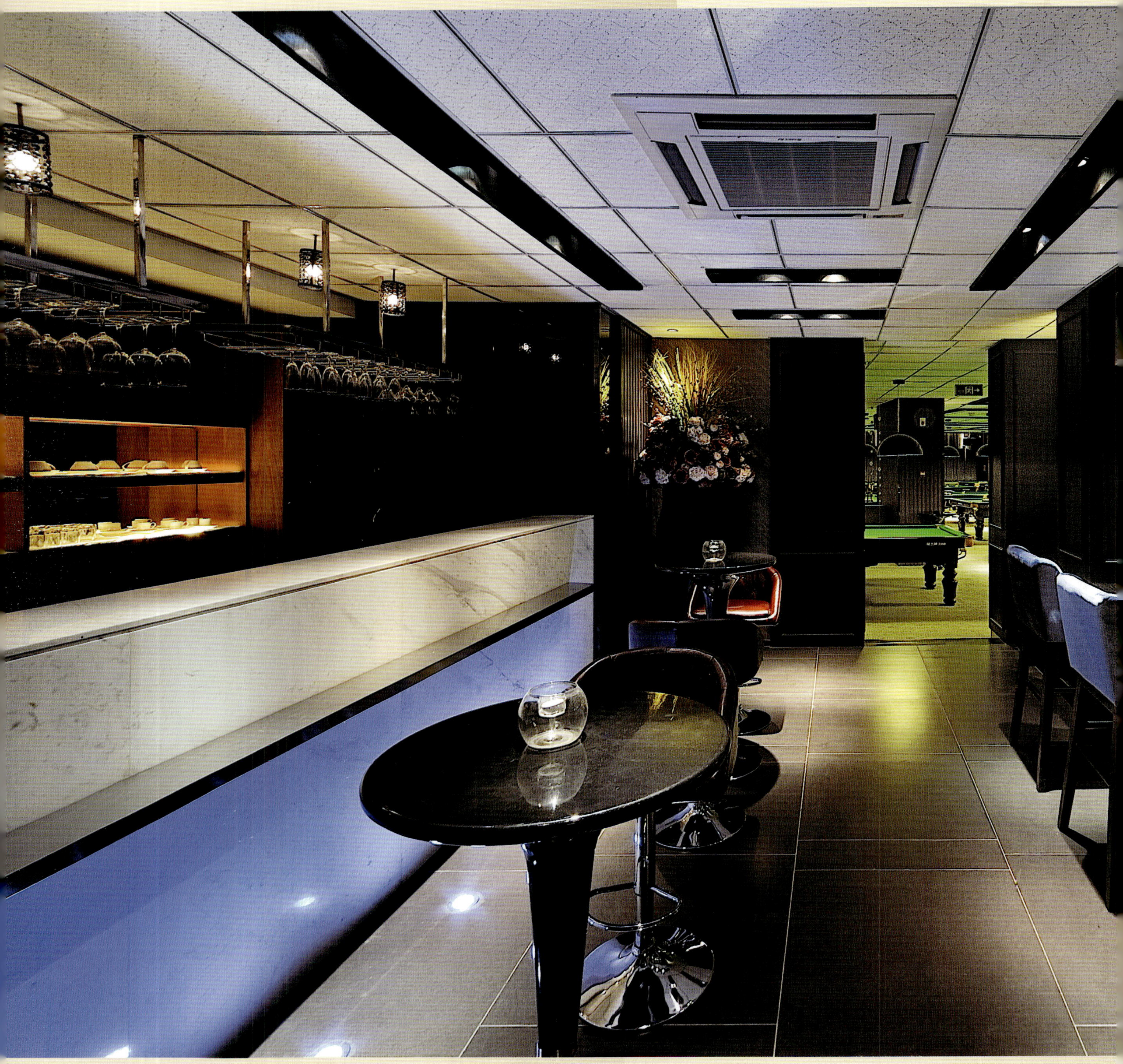

223

Rizon Jet at Biggin Hill airport

Design Agency: SHH
Design Team: Guy Matheson, Emlyn Conlon, Wade Tangney
Creative: Urban Velvet

Architects and designers SHH have completed a luxurious £3m, 2-storey VIP passenger lounge at Biggin Hill airport, for client Rizon Jet, a Middle East- and UK-based private aviation group. Located within a major new-build 130,000 m² hangar and VIP terminal facility at the airport, the lounge - comprised of a 478 m² ground floor space with an additional 186 m² purpose-built mezzanine floor - was launched at the same time as a similar facility in Doha, State of Qatar (created by Doha-based Company Art Line).

Rizon Jet was founded in 2006 and is headquartered in Doha, State of Qatar, with additional operating bases strategically located in the Middle East (UAE) and Europe (UK). Rizon Jet focuses on providing a comprehensive suite of private aviation services, ranging from aircraft charter, aircraft maintenance, aircraft management, FBO/VIP Terminal services to aircraft sales, financing and consulting. Its mission is to deliver top quality services which combine traditional Arabic hospitality with world-renowned aviation standards.

Rizon Jet is part of Ghanim Bin Saad Al Sadd & Sons Holdings (GSSG Holdings), headquartered in Doha, State of Qatar.

225

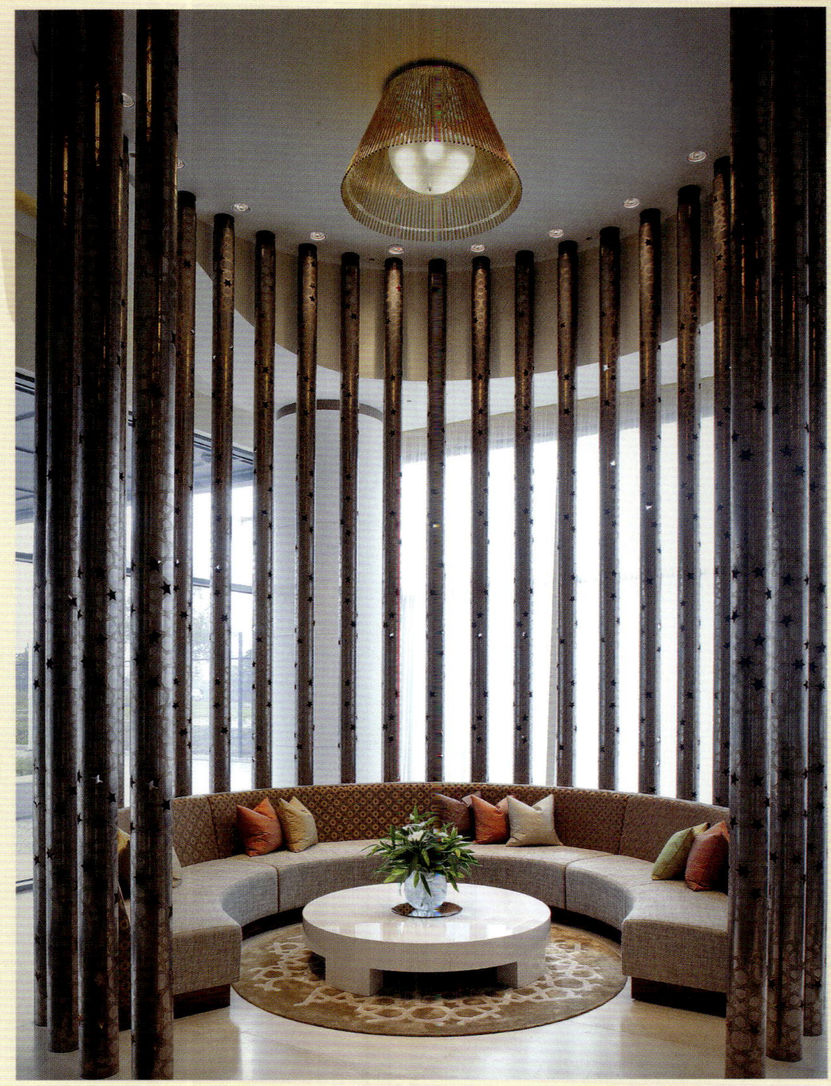

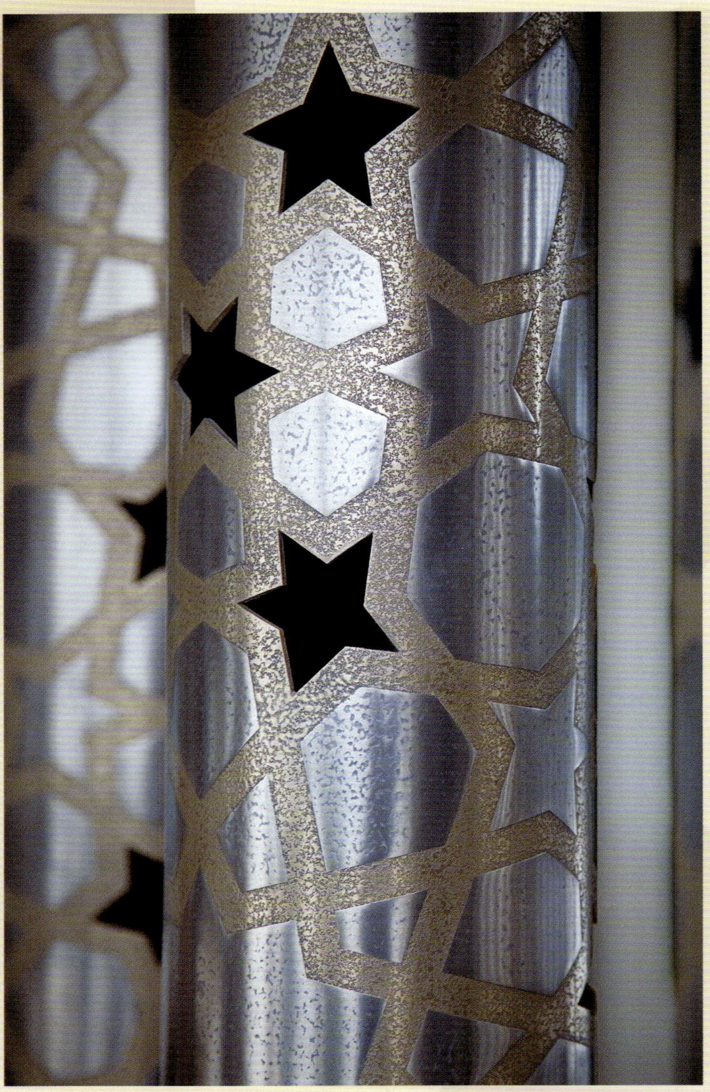

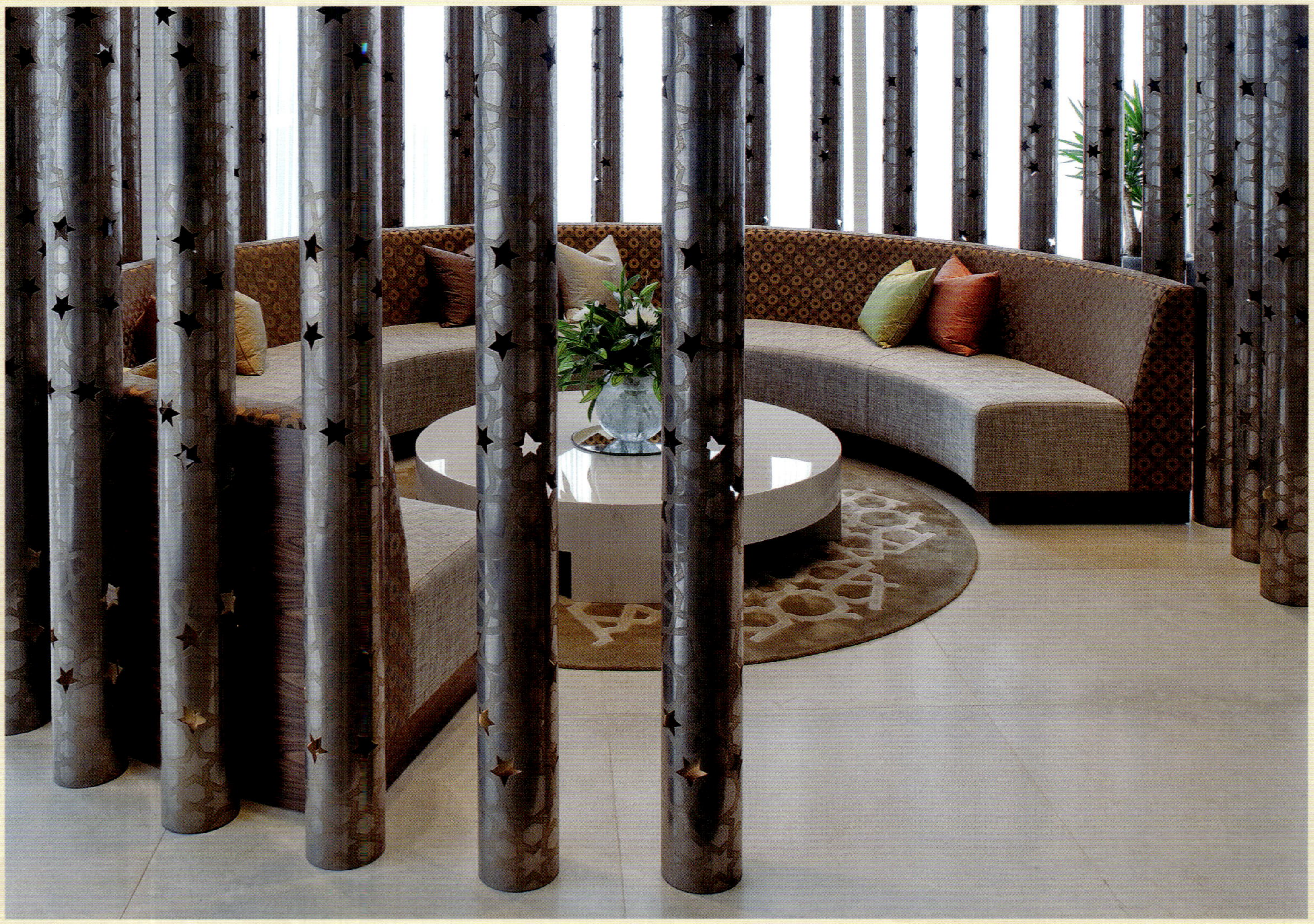

227

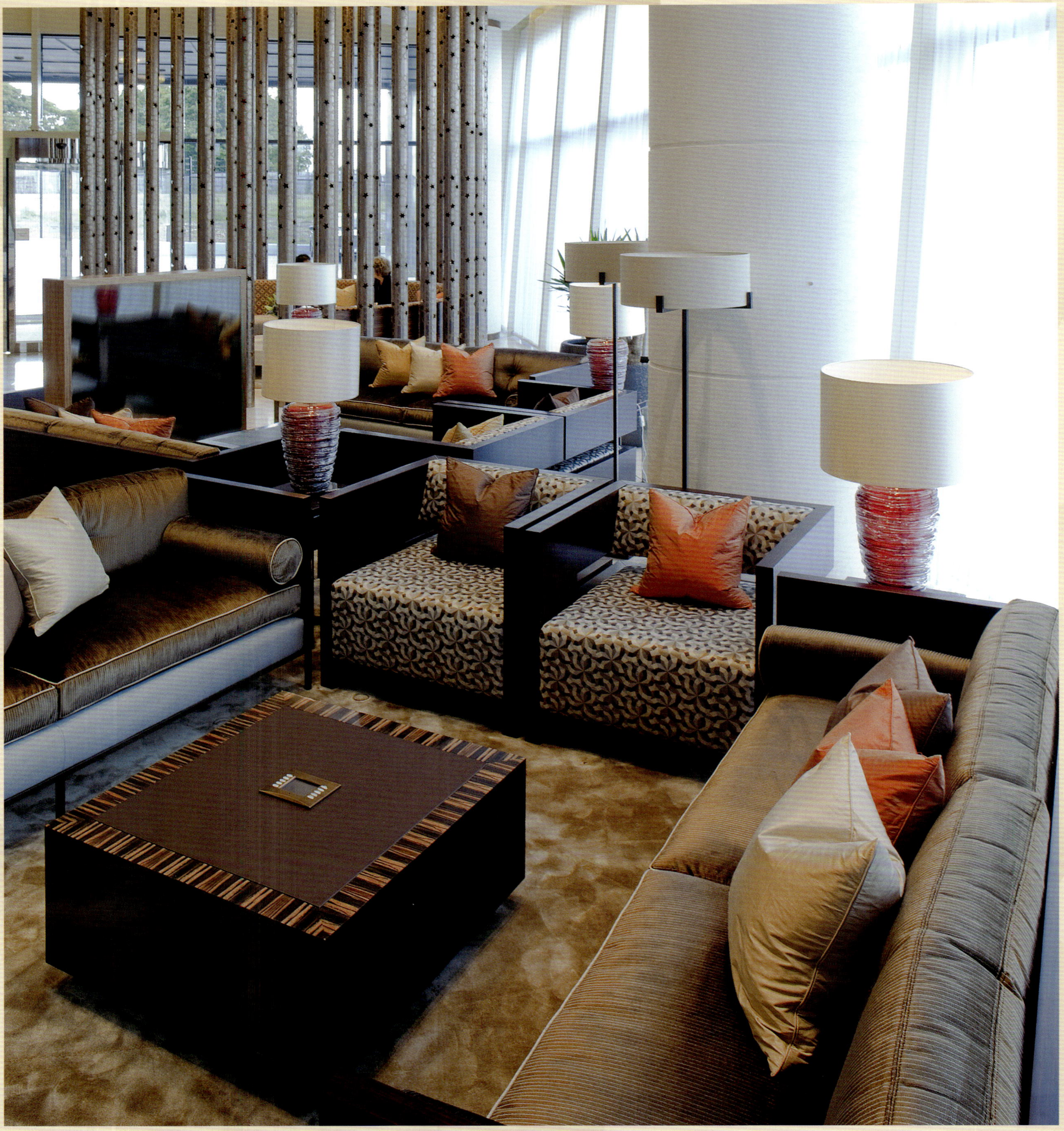

229

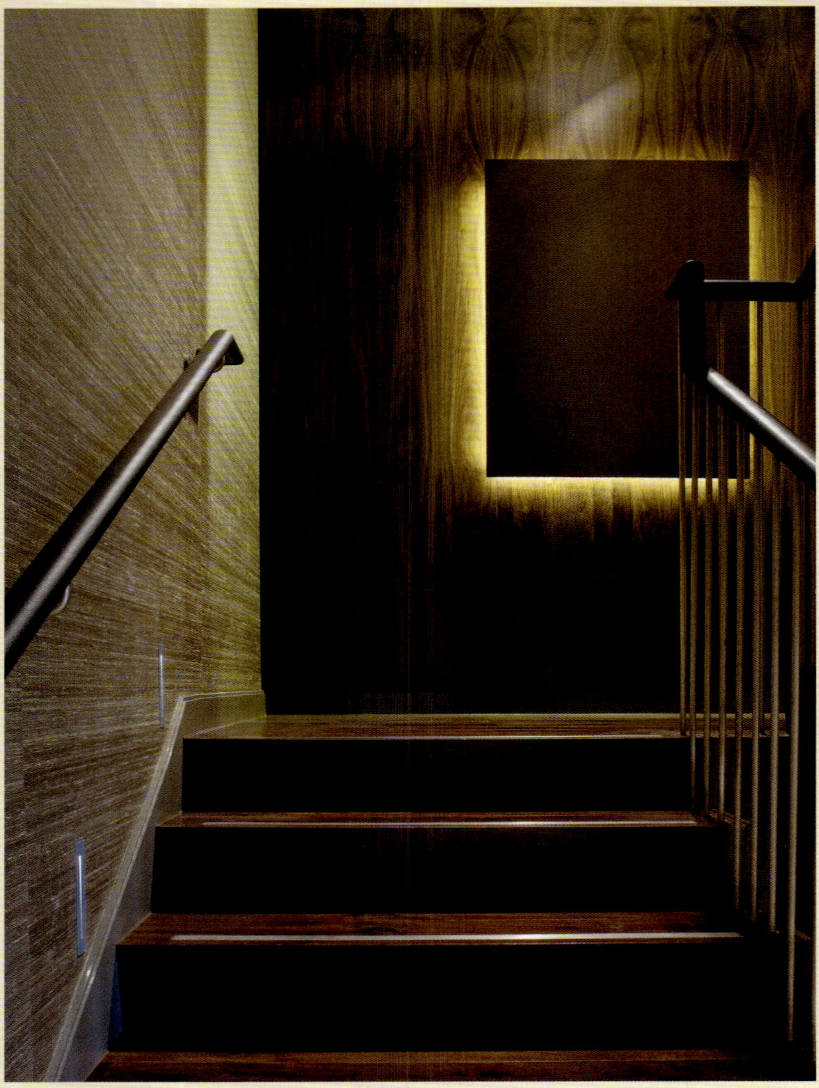
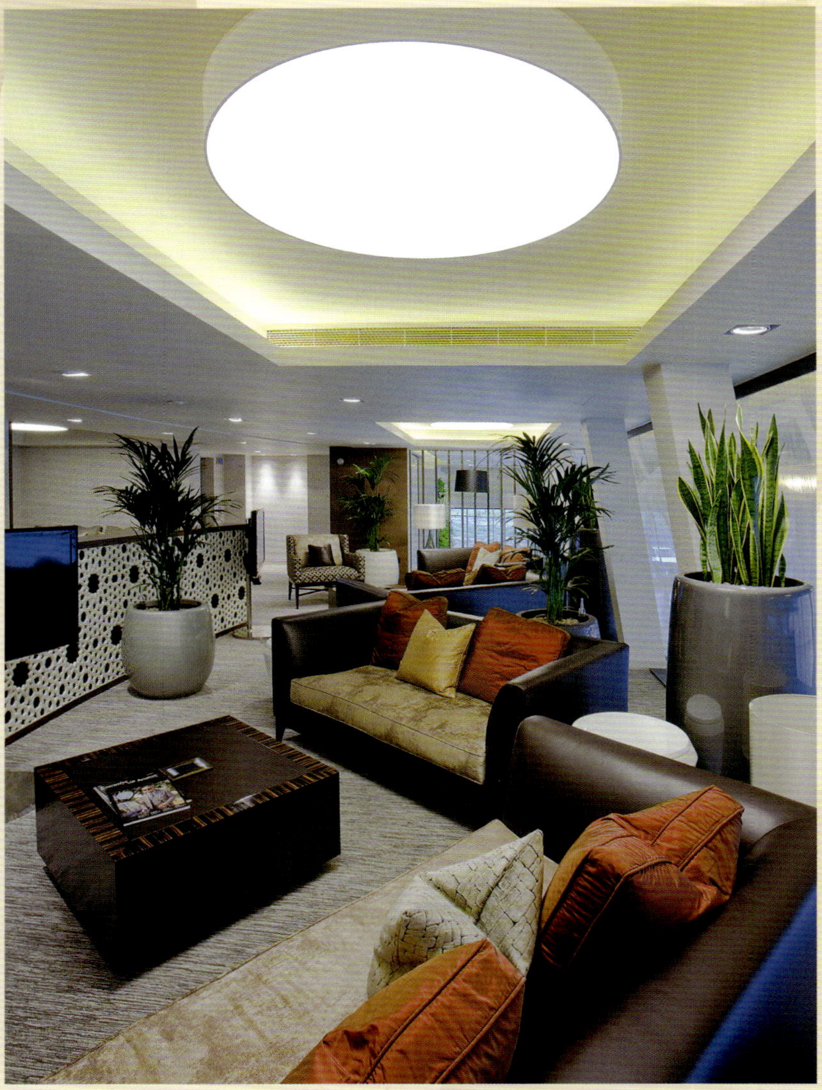
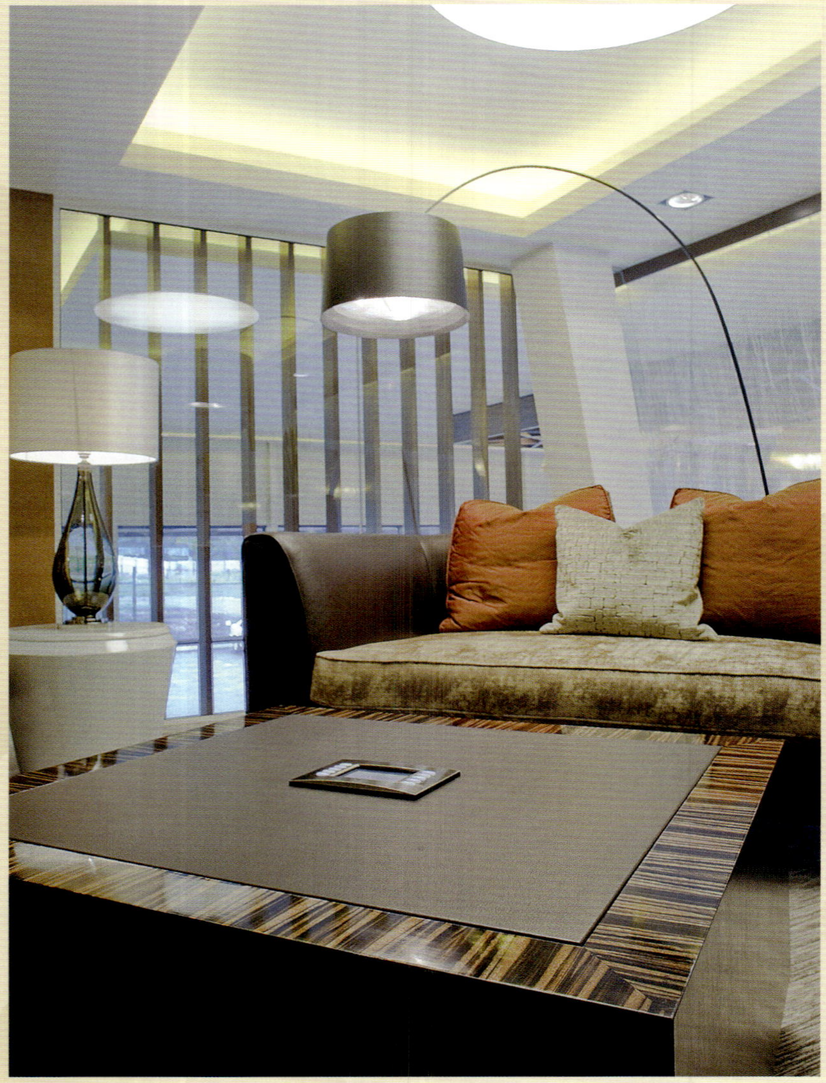
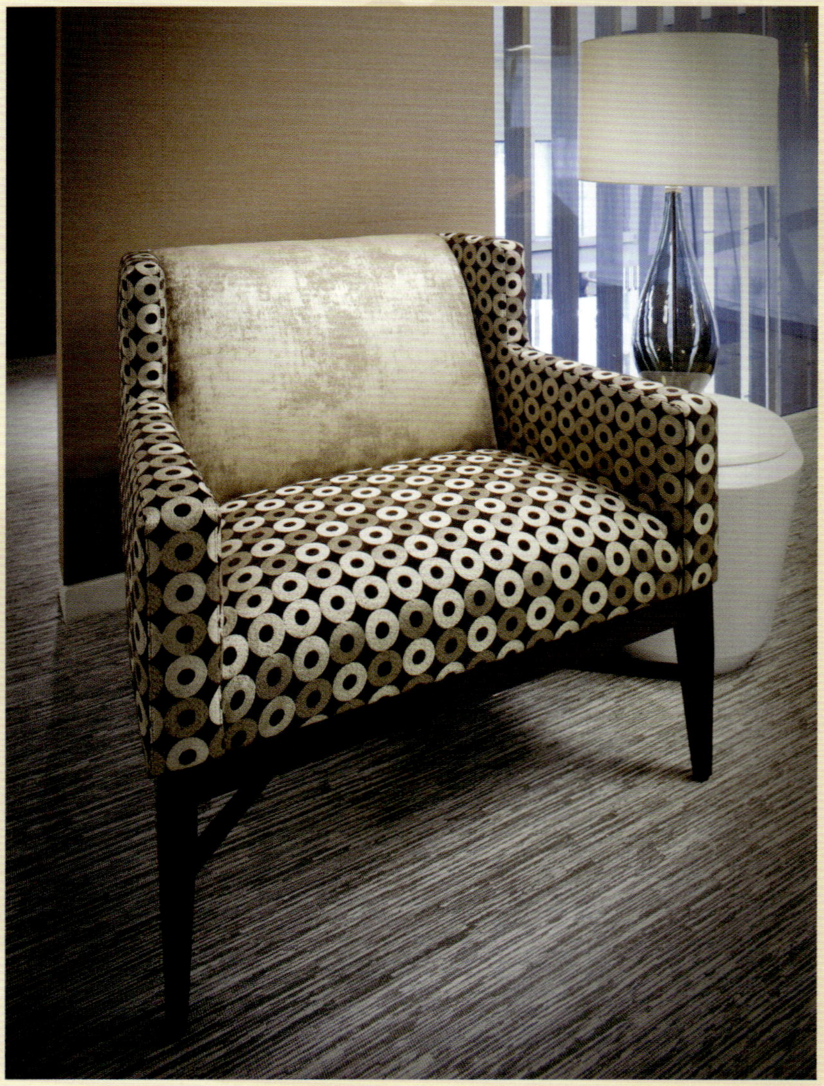

231

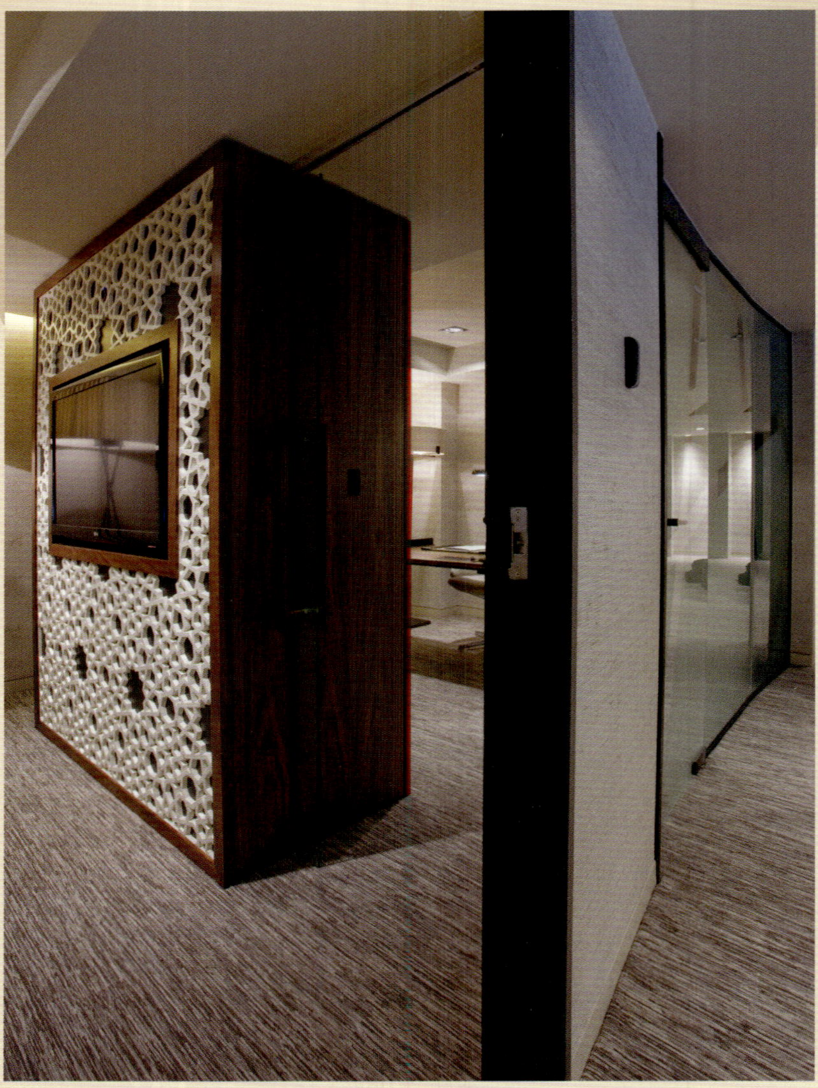
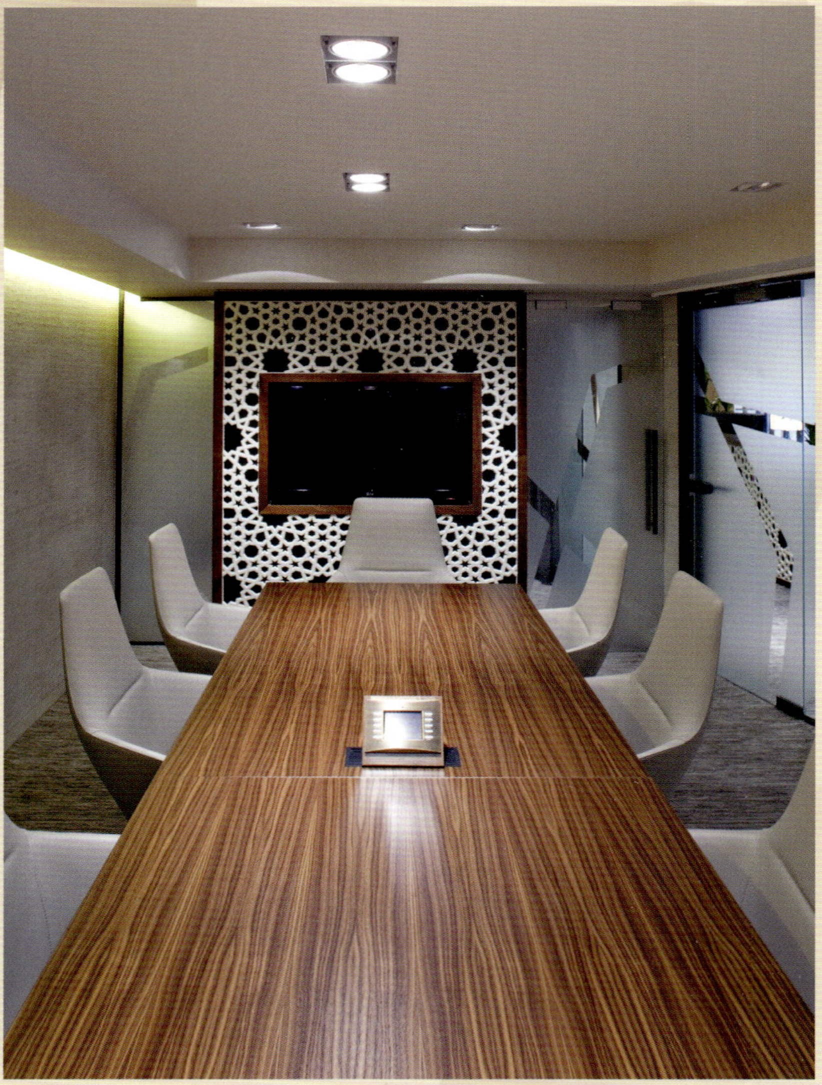
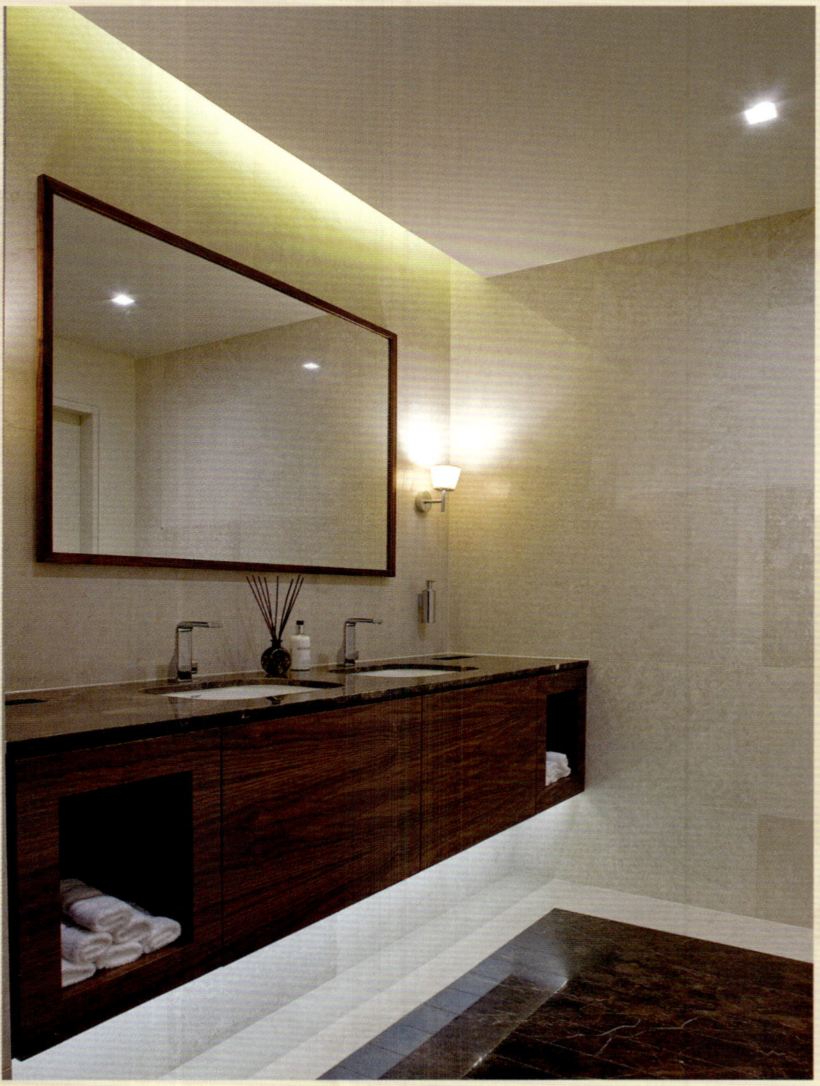
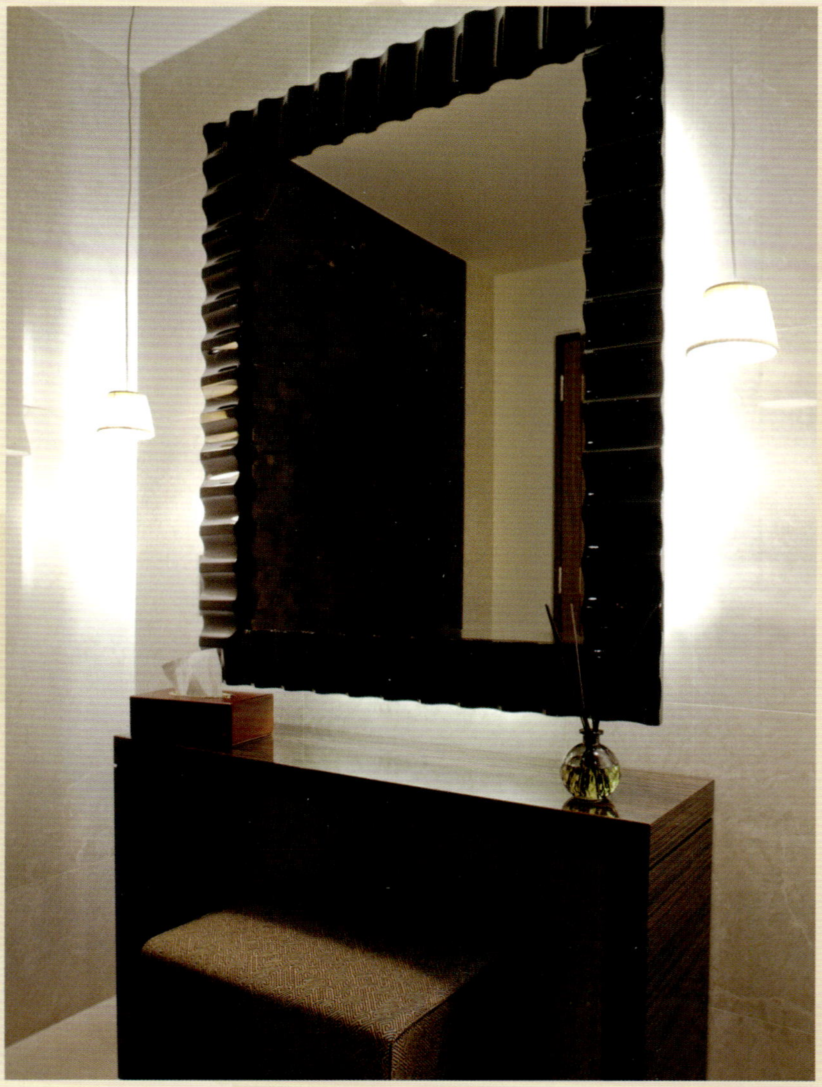

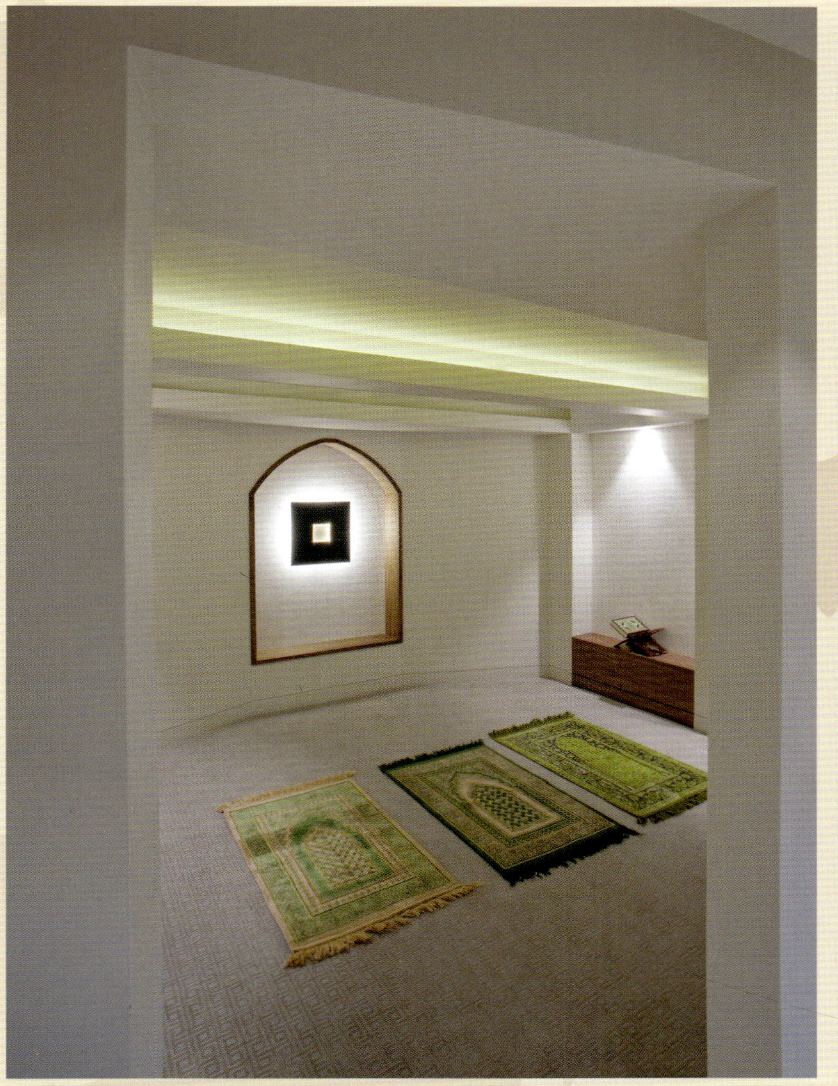
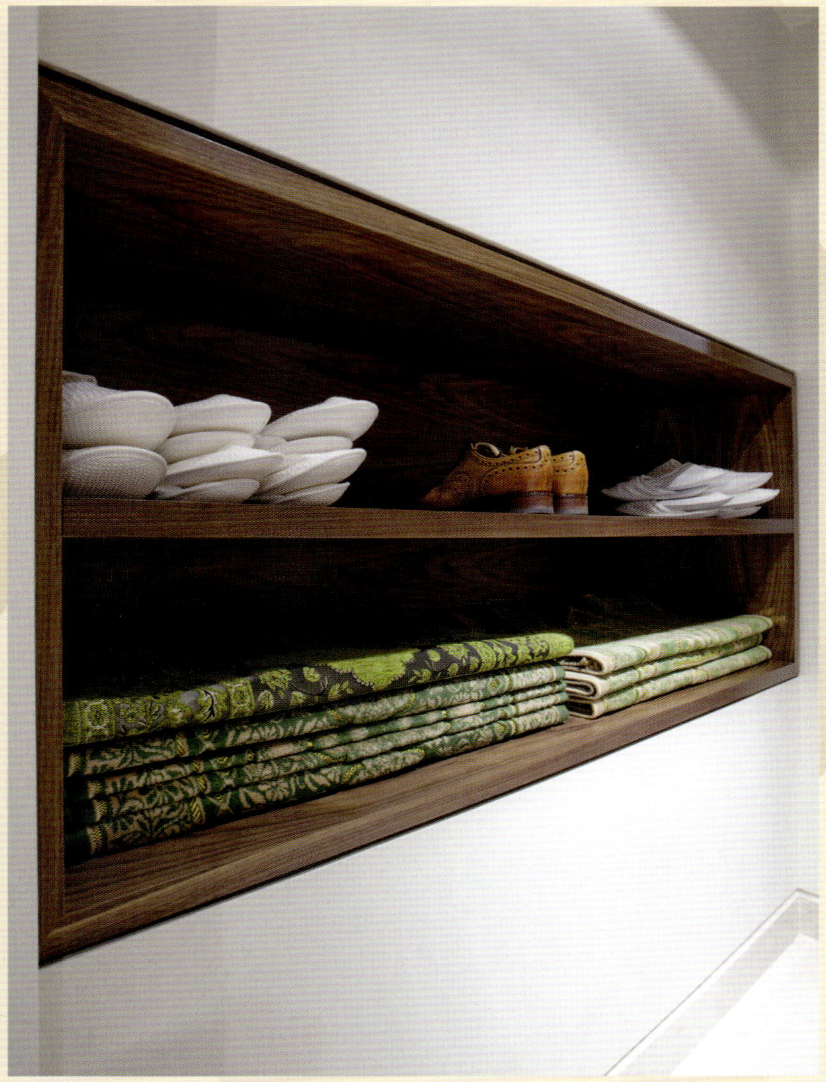

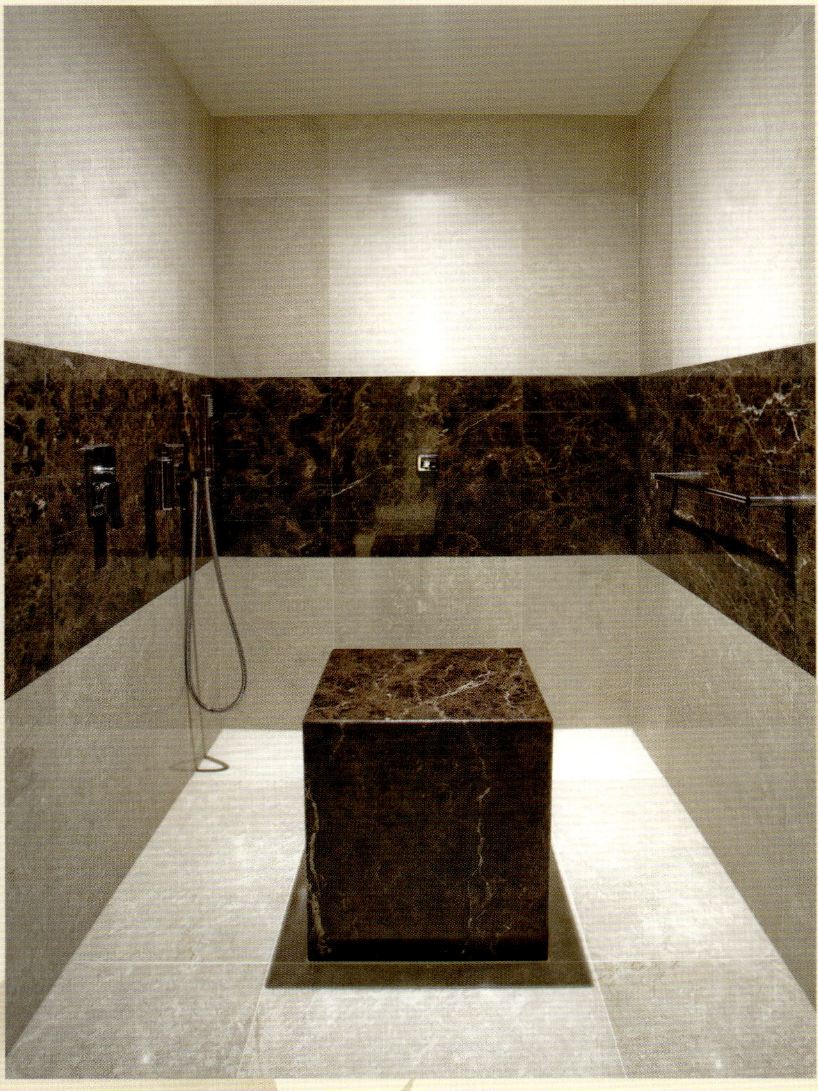

Ru Yi Club — Hidden Luxury

Design Agency: Wisdom Space Design
Designers: Wang Junqin
Location: Beijing, China
Area: 500 m²
Photographer: Sun Xiangyu

Ru Yi Club, graceful and moderate, is neither too avant-garde nor too luxury. It has inherited Japanese fine design and European-style magnificent tradition. The most concise colors and lines have built the simplest yet magnificent lifestyle, which has become the decoder of the art kingdom in Ru Yi Club. The creative design by Wang Junqin, a Taiwanese designer, has brought the owner great visual impact, where the imposing manner of such a gorgeous palace, flowing lines, glittering, and translucent and low-key colors, against the back ground of Bird's Nest, have seamlessly gone with Pangu Seven Star's gorgeous and noble outlook. The luxury of Ru Yi club does not deviate from the human nature; instead, it is the haven for the rich's souls.

Ru Yi Club is positioned at only high-end groups, with the lifestyle and attitude of nobility, privacy and enjoyment hidden. It brings its customers noble feeling and the most wonderful enjoyment due to implicit luxury and tranquility. It offers services compatible with one's status, brings humanistic culture and commercial environment, and provides the highest added value for its customers.

235

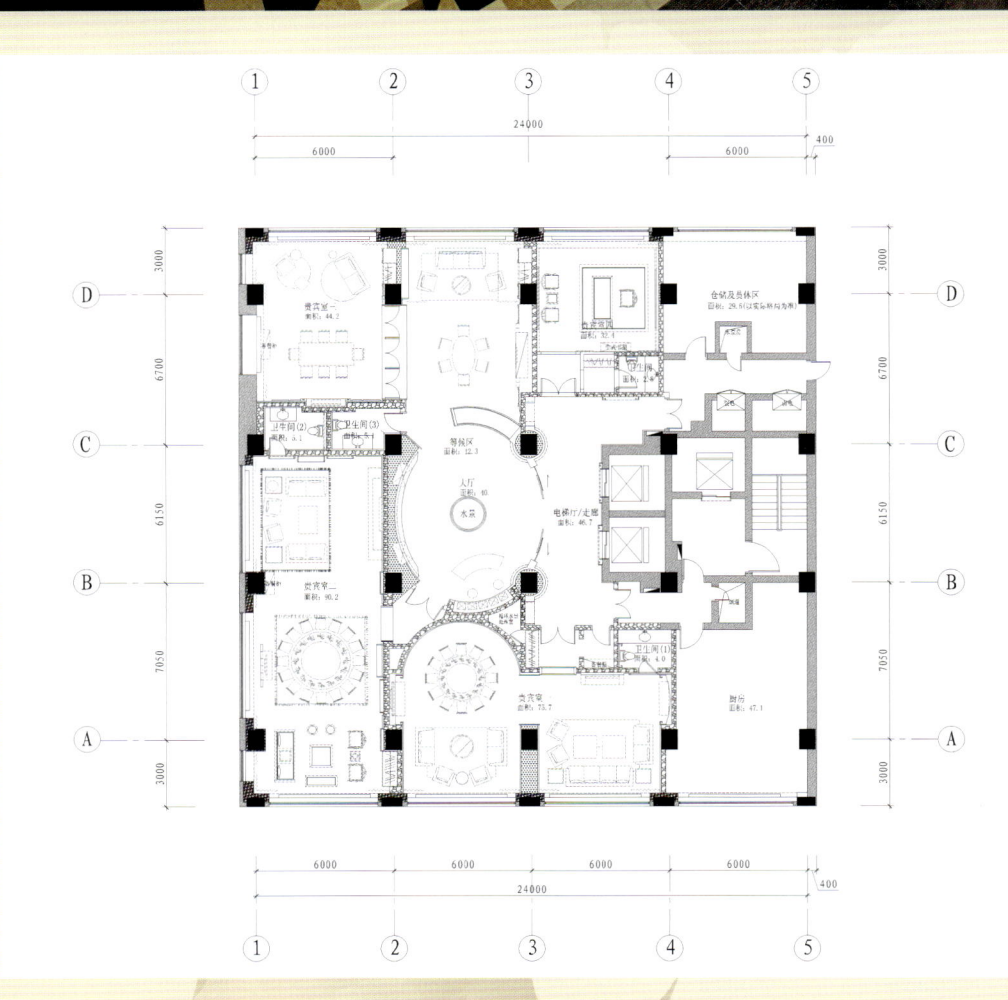

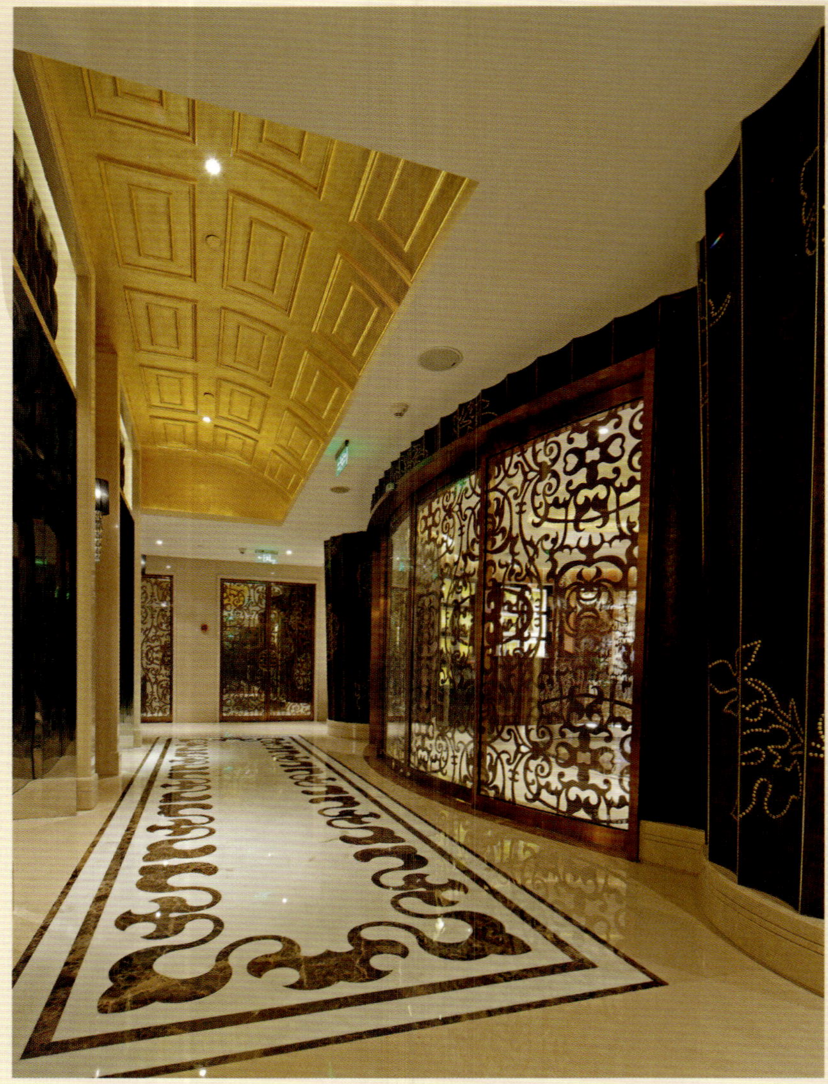

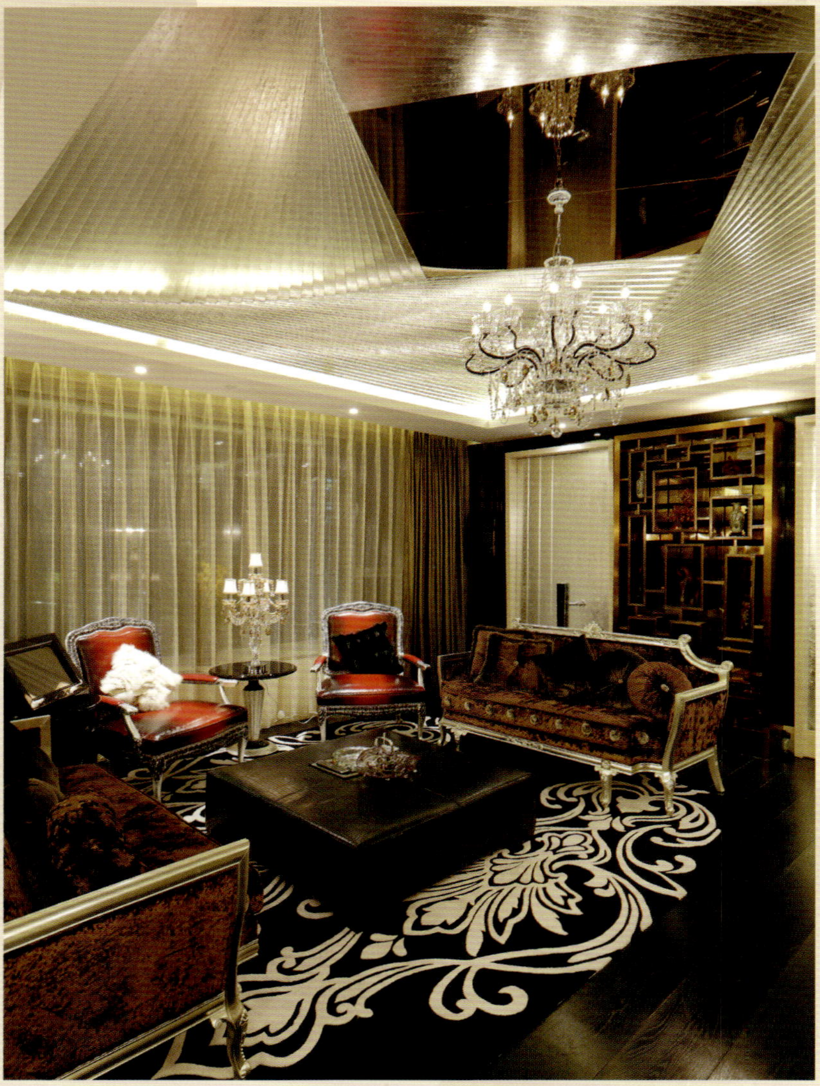

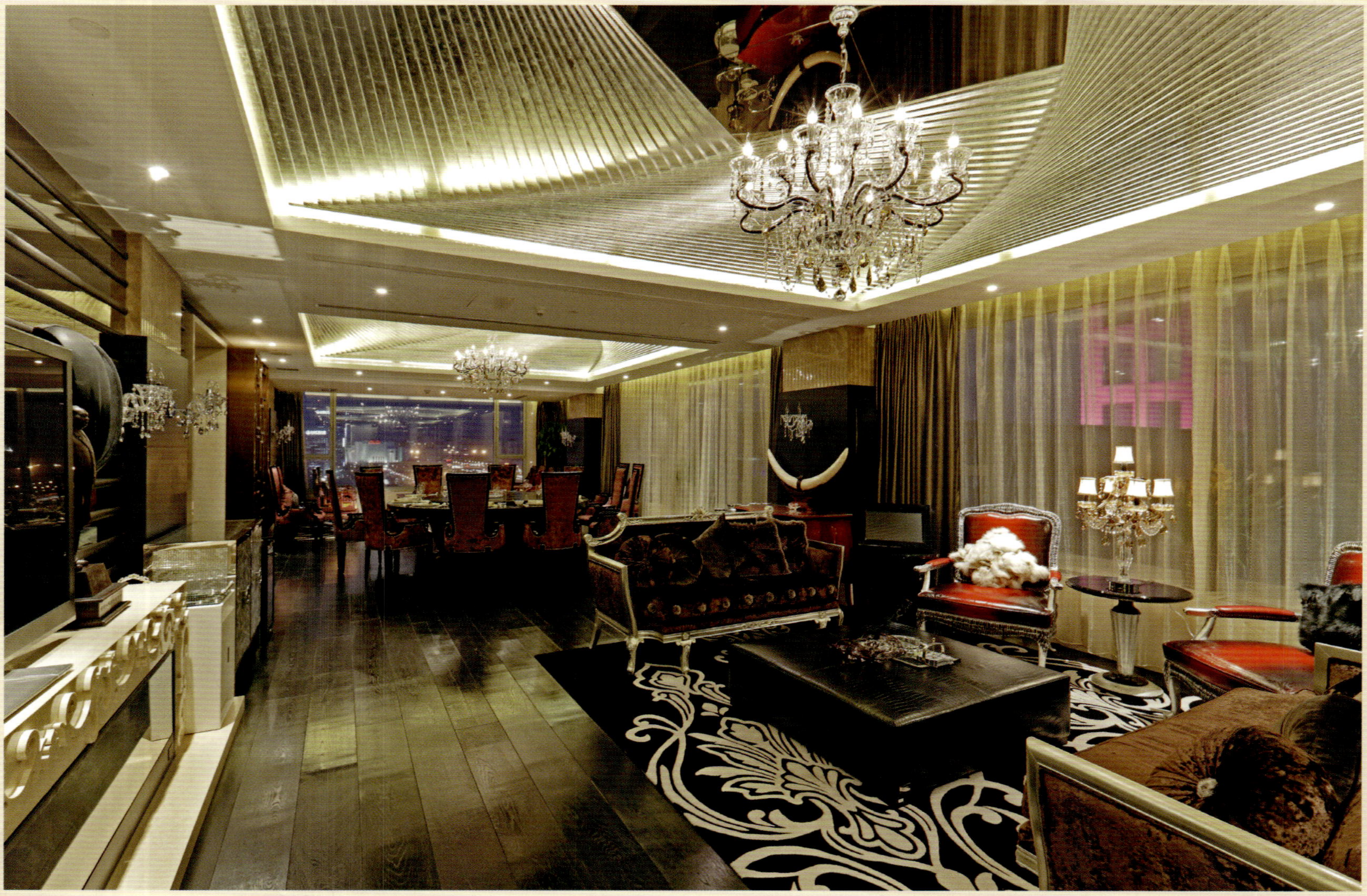

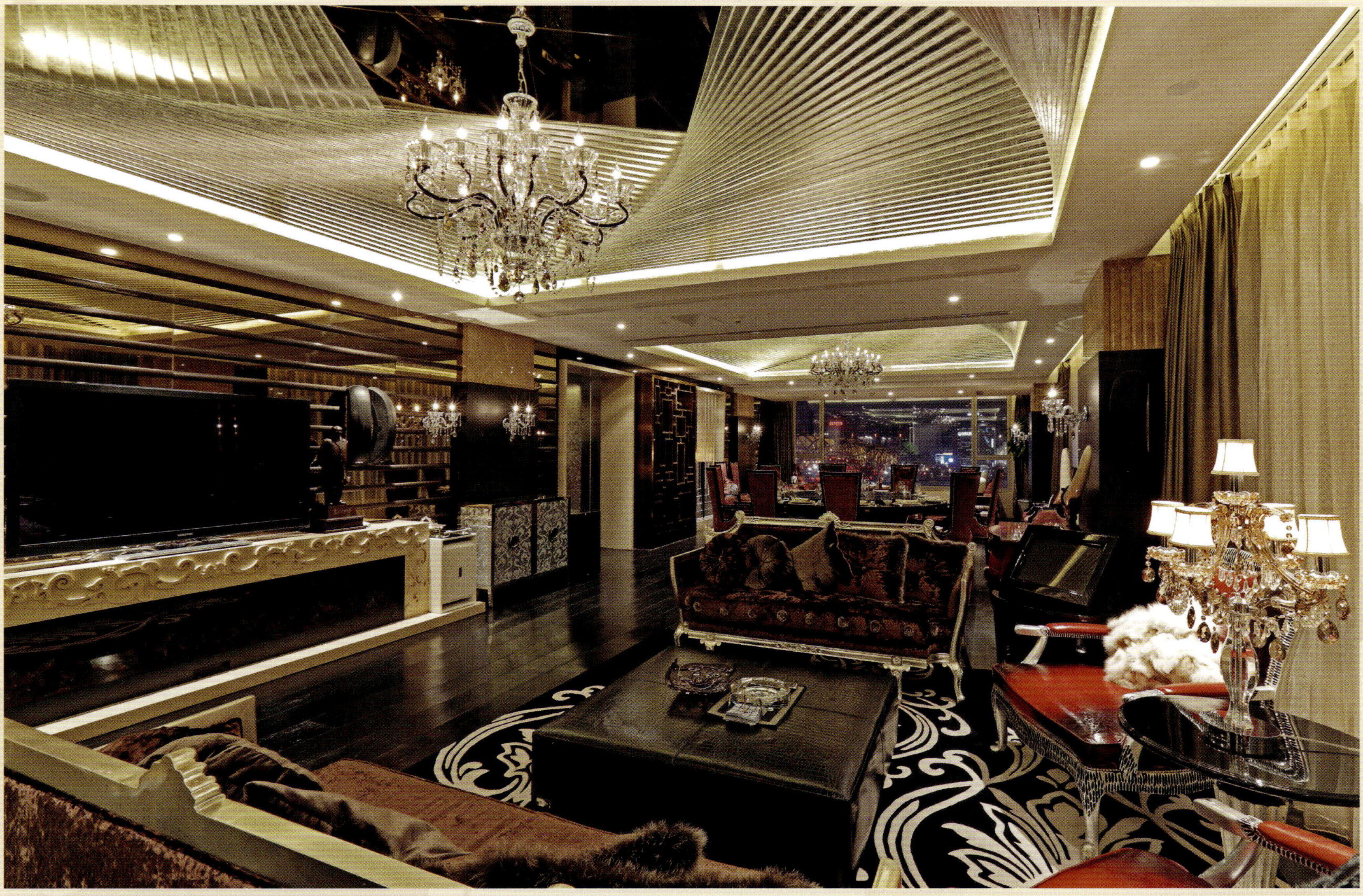

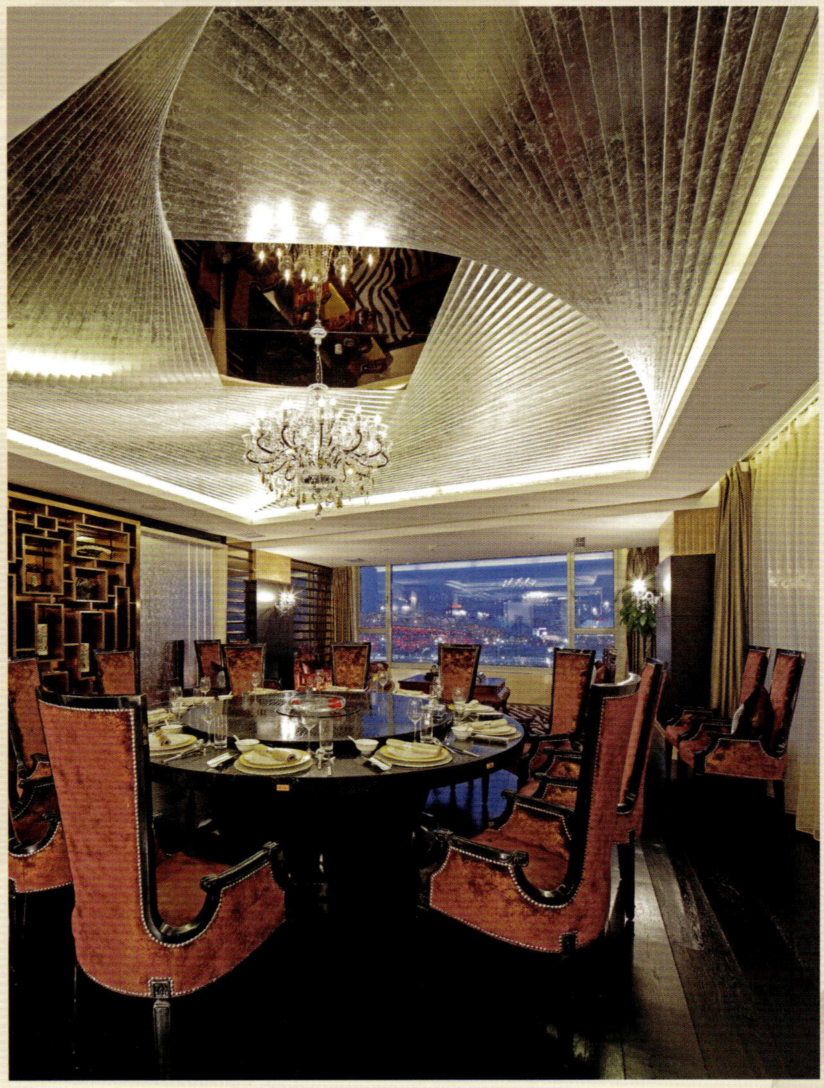

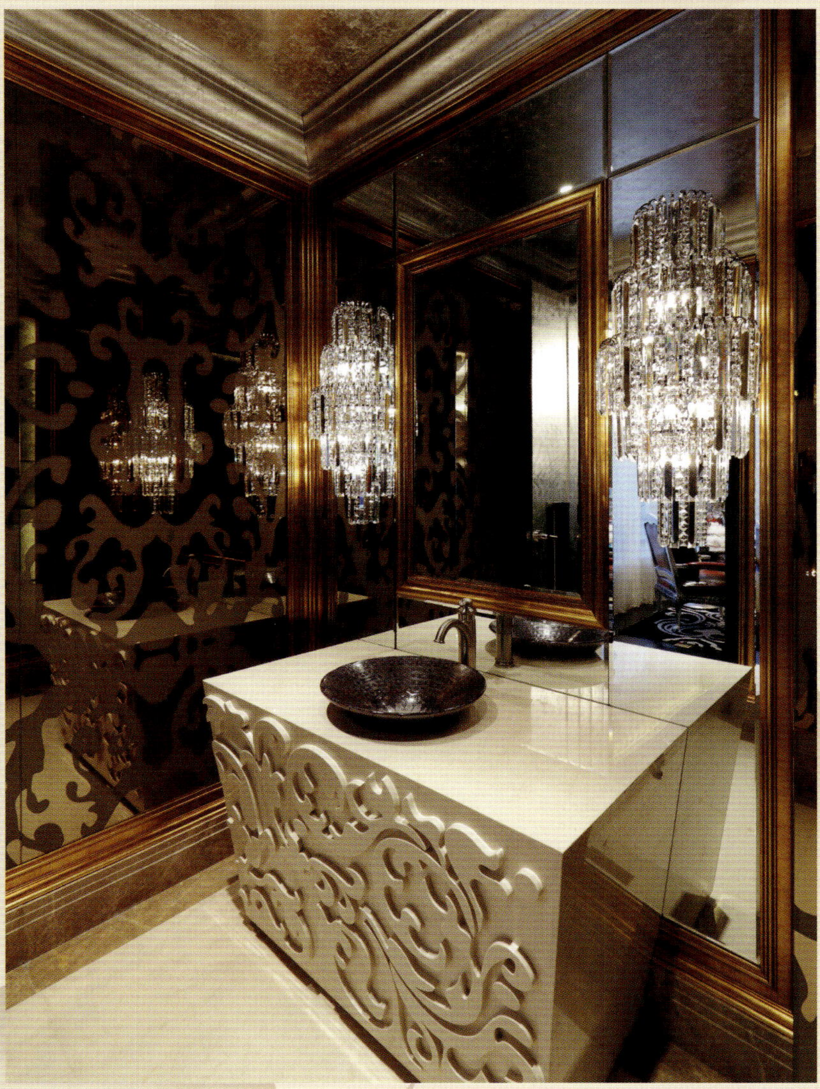

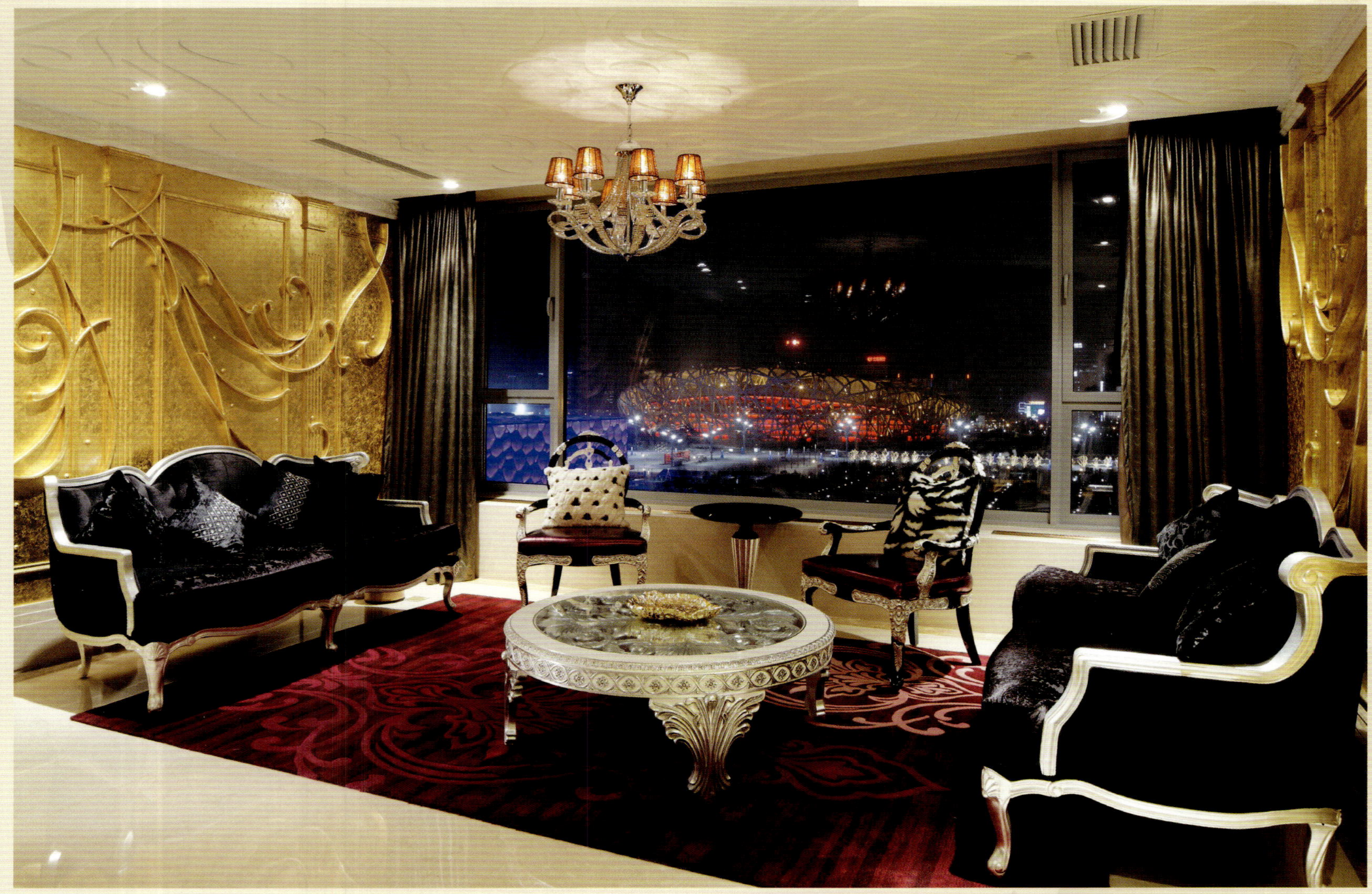

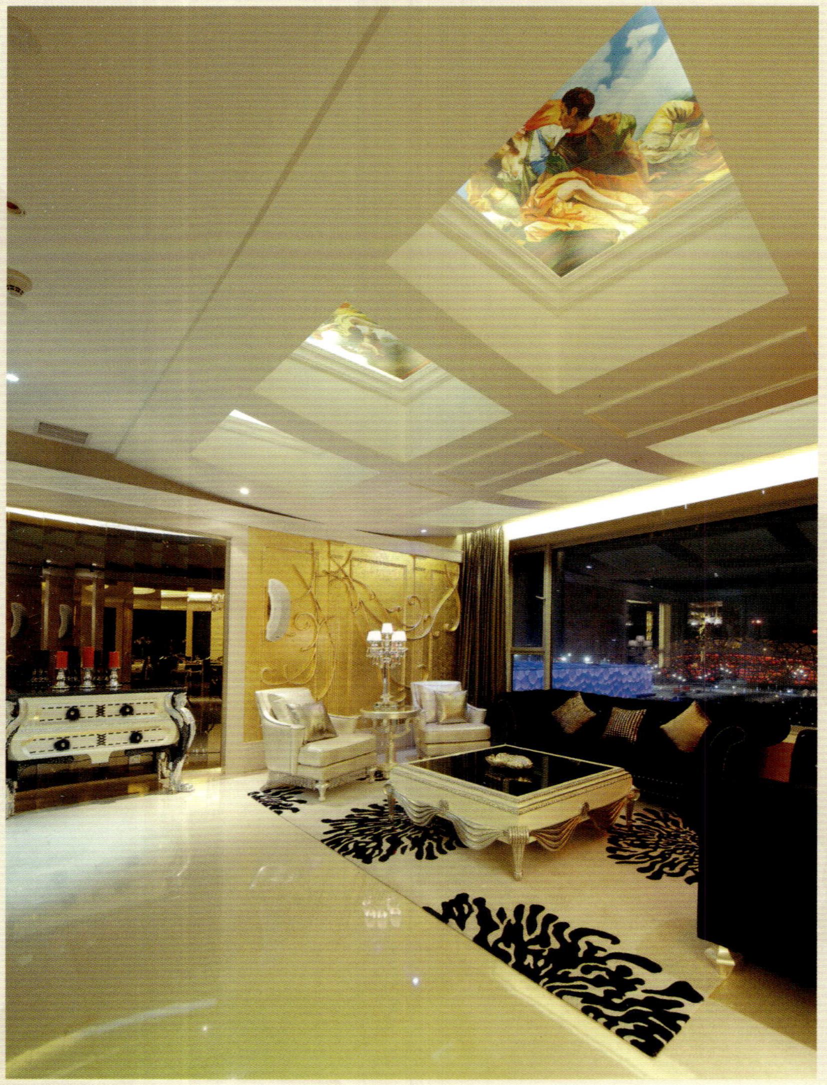

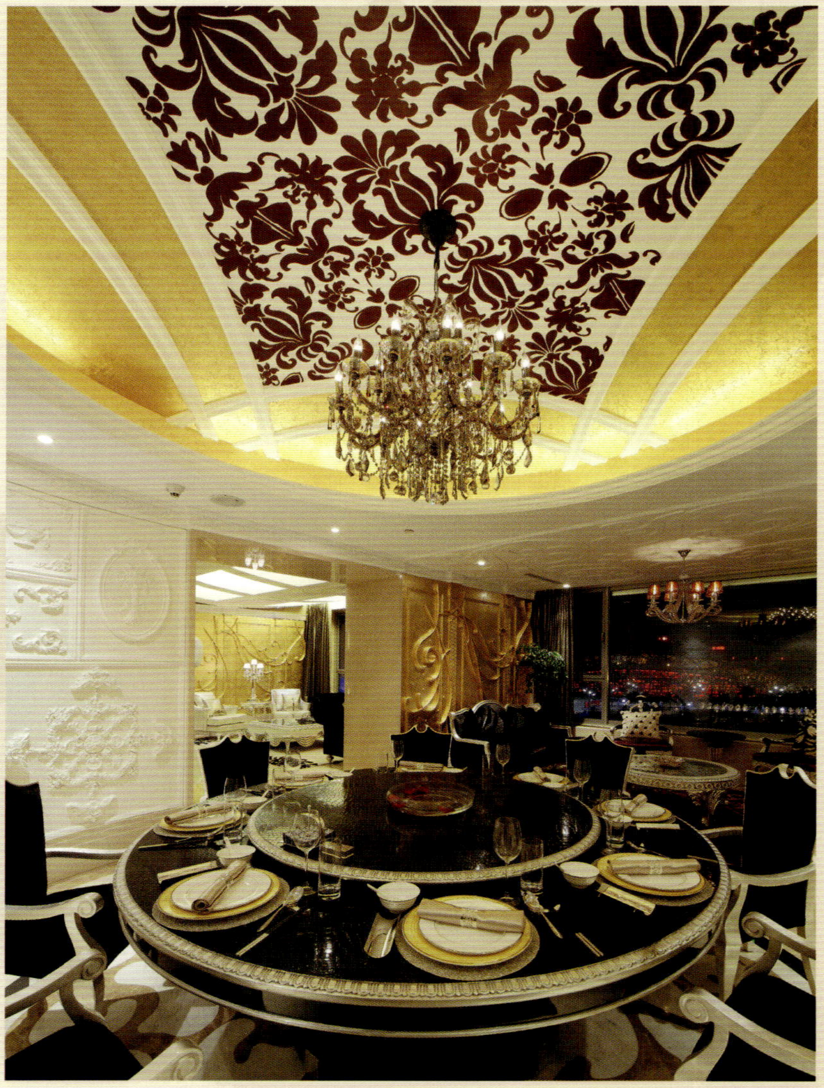

239

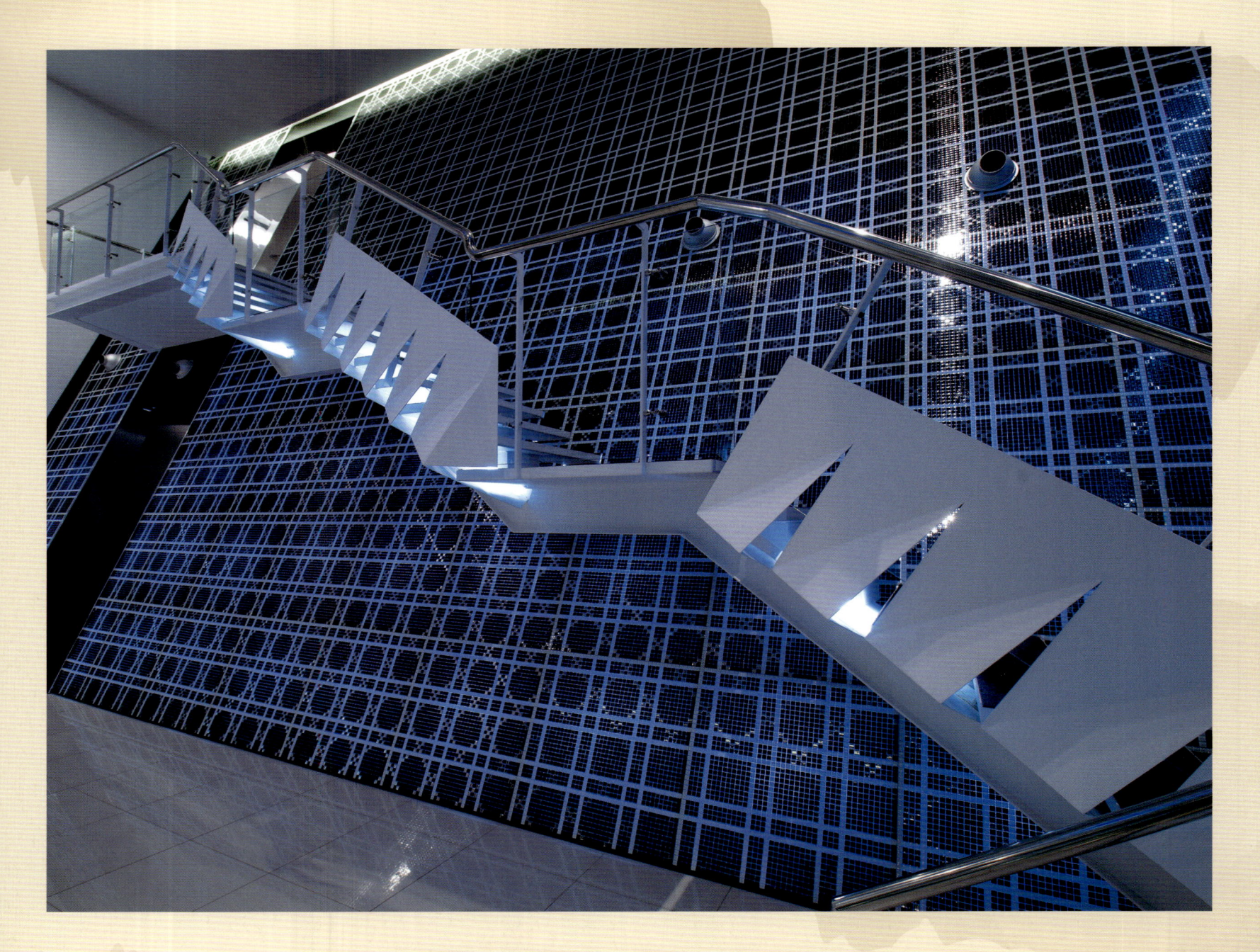

U-PARK Sales Center

Design Agency: Sherwood Design

Designer: Huang Shuheng

Location: Taiwan, China

Area: 1200 m²

Photographer: Wang Jishou

To the Sherwood designer, the most exciting thing is using the unexpected architectural materials and elements, in a limited interior space, to create a conflict but compatible space.

This project is a visual feast: the exterior is like a huge sculpture, and the construction materials make it a splendid architecture and have a strong modern sense.

241

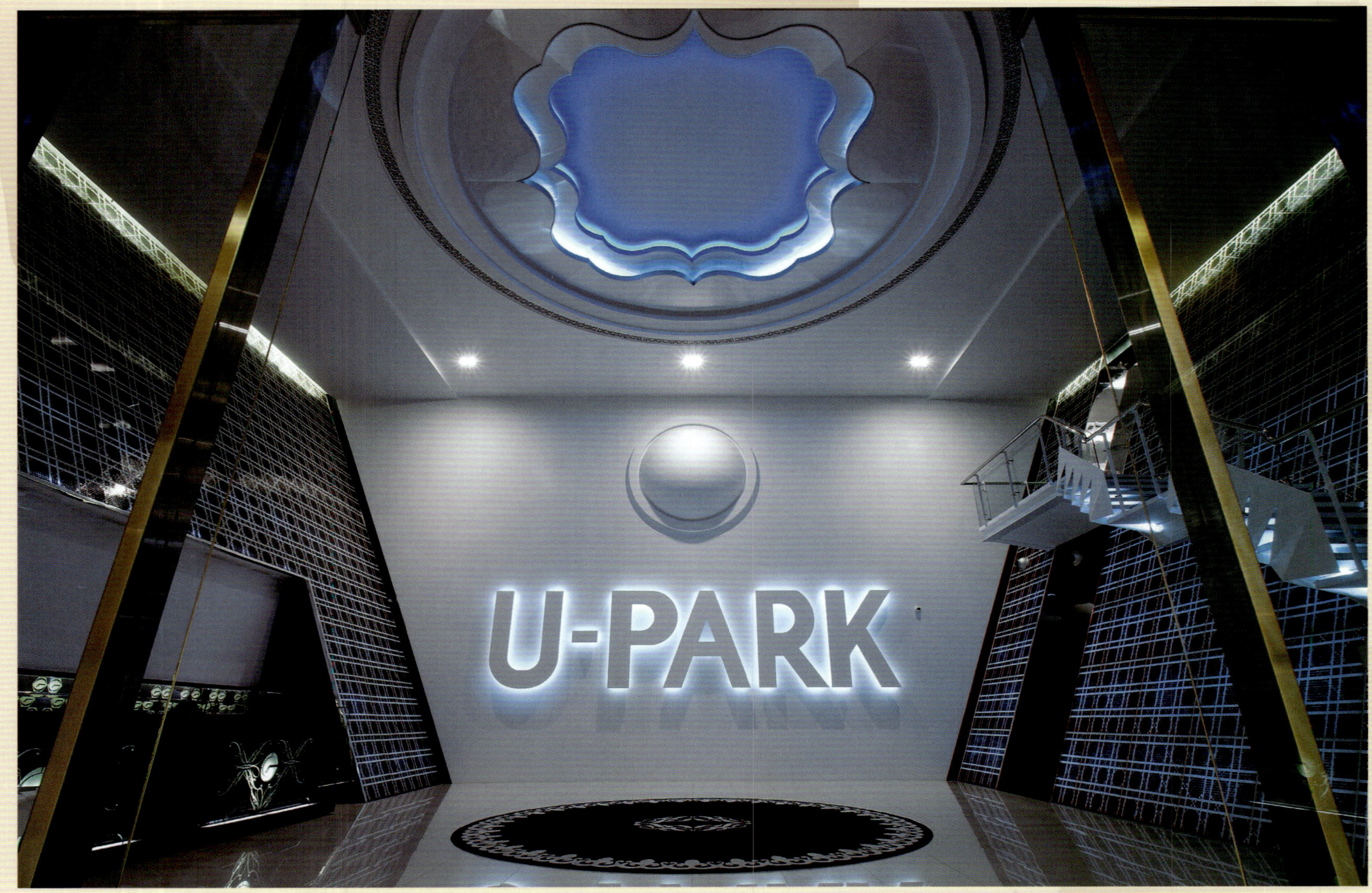
U-PARK

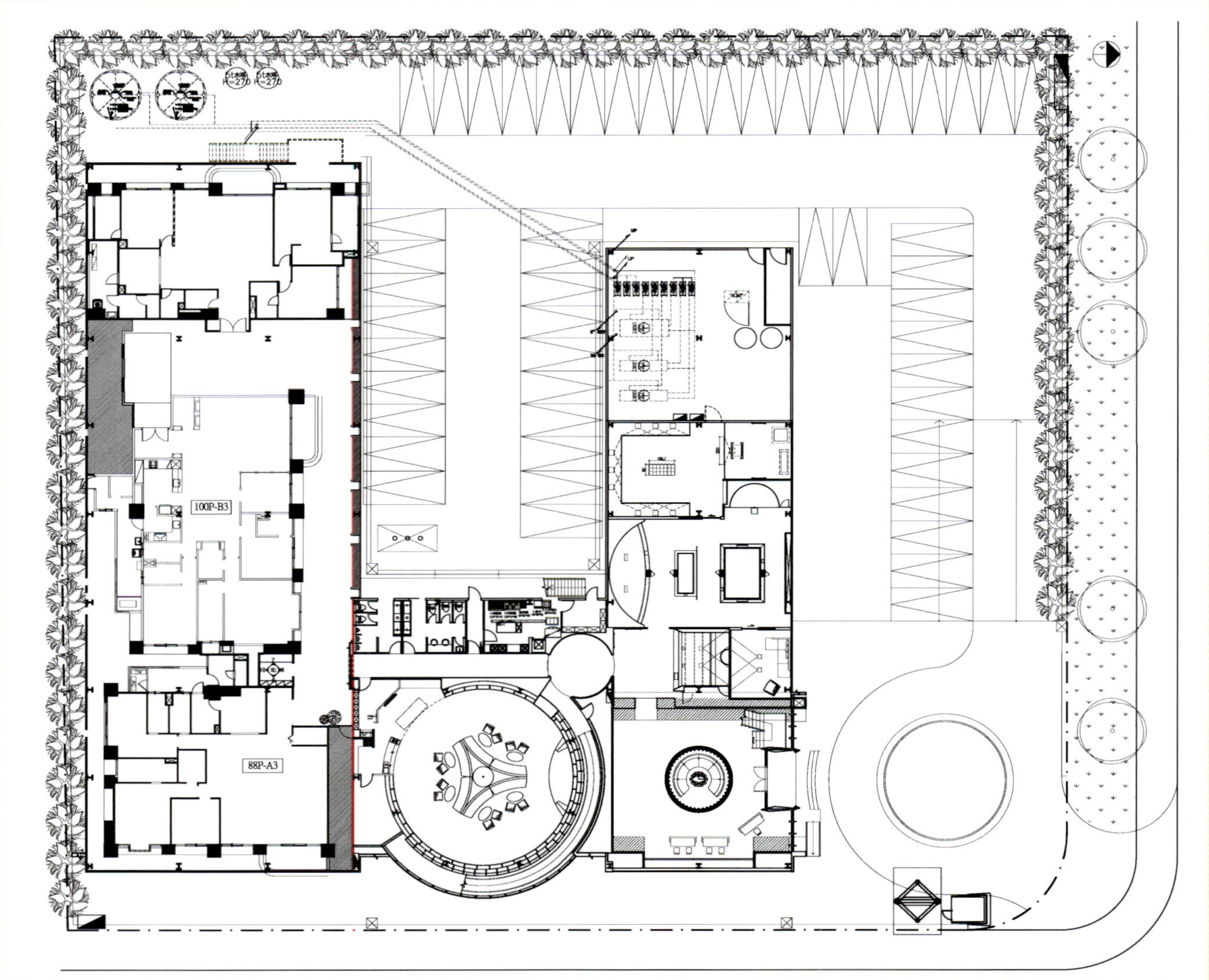
100P-B3
88P-A3

243

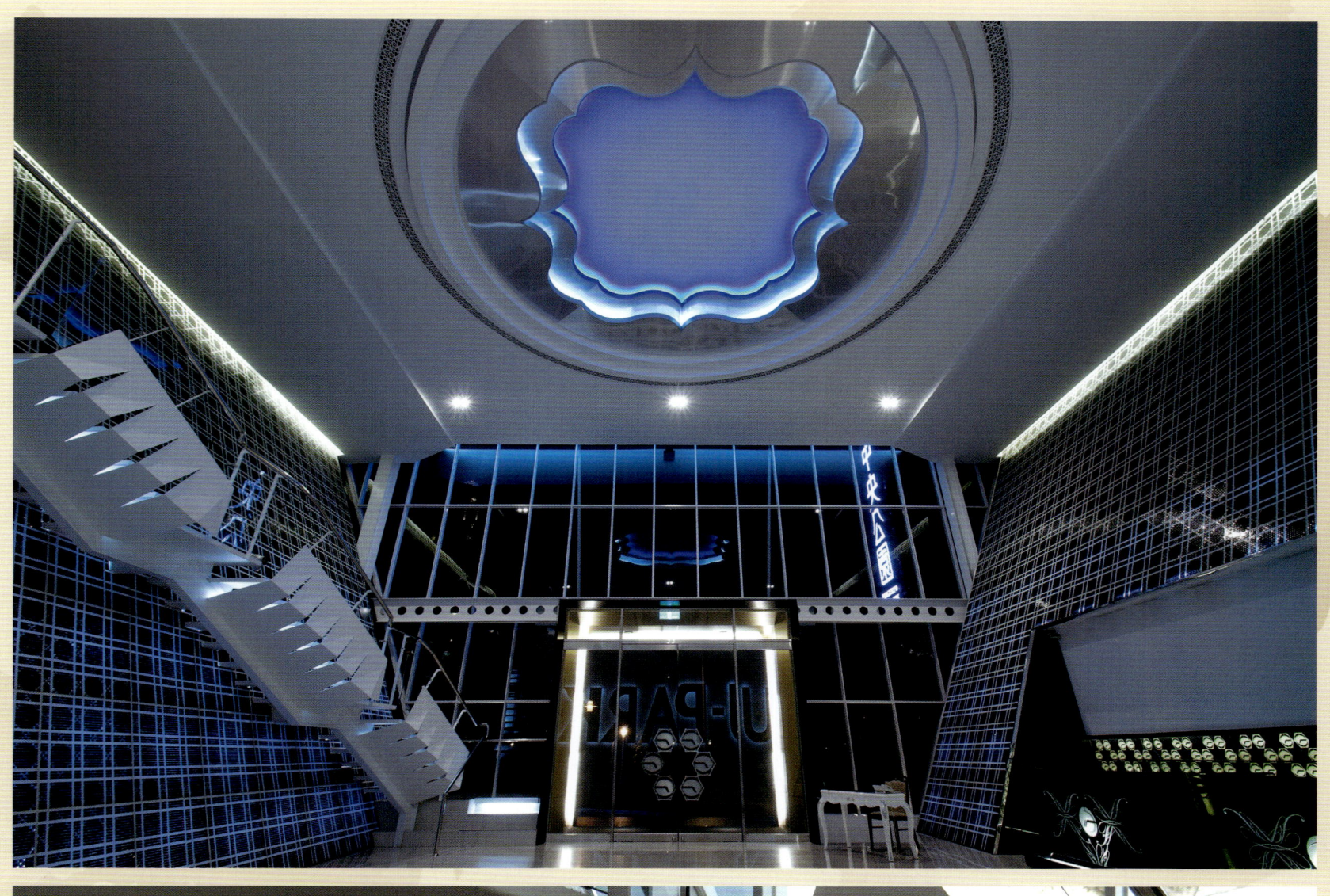

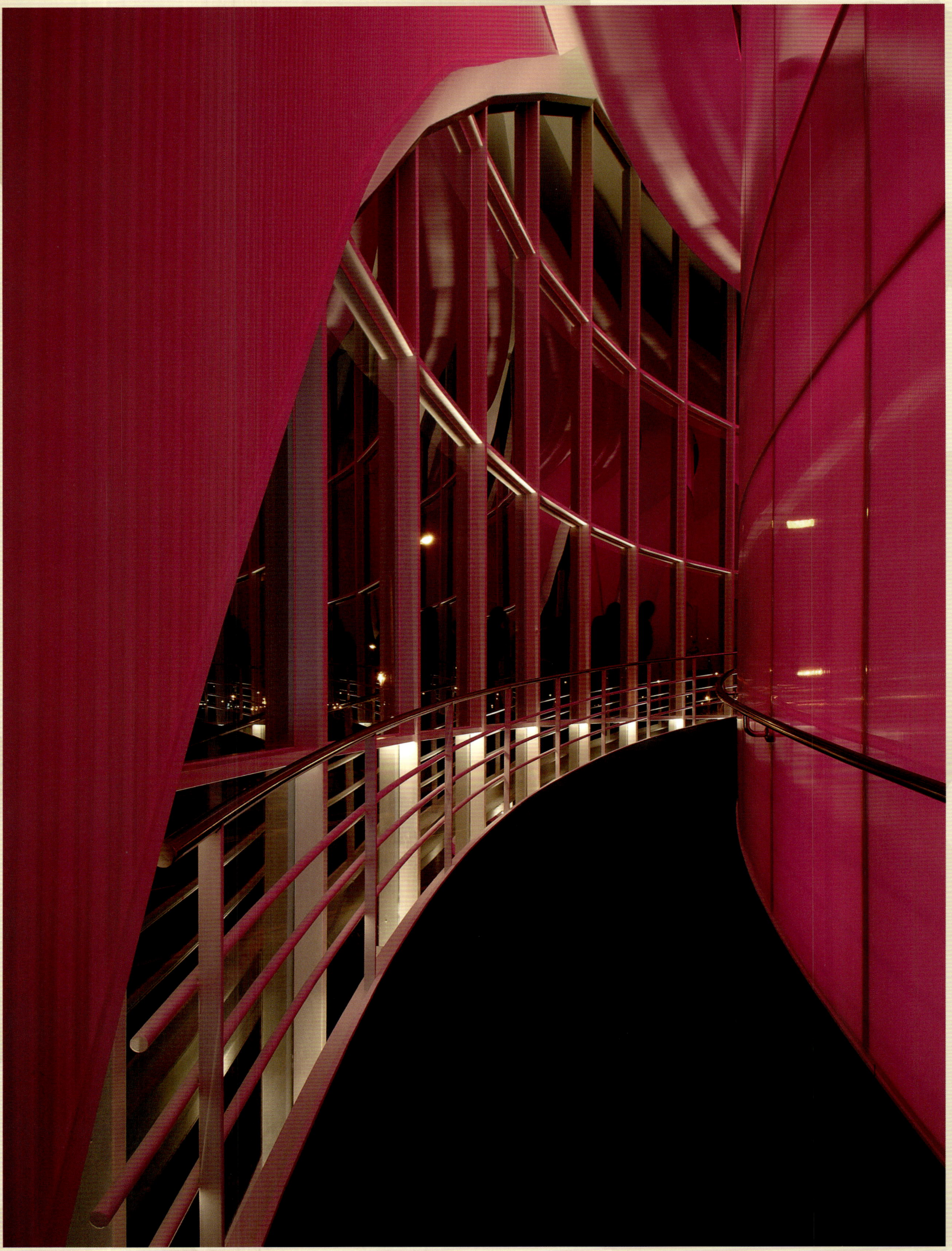

16M昌義街

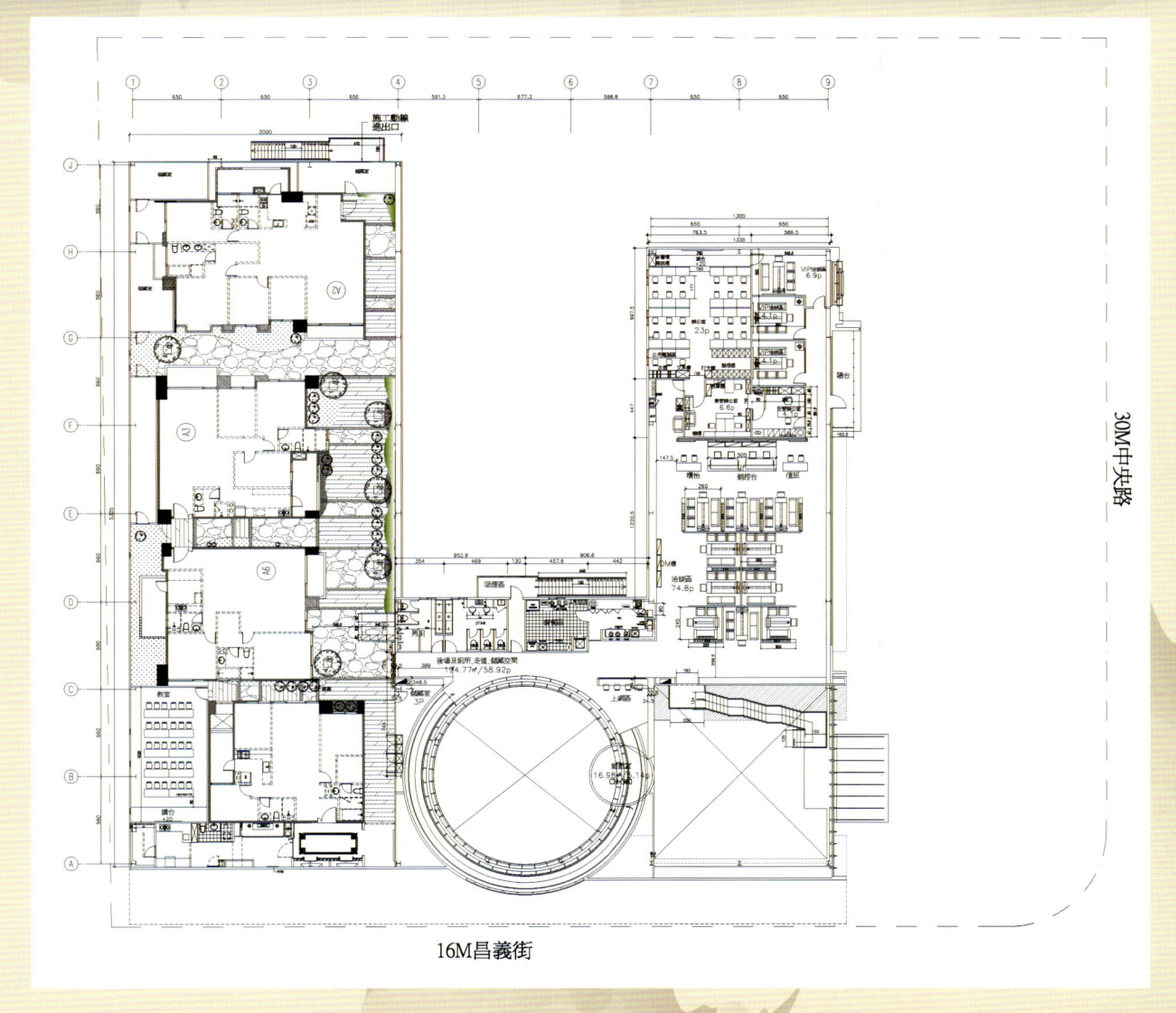

30M中央路

245

246

247

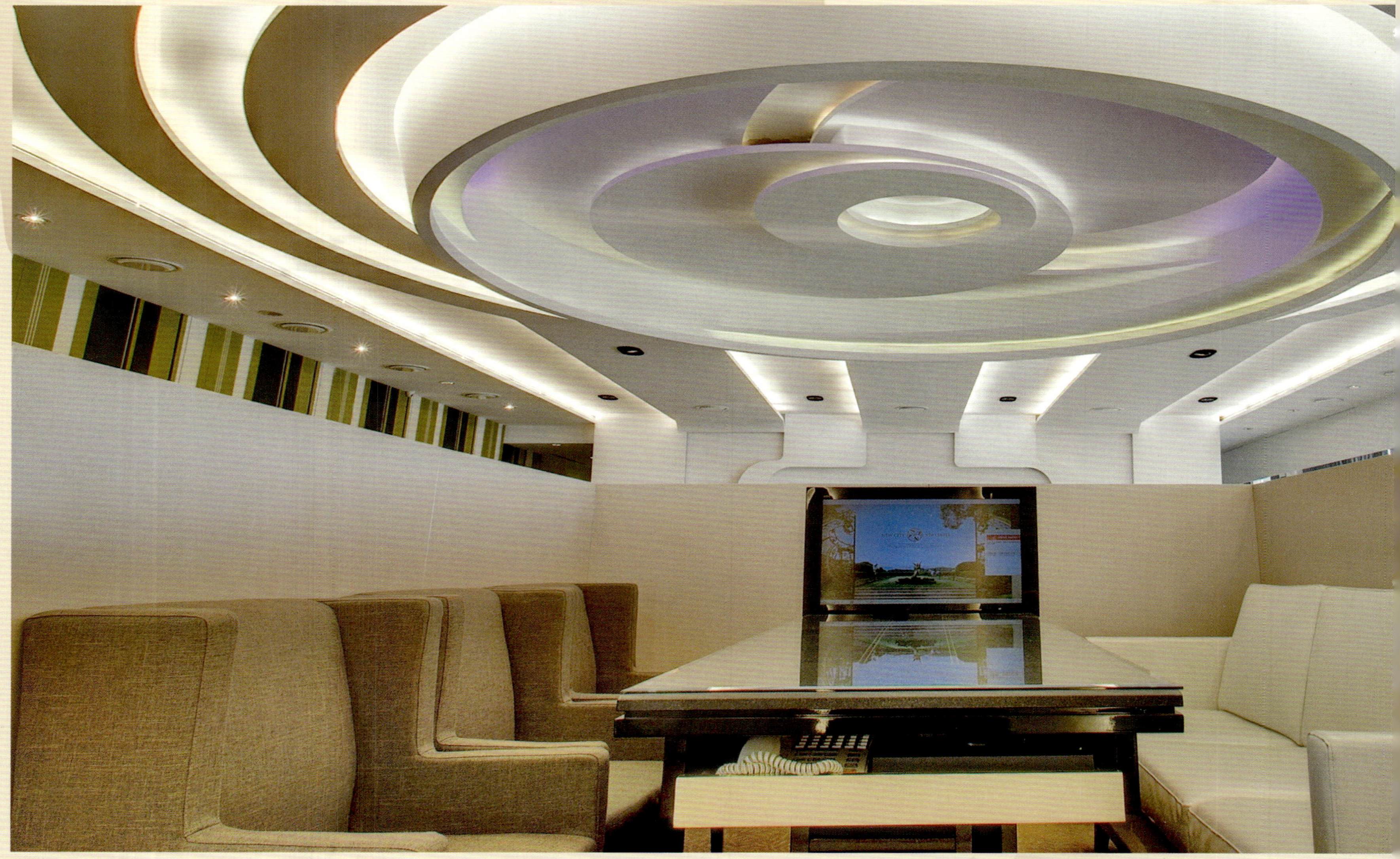

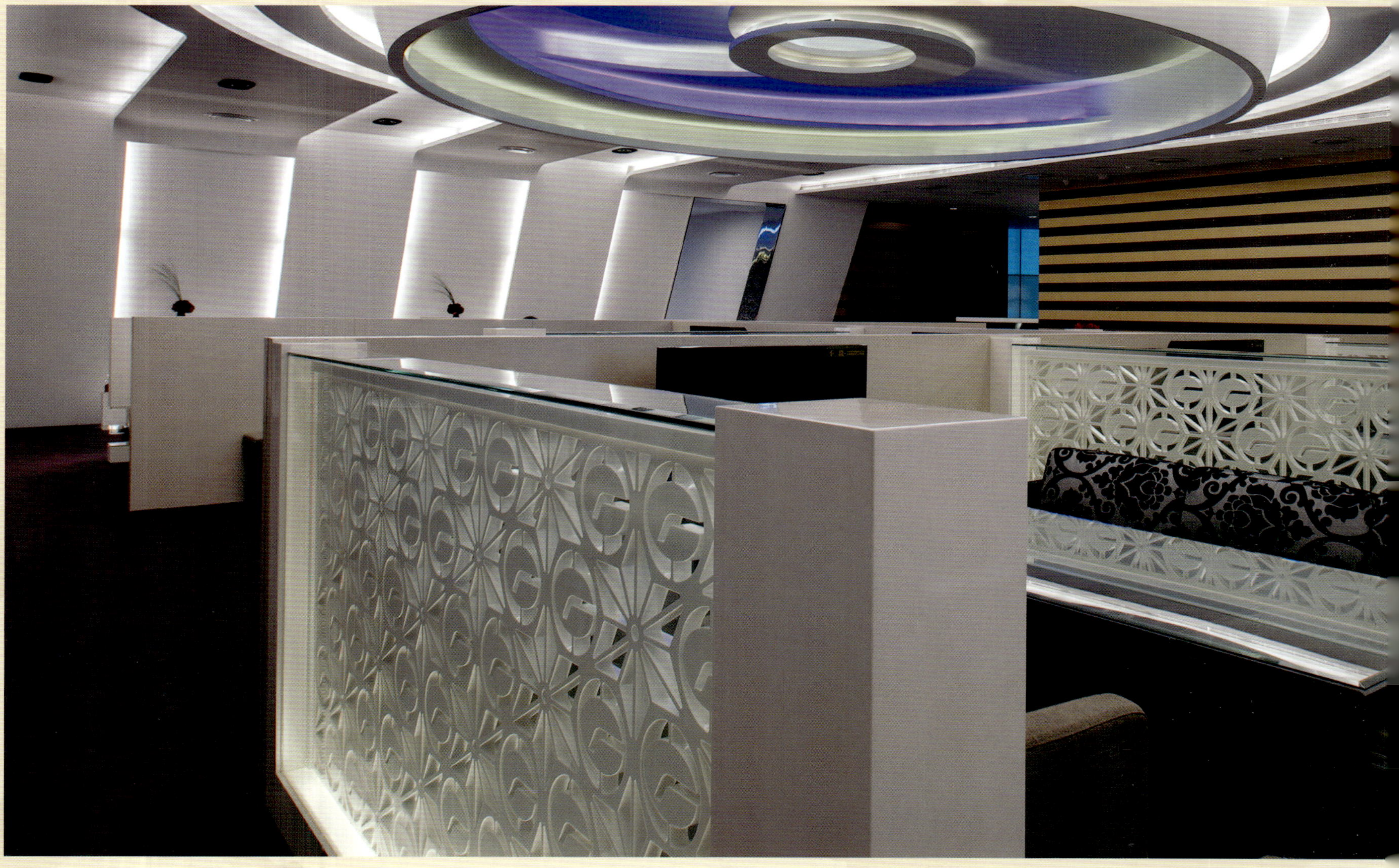

249

Sales Center of Nanning Ronghe MOCO Community

Design Agency: Eric Tai Design Co., Ltd.

Developer: Guangxi Ronghe Co., Ltd.

Location: Nanning, China

What is MOCO? MOCO explains the real meaning of international life of move (movable interaction), own ("I" centered), cool (giving the special feeling for cities and people), and original (originally created) – newly born cells of a city.

"MOCO" is a "modern group" that is in the leading edge of the period and has the gift of fashionable feeling and seeing clearly fresh things of the life.

The designer applies red, white, black, and white bud-shape modeling to express the concept of design; the red color gives us the visual sense for vitality and passion, and the white color reflects pureness of the youth; white acrylic hanging ornaments on the ceiling is like a group of pure white life bodies that are sprouting right now, energetic, youthful, and fashionable.

The design applies modern and simple geometric shape and the color matching with visual impact to convey vitality and passion, creating a charming space. Youth is not a period of time in your life, but it is the word for passion and vitality. Only with youthful mentality, you can stand on the leading edge of fashion, to become one of the "MOCO" group.

251

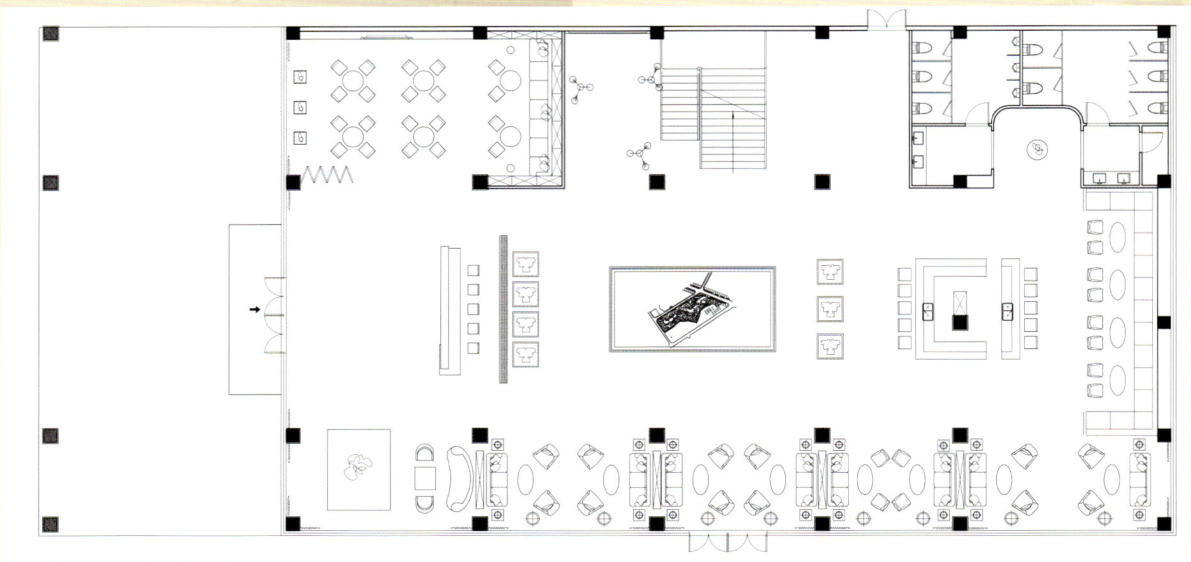

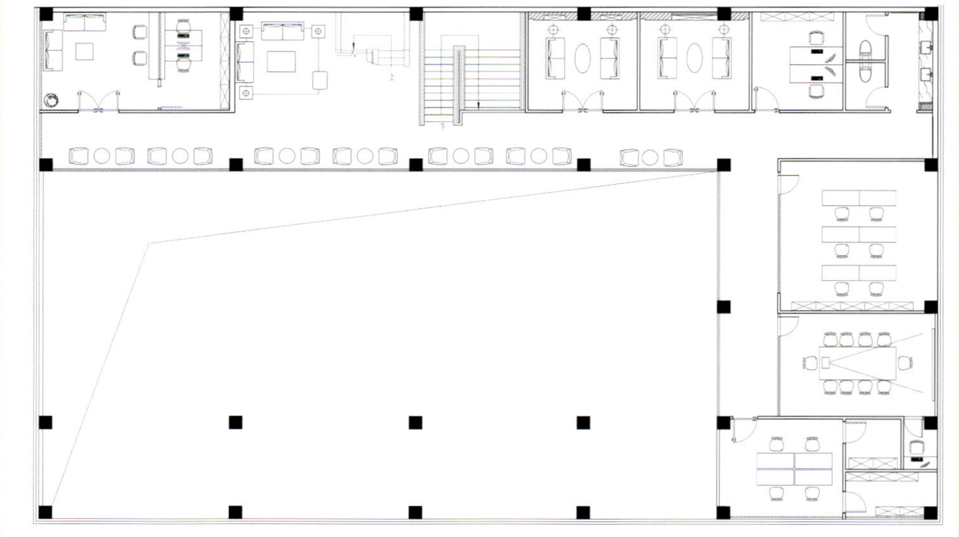

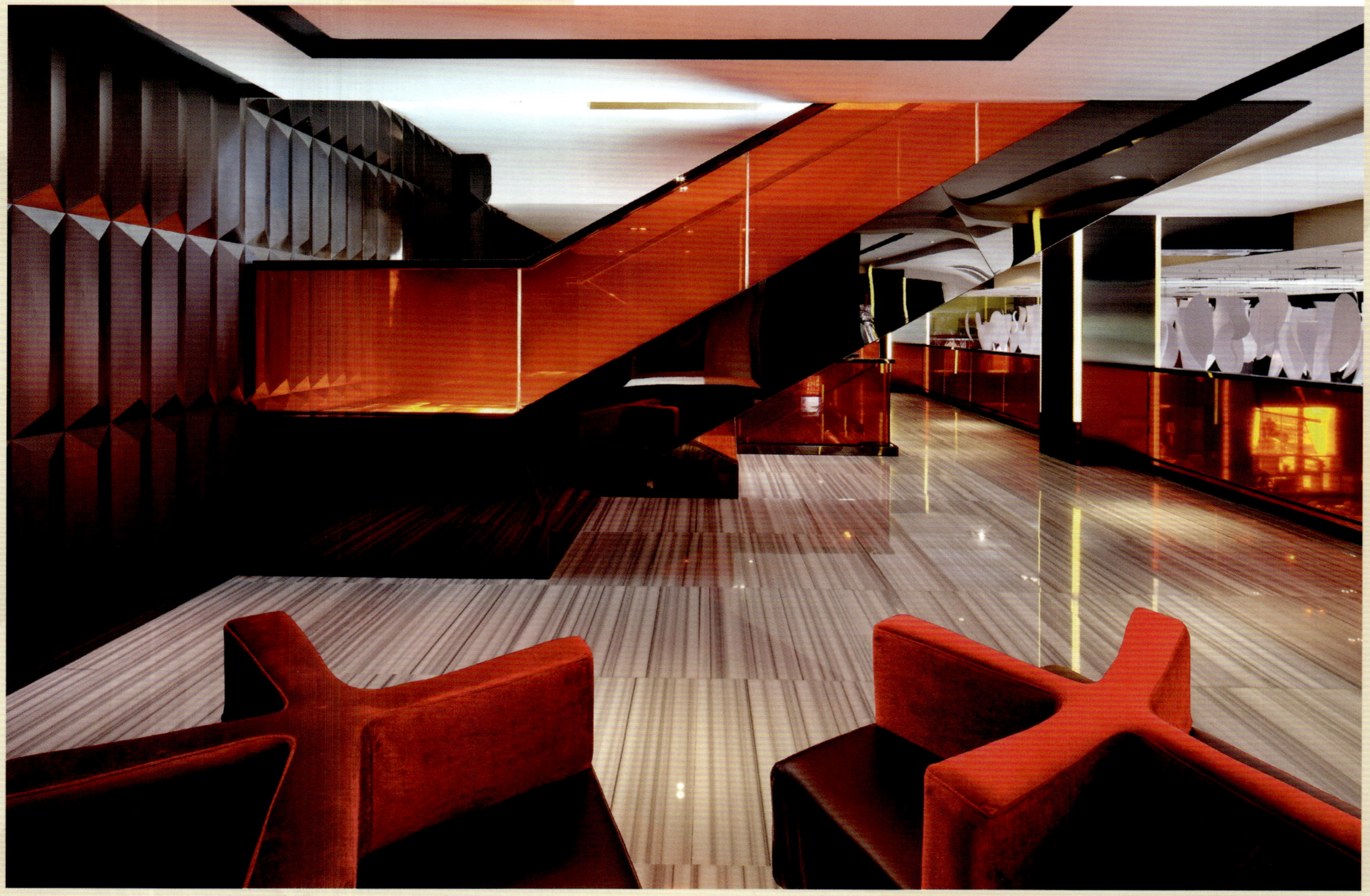

253

254

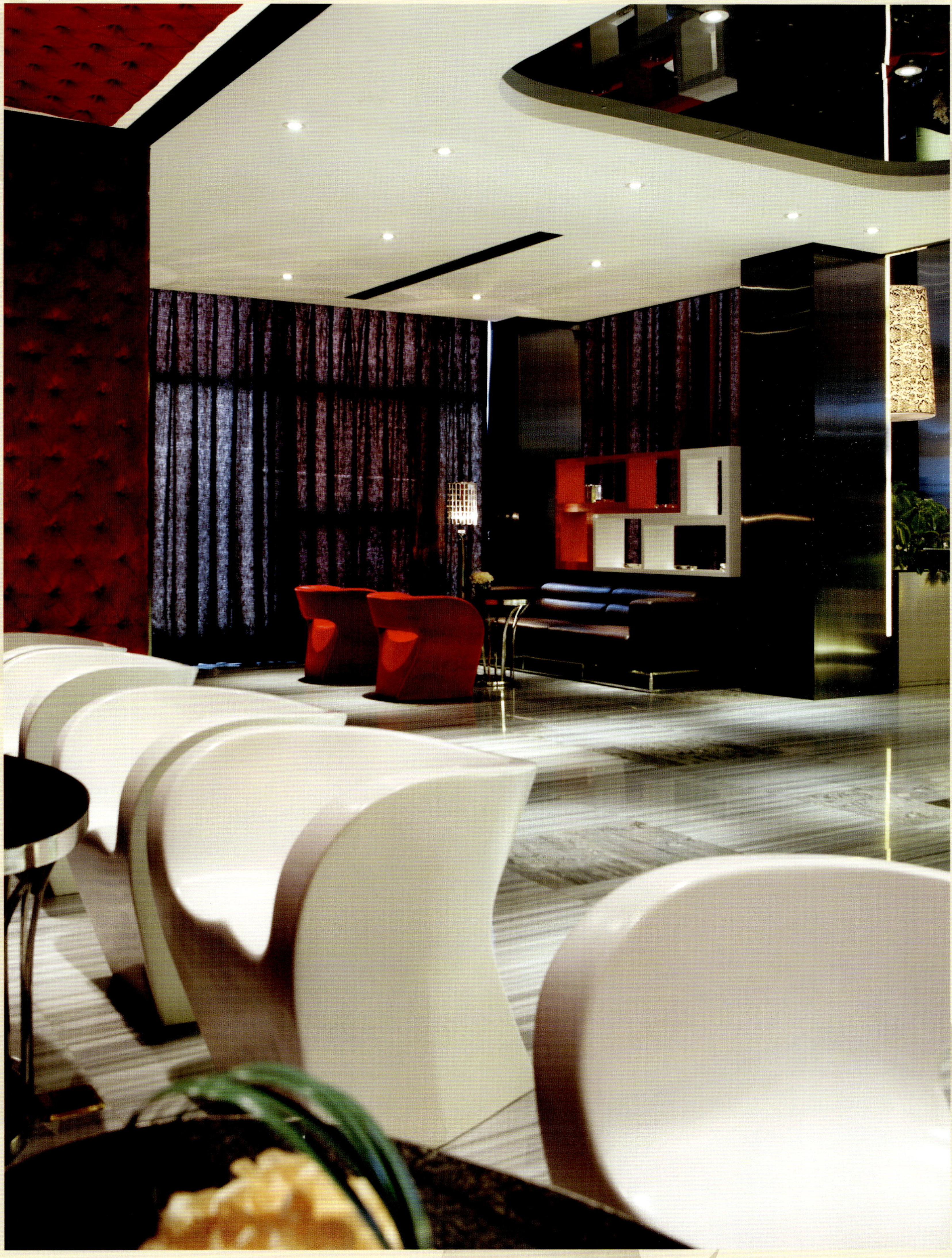

Longhu Shi Ji Feng Jing Club

Design Agency: Hong Kong Fong Wong Architects & Associates
Chief Designer: TSUN FONG
Area: 530m²
Location: Chengdu, China
Photographer: Jiang Guozeng

Although brown expresses a feeling of solemn and fullness, the pine nut brown with a little light gold can outstand from this kind feeling of fullness, creating nobility and grace while at the same time bringing a slight softness and tenderness. People in this atmosphere can not help recalling the landscape of the mountains far away in the early autumn, which is abundant, tranquil and meaningful.

Based on a stable color tone, pine nut brown reveals a potential enthusiasm, especially in the fusion with the cold color like gray and white, which makes it warmer and more lively and elegant.

257

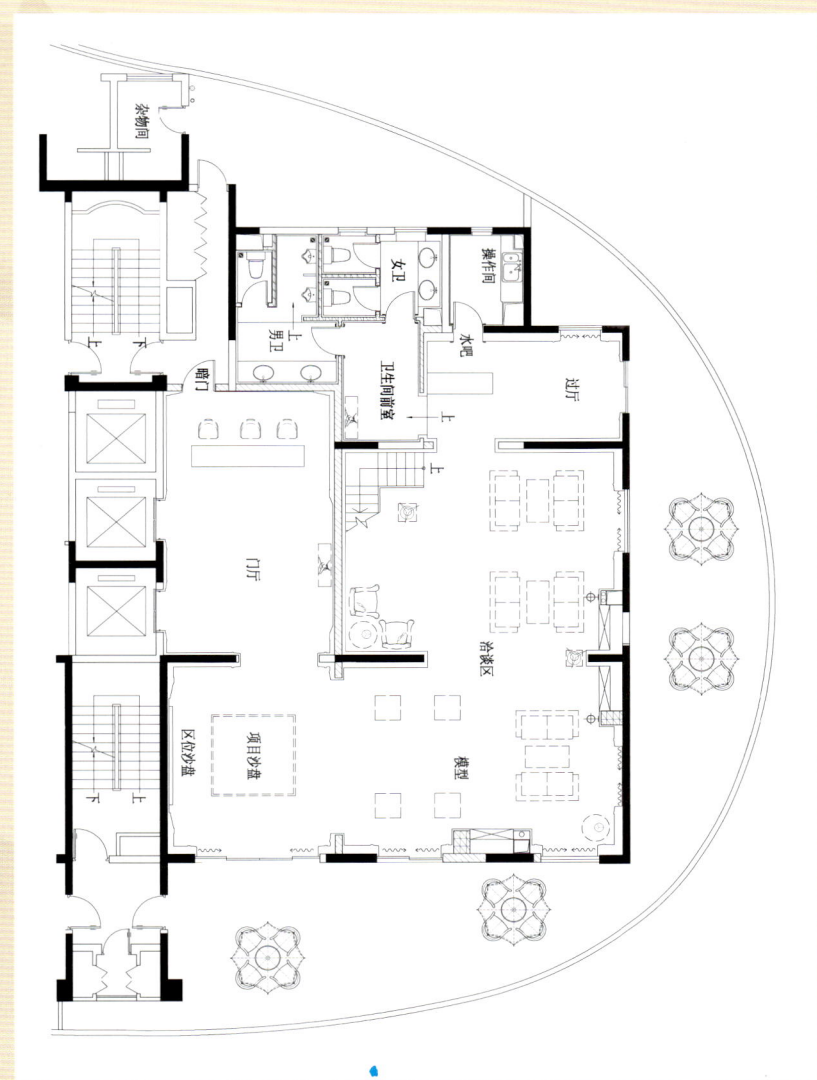

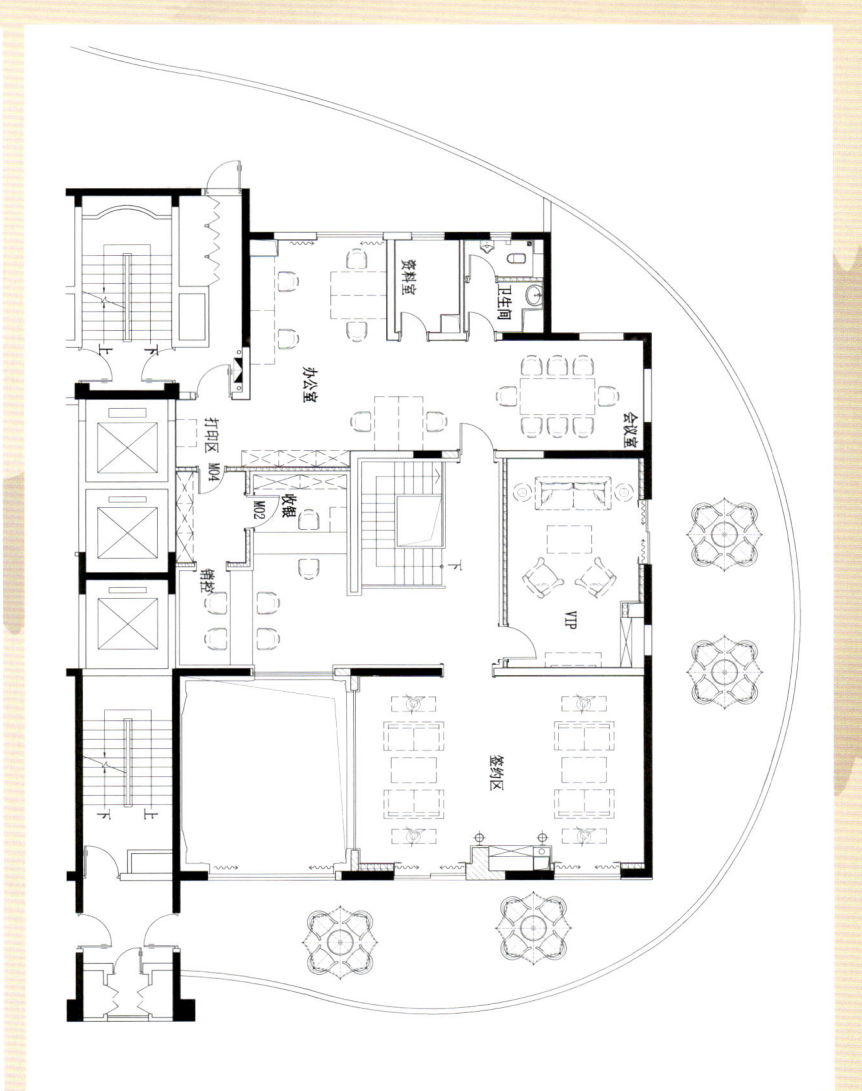

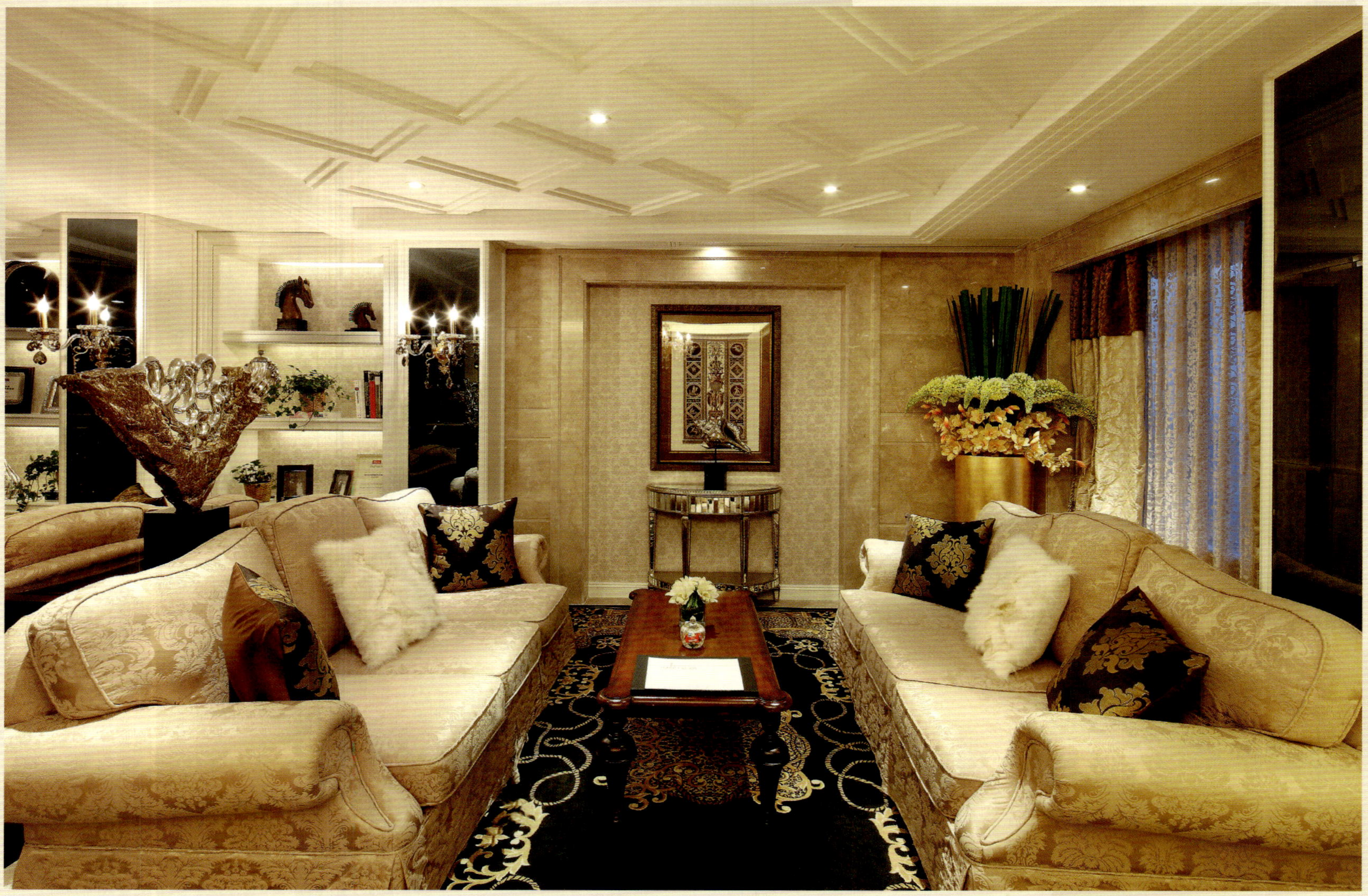

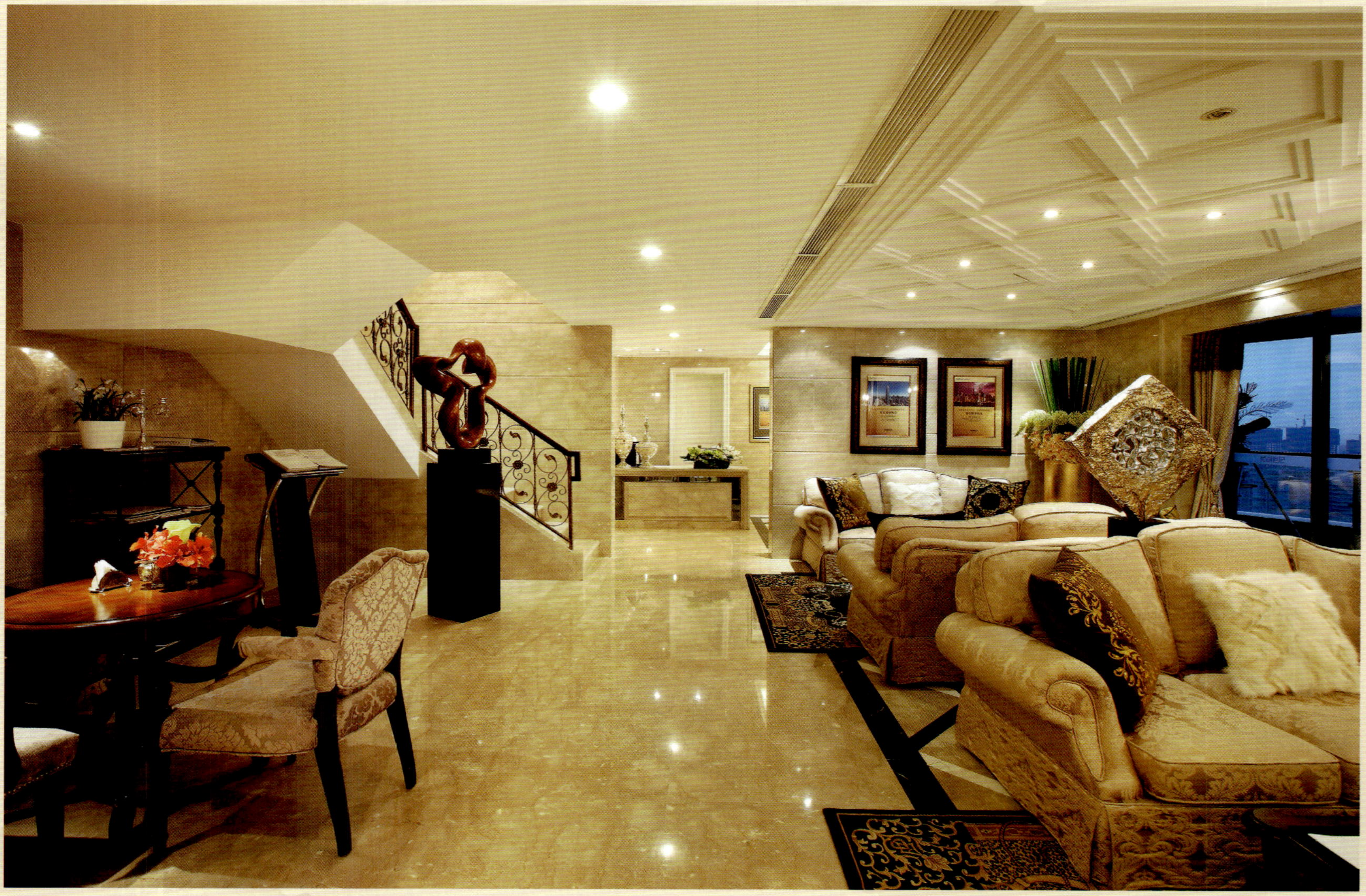

259

Zhengzhou Postal VIP Club

Design Agency: Henan blue Industrial Co., Ltd.
Client: Zhengzhou Postal Office
Location: Zhengzhou, Henan, China
Area: 1500 m²
Photography: Liu Jiafei

Fidelity, one of the five constant virtues, belongs to ethical category of Confucianism. It means people should be honest, trustworthy and veridical. "Mail", here means the post-house to delivery. "The flowing progress of virtue is more rapid than the transmission of royal orders by stages and couriers", excerpts from Mencius Gongsun Chou. How long haven't you received a letter full of scented ink? I can't help thinking of plays of folding a letter in my school days when family, teachers, classmates and friends wrote to each other. That almost becomes a distant memory. Besides folded letter paper, what I send is feeling. Now, with the vigorous development of the economy, our postal VIP club chose "letter" as the theme, and through a simple geometric "fold" interprets the new face of Zhengzhou's postal industry and social value it takes, touching off touch of people. At the entrance, an enormous inclined table-flap combines the ceiling with the ground, leaving the mark of tear, where half extends into the front desk and the other half is made into the surface of the envelope, on which eight points of stamp stick. From here space expands into two sides, one side is a open fitness area, and the other side is the VIP channel. White table-flap corridor is cast shadows of a series of Longman grottoes stamp patterns by projection lamp. In the rounded hall, the postal mark of soaring to great heights is reflected in the still water of the lotus pond, and occasionally ripples with little fish swimming leisurely. Light refracts to the black mirror at the top surface, and white circular wall surrounds it and so on.

We create the human-centered atmosphere of pace, resolve the harmony of man, space and nature, and aim at that you have different view of each step and the scene brings back memories. The postal strives to touch clients and establish a relationship of more mutual trust, stability and cooperation with them, through the space and the enterprise culture connotation it shows. And the design also shows the designers' social responsibility.

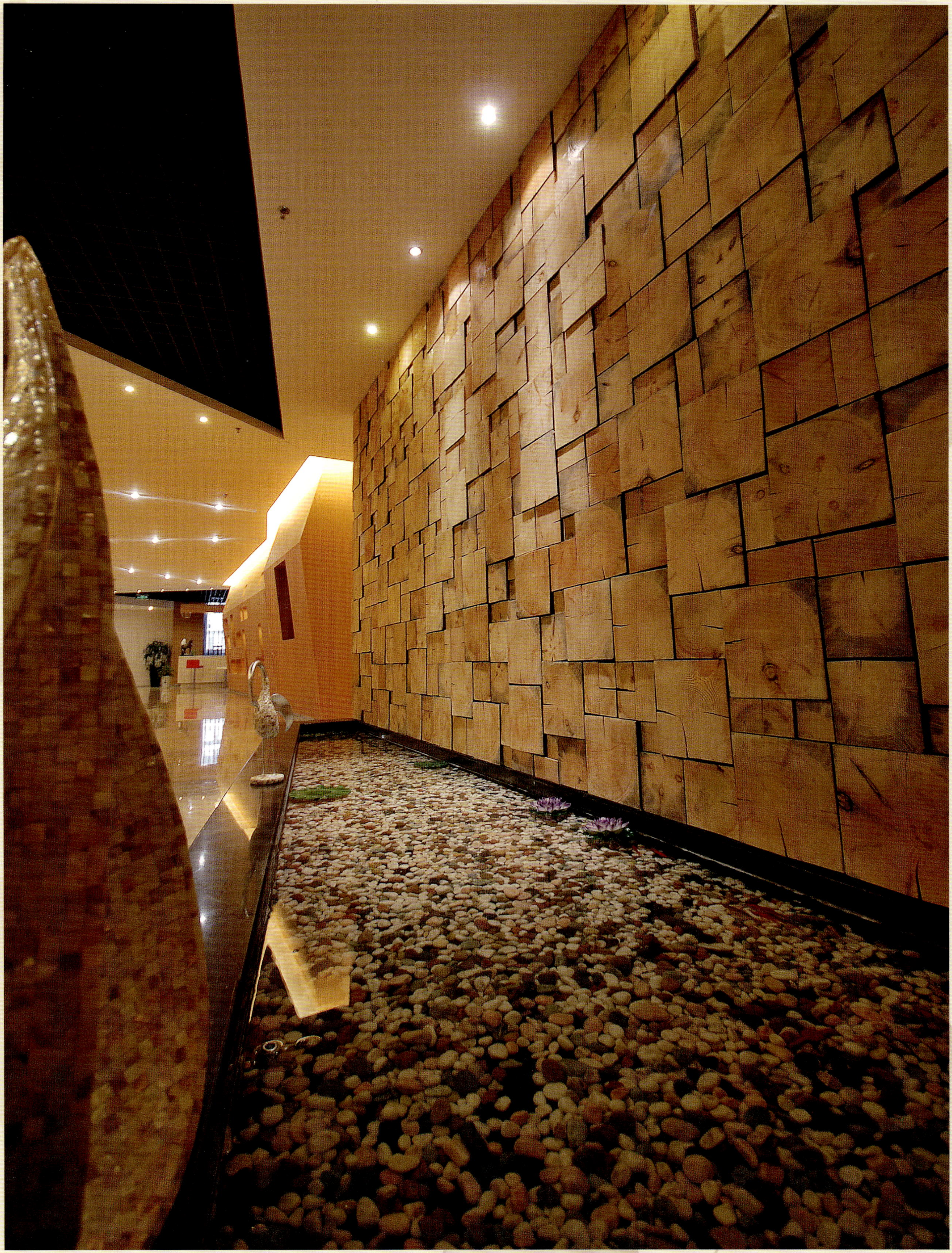

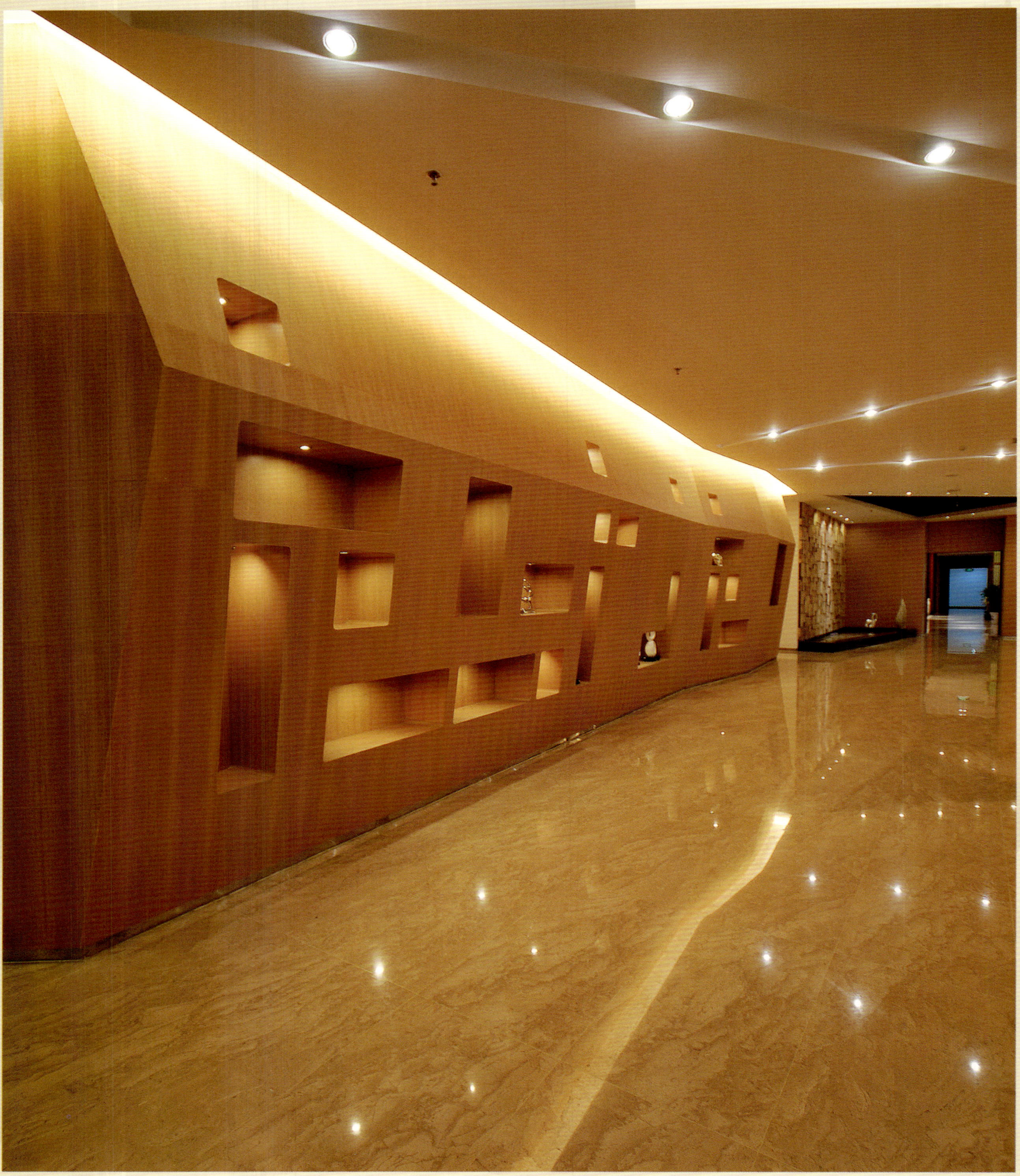

263

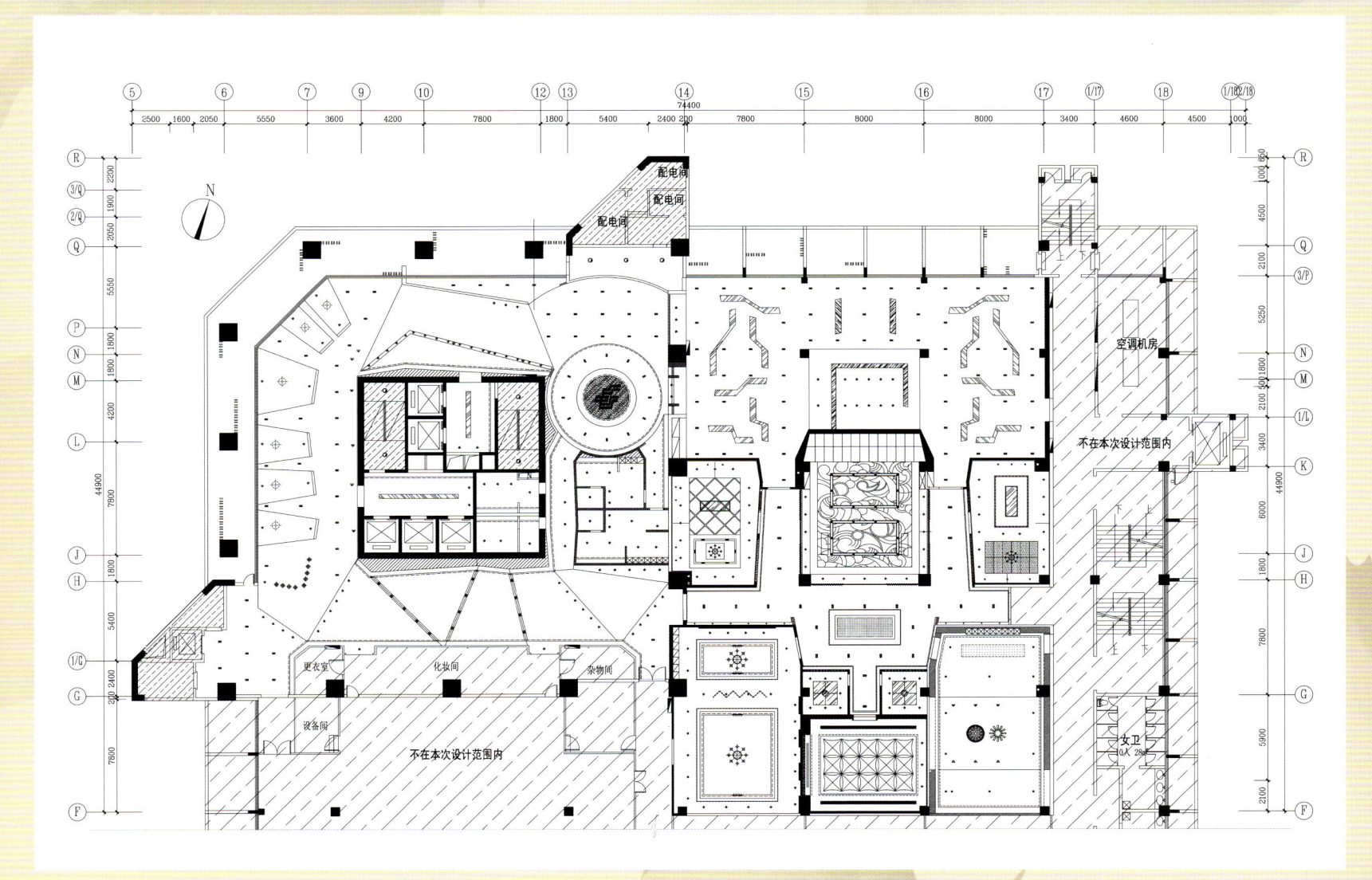

264

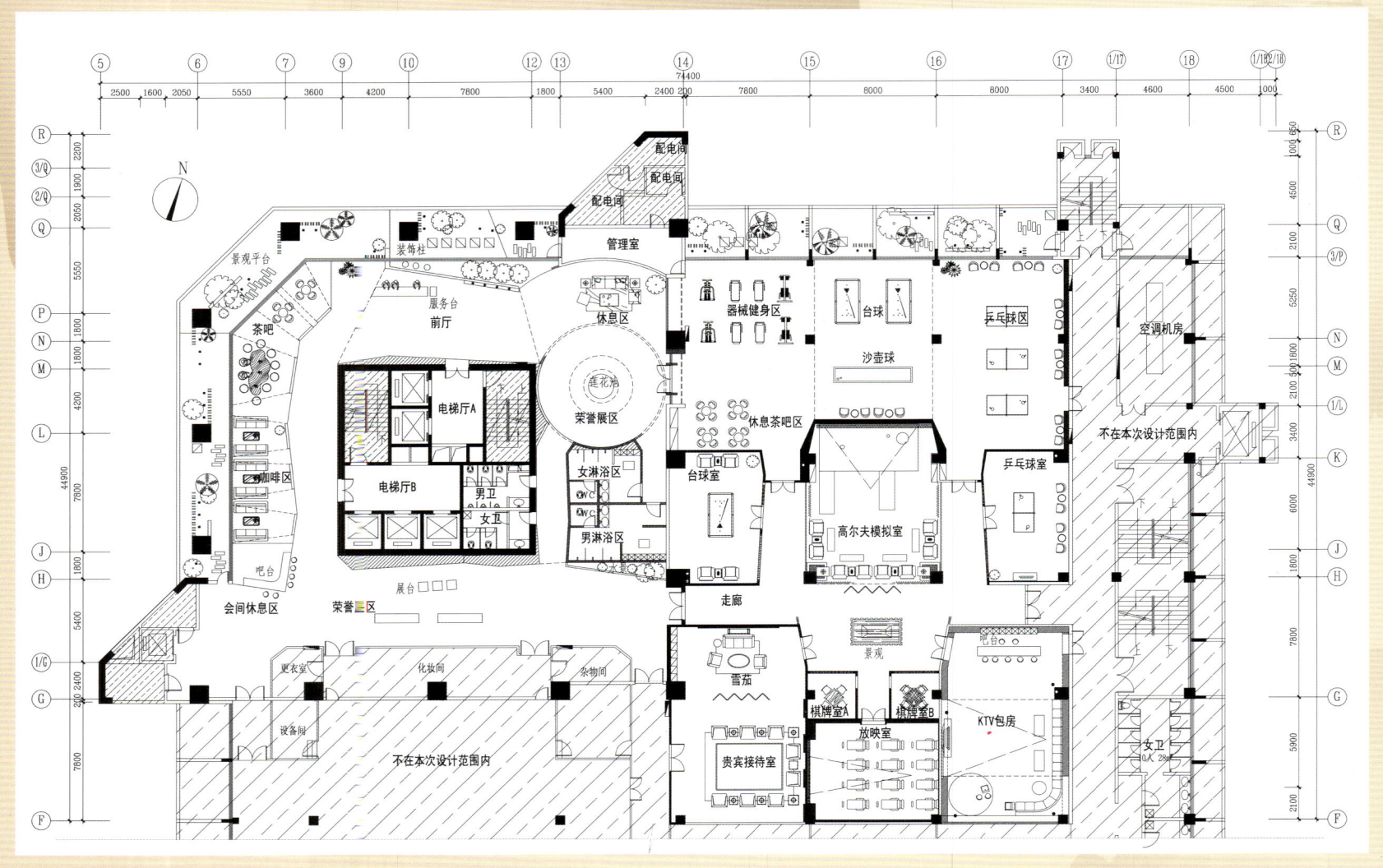

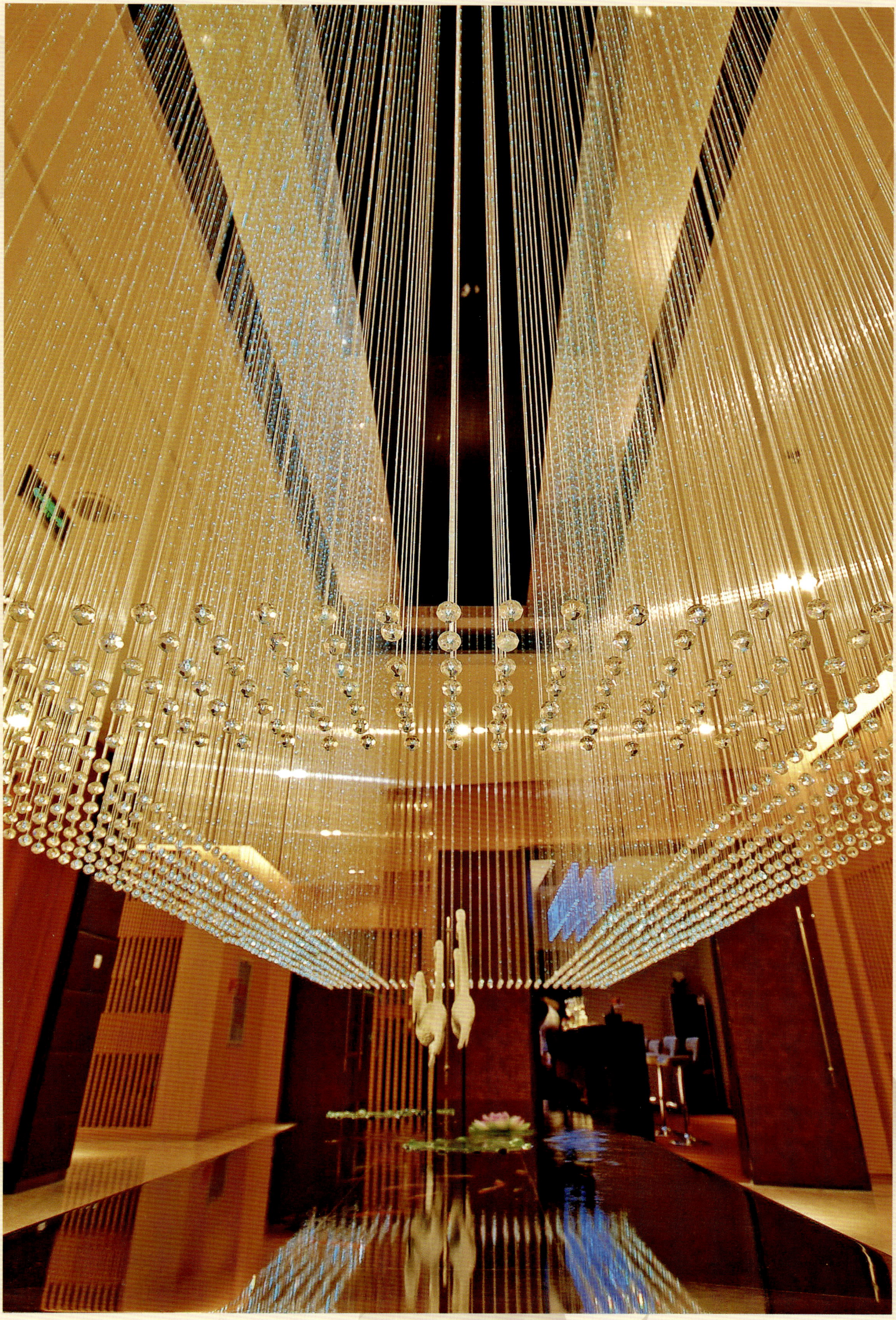

Green Park Club

Design Agency: Sunlay Design
Design Director: Zhang Hua
Designer Team: Fan Li
Location: Beijing, China
Area: 2400 m²
Owner: Fulllink Real Estate
Photographer: Shu He Studio

The club is located on the west bank of the Wenyu River, which twists from long distance and becomes wider here; the club faces the small island in the river, which is covered with dense forest. At the first sight of the place, I was moved deeply by its green. This site decides that the architecture will be the independent standing object, and also can integrate perfectly into the site and reflect its artistic conception.

In the site with strong accommodation, considering that the people the club serves are the group of a variety of cultural backgrounds, the architecture is positioned as collision and blend: the collision of multicultural culture and style; blend cross time and space. It is mild and natural. It tells an ancient and modern story, in which two kinds of aesthetic world encounter.

As the club is located in the slope, combining with the terrain, we design that people enter into the first floor from the west entrance on the slope, and the sun restaurant in the east of the ground floor is located on the bank of the river. The main body of building consists of the two pieces, which looks like isosceles trapezium from the top. Architectural design scheme considers 'axis and symmetry', which are emphasized by classical architectural language; 'fluxion and consistency', which are sought by modern architectural language. Red brick walls and transparent glazing are employed to create coagulated building mass and flowing spaces.

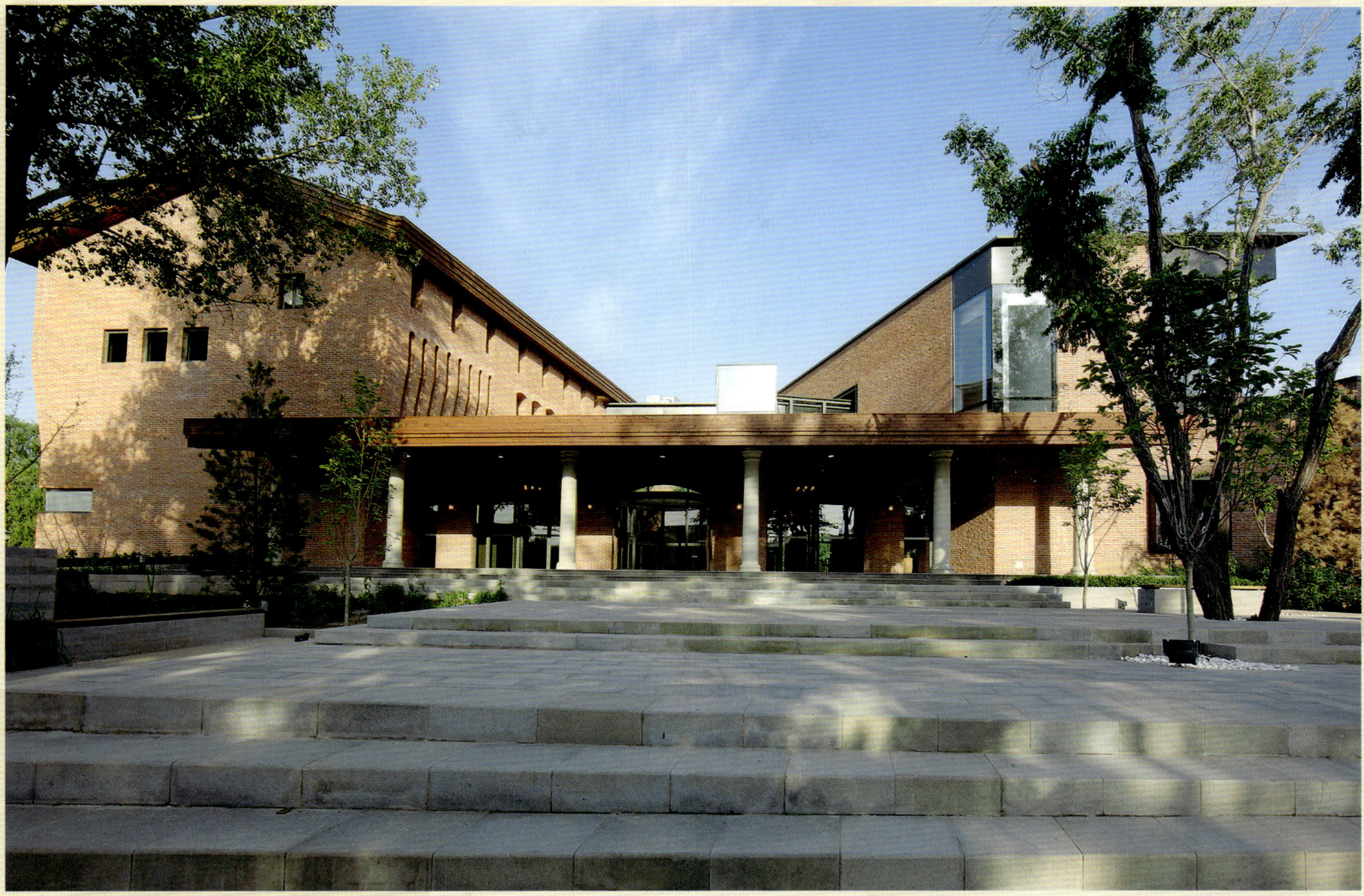

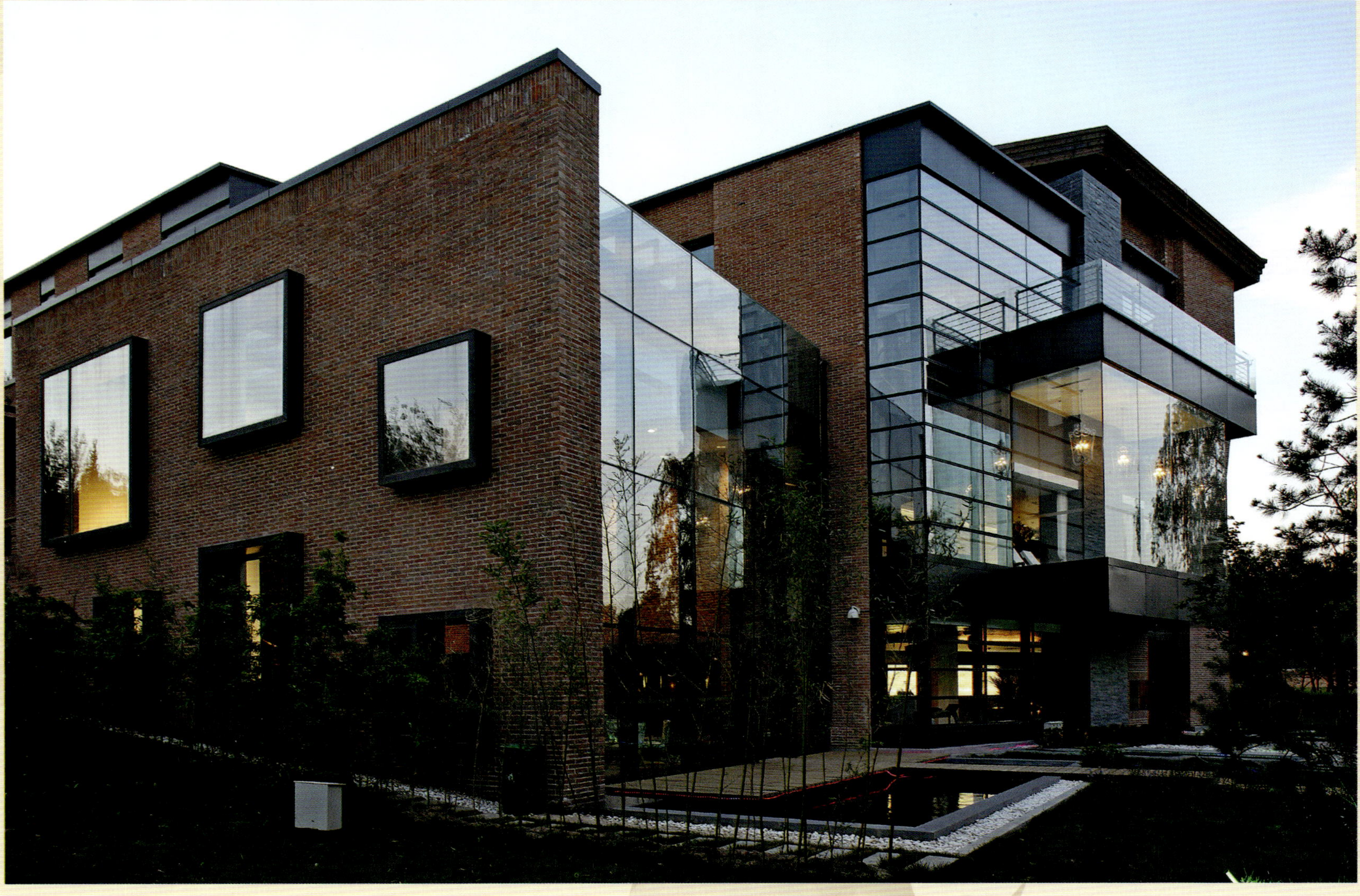

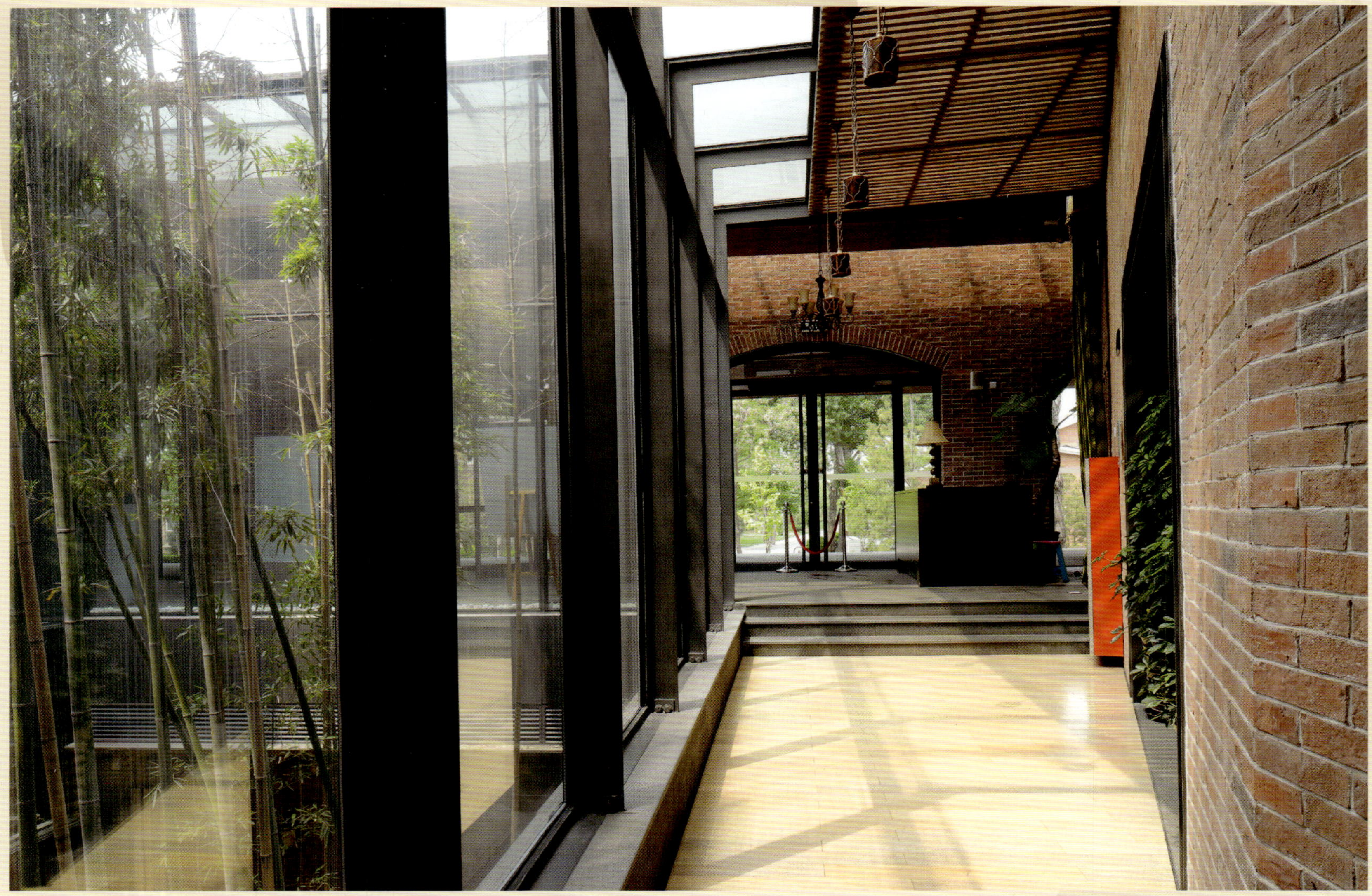

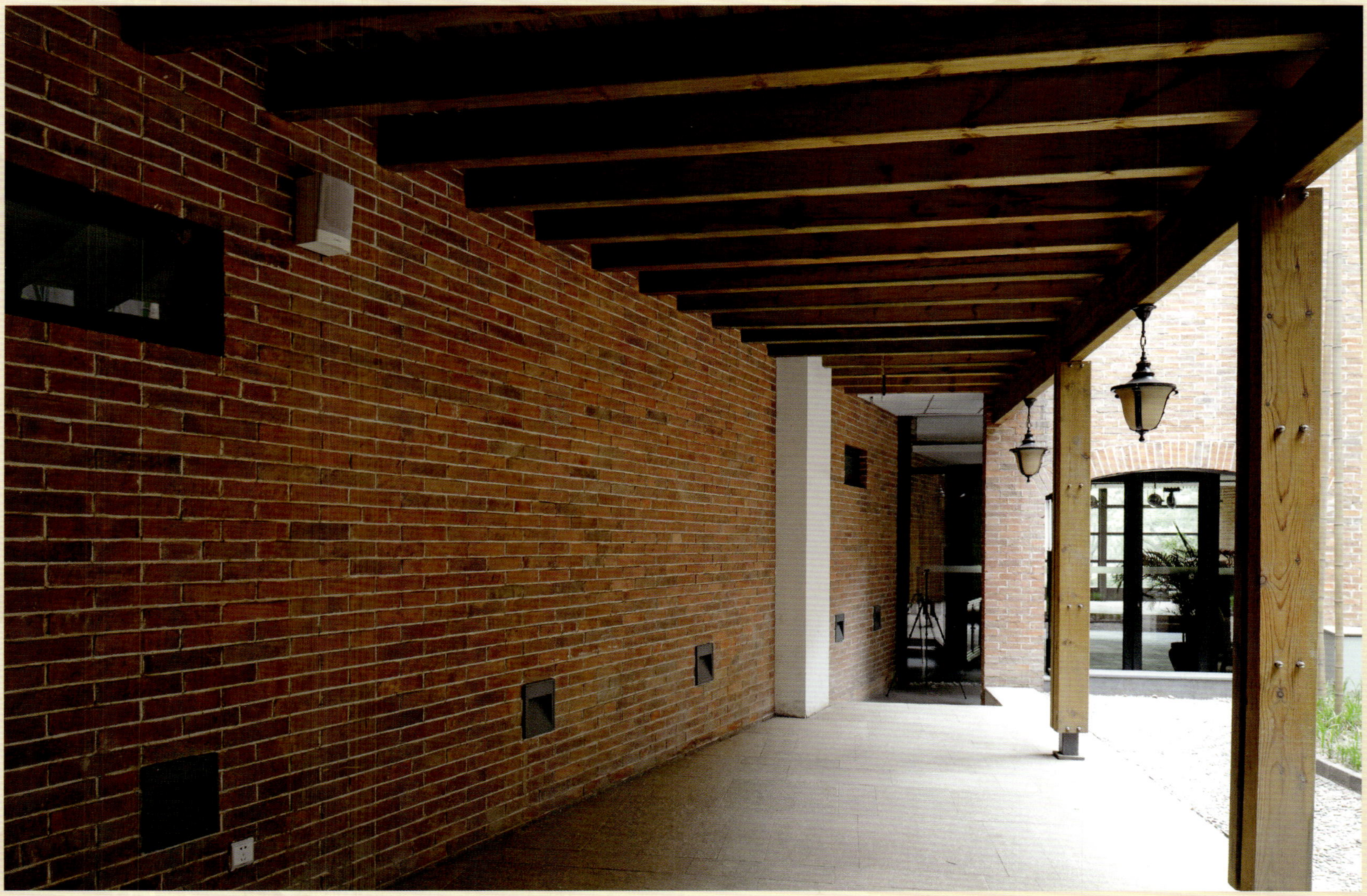

Inside courtyard with comfortable scale are the continuation of greening, water scene and original natural landscape. The rays of sunlight through the windows and the scenes both inside and outside the room become one whole space. First floor of the entrance hall, recreation room, gym, dressing room, ground floor of bars, sun restaurants, and second floor of swimming pools, reading room, roof garden, provide people diverse and different space feeling. It will be great fun walking or staying in the club.

The gap between buildings creates the inner courtyard at the center of the club, which provides attractive landscape for the entrance hall. Then we bring light into the courtyard, and the whole building looks richer and deeper.

Pleasant courtyard of suitable scale constitutes the center of the club. It, together with indoor botanical garden of the sunshine restaurant in the ground floor, the open-air coffee extending outward, artificial greening landscape surrounding the club, river system and original natural landscape, makes green landscape intersperse in the architecture.

270

271

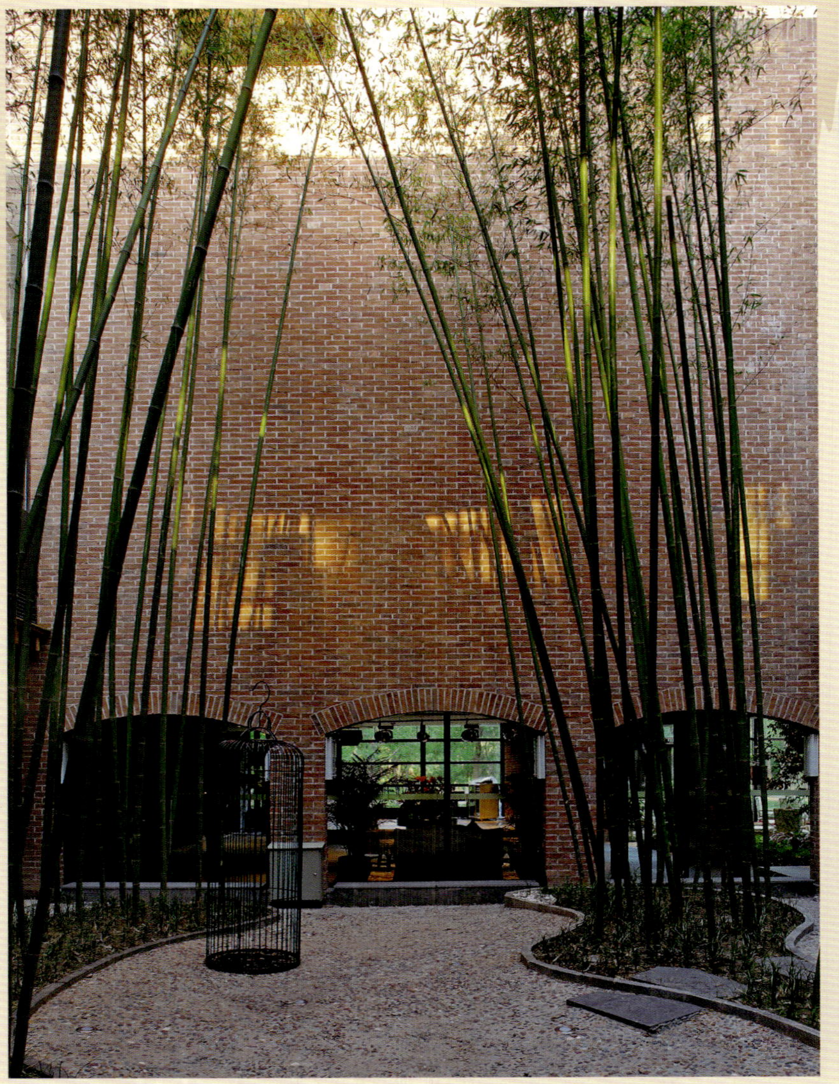

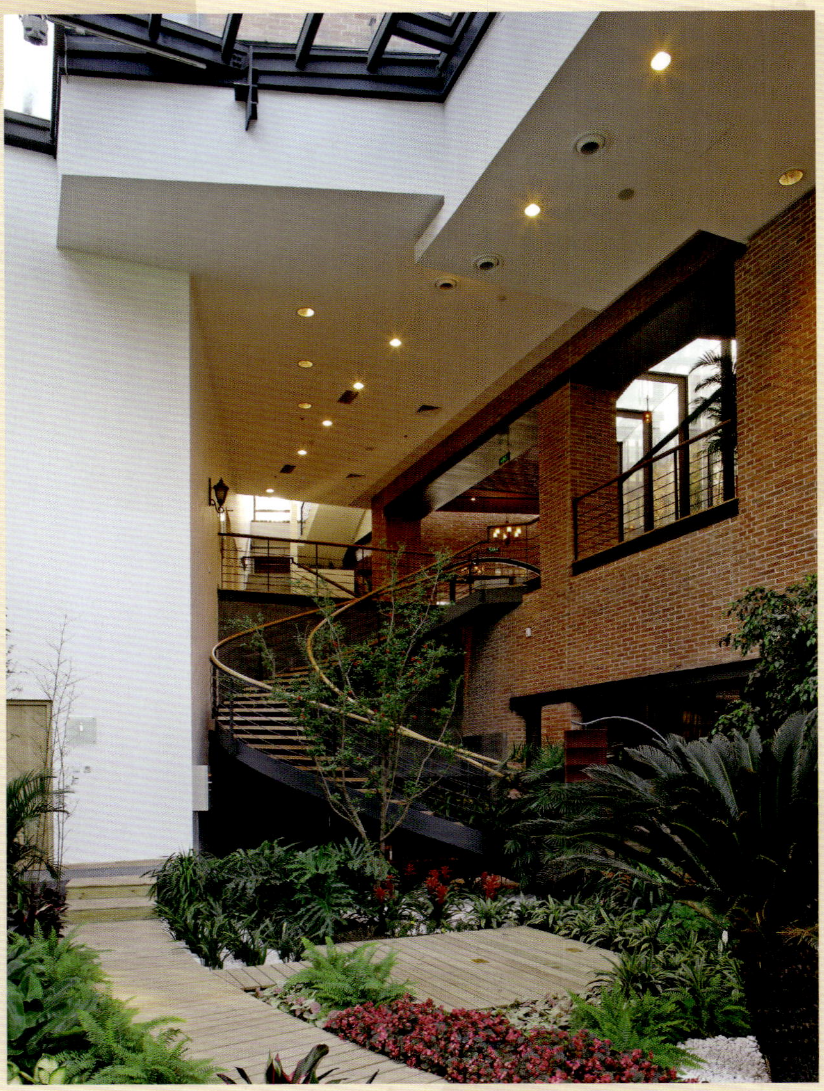

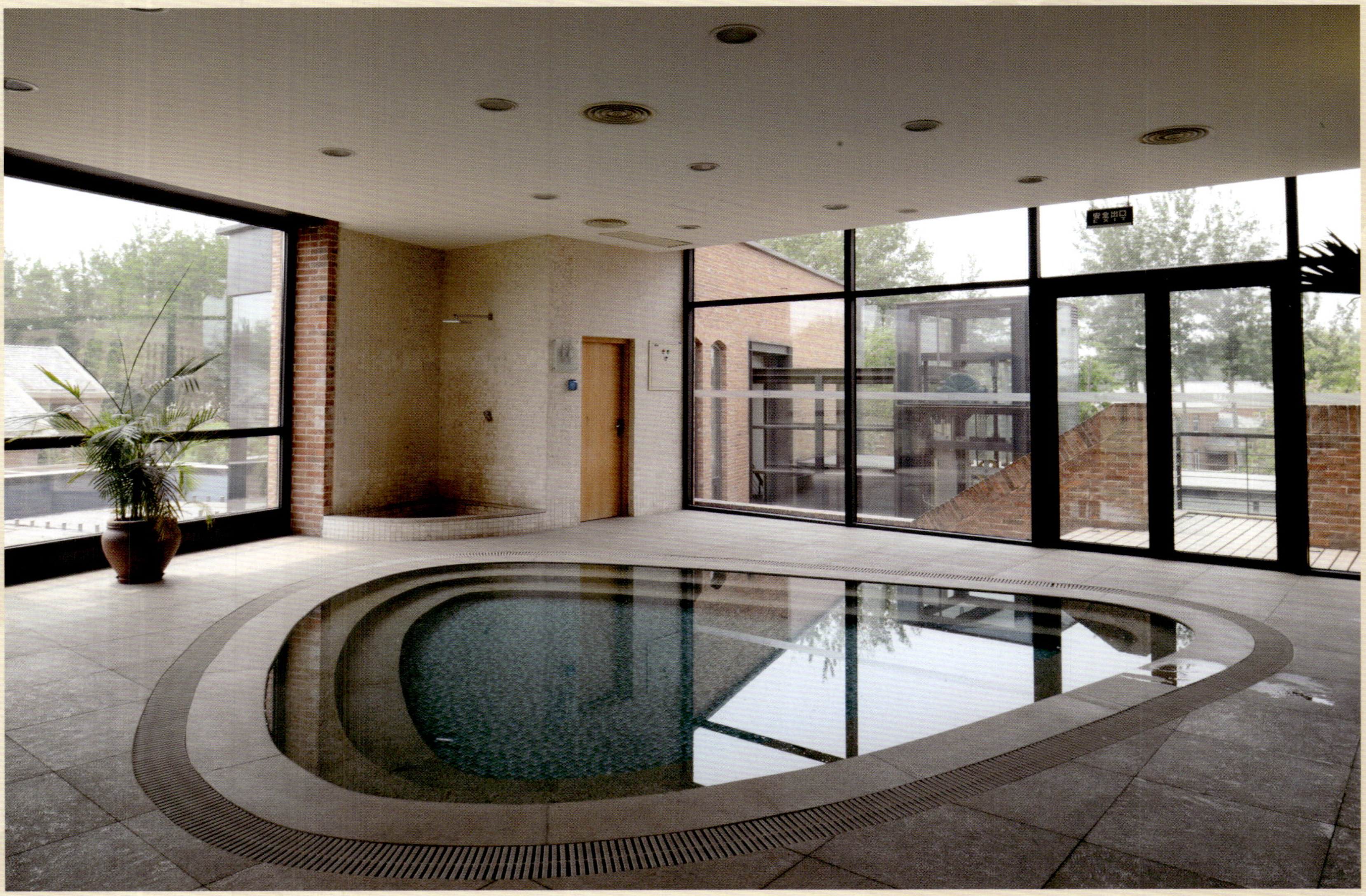

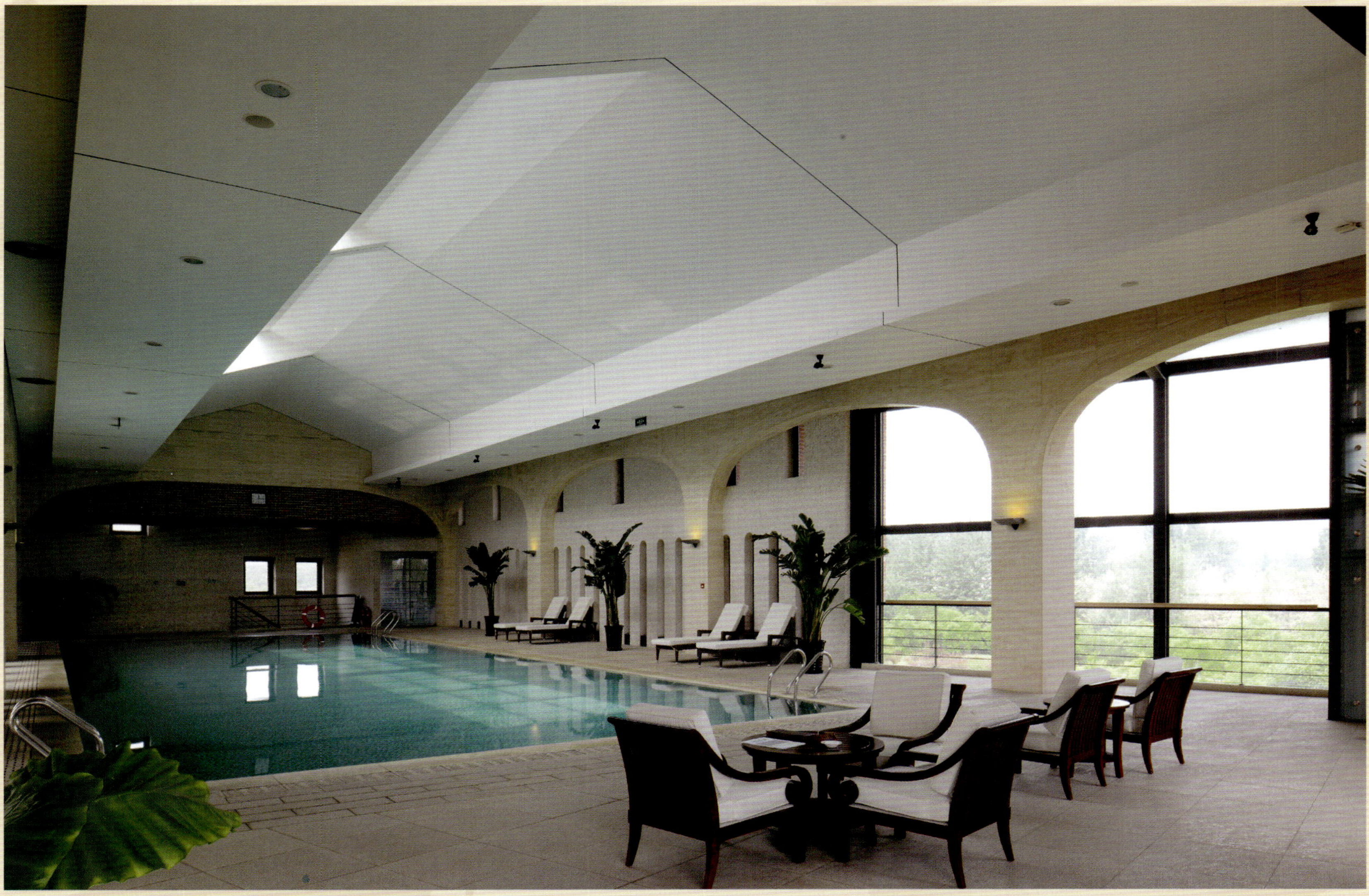

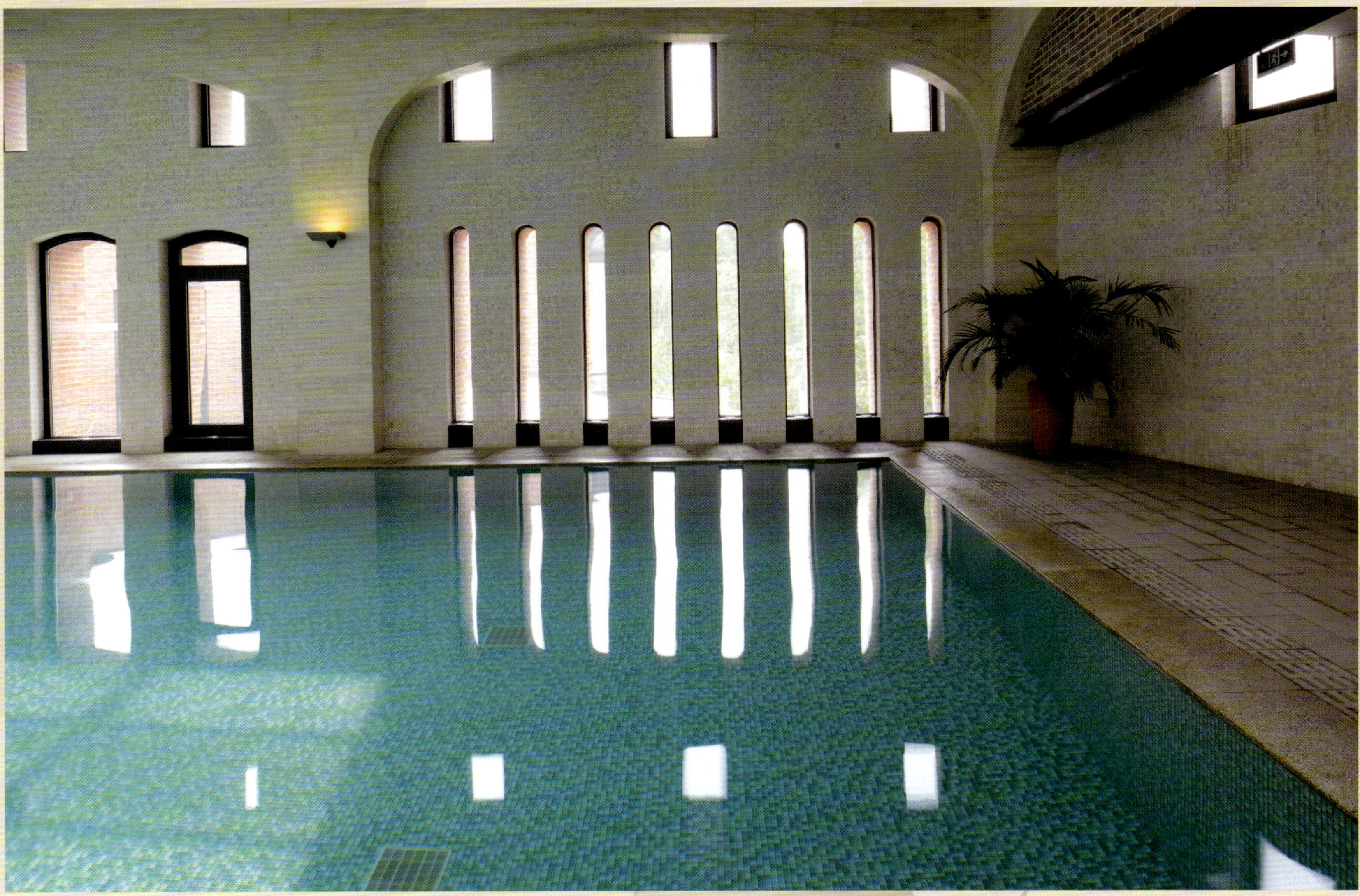

Harbin Bincai Group Sales Center

Design Agency: Beijing Fashion Impression Decoration Co., Ltd.

Leisure and Taste

Settled dust rubbing flower fragrance

Let the worn-out travelers

Feel the fragrance of joy

Let the lonely passengers

Feel the aroma of warm

Let the tired returnees

Feel the aromatic of hope

Elegant and decent color combination is suitable for bright open space, which gives people a kind of quiet and relaxed feeling. In the meantime, it shows a low-key gorgeous sense as well. There are fine beauties everywhere without any exaggeration.

275

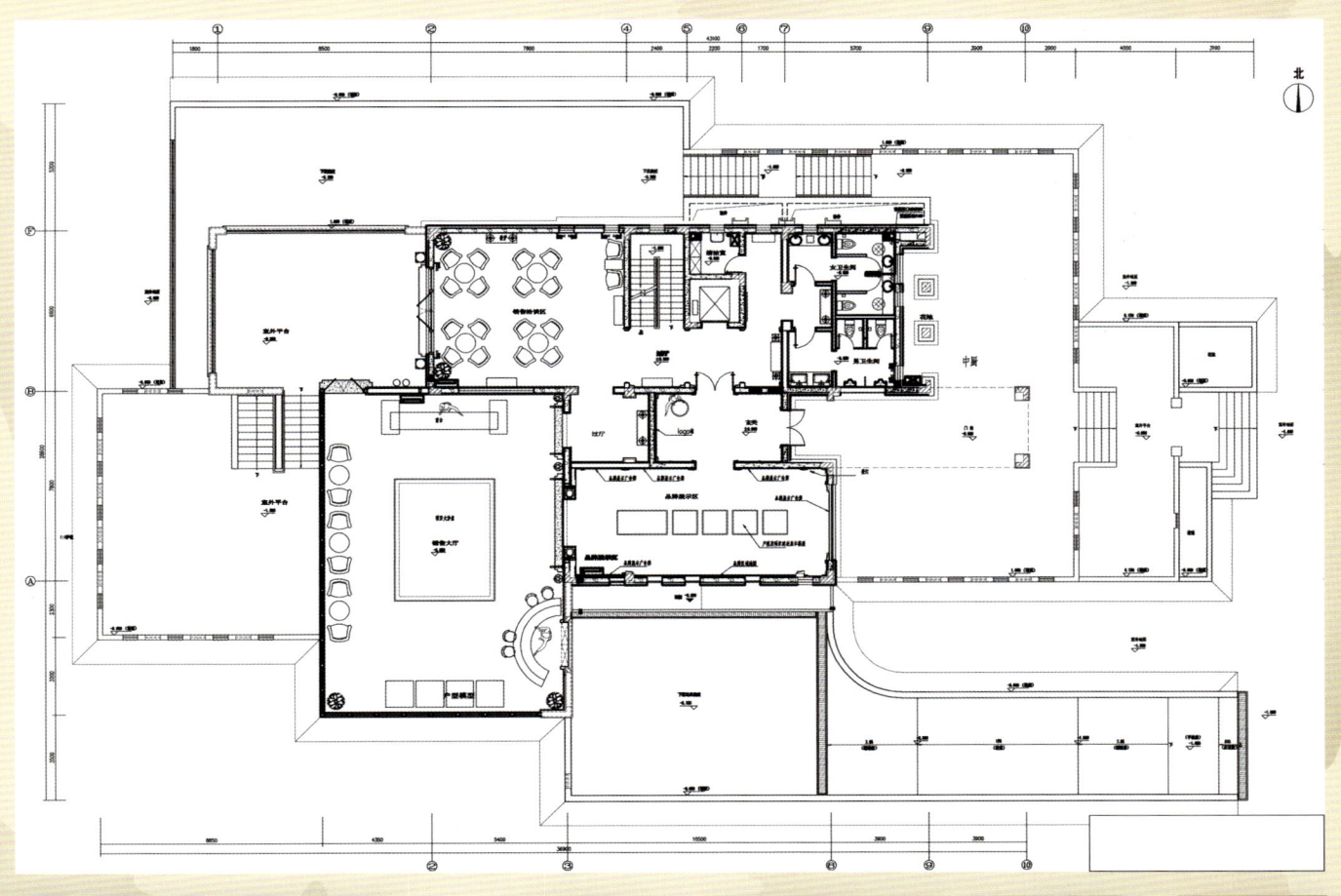

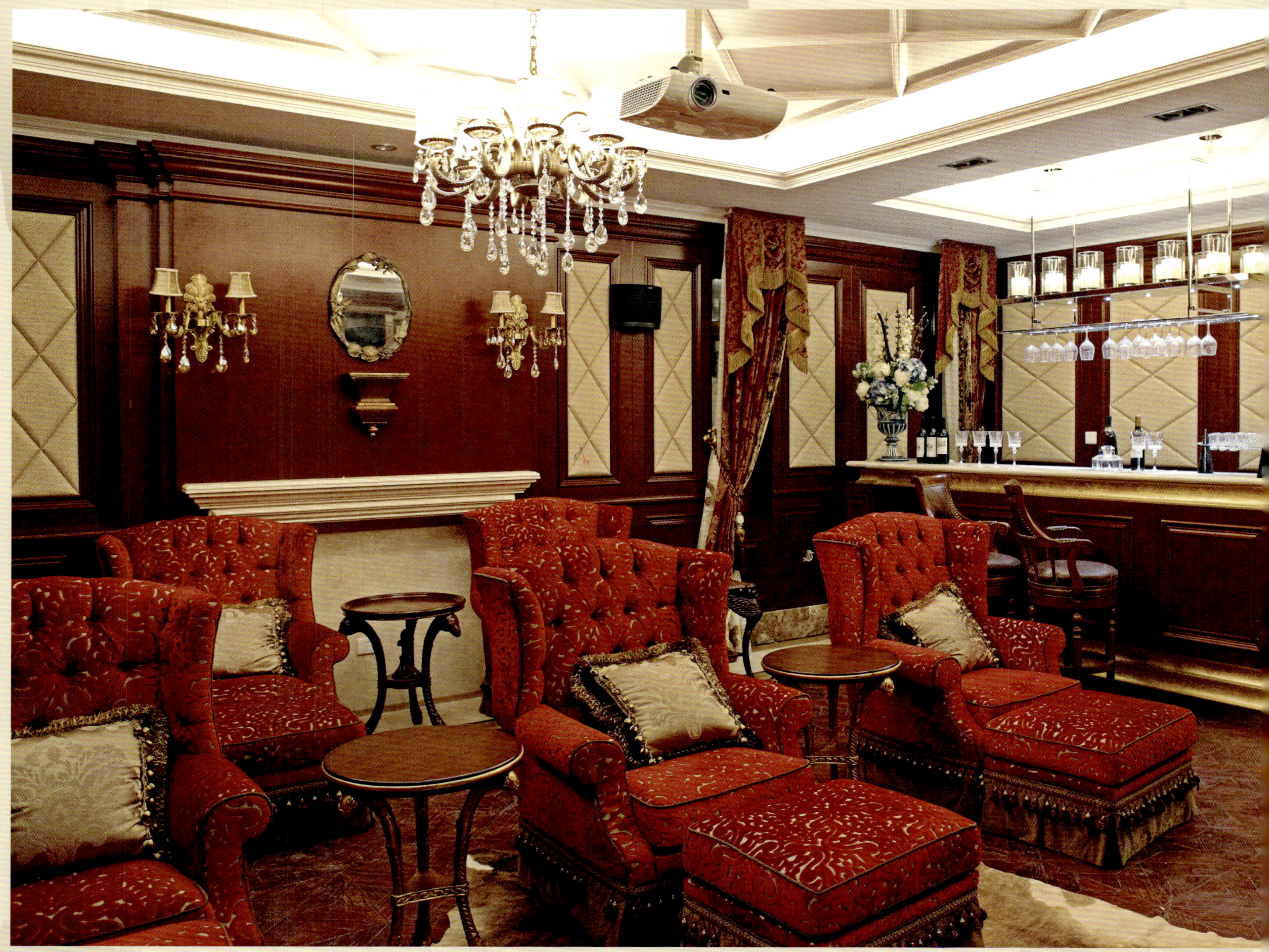

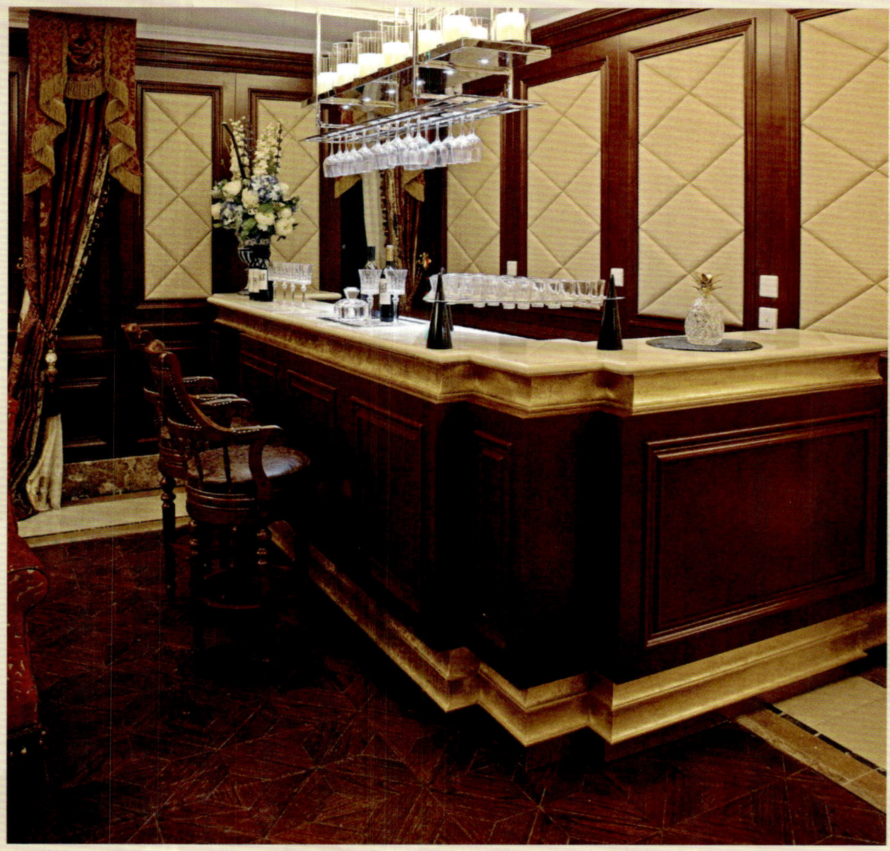

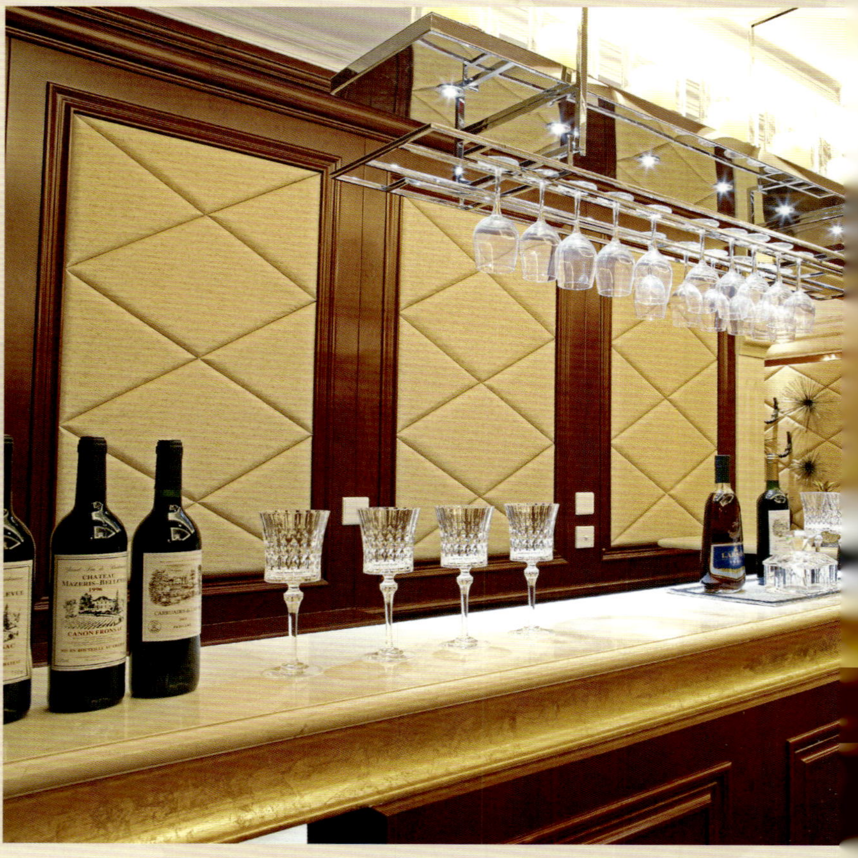

277

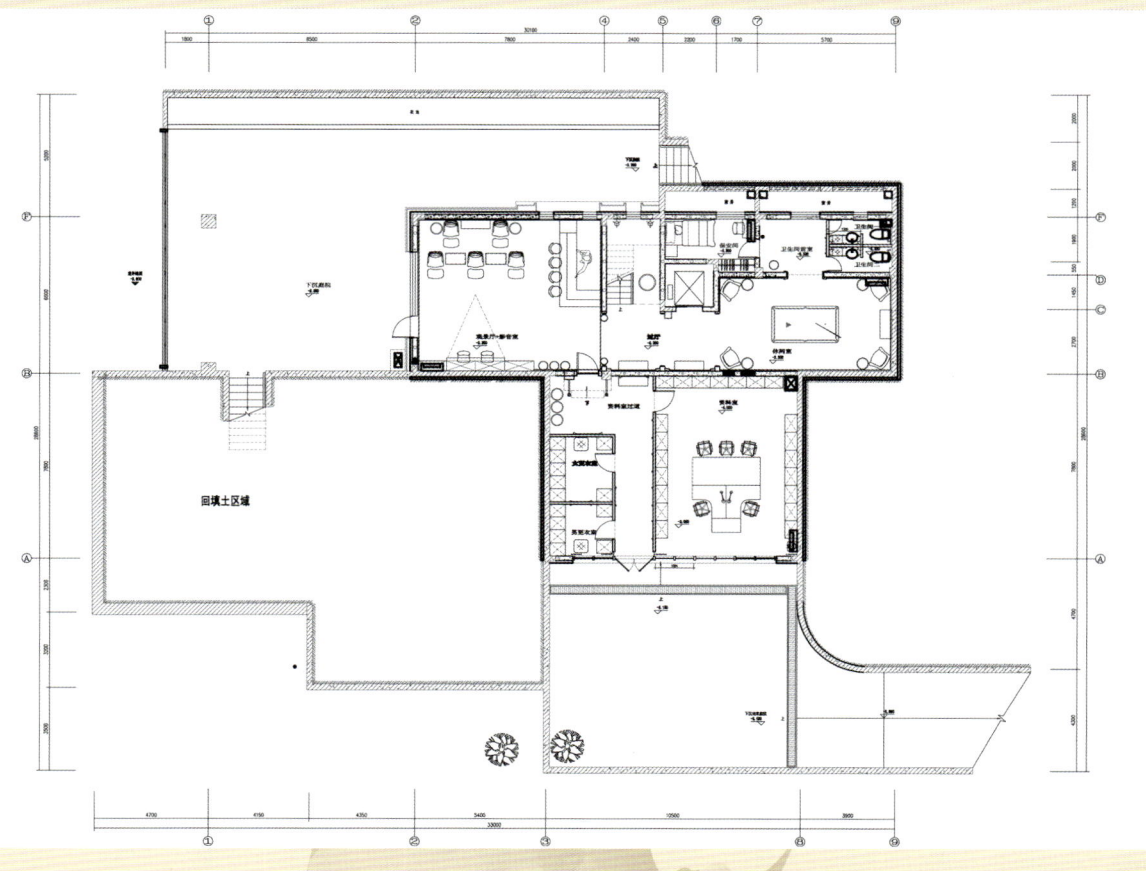

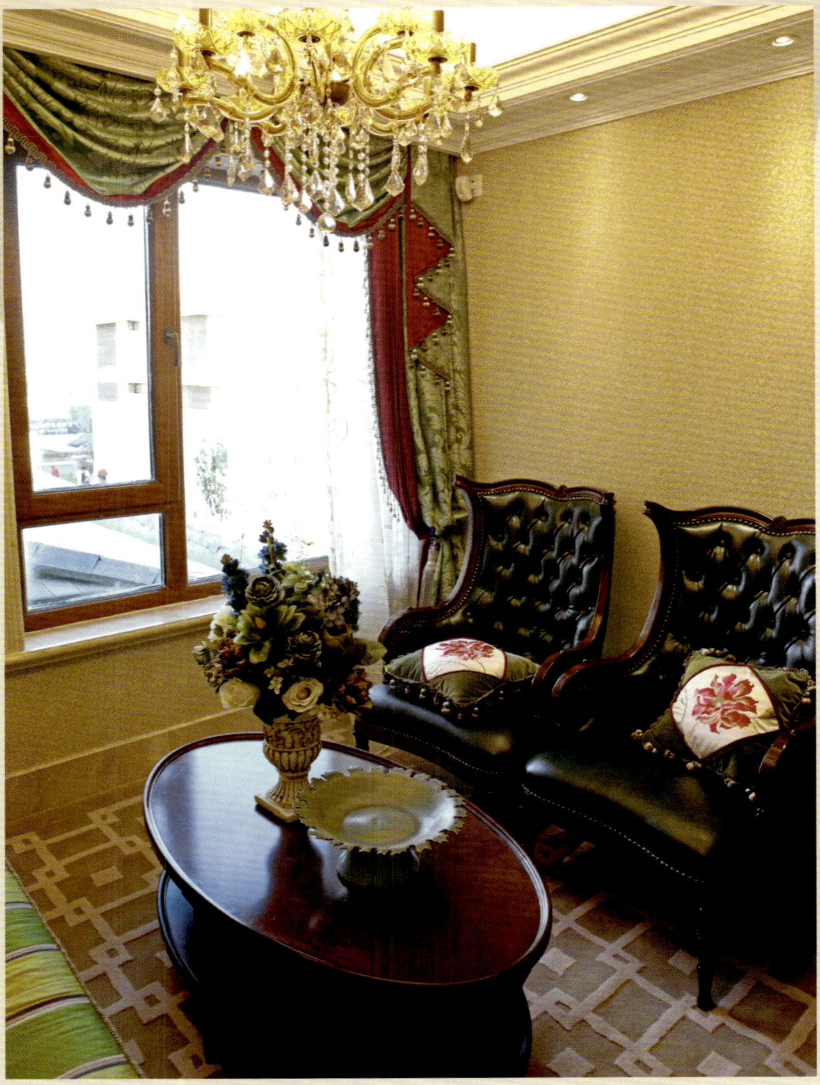
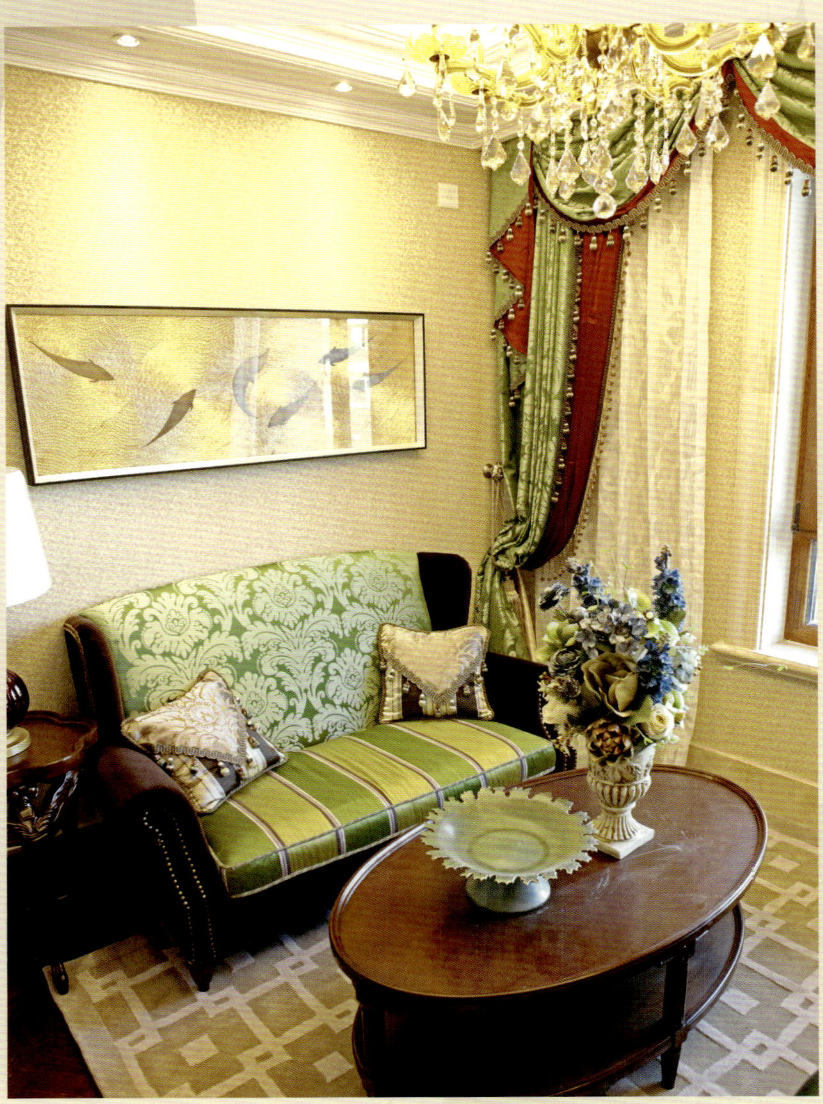
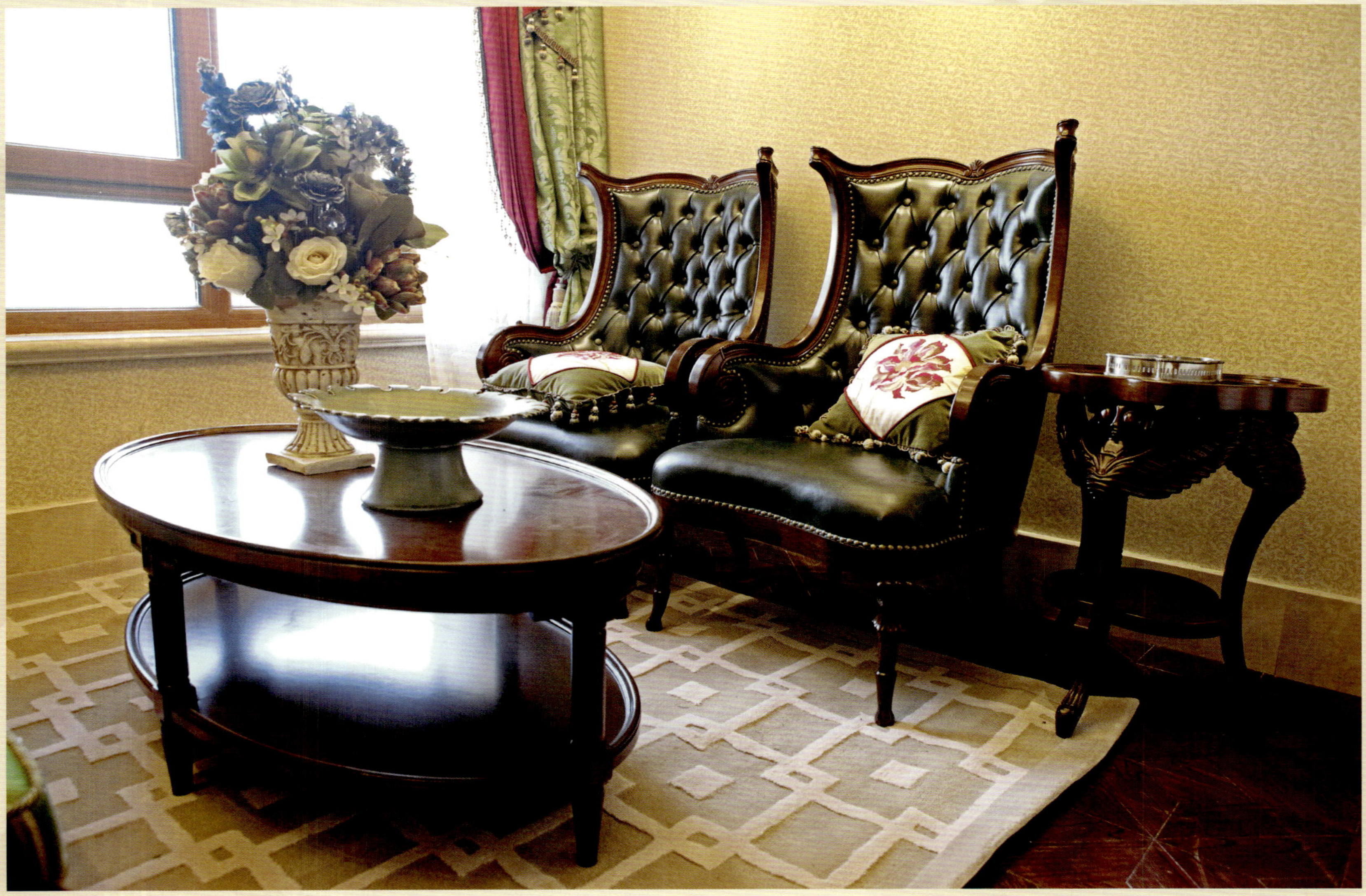

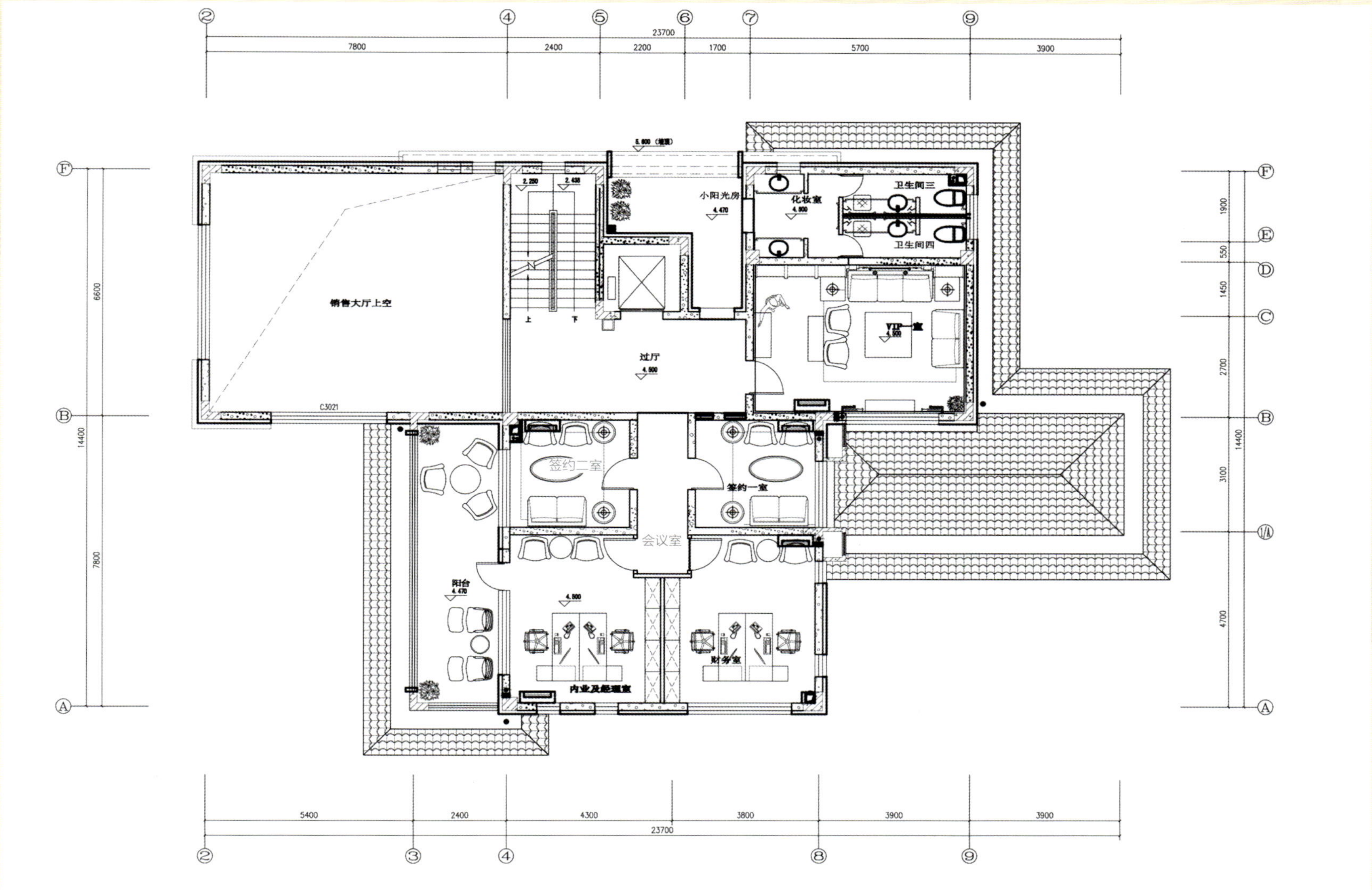

23700
7800
2400
2200
1700
5700
3900
小阳光房
化妆室
卫生间三
卫生间四
销售大厅上空
VIP室
过厅
签约二室
签约一室
会议室
阳台
内业及经理室
财务室
5400
2400
4300
3800
3900
3900
23700

280

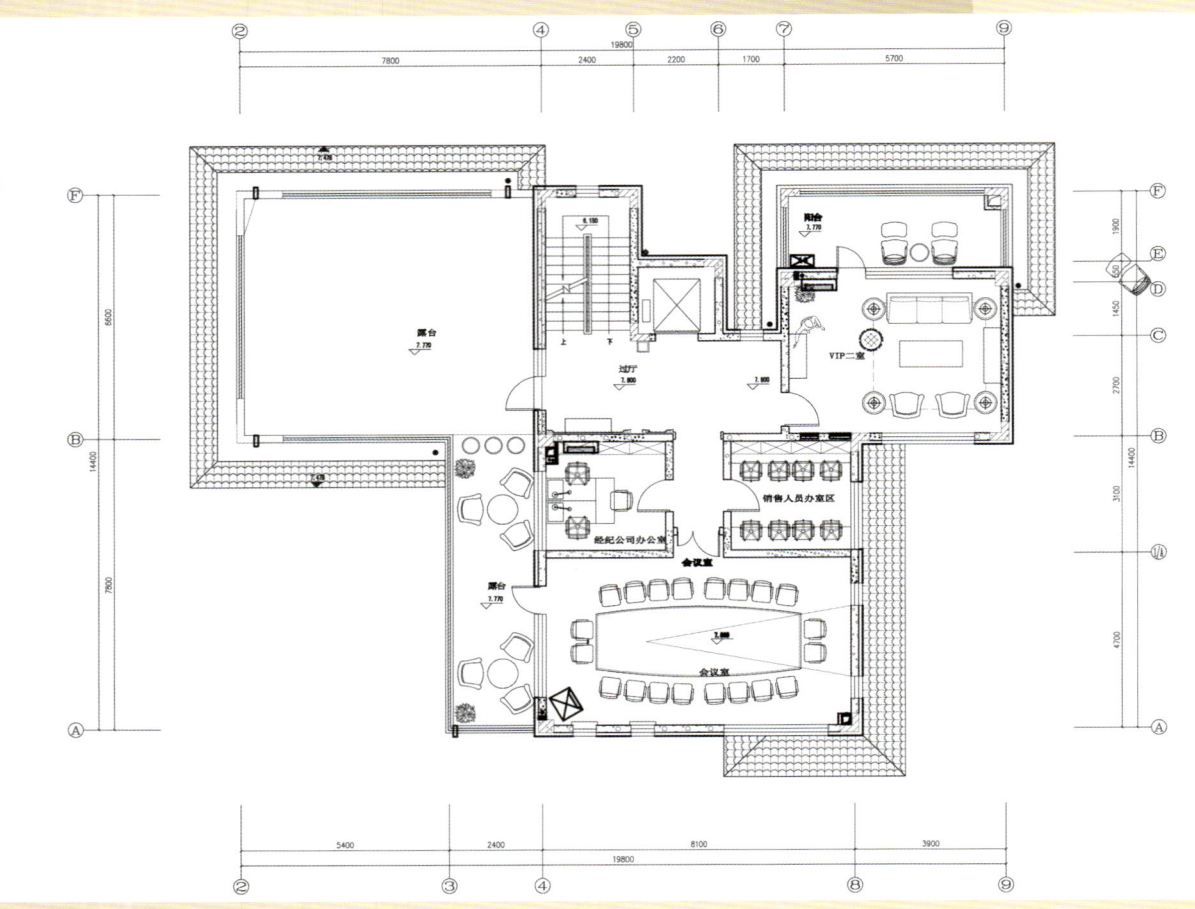

281

282

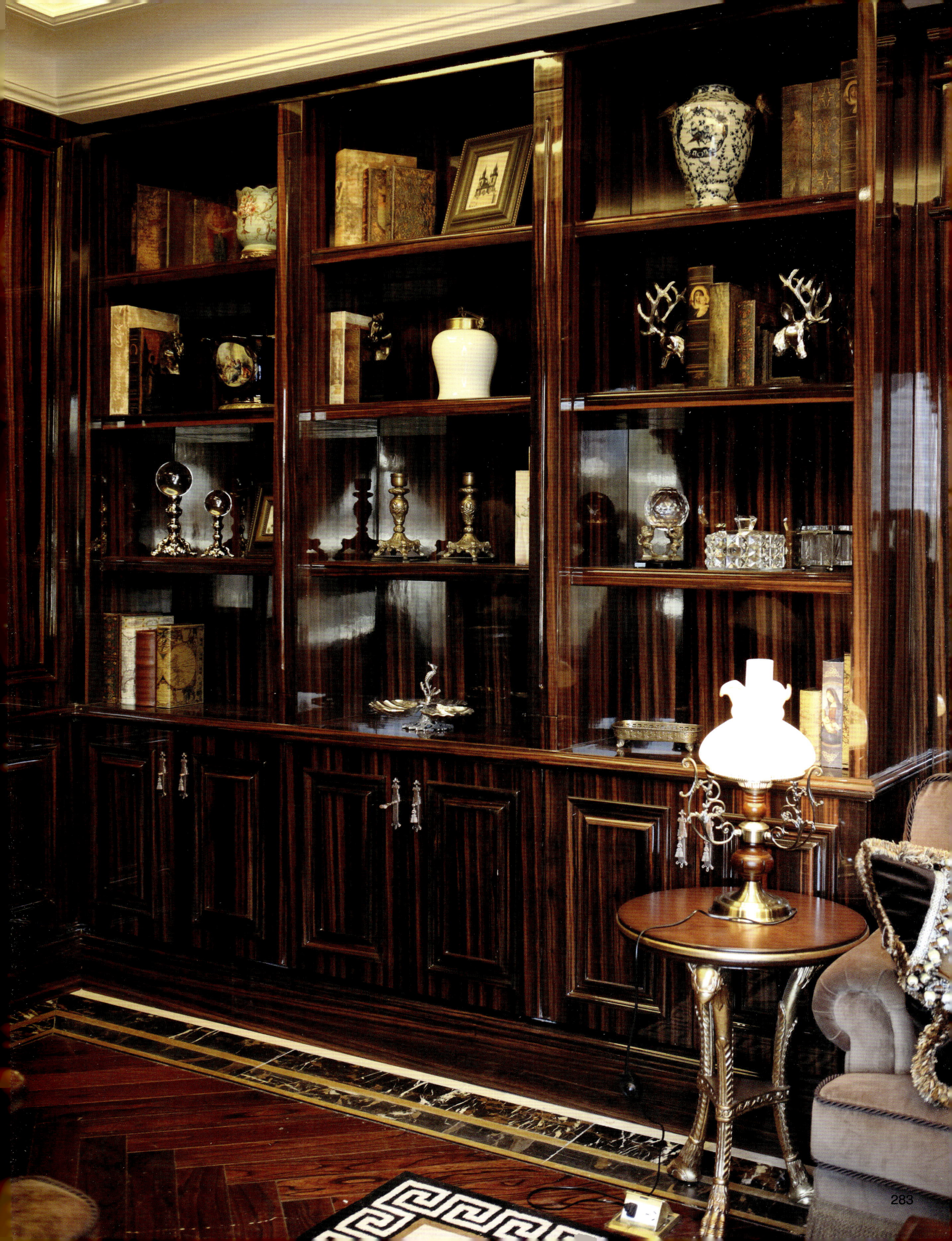

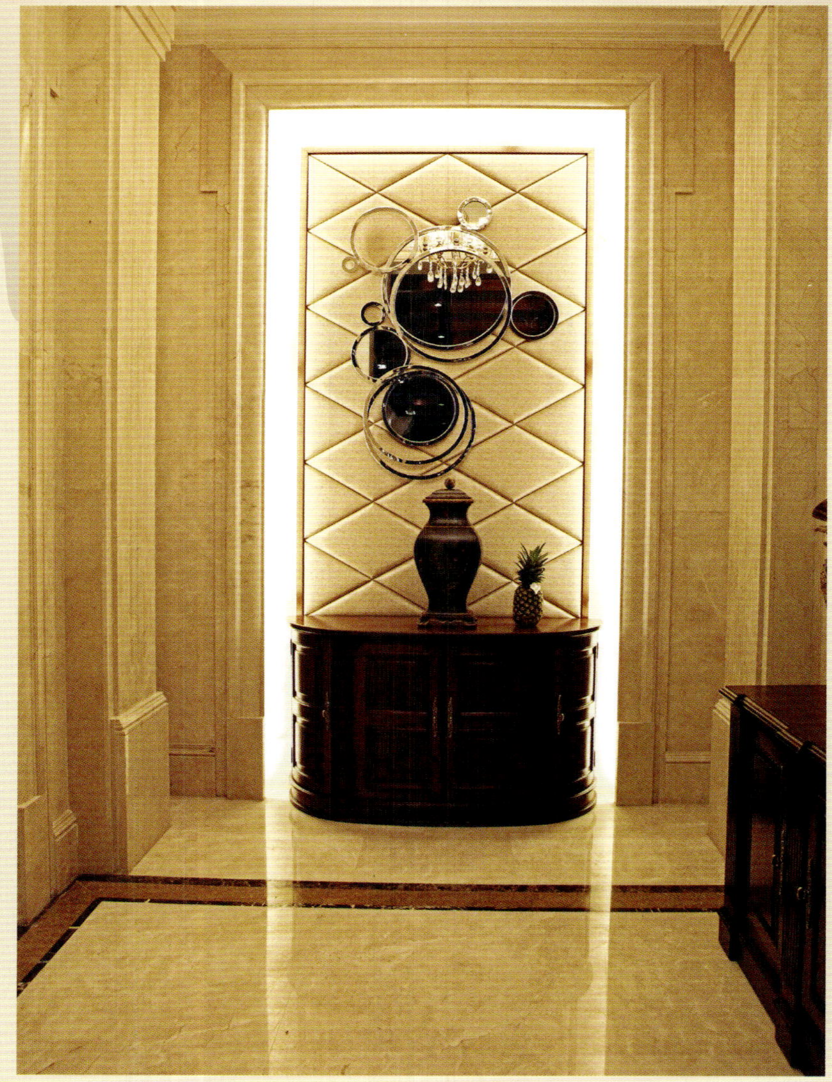
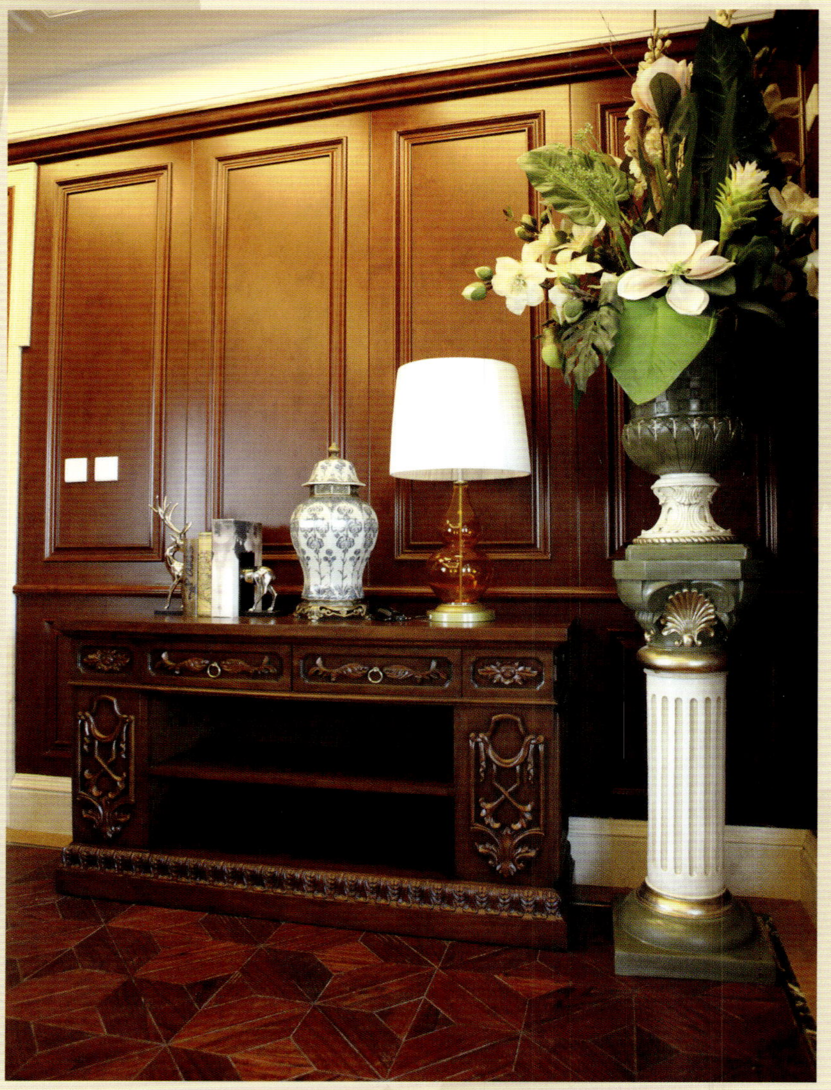
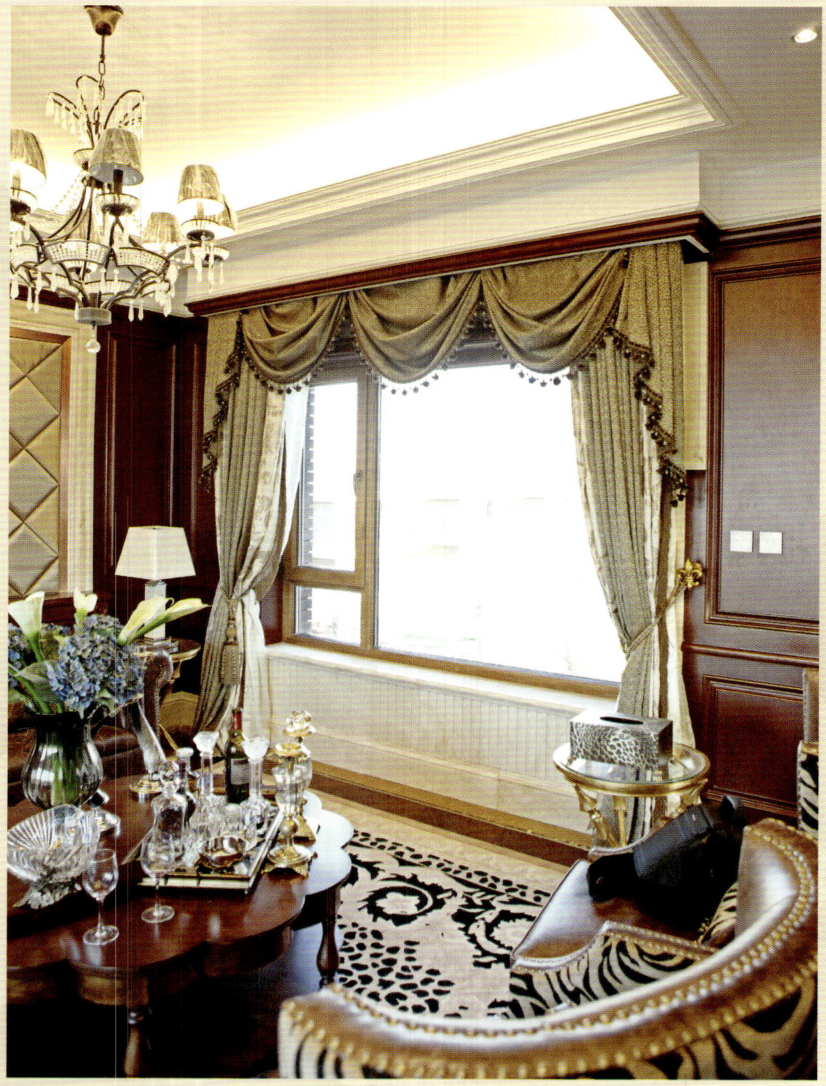
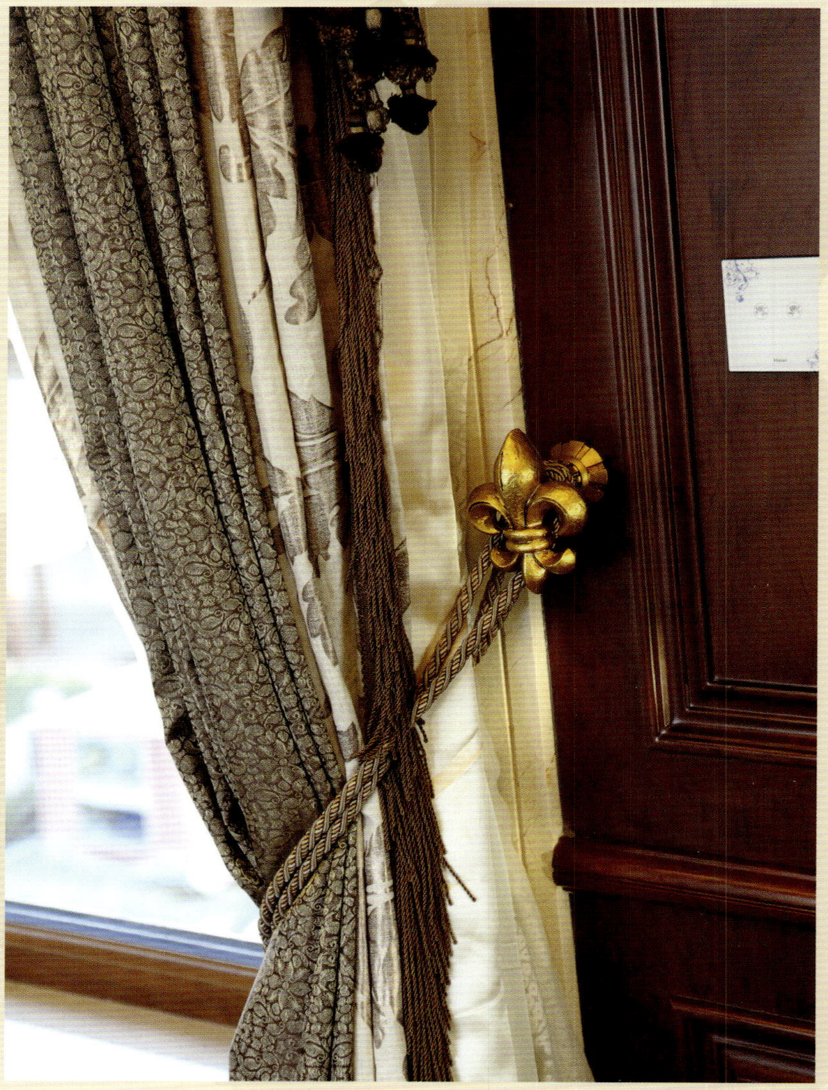

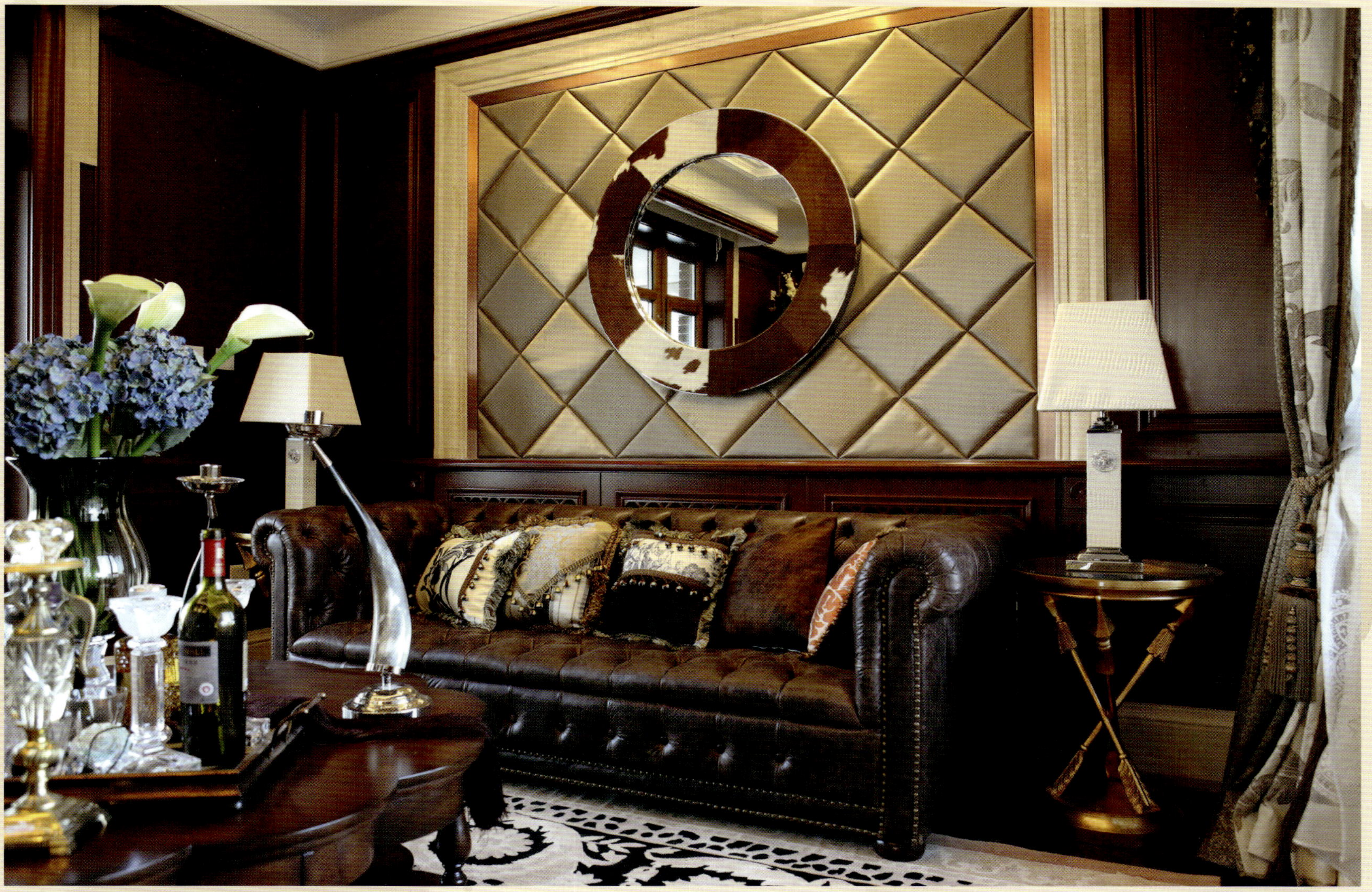

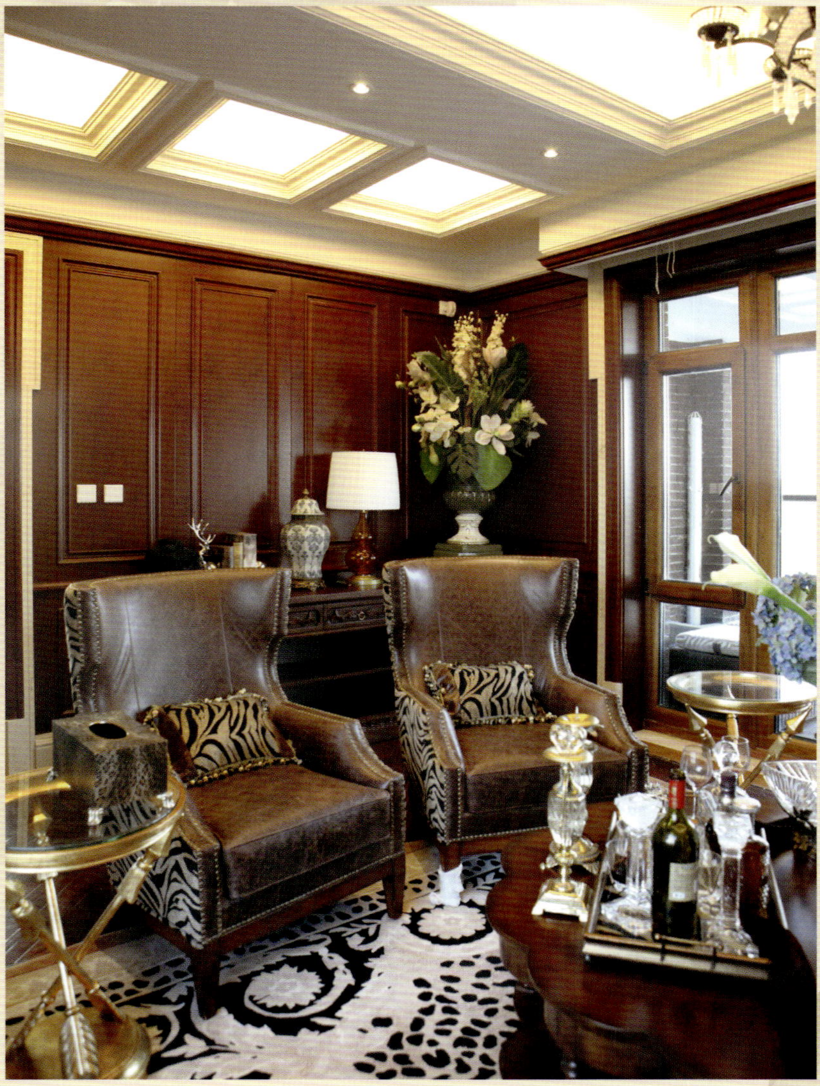

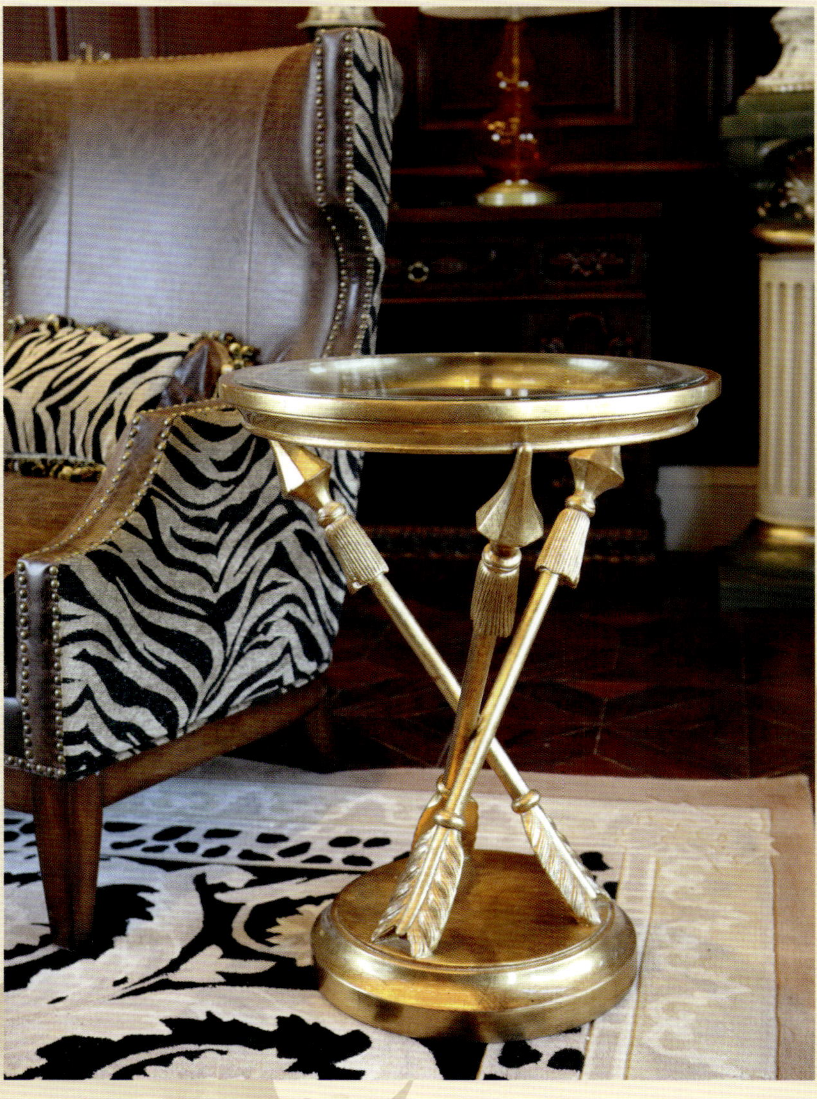

Fuzhou Show Property Beyond Club

Design Agency: Shenzhen Pinki Design Consultant Co., Ltd.
Location: Fuzhou, China
Area: 2100 m²
Design Theme: The Spiritual Dialogue with Space

Through the intersection of point, line and surface, we combined the new fashion elements into our design. It seems that people could have a spiritual dialogue with the space. Our designer used the simple architectural way to shape the overall space, emphasizing the artistic aesthetic of modern architecture. The design object is to not only extend the architectural style of its own, but also add an interactive space, relevant privacy and leading, so as to enrich the visual sense full of rhythm, and overall space with simple, atmospheric modern art beauty; thereby creating a sense of surreal fashion dynamic space.

For some levels, the space can limit our thinking and action. So our designer put all his apperceive into the design, and the design endues with the space, and the space stimulates our user — the spiritual power and creativity. This is our design intention and power source of this case.

一层售楼部原始平面图

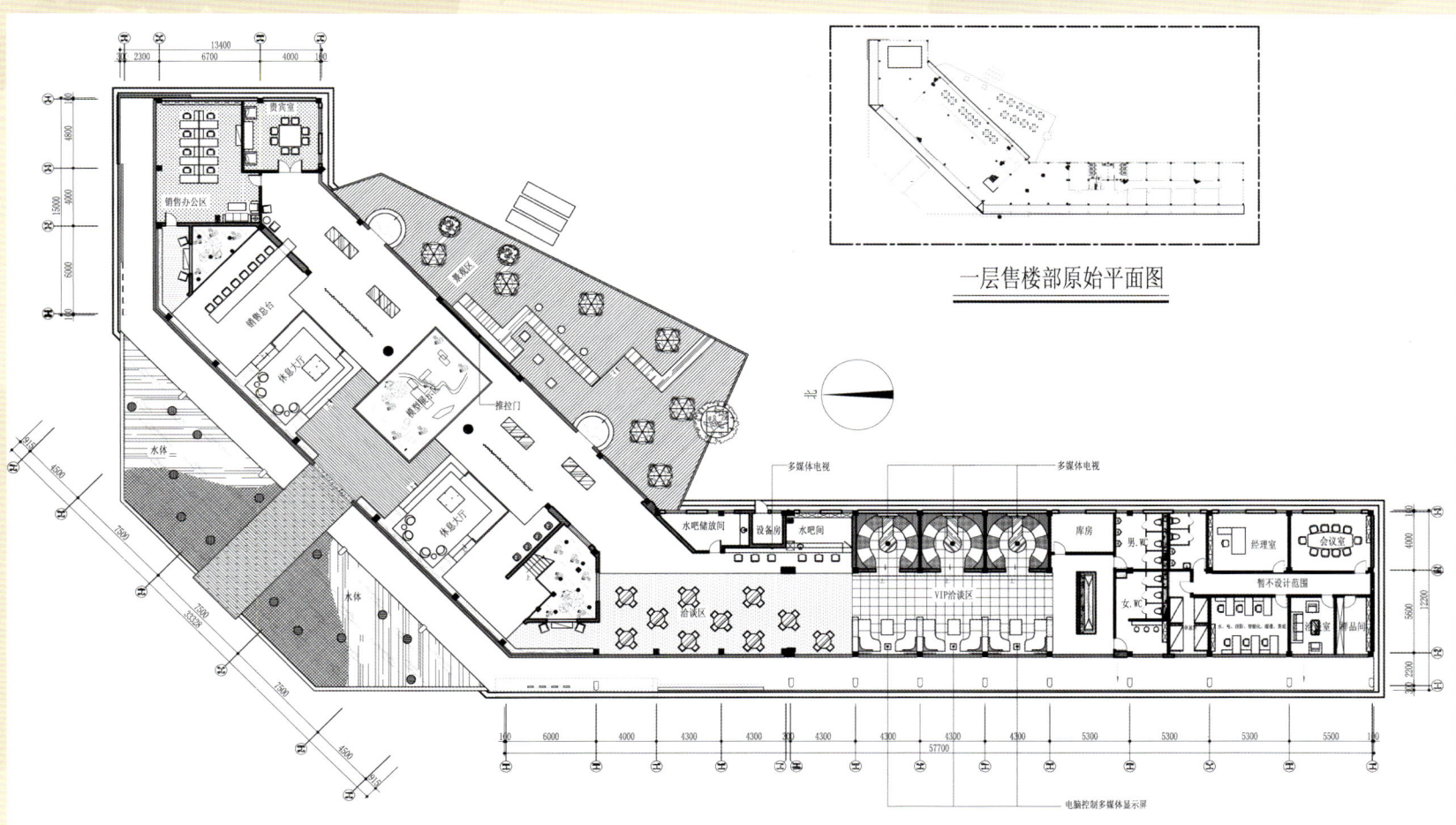

一层售楼处平面布置图
SC: 1:200

288

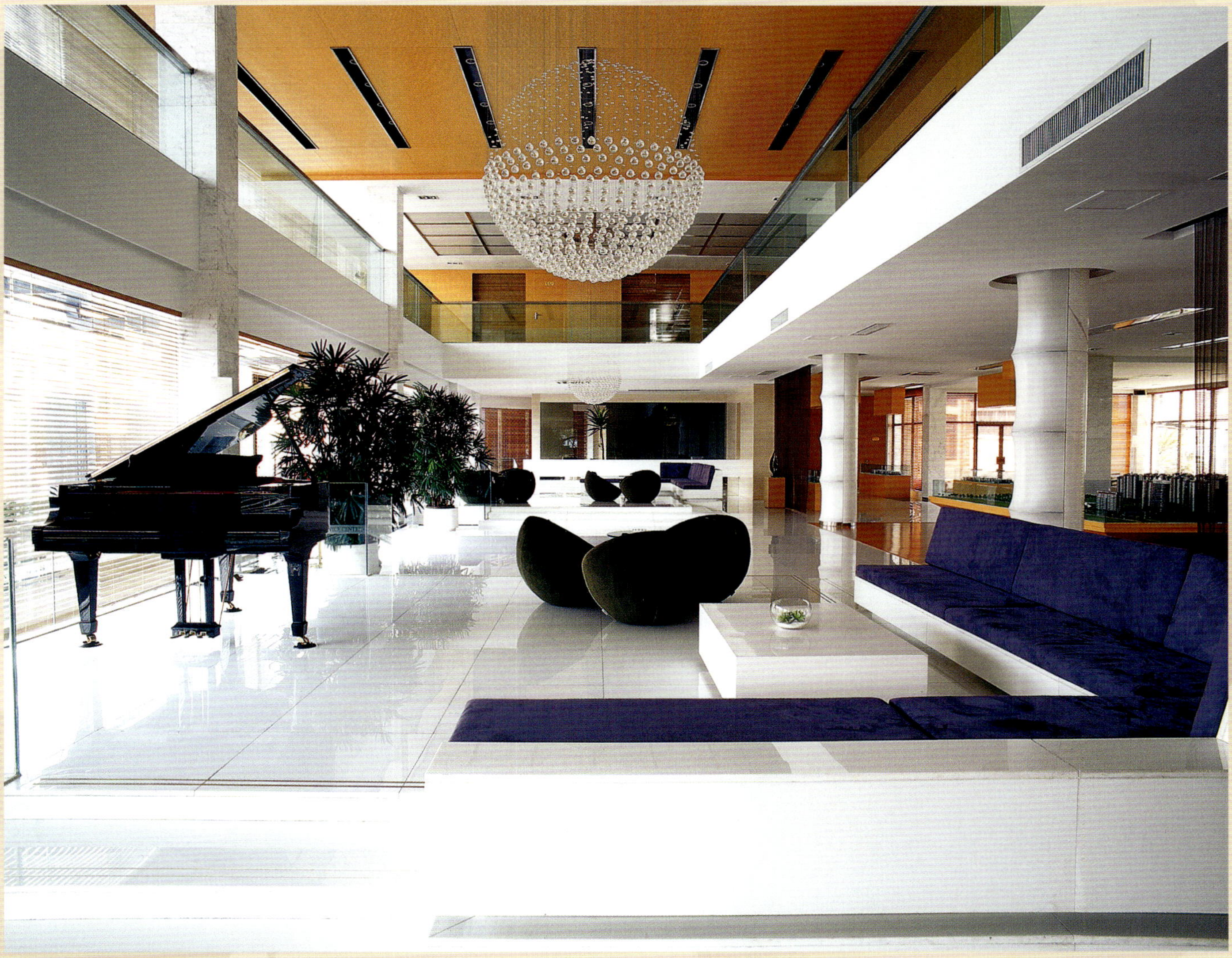

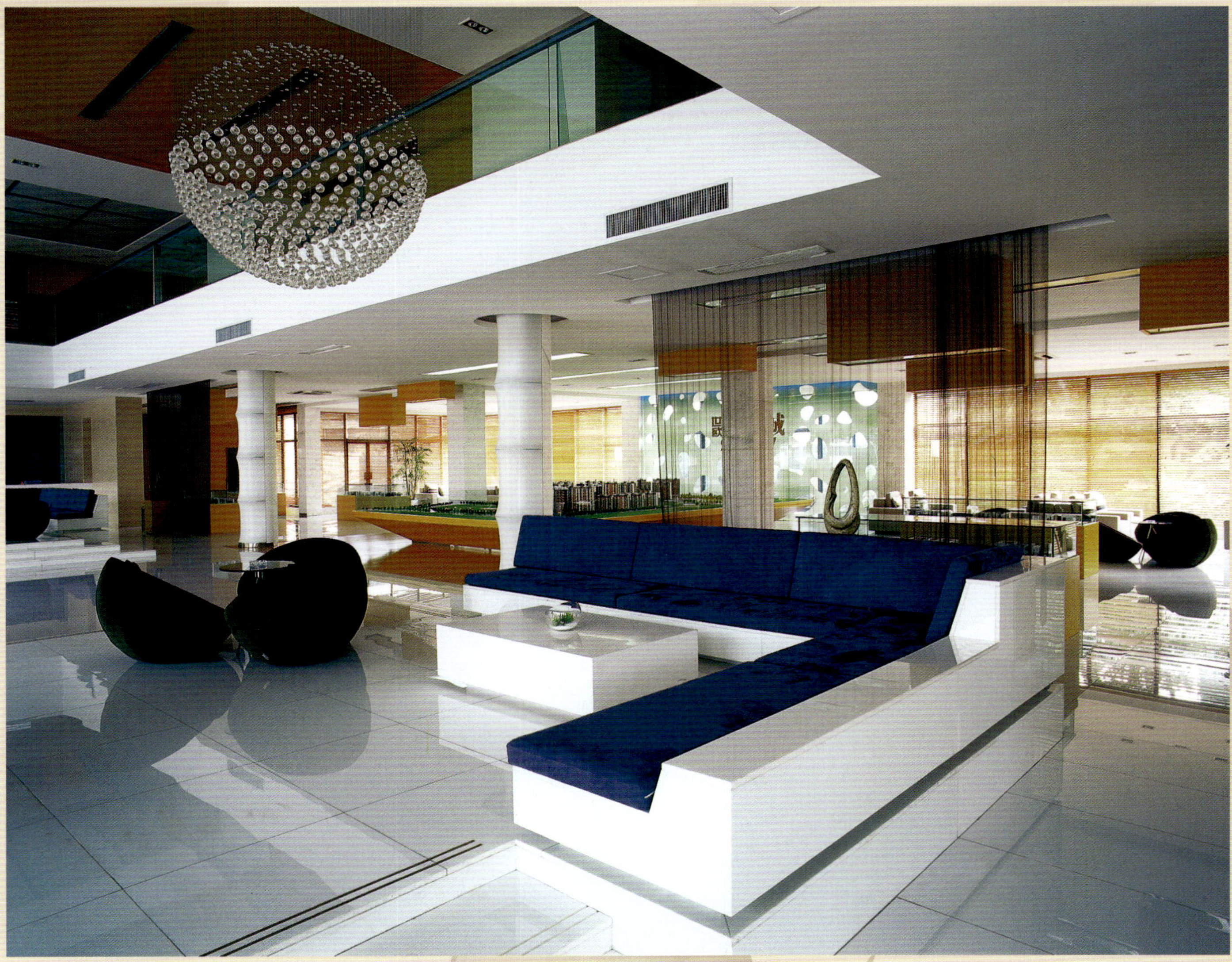

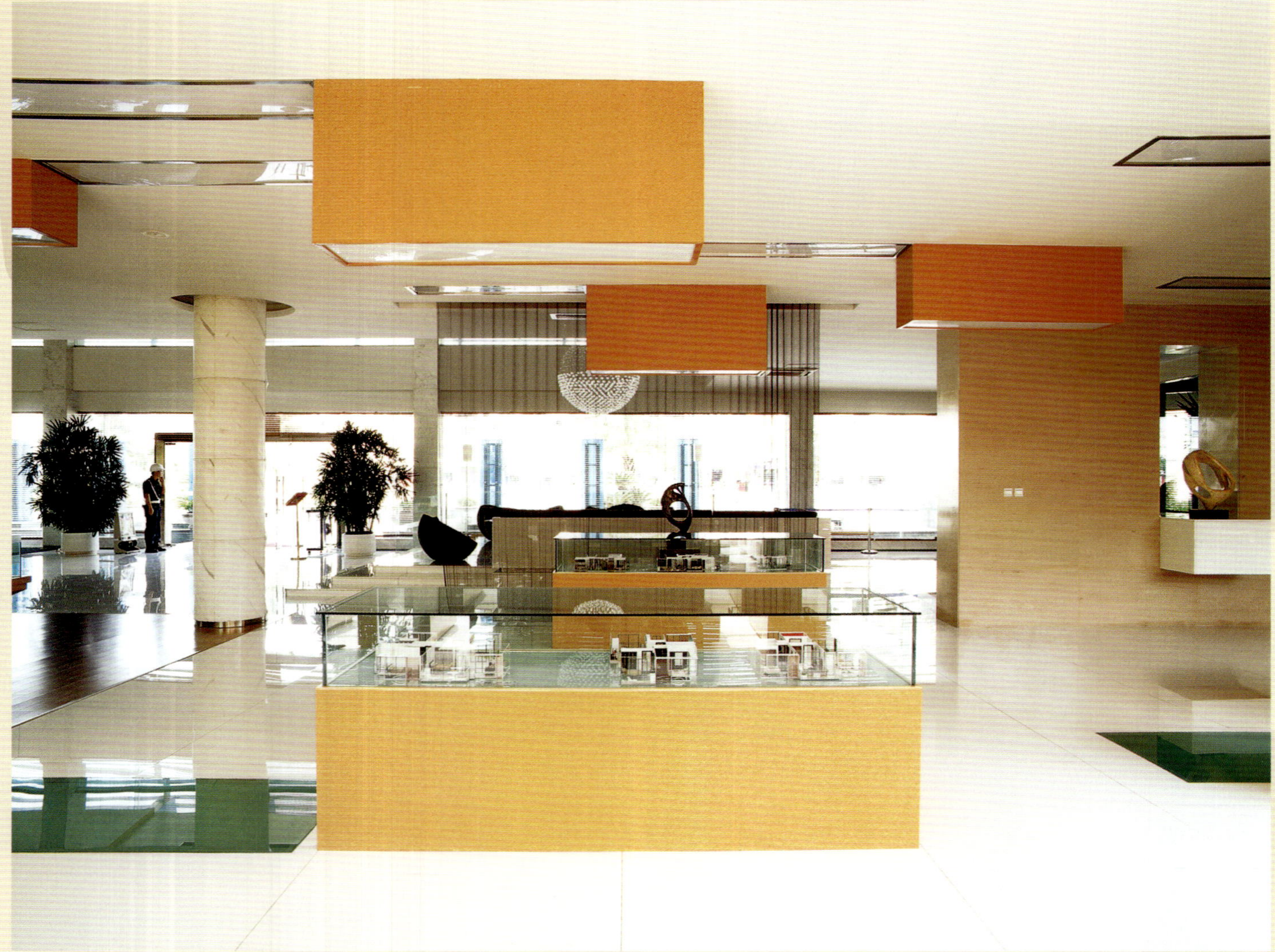

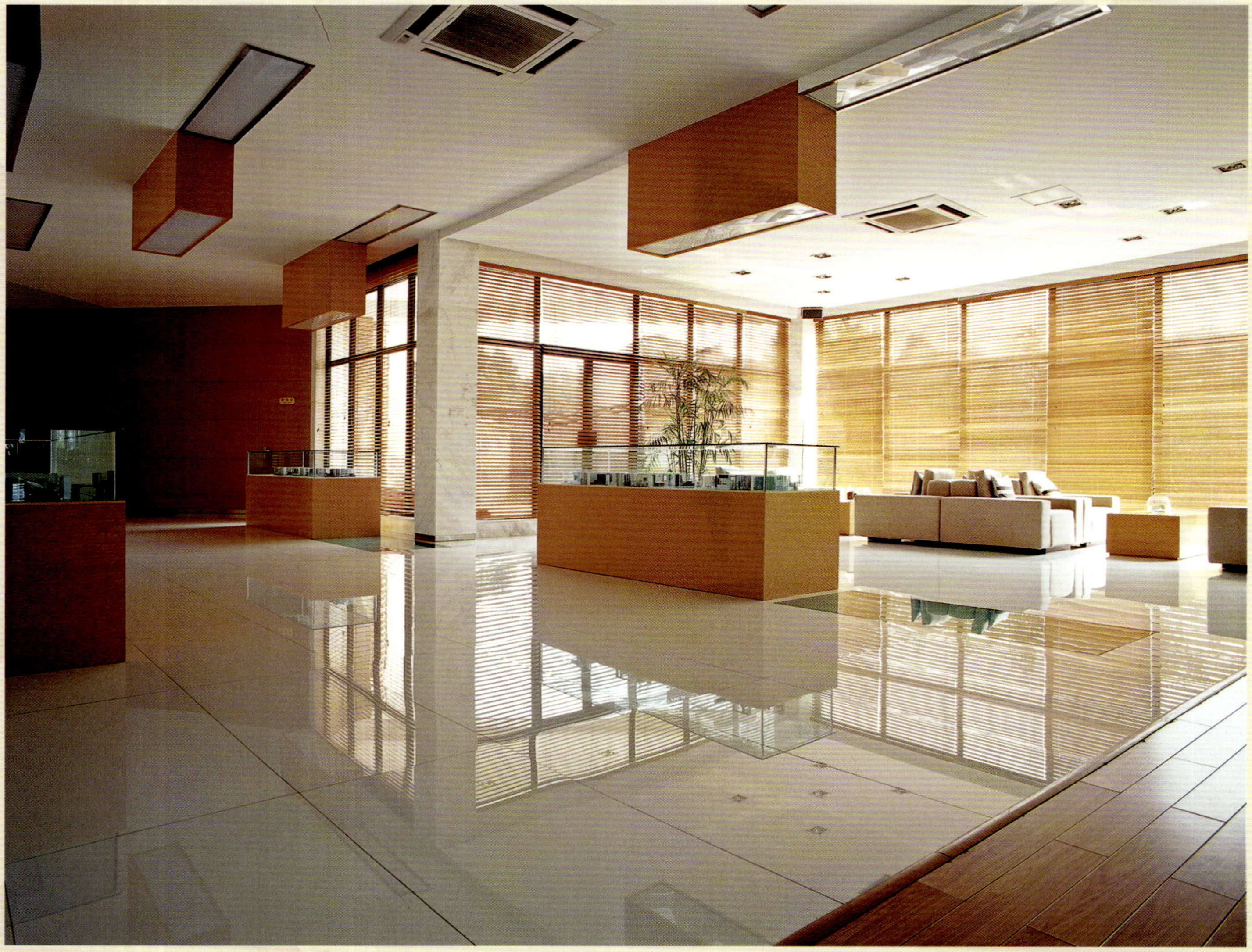

291

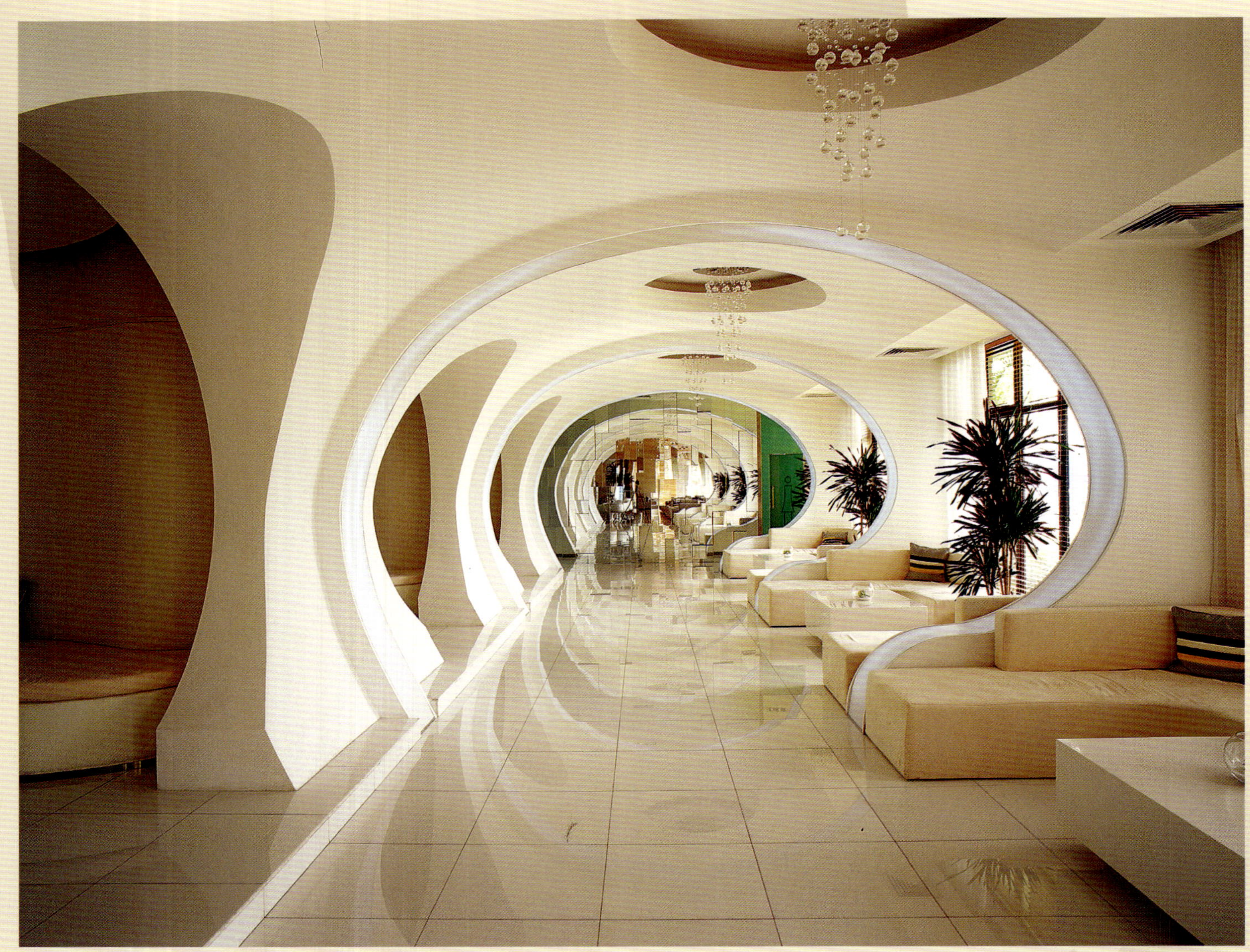

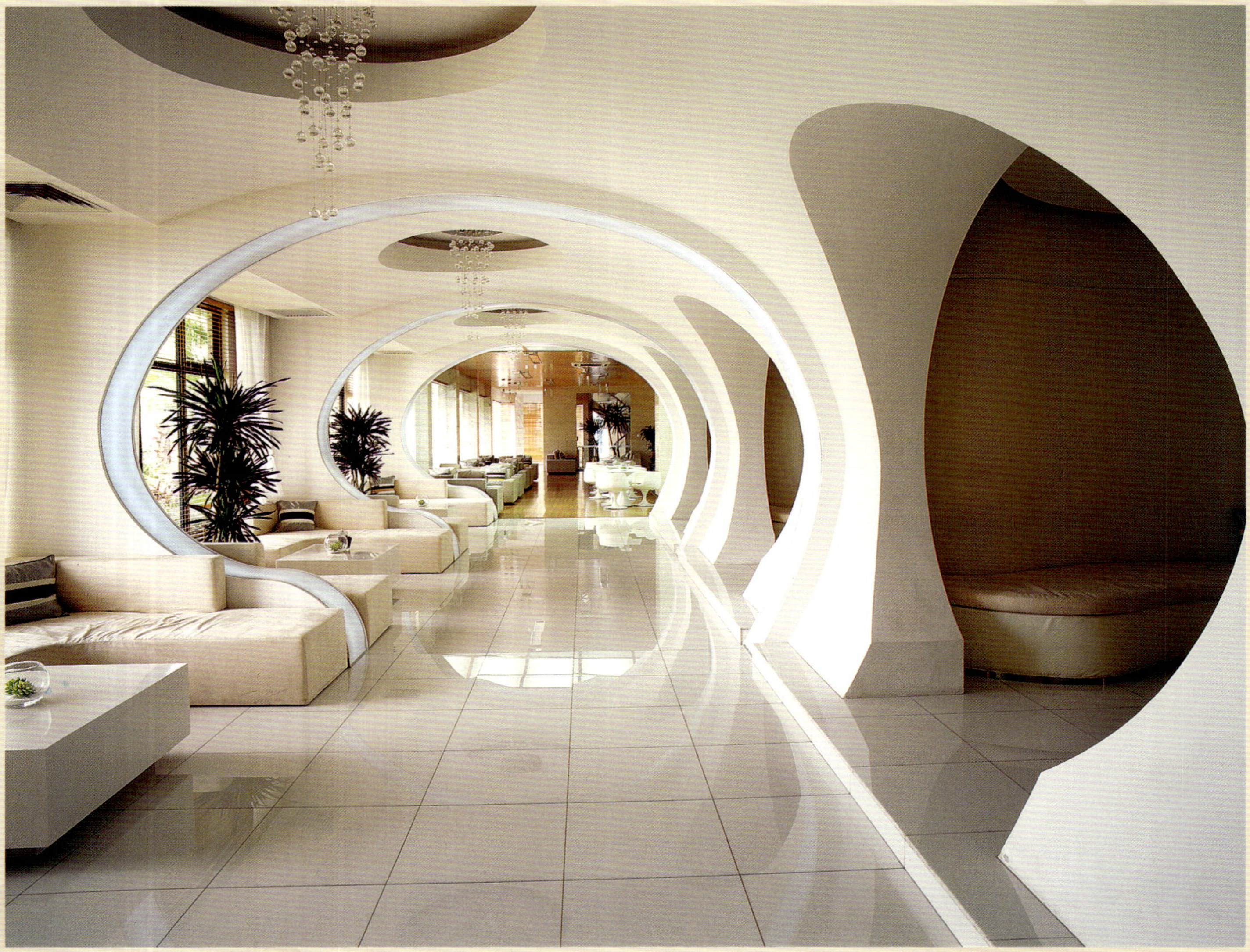

293

Maple Country Club (MCC)

Designer: Zhang Tao
Client: MCC REAL ESTATE SHANGHAI FENGJUN CO., LTD
Area: 2400 m²
Location: Shanghai, China
Photographer: Wu Ruochen

The designer uses various building materials to create an elegant and high-end clubhouse. With a purpose to achieve this point, the hidden reflecting lights along with the spotlight are applied to lighten the surrounding, so as to produce a sense of luxury.

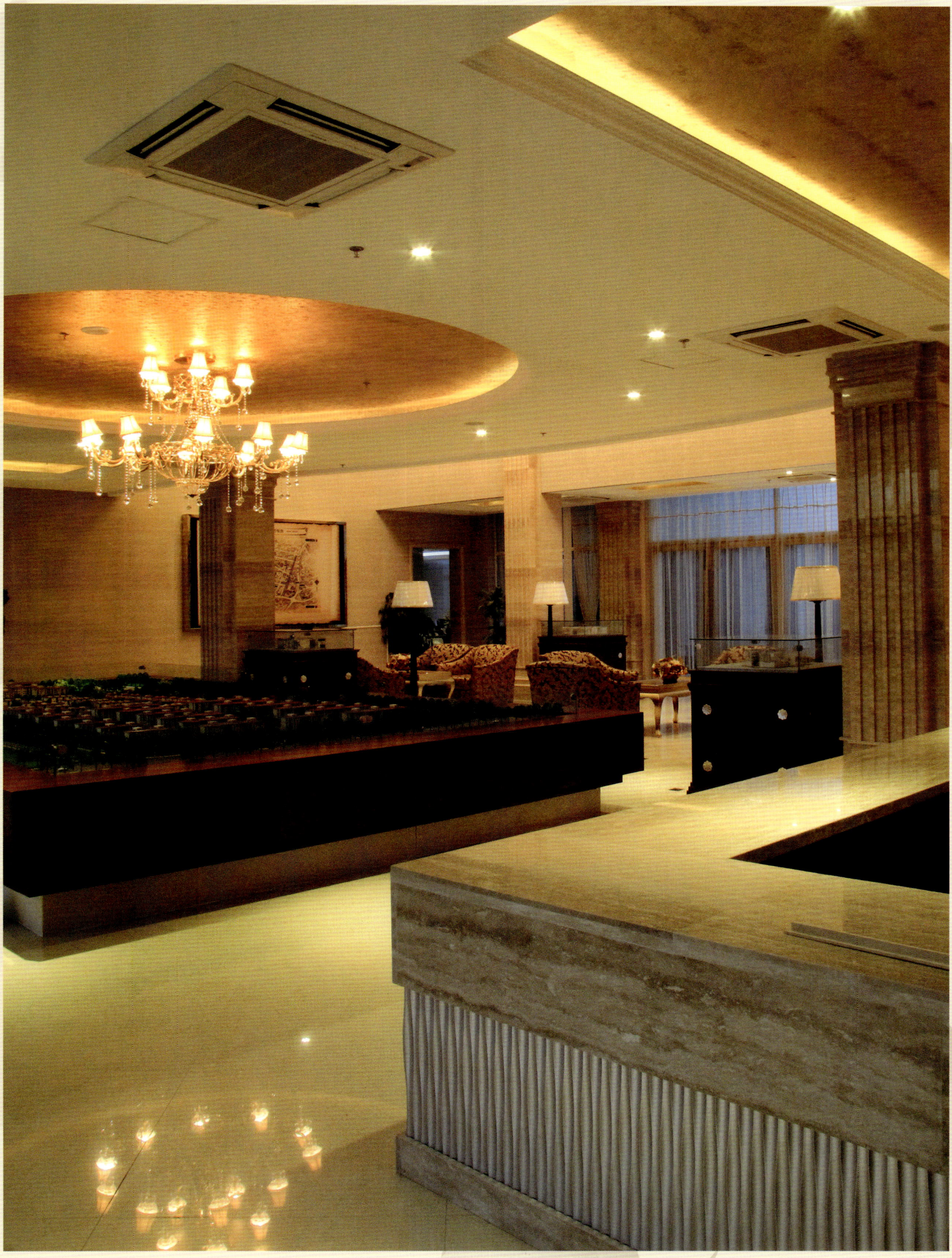

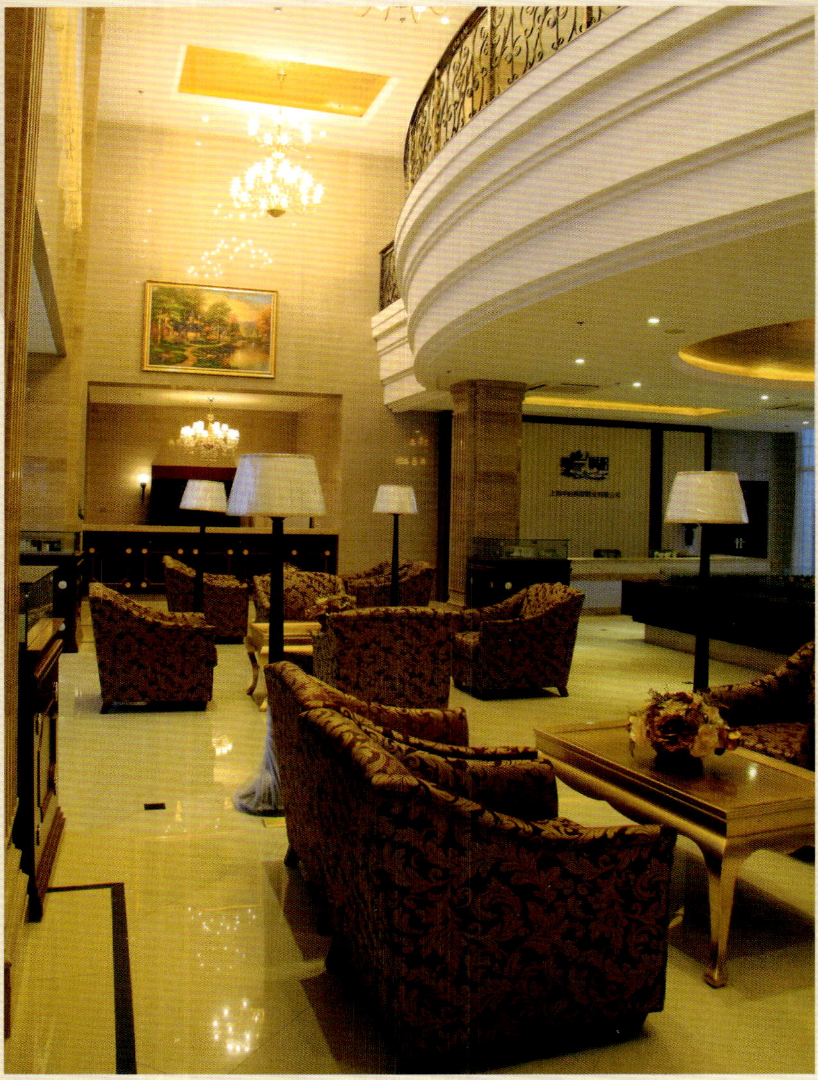

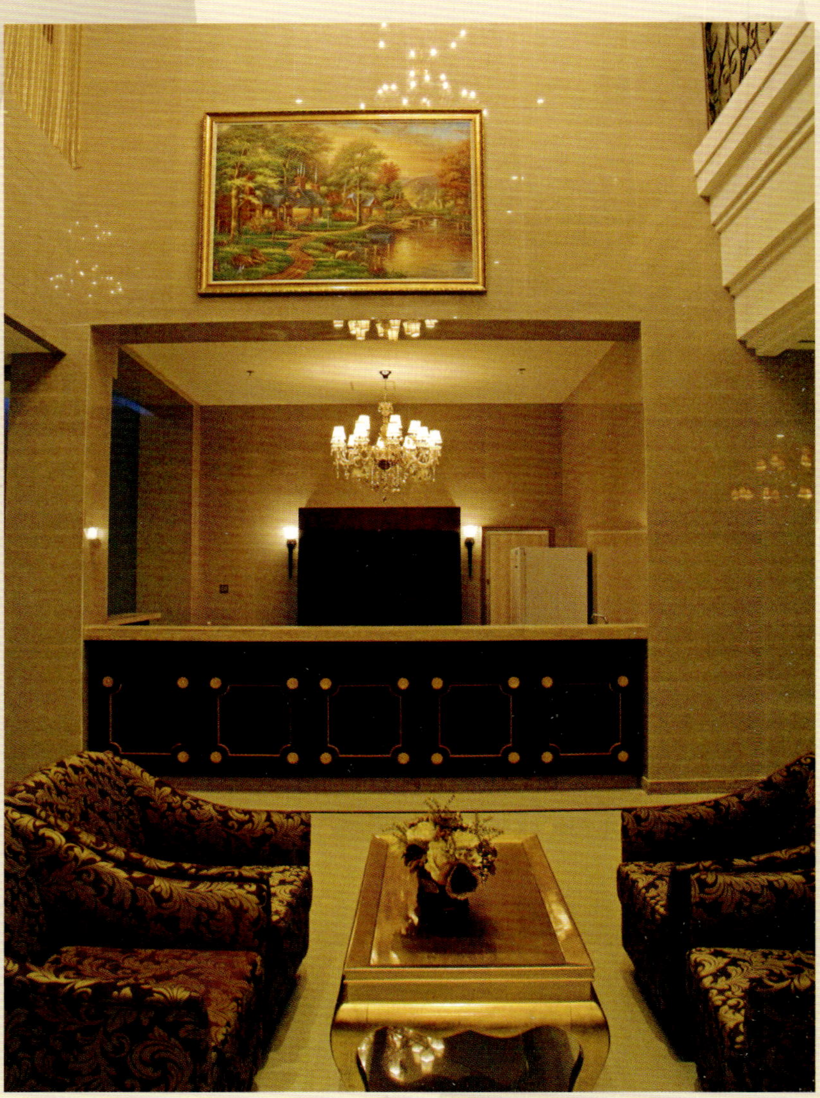

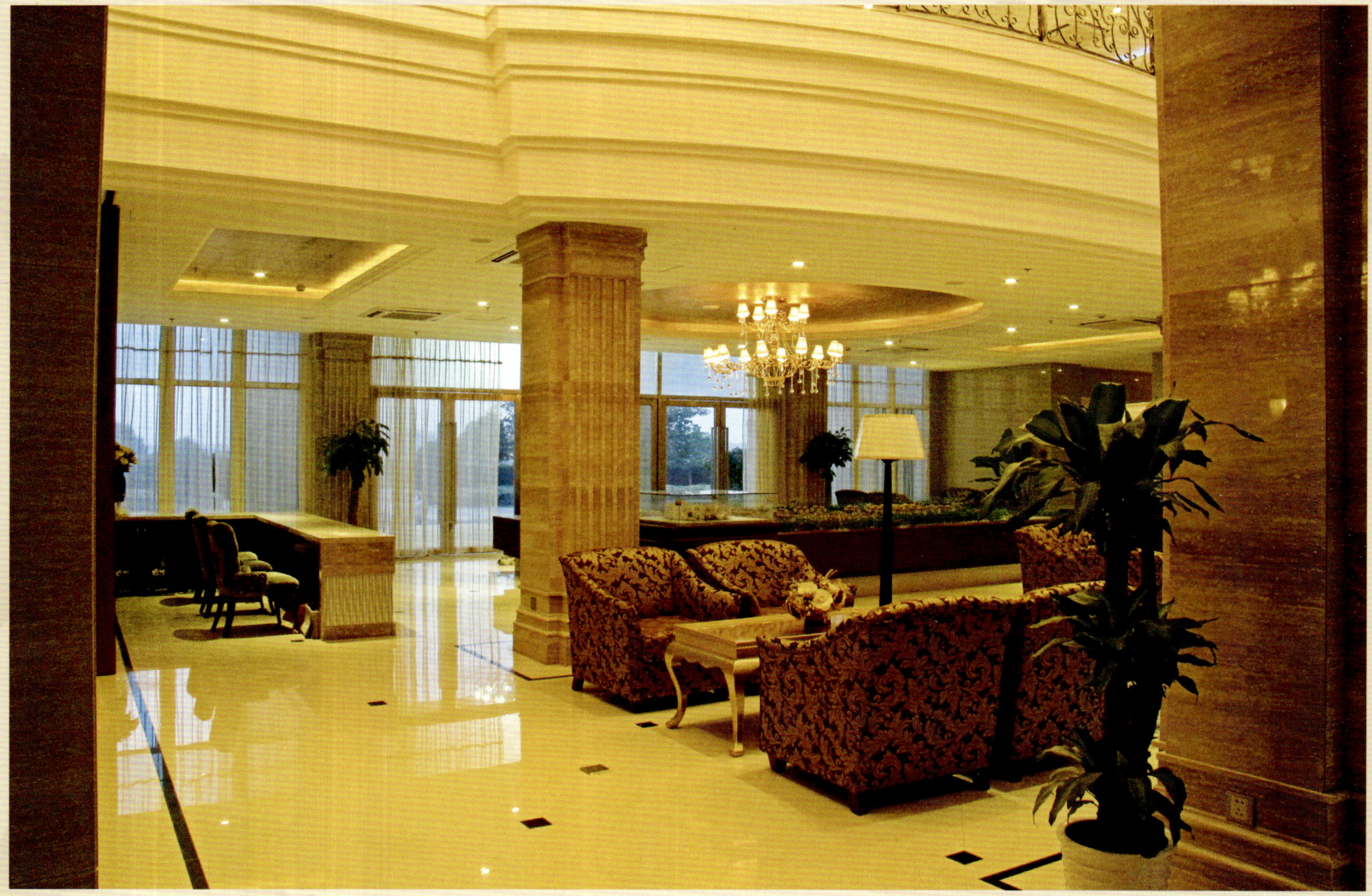

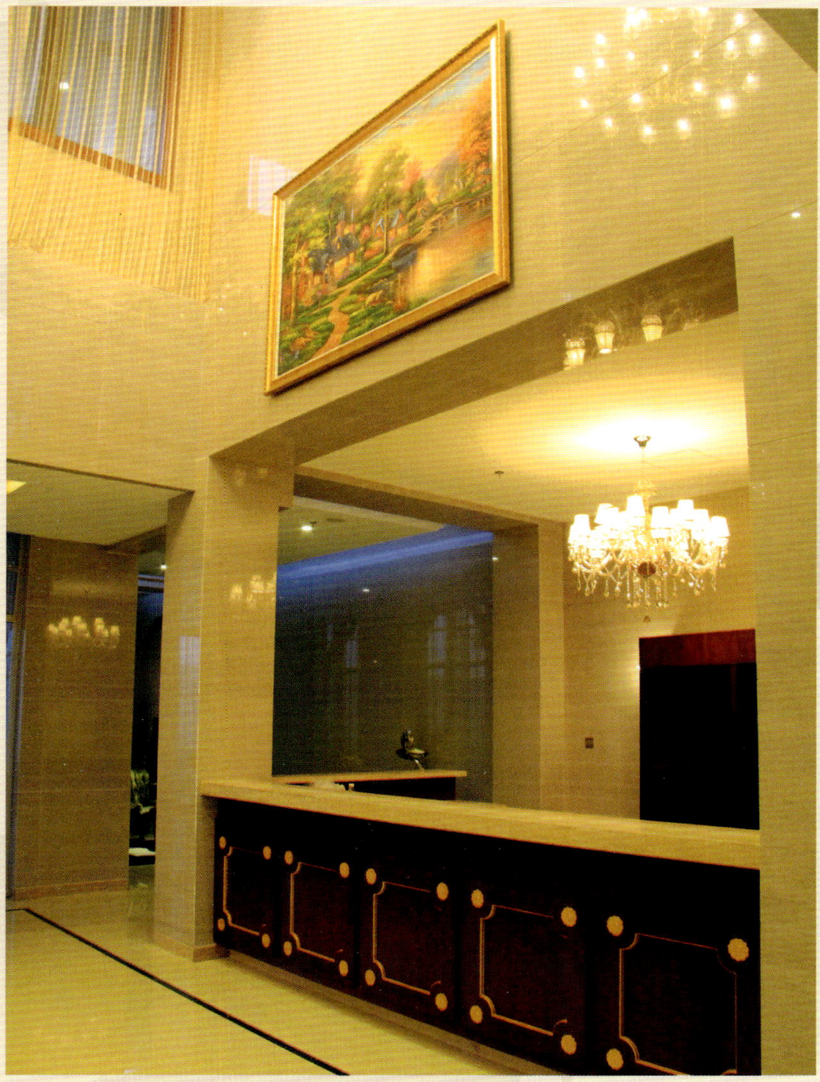
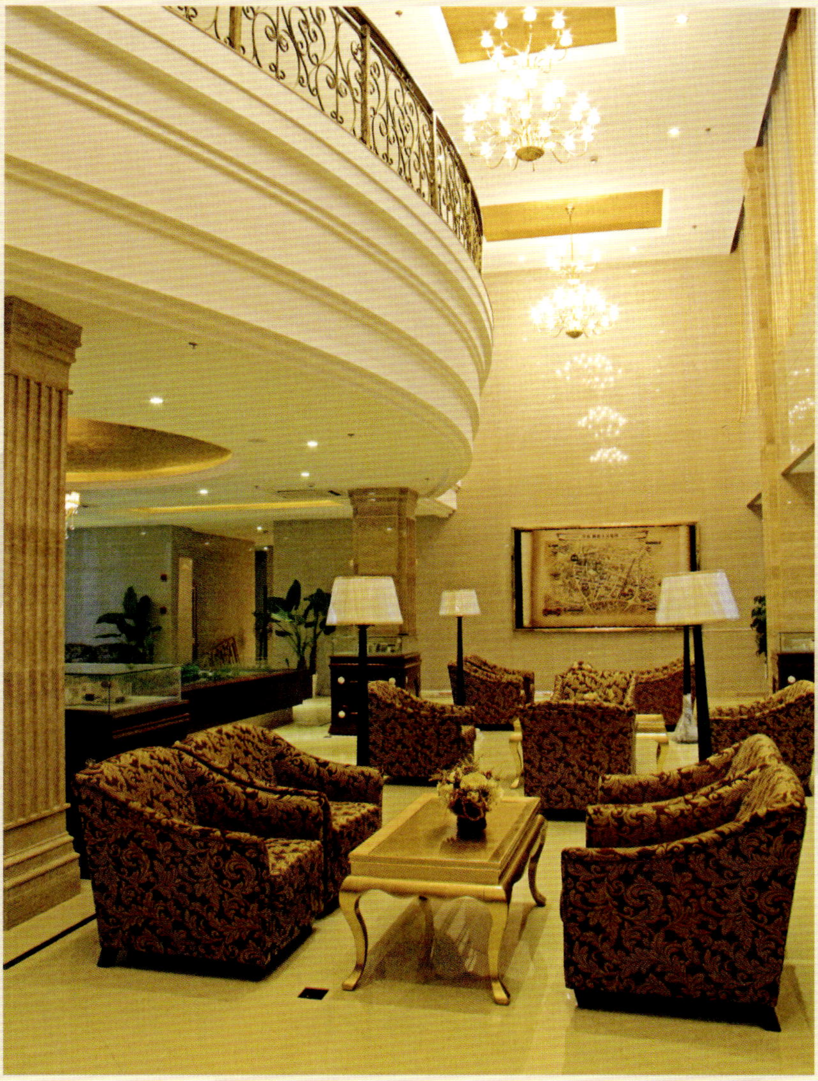
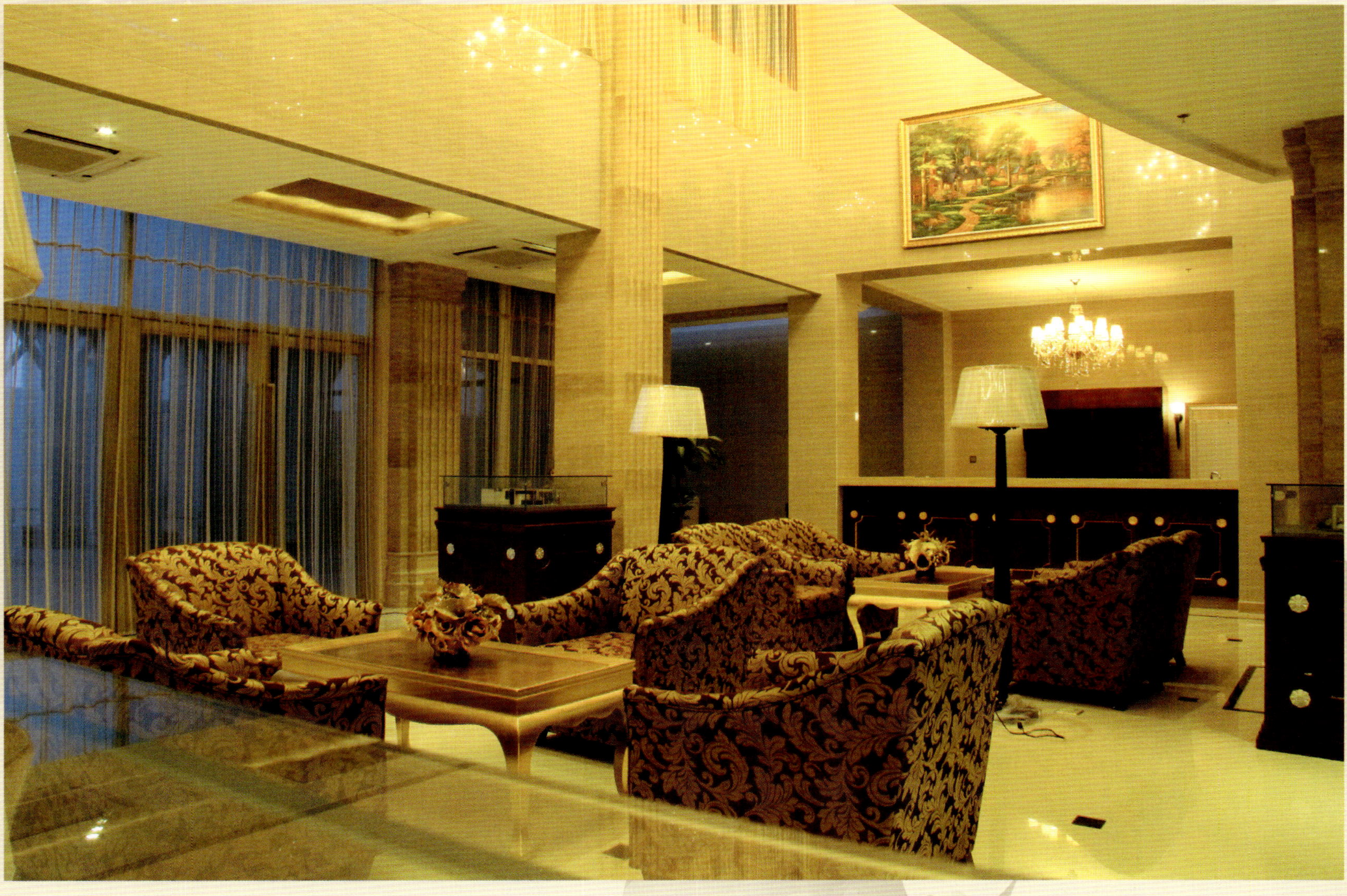

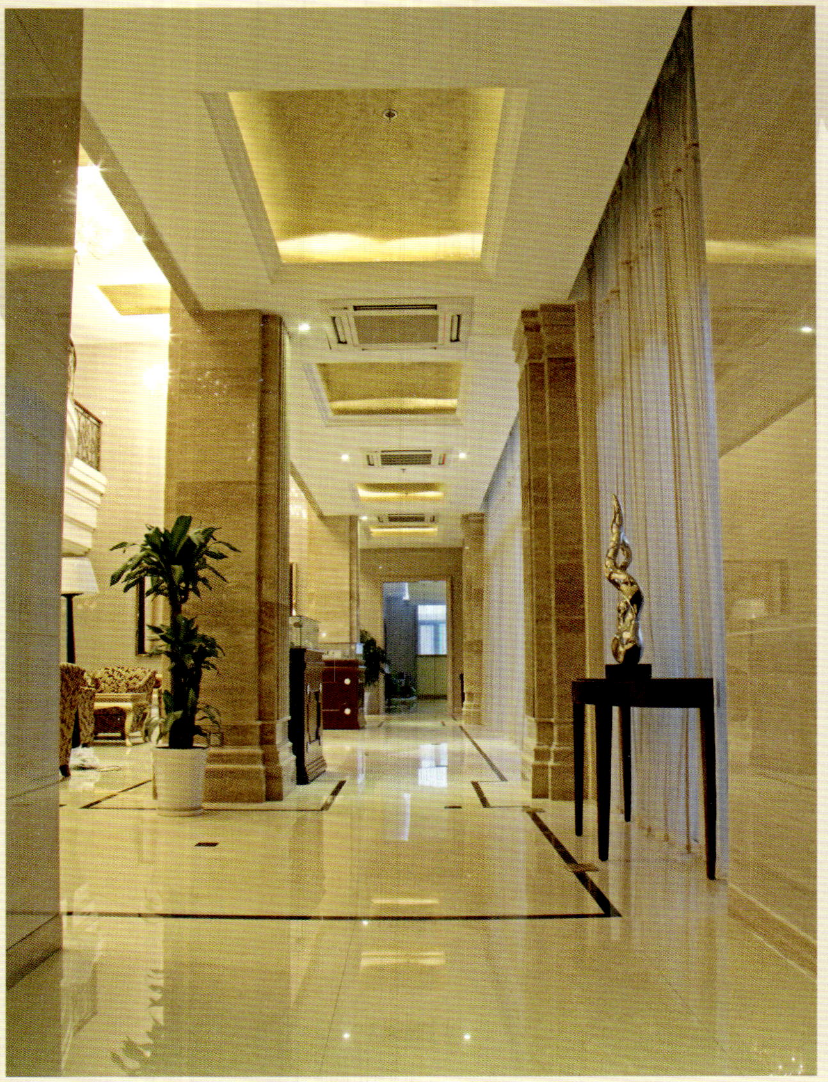

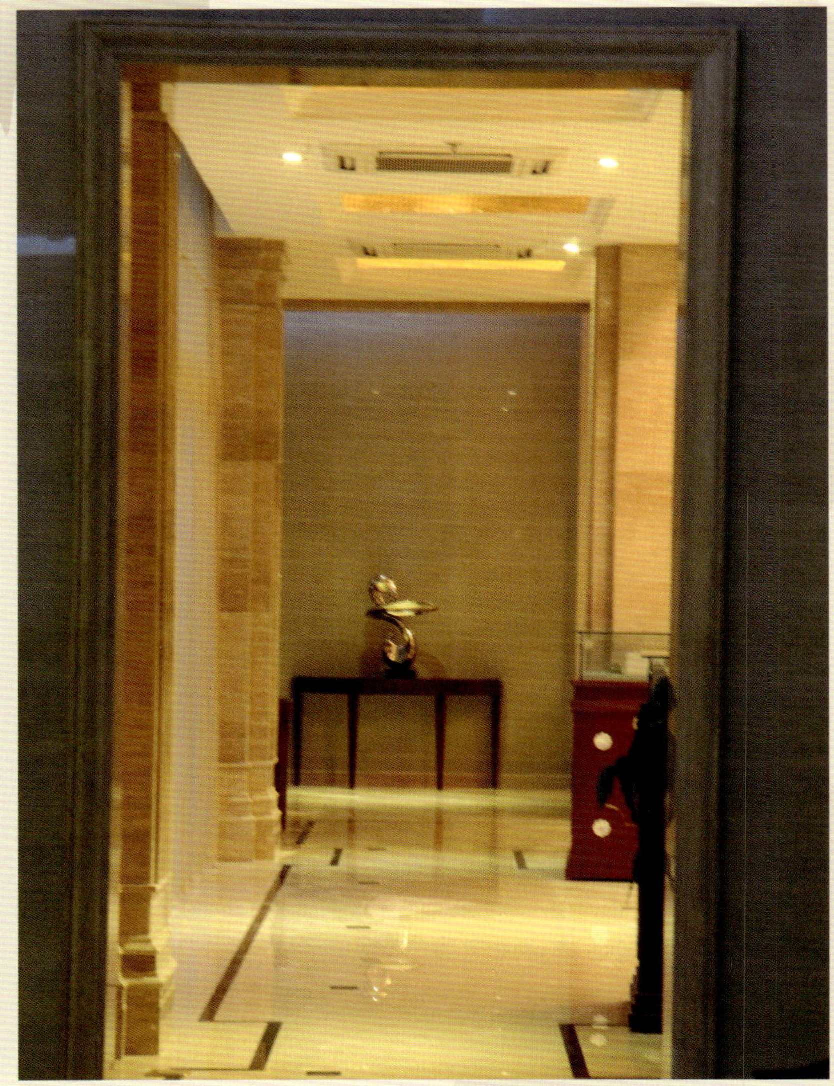

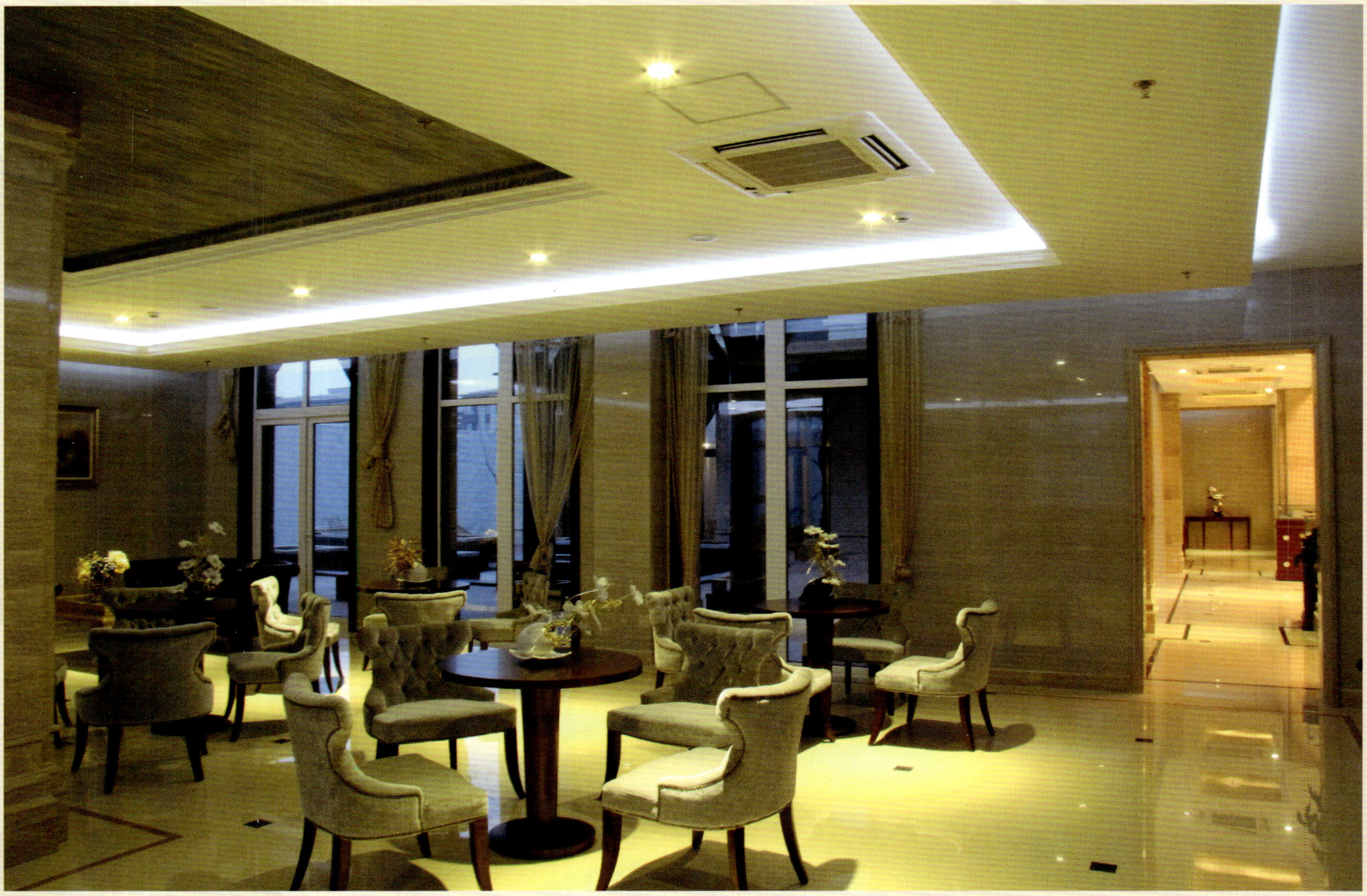

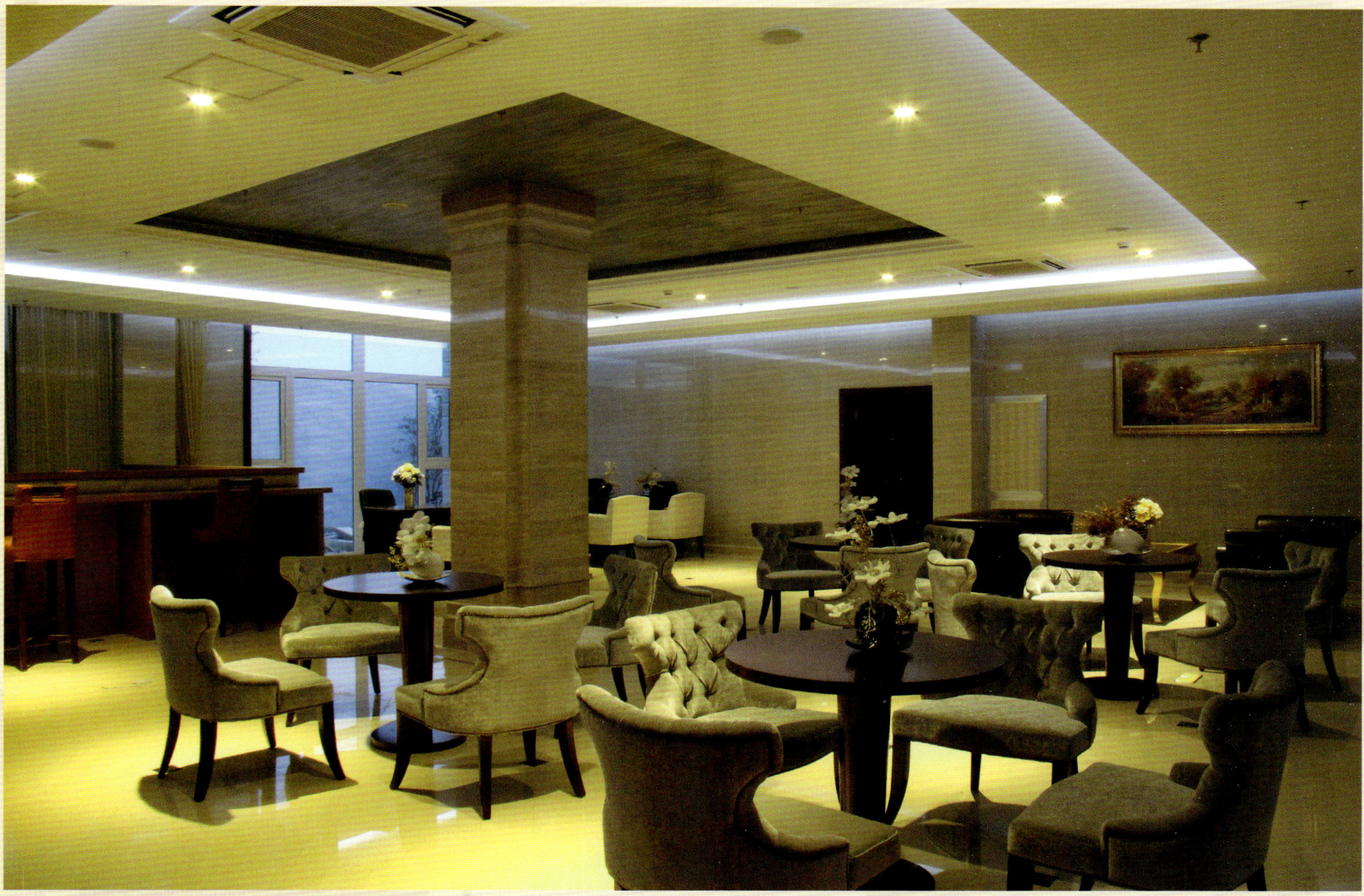

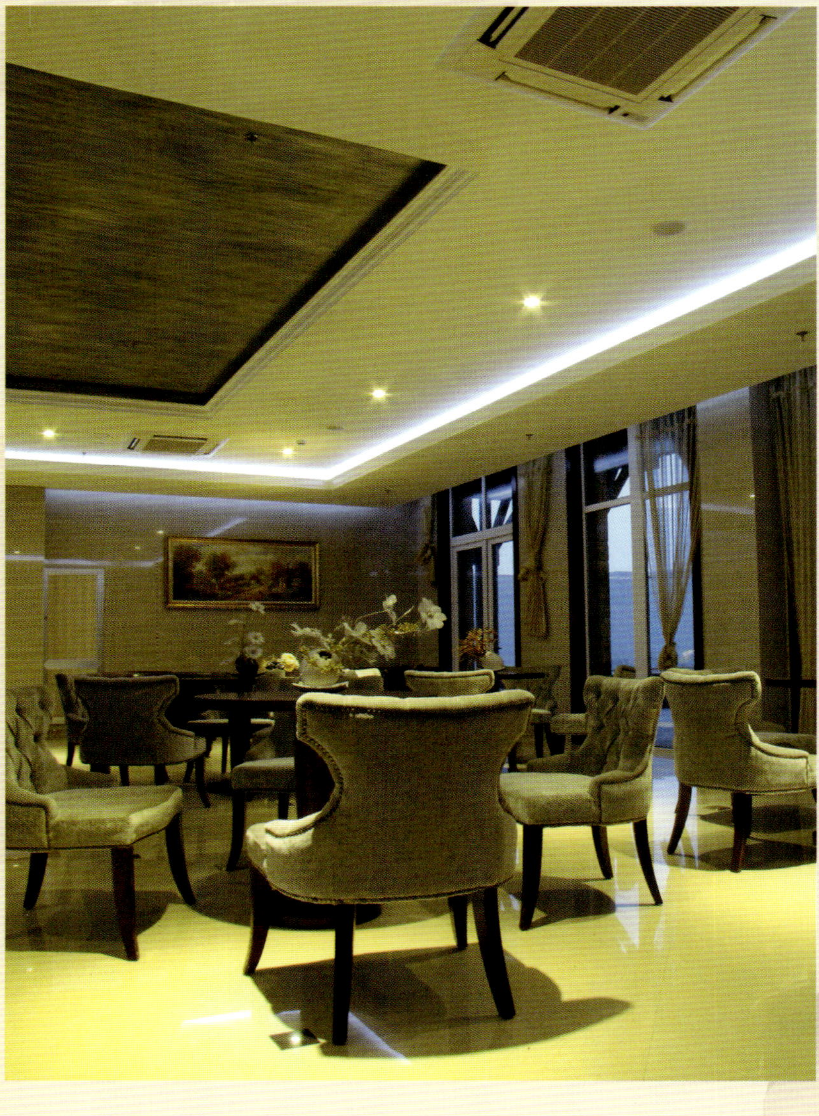

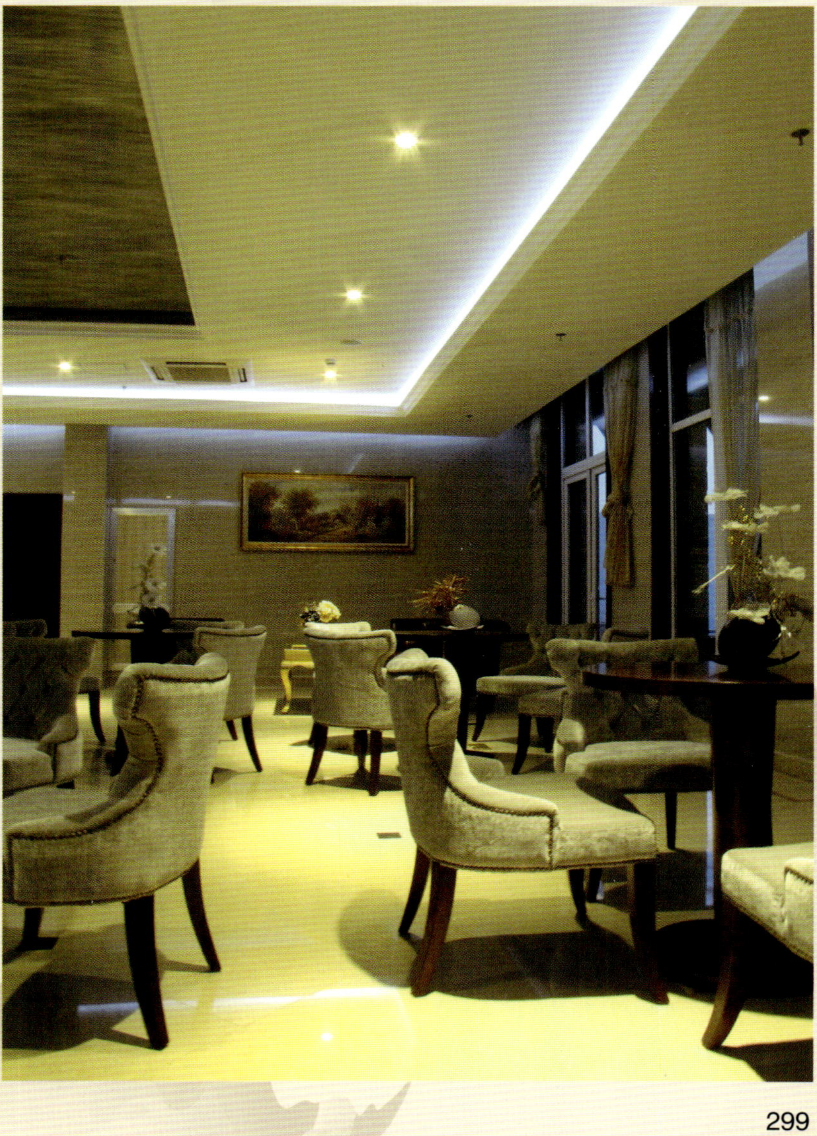

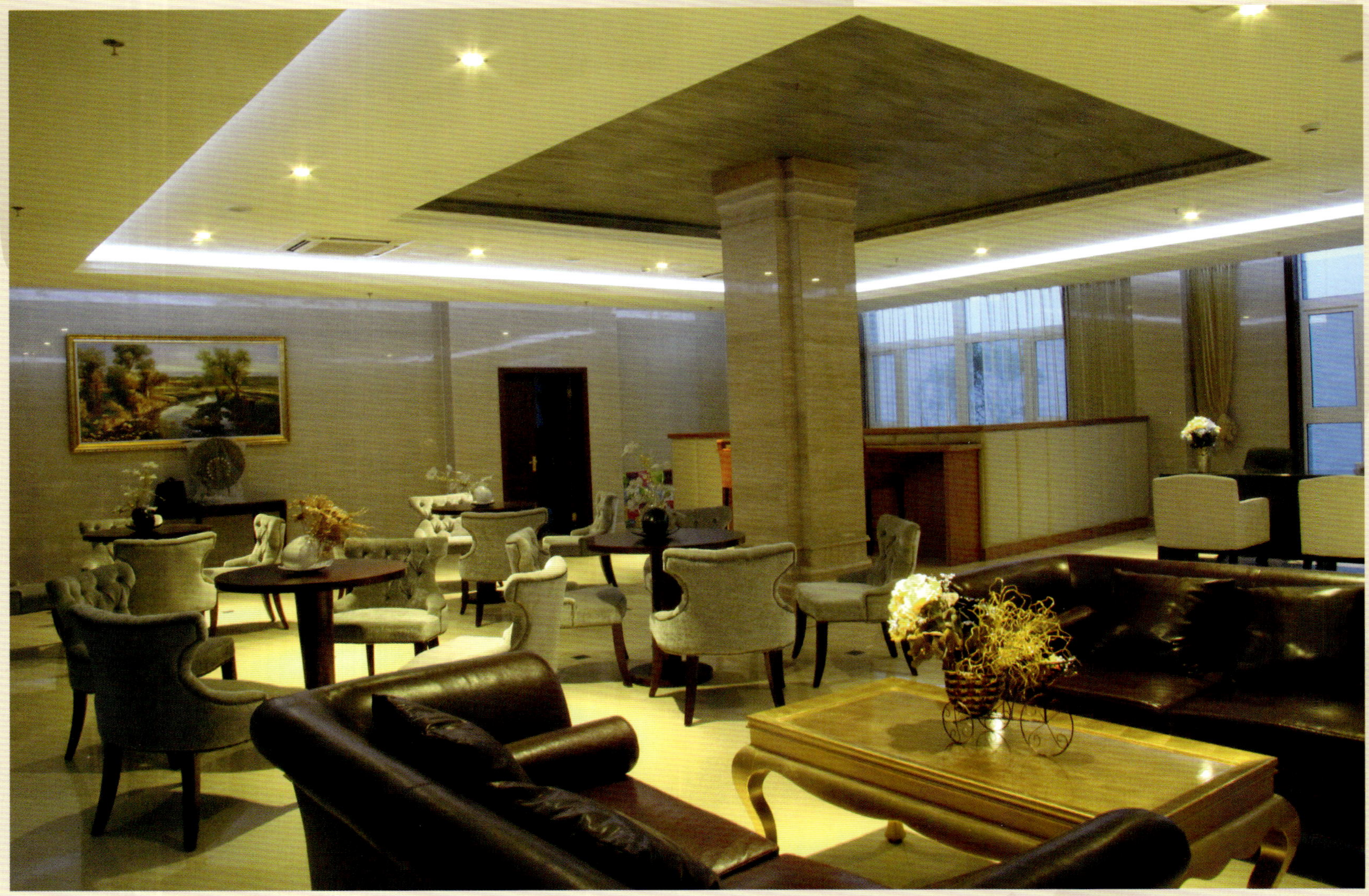

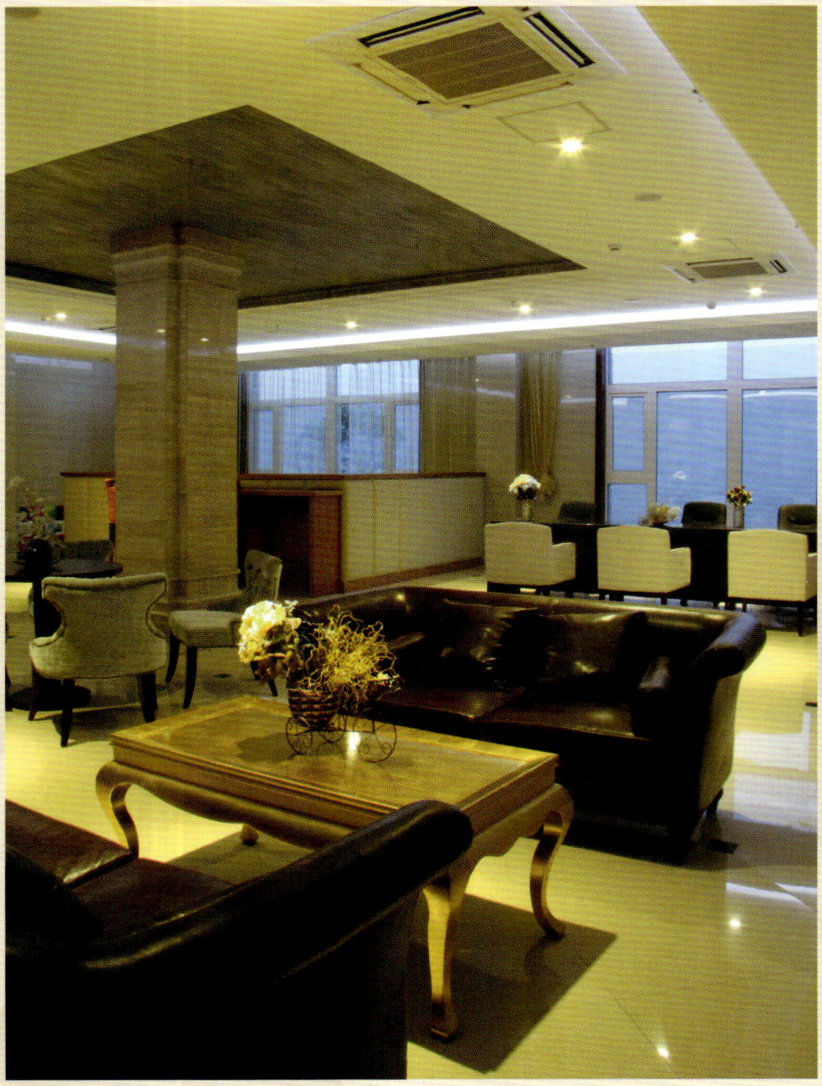

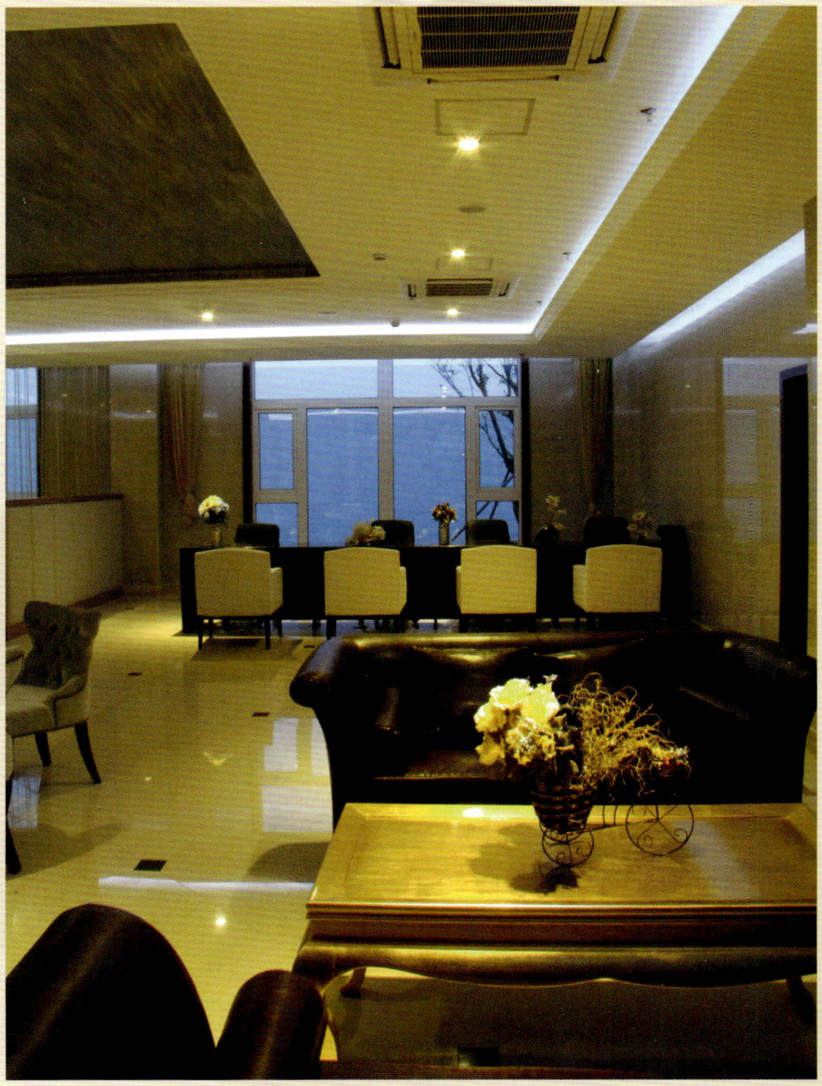

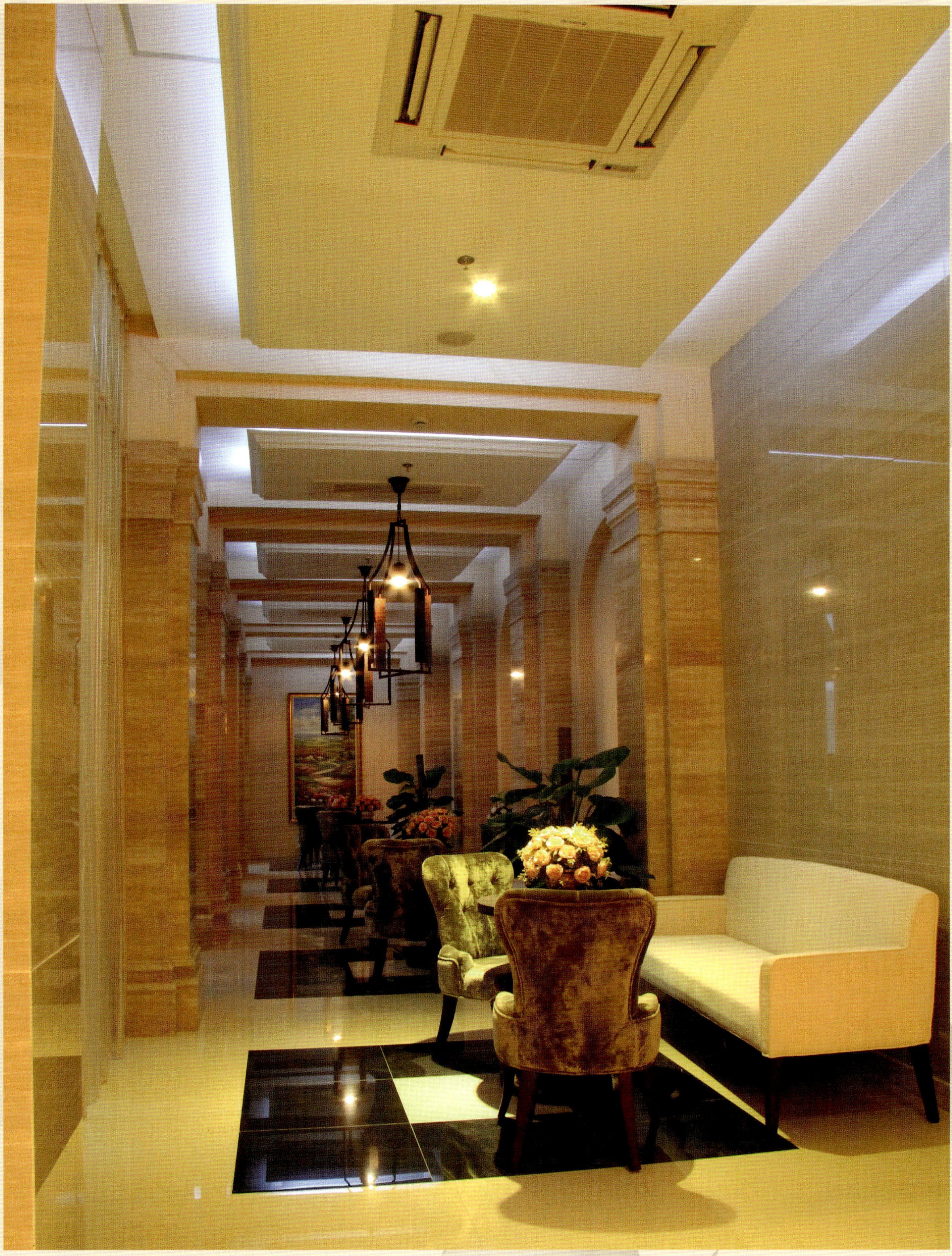

302

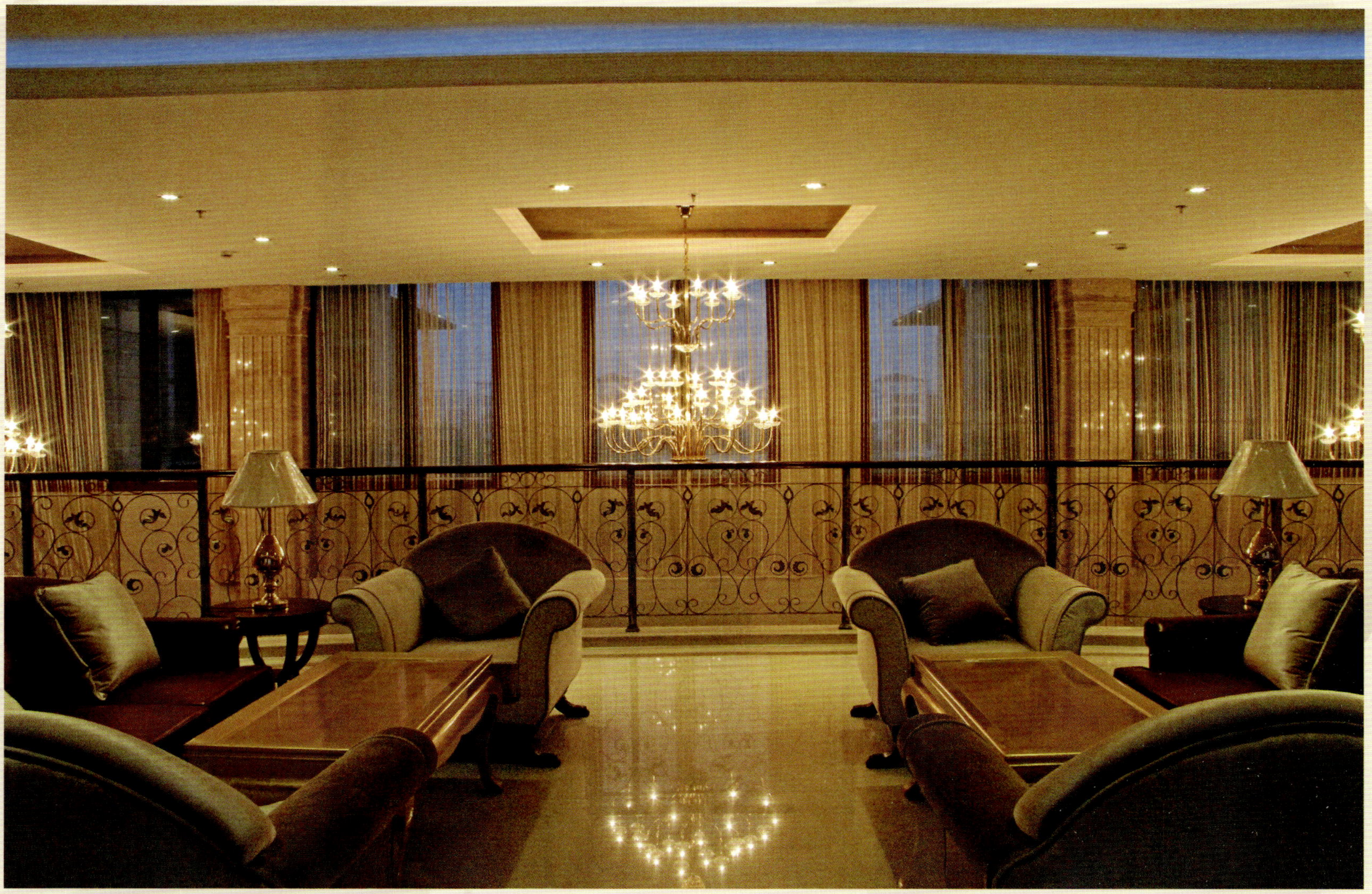

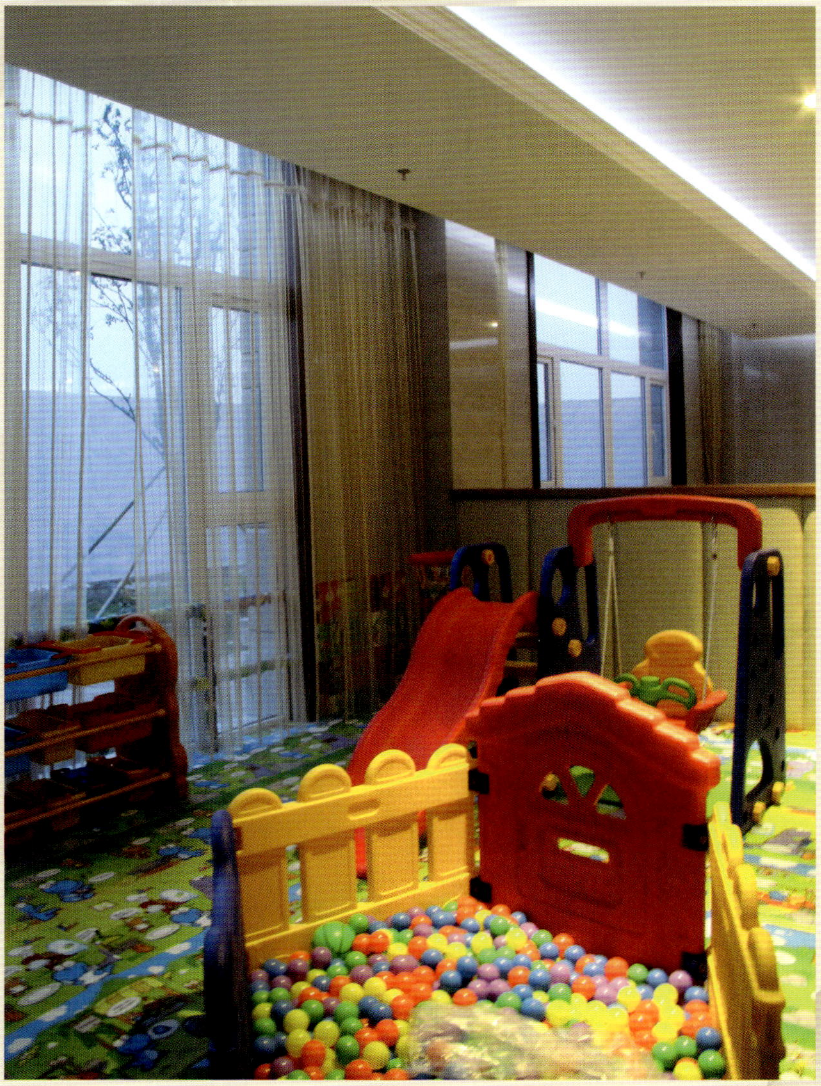

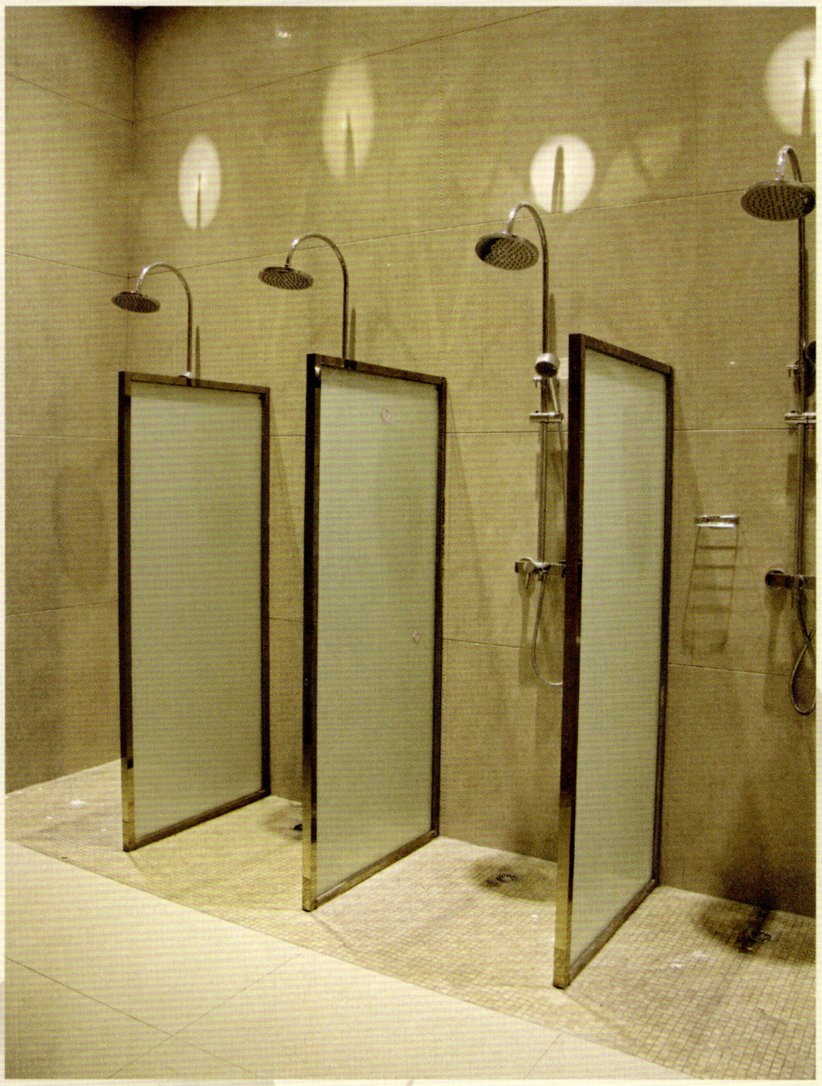

Green Weaving Club House

Designer: Hyunjoon Yoo
Client: Eugeen Group
Collaborators: Sun Planning Architectural Office, Euleem, Eugeen Construction Co., Ltd.
Area: 5670.12 m²
Location: Korea

Golf is a sport that makes people who usually ride on cars and walk on sidewalks or asphalts return to nature and be united with it. In particular, a club house is space where people talk, eat, change clothes, or take a bath in a tub while viewing the nature. The club house provides people who live dry lives in modern times with Utopia-like space before Industrial Revolution.

A long and narrow land was a limitation in designing a club house of this country club. If the necessary rooms are built in a line, a long building over 100 meters which is like the Great Wall of China will cut the golf course in half. To solve the problem, the building was built as short as possible, and cut from here and there so that it looks as if green zones go through the building in between. The building is a straight line from the entrance where people leave their golf bags to the lobby, locker, and finally spa room where privacy is needed most. As the nature penetrates between the rooms, people continually communicate with the nature when they move according to the moving sequence.

This club house was intended to look as if the land was interwoven like bamboo strips interwoven to make bamboo ware. The rooms were designed to look as if being inserted in between the fabric made of warp threads and fillings. The walls were covered with Pachysandra terminalis and ivy to express the feeling of a lifted land. The afforested walls also become an environment-friendly factor that raises energy efficiency of the building.

PLAN

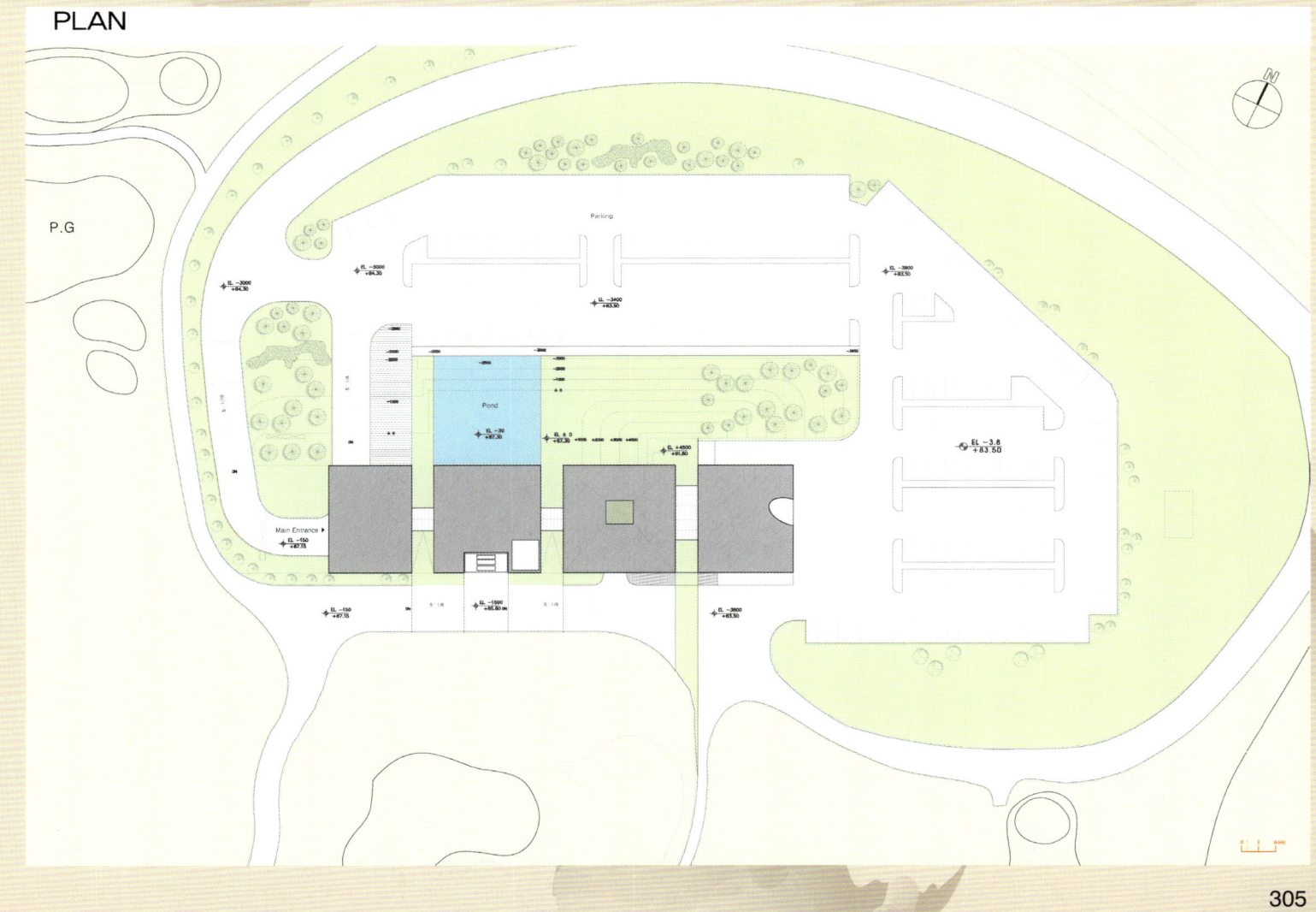

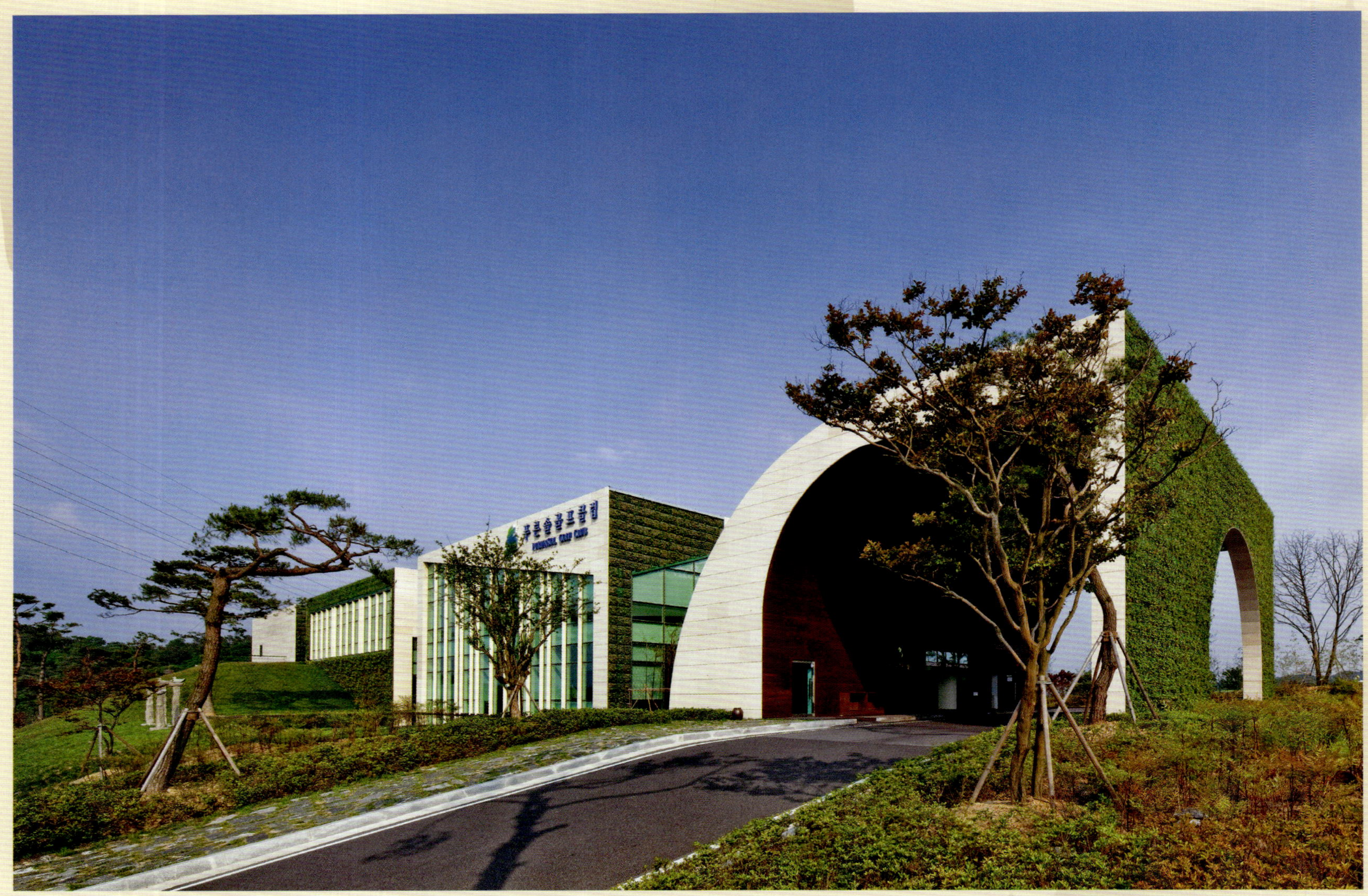
푸른솔골프클럽

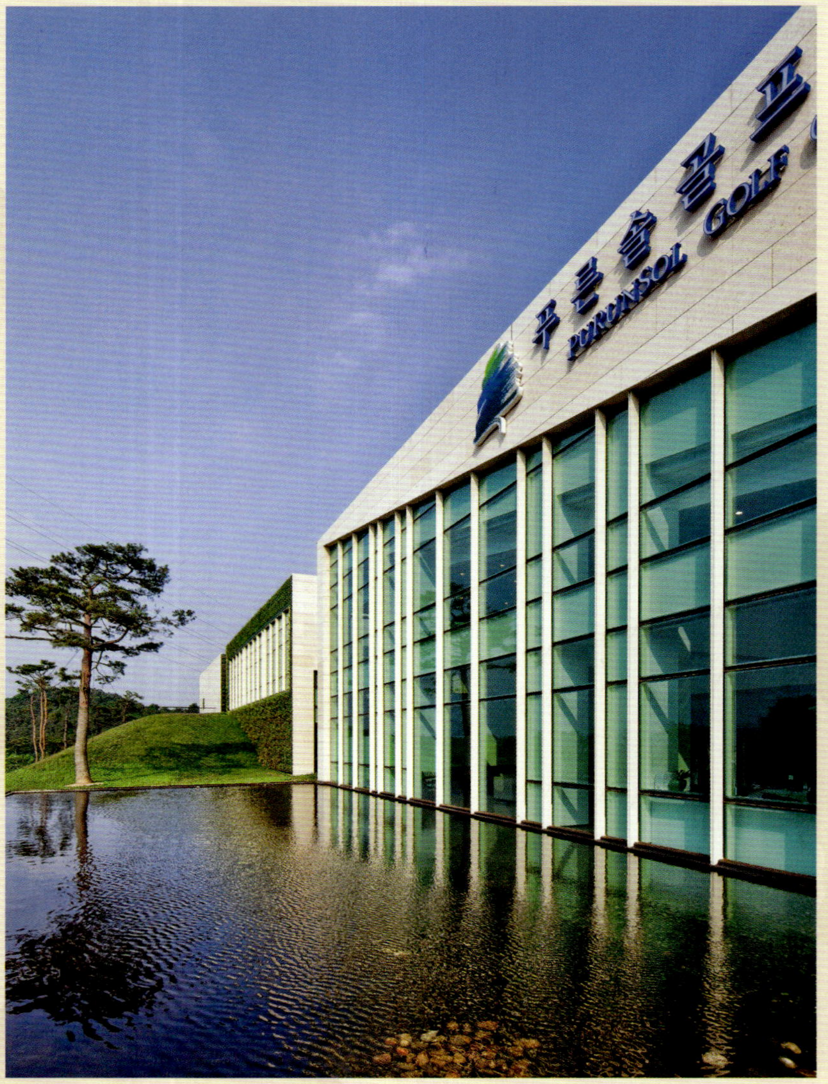
푸른솔골프
PURUNSOL GOLF

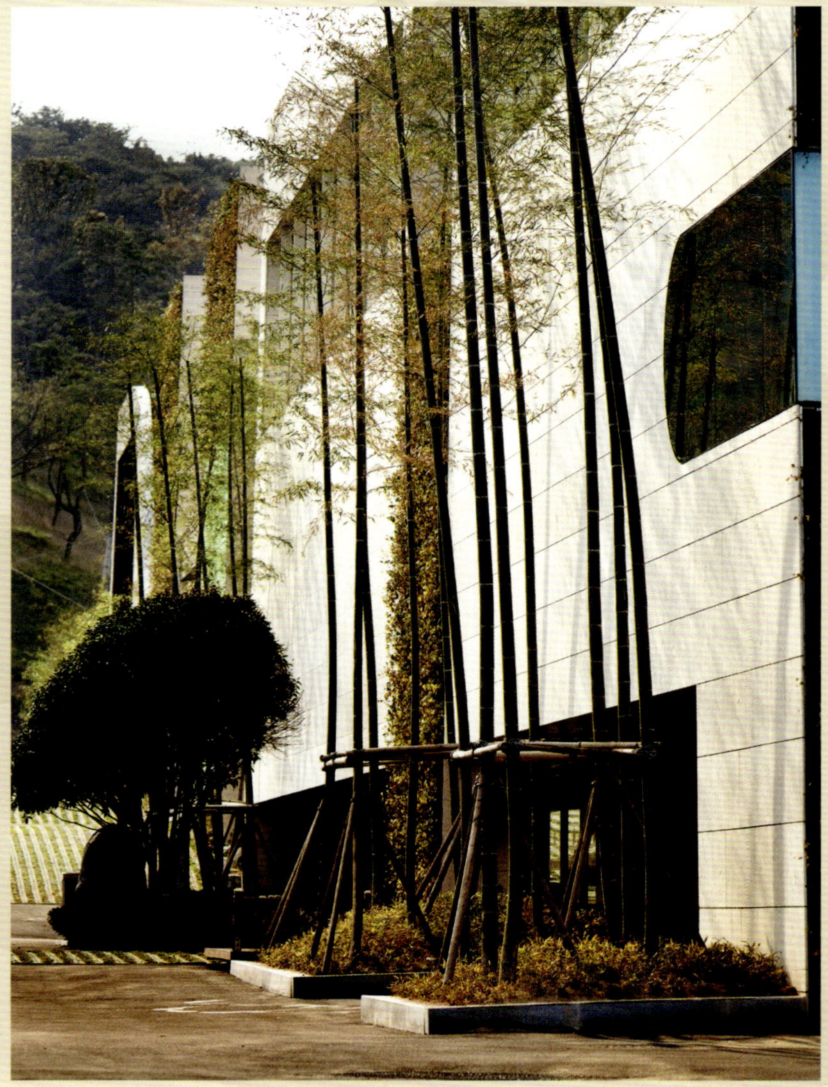

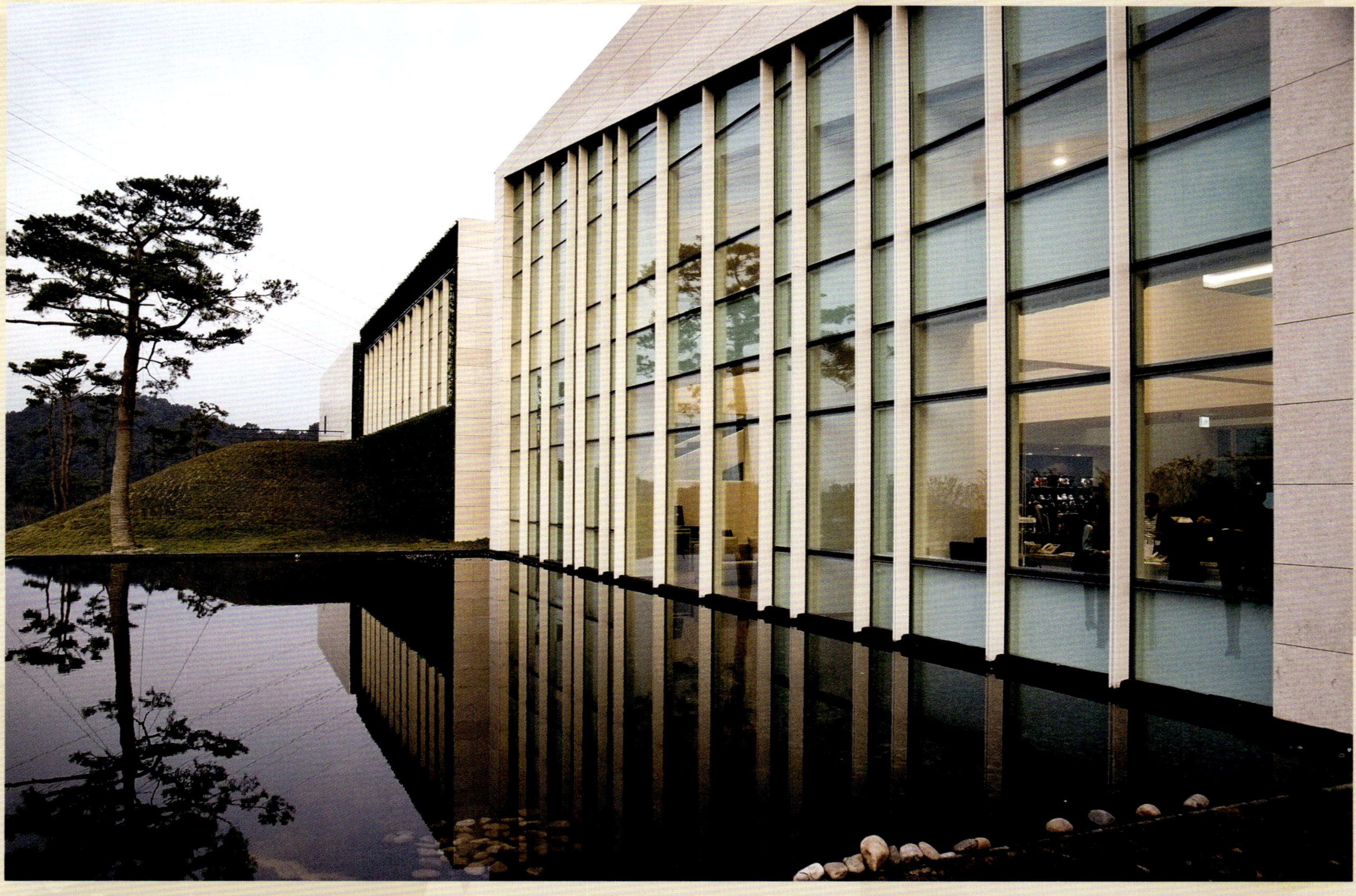

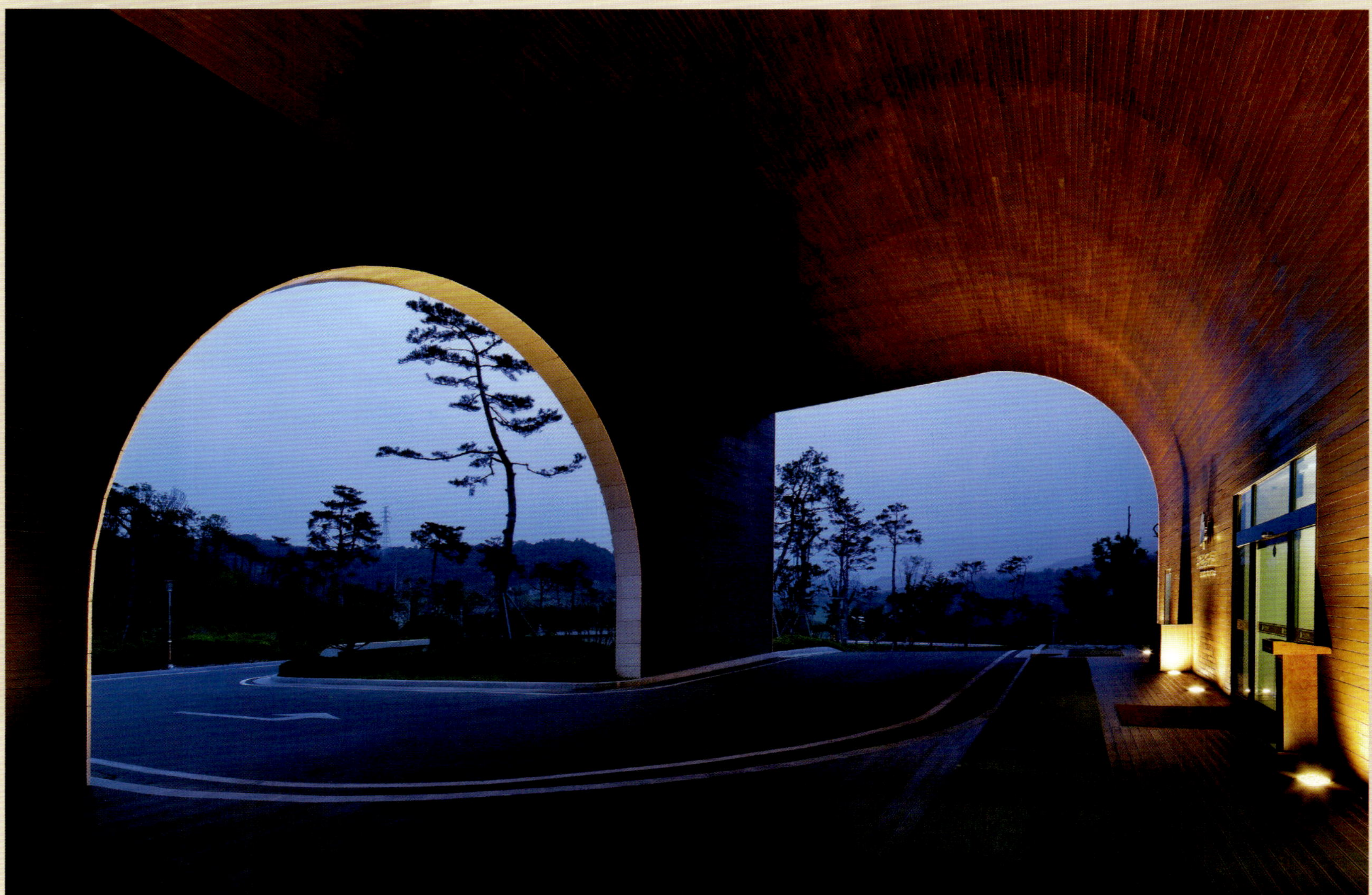

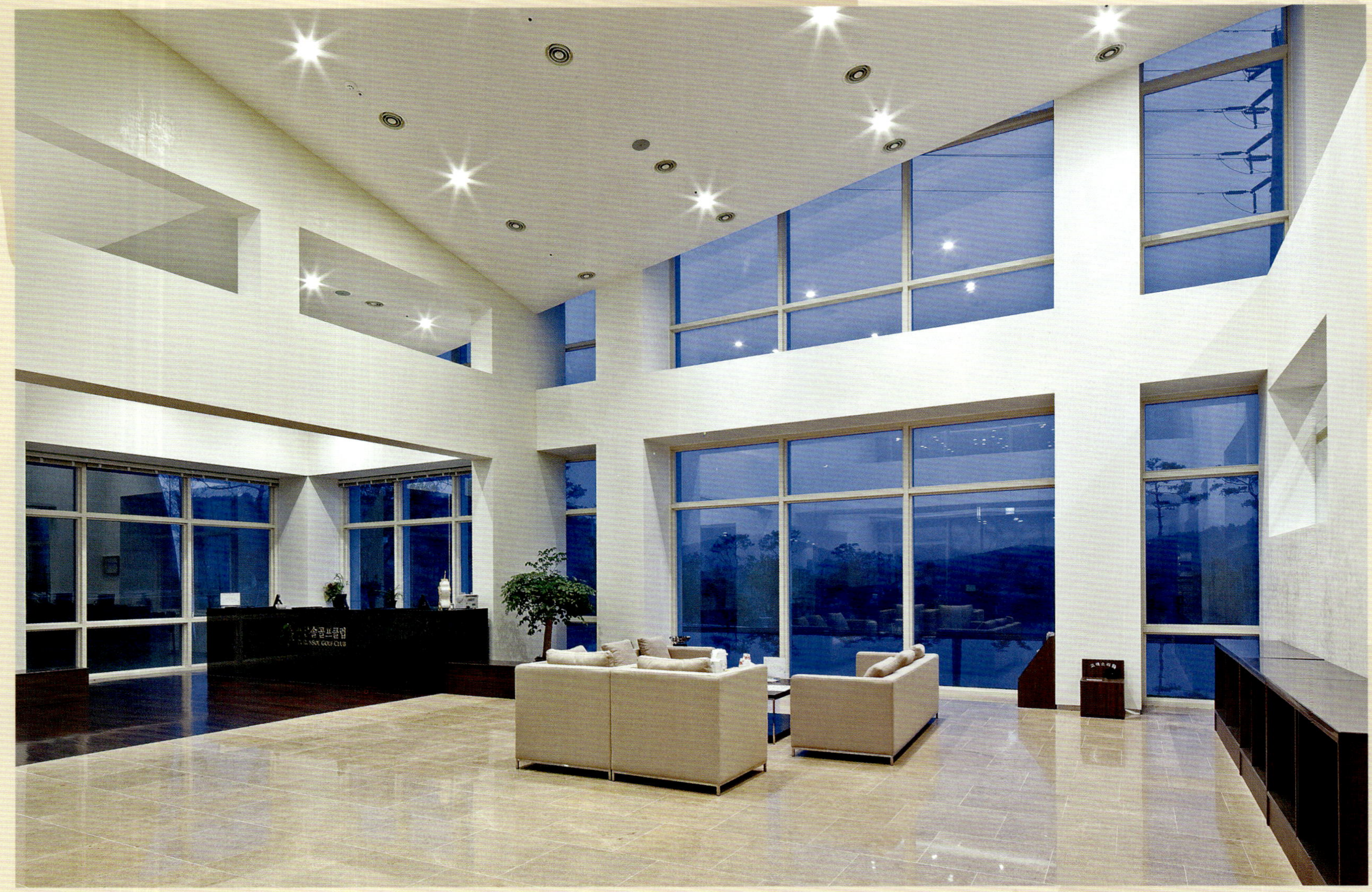

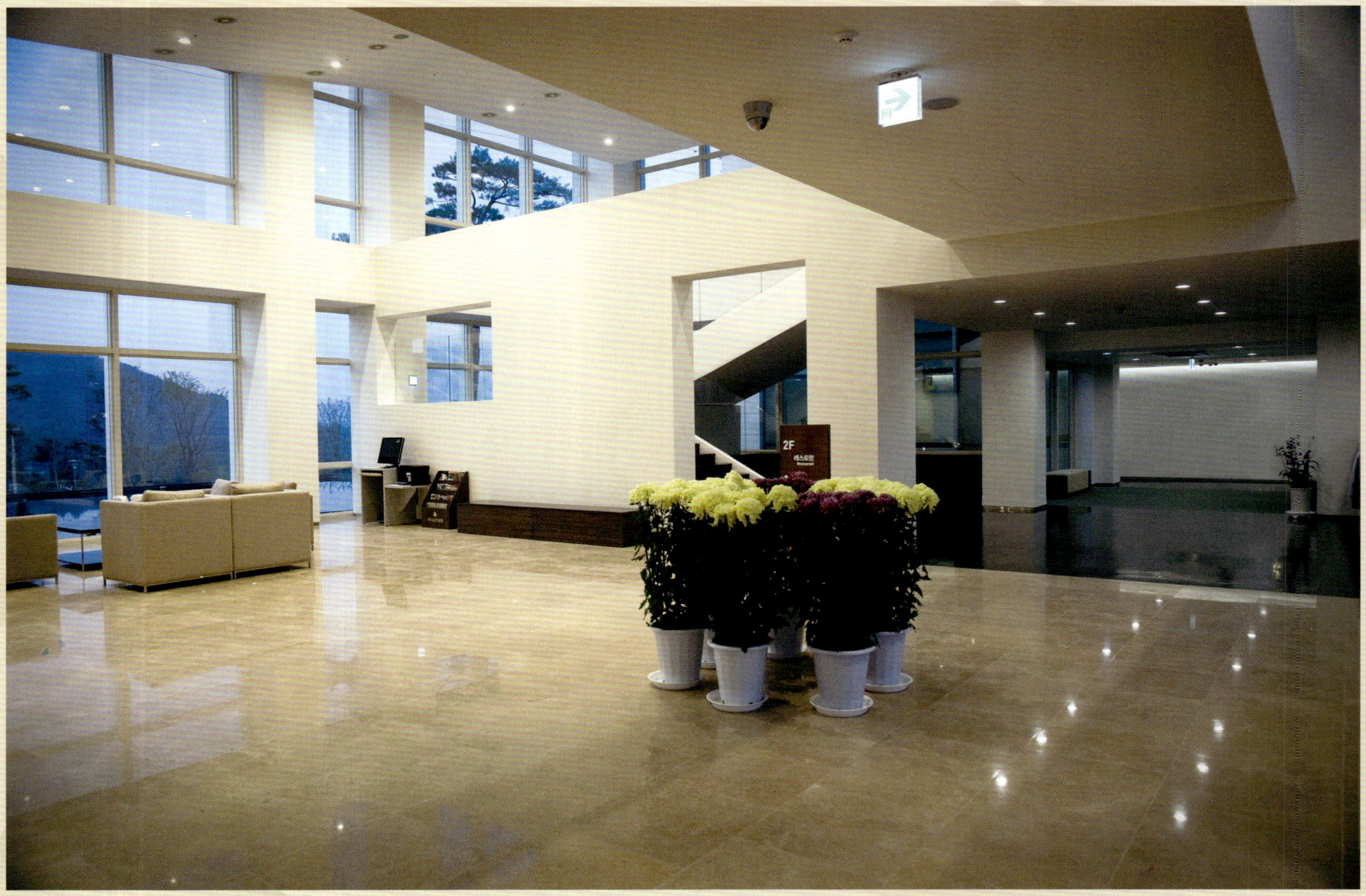
2F

SECTION

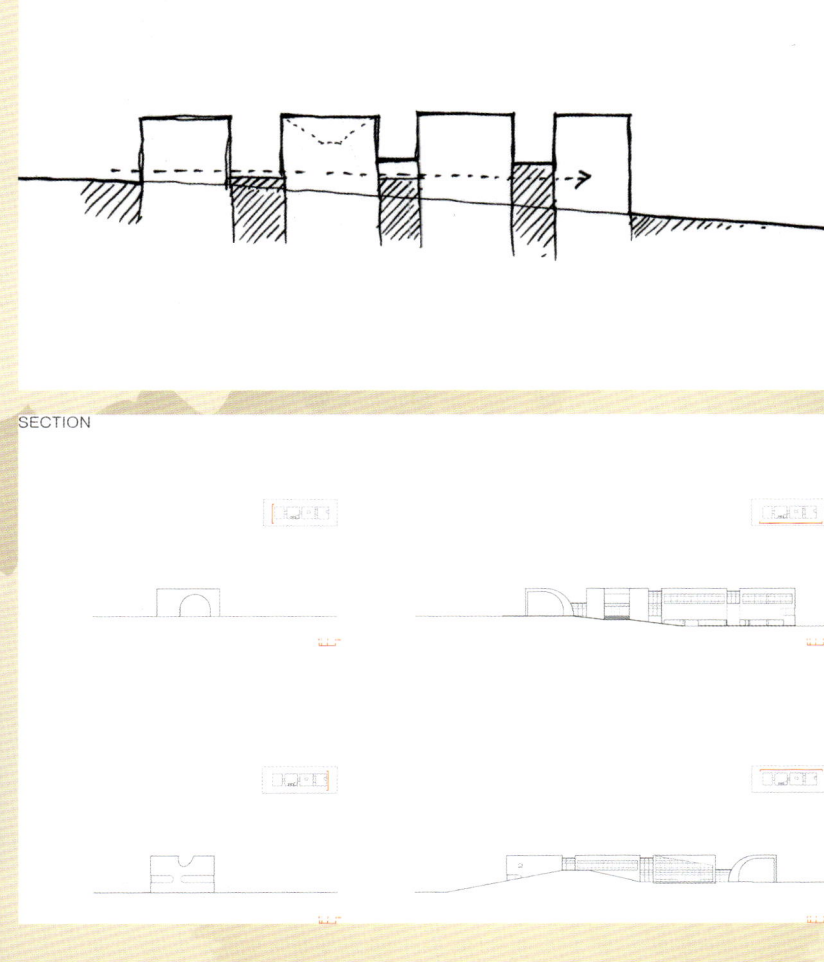

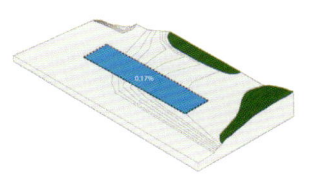

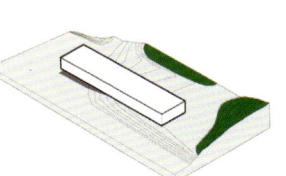

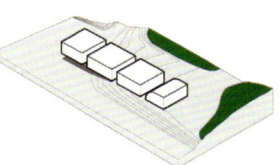

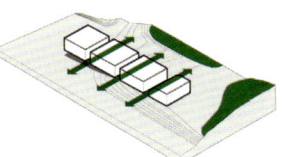

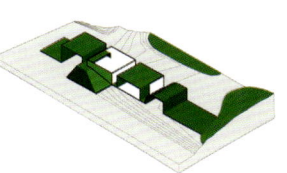

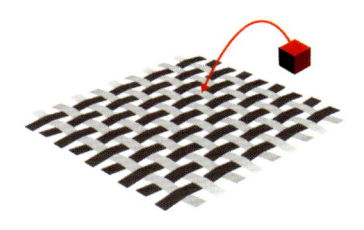

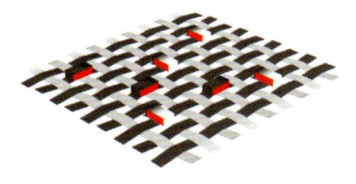

309

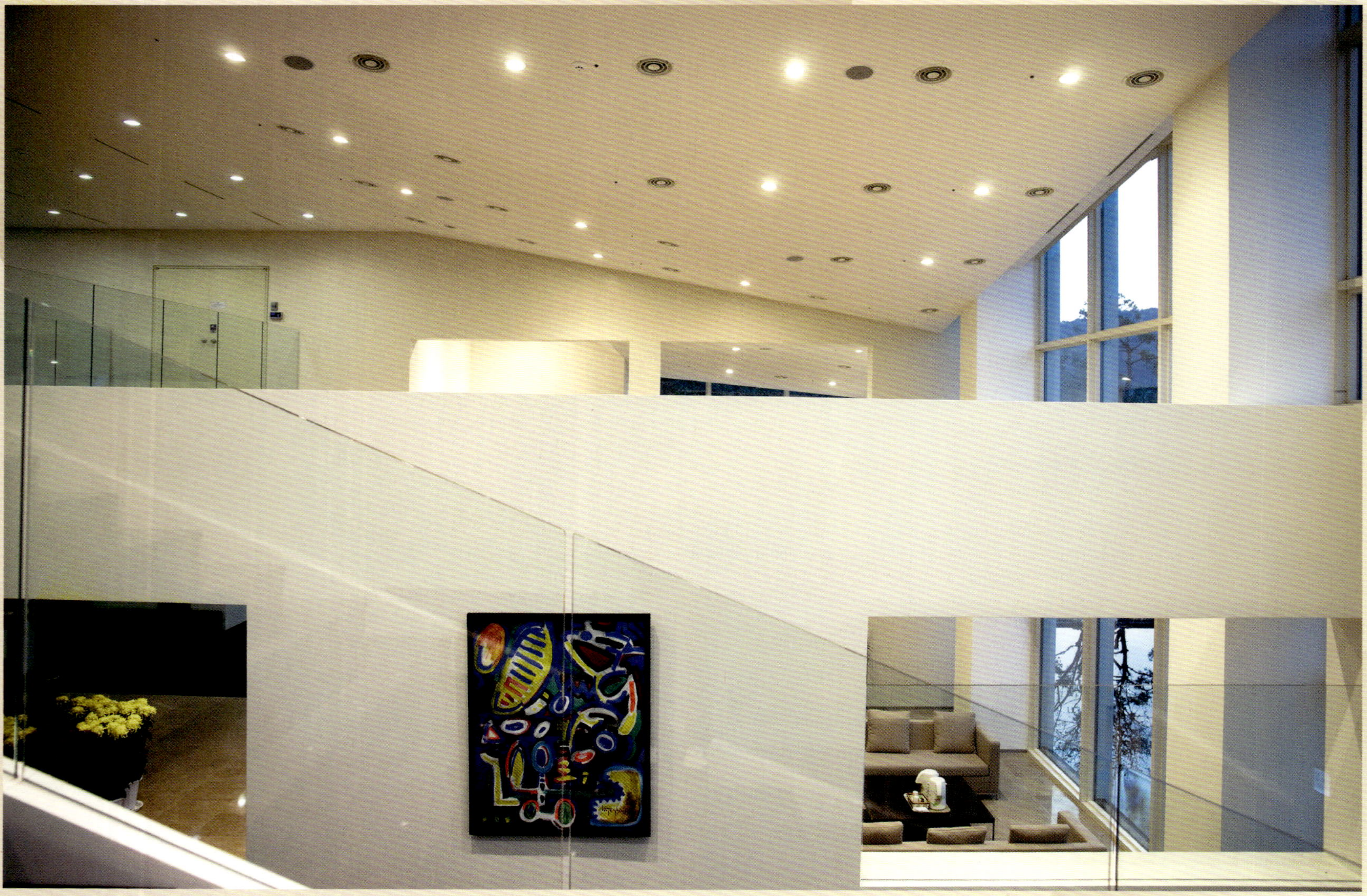

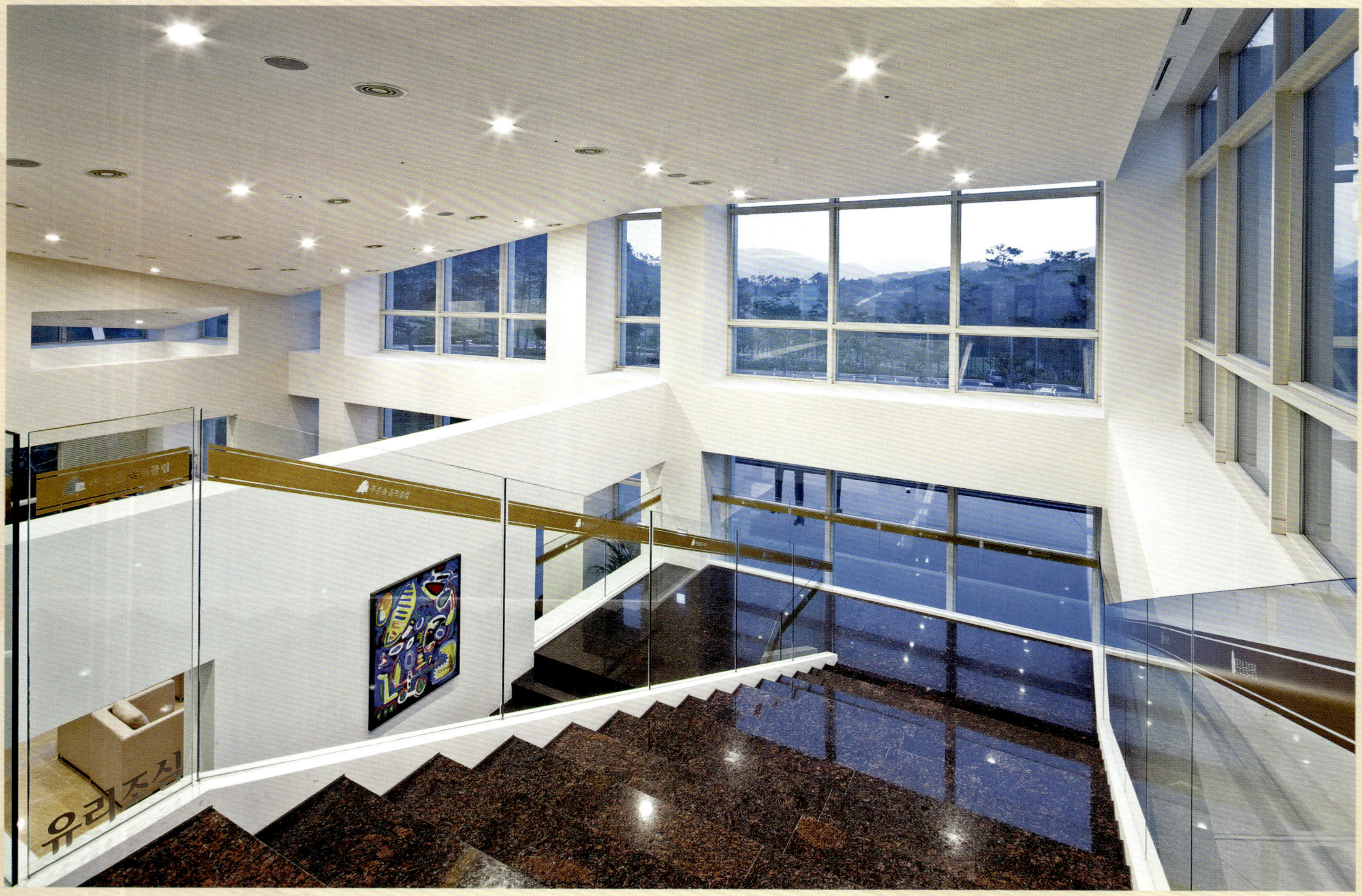

311

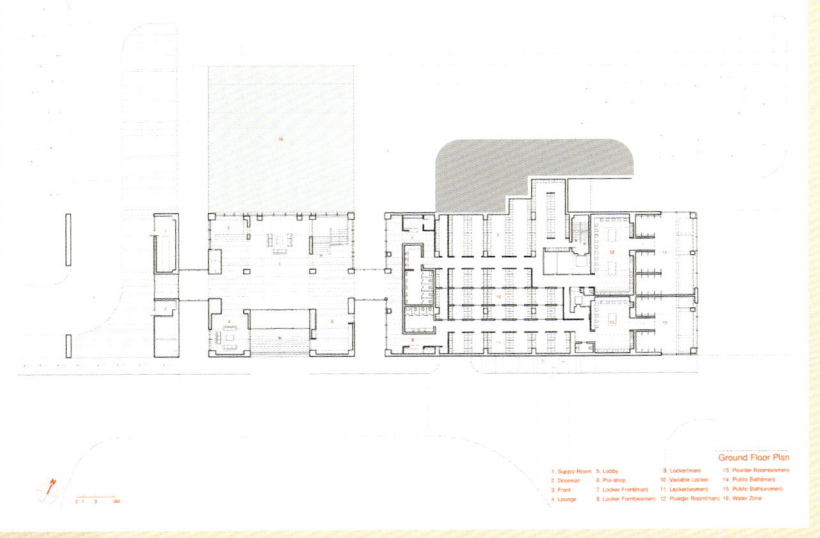

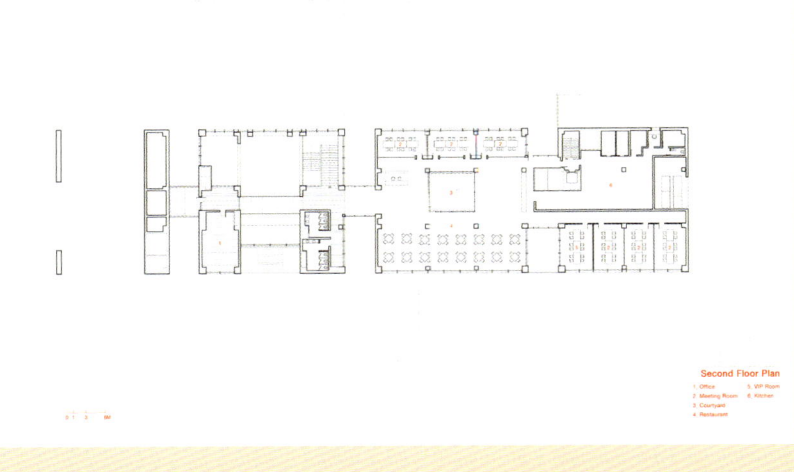

ELEVATION

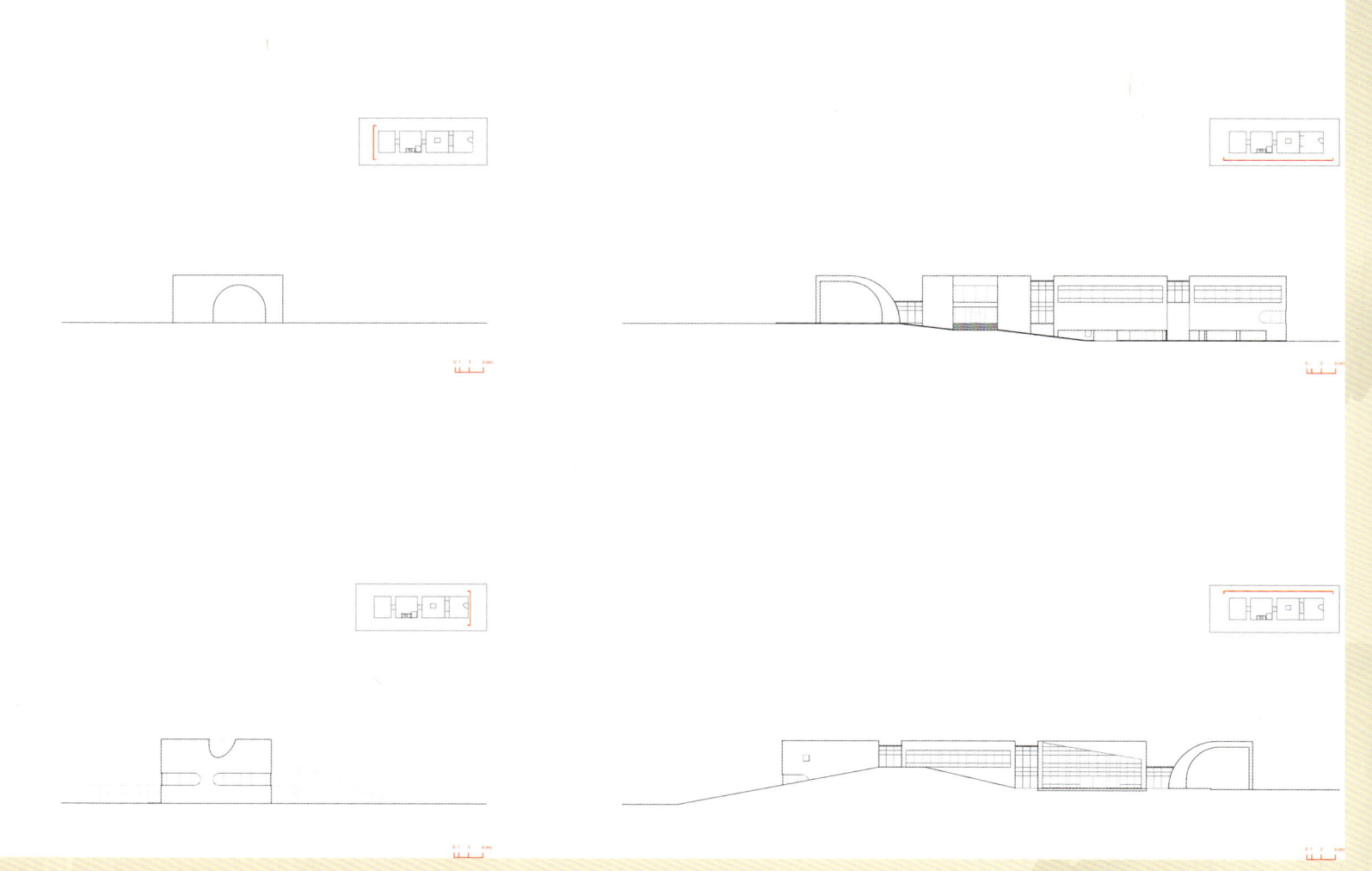

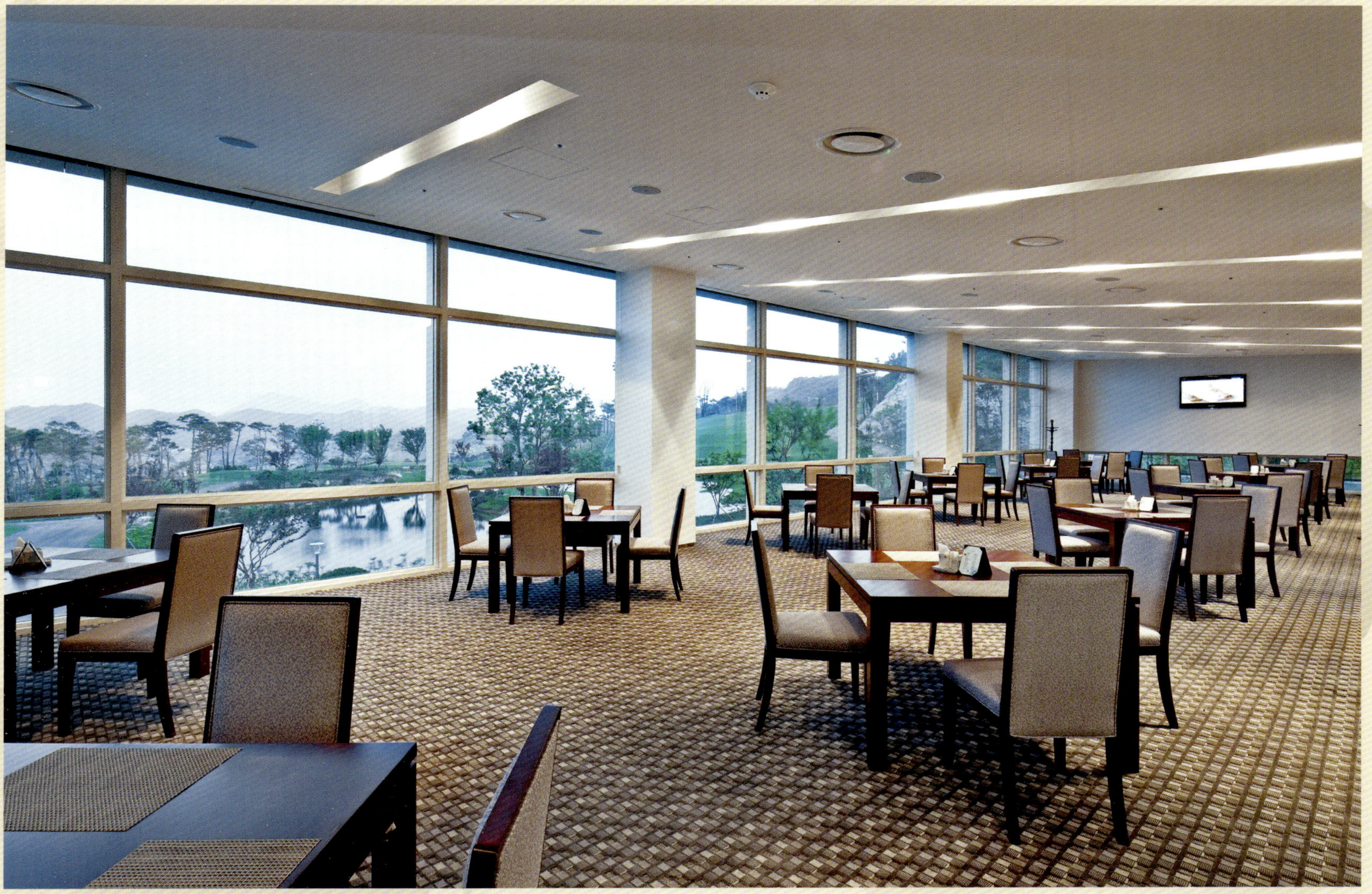

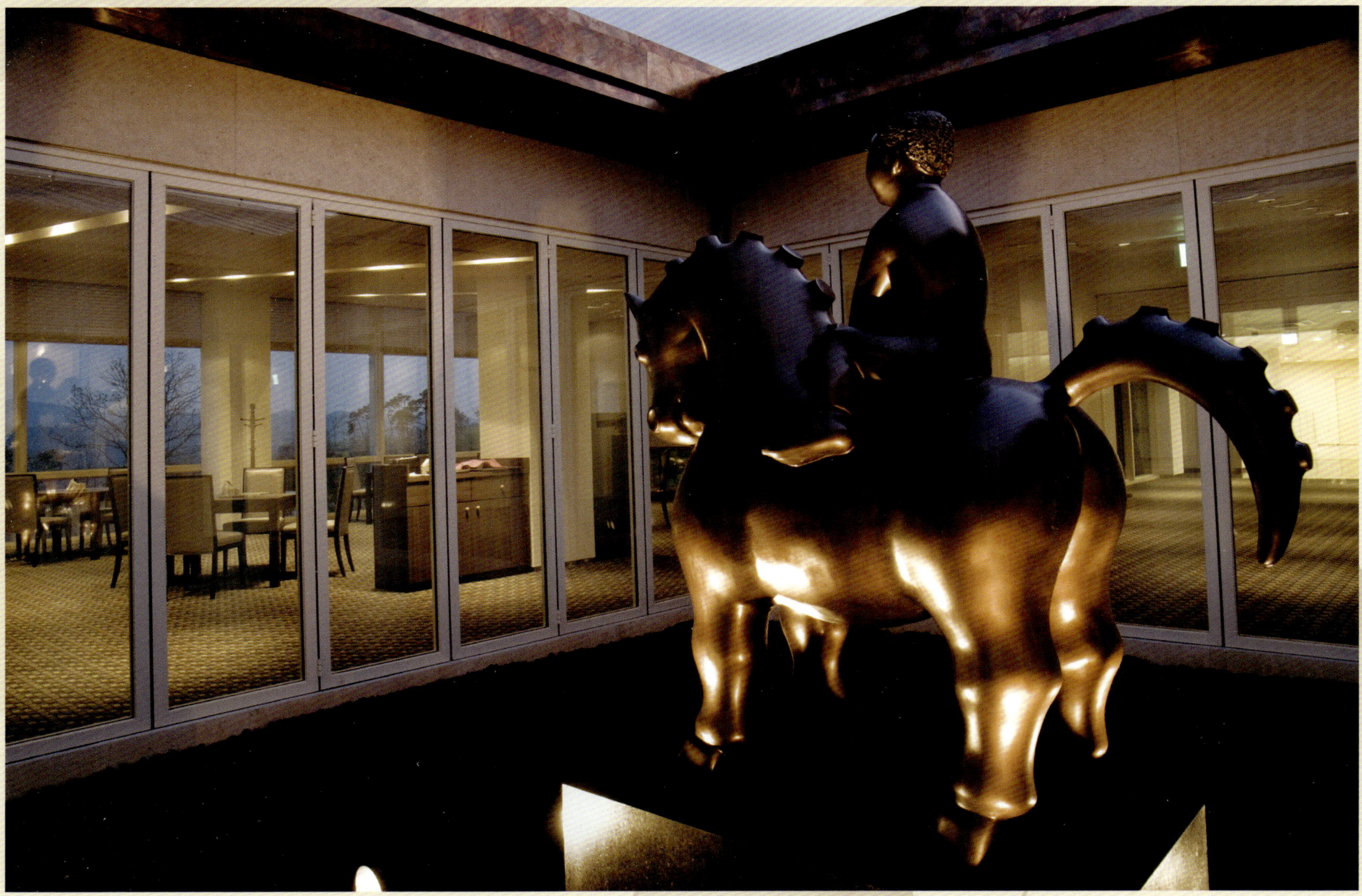

Beijing Fashion Impression Decoration Co., Ltd.

Beijing Fashion Impression Decoration Co., Ltd. is a comprehensive decoration enterprise, with decoration design, engineering construction, furniture and the making of art as its main principal works.

With market segment, our precise position is the supporting facilities of real estate, and our operational targets include sales offices, sample room, club, refined decoration of model house and other real estate supporting facilities. With market and high quality work as the orientation, we are using all the master plan and overall supporting facilities to promote the brand new model of decoration and grow up to the deserved specialist in the specific market.

Concrete

Concrete consists of 5 fundamental building blocks: concrete interiors, concrete architecture, concrete tomorrow, concrete today and concrete heritage. Concrete entire team consists of about 35 professional people. Visual marketers and interior designers, graphic designers and architects work on projects in multidisciplinary teams.

Concrete develops total concepts for businesses and institutions. the agency produces work which is commercially applicable. This involves creating total identities for a company, a building or an area. The work extends from interior design to urban development integration and from the building to its accessories. Concrete, for example, also sets the perimeters for the graphic work and considers how the client can present itself in the market.

This all happens from the one concept philosophy. The designers of Concrete create holistic plans and everything they design is used for the benefit of that total concept: that where their strength and thus the client greatest advantage lies. Concrete is dynamic, and quick on its feet and self-determined. The agency thrives on hard work and the creation of beautiful things. Concrete does not have a pre-determined style and the designers do not simply create designs, interiors or buildings: Concrete devises solutions.

DARA

Patrick Jiang, founder of DARA, was born in the 70s; grew up in the 80s; found his career in the 90s and established himself in the 20th century. He loves painting and art since his childhood. Influences from Chinese and Western culture give him the inspiration to combine these cultures in DARA. He combines the principle of fashion furniture with art to make DARA truly unique. As 2nd generation of Chinese furniture design industry, Patrick establishes the spirit of "Design in China".

DARA, as a practitioner and agent of fashion furniture, has been imitated and praised in the old yet modern Beijing metropolis. The creation of " fusion style" and the application of "mix & match" have made DARA popular with its major customers. DARA, which means elegant, noble, romantic and persona, is a Latin word. It's easy to remember and pronounce, even by those who don't speak English. From ambassadors, celebrities and movies stars to modern young aristocrats, DARA is always their first choice in home design.

Dao He Design Studio

Dao He Design Studio was established in 2011, led by a group of passionate young people. This design studio specializes in architecture design, interior design, visual design and furniture design. By these years' design and research, Dao He Design gained a profound understanding of design. They are not just designers but project managers, too. They remind us that the very best architecture satisfies practical needs while continually challenging us to think outside the circle.

Eric Tai Design Co., Ltd.

Started by Mr. Eric Tai, a renowned interior designer in China, Eric Tai Design Co., Ltd. (hereinafter as Eric Tai Design) and Shenzhen Katha Artwork Co., Ltd. specialize in interior design and decorative furnishing services for clubs, hotels, promotion centers, and sample villa houses, and are among leading interior design providers. Eric Tai Design boasts profound experiences and insights in designs, and is persistent in serving all clients with outstanding design management and wise innovations. It keeps on with far-reaching contributions to continued promotion of the whole interior design industry through unique influences basing on in-depth understanding of world design trends and future developments of the design industry.

For over a decade, Eric Tai Design works on profound understanding of varied styles, expert balance of functional demands with artistic tastes, as well as extraordinary control over visual effects and feel of comforts in a natural fashion. Design principle of ORIGINAL ELEGANCE & NOBLE TASTE is integral into all design works. Eric Tai Design creates paramount values with design services, and meantime harvests greater successes in business, thus winning the company even more opportunities to serve the clients.

Henan blue industrial Co., Ltd.

Found in 1994, Blue Design is officially registered as Henan Blue Industry Co., Ltd.

Blue Design has more than 80 employees. There are over 50 professional designers. Blue Design is good at designing projects of office, club, hotel, restaurant, financial office, etc.

Huang He

The designer has engaged in interior design field since 1995, with main expertise in hotel design. The design concept emphasis on cultural content and the organic integration of the environment brings life and soul to the architectural spaces. His work has won various prestigious awards.

Constantly walks in different countries and cities. Arts tour in France all year round. Good observation and experience. He had visited many hotel architectures in many cities, such as Dubai, Tokyo, Las Vegas, New York, Paris, Venice, as well as cultural restaurants.

These hotels include the Marriott International Hotel Group, Starwood Hotels & Resorts, Hyatt International, and their underline theme hotels. Wide range of knowledge and rich experience bring him more design inspiration. His design style is in line with the international mainstream, with highly individual character.

Works was recorded in "Creative Division in China Year" "50 Best Designs of China's Most Commercially Valuable Works, Fine Business nationally published with distinction in the field.

Hyunjoon Yoo

Hyunjoon Yoo (A.I.A.) is a chair of department at Hongik University School of Architecture, principal architect of Hyunjoon Yoo Architects in Seoul, Korea. He graduated from Yonsei University in Seoul with a bachelor's degree in architectural engineering, followed by a Master of Architecture degree from MIT, and received his Master of Architecture degree with Distinction from Harvard. He worked for Richard Meier & Partners, and for the MIT Architecture Representation & Computation Lab. He was a visiting scholar at MIT in 2010. He has won five awards in international design competitions, including an award and honorable mention at the BSA Unbuilt Architecture Design Awards in the same year. He was awarded as the Korean Young Architects Award in 2009. His work has been selected as one of the Seoul's 15 Architectural Wonders by CNN. He has been a consultant for many projects, including the remodeling project for the Blue House, South Korea's presidential residence. He has also served as judge in competitions such as the Korea National Architecture Competition. Books he has authored include "52 9 12", "The Flow of Contemporary Architecture" and "Modernism: Cultural Hybrid between East and West".

Joey Ho

Joey Ho draws his creative inspiration from the far-reaching corners of Asia. Born in Taiwan, raised in Singapore and gaining his Masters in Architecture from the University of Hong Kong, each of these culturally diverse yet artistically vibrant qualities have played their part in fashioning Joey's unique and avant-garde perspective of the world.

Planting his roots in Hong Kong, Joey set up Joey Ho Design Limited in 2002, attracting a young and energetic team of hugely talented individuals. Their diverse skills, styles and disciplines come together to create dynamic and engaging spaces where people can thrive and blossom. We believe everyone is influenced and inspired by their architectural surroundings and with each new project comes the opportunity to help improve their environment and standard of living. To-date, Joey's designs have garnered more than 90 internationally recognized awards.

Lydia Lu & Zakia Zhang

Lydia Lu is a designer of Symmetry International Space Design. Her major works include COSCO Club, Platinum Bay Zheng's House, etc.

Zakia Zhang is the design director of Symmetry International Space Design. Her major works include Ban Shan Ban Dao club, A Kui Li Ya Sample House, etc.

MOHEN DESIGN INTERNATIONAL

MOHEN DESIGN INTERNATIONAL is an award-winning company creating schemes for residential, contract, office and hospitality design in Shanghai, Tokyo and Taiwan. The practice was initially set up by Mr. Hank M. Chao as a platform for cross-disciplinary collaborations. Today the German, Spanish, American, Japanese, Australian, Taiwanese and Chinese press has reviewed the practice's work.

MOHEN DESIGN INTERNATIONAL projects range from public buildings to individual interiors for private clients. The practice has particular experience in the leisure and hospitality industry, focusing on the design of contemporary bars, clubs and restaurants, hotels and private villas. Using a unique language of color, light and geometry, our interiors are sensuous and eventful. Space is carefully choreographed into stylish environments.

Each design is treated individually and developed with the help of specialist consultants. Traditional architectural services are complemented with concept and brand development. Established contacts to graphic designers, photographers, media consultants, individual artists offer extended interdisciplinary support.

We understand the making of architecture is a multi-layered and collaborative process. Close contact to the client is important to develop optimized design solutions. Each project, regardless of its size, is treated with equal passion and attention to detail. 3-d visualizations allow an immediate insight into an evolving project and form the basis for successful dialogue.

We have diversified practice that focuses on clients wishing to pursue innovative design strategies. The crew are committed to high quality design and have years of experience controlling their craftsmanship skill and design budget.

Neri&Hu Design and Research Office

Founded in 2004 by partners Lyndon Neri and Rossana Hu, Neri&Hu Design and Research Office is a multi-disciplinary architectural design practice based in Shanghai, China. Neri&Hu works internationally providing architecture, interior, master planning, graphic, and product design services. Currently working on projects in many countries, Neri&Hu is composed of multi-cultural staff who speak over 30 different languages. The diversity of the team reinforces a core vision for the practice: to respond to a global worldview incorporating overlapping design disciplines for a new paradigm in architecture.

Pitsou Kedem Architects

Pitsou Kedem Architects was founded in 2002. Today the office employs 8 architects (Irene Goldberg, Nurit Ben Yosef, Raz Melamed, Noa Groman, Ran Broides, Hila Sela, Omer Dagan, and Tamar Berger). The office was established by Pitsou Kedem, a graduate of the Architectural Association in London who also mentors final projects at the Technion's Faculty of Architecture. The office has won, two years in a row, the "Design" award and has been chosen as the Architects Office of the year in the "Private Construction" category by the magazine "Construction and Housing".

The office has designed dozens of private projects as well as commercial projects (Amongst its last projects were the flagship store for B&B italy, a boutique hotel in the prestigious Rothschild Boulevard and an events hall in Ben Avidor Street). The design was one using a minimalistic architectural language based on principals of restricted formality that combine together to produce one clean, coherent and harmonious language. Above all else, the aim is to preserve his architectural language and his own architectural vision in all of his projects.

Shenzhen Horizon Space Design Co., Ltd.

Shenzhen Horizon Space Design Co., Ltd. was founded in August 2005 and committed to the area of interior design. We stick to the principle of "Brain Storm" and "give full scope to the talents" and make our contribution to interior design. We work hard to create harmonious atmosphere of equal competition, mutual respect and make progress together. Creativeness is the source power of the company's development.

There are some high quality technology talents and specialized persons in Horizon Space Design. We started our cooperation with Vanke Real Estate since 2007, and continued the strategic cooperative partnership in model room design in 2008, 2009 and 2010. We accumulated rich experiences during years of cooperation with Vanke.

Shenzhen Pinki Design Consultant Co., Ltd.

Being good at designing hotel, sample house, sales office, restaurants space, club and exhibition; being praised for creating artful space with theme style, he is adept at blending Eastern & Western art and culture in life. Design areas includes: interior design, display & art design, furniture design and landscape architecture.

Liu Weijun is the founder/ executive chairman, the managing director of Shenzhen Pinki Design Consultant Co., Ltd. and the creative director as well as the chief designer of Liu & Associates (IARI) Interior Design Co., Ltd.

Sherwood Design

Ever since the establishment of Huang Shuheng Architect in 1998 and the expansion as well as regroupment in 2004, Sherwood Design has gone through more than ten years and has extended its design field to architecture, interior, exhibition, furniture, etc.

Xuan Wu is an mythological animal in Chinese myth, with the appearance of combining tortoise and snake. It means foresight and permanent. Xuan Wu matches Ren Gui. In ancient Chinese calendar, Ren and Gui are two of the ten Heavenly Stems and they both mean water. Water is the beginning of everything. They name their studio Sherwood after Xuan Wu and expect them as the magic water in heaven and earth, exploring the value of Chinese culture. And they also expect that their minds are flexible like a snake while designing, and that they behave steady like tortoise while they turn ideas into reality.

SHH

SHH is an architects' practice and interiors consultancy, formed in 1992 by its three principals: Chairman David Spence, Managing Director Graham Harris and Creative Director Neil Hogan. With a highly international workforce and portfolio, the company initially made its name in ultra-high-end residential schemes, before extending its expertise to include leisure, workspace and retail. SHH's work has appeared in leading design and lifestyle publications all over the world, including VOGUE and ELLE Decoration in the UK, Artravel and AMC in France, Frame in Holland, Monitor in Russia, DHD in Italy, ELLE Decoration in India, Habitat in South Africa, Contemporary Home Design in Australia, Interior Design in the USA and Architectural Digest in both France and Russia, with over 110 projects also published in 70 leading book titles worldwide plus more than 75 architectural and design award wins and nominations to its name.

Sunlay Design

Founded in 1990, Sunlay Design Group is one of the designing companies which firstly implemented the joint stock system directly under the administration of the Ministry of Construction, and has acquired the top-class designing qualification in 1994. After over a decade's development, it has grown into a medium complex with comprehensive designing capacity, possessing a designing team of over one hundred members.The company has accumulated rich experiences in the civil architecture designing of 7 categories covering urban planning and design, design for residential houses, large public building, commercial building, hotel, educational building as well as interior decoration, while lots of experiences are gained from the construction of the large projects over a decade.For the recent years, with the opening-up of the designing circle, Sunlay Design Group has completed a lot of projects in cooperation with offices from America, Germany, Canada, Spain, Hong Kong and Singapore and as a result, it has been consistently driving its management, research and concepts towards a internationalization development.While deriving strong points from others, Sunlay Design Group will continue its reforms in depth, and maintain the balanced development in research, management and marketing. It will also exert to seek for an innovative mechanism, carry out the training system for the project managers and architects, improve the quality control system as well as the partnership system by holding in mind that the main task of the architect is to resolve the architects' conflicts among aesthetic value, client's interest and public benefit.

Tsun Fong

Tsun Fong: An International designer of Hong Kong, China, born in Guangzhou in 1970 and moved to Hong Kong at the age of 15. He is a PHD student at Inter American University, and has received Master degree of Arts in Interior Design Management from Pole. Design Consorzio dei politecnicodi Milano, Bachelor of Arts in Architecture from the Hong Kong Polytechnic Unversity; he set up his practice "HONG KONG FONG ARCHITECTS&ASSOCIATES" in 1997. He also received several design awards including the gold prize from the First International Architecture, Landscape and Interior design Awards, his works were frequently featured in professional design journals.

Tsung-Jen Lin

Tsung-Jen Lin, director of Crox International, specialized in architecture and urban planning, has a good sense in design and a sharp business understanding in all aspects of a successful project. His practice spans from window display, scenery, interior, to large scale projects like trade show, exhibition and urban landscape. With unique design ability and user-focused approach, Mr. Lin looks into the context for solutions beyond traditional ways. He serves as a cohesive force that fosters an integrated design consulting service at Crox.

Wisdom Space Design

Wang Junqin, as the head of Wisdom Space Design, is a famous interior designer in Taiwan and the international leader of entertainment space design. He has won many national and international awards for his flexible and suitable designs and has been acclaimed as a designer possessing both sense and sensibility, establishing his status in China's design field. The Wisdom Space Design company he founded is famous for its entertainment space design in China's design field, named one of China's top ten most influential catering and entertainment design institutions, and China's most valuable enterprise of interior design, having serviced numerous well-known brands and enterprises. The concept of being prudent, relentless and calm in design is his attitude towards design as well the motivation of his entire team.

Xiao Aibin

Graduated from Sichuan Fine Arts Institute
Senior Chinese interior designer
Senior Chinese architectural interior designer
Member of Chinese woodblock artists association
Director of CIID China Institute of Interior Design
Member of editorial board of Chinese interior design magazine
Executive director of Shanghai Decoration Association
Assistant director of Shanghai Industry Association Design Committee
Sichuan Normal University visiting professor of College of Visual Arts
Chairman and chief designer of Shanghai Xiao's Design Decorating CO., Ltd.

Zhang Tao

Zhang Tao has served in domestic and overseas firms of architectural design and construction successively, such as Taiwan Shen Zubai Architectural Design Firm, World Trade Grape, K. F. Stone Design International Inc. Canada, and so on. He has taken charge of Shanghai Science & Technology Museum, WIO Lakeside Garden, WIO Village, Shell China Exploration and Production Company Limited (Shell), Millennium Hotel, Wuxi and other interior and exterior design projects.

The designer is adopt in using various techniques to build comfortable natural human space, and he pays more attention to the integrity of the design and the unity of finished projects as he is deeply responsible for the project. His finished projects have all won high evaluation from both owners and the industry.

Shenzhen Huge Rock Interior Design Co., Ltd.

Wu Wenli is the board member & design director at Shenzhen Huge Rock Interior Design Co., Ltd. He is a senior commercial space designer who has engaged in the design industry for more than 10 years, committing to the design of hotels, clubs, public spaces, office spaces, villas, sample houses, etc.

Shenzhen Huge Rock Interior Design Co., Ltd. is a professional design corporation specializing in interior and furnishing design for real estate developers, business investment companies, hotels, villas, office spaces, etc.

Huge Rock Design has been adhering to the concept "to promote and enhance the project's quality and value through designing" since its establishment. It has been committed to the development and innovation of design. Till now it has completed over one hundred projects. The design concept of each project was the same, that is, "to promote and enhance the project's quality and value through designing ".

"To serve customers as the priority under market oriented economy" has become Huge Rock Design's consistent service standard and development direction.

ARTPOWER

Acknowledgements

We would like to thank all the designers and companies who made significant contributions to the compilation of this book. Without them, this project would not have been possible. We would also like to thank many others whose names did not appear on the credits, but made specific input and support for the project from beginning to end.

Future Editions

If you would like to contribute to the next edition of Artpower, please email us your details to: artpower@artpower.com.cn